Essentials of MMPI-2 and MMPI-A Interpretation

Second Edition

Essentials of MMPI-2 and MMPI-A Interpretation

Second Edition

James N. Butcher and Carolyn L. Williams

Foreword by Raymond D. Fowler

University of Minnesota Press
Minneapolis · London

Published by the University of Minnesota Press
111 Third Avenue South, Suite 290
Minneapolis, MN 55401-2520
http://www.upress.umn.edu

Printed in the United States of America on acid-free paper

Library of Congress Cataloging-in-Publication Data

Butcher, James Neal, 1933–
    Essentials of MMPI-2 and MMPI-A interpretation / James N. Butcher and
Carolyn L. Williams.—2nd ed.
        p. cm.
Includes bibliographical references and index.
    ISBN 0-8166-3552-8 (hardcover : alk. paper)
1. Minnesota Multiphasic Personality Inventory.   I. Williams, Carolyn L.,
1951–   II. Title.
    BF698.8.M5 B87 2000
    155.2′83—dc21   00-011317

The University of Minnesota is an
equal-opportunity educator and employer.

11 10 09 08 07 06 05 04 03 02 01 00   10 9 8 7 6 5 4 3 2 1

Dedicated to warm and happy memories of
Neal Glynn Butcher
1965–1985

Contents

List of Tables   xi

List of Figures   xv

Foreword by Raymond D. Fowler   xvii

Preface to the Second Edition   xxi

Chapter 1   **Objective Personality Assessment Using the MMPI-2 and MMPI-A**   1

Development of the MMPI   2
The Need to Revise the MMPI   3
The MMPI Restandardization Project   4
Development of the MMPI-2   6
Development of the MMPI-A   8
Highlight Summary: The MMPI-2 and MMPI-A   11

Chapter 2   **Administering, Scoring, and Profiling the MMPI-2 and MMPI-A**   12

Selecting the Proper Form   12
Administering the MMPI-2 and MMPI-A   15
MMPI-2 and MMPI-A Formats   20
Scoring the MMPI-2 and MMPI-A   25
Plotting MMPI-2 and MMPI-A Profiles   26
Coding MMPI-2 and MMPI-A Profiles   32
Highlight Summary: The Case of Alice   35

Chapter 3   **Assessing the Validity of MMPI-2 Profiles**   37

Item Omissions, Inconsistent Responding, and Fixed
    Responding   39
Measures of Random and Exaggerated Responding   44
Measures of Defensiveness and Claims of Extreme Virtue   50
Patterns of Response Invalidity   53
Highlight Summary: Alice's Validity Pattern   58

Chapter 4   **Interpreting the MMPI-2 Standard Scales**   60

Scale Development and Item Content   61
Illustrative Empirical Research and Descriptors   62
Scale 1: Hypochondriasis (Hs)   63
Scale 2: Depression (D)   65
Scale 3: Hysteria (Hy)   68
Scale 4: Psychopathic Deviate (Pd)   71

Scale 5: Masculinity-Femininity (Mf)   76
Scale 6: Paranoia (Pa)   80
Scale 7: Psychasthenia (Pt)   83
Scale 8: Schizophrenia (Sc)   85
Scale 9: Hypomania (Ma)   88
Scale 0: Social Introversion (Si)   91
Case Example of the Standard Scales and Their Subscales   94
Limitations of the Harris-Lingoes Content Interpretation
   Approach   94
Highlight Summary: Alice's Standard Scale Profile   97

Chapter 5   **Interpreting MMPI-2 Profile Types (Code Types)**   99
When and Why to Use Code Types   100
Code-Type Definitions and Stability   100
Similarity of the Traditional MMPI and MMPI-2
   Code Types   101
Research on MMPI/MMPI-2 Code Types   102
Two-Point Code-Type Descriptors   104
Three-Point Code-Type Descriptors   128
Highlight Summary: Analysis of Alice's Code Type   133

Chapter 6   **Interpreting the MMPI-2 Content Scales**   135
MMPI-2 Content Scale Development   136
Psychometric Properties of the MMPI-2 Content Scales   136
An Interpretive Strategy for the MMPI-2 Content Scales   138
MMPI-2 Content Component Scales   147
Case Example of the Utility of the Content Scales   148
Highlight Summary: Alice's Content Scale Performance   153

Chapter 7   **Interpreting the MMPI-2 Supplementary Measures**   155
MacAndrew Alcoholism Scale   155
Addiction Potential Scale   159
Addiction Acknowledgment Scale   159
Marital Distress Scale   162
Hostility Scale   167
Other Scales   169
The Personality Psychopathology 5 (PSY-5) Scales   173
Useful Indexes for the MMPI-2   175
Critical Items   177
Cautions about Other Supplementary Measures   178
Developing and Evaluating New Scales for the MMPI-2
   and MMPI-A   183
Highlight Summary: Alice's Supplementary Measures   184

Chapter 8   **Integrating MMPI-2 Inferences into an Interpretive
Report**   186
A Strategy for Integrating MMPI-2 Information   186
Highlight Summary: Alice's MMPI-2 Interpretation   200
Closing Comments   208

Chapter 9   **The MMPI-A: Extending the Use of the MMPI to Adolescents**   209

Adult-Adolescent Differences on the MMPI   211
The Norm Issue and Adolescents   214
Strategies for Interpreting Adolescents' MMPI Profiles   217
Problems with Using the Original MMPI with
    Adolescents   219
Highlight Summary: Advantages of Using the MMPI-A   222

Chapter 10   **Interpreting the MMPI-A Validity Measures**   226

Overview of the MMPI-A Validity Measures   227
Measures of Defensiveness and Fixed Responding   229
Measures of Random and Exaggerated Responding   237
Highlight Summary: Tony, an Adolescent Case   245

Chapter 11   **Interpreting the MMPI-A Standard Scales**   248

General Interpretive Guidelines for the MMPI-A Standard
    Scales   249
Highlight Summary: Interpretation of Tony's MMPI-A Standard
    Scales   270

Chapter 12   **Using the MMPI-A Content Scales**   273

Development of the MMPI-A Content Scales   273
Comparison of the MMPI-A and MMPI-2 Content Scales   275
Interpretation of the MMPI-A Content Scales   275
The MMPI-A Content Component Scales   297
Highlight Summary: Tony's MMPI-A Content Scales
    Profile   298

Chapter 13   **Interpreting MMPI-A Supplementary Measures**   303

Alcohol and Drug Problem Scales   303
Factor Scales   306
Immaturity Scale   307
Personality Psychopathology 5 (PSY-5) Scales   307
MMPI-A Critical Items   308
Highlight Summary: Tony's MMPI-A Supplementary
    Measures   312

Chapter 14   **Guidelines for MMPI-A Interpretation**   315

Interpretive Questions and Report Outline   317
An MMPI-A Feedback Session   325
Highlight Summary: Integrating Tony's MMPI-A
    Responses   326

Chapter 15   **Computerized MMPI-2 and MMPI-A Interpretive Reports**   330

Automated Interpretation of Personality Tests   331
Options for Obtaining Computer-Based MMPI-2 and MMPI-A
    Reports   333

Computer-Based MMPI-2/MMPI-A Narrative Reports   334
The Minnesota Report™   335
Case Illustration of The Minnesota Report™:
  Adult Clinical System   337
Case Illustration of The Minnesota Report™ for Alcohol and Drug
  Treatment Settings   340
Case Illustration of The Minnesota Report™ for Forensic
  Settings   344
Case Illustration of The Minnesota Report™ for Personnel
  Screening   352
Case Illustration of The Minnesota Report™ for the
  MMPI-A   352
Evaluation of Computer Interpretation Systems   357
Issues concerning Computer-Based MMPI-2 and MMPI-A
  Interpretation   363

Appendix   367
Glossary   371
References   377
Index   395

Tables

1-1.	Reasons for Acceptance of the MMPI-2 and MMPI-A in Psychological Assessment	10
2-1.	Standardized Definitions and Examples for the MMPI-A	19
3-1.	Cannot Say Interpretive Guidelines for the MMPI-2	40
3-2.	VRIN Interpretive Guidelines for the MMPI-2	40
3-3.	TRIN Interpretive Guidelines for the MMPI-2	41
3-4.	F Interpretive Guidelines for the MMPI-2	47
3-5.	F_b Interpretive Guidelines for the MMPI-2	48
3-6.	F_p Interpretive Guidelines for the MMPI-2	49
3-7.	L Interpretive Guidelines for the MMPI-2	51
3-8.	K Interpretive Guidelines for the MMPI-2	52
3-9.	S Interpretive Guidelines for the MMPI-2	53
4-1.	Scale 1 Interpretive Guidelines for the MMPI-2	66
4-2.	Scale 2 Interpretive Guidelines for the MMPI-2	69
4-3.	Scale 3 Interpretive Guidelines for the MMPI-2	72
4-4.	Scale 4 Interpretive Guidelines for the MMPI-2	75
4-5.	Scale 5 Interpretive Guidelines for the MMPI-2	80
4-6.	Scale 6 Interpretive Guidelines for the MMPI-2	83
4-7.	Scale 7 Interpretive Guidelines for the MMPI-2	85
4-8.	Scale 8 Interpretive Guidelines for the MMPI-2	89
4-9.	Scale 9 Interpretive Guidelines for the MMPI-2	92
4-10.	Scale 0 Interpretive Guidelines for the MMPI-2	95
4-11.	Harris-Lingoes D and Pd Subscale Scores for Ann	96
5-1.	General Guidelines for Code-Type Interpretation	104
5-2.	Descriptors for the 1-2/2-1 Code Type	105
5-3.	Descriptors for the 1-3/3-1 Code Type	107
5-4.	Descriptors for the 1-4/4-1 Code Type	108
5-5.	Descriptors for the 1-8/8-1 Code Type	109
5-6.	Descriptors for the 1-9/9-1 Code Type	110
5-7.	Descriptors for the 2-3/3-2 Code Type	111
5-8.	Descriptors for the 2-4/4-2 Code Type	112
5-9.	Descriptors for the 2-7/7-2 Code Type	114
5-10.	Descriptors for the 2-8/8-2 Code Type	115
5-11.	Descriptors for the 2-9/9-2 Code Type	116
5-12.	Descriptors for the 3-4/4-3 Code Type	117
5-13.	Descriptors for the 3-6/6-3 Code Type	118
5-14.	Descriptors for the 3-8/8-3 Code Type	119
5-15.	Descriptors for the 4-6/6-4 Code Type	120
5-16.	Descriptors for the 4-7/7-4 Code Type	121
5-17.	Descriptors for the 4-8/8-4 Code Type	122
5-18.	Descriptors for the 4-9/9-4 Code Type	124
5-19.	Descriptors for the 6-8/8-6 Code Type	125

5-20.	Descriptors for the 6-9/9-6 Code Type	126
5-21.	Descriptors for the 7-8/8-7 Code Type	128
5-22.	Descriptors for the 8-9/9-8 Code Type	129
5-23.	Descriptors for the 1-2-3 Code Type	130
5-24.	Descriptors for the 2-7-4/2-4-7 Code Type	131
5-25.	Descriptors for the 2-7-8 Code Type	133
6-1.	ANX Interpretive Guidelines for the MMPI-2	139
6-2.	FRS Interpretive Guidelines for the MMPI-2	139
6-3.	OBS Interpretive Guidelines for the MMPI-2	140
6-4.	DEP Interpretive Guidelines for the MMPI-2	141
6-5.	HEA Interpretive Guidelines for the MMPI-2	141
6-6.	BIZ Interpretive Guidelines for the MMPI-2	142
6-7.	ANG Interpretive Guidelines for the MMPI-2	142
6-8.	CYN Interpretive Guidelines for the MMPI-2	143
6-9.	ASP Interpretive Guidelines for the MMPI-2	143
6-10.	TPA Interpretive Guidelines for the MMPI-2	144
6-11.	LSE Interpretive Guidelines for the MMPI-2	145
6-12.	SOD Interpretive Guidelines for the MMPI-2	145
6-13.	FAM Interpretive Guidelines for the MMPI-2	146
6-14.	WRK Interpretive Guidelines for the MMPI-2	146
6-15.	TRT Interpretive Guidelines for the MMPI-2	147
6-16.	The MMPI-2 Content Component Scales	148
7-1.	MAC-R Interpretive Guidelines for the MMPI-2	157
7-2.	APS Interpretive Guidelines for the MMPI-2	160
7-3.	AAS Interpretive Guidelines for the MMPI-2	160
7-4.	MDS Interpretive Guidelines for the MMPI-2	163
7-5.	Ho Interpretive Guidelines for the MMPI-2	167
7-6.	Do Interpretive Guidelines for the MMPI-2	170
7-7.	Re Interpretive Guidelines for the MMPI-2	171
7-8.	PK Interpretive Guidelines for the MMPI-2	171
7-9.	Es Interpretive Guidelines for the MMPI-2	172
7-10.	A Interpretive Guidelines for the MMPI-2	173
7-11.	R Interpretive Guidelines for the MMPI-2	173
7-12.	The Item-Scale Membership and Scoring Direction of the PSY-5 Scales	174
7-13.	MMPI-2 Critical Item Sets	179
8-1.	Questions for MMPI-2 Interpretations	187
8-2.	MMPI-2 Treatment Planning Questions	187
8-3.	Means and Standard Deviations by Ethnic Origin for 1,138 Community Adult Men	191
8-4.	Means and Standard Deviations by Ethnic Origin for 1,462 Community Adult Women	192
9-1.	Examples of the Differing Interpretive Strategies Developed for Use of the Original MMPI with Adolescents	218
9-2.	Problems in Using the Original MMPI with Adolescents	221
9-3.	Advantages of Using the MMPI-A	223
10-1.	The MMPI, MMPI-A, and MMPI-2 Validity Indicators	228

10-2.	Cs Interpretive Guidelines for the MMPI-A	231
10-3.	L Interpretive Guidelines for the MMPI-A	232
10-4.	K Interpretive Guidelines for the MMPI-A	233
10-5.	TRIN Interpretive Guidelines for the MMPI-A	236
10-6.	F, F_1, F_2, and F – K Interpretive Guidelines for the MMPI-A	241
10-7.	VRIN Interpretive Guidelines for the MMPI-A	242
11-1.	The MMPI, MMPI-A, and MMPI-2 Standard Scales	249
11-2.	Percentages of Elevated Standard Scale Scores in the MMPI-A Normative and Clinical Samples	250
11-3.	General Guidelines for Interpreting the MMPI-A Standard Scales	252
11-4.	Scale 1 Interpretive Guidelines for the MMPI-A	253
11-5.	Scale 2 Interpretive Guidelines for the MMPI-A	255
11-6.	Scale 3 Interpretive Guidelines for the MMPI-A	257
11-7.	Scale 4 Interpretive Guidelines for the MMPI-A	259
11-8.	Scale 5 Interpretive Guidelines for the MMPI-A	262
11-9.	Scale 6 Interpretive Guidelines for the MMPI-A	264
11-10.	Scale 7 Interpretive Guidelines for the MMPI-A	265
11-11.	Scale 8 Interpretive Guidelines for the MMPI-A	266
11-12.	Scale 9 Interpretive Guidelines for the MMPI-A	269
11-13.	Scale 0 Interpretive Guidelines for the MMPI-A	271
12-1.	Comparison of the MMPI-A and MMPI-2 Content Scales	276
12-2.	General Interpretive Guidelines for the MMPI-A Content Scales	277
12-3.	A-anx Descriptors for the MMPI-A	278
12-4.	A-obs Descriptors for the MMPI-A	279
12-5.	A-dep Descriptors for the MMPI-A	281
12-6.	A-hea Descriptors for the MMPI-A	282
12-7.	A-aln Descriptors for the MMPI-A	283
12-8.	A-biz Descriptors for the MMPI-A	284
12-9.	A-ang Descriptors for the MMPI-A	286
12-10.	A-cyn Descriptors for the MMPI-A	287
12-11.	A-con Descriptors for the MMPI-A	289
12-12.	A-lse Descriptors for the MMPI-A	290
12-13.	A-las Descriptors for the MMPI-A	291
12-14.	A-sod Descriptors for the MMPI-A	293
12-15.	A-fam Descriptors for the MMPI-A	295
12-16.	A-sch Descriptors for the MMPI-A	296
12-17.	A-trt Descriptors for the MMPI-A	297
12-18.	The Content Component Scales for the MMPI-A	299
12-19.	Tony's Content Component Scores	301
13-1.	MAC-R Interpretive Guidelines for the MMPI-A	304
13-2.	ACK Interpretive Guidelines for the MMPI-A	306
13-3.	PRO Interpretive Guidelines for the MMPI-A	307
13-4.	Item Composition of the MMPI-A–Based PSY-5 Scales	308
13-5.	MMPI-A Critical Items Presented by Item Grouping	309
13-6.	Tony's Critical Items	313
14-1.	Questions for MMPI-A Interpretations	317
14-2.	Tony's Content Component Scores	328

Figures

2-1.   MMPI-2 softcover test booklet.   21
2-2.   MMPI-A hardcover answer sheet.   22
2-3a.   MMPI-2 basic scales profile.   27
2-3b.   MMPI-2 supplementary scales profile.   28
2-3c.   MMPI-2 content scales profile.   29
2-4a.   MMPI-A basic scales profile.   30
2-4b.   MMPI-A content and supplementary scales profile.   31
2-5.   Alice's MMPI-2 basic scales profile.   33
3-1.   MMPI-2 validity scales profile.   38
3-2.   All-True pattern: MMPI-2 basic scales profile.   42
3-3.   All-True pattern: MMPI-2 content scales profile.   42
3-4.   All-False pattern: MMPI-2 basic scales profile.   43
3-5.   All-False pattern: MMPI-2 content scales profile.   43
3-6.   Random responding patterns: MMPI-2 validity indicators profile.   46
3-7. F_p elevation: MMPI-2 basic scales profile.   49
3-8.   Fake-good pattern: MMPI-2 validity indicators.   54
3-9.   Defensive pattern: MMPI-2 validity indicators.   55
3-10.   Exaggerated symptom pattern: MMPI-2 validity indicators.   56
3-11.   Exaggerated symptom pattern: MMPI-2 validity indicators.   57
3-12.   Invalid exaggerated symptom pattern: MMPI-2 validity indicators.   58
3-13.   Alice's MMPI-2 validity pattern.   59
4-1.   MMPI-2 K-corrected basic scales profile.   61
4-2.   Uniform T-score distributions for Hs for normative and chronic pain men.   64
4-3.   Uniform T-score distributions for D for depressed inpatients and normals.   67
4-4.   Ann's MMPI-2 basic scales profile.   96
4-5.   Alice's MMPI-2 basic scales profile.   97
6-1.   Rena's MMPI-2 basic scales profile.   149
6-2.   Rena's MMPI-2 content scales profile.   149
6-3.   Alice's MMPI-2 content scales profile.   154
7-1.   Mr. Gabriel's MMPI-2 basic scales profile.   158
7-2.   Mr. Jenkins's MMPI-2 basic scales profile.   161
7-3.   Mr. Jenkins's MMPI-2 selected supplementary scales profile.   162
7-4.   Mr. Levin's MMPI-2 basic scales profile.   163
7-5.   Mr. Levin's MMPI-2 content scales profile.   164
7-6.   Ms. Levin's MMPI-2 basic scales profile.   164
7-7.   Ms. Levin's MMPI-2 content scales profile.   165
7-8.   Mr. Kevin E.'s MMPI-2 basic scales profile.   168
7-9.   Mr. Kevin E.'s MMPI-2 content scales profile.   169
8-1.   Alice's MMPI-2 basic scales profile.   201
8-2.   Alice's MMPI-2 content scales profile.   201
9-1.   Boys' normative sample plotted on three different norms (N = 805).   213

9-2.   Girls' normative sample plotted on three different norms (N = 815).   214
9-3.   Boys' clinical sample plotted on three different norms (N = 420).   215
9-4.   Girls' clinical sample plotted on three different norms (N = 293).   216
10-1.   Russ's MMPI-A basic scales profile.   235
10-2.   Lisa's MMPI-A basic scales profile.   237
10-3.   Jodi's MMPI-A basic scales profile.   243
10-4.   Elizabeth's MMPI-A basic scales profile.   243
10-5.   All-True response set: MMPI-A basic scales profile.   244
10-6.   All-True response set: MMPI-A content scales profile.   244
10-7.   All-False response set: MMPI-A basic scales profile.   245
10-8.   All-False response set: MMPI-A content scales profile.   246
10-9.   Tony's MMPI-A validity scales profile.   247
11-1.   Tony's MMPI-A basic scales profile.   272
12-1.   Tony's MMPI-A content scales profile.   300
13-1.   Tony's MMPI-A supplementary scales profile.   312
14-1.   Form of an MMPI-A interpretive report.   319
14-2.   Tony's MMPI-A basic scales profile.   326
14-3.   Tony's MMPI-A content scales profile.   327
14-4.   Tony's MMPI-A supplementary scales profile.   329
15-1.   Repeat of basic scales profile for Alice (Figure 4-5).   337
15-2.   Repeat of content scales profile for Alice (Figure 6-3).   338
15-3.   Computer-based interpretation of the MMPI-2 for Alice.   339
15-4.   Mr. Jenkins's MMPI-2 basic scales profile.   340
15-5.   Mr. Jenkins's MMPI-2 content scales profile.   341
15-6.   Mr. Jenkins's MMPI-2 supplementary scales profile.   341
15-7.   Computer-based interpretation of the MMPI-2 for Mr. Jenkins.   342
15-8.   Joe's Minnesota Report™ validity scales profile.   345
15-9.   Joe's Minnesota Report™ basic and supplementary scales profile.   346
15-10.   Joe's Minnesota Report™ content scales profile.   347
15-11.   Joe's Minnesota Report™ narrative.   348
15-12.   Eva's Minnesota Report™ basic and supplementary scales profile.   353
15-13.   Eva's Minnesota Report™ content scales profile.   354
15-14.   Eva's Minnesota Report™ personnel selection system
          screening report.   355
15-15.   Tony's Minnesota Report™ validity scales profile.   356
15-16.   Tony's Minnesota Report™ basic and supplementary scales profile.   357
15-17.   Tony's Minnesota Report™ content scales profile.   358
15-18.   Computer-based interpretation of Tony's MMPI-A profile.   359

Foreword
Raymond D. Fowler

Twenty-one years ago on a February afternoon I left my home in Tuscaloosa, Alabama, for St. Petersburg, Florida, to participate in one of the annual MMPI symposia that Jim Butcher has been organizing and directing since 1965. The weather changed from fog to drizzle to rain and finally to an ice storm, causing long delays on all flights connecting through Atlanta. What should have been a 2-hour trip had turned into a 14-hour ordeal by the time I reached the Tampa Bay airport at 3:00 A.M. I woke up the driver of the last taxi still left at the airport, negotiated terms, and settled down for a 35-mile ride to St. Petersburg. The taxi driver, now wide awake, was as eager to talk as I was to get a little sleep.

(Brightly) "What brings you to the Tampa Bay area?" he asked.

(Muttering) "A meeting," I answered.

"What kind of meeting?"

"A psychology meeting."

"What kind of psychology meeting?"

(Irritably) "THE MINNESOTA MULTIPHASIC PERSONALITY INVENTORY!"

(Cheerfully) "Are they ever going to restandardize that thing?"

This story, almost too good to be true (the taxi driver was, of course, a Minnesota graduate), has become a part of the MMPI lore. It seems appropriate to include it in this foreword, since Jim Butcher has told it at dozens of workshops, as have I. Jim and I have been friends and colleagues for almost 30 years, and we have co-authored articles and co-led workshops in various parts of the world. Carolyn Williams, who joined Jim's personal and professional life later, also became my friend and colleague as well a mainstay in the MMPI community. For Jim Butcher and Carolyn Williams, and even for their daughter Holly, the MMPI has been a family affair. A 1964 graduate of the University of North Carolina, where he worked with Grant Dahlstrom, Jim went to the University of Minnesota and initiated a flood of MMPI activities, including an active research program, numerous books, and the now-famous MMPI symposia and workshops that have instructed thousands of psychologists in the interpretation of the MMPI. Carolyn, a University of Georgia graduate, joined the Minnesota faculty in 1981 and began her own MMPI research program with an emphasis on adolescents.

Many people (including my taxi driver) complained for years about the failure to revise the MMPI, but no one did much about it until Jim Butcher began, almost 20 years ago, to encourage serious discussions among MMPI colleagues about the pros and cons of doing so. The need for a revision of the MMPI was apparent. Almost everyone agreed that it had serious flaws. Poor norms, clumsy wording, and outdated nosology were only a few of the charges leveled at the MMPI by friends and enemies alike. How could one justify the continued use of a test standardized 50 years ago on a population that was nonrepresentative even in the 1940s?

The disadvantages of a revision were just as apparent. How could one change the MMPI to any significant degree without jeopardizing the accumulated research and clinical work of a half century? The MMPI was the most widely used and most effective multipurpose instrument in the world, and major revisions could change all that. There was another, entirely understandable source of concern. Because good graduate courses and interpretation manuals were not available, many psychologists had to develop, through self-study and workshops, their own methods of MMPI interpretation. A new MMPI might threaten this painstakingly developed skill. Besides, why change it if it is working well?

Revising the MMPI took more than intelligence and perseverance; it also took raw courage. The task itself was daunting, requiring major time commitments and organizational skills. But even with the completion of the MMPI-2, the job was not over. A few MMPI loyalists hesitated to make the switch. In a discipline with few trustworthy instruments, we do not easily give up a sure thing, but the debates faded as the rapidly developing MMPI-2 literature confirmed the superiority of the revised test beyond question.

When I first began to work with psychological tests almost five decades ago, it was not easy to learn to interpret the MMPI. Neophyte Rorschachers could learn interpretation from excellent books by Walter Klopfer and Samual Beck or choose from numerous interpretive workshops available around the country. Not so for the aspiring MMPI interpreter. There were almost no MMPI courses in graduate programs, and most of the material covered in general personality texts provided little more than did the skimpy manual available at that time. There were few, if any, MMPI workshops, and most internships ignored the MMPI completely.

By the late 1950s, a lively underground information network had developed. Brief manuals prepared by relatively experienced interpreters for their own use and notes taken in the few available MMPI courses began to be circulated, usually as smudged mimeographed or, worse, rapidly fading purple ditto copies. Crude as they were, these humble documents taught most early MMPI interpreters their craft.

Most of these "underground" manuals were built around the concept of code types determined by the most elevated two or three clinical scales. The effectiveness of code types, demonstrated in a 1949 dissertation by George Guthrie, led to their adoption in much of MMPI research as well as in most MMPI interpretation. This method of classifying MMPI profiles was the basis of the majority of clinical, actuarial, and computer-based interpretation systems as well. The two-point code correlates were presented in Dahlstrom and Welsh's *Handbook* in 1960 and in the first two general MMPI texts by John Graham in 1977 and Roger Greene in 1980.

Users of the MMPI-2 and MMPI-A are fortunate that the first book on interpreting both these second-generation MMPI instruments was written by authors so intimately involved in their development. Jim Butcher played a major role in initiating the MMPI-2 and developing its norms, and he has supported it with extensive research. Carolyn Williams participated in the development of the MMPI-2 and, because of her expertise with adolescents, played a key role in the development of the MMPI-A.

Essentials of MMPI-2 and MMPI-A Interpretation should be in the library of every practitioner who uses these instruments. If such a book had been available for the MMPI, the test would probably have become the overwhelming choice of clinicians even sooner and more decisively than it did. Having such an excellent guide to interpretation greatly accelerated the adoption of the MMPI-2 and MMPI-A and continues to be a valuable resource for users of those instruments.

Preface to the Second Edition

Publication of the first edition of this book and the release of the MMPI-A marked the end of a decade of research for the MMPI Restandardization Project. We illustrated how much the Restandardization Project had been a part of our lives in the first edition's preface with a description of a dinner conversation we had with our daughter about a time before she was born. Holly, with all the resoluteness of a 3-year-old, informed us that there never was a time before her birth because she had always existed. Sensing what must have captivated Piaget when he observed his children's cognitive development, we interviewed Holly about the steadfastness of her belief:

"But, Holly, we can remember before you were born, and you were not here."
"I was too!"
"But we didn't see you."
"Well, I was at my office."
"Who was with you?"
"Nick" (her nephew, Jim's grandson).
"What were you doing?"
"Talking about the MMPI!"

This conversation took place 13 years ago. Holly is now 16, and Nick is in his second year of college. Our dinner conversations are less MMPI focused and more relevant to the preoccupations and activities of an enthusiastic and energetic teenager. However, we manage to find other times to discuss the gratifying experiences of the past 18 years of MMPI research since the beginning of the Restandardization Project.

Like the development of the original MMPI, work on the MMPI-2 and MMPI-A was carried out through partnerships among university researchers and practitioners in the field. Many psychologists, other mental health professionals, teachers, and school officials throughout the United States contributed to our studies. They recognized the MMPI's value in understanding and helping individuals in trouble and were quite willing to participate in research to modernize the long-established standard. We hope that this second edition of our book will benefit our partners in the field as continuing appreciation for their efforts in our research programs. We are also indebted to the thousands of people who volunteered their time as subjects in the many studies that served to develop the MMPI-2 and MMPI-A.

We are pleased to have been able to follow the steps of Starke Hathaway, J. C. McKinley, and Elio Monachesi. With each passing year of the MMPI Restandardization Project, we became more appreciative of the magnitude of their contributions to psychological assessment. That they did it without personal computers, word processing, and fax machines amazes us.

The University of Minnesota Press recognized that the MMPI was no longer just a "Minnesota test" when the MMPI Restandardization Committee was appointed in 1982. W. Grant Dahlstrom of the University of North Carolina and John R. Graham of Kent State University joined a Minnesotan on the committee, James N. Butcher. Auke Tellegen, also from the University of Minnesota, was appointed to the committee in 1986. This committee guided the research that resulted in the publication of the MMPI-2 and eventually the MMPI-A. In 1990, Beverly Kaemmer appointed the Adolescent Project Committee to advise the University of Minnesota Press on the final development of the MMPI-A. Robert Archer of the Eastern Virginia Medical School joined James Butcher and Auke Tellegen on this committee.

We greatly appreciate the assistance of our colleague Auke Tellegen, not only for his substantial contribution to the development of the MMPI-2 and MMPI-A with his uniform T scores and the VRIN and TRIN inconsistency scales but also for his assistance in the preparation of sections of this book dealing with those topics.

Our work on the MMPI-2 and MMPI-A content scales follows a recent tradition in personality assessment that Jerry S. Wiggins so ably pioneered with the Wiggins content scales for the original MMPI. His gracious welcome to our new scales and farewell to his own in the foreword of our MMPI-2 content scales monograph was moving. Likewise, Craig MacAndrew provided the legacy for our work by developing new alcohol and drug problem scales for the MMPI-2 and MMPI-A.

Our computerized interpretive systems for the MMPI-2 and MMPI-A were substantially influenced by Raymond Fowler's innovations in this area. He has contributed in many other ways as well. Over the years, he has always been supportive, encouraging, and someone we could rely on.

Many students volunteered their time in our research projects, worked long hours as research assistants (would you do just one more analysis? How about proofing this table again?), and chose to do their doctoral theses on topics related to the MMPI Restandardization Project. We are very grateful for their contributions. Their intellect, curiosity, and eagerness brought pleasure to our work. We say this even with memories like the time a research assistant neglected to make backup copies of a data file and left the diskette on the roof of a car driven through the streets of Minneapolis! The student was there afterward, helping us search through streets, alleys, and dumpsters looking for the missing floppy disk. We can laugh now.

We began the revision of this book not quite realizing how much research had been completed by other psychologists since the release of the MMPI-2 in 1989 and the MMPI-A in 1992. The extent of research on MMPI-2 and MMPI-A since their publication has been astounding. Hundreds of research papers were available for us to draw on in developing this revision. We very much appreciate Reneau Kennedy for providing some additional case material included in this edition.

We have two very special colleagues, collaborators, and friends who were very much part of our research on the MMPI-2 and MMPI-A. John R. Graham, in addition to being on the Restandardization Committee, served many other roles, and we benefited greatly from his efforts and thoughtfulness. It would be hard to imagine how these projects could have been completed without him. Yossef S. Ben-Porath joined the MMPI Project a bit later as an exceptionally talented student, quickly becoming an indispensable colleague. They are not only respected colleagues but also two of our closest friends and only an e-mail or MMPI meeting away.

We end our revision of this book with satisfaction (and relief), although it is likely that the future will see us again "talking about the MMPI."

Chapter 1

Objective Personality Assessment Using the MMPI-2 and MMPI-A

According to Starke Hathaway (1965), sheer frustration led him and J. C. McKinley to begin research in 1939 that eventually resulted in the publication of the MMPI. They developed the MMPI to assist themselves and others at the University of Minnesota Hospitals in the routine tasks of assessing and diagnosing patients with mental disorders. Other objective inventories of his day were too tied to psychological theories about the structure of personality to be useful, were developed with college students, or measured variables unrelated to psychopathology and thus were of little benefit to Hathaway in his work on an adult psychiatric service.

Despite the MMPI's origins in a single psychiatric service in Minnesota, it became the most widely used and researched objective personality inventory in the world (Lees-Haley, Smith, Williams & Dunn, 1996; Lubin, Larsen & Matarazzo, 1984; Piotrowski & Keller, 1992). Its use extended far beyond the University of Minnesota Hospitals into psychiatric clinics and hospitals across the United States. Very soon after its development, the MMPI was employed with patients in general medical settings, adolescents in schools, inmates in correctional facilities, individuals in alcohol and drug problem treatment units, military personnel, and eventually applicants in industrial settings who applied for highly responsible or stressful positions, such as airline pilot, police officer, or nuclear power plant operator. It also became the most widely used measure of psychopathology in psychological, psychiatric, and medical research studies.

The late 1940s and early 1950s saw the MMPI crossing national boundaries as well. Some of the first translations of the MMPI were developed for Italy, Germany, and Puerto Rico (Butcher, 1985). By 1976, over 50 foreign-language translations were available (Butcher & Pancheri, 1976). Cheung (1985; Cheung & Song, 1989), reporting her work on a Chinese version of the MMPI, described the advantages of using the MMPI in places such as Hong Kong or Beijing, where few standardized Chinese instruments existed to assist clinical psychologists in their work. Adopting and adapting a well-established instrument such as the MMPI was made possible by others' prior conceptual work and investigations into the test's psychometric properties. Given that other translations of the MMPI had passed cross-cultural methodological scrutiny (Butcher & Pancheri, 1976), Cheung (1985) indicated that adapting and validating the MMPI was more efficient than constructing entirely new indigenous instruments. This was particularly true in less industrialized places where professional resources were more limited. Others obviously felt the same because by 1989 there were over 140 MMPI translations in 46 countries.

What has contributed to the remarkable success and durability of the MMPI? One obvious answer is that the MMPI provides a useful and practical technique for assessing individuals who report mental health symptoms and problems. This likely accounts for the large number of research studies documenting the MMPI's reliability and validity. Because it provides information useful in predicting individual clients' problems and behaviors cost-effectively, clinicians are willing to cooperate in research projects using the MMPI. In fact, they frequently contribute to the MMPI research literature.

Starke Hathaway (1965) listed several structural features of the MMPI, in addition to its validity, that he thought accounted for its popularity:

> the provisions for some control over undesirable response patterns, detection of invalid records such as those from nonreaders, the use of simple language, the simplicity of administration and scoring, and, finally, the general clinical familiarity of the profile variables. (p. 463)

Other qualities contributed to the MMPI's reputation as a sound psychological assessment procedure. It provided reliable evaluations; that is, its scores were consistent across administrations. As Hathaway (1965) indicated, the MMPI also made it possible to evaluate the credibility of the person's self-report through the use of validity scales. Another important characteristic was that a person's score on an MMPI scale could be interpreted within a normative framework (e.g., the individual under consideration could be compared with others to determine whether his or her scores were low or high, whether the scores were extreme compared with normals, or whether his or her scores matched the pattern of known groups, such as those with depression or schizophrenic disorders).

Development of the MMPI

Hathaway and McKinley believed the best way to learn what was troubling an individual was to ask him or her. Consequently, they chose for their inventory statements with which the client could agree or disagree, using a "True" or "False" response. This approach involved a straightforward self-administered task that could be completed by individuals with a relatively low reading level (sixth grade) in a relatively brief time, usually an hour and a half. Hathaway and McKinley thought that patients who endorsed similar symptoms or items in the MMPI pool were diagnostically more alike than they were different. For example, an individual endorsing many symptoms related to having a depressed mood was likely to be more similar to other depressed patients than to other clinical groups. Hathaway and McKinley also thought that individuals endorsing more symptoms of a particular kind could be viewed as experiencing a more serious problem than those reporting fewer symptoms. To quantify this relationship between number of psychological symptoms and diagnostic similarity, they developed scales by which individuals could be compared on particular variables. A group of items endorsed in a defined direction constitutes a *scale*. The MMPI scales were conceived as measurable dimensions that reflect particular problems, such as depression or hypochondriasis.

Hathaway and McKinley rejected the view that items should be selected for specific personality scales according to content obviously related to the various personality attributes or symptom clusters. They considered the selection of scale items based on face validity, the general practice of test developers at the time, to be too subjective. Instead, Hathaway and McKinley developed the MMPI on the basis of item and scale validity. That is, they required that any item on a scale be assigned to a scale only if it objectively discriminated a given criterion group (e.g., individuals with depression) from their normative sample (i.e., healthy visitors to the University of Minnesota Hospitals). This approach was referred to as an *empirical scale-construction strategy.*

Hathaway and McKinley compiled a large pool of potential items (about 1,000) that were, for the most part, indicative of symptoms of mental disorders or other problems treated on their psychiatric service. They had no preconceived notion of whether a particular item was related to the constructs of interest. Instead, they empirically compared the responses of the normal subjects with those of groups of well-classified patients to determine which items would be included on a particular scale. Their objective approach came to be referred to as *blind,* or *dustbowl, empiricism.* It is important to realize, because it is often overlooked, that Hathaway and McKinley took great care in initially writing and ultimately choosing items for their pool as well as in selecting their criterion groups. These two important aspects of their procedure should not be considered "blind."

Hathaway and McKinley's empirical scale-construction method produced MMPI clinical scales that have high generality across diverse settings (Butcher, 1999; Graham, 1990) and across national boundaries (Butcher, 1996; Butcher & Pancheri, 1976). As mentioned before, the MMPI also became an important criterion measure in the objective study of psychopathology.

The Need to Revise the MMPI

The MMPI was not without problems. Hathaway (1965) indicated that the MMPI could be criticized for "its perpetuation of the Kraepelin-derived diagnostic nosology" (p. 462). These problems became more evident with the changes in psychiatric diagnosis, particularly with the transformations in the *Diagnostic and Statistical Manual of Mental Disorders* (American Psychiatric Association, 1952, 1968, 1980, 1987). Hathaway (1965) also noted problems with their method of selecting items for scales, but he but did not elaborate.

Over time, others noted problems with the original MMPI. Butcher (1972), Butcher and Owen (1978), and Butcher and Tellegen (1966) concluded that many of the items in the inventory were out of date or objectionable and recommended that the instrument be revised by deleting obsolete items and broadening the item pool to include more contemporary themes. Use of the original MMPI norms was also questioned. Butcher (1972) pointed out that the normative sample on which the original MMPI scales were based was not appropriate for many contemporary comparisons. The original normative sample was composed essentially of white, rural subjects from Minnesota, whereas the instrument was used across the United States with broadly diverse clients. Colligan, Osborne, Swenson, and Offord (1983) and Parkison and Fishburne (1984) conducted studies showing that the original MMPI norms were inappropriate for use with today's subjects.

Perhaps because the instrument worked so well and was used so widely, these problems were overlooked for over 40 years despite calls for a revision. During these years, other objective personality inventories were developed, although none gained the acceptance attained by the MMPI. With the passage of time and a growing awareness of the limitations of the original instrument, the University of Minnesota Press, the copyright holder, decided to revise the MMPI. This revision was framed as a modernization and restandardization of an instrument of demonstrated reliability and validity. Given the extensive research base supporting the use of the MMPI in psychological assessment, an adaptation or restandardization seemed much more appropriate than a radical revision. One of the goals of the restandardization was to maintain the acceptability of the original instrument in its restandardized versions: the MMPI-2 for adults and the MMPI-A for adolescents.

The MMPI Restandardization Project

In 1982, Beverly Kaemmer, MMPI manager at the University of Minnesota Press, appointed a committee to undertake the restandardization of the MMPI. James N. Butcher (University of Minnesota) and W. Grant Dahlstrom (University of North Carolina) began the work, joined later that year by John R. Graham (Kent State University) and in 1986 by Auke Tellegen (University of Minnesota). Beverly Kaemmer represented the University of Minnesota Press. The Restandardization Project's tasks were to modify the original test booklet and to conduct studies to develop new norms for the instrument. Funding for the project was provided by the University of Minnesota Press out of income from the sale of MMPI materials and from scoring and interpretive services.

In the first year of the project, the committee decided to develop two separate experimental booklets, one for adults (Form AX) and one for adolescents (Form TX), for use in data collection. Each experimental booklet included all the original MMPI items, some with minor wording improvements (Butcher, Dahlstrom, Graham, Tellegen & Kaemmer, 1989; Butcher et al., 1992). Items measuring new content (e.g., suicidal behavior, treatment readiness, Type A behaviors, and problematic alcohol and other drug use) were added to both experimental booklets. In addition, developmentally relevant items were added to the appropriate booklets (e.g., work adjustment items were added to Form AX and school adjustment items to Form TX). James Butcher, Grant Dahlstrom, and John Graham, with consultation from other MMPI experts, wrote the new items for Form AX. James Butcher and John Graham invited Carolyn Williams, experienced in work with adolescents, to participate with them in writing items for the Form TX booklet.

The MMPI Restandardization Committee decided that maintaining the integrity of the instrument during its restandardization could best be accomplished by keeping the MMPI validity and standard scales relatively intact. Otherwise, the half century of research supporting the use of these scales would not be relevant to the restandardized versions. Items constituting the validity and standard scales, except for a few objectionable items on four scales (four items on F, one on Hs, three on D, four on Mf, and one on Si), were retained in the MMPI-2. New items measuring additional clinical problems and applications were added to the inventory, replacing the items from the original booklet that did not score on the validity or standard scales. Thus, broader content coverage, allowing for new scale development, was accomplished without altering the original scales.

To modernize the MMPI, committee members and their collaborators collected extensive normative and clinical data using Form AX with adults and Form TX with adolescents. Data collected during the restandardization allowed committee members to assess what changes needed to be made in the instrument. These data also served as validity information for both the original and the newly developed scales. The decision to develop a separate version for adolescents was also based on data collected during the project. The MMPI Restandardization Committee established several major goals for the project:

1. Revise and modernize the MMPI items by deleting those that are objectionable, nonworking, or outdated and replace them with items addressing contemporary clinical problems and applications. Include items on the original validity and standard scales in the first part of the booklet.

2. Ensure continuity with the original instrument by keeping the MMPI validity, standard, and several supplementary scales virtually intact. (Studies show that the MMPI-2 versions of these scales are comparable to the original MMPI versions and thus can be considered equivalent scales [Ben-Porath & Butcher, 1989a, 1989b]).

3. Develop new scales to address problems that were not covered in the original MMPI.

4. Collect new, randomly solicited samples of adults and adolescents, representative of the population of the United States, to develop age-appropriate norms.

5. Develop new normative distributions for the adult and adolescent scales that would better reflect clinical problems and would resolve the problem of nonuniformity in percentile classification that occurred with the original MMPI scales (i.e., T scores at a given value were not equivalent percentiles across scales).

6. Collect a broad range of clinical data for evaluating changes to be made in the original scales and for validating the new scales.

After the publication in 1989 of the MMPI-2 for adults (Butcher et al., 1989), Beverly Kaemmer of the University of Minnesota Press appointed a new committee to determine whether an adolescent form of the MMPI was needed. James N. Butcher, Auke Tellegen, and Robert Archer (Eastern Virginia Medical University) formed this committee. John R. Graham, Carolyn L. Williams, and Yossef S. Ben-Porath continued to work as Butcher's collaborators on several research projects related to the development of the MMPI-A. The MMPI-A manual was published in 1992 (Butcher et al., 1992).

Development of the MMPI-2

The MMPI-2 normative sample consists of 2,600 subjects (1,462 women and 1,138 men, ages 18 through the adult years), sampled from seven regions of the United States (California, Minnesota, North Carolina, Ohio, Pennsylvania, Virginia, and Washington). The normative sample was balanced for gender and demographic characteristics, such as ethnic group membership. Normative subjects were randomly solicited, initially contacted by letter, and asked to come to a prearranged testing site for completion of the test battery. All subjects were administered the 704-item experimental Form AX of the MMPI, a biographical questionnaire, and a questionnaire assessing significant life events in the past 6 months.

Heterosexual couples (N = 800) were also included in the normative sample. Each member of the couple was administered Form AX, the Dyadic Adjustment Questionnaire (Spanier & Filsinger, 1983), and a revised version of the Katz Adjustment Scale (Katz, 1968). This information provided validity descriptors for the MMPI-2 scales with nonclinical samples.

In addition to the normative study described in the manual for the MMPI-2, a number of other normative and clinical studies provided validation for the MMPI-2 standard scales and the new content scales. These included studies in inpatient psychiatric facilities (Ben-Porath, Butcher & Graham, 1991), alcohol treatment settings (Greene, Weed, Butcher, Arredondo & Davis, 1992; Levenson et al., 1990; Weed, Butcher, Ben-Porath & McKenna, 1992), mothers at risk for child abuse (Egeland, Erickson, Butcher & Ben-Porath, 1991), outpatients in marital distress (Hjemboe & Butcher, 1991), antisocial personalities (Lilienfeld, 1991), posttraumatic stress–disordered veterans (Litz et al., 1991), older men (Butcher et al., 1991), military personnel (Butcher, Jeffrey, et al., 1990), and college students (Butcher, Graham, Dahlstrom & Bowman, 1990).

Present-day subjects, including individuals from the new normative sample, tend to endorse more items in the pathological direction, thus producing higher mean scores (approximately 5 T-score points on each scale) than the original MMPI normative sample. This probably occurs because a somewhat different set of instructions are used today. Originally, item omissions were allowed, even encouraged. In current practice, test administrators tend to encourage completing all the items. Consequently, the original MMPI norms are inaccurate for today's test usage. The new norms, based on responses obtained using contemporary instructions, should allow for more accurate assessment.

The original MMPI norms were developed using a linear T-score transformation (Hathaway & McKinley, 1940, 1942a). In an effort to make the scales comparable, the T-score distributions were assigned a mean of 50 and a standard deviation of 10. This approach was followed during the restandardization, with an important modification that solved the problem of nonequivalency of percentile values across scales that occurred with the original linear T scores.

The MMPI-2 T scores, referred to as *uniform T scores*, were developed by Auke

Tellegen (Tellegen & Ben-Porath, 1992) using the eight clinical scales (1, 2, 3, 4, 6, 7, 8, and 9) to constitute a composite distribution. For these scales, raw scores were converted into the corresponding uniform T scores by regressing raw scores on percentile-equivalent uniform T scores. Then uniform T scores were derived, separate for men and women, for the 8 clinical scales and the 15 MMPI-2 content scales (Butcher et al., 1989).

In interpreting original MMPI profiles, clinicians followed the strategy of considering a T score of 70 the point at which an elevation was clinically significant. This cutoff was selected because it was thought to fall at a percentile rank of 95 for each MMPI scale. However, in practice, percentile equivalents for a given T score varied across scales. In clinical studies with the MMPI-2, a T score of 65 proved to be the optimal score level for separating known clinical groups from the MMPI-2 normative sample (Butcher, 1989c; Keller & Butcher, 1991). Consequently, a T score of 65 or greater was chosen to demarcate the "clinical range" on the MMPI-2 (Butcher et al., 1989). On the MMPI-2, a T score of 65 falls uniformly at the 92nd percentile for the eight clinical scales and the MMPI-2 content scales.

Even though the MMPI Restandardization Committee sought to maintain continuity with the original MMPI by keeping the validity and clinical scales relatively intact, the MMPI-2 is a different instrument in several other respects. The revised instrument contains new items and fewer items that are objectionable to test takers. The MMPI-2 norms are based on a more diverse and ethnically balanced sample and are more appropriate for present-day test users. A number of new scales were added to aid in psychological assessment. New validity scales assessing test-taking attitudes have been incorporated, and several new measures focus on clinical problems (e.g., Addiction Acknowledgment scale and Marital Distress scale) not assessed in the original MMPI.

A person's endorsement of content about him- or herself is an important source of clinical information in MMPI-2 and MMPI-A interpretation. Reliance on MMPI item content has increased over the last 20 years despite the "dustbowl empiricism" characterizing its original development. Content scales (i.e., homogeneous groupings of items measuring single dimensions such as anger or bizarre thinking) are relatively easy to understand, to interpret, and to explain to others (Burisch, 1984). Wiggins (1966) developed a set of homogeneous scales for assessing the content dimensions contained in the original MMPI. However, a number of items on several of these scales were deleted in the MMPI revision process. Moreover, the MMPI-2 contains many new items not represented in the original Wiggins scales.

Content scales for the MMPI-2, described more fully in Chapter 7, were developed by Butcher, Graham, Williams, and Ben-Porath (1990) to assess the main content dimensions in the revised inventory. The MMPI-2 content scales were derived by a multimethod, multistage scale-construction strategy employing both rational and statistical procedures to ensure content homogeneity and strong statistical properties. The MMPI-2 content scales assess symptomatic behavior (Anxiety, Fears, Obsessiveness, Depression, Health Concerns, Bizarre Mentation), personality factors (Type A Behavior, Cynicism), externalizing behavior (Anger, Antisocial Practices), negative self-view (Low Self-Esteem), and clinical problem areas (Family Problems, Work Interference, Negative Treatment Indicators).

The MMPI-2 content scales have been shown to have strong internal psychometric properties along with external validity. For example, comparisons between the MMPI-2 content scales and the clinical scales using the same behavioral descriptors show the content scales to be of equal or greater external validity than the original MMPI clinical scales (Ben-Porath et al., 1991; Butcher, Graham, Williams & Ben-Porath, 1990).

Development of the MMPI-A

When the MMPI Restandardization Committee initiated the revision of the original MMPI in 1982, they did not immediately decide to develop a separate version of the instrument for adolescents. There was a consensus at the time that several problems limited the use of the original instrument with adolescents. For example, the MMPI items were written from an adult perspective and were administered to adolescents with no modifications, the MMPI scales were not developed using samples of adolescents or considering developmental issues but were simply assumed to be appropriate for adolescents even though they were derived from samples of adults, originally there were no adolescent norms for the MMPI, and interpretations for adolescents were often based on research with adults. The history of the MMPI's use with adolescents and the problems that arose are discussed in more detail in Chapter 9. Despite these problems, committee members recognized that the instrument was used extensively with adolescents. In fact, Starke Hathaway administered the MMPI to over 10,000 adolescents in Minnesota schools, demonstrating its ability to predict delinquency and other problems in youth (e.g., Hathaway & Monachesi, 1953a, 1957, 1963; Hathaway, Reynolds & Monachesi, 1969).

Committee members decided to study whether a separate version of the MMPI for adolescents would prove useful and valid through the use of the experimental Form TX for adolescents. Because the adolescent normative sample for the original MMPI (Marks, Seeman & Haller, 1974) was not representative of the ethnic diversity in the United States, an important goal of data collection was to obtain a large, diverse normative sample of youth from several regions of the United States. The subjects for the adolescent MMPI norms were obtained through schools in several regions of the United States, including California, Minnesota, Ohio, North Carolina, New York, Pennsylvania, Virginia, and Washington. These testing locations were chosen to maximize the possibility of obtaining a balanced sample of subjects according to geographic region, rural-urban residence, and ethnic background.

The 704-item Form TX was administered to 815 girls and 805 boys in the normative sample and was also employed in an extensive clinical evaluation study (see Williams & Butcher, 1989a, 1989b; Williams, Butcher, Ben-Porath & Graham, 1992). The final MMPI-A normative and clinical samples were more diverse in background than were the previous ones that included only white subjects (Marks et al., 1974). The MMPI-A normative sample consisted of 805 boys and 815 girls, ages 14 to 18.

The decision to develop MMPI-A norms beginning at age 14 was pragmatic. Although efforts were made to include youth as young as 12 and 13 in the sample, some school administrators were reluctant to grant permission to test these younger individuals with Form TX for several reasons, including its length, general adult orientation, and objectionable content (particularly items about sexual behavior). Data obtained from the limited sample of 12- and 13-year-olds who were tested revealed more invalid test protocols in this age range. Rather than delaying the publication of the MMPI-A until a larger and more representative sample of 12- and 13-year-olds could be obtained, the committee decided to use the data available to develop the test for 14- to 18-year-olds. Chapter 2 presents more information about using the MMPI-A with 12- and 13-year-olds.

The MMPI-A booklet consists of 478 items, many of which were on the original MMPI and were also included in the MMPI-2. However, a number of new items were added to the booklet to address adolescent problems and behaviors, such as attitudes about school and parents, peer-group influence, and eating problems. These items were distributed throughout the booklet in order to make the instrument more relevant to adolescents. Furthermore, items about youthful behaviors that were worded in the past tense on the MMPI and MMPI-2 were changed to the present tense for the MMPI-A.

Several item level changes were made in the MMPI-2 and the MMPI-A. Of the original items, 82 with problematic wording were rewritten for the MMPI-2; 70 items in the MMPI-A booklet are rewritten versions of original items. MMPI-2 items used to develop the Negative Treatment Indicators content scale were included in the MMPI-A, as were additional items about alcohol and drug problems. The objectionable items eliminated from the MMPI-2 were also eliminated on the MMPI-A. In addition, items referring to sexual behavior, objectionable in school settings and not necessarily having the same psychological meaning for adolescents as for adults, were eliminated. Finally, to shorten the MMPI-A booklet, items unique to the Fears content scale were eliminated (resulting in this scale's deletion from the MMPI-A), as were some scale 5 and scale 0 items.

Continuity was maintained between the MMPI and MMPI-A for validity scales L and K, the standard scales (the eight clinical scales and scales 5 and 0), the Mac-Andrew Alcoholism Scale (MAC-R), and supplementary scales A and R (Butcher et al., 1992). However, the psychometric properties of the adult-derived scales were investigated using adolescent samples, resulting in some scale changes. The F scale required extensive revision to ensure that it performed as an infrequency measure for adolescents. Statistical analyses using adolescent samples and rational procedures that included a developmental perspective were used in developing the MMPI-A content scales and the VRIN and TRIN inconsistency scales. Three of the MMPI-A content scales were developed primarily using the new adolescent-specific items (School Problems, Low Aspirations, and Alienation). The Family Problems (A-fam) scale was improved with the addition of adolescent-specific content. A new scale, Conduct Problems (A-con), was substituted for the MMPI-2 Antisocial Practices (ASP) scale on the MMPI-A when inadequate empirical validity was found for ASP with adolescents (Williams et al., 1992).

MMPI-A norms, like the MMPI-2 norms, were based on the uniform T-score transformation developed by Auke Tellegen, which ensured percentile equivalence across the different MMPI scale scores (Butcher et al., 1992). Both the MMPI-2 and the MMPI-A norms were developed using the same target distribution, ensuring

Table 1-1. Reasons for Acceptance of the MMPI-2 and MMPI-A in Psychological Assessment

The MMPI-2 and MMPI-A are easy to administer and are available in printed booklets, on cassette tapes, and by computer administration. It usually takes between 1 and 1½ hours for adults to complete and 1 hour for adolescents.
Individuals self-administer the test by simply responding T (True) or F (False) to items on the basis of whether the statement applies to them. The items are written so that individuals with a sixth-grade reading level can understand them.
Many foreign language versions of the MMPI-2 and MMPI-A are in use.
The MMPI-2 and MMPI-A are relatively easy to score. Item responses for each scale are tallied and recorded on profile sheets. Scoring can be delegated to clerical staff to conserve more costly professional time. Computerized scoring programs are available that enhance the scoring process (i.e., they reduce errors and score the numerous available scales quickly).
The MMPI-2 and MMPI-A provide several response attitude measures that appraise the test-taking attitudes of the client, including several not available on the original MMPI. Any self-report instrument is susceptible to manipulation, either conscious or unconscious; thus, it is imperative to assess what the client's test-taking attitudes were at the time the answer sheet was completed.
The MMPI-2 and MMPI-A are objectively interpreted instruments. Empirically validated scales possess clearly established meanings. A high score on a scale is associated with behavioral characteristics. These scale "meanings" are easily taught and objectively applied to clients. The established correlates for the scales allow them to be interpreted objectively, even by computer.
MMPI-2 and MMPI-A scales have good reliability (i.e., are quite stable over time). With well-established scale reliability, these revised instruments are considered effective in settings, such as forensic assessments, where good test reliability is a necessary characteristic.
The MMPI-2 and MMPI-A provide clear, valid descriptions of people's problems, symptoms, and personality characteristics. Scale elevations and code-type descriptions provide a terminology that enables clinicians to describe patients clearly. To say that a client possesses "high 4 characteristics" or exhibits features of a "2-7" communicates very specific information to other psychologists.
MMPI-2 and MMPI-A scores enable the practitioner to predict future behaviors and responses to different treatment approaches, as was the case for the original MMPI. For example, if the client's MMPI-2 profile is defined most prominently by scale 2 (Depression), it is likely that treatment, such as cognitive-behavioral therapy or antidepressant medication, will bring about positive change and a commensurate lowering of the scale 2 score.
The MMPI-2 and MMPI-A profiles provide a valuable method for providing test feedback about personality characteristics, symptoms, and so on to clients.

percentile equivalence across the two forms. Thus, as a person ages, his or her MMPI-A and MMPI-2 T scores can be compared directly. The same cutoff for clinical interpretations (i.e., a T score of 65) is recommended for the MMPI-A as for the MMPI-2. However, for adolescents, clinicians are advised to consider scales elevated in the 60 to 64 T-score range as yielding potentially useful descriptors.

The remainder of this book provides information about using and interpreting the MMPI-2 and the MMPI-A. The original MMPI is no longer available for clinical use. Publication was discontinued in September 1999 to avoid interpretive confusion that can result from having available two versions of the same test. Table 1-1 provides the reasons the MMPI-2 and MMPI-A are so widely accepted in psychological assessment. Chapter 2 addresses both MMPI-2 and MMPI-A concerns. However, the MMPI-A is sufficiently different from the MMPI-2 that it is dealt with separately in Chapters 9 to 14.

Highlight Summary: The MMPI-2 and MMPI-A

The MMPI was originally developed by Hathaway and McKinley to aid in diagnostic screening. Hathaway and Monachesi (1953a) provided the following description:

> The MMPI is a psychometric instrument designed ultimately to provide, in a single test, scores on all the more clinically important phases of personality. In devising the instrument, the point of view determining the importance of a trait was that of a clinical or personnel worker who wishes to assay those traits commonly characteristic of psychological abnormality. (p. 13)

The instrument became the most widely used personality instrument in psychological assessment. Its adoption in numerous countries outside the United States indicates a strong generalization of validity across cultural settings.

Problems with the original MMPI became obvious as the years advanced and as the applications expanded beyond the original purpose of the instrument. In 1982, the test publisher, the University of Minnesota Press, began a program of research and revision that culminated in two separate but overlapping and parallel forms of the MMPI: the MMPI-2 for adults and the MMPI-A for adolescents.

The MMPI-2 is a revised version of the instrument in which the validity and standard scales have been kept virtually intact. In addition, a number of new scales for expanded clinical applications have been developed. New norms, based on a large, representative sample of normals (N = 2,600), provide a more relevant comparison sample for today's test applications. A number of validity studies have documented the MMPI-2's effectiveness as a replacement for the original MMPI in the assessment of adults.

The adolescent version of the MMPI, the MMPI-A, was developed to eliminate many of the problems psychologists found in using the original MMPI with adolescents, such as too few items with adolescent-specific content, absence of specific scales for adolescents, and norms that were out of date and not representative. The item pool for the MMPI-A does not contain objectionable items, and it includes content relating specifically to adolescent problems. Several new scales, such as School Problems and Conduct Problems, were developed to address difficulties that adolescents experience. Finally, new norms were developed on a contemporary sample of adolescents from several regions of the United States to provide a more relevant comparison group for adolescents.

Chapter 2

Administering, Scoring, and Profiling the MMPI-2 and MMPI-A

The selection of test administration and processing options for the MMPI-2 and MMPI-A depend on the practitioner's preference, facilities, and equipment and the time available for processing test results. This chapter provides an overview of the various test administration and processing procedures, detailing the relative merits of each format and indicating possible limitations. Because MMPI-A procedures generally parallel those for the MMPI-2, separate descriptions are provided only when they differ, as they do in administering the test to adolescents.

Selecting the Proper Form

The MMPI-A is recommended for adolescents ages 14 through 18; the MMPI-2 is recommended for use with adults from age 18 onward. An important question arises when the individual to be tested is 18, when either the MMPI-A or the MMPI-2 can be used. The practitioner needs to determine which form to administer, depending on the individual's life circumstances (e.g., whether he or she is still in high school, in college, in the military, or living independently from parents) and the questions to be addressed in the assessment. The psychologist may administer either form with confidence, but the individual's T scores and interpretation will vary for a given set of raw scores, depending on which comparison group is chosen. Clinicians working with 18-year-olds should be aware of how the MMPI-2 and MMPI-A norm sets can produce different T scores based on the same raw score. In general, use of the MMPI-2 norms will result in slightly higher T scores for the standard scales than would the use of the MMPI-A norms (Gumbiner, 1997; Shaevel & Archer, 1996). For example, a young man's raw score of 24 on the Pd scale will give a T score of 66 on the MMPI-2 and a T score of 57 on the MMPI-A. This should be considered when interpreting the test for 18-year-olds and may reflect how the persistence of some behaviors from adolescence into early adulthood may signify greater likelihood of problems. On the other hand, there are significant changes in life circumstances and development for most 18-year-olds, and pathology suggested by MMPI-2 results may be more transitory for these younger adults. We do not recommend plotting MMPI-2 or MMPI-A scores on both norm sets for 18-year-olds, as have others (Archer, 1997a; Shaevel & Archer, 1996). Although some scales have essentially the same items on both forms, not all do.

Clinicians should make the decision of which version is most appropriate for a given 18-year-old and use the norms derived for that version. In general, the MMPI-A item content is more appropriate for 18-year-olds still living at home with parents and attending high school. The MMPI-2 is more appropriate for 18-year-olds living away from their parents' home, either in college or employed full time, although Gumbiner (1997) argues that the MMPI-A may be more useful for 18-year-old college men because of possibly delayed maturation and the greater pathology observed on the MMPI-2 in volunteer men compared to 18-year-old women. However, because 18-year-olds are included in the norms for both instruments, either version can be used; the decision lies with the clinician.

There may be circumstances when practitioners are asked to interpret an MMPI-2 or MMPI-A profile when they are not available to ensure that the age-appropriate version is administered. If the individual being evaluated is not available for retesting with the appropriate version, the first step is to inform the referral source of this problem so that it is not repeated with other clients. Next, the client's raw scores can be converted to the age-appropriate version by plotting them on the profile sheet of the appropriate form using the following procedures.

MMPI-2 raw scores can be converted to usable MMPI-A raw scores by dropping MMPI-2 items that do not appear in the MMPI-A and plotting the standard scale scores on the MMPI-A profile sheet. The F score presents the greatest complication for the basic scales (see Chapters 9 and 10). In this case, the F items on the MMPI-A, appearing mostly on F_1, should be used as the infrequency measure. Remember that the K correction is not used on the MMPI-A profile. A similar process can be followed for some of the supplementary scales and content scales appearing on both versions of the instrument (see Chapters 12 and 13). However, the supplementary scales and content scales specific to the MMPI-A will not be available (e.g., Alcohol and Drug Problem Proneness, Adolescent-Conduct Problems, Adolescent-School Problems, Adolescent-Low Aspirations, Adolescent-Alienation). The MMPI-2 and MMPI-A manuals provide information about the item-scale membership needed to accomplish these MMPI-2 to MMPI-A conversions.

The conversion process from MMPI-A to MMPI-2 is more complicated. Raw scores from some MMPI-A scales will be the same as raw scores for the MMPI-2 (see Tables 9-4 to 9-6). However, scores for scales L, F, Pd, Mf, Sc, and Si need to be prorated because there are fewer items on these scales in the MMPI-A than there are in the MMPI-2. Again, the MMPI-2 and MMPI-A manuals provide the information needed to determine item-scale memberships. The raw score for F_1 on the MMPI-A should be prorated to become the F scale on the MMPI-2; F_2 cannot be converted because many of the items are not in the MMPI-2. However, if F_2 is elevated, the supplementary scales and content scales should not be interpreted (see Chapter 10). If MMPI-A scores are used to estimate MMPI-2 scores, it is important to K-correct the scores before plotting them on the MMPI-2 profile. Only the supplementary scales and content scales with substantial item overlap (see Chapter 9) should be converted. Many important scales cannot be converted because of insufficient item overlap. These conversion procedures are cumbersome and have the potential for introducing error into the assessment process, arguing for appropriate instrument choice at the time of administration, not later.

Questions may also arise about the appropriateness of administering the

MMPI-2 or MMPI-A to individuals outside the age range used to develop the instrument. Is it appropriate to use the MMPI-2 for adolescents 17 years and under or the MMPI-A for adults 19 years and older? In some cases, convenience may argue for substituting the MMPI-2 for the MMPI-A (or vice versa)—for example, when clinics serving adults occasionally get a younger adolescent for assessment and do not have an MMPI-A booklet or answer sheet available. Others may have more substantive arguments for substituting for the age-appropriate version of the instrument for a particular client. Consider the case of a 16-year-old boy being tried as an adult for a capital crime. If the courts determine that the youth is to be treated as an adult in their procedures, should he be evaluated with the MMPI-2? What about a 23-year-old brain-injured woman whose cognitive abilities and emotional development are estimated to be at a 12- to 13-year-old level? Is the adolescent-based MMPI-A more appropriate?

The test manuals for each instrument are very clear about recommending the use of the MMPI-2 with adolescents or the MMPI-A with adults:

> It is inappropriate to use either instrument to make individual predictions for those outside the age range of the instrument.

Although the MMPI-2 and MMPI-A are comparable measures of psychopathology, they are not substitutes for each other. Earlier MMPI research (e.g., Archer, 1987; Hathaway & Monachesi, 1953a, 1963; Marks, Seeman & Haller, 1974) and information from the MMPI Restandardization Project pointed to the need for separate versions of the MMPI for adults and adolescents (e.g., Butcher, Dahlstrom, Graham, Tellegen & Kaemmer, 1989; Butcher et al., 1992; Williams & Butcher, 1989b; Williams, Butcher, Ben-Porath & Graham, 1992).

A final age-related question is whether the MMPI-A can be administered to those younger than 14 years of age. We have used the MMPI with adolescents as young as 12 and 13 years (Williams, 1986; Williams & Butcher, 1989a, 1989b). However, 12- and 13-year-old adolescents were excluded from the MMPI-A Restandardization Project's normative sample because they produced a greater number of invalid profiles than did older adolescents and we did not have an adequate number to include them in the normative sample (see Chapter 1). We recommend that clinicians consider whether a 12- or 13-year-old has the reading ability, breadth of experiences, and patience to complete an MMPI-A. If it is successfully administered to a 12- or 13-year-old, it should be scored using the norms provided in the test manual (Butcher et al., 1992).

We recommend that the norms for 13-year-old boys and girls developed by Archer (1997a) not be used for clinical decision making for several reasons. They were derived from a very small sample (81 boys and 144 girls), with no descriptions provided of the data collection methods or demographic characteristics of the sample. The T scores used linear rather than the uniform T-score transformations for scoring the MMPI-A scales. No studies suggest that separate norms are needed for 12- and 13-year-olds. The MMPI-A Project Committee did not endorse the development of separate norms for 13-year-olds.

Chapter 9 presents more information about the differences in adult and adolescent responses to the MMPI leading to the decision to develop a separate version for adolescents. The descriptors and other interpretive information presented in this book are based on the assumption that an age-appropriate version of the instrument is used. There is no evidence supporting the accuracy of these descriptors and interpretations when the age-inappropriate version of the instrument is used. Convenience, judicial decisions to try an adolescent in an adult court, brain-injured adults, and similar rationales do not provide the necessary empirical support for making predictive statements about the individuals being assessed with an age-inappropriate MMPI version.

One final consideration with respect to choice of instrument to use is the question of whether the client can read and understand English well enough to respond to the items. A sixth-grade English-language reading level is required to comprehend the item content. Many individuals for whom English is a second language can read and understand the MMPI-2 and MMPI-A items. For those who cannot, a number of foreign-language versions are available for use. For example, Hispanic test booklets are available for use with adults and adolescents from Spanish-speaking countries who have recently arrived in the United States or who, for other reasons, are fluent only in Spanish.

Administering the MMPI-2 and MMPI-A

Some general test administration issues warrant discussion before we turn to specific aspects of MMPI-2 and MMPI-A test administration. The test should be administered in a professional manner to encourage a serious, task-oriented attitude on the part of the test taker. Whether the inventory is being administered individually or in a group setting, care needs to be taken to ensure that the individual knows what is expected of him or her in the test situation.

A comfortable, private, and supervised setting should be provided for the client taking the MMPI-2 or MMPI-A. Although space limitations may require modifications of test administration procedures, clients should have enough work space to feel that their responses can be made privately, without concern about their answers being observed. This is especially important if the tests are group administered. The inventory should not be given to individuals to complete in an unsupervised setting because it is not possible to ensure that the person being tested actually took the test (Pope, 1990). It is never appropriate to send an MMPI-2 or MMPI-A booklet home with an individual because it is impossible to ensure accuracy, privacy, and confidentiality of the responses.

It is desirable to explain the reasons for administering the MMPI-2 or MMPI-A before this is done. In some clinics, testing may be performed by trained personnel before the patient is actually seen by a psychologist or psychiatrist. In such settings, care must be taken to ensure that the person responsible for the assessment communicates clearly to the client the reason for testing. Clients who are simply handed the booklets and told to respond to the test items may misconstrue the purposes of the testing, which could compromise the validity of their self-report.

The test should be administered by someone trained in giving standardized test instructions. Problems in profile interpretation arise if the test taker has received vague or nonstandard instructions. Deviating from the instructions on the booklet should be avoided or carefully evaluated before decisions based on the test results are made. Consult the MMPI-2 and MMPI-A booklets for test instructions.

Special Administration Considerations for Adults

In some settings, such as personnel screening, use of the MMPI-2 is complicated by defensive response styles or the natural desire for applicants to present themselves in a positive light. For example, applicants for jobs as airline pilots typically do not endorse many psychological problems, tending to be quite defensive. When encountering defensive profiles, some assessors attempt to obtain more valid records by having applicants retake the test after alerting them to the fact that they were initially "too defensive" and produced unusable results. Characteristically, when retested with these instructions, applicants produce less defensive profiles.

In an effort to obtain more cooperative response attitudes in a personnel screening situation, Fink and Butcher (1972) conducted a study with college students taking the MMPI in a simulated personnel situation in which they altered the test instructions as follows:

> The following personality inventory is made up of many statements; you are to decide whether the statements are mostly true as applied to you or mostly false, and then fill in the appropriate spot on your answer sheet. In taking the test, some people have been concerned about certain things. For example, some people wonder how honest they have to be in responding to the items. In the development of the inventory, several scales were constructed to allow the interpreter to evaluate test-taking attitudes. In other words, people who give an overly virtuous picture of themselves or people who try to appear more psychologically disturbed than they are, are easily detected. Thus, their test protocols are invalid and have to be discarded.
>
> It is also important to realize that this inventory was developed as a way of measuring individual personality traits not just to detect if a person is insane or not. We all know that every person is different, that is, has a different personality, and that they are better suited for certain things because of this. This test helps a psychologist understand what an individual's personality is like, and, by this, enable him (or her) to advise and help in a more efficient manner.
>
> Some of the statements may seem unrelated to anything about your personality, and other items may seem too personal. A word then, about how these items were chosen. A large list of statements was given to a group of normal people and to people suffering from many kinds of personality problems. Then, the statements that were answered with different frequency by the two groups were selected as a scale, and it was shown that people who have certain kinds of personality structures will answer these items in similar ways. . . . So the important thing to remember is that test interpretation does not involve reading your specific responses. Scoring involves simply placing a scoring stencil over the answer sheet and counting the responses for each personality scale. This allows us to compare your total responses on each scale with other people.

We hope that you will answer all the items, unless they really do not apply to you.

The experimental group of subjects was given these altered instructions, and a second group of control subjects was given traditional instructions before testing. In addition, subjects were given a follow-up questionnaire:

Imagine that you had been asked to take this test as part of the selection procedure in a job application.
1. Would you have felt that some of the items were (highly offensive, mildly offensive, not offensive)? Circle one.
2. In your opinion, would this test constitute an invasion of privacy? (Yes, No, Unsure)
3. Would you feel (highly anxious, mildly anxious, not anxious) about the results of the test?

The results of the study indicated no significant mean MMPI standard scale differences between the two conditions, suggesting that the indicators of psychopathology did not differ significantly. However, the subjects in the special instructions experimental group were less defensive and acknowledged greater willingness to report problems than did the subjects who received traditional instructions. In addition, the special instructions experimental group, in posttest questionnaires, reported that they viewed the test as less offensive, and fewer of them thought the test was an invasion of privacy.

In a more recent study, Butcher, Morfit, Rouse, and Holden (1997) extended the Fink and Butcher study in a personnel screening context. Airline pilot applicants for a major airline who presented themselves as extremely defensive (e.g., high L or K scores) on the test were given the opportunity to retake the test. Those choosing to retake the test were given further information about the test; for example, they were informed that the MMPI-2 has measures that appraise test defensiveness and that they had produced an invalid record. They were encouraged to retake the test and provide a more frank self-appraisal. On the second administration, the majority of applicants produced valid profiles without significantly increasing their elevations on clinical scales. However, 14 percent of the applicants did produce significant scale elevations the second time. These results showed that some applicants do apparently "mask" psychological problems in the application process that can be detected on retest under conditions of altered instructions.

Overall, the results of these studies have shown that special instructions explaining the psychological test procedures for detecting "self-protective" responding and giving reassurance regarding its use can decrease defensiveness and lower resentment toward the test-taking situation. However, a recent study by Butcher, Atlis, and Fang (1999) found that simply altering the MMPI-2 instructions on the test booklet to try to promote more frank responding did not by itself produce profiles that were substantially different from those taken under standard conditions. In an analog study with college students, the authors altered the MMPI-2 instructions to inform the subjects of the presence of measures to detect defensive or faked responding and encouraging them to respond honestly. The study compared the responses of people who had no inherent motivation to deceive the examiners who were administered the test under altered instructions with people who took the test under standard instructions. The results showed that the altered instructions did not result in appreciable profile differences in a sample of individuals who had no apparent motivation to present in a particular way, such as in a personnel screening context or a family custody evaluation.

The use of altered instructions can serve to detect some problems in defensive clients. In clinical populations where the practitioner might be interested in detecting invalidating response motivation, it should be remembered that the norms for the test were collected using standard instructions. If altered instructions are used, the practitioner needs to address the possible influences of this change in the test interpretation.

Special Administration Considerations for Adolescents

As noted earlier, testing with adolescents presents some special problems. Additional care needs to be taken to ensure that an adolescent approaches the test situation with an appropriate, task-oriented mind-set and a clear understanding of what is expected. Moreover, it is important to ensure that the testing atmosphere, especially in group testing, is conducive to concentration. The following procedures are recommended:

1. Ensure that the adolescent is a willing participant in the testing and approaches the task in a cooperative manner. The test administrator should take time in the beginning to explain the reasons for the testing and answer any questions the adolescent might have.

2. Ensure that the testing situation is private and free from intrusions, for example, from distractions created by other adolescents in the testing room. The adolescent should be given ample time and freedom from interference to concentrate on the questions.

3. Ensure that the adolescent understands the test instructions. The proctor should go over the test instructions carefully, making certain that the adolescent has the directions clearly in mind. It is very important to monitor the adolescent's responses to the questions to ensure that the young person is recording them in the proper place.

4. Ensure that the adolescent understands the MMPI-A items. The MMPI-A requires about a sixth-grade reading level. However, a few items in the booklet may require more than a sixth-grade reading level. Table 2-1 lists the words we received the most questions about in large testing sessions with young adolescents. We developed these definitions and examples for use in test administration. The table can be used and expanded as necessary for your use.

5. Provide sufficient breaks and reinforcement (both social and tangible) to maintain cooperation. In some settings, points are given when sections of the MMPI-A are completed. Candy and praise were frequently

Table 2-1. Standardized Definitions and Examples for the MMPI-A

Word/phrase	Definition	Example
Anxiety	Nervous, jumpy, upset	I feel nervous or upset about something or someone almost all the time.
Apt	Likely	I am likely to go home after school.
Benefit	To do good for, to help	If given the opportunity, I could do something that would do great good for the world. If I was allowed, I could do something that would greatly help the world.
Brood	Worry	I worry a great deal.
Condemned	Doomed, ruined	I believe I am a doomed person. I believe I am a ruined person.
Crowd	A large number of people	I avoid being with a large number of people.
Disturbed	Interrupted, upset	My sleep is interrupted and upset.
Editorial	Opinion by an editor	I like to read opinions by editors in newspapers.
Excessively	Too much or too great	I have used too much alcohol.
Fault	Problems, criticisms	My parents find more problems with me than they should. My parents criticize me more than they should.
Fitful	Restless	My sleep is restless and disturbed.
Have it in for me	Are unfair, out to get me, treat me worse than others	My teachers are unfair to me.
Judgment	Ability to decide what is right	My ability to decide what's right is better than it ever was.
Lacking in	Do without, do not have	I am certainly without self-confidence. I do not have self-confidence.
Law enforcement	Police, police force	I believe in the police.
Laxative	A mild drug used to relieve constipation or to help a person have a bowel movement (Ex-lax, Feen-a-mint)	Sometimes I use Ex-lax or another medicine so I won't gain weight.
Lecture	An informative talk	I like to attend informative talks on serious subjects.
Loud fun	Noise, activity	I like to go to parties and other affairs where there is lots of noise and activity.
Object	Disapprove of	My parents often disapprove of the kind of people I go around with.
Plotted against	Involves people making secret plans against someone else	I believe others are making secret plans about me.
Quarrels	Disagreements, arguments, fights	I have very few disagreements with members of my family.
Self-confident	Belief in one's own abilities, certainty about one's capability	I am entirely certain about my abilities.
Shrink	Avoid	I avoid facing a crisis or difficulty.
Sociable	Outgoing, friendly	I am a very outgoing and friendly person.

Table 2-1. Standardized Definitions and Examples for the MMPI-A, Continued

Word/phrase	Definition	Example
Soul	Spiritual part of a person, the mind or thinking part	My spirit sometimes leaves my body. My mind sometimes leaves my body.
Spirits	Supernatural beings or creatures like ghosts	Evil ghosts possess me at times. Bad creatures sometimes control me.
Stranger	Outsider, newcomer, someone you do not know	I do not mind meeting newcomers or people I do not know.
Stress	Mental or physical tension	I am not feeling much mental or physical tension these days.
Success	To turn out as hoped for	If people had not had it in for me I would have turned out better.
Tender	Sensitive to pain, frail, weak	The top of my head is sometimes sensitive to pain. The top of my head sometimes feels weak.
Unpardonable	Cannot be forgiven	I believe my sins cannot be forgiven.

used with subjects in the MMPI Restandardization Project samples. It may be useful to administer the MMPI-A in 20- to 30-minute sessions rather than one session.

MMPI-2 and MMPI-A Formats

One of the values of the MMPI-2 and the MMPI-A is that they are relatively easy to administer. A number of different administrative formats have been developed to make the test situation conform to particular patient limitations or to take advantage of particular setting requirements. The item order of the inventory is the same for all forms of the test except for the special research form to be discussed later (i.e., the adaptively administered test).

Paper-and-Pencil Versions

The printed MMPI-2 and MMPI-A booklets are perhaps the most frequently used forms of the test. The separate booklets are available in softcover and hardcover. Each has advantages and limitations. The softcover booklet (see Figure 2-1) can be administered in individual or group sessions. It is durable and reusable. A limitation of the softcover booklet is that it requires a hard writing surface, such as a desk or a table.

The hardcover booklet was developed to provide a "laptop" administration form. The hardcover booklet is held together by a spiral binding, allowing the client to use the cover as a writing surface. This form requires a specially designed answer sheet (see Figure 2-2) that is attached to the back cover by pegs to prevent it from slipping. The booklet and answer sheet are staged by having the statements printed on pages of gradually decreasing width. The answer sheet is fixed to the back of the booklet so that the appropriate columns of the answer sheet are exposed to view as the booklet pages are turned.

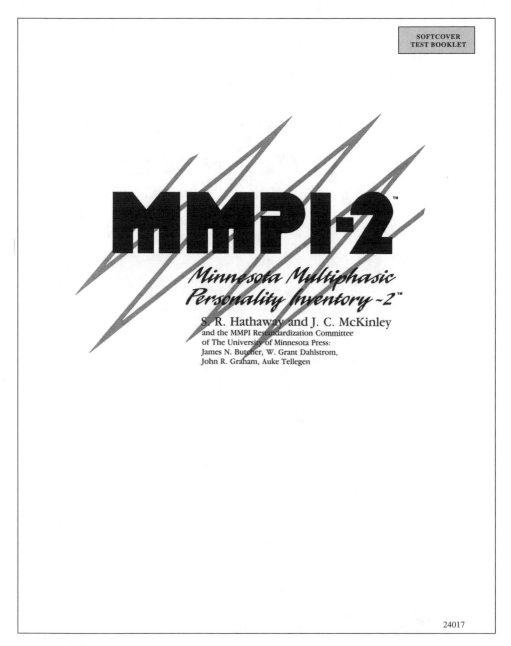

Figure 2-1. MMPI-2 softcover test booklet.

In using the hardcover version, test administrators need to make certain that the answer sheet remains fixed in the appropriate position because the answer sheets can slip out of alignment, resulting in incorrect answer columns being used and thereby invalidating the test. Another setting-specific disadvantage has been noted. A psychologist in a correctional facility pointed out that his prison system was

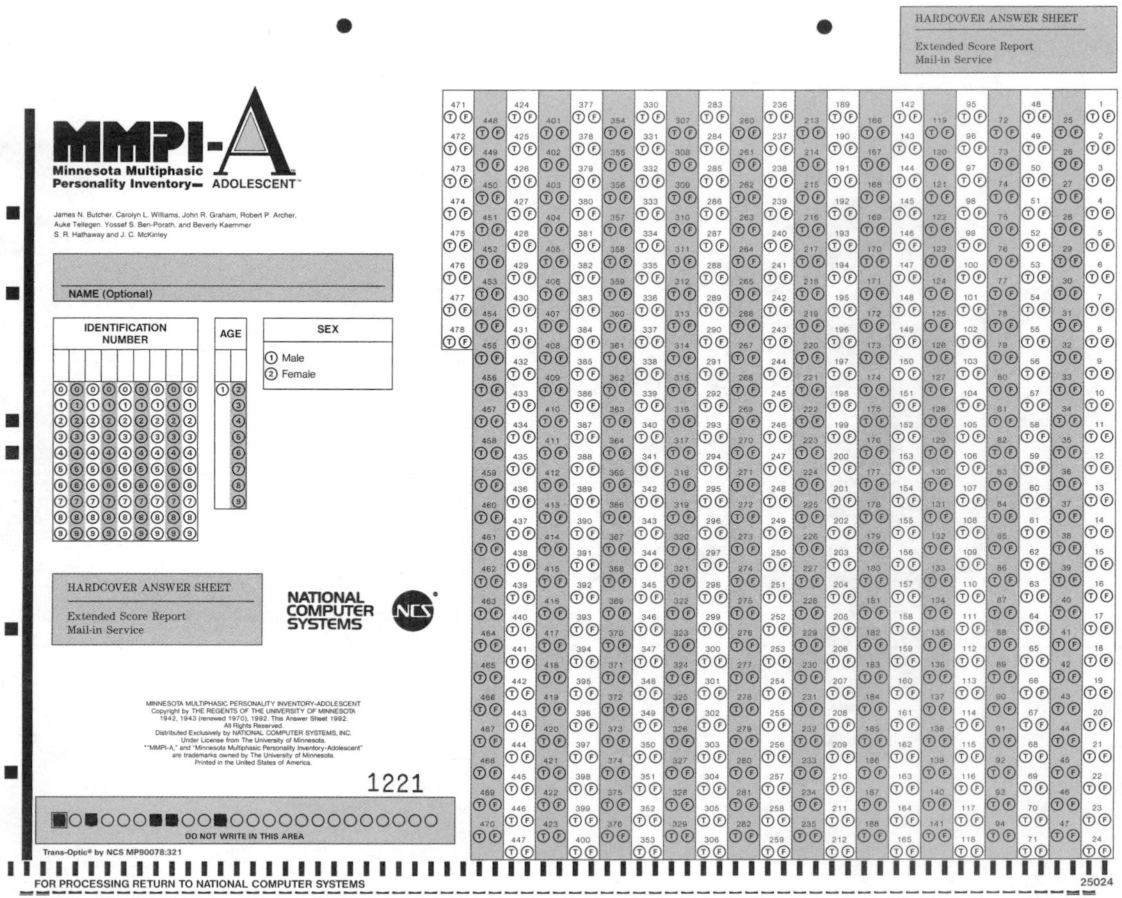

Figure 2-2. MMPI-A hardcover answer sheet.

not able to use the hardcover MMPI-2 booklet because the wire spiral binding was removable and provided a weapon for inmates to attack others or harm themselves!

Whether the softcover or hardcover version is used, the examiner should check each booklet before use to ensure that previous clients have not left messages, complaints, obscenities, and so on in the margins. One of the authors once found a booklet in which a number of MMPI statements had been "edited" to suit the previous user and express his generally cynical philosophy of life. Entertaining though it was, it altered the sentence meanings too much to obtain a valid test with other clients. Adolescents seem particularly prone to writing messages in the booklets.

Audiocassette Versions

Audiocassette versions of the MMPI-2 and MMPI-A provide alternative administration formats for individuals with visual problems or reading difficulties as well as for individuals who are unable to use the booklets and answer sheets because of physical disability. Audio versions of the MMPI-2 are currently available in Spanish and Hmong, as well as in English. The audio form presents each item twice, allowing sufficient time for an individual to record his or her response. Research has shown that the audio version of the MMPI is comparable to the booklet version (Dahlstrom & Butcher, 1964; Reese, Webb & Foulks, 1968; Urmer, Black & Wendland, 1960; Wolf, Freinek & Shaffer, 1964). The use of professionally developed audiocassettes is preferable to reading items to clients. Reading the items increases the likelihood of deviation from standardized item presentations. The audiotapes can seem slow and boring, particularly for adolescents. Careful monitoring with frequent breaks may be necessary to maintain motivation to complete the assessment.

Computer-Administered Versions

The MMPI-2 and MMPI-A can be administered on-line by computer. The test items are presented on a video screen, and the responses are recorded by the individual pressing the appropriate keys, designated as "True" and "False," on a standard keyboard. The computer initially presents all items in their standard order to each subject. If a response is not given in the allotted time, the item is skipped and presented again later in the sequence.

There are several advantages to this administration format:

1. Many individuals, particularly younger adolescents, enjoy working at a computer terminal and feel comfortable with this format. Those who have never used a computer can be taught quickly and appreciate having the opportunity to get experience with a computer.

2. It actually requires less time to take the standard MMPI-2 by computer than by booklet. Many people can finish the full MMPI-2 in an hour to an hour and 15 minutes because the response required is simply pressing a key rather than manipulating answer sheets, checking one's place,

and marking with a pencil. Even less time is required for the MMPI-A in this format.

3. The scales can be readily scored and computer interpreted immediately after the individual has completed the test. For example, it is possible to have a complete computer-generated personality report immediately after the individual finishes responding.

The administration of test items by computer produces comparable results to administration by test booklet. Finger and Ones (1999) conducted a meta-analysis of research comparing computer-administered MMPI scores with those obtained by booklet administration. They found that the two administrative formats were comparable. One disadvantage of computer administration is that it may not be cost-effective because only one person can be tested on a given machine at a time. Testing may tie up a computer for too long or require that an expensive computer be dedicated solely to test administration. Psychologists in some settings find it more cost-effective to have the client use the booklet version and have a clerk key-punch the answers (requiring about 8 minutes) into the computer.

Abbreviated and Short Forms for the MMPI-2 and MMPI-A

Even though experts (Dahlstrom, 1980; Lachar, 1979) point out that testing time is a less important consideration than obtaining sufficient clinical information, some researchers attempted to develop effective shortened versions of the original MMPI to reduce the testing time for clients. However, none were found to provide sufficient information and were not recommended for clinical use (Graham, 1987; Greene, 1982; Hart, McNeill, Lutz & Adkins, 1986; Helmes & McLaughlin, 1983; Hoffmann & Butcher, 1975; Streiner & Miller, 1986; Wilcockson, Bolton & Dana, 1983). The MMPI has been considered too long and tedious for many patients to complete, and in some clinical settings, time for test administration can be scarce. The stated reason for using short forms (i.e., the need to reduce patient testing time) is not well founded. The idea that patients are too busy to respond to the full MMPI, MMPI-2, or MMPI-A or are otherwise unable to complete the inventory is questionable (Graham, 1987). For most individuals in inpatient units, taking the full MMPI-2 or MMPI-A does not usually detract from their ongoing activities. Even in outpatient settings, complete assessments can usually be arranged if the staff and patients are informed of the importance of the information. Patients are willing to share information about themselves if they view the questions as relevant to understanding their problems and know that they will be given extensive feedback about the test results. Rarely will clients object to testing if a clinician or staff person explains the purpose of the test. This is especially true if clients are informed that the results will be valuable in treatment planning and that they will be given feedback about test results.

The abbreviated form is created by presenting only the items contained on desired scales. For example, scores for the traditional validity scales (L, F, and K) and the standard scales can be obtained by administering only the first 370 items in the MMPI-2 or the first 350 items in the MMPI-A. This is possible because all the items constituting the original standard and validity scales are in the first part of the booklet. The actual number of items administered for each scale (e.g., the Depression scale) remains the same as when the full test is administered. The scales containing items in the back of the booklet (e.g., the new validity scales and the content scales) are not scored. Accurate assessments, although limited to the standard scales, can be obtained with the abbreviated forms. However, it is important to note that many of the adolescent-specific scales of the MMPI-A are not available when the abbreviated version is used.

Computer Adaptive Administration

When a clinician conducts a clinical interview, he or she does not ask the same questions in the same order for all clients. An inflexible interview format would be highly inefficient and would quickly alienate even the most tolerant clients. Practitioners usually vary their interview for each client, depending on the person's response to previous questions. For example, if the client responds "no" to the question "Are you married?," the clinician does not follow with questions about the individual's spouse but moves to a different topic.

Yet personality inventories traditionally pose the same questions, in the same order, to all people regardless of whether they are relevant to the individual tested. Until recently, it has not been technically possible to vary item presentation in fixed inventories such as the MMPI-2 or MMPI-A. Item administration contingent on previous responding is now technically possible with personal computers, and research has demonstrated the comparability of the adaptive approach with the booklet version (Roper, Ben-Porath & Butcher, 1991). This format has not yet been developed for clinical use.

Scoring the MMPI-2 and MMPI-A

Many types of answer sheets are available for the MMPI-2 and MMPI-A because different scoring methods (e.g., hand scoring and optical scanning) require different answer forms. The test administrator should determine in advance which scoring option is to be used in order to employ the proper answer sheet. The most frequently used answer sheets are hand scored, optically read, and computer-processed or keypunched versions.

Hand Scoring

Many practitioners and small clinics have a trained individual hand score the answer sheet and draw profiles by hand, a time-consuming procedure taking from 15 to 40 minutes, depending on the number of scales scored and the care with which the task is completed. If the practitioner wishes to take advantage of the full range of MMPI-2 or MMPI-A measures (i.e., validity scales, standard scales, supplementary scales, content scales, Harris-Lingoes and Si subscales, and content component scales), scoring requires substantially more time. Consequently, those using the hand-scoring option typically score only the validity and standard scales, limiting the interpretation that can be made from the MMPI-2 or MMPI-A.

All MMPI-A and MMPI-2 scales, with the exception of the VRIN and TRIN inconsistency scales, are scored by simply counting the number of items endorsed on the particular scale. Scoring templates are placed over the answer sheet, allowing the scorer to visually check the responses for each scale. The responses are then recorded on the appropriate place on the profile sheet. (For VRIN and TRIN, scoring templates are placed over a recording grid rather than directly over the answer sheet.) Several problems commonly occur with hand scoring. Templates are used improperly, for example, by failing to correctly align them. Counting errors are made, so it is a good idea for the scorer to count the items twice to ensure accuracy.

Computer Scoring

Several options are available for computer processing of MMPI-2 and MMPI-A protocols. Computer processing is covered briefly here, and computer interpretation is discussed in more detail in Chapter 14. The official MMPI-2 distributor, National Computer Systems (NCS) in Minneapolis, provides a number of scoring options for the MMPI-2 and MMPI-A. For on-line administration of the MMPI-2 and MMPI-A, the client responds to the items by pressing keys designated "True" or "False." Or the client responds to the items on an answer sheet, and the responses are key entered into the computer or onto a disk. In both cases, the computer scores the item responses and draws profiles.

Computer processing of personality test protocols has become a widely used, cost-effective, and very accessible means of facilitating the use of psychological tests. A note of caution: The MMPI-2 and MMPI-A are copyrighted instruments. Any duplication of the items, and the scored direction of the items and the T scores requires permission of the publisher.

Mail-in Scoring

Another approach to computer scoring is to have the test taker use an optically scannable answer sheet that is mailed to NCS for processing. The scored and interpreted test is then returned by mail to the practitioner. This service is useful for those who can wait for mailed responses. Scanners are also available for in-office scoring.

Plotting MMPI-2 and MMPI-A Profiles

To facilitate interpretation, the MMPI-2 and MMPI-A scale scores are plotted on profile sheets that provide a visual summary of the scale elevations and patterns of scores. Separate profiles are used for males and females. The profile sheets are designed so that raw scores, once computed, can be plotted directly in the appropriate place on the graph, thereby converting the raw scores to T scores. There are a number of profile sheets available to facilitate scoring of a broad range of MMPI-2 and MMPI-A scales. The hand-scoring profile sheets most commonly used for the MMPI-2 are shown in Figure 2-3 and for the MMPI-A in Figure 2-4.

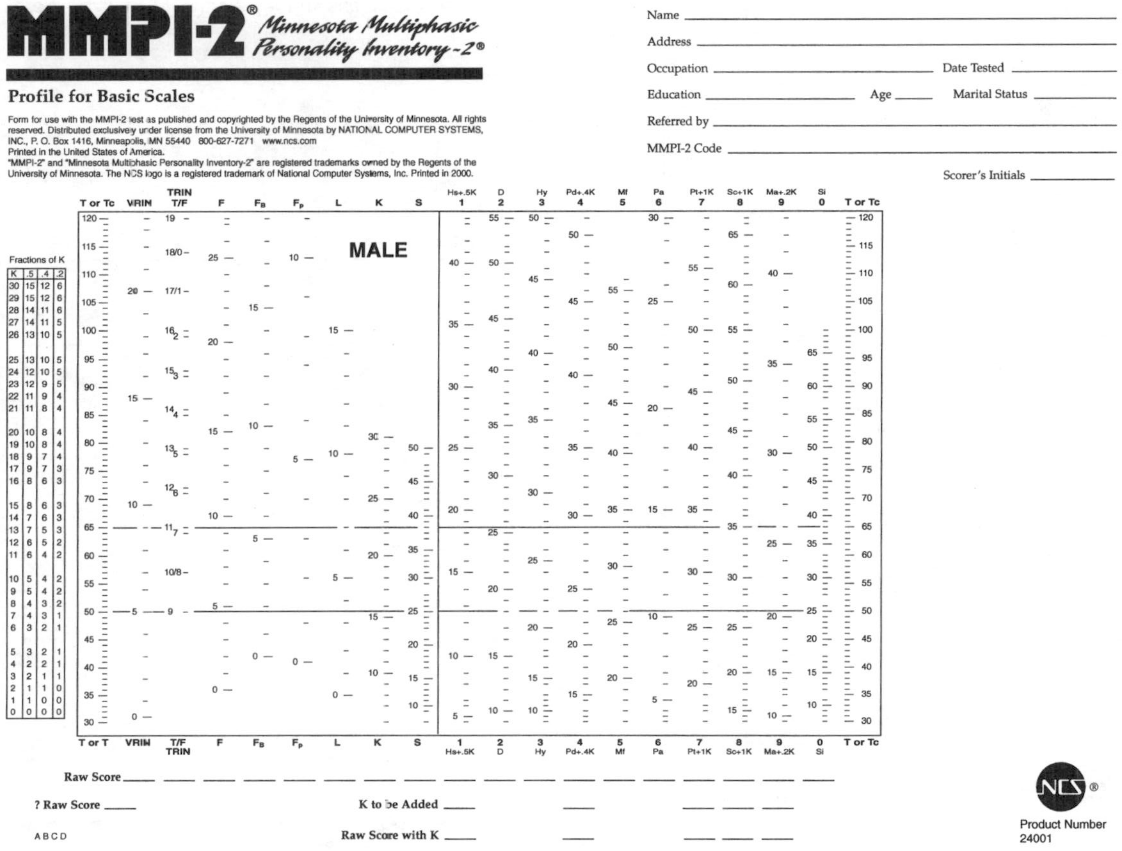

Figure 2-3a. MMPI-2 basic scales profile.

Figure 2-3b. MMPI-2 supplementary scales profile.

MMPI-2® *Minnesota Multiphasic Personality Inventory-2®*

Profile for Content Scales

Form for use with the MMPI-2 test as published and copyrighted by the Regents of the University of Minnesota. All rights reserved. Distributed exclusively under license from the University of Minnesota by NATIONAL COMPUTER SYSTEMS, INC., P. O. Box 1416, Minneapolis, MN 55440 800-627-7271 www.ncs.com
Printed in the United States of America.
"MMPI-2" and "Minnesota Multiphasic Personality Inventory-2" are registered trademarks owned by the Regents of the University of Minnesota. The NCS logo is a registered trademark of National Computer Systems, Inc. Printed in 2000.

Name
Address
Occupation
Education   Age   Marital Status
Referred by
MMPI-2 Code

Date Tested

Scorer's Initials

MALE

T	ANX	FRS	OBS	DEP	HEA	BIZ	ANG	CYN	ASP	TPA	LSE	SOD	FAM	WRK	TRT	T

Raw Score

A B C D

Product Number
24002

Figure 2-3c. MMPI-2 content scales profile.

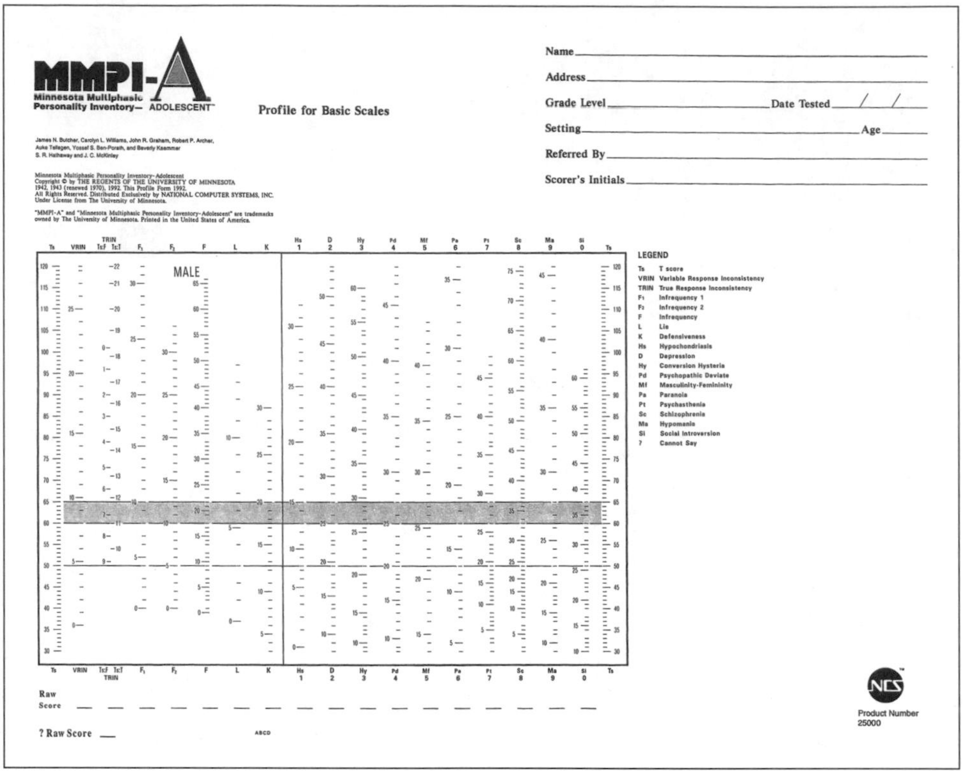

Figure 2-4a. MMPI-A basic scales profile.

The MMPI Restandardization Committee decided to make both K-corrected and non–K-corrected profile sheets available for the MMPI-2 to encourage research on the correction because there is some indication that it is not the most appropriate correction to use for all settings and applications (Weed, Ben-Porath & Butcher, 1990). For current clinical use, it is important to keep in mind that most of the validity research on the MMPI was conducted with K-corrected scale scores. The K correction is not used on the MMPI-A and thus is not included on the MMPI-A profile sheet.

Uniform T Scores

The T scores in the original MMPI were somewhat problematic in that they were not uniform across the scales; that is, a T score of 70 would fall at different percentile ranks across the scales. Moreover, T scores were based on the 1930s normative sample gathered by Hathaway and McKinley and a somewhat later but still dated adolescent normative sample. The MMPI Restandardization Committee developed norms based on contemporary samples of individuals and followed a procedure, developed by Auke Tellegen and referred to as uniform T scores, that would allow all the scale scores to fall at equivalent percentile ranks.

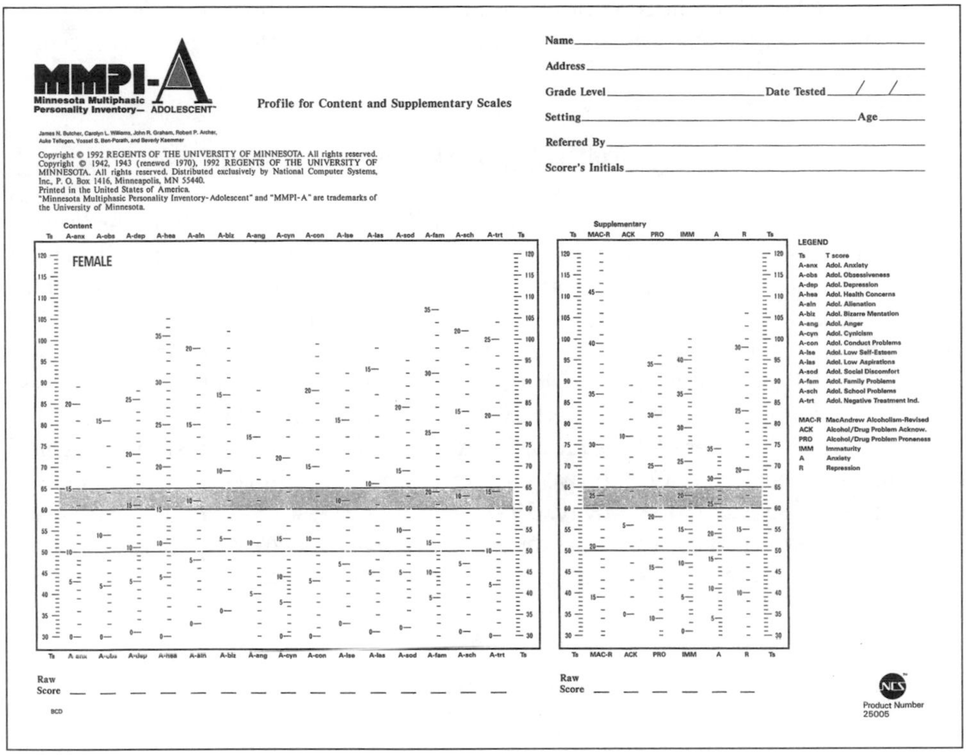

Figure 2-4b. MMPI-A content and supplementary scales profile.

The uniform T scores involved deriving a composite (or average) distribution of the raw scores on the eight clinical scales and adjusting the distribution of each scale to match the composite distribution. This procedure produced percentile equivalent scales because they are based on distributions that are comparable in terms of skew and kurtosis. This procedure allowed MMPI-2 and MMPI-A scale distributions to retain some of the familiar features of the original MMPI.

The K Correction

Five of the MMPI-2 raw scores on the basic scales profile sheet—Hs, Pd, Pt, Sc, and Ma—are adjusted by adding a correction, based on the K score, in an effort to compensate for test defensiveness. Again, the correction is not used for adolescents.

Cautions in Plotting MMPI-2 and MMPI-A Profiles

Profiles should be plotted carefully because a number of errors can occur. Before interpreting an MMPI-2 or MMPI-A profile that someone else has plotted, the interpreter should check the profile for possible errors. Some common plotting errors are incorrect application of the K correction, using the wrong profile sheet (e.g., the form for men instead of the form for women), and plotting the scale scores on the wrong scale.

Coding MMPI-2 and MMPI-A Profiles

Profile coding was developed early in the MMPI's history as a shorthand technique for communicating the main facets of an MMPI configuration and is still useful in interpreting profiles today. Coding facilitated grouping of similar profile codes by researchers. Coding systems summarize scores from the original MMPI validity and standard scales. Information from other MMPI-2 and MMPI-A scales (e.g., TRIN, VRIN, and the content scales) are not available from these coding systems. The profile codes are obtained by rank ordering the MMPI-2 and MMPI-A standard scales in order of scale elevation and using symbols to designate level of elevation for each scale. Of the two coding systems that have been published—the Hathaway System (Hathaway, 1947) and the Welsh System (Welsh, 1948, 1951)—the Welsh coding system is the most widely used. We begin by describing the original Welsh coding system and later discuss modifications for coding the MMPI-2 and MMPI-A.

The Welsh Code

Each of the MMPI-2 and MMPI-A standard scales has a number that serves as the basis for coding. Many MMPI-2 and MMPI-A users routinely refer to the scale numbers rather than to scale names or abbreviations to avoid the negative implications that may follow in nonpsychiatric settings. (We use scale numbers, names, and abbreviations interchangeably in this book.) In coding a profile according to the Welsh system, each standard scale is represented by its number, so that Hs becomes 1; D, 2; Hy, 3; Pd, 4; Mf, 5; Pa, 6; Pt, 7; Sc, 8; Ma, 9; and Si, 0 (zero). Much of the early research on MMPI codes did not incorporate the Mf or Si scales because these were not considered clinical scales.

Figure 2-5 presents the MMPI-2 validity and standard scale profile for a young woman named Alice. We use Alice's MMPI-2 profile to illustrate the Welsh coding system. The first step in coding Alice's MMPI-2 profile is to write down the numbers representing the scales in order of T-score elevation, from highest to lowest. The highest scale is Pt with a T score of 72, so 7 will be the first number in the code. The second highest scale is Sc, or scale 8, at 67; the code is now 78. The third highest is Hy, and the code becomes 783. This procedure is followed until all the scales are listed by number in descending order of T scores. The digit sequence for the figure is 7 8 3 4 1 6 2 5 9 0. It may be useful to place a small tally mark on the profile form near the T score as the scale number is written down to ensure that all scales are included in the code. Another check for accuracy involves reading through the completed code series in numeric order to determine whether a scale has been repeated or omitted.

The second step in coding is to enter the appropriate symbols to denote scale

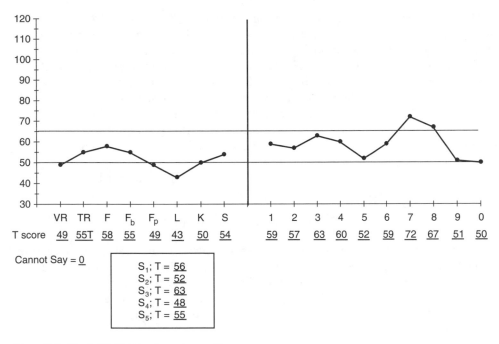

T score   49 55T 58 55 49 43 50 54   59 57 63 60 52 59 72 67 51 50

Cannot Say = 0

$S_1; T = 56$
$S_2; T = 52$
$S_3; T = 63$
$S_4; T = 48$
$S_5; T = 55$

Figure 2-5. Alice's MMPI-2 basic scales profile.

elevation. The following elevation symbols are used to denote the elevation level for the scales in the code. It should be noted that with the publication of the MMPI-2 and MMPI-A, the Welsh system, based on increments of 10 T-score points, becomes somewhat cumbersome in representing the "critical elevations" in MMPI-2 and MMPI-A profiles. The T-score level at which interpretation is recommended is now at 65, a point at which no Welsh code system is available. Consequently, we have been employing a slight modification of the Welsh code so that the 65 T-score level is immediately recognizable in the profile code. We recommend that a "+" sign be used to demarcate the 65 to 69 T-score level. Profile coding proceeds as follows:

100 or more	**
90–99	*
80–89	"
70–79	'
65–69	+
60–64	-
50–59	/
40–49	:
30–39	#
29 or less	There are no T scores below 30.

When two or more scales fall in the same range of 10 T-score points, the elevation symbol follows the digit for the lowest scale. These symbols were selected because they appear on standard typewriters and are familiar to most people.

For Alice's profile, the highest elevation is 72 on the Pt scale, indicating that the scale digit 7 should be followed by ' . The Sc scale follows at a T score of 67, so the + symbol is inserted after scale 8. Next come the Hy scale at 63 and the Pd scale at 60. These are followed by -. The next six scales fall in the same range (between 50 and 59) and are followed by a slash (/:#) (the Hs scale and the Pa scale are at 59, the D scale is at 57, the Mf scale is at 52, the Ma scale is at 51, and the Si scale is at 50). The code is now 7'8+ 34-16259 0/: #.

In addition to the standard scales, the validity scales should be coded and placed separately to the right of the clinical scales. The code is now as follows:

*" 7' 8 + 34-162590/:# FK/L:

Another refinement in the code is sometimes used. Some practitioners choose to begin and end each code with an elevation symbol. Even though the beginning and ending symbols are redundant, their use may allow the practitioner to easily locate cases by the highest (or lowest) score. Because no elevations fall in the ranges of 80 to 89, 90 to 99, and 100 and above, if we were using this refinement, the code for Alice's MMPI-2 profile would appear as follows:

*" 7' 8 + 3 4-1 6 2 59 0/:# FK/L:

Note that we have added underlining. Customarily, when two or more scales are within 1 T-score point of each other, both code digits are underlined. Thus, Alice's scores on scales 2 (T = 59), 1 (58), and 9 (58) are underlined, as are 5, 9, and 0. When two or more scales have the same T score, they are placed in the usual ordinal sequence and underlined. Another example: If both D and Pt are 65, the code will be 27- rather than 72-. If scales fall into two different ranges but are still within 1 T-score point, they and the elevation symbol will all be underlined: D = 70 and Pt = 69 will be 2'7. Some MMPI users have felt that this use of underlining to indicate equivalence of T-score values is arbitrary and overly precise and choose not to employ the procedure.

Other elevation symbols are sometimes used to denote very high scores. Scores from 100 to 109 are followed by **, 110 to 119 by !, and 120 by !!. This practice may be useful if a large number of cases are seen with extreme elevations, for example, in an inpatient facility. Profile codes may contain gaps because no scale falls in some elevation ranges. The appropriate elevation symbol for the missing range must be included. If, for example, a 20-point range is skipped, all the symbols marking that range should be included even though the middle symbol is actually redundant.

A further refinement of the traditional coding system takes into consideration the relative stability of the code type. Graham, Smith, and Schwartz (1986) recommended that the stability of a particular MMPI score or index be determined, in part, by its distinctiveness. They defined distinctiveness in terms of the distance between the highest score or index and the next elevated scores in the profile code.

They proposed three levels of "definition" that described the distinctiveness of a score or index as follows:

1. An MMPI-2 score or index that is 10 T-score points or greater than the next highest score in the profile code is "Very Well Defined" and is likely to be highly stable on retest.

2. An MMPI-2 score or index that is 5 to 9 T-score points greater than the next highest score in the profile code is "Well Defined" and is likely to be stable on retest.

3. An MMPI-2 score or index that is 0 to 4 T-score points greater than the next highest score in the profile code is "Not Well Defined" and may not be stable on retest.

In coding the profile, an additional set of symbols is included at the end of the code to indicate how well defined the code type is for the profile. More is said about this important property of code types in Chapter 5; it is sufficient at this point to indicate that the rating of the profile, in terms of profile definition, is included in parentheses at the end of the code type as follows:

"Very Well Defined" code   (D/2)
"Well Defined" code   (D/1)
"Not Well Defined" code   (D/0)

The complete code for Alice's profile is as follows:

$$*" 7' 8 + \underline{3\ 4\text{-}1}\ 6\ 2\ \underline{59}\ \underline{0}/:\# \text{FK}/\text{L}: (\text{D}/0)$$

The same process is used for coding an MMPI-A profile.

Highlight Summary: The Case of Alice

We use clinical cases to illustrate elements of MMPI-2 and MMPI-A interpretation throughout this book. Beginning with this chapter and continuing throughout the chapters dealing with the MMPI-2, one case, Alice, is featured at the end of each relevant chapter to summarize or illustrate the information presented in the chapter. An adolescent boy, Tony, is highlighted in Chapters 10 to 14. Both cases are included in Chapter 15 about computerized testing.

Alice, the case used to illustrate the elements of MMPI-2 interpretation, is an 18-year-old, unemployed, white woman who was referred to a mental health center by her family physician following an intense episode of extreme anxiety and panic. The physician previously evaluated Alice's physical complaints and recommended a psychological evaluation. Alice's anxiety episode occurred after the loss of her most recent job and included feelings of having disappointed her parents. The psychologist's choice of test forms, processing, scoring, and profile coding for Alice illustrates the information provided in this chapter. Alice, at age 18, could have been tested with either the MMPI-2 or the MMPI-A. Even though Alice still lived with her parents (making the MMPI-A family content somewhat more relevant), she had graduated from high school several months earlier and was experiencing work-related problems. Because of this, the psychologist chose to administer the MMPI-2 rather than the MMPI-A. The NCS scoring and interpretation service was used (see Chapter 15 for more details).

Alice's basic profile was coded according to both the MMPI-2 norms. Relevant extratest information about Alice is described in Chapter 8 on integrating MMPI-2 descriptors. Similar information for Tony, our adolescent case, is presented in Chapters 10 to 14.

Chapter 3

Assessing the Validity of MMPI-2 Profiles

Because the MMPI-2 and MMPI-A are self-report personality measures, their validity and utility depend on the cooperativeness of the individual taking them. If an individual wishes to distort responses to the test items to present a particular picture (e.g., one of a seriously disturbed person or of a person in good psychological health), he or she can readily do so. Thus, personality questionnaires would be very difficult to use and unreliable if there were no means of knowing whether a particular test protocol was valid. Fortunately, a number of measures have been developed for the MMPI-2 and MMPI-A to provide the interpreter with information about the individual's cooperativeness, openness, and willingness to share personal information through responses to the test items. The answer to the question "Can the MMPI-2 or the MMPI-A be faked?" is, of course, yes. However, in most cases in which we know that an individual is attempting to distort responses, we are able to appraise the person's message and the extent of the response distortion.

Using the measures of response invalidity that have been developed, we can judge whether the individual has distorted the responses to the point of invalidating the test, or, in some cases, we can correct for test defensiveness to arrive at a more accurate symptom picture. Knowing that there is a tendency for some individuals in some settings to produce invalid MMPI-2 and MMPI-A protocols can be useful information in the interpretive process. For example, individuals who claim damages in a court case because of "psychological maladjustment" may endorse an excessive number of items reflecting problems, producing very exaggerated symptom patterns that are unbelievable. Some parents in domestic court-custody battles tend to present an overly favorable pattern on the MMPI-2 by excessively denying minor faults that most people would admit to (Bathurst, Gottfried & Gottfried, 1997; Postuma & Harper, 1998). This response distortion can provide clues about the test taker's motivations that might prove valuable in the overall psychological evaluation.

In this chapter, we discuss the MMPI-2 patterns that provide the interpreter with information about whether the client's profile is valid and interpretable. We illustrate each of the validity indicators and summarize the conclusions that can be made from them. In discussing a topic that has as many facets or components as the MMPI-2 validity indicators do, we are faced with the question "Where do we begin?" There is no right or wrong starting point because as the interpreter gains experience with MMPI-2 profile interpretation, he or she will look "simultaneously" at several measures or examine one peak elevation in conjunction with others. For our purposes, we plan to follow an initial sequence of examining several indexes that address invalidating test-taking approaches sometimes adopted

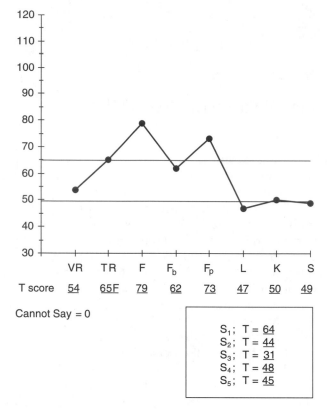

Figure 3-1. MMPI-2 validity scales profile.

by uncooperative clients—item omitting, responding inconsistently, and responding all True or all False. Next, we focus our attention on several ways that have been developed for examining symptom exaggeration or claiming an unlikely number of problems—the three infrequency scales, F, F_b, and F_p. Finally, we address three measures of impression management through such tactics as test defensiveness, problem denial, or claiming extreme virtues—the Lie scale (L), the Defensiveness scale (K), and the Superlative Self-Presentation scale (S). In the discussion that follows, we describe the validity indicators by proceeding from left to right on the profile form shown in Figure 3-1. This profile order is followed in most of the MMPI-2 profile forms available from the test publisher. However, this order may not always be present because some clinics or mental health facilities may be using an earlier version of the MMPI-2. Similar information is presented in Chapter 10 about the MMPI-A validity indicators and scales.

The determination of scale invalidity from a test score is a somewhat arbitrary judgment. The scores on a particular scale are continuous distributions, whereas a determination of "Valid" versus "Invalid" is a dichotomous process—a judgment that scores in a particular range fall into one of these categories. In clinical interpretation, it is customary to use "cutoff scores" to suggest a valid or invalid performance on a validity scale. Appropriate cutoff scores are somewhat arbitrary but represent the "best guess" estimates based on the available empirical research for a particular application.

Item Omissions, Inconsistent Responding, and Fixed Responding

Cannot Say Score (?)

The MMPI-2 contains a Cannot Say score (?) that gives the interpreter information about the subject's cooperativeness with the psychological evaluation. The Cannot Say (Cs) score is simply the total number of items the test taker did not answer. Uncooperative or defensive individuals may fail to respond to some of the test items; this situation attenuates the scale scores, producing an underestimation of psychological problems (Brown, 1950). Recently, Berry et al. (1997) found that high numbers of Cannot Say scores resulted in the attenuation of MMPI-2 profiles. If the individual has omitted more than 30 items within the first 370 items, the protocol is considered invalid. (Remember that the original validity scales, L, F, and K, and the standard scales can be scored from items 1 to 370.) If the item omissions occur beyond item 370—if, for example, the individual did not complete the full MMPI-2—the original basic scales can be interpreted, but scores on the newer validity indicators, the content scales, and some supplementary scales will likely be attenuated and should not be interpreted.

As noted, computer scoring of the MMPI-2 can enable a thorough evaluation of omitted items. Scoring services such as The Minnesota Report™ (available through National Computer Systems) provide a list of every omitted item, and the percentage of items that the client responded to on each scale is noted on the profile. The omitted items can be examined to determine how any patterns of nonresponding have influenced scale elevations. If the client has responded to 95% or more of the items on any scale (regardless of the overall Cannot Say score), that scale can be interpreted. Clinically significant elevations on scales with greater than 6% missing items can also be interpreted; however, the absence of problems should not be inferred in the absence of scale elevation on scales missing greater than 6% of their items. Possible reasons for item omissions include test defensiveness, indecisiveness, fatigue, low mood, carelessness, poor reading skill, or a perception on the part of the client that the item is irrelevant. The Cannot Say interpretive guidelines are summarized in Table 3-1.

Variable Response Inconsistency (VRIN)

The Variable Response Inconsistency (VRIN) scale, developed by Tellegen (1982, 1988), is made up of 67 pairs of items for which one or two of four possible configurations (True-False, False-True, True-True, False-False) represent inconsistent responses. For example, answering True to "I find it hard to talk when I meet new people" and False to "When in a group of people I have trouble thinking of the right things to talk about," or vice versa, are inconsistent responses. The scale is scored by summing the number of inconsistent responses. The VRIN scale,

Table 3-1. Cannot Say Interpretive Guidelines for the MMPI-2

☐ Cannot Say scores (Cs) ≥ 30 indicate that the Individual has produced an invalid protocol that should not be interpreted except under the circumstances noted below. No other MMPI-2 scales should be interpreted.

☐ If most of the Cs items occur toward the end of the booklet (after item 370), the original validity scales (L, F, and K) and the standard scales can be interpreted. However, the newer validity indicators, the supplementary scales, and the content scales, containing items later in the booklet, should not be interpreted.

☐ Computer scoring services such as The Minnesota Report ™ available from National Computer Systems provide a list near the end of the report of every item omitted, and the percentage of items endorsed on each scale (response percentage) is noted on the profile sheet. The omitted items can be examined to determine how patterns of nonresponding have influenced scale elevations. Furthermore, scores on scales with ≥ 95% endorsements can be interpreted. Clinically significant elevations on scales with > 6% missing items can also be interpreted; however, the absence of problems should not be inferred in the absence of scale elevation on scales missing > 6% of their items.

☐ Possible reasons for item omissions:
  • Defensiveness
  • Indecisiveness
  • Fatigue, low mood
  • Carelessness
  • Low reading skill
  • Perceived irrelevance of items

Table 3-2. VRIN Interpretive Guidelines for the MMPI-2

☐ VRIN T scores ≥ 80 indicate inconsistent random responding that invalidates an MMPI-2 protocol.

☐ VRIN T scores of 70 through 79 suggest a possibly invalid profile owing to inconsistent responding.

---

unconfounded by content, provides an assessment of random responding or confusion. VRIN interpretive guidelines are provided in Table 3-2.

True Response Inconsistency (TRIN)

Tellegen (1982, 1988) developed the True Response Inconsistency (TRIN) scale to assess the tendency for some individuals to respond in an inconsistent manner to items that should, to be consistent, be endorsed in a particular way. TRIN is made up of 23 pairs of items to which the same response is inconsistent. For example, answering True to both "Most of the time I feel blue" and "I am happy most of the time" is inconsistent. Fourteen of the 23 item pairs are scored inconsistent only if the client responds True to both items. Nine of the item pairs are scored inconsistent only if the client responds False to both items.

The scoring for TRIN is somewhat more complicated than the scoring of other MMPI-2 scales. First, the number of True and False inconsistent responses is

Table 3-3. TRIN Interpretive Guidelines for the MMPI-2

☐ TRIN T scores ≥ 80 indicate inconsistent responding because of "yea-" or "nay-saying."

☐ TRIN scores of 70 through 79 suggest possible inconsistent responding.

☐ A "yea-saying" response set is indicated by a TRIN score in the inconsistent True direction (TRIN ≥ 80T).

☐ A "nay-saying" response set is indicated by a TRIN score in the inconsistent False direction (TRIN ≥ 80F).

determined. One point is added to the subject's score for each of the 14 item pairs in which a True response is inconsistent. One point is subtracted for each of the 9 item pairs if a False response is endorsed. Next, a constant of 9 points is added to the scale to avoid negative numbers. For example, if a subject endorsed 4 of the True item pairs and 6 of the False item pairs on TRIN, his or her score would be 4−6 + 9, or 7(F). This suggests a tendency to say False to items rather than to pay attention to content. If a subject endorsed 12 of the True pairs and 2 of the False pairs inconsistently, the score would be 12−2 + 9, or 19(T)—suggesting that there is a tendency to say True in an inconsistent manner. Extreme scores on either end of this range reflect a tendency to indiscriminately answer either False— nay-saying—at the low end of the range or True—yea-saying—at the upper end of the distribution. Raw scores are converted to linear T scores based on the normative sample. When scoring TRIN, the score is designated as T or F to indicate the direction of the indiscriminate responding. Table 3-3 provides guidelines for interpreting TRIN.

All-True or All-False Pattern

Another useful index for assessing the invalidity of MMPI-2 profiles is the percentage of True or False responses in the record. An extremely low True or False percentage, less than 20%, reflects a highly distorted response pattern, such as conscious manipulation or careless responding to the items. Records with such a low percentage of True or False responses produce uninterpretable profiles. The effect of an all-True response pattern is shown in Figure 3-2 for the clinical scales and Figure 3-3 for the content scales. The effect of an all-False pattern on the clinical scales is provided in Figure 3-4 and for content scales in Figure 3-5.

The all-True response pattern provides an invalid and uninterpretable clinical profile with extreme elevation on the scales measuring severe psychopathology (Pa, Pt, Sc, and Ma). The resulting validity scale pattern is of interest. Notice that the F scale elevation is very high (a T score of 120), reflecting a clearly uninterpretable profile. The L and K scores are extremely low, reflecting the fact that the items on these two scales are predominantly endorsed in the False direction. The all-True response pattern also significantly affects the scores on the content scales. All scales but one (SOD) are significantly elevated because many of the content scale items are endorsed True.

The all-False response pattern produces a somewhat different, though equally

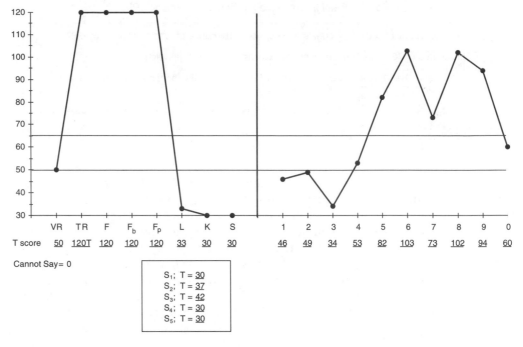

Figure 3-2. All-True pattern: MMPI-2 basic scales profile.

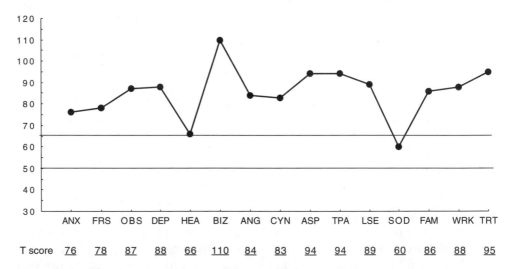

Figure 3-3. All-True pattern: MMPI-2 content scales profile.

invalid, profile. The L and K scores are extremely elevated, showing a clearly in-valid configuration. It is interesting that the F scale is also elevated (a T score of 95), suggesting an unselective response to the items. Notice too that the all-False response pattern produces a more "neurotic" appearing profile with very high elevations on the Hs and Hy scales and high elevations on most of the scales

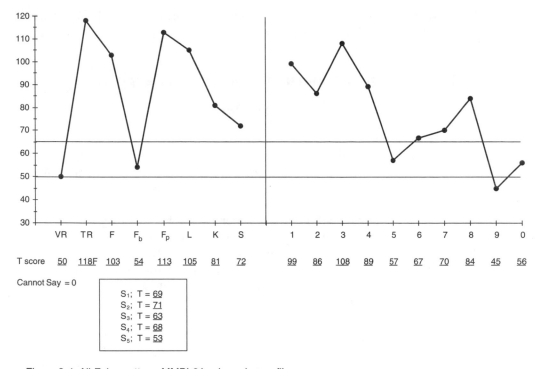

T score	50	118F	103	54	113	105	81	72		99	86	108	89	57	67	70	84	45	56

Cannot Say = 0

S_1; T = 69
S_2; T = 71
S_3; T = 63
S_4; T = 68
S_5; T = 53

Figure 3-4. All-False pattern: MMPI-2 basic scales profile.

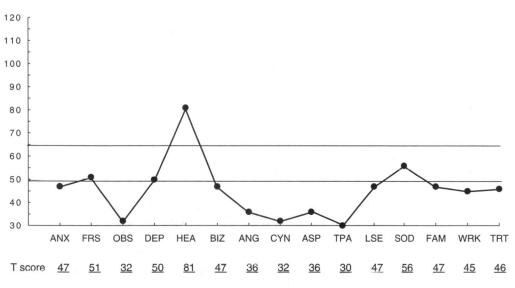

T score	47	51	32	50	81	47	36	32	36	30	47	56	47	45	46

Figure 3-5. All-False pattern: MMPI-2 content scales profile.

employing a large K correction, such as Sc and Pt. Most of the MMPI-2 content scales are attenuated with an all-False response pattern; only HEA is elevated.

Measures of Random and Exaggerated Responding

The Infrequency (F) Scale

Hathaway and McKinley (1942b) considered symptom exaggeration or faking an important response tendency to detect in self-report assessment. They developed a simple yet highly effective means of detecting the tendency to claim an inordinate number of psychological symptoms or to exaggerate one's adjustment problems. The idea underlying the F, or Infrequency, scale was that individuals who are attempting to claim psychological adjustment problems that they do not have will actually go to extremes and endorse symptoms from broad and inconsistent problem areas. Moreover, the exaggerated responding is actually in excess of what most patients would endorse. To assess this tendency of claiming excessive symptoms, originally referred to as "plus-getting," Hathaway and McKinley developed a scale made up of a broad range of psychological symptoms covering such a wide range of problems that they did not reflect actual clinical syndromes or disorders. Hathaway and McKinley conducted an item analysis and selected items that were infrequently endorsed in the normal adult sample, usually by less than 10% of respondents. The authors assumed that an individual who subscribed to a large number of these rarely endorsed symptoms was claiming too many problems. Patients do not usually endorse a broad range of F items but more selectively respond to symptoms.

The F scale in the MMPI-2 contains 60 items representing a wide range of symptoms and aberrant attitudes. Adults from normal samples usually endorse fewer than five items. If test takers endorse a large number of these extreme items, they are presenting an extreme symptomatic picture not found in the general population. As we will see in Chapter 10, the F scale for adults did not work as intended with adolescents.

The F scale also provides a good indication of random responding to MMPI-2 items. If an individual has endorsed approximately 30 items in the scored direction, the possibility of random item endorsement or an error in response recording (i.e., putting answers in the wrong place on the answer sheet) should be suspected. Thirty items are indicative of random responding because there are 60 items on the F scale; if a two-choice response format such as True or False is provided, and if the individual is responding randomly, he or she will endorse about 30 items by chance.

The F score can provide a valuable index of the individual's cooperativeness and ability to provide useful information about him- or herself. Suggested meanings of F scale elevations include the following:

T < 50:   Little symptom expression. No symptom exaggeration.

T 51–59:   Accessible and open to discussion of problems if F is higher than L and K.

T 60–64:   Valid profile; some symptom expression.

T 65–80:   Likely a valid profile, but some symptom exaggeration is possible; presenting a wide range of psychological problems; the subject is open and accessible to discussing problems.

T 81–90:   Borderline validity; suggests possibly confused and disoriented pattern; likely exaggeration of complaints; use of symptoms to gain services, sympathy, etc.

T 91–99:   High-ranging profiles, which should be interpreted very cautiously.

T 100–109:   Probably invalid, but some profiles of inpatient psychiatric patients and incarcerated felons who have recently been admitted can be interpreted up to 109 if VRIN is in the valid range.

In sum, high-ranging F scores may reflect any of the following conditions. The interpreter should evaluate the situation further to determine which condition is most likely for a given client:

1. *Possible recording error.* The individual may have produced an invalid profile owing to improper recording of answers.

2. *Random responding.* The individual may have responded randomly to the test items. Some uncooperative subjects may take the easy way of completing the MMPI-2 by random or near random responding. The MMPI-2 F scale detects this response pattern well (Berry et al., 1991). See Figure 3-6.

3. *Possible disorientation.* The individual may be confused and disoriented and unable to follow directions or track the meaning of the items, perhaps owing to toxicity, organic brain syndrome, or extreme anxiety. However, in some settings, high-ranging profiles, between 90 and 109, may occur and should not be treated as invalid. For example, in inpatient psychiatric settings or in prison settings, new admissions often present with a highly exaggerated but interpretable pattern of symptoms.

4. *Severe psychopathology.* In some cases, particularly among newly admitted inpatients and inmates in correctional facilities, intense problems and disorientation may be suggested. Gynther (1961); Gynther, Altman, and Warbin (1973d); Gynther and Petzel (1967); and Gynther and Shimunkas (1965) have provided a great deal of information about high F-scoring inpatients. Megargee and Bohn (1977) have shown that incarcerated felons taking the MMPI at admission to prison often produce high F scores that have interpretable utility. Consequently, they recommend the cutoff score for suggesting invalidity for F to be 100+. Graham, Watts, and Timbrook (1991) suggest that it may be useful to interpret profiles up to a T score of 109 in inpatient settings.

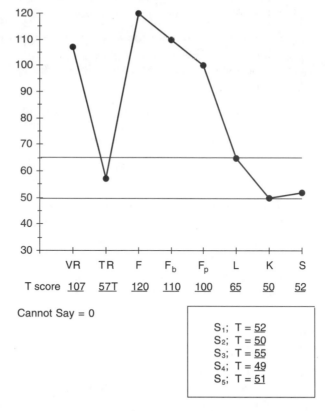

Figure 3-6. Random responding patterns: MMPI-2 validity indicators profile.

5. *Possible malingering.* The individual may be consciously exaggerating to present the view that he or she is seriously disturbed in order to benefit from services. High F responding occurs frequently among individuals who want to convince professionals that they need psychological services. This pattern is also found among individuals who claim problems in order to influence the court (Pope, Butcher & Seelen, 1999; Schretlen, 1988). Grossman, Haywood, Ostrov, Wasyliw, and Cavanaugh (1990) found that police officers who did not want to return to work produced higher F scores than those who wanted to return to duty. Several recent studies have reported the effectiveness of MMPI-2 test indicators (such as the F scale) in detecting malingering (Gallagher & Ben-Porath, 1999; Iverson, Franzen & Hammond, 1995; Rogers, Sewell & Salekin, 1994).

6. *Different cultural background.* Cross-cultural research with the original MMPI showed that individuals whose cultural backgrounds were very different from the MMPI normative group, particularly those from Asia, may produce higher F scale scores. This higher F elevation occurred even in samples of individuals who were motivated and coop-

Table 3-4. F Interpretive Guidelines for the MMPI-2

☐ T scores ≥ 110 indicate uninterpretable profile because of extreme item endorsements.

☐ T scores of 90 through 109 are indicators of a possibly invalid protocol. Some high F profiles are obtained in inpatient settings and reflect extreme psychopathology. VRIN T scores ≤ 79 can be used to rule out inconsistent responding.

☐ T scores of 80 through 89 indicate an exaggerated response set, which probably reflects an attempt to claim excessive problems. VRIN T scores ≤ 79 can be used to rule out the inconsistent responding.

☐ T scores of 60 through 79 indicate a problem-oriented approach to the items.

☐ Interpretive hypotheses for elevated F scores:
- Possible symptom exaggeration
- Faking psychological problems
- Malingering
- Confusion, reading problems (If VRIN is below a T score of 80, this hypothesis is ruled out.)
- Random responding (If VRIN is below a T score of 80, this hypothesis is ruled out.)
- Severe psychopathology

erative with the testing (Butcher & Pancheri, 1976). Although inadequate test translation could be a factor, these F scale differences might also have resulted from cultural factors. Cheung, Song, and Butcher (1991), in a study of the MMPI in Hong Kong and mainland China, found that several of the traditional F items did not operate as infrequency items in Chinese samples. That is, their endorsement percentages were very different from those in the United States. Some items were found to work in the opposite direction than they do in the United States. Cheung et al. (1991) developed a more effective infrequency scale for use in China following item-response criteria similar to those Hathaway and McKinley used with the original MMPI items. Test translators should be aware that F items need to be carefully evaluated for possible cultural influences in other countries. Interpretive guidelines for F are provided in Table 3-4.

The Infrequency Back (F$_b$) Scale

An additional index of test invalidity, the F$_b$, or F Back, scale was developed for the MMPI-2 to detect possibly deviant or random responding in the latter part of the booklet. Because the items on the F scale occur before item number 370, the F scale does not detect random responding to items in the second half of the booklet. The F$_b$ scale was developed using the same method that Hathaway and McKinley employed to develop the original F scale, that is, by including items infrequently endorsed by the normal population.

Suggested interpretations of the F$_b$ scale include the following:

1. If both the F$_b$ and the F scales are elevated above T = 110, no additional interpretation of F$_b$ is indicated because the clinical and content scales may be invalid by F scale criteria.

Table 3-5. F_b Interpretive Guidelines for the MMPI-2

☐ Like the F scale, F_b assesses exaggerated responding by examining infrequent responses to items in the latter part of the MMPI-2 booklet.

☐ If the F scale is valid and $F_b \geq 90$, the standard scales are probably interpretable, but the scales containing items in the latter part of the booklet (e.g., the content scales) should not be interpreted.

☐ Interpretive hypotheses for elevated F_b scores:
- Possible symptom exaggeration
- Faking psychological problems
- Malingering
- Confusion, reading problems (If VRIN is below a T score of 80, this hypothesis is ruled out.)
- Random responding (If VRIN is below a T score of 80, this hypothesis is ruled out.)
- Severe psychopathology

2. If the T score of the F scale is valid (i.e., below 89) and F_b is below T = 89, then a generally valid approach throughout the booklet is indicated.

3. If the T score of the F scale is valid (i.e., below 89) and F_b is above 90 (i.e., the individual may have dissimulated on later responses), then an interpretation of F_b is needed. In this case, interpretation of the original validity scales (L, F, and K) and standard scales is possible, but interpretation of scales that require valid responses to later items, such as the new validity indicators and MMPI-2 content scales, needs to be deferred. The F_b interpretive guidelines are provided in Table 3-5.

The Psychopathology Infrequency F_p Scale

The F_p, or Psychopathology Infrequency, scale is a measure of infrequency that has been added to the basic profile and that provides a valuable perspective on the veracity of the client's symptom claiming (Arbisi & Ben-Porath, 1995, 1997). Remember that the original F scale was developed by examining extreme endorsements in a normal population. The resulting "rare" response items thus reflect exaggerated responding in a normal population. A perhaps more useful scale is one that assesses extreme responding in a psychiatric setting. This approach to response infrequency was taken by Arbisi and Ben-Porath (1995, 1997). The items on F_p are rare or extreme within a sample of people with severe psychological disability. The F_p scale assesses the extent to which a person taking the test is claiming more psychological problems than people in an inpatient psychiatric facility (see Figure 3-7 and Table 3-6).

The F–K Index

Another way of evaluating symptom exaggeration is to contrast the client's performance on the F scale with performance on the K scale (a measure of defensiveness to be discussed shortly). Gough (1950) developed the F–K, or Dissimulation Index, for the original MMPI to assess the extent to which an individual dissimulated or

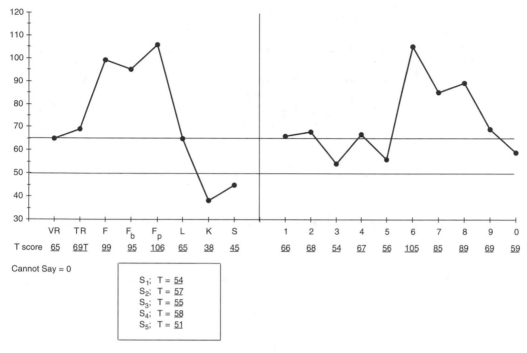

Cannot Say = 0

S_1; T = 54
S_2; T = 57
S_3; T = 55
S_4; T = 58
S_5; T = 51

Figure 3-7. F_p elevation: MMPI-2 basic scales profile.

Table 3-6. F_p Interpretive Guidelines for the MMPI-2

☐ T scores ≥ 110 clearly reflect an uninterpretable profile, suggesting that the person likely has malingered psychiatric symptoms.

☐ T scores of 90 through 109 indicate a likely invalid test protocol resulting from symptom exaggeration—claiming more symptoms than most psychiatric patients in an inpatient setting do. VRIN T scores ≤ 79 can be used to rule out inconsistent responding.

☐ T scores of 80 through 89 show a high degree of symptom claiming—probably an invalid protocol because of the tendency to claim excessive problems. VRIN T scores ≤ 79 can be used to rule out inconsistent responding.

☐ Interpretive hypotheses for elevated F_p scores:
  • Exaggerated claims of extensive, unusual psychiatric problems
  • Faking psychological problems to gain services
  • Malingering
  • Confusion, reading problems (If VRIN is below a T score of 80, this hypothesis is ruled out.)
  • Random responding (If VRIN is below a T score of 80, this hypothesis is ruled out.)

claimed nonexistent problems and the tendency to exaggerate complaints. Gough thought that extremely high symptom checking (i.e., high F elevation) along with low defensiveness (i.e., low K) suggested an invalid or dissimulated performance. This index is determined by subtracting the raw score of the K scale from the raw score of the F scale. Gough recommended an F–K score of 9 or greater as an indication that the profile was invalid because of symptom exaggeration. Others (e.g., Lachar, 1974) recommended an F–K score of 12 or higher as invalid because the score suggested by Gough (9) was so low that it eliminated too many interpretable profiles.

The F–K index works well in differentiating individuals who have endorsed an inordinate number of psychological symptoms through the F scale. Although the F–K index works well in the detection of invalid records, it may be a superfluous index because F alone detects invalid records in most cases. The index K–F (subtracting F when K is the higher scale) to assess "fake good" profiles has not worked well in practice and is not recommended for clinical use. Too many valid and interpretable protocols are rejected by this index when K is greater than F.

Measures of Defensiveness and Claims of Extreme Virtue

The Lie (L) Scale

The L, or Lie, scale is a measure of the tendency of some individuals to distort their responses by claiming that they are excessively virtuous. The scale is based on the idea that individuals who are attempting to claim excellent psychological adjustment will endorse items that indicate extremely high moral character—more than most individuals would claim. The 15 items constituting this scale are obvious in content and center around the assertion of great virtue, for example, "At times I feel like swearing" (False) and "I do not always tell the truth" (False). Scores elevated above a T score of 65 suggest individuals who are presenting themselves in an overly positive light by attempting to create an unrealistically favorable view of their moral character and psychological adjustment.

The L scale is a measure of cooperativeness and willingness to endorse negative self-views. Individuals who score high on this scale, T greater than 60, are presenting themselves as having no faults. If the L score is greater than 65, the individual is claiming virtue not found among people in general. In addition to serving as an indicator of response distortion or invalidity, the L scale is associated with personality characteristics that suggest naïveté, lack of psychological mindedness, rigid thinking, an unrealistic self-image, and neurotic defensiveness. Table 3-7 summarizes the guidelines for interpreting L.

The K Scale

The K scale (often referred to as a suppressor scale because it is associated with lowering psychopathology on the clinical scales) was developed as a measure of test defensiveness. This scale, developed empirically by Meehl and Hathaway (1946) to improve the classification of patients who were defensive on the MMPI, is used both as an indicator of test defensiveness and as a correction for the tendency to deny problems. As a corrective factor, K modifies five MMPI scales: Hs, Pd, Pt, Sc, and Ma. The fractions of K to be added to the clinical scales were empirically determined to improve test-based diagnostic assessment.

Table 3-7. L Interpretive Guidelines for the MMPI-2

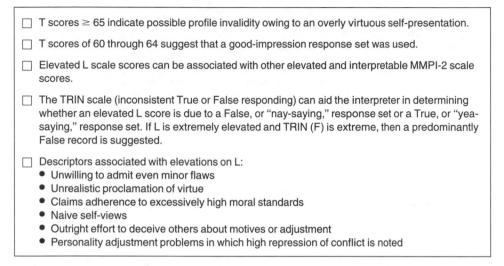

☐ T scores ≥ 65 indicate possible profile invalidity owing to an overly virtuous self-presentation.

☐ T scores of 60 through 64 suggest that a good-impression response set was used.

☐ Elevated L scale scores can be associated with other elevated and interpretable MMPI-2 scale scores.

☐ The TRIN scale (inconsistent True or False responding) can aid the interpreter in determining whether an elevated L score is due to a False, or "nay-saying," response set or a True, or "yea-saying," response set. If L is extremely elevated and TRIN (F) is extreme, then a predominantly False record is suggested.

☐ Descriptors associated with elevations on L:
  • Unwilling to admit even minor flaws
  • Unrealistic proclamation of virtue
  • Claims adherence to excessively high moral standards
  • Naive self-views
  • Outright effort to deceive others about motives or adjustment
  • Personality adjustment problems in which high repression of conflict is noted

The K scale contains items that are much less "obvious" in content than the L scale, such as "Criticism or scolding hurts me terribly" (False), "I frequently find myself worrying about something" (False), and "At times I feel like swearing" (False). Most of the items on the scale are endorsed False, reflecting the scale's function as a measure of problem denial.

The K scale has been shown to assess an individual's willingness to disclose personal information and discuss his or her problems. High scores (above 65) reflect an uncooperative attitude and reluctance to disclose personal information. Low scores (below a T of 45) suggest openness and frankness.

The K scale appeared to operate for MMPI-2 normative subjects much as it did for original MMPI subjects. Consequently, the K weights originally derived by McKinley, Hathaway, and Meehl (1948) were maintained in the MMPI-2. This scale is positively correlated with intelligence and educational level, which should be taken into account when interpreting the scores. A change in the norms for K in the MMPI-2 makes the scale somewhat less elevated for individuals of higher socioeconomic status (SES) than it was in the original MMPI. In the past, interpreters had to take SES into account and mentally adjust scores for the SES level of the individual. Because the new normative sample has a generally higher SES level, adjustment of higher-SES subjects' scores is not necessary. Some adjustment is probably necessary for individuals who have less than a high school education—modulating the interpretation of low K scores for individuals in this range is suggested (Butcher, 1990b).

Some debate has been waged over whether the K score actually improves discrimination in the way that Hathaway and Meehl had hoped (Colby, 1989; Silver & Sines, 1962; Weed, Ben-Porath & Butcher, 1990). It is likely that future research will further examine K as a suppressor variable. In the meantime, both K-corrected

Table 3-8. K Interpretive Guidelines for the MMPI-2

☐ T scores > 65 suggest possible defensive responding. Elevations in the 65 to 69 range are fairly common in settings in which the individual is motivated to present a favorable image (e.g., family custody evaluations or personnel screening).

☐ Scores on the K scale are used to correct for defensive responding on several MMPI-2 scales (Hs, Pd, Pt, Sc, and Ma). Further research needs to clarify whether the K correction is appropriate for particular settings.

☐ Absence of psychopathology should not be assumed in profiles with an elevated K score and normal-limits scale scores.

☐ Interpretive hypotheses with elevated K scores:
  ● Defensiveness
  ● Possessing a great need to present oneself as very well adjusted
  ● A "nay-saying" response set (If TRIN is extremely elevated, the individual may be presenting a "nay-saying" response set.)

and non–K-corrected hand-scoring profiles are available for the MMPI-2 because some psychologists might be interested in examining the impact of using non–K-corrected scores. Non–K-corrected scores are not recommended for clinical interpretation because most of the research has been published on K-corrected scores. Table 3-8 summarizes the K interpretive guidelines.

The Superlative Self-Presentation (S) Scale

The inclusion of new items in the MMPI-2 item pool made it possible for Butcher and Han (1995) to construct an additional measure of test defensiveness, the S, or Superlative Self-Presentation, scale. A highly defensive sample of men (applicants for airline pilot positions with a major air carrier) were tested. Only men were used in this initial stage because most airline pilot applicants are men. Their responses to MMPI-2 items were contrasted with those of the MMPI-2 normative male sample. This item analysis resulted in a 50-item scale. Both men and women were included in later stages of scale development. The norms for the S scale were developed on the male normative sample ($N = 1,138$) and the female normative sample ($N = 1,462$). The S scale has subsequently been shown to assess test defensiveness (it is highly correlated with the K scale, in the low 80s) and is elevated substantially in test situations employing instructions to "look good" (Baer, Wetter, Nichols, Greene & Berry, 1995; Lim & Butcher, 1996). See Table 3-9 for interpretive suggestions for S.

In addition to serving as a general measure of test defensiveness, the S scale can provide clues to the possible reasons underlying defensive attitudes. Five subscales provide a breakdown of item content:

S_1—Beliefs in Human Goodness. Item content concerns basic human goodness such as "Most people are honest chiefly through fear of being caught" (False).

Table 3-9. S Interpretive Guidelines for the MMPI-2

☐ T scores ≥ 65 suggest possible defensive responding or a tendency to claim only very positive characteristics and present an overly positive self-portrayal. Elevations in the 65 to 69 range are relatively common in settings in which the individual is motivated to present a favorable image (e.g., family custody evaluations or personnel screening).

☐ Subscale scores on the S scale may provide important information about the ways in which a person is expressing defensiveness:

    S_1 Beliefs in Human Goodness
    S_2 Serenity
    S_3 Contentment with Life
    S_4 Patience/Denial of Irritability
    S_5 Denial of Moral Flaws

☐ Absence of psychopathology should not be assumed in profiles with an elevated S score and normal-range standard scale scores.

☐ Interpretive hypotheses with elevated S scores:
    • Defensiveness
    • Possessing a great need to present oneself as very well adjusted
    • A "nay-saying" response set (If TRIN is extremely elevated in the False direction, the individual may be presenting a "nay-saying" response set.)

S_2—Serenity. The items on this scale center on content such as "I have never felt better in my life than I do now" (True) or "I always have too little time to get things done" (False).

S_3—Contentment with Life. The items on this subscale deal with morale, for example, "I am satisfied with the amount of money that I make (True) or "I work under a great deal of tension" (False).

S_4—Patience/Denial of Irritability. Endorsing the content on this scale suggests that the respondent is calm, cool, and patient. Items include "At movies, restaurants, or sporting events, I hate to have to stand in line" (False) and "I easily become impatient with other people" (False).

S_5—Denial of Moral Flaws. The content on this subscale deals with denial of flaws such as "I never used alcohol excessively" (False) and "I have done some bad things in the past that I never tell anyone about" (False).

Elevations on these subscales may reveal particular content areas in which the client is denying difficulty. For example, persons taking the MMPI-2 in personnel screening situations are typically defensive on all five content subscales, whereas parents being evaluated in family custody cases tend to have high elevations on S4 (Patience/Denial of Irritability) and S5 (Denial of Moral Flaws) (Butcher, 1998a).

Patterns of Response Invalidity

In assessing an individual's attitude toward responding to MMPI-2 items, it is valuable to view the configuration of validity scale scores. Very distinctive validity scale patterns emerge with different invalidating response sets. We examine several of the most common invalidating patterns to discern the conditions under which such response patterns are frequently produced.

Fake-Good Profile

The profile shown in Figure 3-8 provides a good example of a relatively unsophisticated effort to distort MMPI-2 results by presenting an overly favorable self-view or a "good impression" pattern.

In this configuration, the elevation on L is prominent, suggesting that the individual has, perhaps consciously, endorsed many items that claim highly virtuous personality characteristics that, in their extreme, are very unlikely and create suspicion about the individual's willingness to cooperate with the evaluation. Assessment situations that frequently produce this pattern include child-custody evaluations, personnel screening, and physical injury litigation in which the individual is attempting to claim a great deal of personal virtue and acknowledge few or no psychological symptoms. The response set claiming excessive personal virtue is

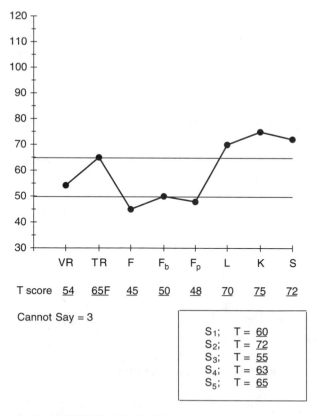

Figure 3-8. Fake-good pattern: MMPI-2 validity indicators.

associated with an unwillingness to endorse psychological problems on the clinical scales; however, in some settings (workers' compensation evaluations) physical problems may be claimed readily.

Defensive Profile

The configuration presented in Figure 3-9 shows high K and S scale elevations, with the individual not responding to the rather obvious L items or endorsing psychological symptoms through the F scale. This response pattern is more consistently found among individuals who are psychologically inaccessible or unwilling to disclose much personal information about themselves—for example, reluctant therapy cases or individuals being assessed against their will.

This type of defensive profile does not provide a clear picture of the individual's adjustment problems, and both the basic and the content scale profiles are likely to reflect few problems. A cautious statement about the individual's reluctance to report problems should be made in the report.

However, it is possible for some individuals to produce basic or content scale

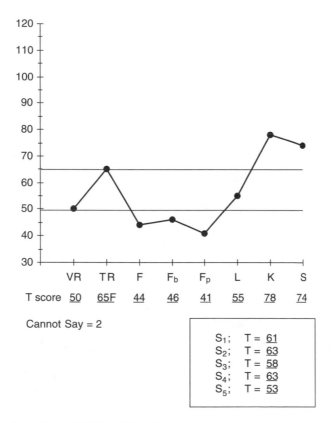

Figure 3-9. Defensive pattern: MMPI-2 validity indicators.

elevations even with this defensive response set. In these cases, when basic or content scale elevations occur in the context of a defensive record, the results should not be considered invalid but should be interpreted with the understanding that the test profiles are likely to underrepresent psychological problems.

Exaggerated Symptom Pattern

The validity configuration shown in Figure 3-10 is a marginally valid profile that should be interpreted only with great caution. As noted earlier, the F scale should be below a T score of 79 to reflect a selective problem orientation. When the F score exceeds 80, the individual probably has endorsed an excessive number of psychological problems and is likely to be confused about the task or exaggerating psychological symptoms. However, this profile is valid and interpretable, though any discussion of the case should be prefaced with the caution that the individual clearly intended to present more problems or to appear more psychologically disturbed than he or she may be.

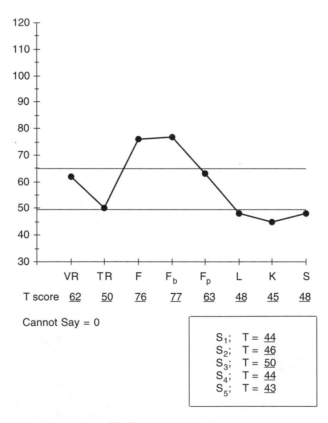

Figure 3-10. Exaggerated symptom pattern: MMPI-2 validity indicators.

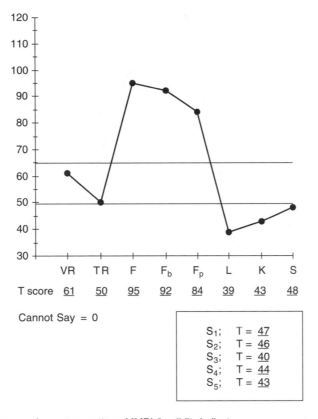

Figure 3-11. Exaggerated symptom pattern: MMPI-2 validity indicators.

The highly exaggerated profile shown in Figure 3-11 was obtained in a workers' compensation case in which the individual was claiming a physical injury (neurological symptoms assumed to be related to toxic exposure) when no work-related-injury incident had been reported and no organic basis could be discerned for the injury in the physical examination. The individual presents a rather mixed and confused clinical picture in which a number of extreme and perhaps unrelated symptoms are endorsed.

Invalid Exaggerated Pattern

The extremely exaggerated profile shown in Figure 3-12 is an invalid pattern that should not be interpreted except to indicate that it is likely to be an exaggerated or faked record. The individual has endorsed a broad range of unrelated symptoms that do not reflect a clear and consistent pattern of psychopathology. The high score on the VRIN scale (T = 92) further supports the interpretation that he or she has not responded in a consistent, selective, task-oriented manner on the test.

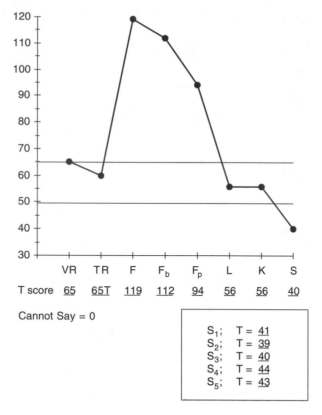

Figure 3-12. Invalid exaggerated symptom pattern: MMPI-2 validity indicators.

Highlight Summary: Alice's Validity Pattern

As we have seen in this chapter, the validity and utility of the MMPI-2 are dependent on the cooperativeness of the individual taking the inventory. To appraise the individual's test-taking attitudes, a number of measures have been developed to provide the interpreter with information about the individual's cooperativeness, openness, and willingness to share personal information through responses to the test items. We evaluate Alice's validity scale scores to determine whether her approach to the items provides a clear picture of her current personality functioning and symptoms. (See Alice's Validity scale pattern repeated in Figure 3-13).

The Cannot Say score provides information about how well a person cooperates with the evaluation and complies with the instructions. Alice answered all the MMPI-2 items. Moreover, her approach appears to be honest, based on her responses to the L scale. Her average L score suggests that she did not attempt to claim an unrealistic amount of rectitude. Her K- and S-scale scores reflect a lack of defensiveness.

The F scale, a measure of response infrequency, needs to be evaluated to determine whether the individual has endorsed an unrealistic number of problems. Alice has endorsed a few F items, indicating that she reports some extreme symp-

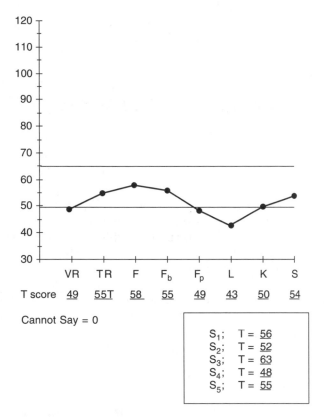

T score   VR   TR   F   F_b   F_p   L   K   S
          49   55T   58   55   49   43   50   54

Cannot Say = 0

S_1;   T = 56
S_2;   T = 52
S_3;   T = 63
S_4;   T = 48
S_5;   T = 55

Figure 3-13. Alice's MMPI-2 validity pattern.

toms. Her T score of 80 on the F scale is considered consistent with appropriate problem expression (most patients endorse some items on F) and does not reflect a tendency to exaggerate or falsely claim mental illness. Alice's response to the VRIN and TRIN scales shows a pattern of consistent responding to test items. These validity scale scores and their relative elevations indicate that Alice's approach to the MMPI-2 items was valid and cooperative and that her test protocol is likely to be a good indication of her present personality functioning and symptoms.

Chapter 4

Interpreting the MMPI-2 Standard Scales

After determining whether an MMPI-2 profile is valid, the next step in interpretation is to evaluate the client's scores on the standard scales (clinical scales 1, 2, 3, 4, 6, 7, 8, and 9 and scales 5 and 0). This step involves comparing the client's raw scores to those of people in general (i.e., to the MMPI-2 normative sample) by converting them into standard T scores. Scale interpretation involves assessing the elevation of each of the standard scales in the profile (see Figure 4-1) and applying the appropriate, established descriptors or correlates for the scale.

As noted, converting the raw scores to T scores allows the interpreter to compare a client's score with the scores of the normative sample. Each T-score distribution has a mean score of 50 and a standard deviation of 10. The dark line on the profile sheet at the 65 T-score level, which uniformly across scales corresponds to the 92nd percentile, is the point at which elevation takes on clinical meaning. For example, in Figure 4-1 the highest standard scale score (and the only scale elevation in the clinically interpretable range) is on scale 2, the Depression (D) scale, at a T score of 70, which falls at the 96th percentile of the normative group. Because the client's score on the Depression scale is significantly elevated above the norm, the correlates of this scale could be applied to this individual with considerable confidence. An elevation on a particular scale reflects the likelihood that the individual "belongs" to the criterion group. A T score of 70 on scale 2 indicates that less than 4% of the population will score that high (at that degree of scale elevation) and the individual responds in a manner similar to the criterion group of depressed patients.

Low scores on most standard scales are not interpreted as possessing particular meaning. Exceptions to this interpretive rule are scales 0 (Social Introversion, Si) and 5 (Masculinity-Femininity, Mf), which are bipolar in nature. (To some extent, low scores on the Ma scale have been related to the expression of a number of problems [Graham, Ben-Porath & McNulty, in press].) Low scores on Si reflect introverted behaviors, the opposite of high scores, that are correlated with extroverted behaviors. Low scores on Mf in men can reflect a negative attitude toward treatment. Linear T scores, not the uniform T scores of the clinical scales, are used to interpret scales 5 and 0, another reflection of the bipolar nature of these two scales.

To interpret the MMPI-2 standard scales effectively, it is necessary to understand and appreciate how the scales derive their meaning from the network of empirical correlates. Our discussion of each standard scale will highlight how the scale operates in describing clients' behavior: (1) scale development procedures, (2) item content, (3) illustrative research underlying the scale, and (4) a summary of the descriptors found to be associated with it. Points 1 and 2 are relevant for

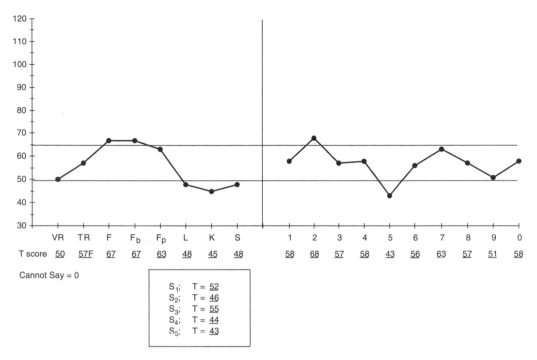

Figure 4-1. MMPI-2 K-corrected basic scales profile.

both the MMPI-2 and the MMPI-A. MMPI-A standard scale descriptors are described in Chapter 11.

Scale Development and Item Content

An adequate understanding of the MMPI-2 standard scales depends, in part, on the interpreter's awareness of how they were developed. In most cases, the MMPI standard scales were derived using an empirical-contrast method. The original test authors, Hathaway and McKinley, collected a sample of "normal" subjects and a sample of patients fitting a clear, homogeneous diagnostic pattern. Items that differentiated the clinical from the normal group were included on a scale to define membership in a clinical-diagnostic group. In some cases noted in the following, further refinement of the scale was necessary to improve prediction.

Most of the MMPI-2 standard scales contain heterogeneous item content. This complexity of the scales makes it difficult to interpret them strictly from the perspective of content. The task of interpreting the standard scales is made easier by evaluating the relative contribution of the specific content subscales, developed by Harris and Lingoes (1955), to the total elevation on a scale. Harris and Lingoes developed their content themes for scales 2, 3, 4, 6, 8, and 9 by rationally placing the items on the scale into similar content groups. This strategy was developed to enable the interpreter to understand a particular scale elevation by evaluating the individual's response to specific item content. Many of the Harris-Lingoes subscales have been found to be good predictors of personality correlates (Wrobel, 1992). A similar set of subscales was more recently developed for scale 0 (Ben-Porath, Hostetler, Butcher & Graham, 1989).

Although content interpretation is discussed more fully in Chapter 7, we introduce the content homogeneous subscales here because they help the MMPI-2 interpreter understand how specific item content can contribute to standard scale elevations. Many of the Harris-Lingoes subscales are too small to rely on for psychometric prediction, even though T scores are available for them. The subscales are also problematic measures because of the item overlap among them. However, they can be indicators of the relative weight of specific item content groups on the standard scales but should be consulted only if the T score on the parent standard scale (2, 3, 4, 6, 8, and 9) is at least moderately elevated (i.e., ≥ 60). The Harris-Lingoes subscales should not be used if the T score on the standard scale is 59 or less. Likewise, the Si subscales should be consulted only when the Si score is greater than or equal to 60. Harris-Lingoes subscales are interpreted at high elevations only (i.e., T scores greater than or equal to 65) because many of them are short. The relative elevation on the various subscales on a clinical scale can provide the interpreter with clues as to which of the empirical correlates for an elevated scale are likely to be prominent in the interpretation.

Illustrative Empirical Research and Descriptors

As previously noted, an MMPI-2 standard scale obtains its meaning from the research studies that relate scale elevations to measured behavior. Several studies illustrating the characteristics that define each scale are discussed. Numerous other general resources are available (e.g., Butcher, Rouse & Perry, in press; Dahlstrom, Welsh & Dahlstrom, 1975; Graham, 1990; Graham et al., 2000; Greene, 1991; Hedlund, 1977).

The correlates for each of the scales were adapted from research findings and written in a style that can be used for generating interpretive statements from elevated scale scores. In our discussion of scale elevations, we refer to a T score of 65 or greater as a high elevation, unless otherwise specified. A T-score elevation between 60 and 64 is considered to be moderately elevated.

Much of the information presented in this chapter is also relevant to the MMPI-A standard scales, discussed in more detail in Chapter 11. The previous descriptions of the meaning of T-score elevations, scale-development procedures, and item content apply equally well to the MMPI-A standard scales. As we will see in Chapter 11, the standard scales are relatively intact in both restandardized versions of the instrument. For many years, research and empirical descriptors derived from studies of adults were simply assumed to apply to adolescents. In some cases, this assumption has been substantiated (e.g., Archer, Gordon, Giannetti & Singles, 1988; Williams & Butcher, 1989a), in other cases it has not (e.g., Williams & Butcher, 1989b). This results in somewhat different interpretive guidelines for the MMPI-2 standard scales, which are covered in the present chapter, and the MMPI-A standard scales, described in Chapter 11.

Scale 1: Hypochondriasis (Hs)

Scale Development

McKinley and Hathaway (1940) chose to use the clinical construct of hypochondriasis to develop the first scale of their multiphasic inventory because of the pervasiveness of this problem in medical and mental health settings and because the disorder is clear-cut and relatively easy to diagnose. They defined hypochondriasis as "abnormal, psychoneurotic concern over bodily health." Most of the patients included in the criterion group were adults who were excessively concerned about bodily processes even though there was no organic basis to their problems. Because the authors were particularly interested in cases in which hypochondriacal concern was central to the clinical picture, they excluded those individuals whose somatization symptoms were part of a psychotic process.

Hathaway and McKinley (1940) were able to identify 50 cases of relatively "pure" hypochondriasis for the initial scale development. The patients included in the criterion group were homogeneous, selected to exclude individuals at age extremes and those who were actively psychotic. The "normal" control samples were composed of two groups. One included 109 men and 153 women ages 26 to 43 years. All were married and were visitors to the University of Minnesota Hospitals. A second group of 265 normal college students served as a control sample for the item selection to compensate for differences obtained in marital status, age, or socioeconomic level. Items initially selected for the scale were those that empirically differentiated the hypochondriacal patients from the normals. The authors also included a correction factor for individuals suffering from severe psychiatric disorders who presented with somatic symptoms. Originally, there were 33 items on the Hs scale. Scale 1 of the MMPI-2 contains 32 of these original items; one item was deleted during the revision because of objectionable content. This same item was deleted from the MMPI-A.

Item Content

The items on Hs represent a broad range of physical symptoms. Scale 1 items are obvious and overlap primarily with the other neurotic scales (i.e., scales 2, 3, and 7), particularly scale 3, which includes 20 Hs items. The items are not restricted to one body system or symptom pattern; rather, they include general aches, pains, weakness, fatigue, and ill health; stomach problems; breathing difficulties; poor vision and other sensory problems; coughing; sleep difficulties; dizziness; and numbness. Because its item content is so homogeneous, centering strictly around somatic complaints, Harris and Lingoes (1955) did not develop subscales for scale 1.

Illustrative Empirical Research

Hs has been widely researched and found to be related to excessive medical complaints, chronic pain, and extreme hypochondriacal concern. Although some

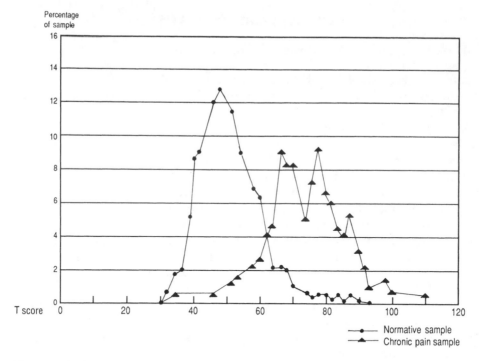

Figure 4-2. Uniform T-score distributions for Hs for normative and chronic pain men.

research suggests that patients with actual physical disorders score with moderate elevations (i.e., T scores of 60–64) on Hs (Greene, 1954), elevated scores (i.e., T scores ≥ 65) generally reflect excessive somatic responding without a physical basis. Several recent studies support the traditional correlates of Hs as a measure of somatization. Lichtenberg, Skehan, and Swensen (1984) found that personality, as measured by Hs, was the most powerful predictor of pain compared with other measures, such as arthritic severity or life stress. In a prospective study, Fordyce (1987) found that scale 1 and job dissatisfaction were more significantly related to employees' later development of low back pain than other personality, ergonomic, or life-event variables.

Individuals in a psychiatric inpatient facility who score high on Hs may be experiencing severe cognitive symptoms centering around hypochondriacal problems. Graham and Butcher (1988) found that psychiatric inpatients obtaining high scores on the Hs scale were rated by clinicians as showing somatic concern, having unusual thought content, and exhibiting hallucinatory behavior.

Keller and Butcher (1991) found that MMPI-2 scale 1 was a prominent elevation among chronic pain patients. Scale 1 discriminated well between clinical groups characteristically having a great deal of somatic concern. Figure 4-2 shows how chronic pain patients responded to the Hs items in contrast with the MMPI-2 normative sample. The two groups produce very distinct response distributions. The level of scale elevation providing optimal group separation appeared to be at about a T score of 65.

The traditional interpretation of elevations on scale 1 as indicating somatic concern among general population subjects was confirmed in the couples rating study of the MMPI Restandardization Project (Butcher, Dahlstrom, Graham, Tellegen & Kaemmer, 1989) and in the recent behavioral correlates study of outpatients by Butcher et al. (2000) and by Graham, Timbrook, Ben-Porath, and Butcher (1991). The correlates of Hs for men and women in the normative sample, as rated by their spouses, centered around worries over health, reporting headaches, stomach trouble, and other ailments and appearing generally worn out.

Descriptors

High scorers have excessive bodily concerns, numerous vague somatic symptoms, and undefined complaints, such as gastric upset, fatigue, pain, and physical weakness. Their long-standing health concerns result in periods of reduced efficiency even though they are not incapacitated with a major illness. In addition to these physical complaints, they are likely to be selfish, self-centered, and narcissistic. Pessimism, a defeatist attitude, and cynicism also characterize them. They typically are dissatisfied and unhappy, tending to make others feel miserable with their complaining, whining, demanding, and critical behavior. They appear to lack manifest anxiety though they may report feeling tense. These individuals may express hostility indirectly, rarely acting out. Others may view them as dull, unenthusiastic, unambitious, and ineffective in verbal communication. Individuals who score high on scale 1 are viewed as not very responsive to psychological therapy, tend to seek only "medical" treatment, and tend to terminate therapy because the therapist is seen as not giving them enough attention and support. Table 4-1 summarizes the interpretive guidelines for scale 1.

Scale 2: Depression (D)

Scale Development

The second standard scale on the basic profile sheet, the Depression (D) scale, provides the interpreter with a measure of symptomatic depression. The clinical picture assessed by the D scale is that of a generally negative frame of mind in which the individual has reported poor morale, lack of hope in the future, dissatisfaction with life, and a low mood.

In developing the original MMPI D scale, Hathaway and McKinley (1942a) obtained 50 patients who were mostly in the depressed phase of a manic-depressive disorder. They used several contrast groups to develop scale 2, including 139 normal married men and 200 normal married women between the ages of 26 and 43 years, 265 college students, and 50 patients without clinical depression. Initially, scale 2 was developed by determining which of the MMPI items significantly discriminated the depressed patients from the normal group. A number of additional items were included in the scale to minimize elevations on the scale for patients who were not diagnosed as depressed but suffered from some other disorder. In the MMPI-2, three objectionable items were deleted from scale 2. The same deletions were made on the MMPI-A version of D.

Table 4-1. Scale 1 Interpretive Guidelines for the MMPI-2

☐ High elevations on scale 1 are T scores ≥ 65. The probability that the descriptors listed below apply to a given individual increases with higher scale elevations.

☐ Moderate elevations on scale 1 are T scores of 60 to 64, inclusive. Elevations in this range may be associated with some of the descriptors listed below. Many individuals with known medical disorders also obtain scores in this range.

☐ Descriptors for elevated scores:
  - Excessive bodily concerns
  - Vague somatic symptoms
  - Epigastric complaints, fatigue, and pain
  - Selfish, self-centered, and narcissistic
  - Pessimistic, defeatist, and cynical outlook on life
  - Dissatisfied and unhappy
  - Whining and complaining
  - Attention demanding
  - Critical of others
  - Expresses hostility indirectly
  - Rarely acts out
  - Functioning at a reduced level of efficiency but without major incapacity
  - Complains about health to the extent that it may make others feel miserable
  - Tends to be difficult to engage in psychological therapy
  - Lacks insight into symptoms

Item Content

Most of the items on D contain content that is obviously related to low mood, low self-esteem, lack of interest in things, and feelings of apathy. Harris and Lingoes found several distinct subsets of item content on the MMPI D scale. They suggested the following subcategories of item content to help interpreters understand the meaning of scale 2 elevations. Again, these Harris-Lingoes subscales are interpreted only if the elevation on scale 2 is greater than or equal to 60 and the subscale's score is greater than or equal to 65:

D_1—*Subjective Depression* (32 items)
High scorers on this subscale endorse content indicating that they feel depressed, unhappy, or nervous; lack energy; and have few interests. They feel that they do not cope well with problems and have difficulties concentrating and giving attention to daily tasks. They feel inferior, lack self-confidence, and are often shy and uneasy in social situations.

D_2—*Psychomotor Retardation* (14 items)
High scorers on this subscale report being immobilized, listless, and withdrawn; lacking energy; and avoiding people.

D_3—*Physical Malfunctioning* (11 items)
High scorers on this subscale report that they are preoccupied with physical functioning, deny good health, and have a wide variety of somatic complaints.

D₄—*Mental Dullness* (15 items)

High scorers endorse items suggesting lack of energy, tension, concentration problems, and attention deficits. They seem to lack self-confidence and feel that life is empty. They are apathetic.

D₅—*Brooding* (10 items)

High scorers tend to brood and ruminate a great deal and deny feeling happy. They feel inferior and report that life is not worth living. They feel easily hurt by criticism and feel that they are losing control of their thought processes. They report feeling useless.

Illustrative Empirical Research

The MMPI D scale has been found to be related to the presence of mood disorder (Endicott & Jortner, 1966; Nelson, 1987; Nelson & Cicchetti, 1991). Butcher (1989d) showed that the MMPI-2 D score clearly differentiated depressed inpatients from normals, with a T score of 65 providing good separation between the two groups (see Figure 4-3).

In an inpatient psychiatric sample, Graham and Butcher (1988) found that psychiatric patients scoring high on the MMPI-2 D scale were rated by clinicians as having a depressed mood, feeling low, experiencing guilt feelings, and having hallucinations. Ben-Porath, Butcher, and Graham (1991) found that the MMPI-2 D score was the most effective standard scale for differentiating depressives from schizophrenics in an inpatient population.

Interpretation of elevated scale 2 scores for individuals from the general population received substantial empirical support from the couples rating study in the

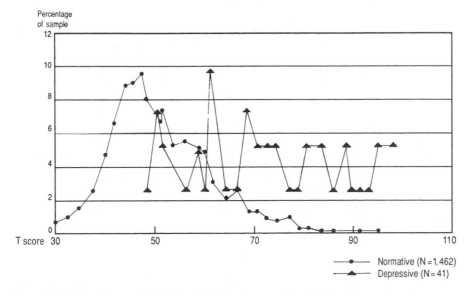

Figure 4-3. Uniform T-score distributions for D for depressed inpatients and normals.

MMPI Restandardization Project (Butcher et al., 1989). Men and women who scored high on D were viewed by their spouses as generally maladjusted, lacking energy and self-confidence. Their spouses reported that they tended to get sad or blue easily, give up on tasks too quickly, and were overly concerned that something bad was going to happen. They were seen as lacking an interest in things and tended to be viewed as bored and restless. The correlates for the Depression scale were reaffirmed in two recent empirical studies (Butcher et al., 2000; Graham et al., in press).

Descriptors

High scorers are seen as depressed, unhappy, dysphoric, pessimistic, self-deprecating, guilt prone, and sluggish. They report having somatic complaints, weakness, fatigue, low energy, and tension. These individuals are prone to worry, indecisive, and low in self-confidence. They report feeling useless and are unable to function effectively much of the time. They feel inadequate and report feeling like a failure at school or on the job. Individuals with high scores on D are viewed as introverted, shy, retiring, timid, reclusive, and aloof. They tend to maintain psychological distance and avoid interpersonal involvement. They are seen as cautious, not impulsive, and conventional. They are usually viewed as passive and unassertive and tend to make concessions in interpersonal relations to avoid conflict. High scorers tend to be motivated to receive treatment. Table 4-2 summarizes the interpretive guidelines for scale 2.

Scale 3: Hysteria (Hy)

Scale Development

In developing the original MMPI, Hathaway and McKinley were interested in providing an objective measure of a complex clinical phenomenon referred to as conversion hysteria, which today we call conversion disorder. Conversion disorder patients often manifest an unusual pattern of personality characteristics composed of denial and flamboyant social assertiveness. Yet under environmental or relationship stress, the individual may become suddenly disabled by physical problems, usually vague and of unknown origin. The patients used in the development of this scale were 50 cases with a clinical diagnosis of psychoneurosis (hysteria). Most were diagnosed as conversion hysteria (e.g., aphonia or anesthesia). The normal group employed in the item analysis to develop the Hy scale included 139 men and 200 women from the original MMPI normative sample and 265 college students. The final Hy scale contained 60 items, all of which were carried over into MMPI-2 and MMPI-A.

Item Content

The content of scale 3 is complex, composed of several seemingly unrelated item clusters. The items describe somatic complaints, denial of psychological problems,

Table 4-2. Scale 2 Interpretive Guidelines for the MMPI-2

☐ High elevations on scale 2 are T scores ≥ 65. The probability that the descriptors listed below apply to a given individual increases with higher scale elevations.

☐ Moderate elevations on scale 2 are T scores of 60 to 64, inclusive. Elevations in this range may be associated with some of the descriptors listed below.

☐ Descriptors for elevated scores:
  - Depressed, unhappy, and dysphoric
  - Pessimistic about the future
  - Self-deprecating, lacking in self-confidence
  - Often feels guilty
  - Sluggish, weak, easily fatigued, and reporting low energy
  - Having many somatic complaints
  - Agitated, tense, high-strung, and irritable
  - Prone to worry
  - May have a sense of dread over future problems
  - Feels useless, unable to function, and like a failure
  - Typically introverted, shy, retiring, and timid
  - Aloof, withdrawn, or distant
  - Avoids interpersonal involvement
  - Cautious and conventional
  - Shows concentration difficulties
  - Difficulty making decisions
  - Nonaggressive, overcontrolled, nonimpulsive
  - Makes concessions to avoid conflict
  - Typically motivated for therapy

☐ Elevations on scale 2 can be more fully understood by examining the item content, as assessed by the Harris-Lingoes subscales, contributing to the scale elevation. The Harris-Lingoes subscales for scale 2 are:
  - Subjective Depression
  - Psychomotor Retardation
  - Physical Malfunctioning
  - Mental Dullness
  - Brooding

---

and social extroversion or social facility. Scale 3 items were grouped by Harris and Lingoes into five subscales, which are interpreted only when scale 3 is moderately or highly elevated (T score of 60) and the subscale score is high (T score of 65):

Hy$_1$—*Denial of Social Anxiety* (6 items)
High scorers endorse items indicating that they are socially extroverted and comfortable in social settings. They deny being shy or having difficulty talking to others.

Hy$_2$—*Need for Affection* (12 items)
High scorers report having strong needs for attention and affection. They feel that they are sensitive, optimistic, and trusting of others. They indicate that they tend to avoid confrontations and deny negative feelings toward others.

Hy₃—*Lassitude-Malaise* (15 items)

High scorers feel physically uncomfortable and in poor health. They deny being happy. They endorse feeling tired, weak, and fatigued and report having concentration difficulties. They may claim to have a poor appetite and sleep disturbance and feel vaguely unhappy.

Hy₄—*Somatic Complaints* (17 items)

High scorers report multiple somatic complaints, such as headaches, dizziness, or problems with balance. They tend to use repression and conversion of affect in conflict situations.

Hy₅—*Inhibition of Aggression* (7 items)

High scorers deny hostile and aggressive impulses. They feel that they are sensitive toward others and deny irritability.

Several items on Hy may seem contradictory or inconsistent, but they reflect the incongruities in the conversion disorder itself. In nonclinical cases, these seemingly conflicting item groups are usually not endorsed together. However, in some clinical cases in which the individual possesses these seemingly disparate characteristics, a particular clinical pattern emerges. This clinical pattern, made up of psychological denial, social facility, and manifestation of vague somatic complaints, is seen as a distinctive clinical syndrome centering around somatization. For example, in diagnostic disorders such as conversion disorder or psychogenic pain disorder, many of these disparate items are endorsed together, resulting in marked elevations on scale 3.

Illustrative Empirical Research

Moderate elevations on Hy (T score of 60–64) are commonly produced by individuals who are attempting to put their best foot forward in a job application. They likely are not responding to content related to physical symptoms but, instead, endorse the items on Hy related to social facility and denial of problems (Butcher, 1979). However, when Hy scores are highly elevated (T score of 65), the meaning of the scale changes, reflecting the likely endorsement of vague physical problems and health concerns. High elevations on Hy reflect a proclivity toward developing somatic complaints in response to stressful events. Individuals with elevated Hy scores are usually presenting somatic symptoms of a vague undefined nature. Research has found that a subtype of patients in chronic pain programs produce high Hy scores often paralleling the elevation on Hs (Keller & Butcher, 1991). Thus, the Hy scale often forms an interesting configuration with other scales (to be discussed in the next chapter) in which both denial of psychological problems and manifestation of vague somatic complaints occur together. This pattern is sometimes associated with malingering, either conscious or unconscious, and physical problems (Butcher & Harlow, 1985).

Graham and Butcher (1988) found that psychiatric inpatients obtaining high scores on the MMPI-2 Hy scale showed other psychological problems in addition to their somatic concerns, which included clinician ratings of depression and low self-esteem. Graham et al. (2000) reported somatization to be the most prominent correlate for Hy in an outpatient sample.

Descriptors

Individuals who score high on Hy tend to react to stress by developing physical symptoms such as headaches, chest pains, weakness, and tachycardia. Symptoms appear suddenly and abate relatively quickly. Individuals with high Hy scores are seen as lacking in insight about the underlying etiology of their symptoms and about their own motives and feelings. They also tend to lack anxiety, tension, and depression, although in some settings and when other scales (such as D and Pt) are elevated, these symptoms can appear.

Individuals with Hy as their highest score are found to be psychologically immature, childish, infantile, self-centered, narcissistic, and egocentric. They seek and expect attention and excessive affection from others and use indirect and manipulative means to get it. They are interpersonally indirect and do not express hostility and resentment openly. They tend to be socially extroverted, friendly, talkative, and enthusiastic, though somewhat superficial in interpersonal relationships. They may occasionally act out in a sexual or aggressive manner with little apparent insight into their behavior. High Hy scorers rarely report delusions, hallucinations, or suspiciousness. They may show initial enthusiasm about treatment, but efforts to change their behavior are often ineffective. They are seemingly slow to gain insight into the causes of their own behavior and are resistant to psychological interpretations. They have been found to respond well to direct advice or suggestion if their defenses are not threatened. Table 4-3 summarizes the interpretive guidelines for scale 3.

Scale 4: Psychopathic Deviate (Pd)

Scale Development

This scale was developed by McKinley and Hathaway (1944) as a measure of antisocial tendencies or psychopathic behavior. The criterion groups that McKinley and Hathaway used in the original scale development were composed of young men and women (N = 78) from an inpatient university hospital and 100 inmates from a federal prison reformatory (all had received a psychiatric diagnosis of psychopathic personality). Their offenses included such acts as truancy, promiscuity, runaway, and theft. Their responses to the MMPI items were contrasted with 294 normal men and 397 normal women. The items on the MMPI-2 Pd scale are the same items (with minor rewording) as on the original MMPI Pd scale. One item ("My sex life is satisfactory."), deemed inappropriate for adolescents, was dropped from the MMPI-A Pd scale.

Item Content

The item content of Pd is quite heterogeneous, making interpretation of the scale somewhat complex. However, the total score is highly correlated with external behaviors indicating family or behavior problems of an aggressive, interpersonally manipulative, and impulsive nature. The Harris-Lingoes subscales can help facilitate the interpretation of elevations on scale 4:

Table 4-3. Scale 3 Interpretive Guidelines for the MMPI-2

☐ High elevations on scale 3 are T scores ≥ 65. The probability that the descriptors listed below apply to a given individual increases with higher scale elevations.

☐ Moderate elevations on scale 3 are T scores of 60 to 64, inclusive. Elevations in this range may be associated with some of the descriptors listed below for scale 3.

☐ Descriptors for elevated scores:
  • Reacts to stress and avoids responsibility through development of physical symptoms
  • Has headaches, chest pains, weakness, and tachycardia
  • Symptoms often appear and disappear suddenly
  • Lacks insight about causes of symptoms
  • Lacks insight about own motives and feelings
  • Shows low anxiety, tension, and depression
  • Rarely reports delusions, hallucinations, or suspiciousness
  • Psychologically immature, childish, and infantile
  • Typically self-centered, narcissistic, and egocentric
  • Expects attention and demands affection from others
  • Uses indirect and devious means to get attention
  • Does not express hostility and resentment openly
  • Socially involved, friendly, talkative, and enthusiastic
  • Superficial and immature in interpersonal relationships
  • Typically slow to gain insight into causes of own behavior
  • May be resistant to psychological interpretations
  • May be initially enthusiastic about treatment and might respond to direct advice or suggestion

☐ Elevations on scale 3 can be more fully understood by examining the item content, as assessed by the Harris-Lingoes subscales, contributing to the scale elevation. The Harris-Lingoes subscales for scale 3 are:
  • Denial of Social Anxiety
  • Need for Affection
  • Lassitude Malaise
  • Somatic Complaints
  • Inhibition of Aggression

Pd₁—*Familial Discord* (11 items)

High scorers endorse items suggesting that they view their home situation as unpleasant and lacking in love, support, and understanding. They view their family as critical and controlling. They indicate a desire to leave home.

Pd₂—*Authority Problems* (10 items)

High scorers report that they resent authority and have had trouble with the law. They report definite opinions about right and wrong and tend to stand up for their beliefs. They report a history of behavior problems in school. They admit stealing, problematic sexual behavior, and problems with the law.

Pd₃—*Social Imperturbability* (12 items)

High scorers report feeling comfortable and confident in social situations. They acknowledge being exhibitionistic and opinionated.

Pd₄—*Social Alienation* (18 items)

High scorers report feeling misunderstood, alienated, isolated, and estranged from others. They report loneliness and unhappiness and being uninvolved.

They blame others for their problems. They report being self-centered, insensitive, and inconsiderate. They may also indicate some regret and remorse over their past actions.

Pd$_5$—*Self-Alienation* (15 items)

High scorers report feeling uncomfortable and unhappy with themselves. They seem to have problems in concentration. They report finding life uninteresting or unrewarding. They find it hard to settle down to life. They may report excessive use of alcohol.

Illustrative Empirical Research

High Pd elevations have been found to be related to membership in many deviant groups, including psychopathic personalities (Guthrie, 1952), delinquents (Rempel, 1958), shoplifters (Beck & McIntyre, 1977), prisoners (Panton, 1959), and drug addicts (Hill, Haertzen & Glaser, 1960). These individuals tend to manifest considerable antisocial features. However, research has also shown the Pd score to be related to personality characteristics in normal groups as well. Moderate scale elevations occur among diverse groups, such as applicants for police department positions (Saccuzzo, Higgins & Lewandowski, 1974), individuals with poor driving records (Brown & Berdie, 1960), skydivers (Delk, 1973), and actors (Taft, 1961). Assuredly, these moderate elevations appear to be due to a willingness to take risks and to unconventional or extroverted lifestyles among these individuals.

The Pd scale has also been shown to be associated with significant behavioral problems in longitudinal research. Garfinkle, Bagby, Waring, and Dorian (1997) studied personality problems in psychiatrists who had become sexually involved with their patients. They examined the results of a test battery, including the MMPI, that had been administered to 120 psychiatric residents who had been tested during the first year of their residency. The residents were followed up between 13 and 17 years after they had completed their residency. The residents who had been disciplined by the Canadian licensing board for boundary violations with patients had markedly more elevated scores on the Pd and Ma scales than did the other residents. In another study, Loper, Kammeier, and Hoffman (1973) examined earlier MMPI scores of a group of men who had been treated for alcoholism in alcohol treatment facilities in Minnesota. All these alcoholics had been students at the University of Minnesota 17 years earlier and had been tested with the MMPI on a routine basis when they were college freshmen. These investigators found that the men who later became alcoholic had prominent, significant elevations on the Pd scale compared with their classmates at the earlier testing.

Several recent studies have been devoted to refining the characteristics measured by scale 4 in the MMPI-2. Lilienfeld (1991), using a sample of college students who had been assessed for the presence of *DSM III-R* characteristics of antisocial personality, reported that Pd was more closely associated with negative emotionality, especially alienation, than it was with other aspects of antisocial behavior. It is interesting that content scale ASP (to be discussed in Chapter 7) is only modestly correlated (.37) with Pd (Butcher, Graham, Williams & Ben-Porath, 1990), indicating that Pd and ASP are not assessing the same personality dimension. As noted previously, scale 4 is a very heterogeneous scale containing many behaviors that are not antisocial, whereas ASP is a more direct measure of antisocial behaviors and attitudes. Two other recent studies provide additional information about the meaning of elevations on scale 4. Pd was found to be highly related to the presence of marital problems. Couples in marital therapy had significantly higher MMPI-2 scale 4 elevations than did normal couples (Hjemboe & Butcher, 1991). Pd was also found to be prominent in mothers who were at risk for abusing their children (Egeland, Erickson, Butcher & Ben-Porath, 1991).

Research subsequent to the publication of the MMPI-2 has supported the conclusions of the initial MMPI-2 studies. Interpretation of elevated scale 4 scores for individuals from the general population received empirical substantiation from the couples rating study in the MMPI Restandardization Project (Butcher et al., 1989). Subjects from the MMPI-2 normative sample who scored high on Pd were viewed by their spouses as antisocial, impulsive, moody, and resentful. They were reported to take drugs other than those prescribed by a doctor, have sexual conflicts, and show negative behavior, such as swearing.

Descriptors

High scorers on scale 4 are found to engage in antisocial behavior, have rebellious attitudes toward authority figures, have stormy family relationships, tend to blame their parents for their problems, and show a history of underachievement in school or poor work history. If married, they tend to have marital problems. The high Pd scorer is viewed as impulsive, strives for immediate gratification of impulses, does not plan well, acts without considering the consequences, is impatient, shows limited tolerance of frustration, has poor judgment, and takes risks that others avoid. Moderate range scores on Pd (T score of 60–64) should not be interpreted as reflecting the more extreme antisocial personality features.

High Pd people are viewed as immature, childish, narcissistic, self-centered, and selfish. In social situations, they are seen as ostentatious, exhibitionistic, and insensitive. They seem to be interested in others only in terms of how they can use them for their own purposes. They usually are likable and create a good first impression, although they are shallow and superficial in relationships. They seem unable to form warm attachments to others. They are viewed as extroverted, outgoing, talkative, active, energetic, spontaneous, and self-confident.

High Pd scorers are found to be hostile, aggressive, sarcastic, cynical, resentful, rebellious, and antagonistic. They may display aggressive outbursts, engage in assaultive behavior, and show little guilt over their negative behavior. Many individuals with this profile type may feign guilt and remorse when in trouble. They are usually seen as being free from disabling anxiety, depression, and psychotic symptoms. Those with high elevations are likely be diagnosed as personality disordered (antisocial or passive-aggressive).

As to potential for change, high scorers on scale 4 are viewed as unable to profit from experience and lacking in definite goals. They show an absence of deep emotional response and may not form a treatment relationship. They tend to be unmotivated and report feeling bored and empty. Their treatment prognosis is

Table 4-4. Scale 4 Interpretive Guidelines for the MMPI-2

☐ High elevations on scale 4 are T scores ≥ 65. The probability that the descriptors listed below apply to a given individual increases with higher scale elevation.

☐ Moderate elevations on scale 4 are T scores of 60 to 64, inclusive. Elevations in this range may be associated with some of the descriptors listed below for scale 4.

☐ Descriptors for elevated scores:
- Antisocial behaviors
- Appears not to have incorporated values and standards of society
- Rebellious toward authority figures
- Stormy family relationships
- Blames others for problems
- History of underachievement or work problems
- Marital or other relationship problems
- Impulsive behavior
- Strives for immediate gratification
- Does not plan well, acts without considering consequences of actions
- Impatient, limited frustration tolerance
- Poor judgment, takes many risks
- Does not seem to profit from experience
- Reportedly immature, childish, and self-centered
- Often ostentatious and exhibitionistic
- Insensitive to the needs of others
- Has shallow interpersonal relationships
- Tends to use other people for own gain
- May be initially likeable but tends to be superficial in relationships
- May be unable to form warm attachments
- Extroverted, outgoing, talkative, active, and spontaneous
- Lacks definite goals
- May be hostile, aggressive, sarcastic, cynical, resentful, and rebellious
- May act out in an aggressive manner
- Shows little guilt over negative behavior but may feign guilt and remorse when in trouble
- Usually free from disabling anxiety, depression, and psychotic symptoms
- Dissatisfied with life and feels bored and empty
- Absence of deep emotional response to others
- Poor prognosis for change in therapy

☐ Elevations on scale 4 can be more fully understood by examining the item content, as assessed by the Harris-Lingoes subscales, contributing to the scale elevation. The Harris-Lingoes subscales for scale 4 are:
- Familial Discord
- Authority Problems
- Social Imperturbability
- Social Alienation
- Self-Alienation

---

usually considered poor because they are resistant to change in therapy. They tend to blame others for problems and to intellectualize their problems. Although they may agree to treatment to avoid punishments such as jail or some other unpleasant outcome, they are likely to terminate psychological therapy before change is effected. Table 4-4 summarizes the interpretive guidelines for scale 4.

Scale 5: Masculinity-Femininity (Mf)

Scale Development

The Masculinity-Femininity scale is different from the other standard scales in several ways. The construct underlying its development is not a clinical syndrome. Instead, scale 5 was designed to identify personality features of "male sexual inversion" or homosexual men who had a feminine interest pattern (Dahlstrom & Welsh, 1960; Hathaway, 1956). The criterion group used in the scale's development was quite small compared to the other standard scales and included only 13 homosexual men with gender identification problems (i.e., "male sexual inverts"). Hathaway (1956) was somewhat unclear about the procedures used for item selection, but Constantinople (1973) suggested the following progression:

1. Retention of all items from the original MMPI pool that discriminated men from women

2. Deletion from this subpool of all items which failed to discriminate the responses of the 13 homosexual men forming the criterion group, as well as an unspecified number of men with high inversion scores on the Terman Inversion Scale, from 54 "normal" soldiers (all men)

3. A check for men-women discrimination using both the original group of normals and smaller groups of soldiers (men) and airline employees (women)

The original MMPI Mf scale consisted of 60 items: 37 from the MMPI item pool and 23 suggested by the work of Terman and Miles (1936).

Hathaway attempted to improve Mf by using a criterion group of women "whose personal problems included homosexuality" (Hathaway, 1956) to form another scale. It was derived using a process similar to the procedures used for scale 5 and was designated Fm. However, Fm was highly correlated with Mf and did not perform well on cross-validation. Fm was abandoned in favor of using Mf for both men and women by reversing the T-score conversions for women. Thus, high T scores for men and women indicated a deviation from the interest patterns assumed to be typical for their gender (i.e., feminine interests in men and masculine interests in women).

Scale 5 was maintained on the MMPI-2 with four item deletions to eliminate objectionable content (i.e., those with religious themes) or irrelevant content (e.g., the item asking about "drop-the-handkerchief"). Additional item deletions on Mf were made on the MMPI-A, as described in Chapter 11.

Perhaps because of the basic assumptions underlying scale 5's development and the procedures followed, it is one of the more difficult standard scales to interpret. Homosexuality is no longer in the psychiatric nomenclature, nor are homosexuals considered more likely to have mental disorders than others. Thus, there is no need for a clinical measure to identify homosexuals. However, some, including the test authors, indicated that scale 5 also was a measure of "the tendency toward masculinity or femininity of interest pattern" (Hathaway & McKinley, 1942b).

Constantinople (1973) provided cogent arguments against the use of scale 5 as a measure of masculine and feminine interests that we believe remain valid. First of all, the scale's item selection and validation procedures demonstrate that its major aim was to identify sexual inversion in men:

> Its derivation should produce some caution since homosexuality is explicitly included in the definition of the construct. (p. 395)

Constantinople also questioned the scale's underlying assumptions of unidimensionality and the bipolarity of its construct. Scale 5 assumes that masculinity-femininity is a single bipolar dimension ranging from extreme masculinity at one end to extreme femininity at the other. Furthermore, the Mf scale is based on the hypothesis that masculinity-femininity is a unitary rather than a multidimensional trait. Constantinople (1973) reviewed several studies demonstrating that both rationally derived categories (Dahlstrom & Welsh, 1960) and factor analyses of scale 5 items (Graham, Schroeder & Lily, 1971) indicate that the Mf-defined constructs of masculine and feminine interests are not opposite ends of a single bipolar continuum but, rather, separate categories or factors. She also points to Cronbach's (1960) assessment of the overall weakness of scale 5.

Our concerns about the use of scale 5 in contemporary assessment are not limited to those expressed almost 20 years ago. Scale 5 items are not substantially different in the revisions of the MMPI because of the decision to maintain continuity in the standard scales between the MMPI and its successors, the MMPI-2 and MMPI-A. However, masculine and feminine interests have not remained stagnant since the Mf items were written in the 1930s and 1940s. Items would have to be added to the MMPI item pool to adequately assess this construct. Furthermore, as indicated in the previous discussion, responses from homosexual men were the predominant method of selecting items defining feminine interests in the original item pool. Decades of research on gender differences indicate that this is no longer an acceptable scientific practice.

Item Content

Scale 5 items are heterogeneous, most of them relating to interests and occupational choices, with very few indicating psychological problems or symptoms. Only 5 of the original 60 items deal with sexual concerns or practices. The occupational choices are very stereotypically feminine (e.g., librarian, nurse, artist who draws flowers) or masculine (e.g., soldier, sports reporter, forest ranger). Scale 5 item content is quite obvious to the test taker, who can readily choose whether to admit to items indicating gender-based interests or sexual concerns.

A factor analysis by Graham et al. (1971) revealed six separate factors for this 60-item scale. A set of subscales for Mf using the results of this factor analysis was presented by Serkownek (1975) and gained popularity among users of the original MMPI. However, Graham (1990) described several methodological problems in the development of these subscales that resulted in their deletion from the MMPI-2.

Peterson (1989) developed two gender-role scales for the MMPI-2: GM (Masculine Gender Role) and GF (Feminine Gender Role). GM and GF were developed using the experimental item pool for the MMPI-2. However, this experimental item pool did not include new items designed to assess contemporary gender issues. These scales have not been sufficiently validated to use in clinical assessment.

Illustrative Empirical Research

Scale 5 has not been as extensively researched as many of the other standard scales. Constantinople (1973) indicated that several studies documented consistently large mean score differences between men and women. However, Murray (1963) found that 20 of the 60 items did not discriminate between the genders and that deletion of those items brought men's scores largely into the normal range. Although extreme Mf scores have been interpreted as a possible indication of gender-identity problems or homosexuality in men, no support for such an interpretation for women has been documented (Constantinople, 1973).

Some of the earliest research findings demonstrate the influence of education on scale 5 scores. Goodstein (1954), for example, showed that college men scored one-half to one standard deviation above the mean reported for the Minnesota normals. Other characteristics such as intelligence and socioeconomic status have also been found to relate to Mf scores (Graham, 1990), which further complicates the scale's ability to predict gender-identity concerns.

Education remains important in the interpretation of MMPI-2 scale 5. The correlation between years of education and scale 5 T scores is .35 for men and −.15 for women (Butcher, 1990b). Mf scores range, on average, about 5 points lower for men with less than a high school education and 5 points higher for men with postbaccalaureate degrees (Butcher, 1990b). Long and Graham (1991) failed to find any useful correlates for the MMPI-2 Mf scale. Greene (1991) also noted the relative paucity of behavioral correlates for scale 5.

Descriptors

The previous descriptions of the development, content, and supporting research base for scale 5 indicate that a different interpretive approach is needed for this scale. Since the publication of the MMPI-2, we have begun to question the appropriateness and utility of continuing this scale on newer versions of the MMPI. As discussed in Chapter 11, we recommended that it be considered for deletion from the MMPI-A (Williams & Butcher, 1989a). However, this was thought to be too radical a departure from the original MMPI by several committee members. In any event, a cautious interpretive strategy is warranted unless additional research suggests otherwise.

The Mf scale is not a "symptom scale," as are most of the other standard scales. Elevations on this scale reflect interests, values, and personality characteristics. It can have meaning with both high and low scores, whereas most of the standard scales are interpreted at high elevations only. Interpretation of scale 5 differs by gender, educational level, socioeconomic status, and elevation levels. The meaning of elevated scores differs somewhat on scale 5 compared with the other standard scales. The more items endorsed by a male in the deviant direction, the greater his interests differ from the stereotypically defined masculine pattern. Because the feminine end of the scale has been defined primarily by responses from men, we refrain from making a similar statement for women.

College-educated men often obtain scores in the 60 to 65 T-score range. A moderately elevated MMPI-2 score for men with college backgrounds would be between 65 and 70. More extreme scores would be greater than or equal to 70. Greene (1991) suggests that these highly elevated scores in college men cannot be attributed solely to a humanistic and liberal arts background but include gender conflicts as well.

Men with a high school education or less typically achieve lower elevations. Thus, elevations that are considered moderate for men with a college education would be more extreme for those without such experiences. Low scores in men are defined as less than a T score of 40.

Elevated scores are somewhat unusual in women from the general population (e.g., only 6.6% of the women from the MMPI-2 normative sample score a T score of 65 or higher on Mf). Elevated scores may be more likely for women in psychiatric settings. We observed that 14.7% of 191 women in a psychiatric setting had T scores of 65 on scale 5. Low scores typically are defined for women as less than a T score of 40. However, it is important to keep in mind that highly educated women often score between 40 and 50.

Descriptors for Men

High elevations on scale 5 in men traditionally are interpreted as indicating more feminine interest patterns and behaviors and a denial of stereotypically masculine interests. This interpretation must be tempered by the man's educational background and socioeconomic level. With more extreme elevations, high-scoring men may have conflicts about sexual identity, may be insecure in masculine roles, or may be effeminate in manner. The high scorer likely endorses a variety of aesthetic and artistic interests. He may be seen as intelligent and valuing cognitive pursuits. Sensitivity, tolerance of others, and nurturance are other likely characteristics of high-scoring men. Submissive qualities may be apparent, and acting-out behaviors are unlikely.

Low-scoring Mf men can be characterized as "macho." They endorse extremely masculine values, overemphasizing strength and physical prowess. They may be viewed as inflexible, coarse, crude, or vulgar. It has been suggested that extremely low scores indicate those with doubts about their masculinity, limited intellectual ability, narrow range of interests, and inflexible and unoriginal problem-solving abilities. However, low scores should not be overinterpreted in men without a high school education.

Descriptors for Women

Women who score high on scale 5 are unusual compared with other women. They endorse items that some see as representing extremely masculine interests. Women with lower Mf scores endorse more items indicative of what have been described as stereotypically feminine interests. Given the lack of studies, the questionable developmental strategy of Mf as a measure of feminine interests in women, and the conflicting findings with educated women (Graham, 1990), we

Table 4-5. Scale 5 Interpretive Guidelines for the MMPI-2

☐ Interpretation of scale 5 differs by gender, educational level, socioeconomic status, and elevation levels. It is not a symptom scale, and elevations reflect interests, values, and personality characteristics.

☐ College-educated men often obtain scores in the 60 to 65 T-score range. A moderately elevated MMPI-2 score for men with college backgrounds is 65 to 70. More extreme scores would be > 70.

☐ Men with less than a high school education typically achieve lower elevations. Thus, elevations that are considered moderate for college-educated men are more extreme for those without such experiences. Low scores in men are defined as less than a T score of 40.

☐ High elevations on scale 5 in men are interpreted as indicating more stereotypically feminine interest patterns and behaviors and a denial of stereotypically masculine interests. With more extreme elevations, high-scoring men may have conflicts about sexual identity, be insecure in masculine roles, or be effeminate in manner. The high scorer likely endorses a variety of aesthetic and artistic interests. He may be seen as intelligent and valuing cognitive pursuits. Sensitivity, tolerance of others, and nurturing are other likely characteristics. Submissive qualities may be apparent and acting-out behaviors are unlikely.

☐ Low-scoring men endorse extremely stereotypically masculine values, overemphasizing strength and physical prowess, often called "macho." They may be viewed as inflexible, coarse, crude, or vulgar. Lower scores suggest possible doubts about masculinity, limited intellectual ability, narrow range of interests, and inflexible and unoriginal problem-solving abilities.

☐ Elevated scores in women are somewhat unusual and can be defined as T scores ≥ 65. Low scores in women typically are defined as T scores < 40. Highly educated women often have T scores of 40 to 50.

☐ Until there is more evidence supporting the use of scale 5 with women, the scores should be interpreted cautiously:
  • Women who score high on scale 5 describe interests that are typically seen as stereotypically masculine or "macho." This pattern is unusual compared to other women.
  • Low-scoring women endorse more items reflecting interests that historically have been described as stereotypically feminine.

recommend considerable caution in making interpretive statements for women unless more adequate studies are completed that demonstrate Mf's validity with women. At present, we recommend only the interpretive statements appearing in Table 4-5.

Scale 6: Paranoia (Pa)

Scale Development

Scale 6 assesses the behavior pattern of suspiciousness, mistrust, delusional beliefs, excessive interpersonal sensitivity, rigid thinking, and externalization of blame commonly found in paranoid disorders (Hathaway, 1956). These symptoms often occur with paranoid states, paranoid schizophrenia, or other severe paranoid disorders. The 40 items constituting Pa were obtained by empirical discrimination between a group of individuals diagnosed as having paranoid disorders or paranoid features in their clinical picture and a group of normal individuals.

Scale 6 was initially found to work well in identifying many individuals in clinical settings with paranoid behavioral features. However, one problem that has been observed with Pa is that some individuals with clear paranoid features may second-guess the test and not endorse items that would produce a high Pa score. Instead, they answer the items in a wary, excessively sensitive, and mistrustful manner in keeping with their symptomatic behavior, actually producing low scale 6 scores.

The fact that some highly suspicious and mistrustful individuals do not score high on this scale raises the need for interpretive caution. If the Pa score is elevated above a T score of 65, interpret the profile as suggesting suspicion, mistrust, and possible paranoid ideation. However, the absence of scale elevation does not indicate the opposite, especially in inpatient facilities, where low Pa scores can be found in individuals with paranoid disorders. The item content of Pa was not changed in the MMPI-2 or MMPI-A.

Item Content

Harris and Lingoes (1955) identified three subgroups of item content in Pa. These subscales can be used to clarify elevated scores on scale 6:

Pa_1—*Persecutory Ideas* (17 items)
High scorers report that their world is threatening and have feelings of being misunderstood, unfairly blamed, or punished. They feel suspicious, distrust others, and tend to blame others for their problems. Elevations above 65 suggest delusions of persecution.

Pa_2—*Poignancy* (9 items)
High scorers see themselves as high-strung and sensitive. They seem to feel more intensely than others. They feel lonely, misunderstood, and distant from others. They may look for risk and excitement.

Pa_3—*Naïveté* (9 items)
High scorers endorse extremely naive and optimistic attitudes about others. They seem to feel overly trusting and vulnerable to being hurt. They report having high moral standards and deny hostility.

Illustrative Empirical Research

Research on the MMPI in clinical samples indicates that Pa is related to severe psychopathology. Guthrie (1952) found that paranoid schizophrenics produce high elevations on Pa. Graham and Butcher (1988) found that psychiatric inpatients obtaining high scores on scale 6 were rated by clinicians as suspicious, having unusual thoughts, being anxious, and showing emotional withdrawal.

Interpretation of elevated Pa scale scores for normals received empirical substantiation from the couples rating study in the MMPI Restandardization Project (Butcher et al., 1989). As viewed by their husbands, women from the MMPI-2 normative sample who scored high on Pa were moody, tended to get sad and blue, lacked emotional control, cried easily, and had bad dreams.

The Pa scale may be moderately elevated in situations in which the individual is being evaluated under duress, such as family custody or pretrial criminal assessments. The person may be wary about responding openly and may try to avoid responsibility for problems. Such situations can result in elevations up to about a T score of 69. However, scale elevations greater than 70 are interpreted as reflecting more chronic or personality-based problems and not simply situational duress.

Descriptors

The correlates for Pa change markedly at different levels of elevation, which differs somewhat from many of the other standard scales. Individuals with very high elevations (T > 80) often show frankly psychotic behavior, disturbed thinking, delusions of persecution or grandeur, and ideas of reference. They tend to feel mistreated and picked on and are angry and resentful. They harbor grudges toward others and use projection as a defense mechanism. The most frequently applied diagnoses of extremely high Pa individuals are schizophrenia, paranoia, or paranoid personality.

Individuals with high elevations (T = 65–79) often manifest a paranoid predisposition. They are hypersensitive and overly responsive to reactions of others, feel that they get a raw deal from life, rationalize and blame others, are suspicious and guarded, and are hostile, resentful, and argumentative. High scorers are viewed as moralistic and rigid and tend to overvalue rationality. They are viewed as having a poor prognosis for therapy because they do not like to talk about emotional problems and usually have difficulty establishing rapport with a therapist.

Individuals with moderate elevations (T scores of 60–64, inclusive) show no specific correlates. It should be noted that some individuals obtain scores in this range on the basis of endorsing the interpersonal sensitivity items on the scale. Interpretation of elevations in this range can be clarified by reference to the Harris-Lingoes subscales.

Very low scores (T < 35) should be interpreted with caution because some individuals with paranoid problems can obtain scores in this range. Low Pa scores (especially in an inpatient context) are viewed as functionally paranoid if the following conditions are found:

1.   The Pa score is below a T score of 35.

2.   The Pa score is the lowest scale on the profile.

3.   At least one standard scale score is above a T score of 65.

4.   The validity configuration is defensive (i.e., both L and K are above a T score of 60 and above F).

Under these conditions, low Pa scores suggest a frankly psychotic disorder, delusions, suspiciousness, ideas of reference, and symptoms that are less obvious than for high scorers. They tend to be evasive, defensive, guarded, shy, secretive, and withdrawn. Table 4-6 summarizes the interpretive guidelines for scale 6.

Table 4-6. Scale 6 Interpretive Guidelines for the MMPI-2

☐ Very high elevations on scale 6 are T scores > 80. High elevations on scale 6 are T scores of 65 to 79, inclusive.

☐ In some cases (see text for more details), individuals with extremely low T scores (< 35) may have paranoid disorders and are so suspicious and distrustful that they respond evasively to the scale 6 items. In clinical settings, these low scores, coupled with a defensive validity pattern, suggest:
  • Frankly psychotic disorder, delusions, or suspiciousness
  • Ideas of reference
  • Symptoms are usually less obvious than for high scorers
  • Evasive, defensive, guarded
  • May be shy, secretive, withdrawn

☐ Descriptors for very high elevations:
  • May show frankly psychotic behavior and disturbed thinking
  • Delusions of persecution and/or grandeur likely
  • Ideas of reference
  • Tends to feel mistreated and picked on
  • Tends to be angry, resentful, and harbors grudges
  • Uses projection as a defense
  • Most frequently diagnosed as schizophrenia or paranoid state

☐ Descriptors for high elevations:
  • Paranoid predisposition
  • Overly sensitive and responsive to reactions of others
  • Feels that he or she is getting a raw deal from life
  • Tends to rationalize and blame others
  • Shows suspicious and guarded behavior
  • Hostile, resentful, and argumentative
  • Tends to be moralistic and rigid
  • May be overly "rational"
  • Does not like to talk about emotional problems
  • Has difficulty establishing rapport with therapist
  • Tends to have a poor prognosis for therapy

☐ Elevations on scale 6 can be more fully understood by examining the item content, as assessed by the Harris-Lingoes subscales, contributing to the scale elevation. The Harris-Lingoes subscales for scale 6 are:
  • Persecutory Ideas
  • Poignancy
  • Naïveté

Scale 7: Psychasthenia (Pt)

Scale Development

Scale 7 was originally developed to assess a psychological disorder (psychasthenia) that today we would describe as anxiety disorder with obsessive-compulsive features. Hathaway and McKinley (1942b) obtained a criterion group of patients (20 patients with clear diagnoses) who possessed behavioral features of anxiousness, severe ruminations, and obsessive-compulsive features. The patients' MMPI responses were contrasted with those of the normal Minnesota sample (139 men and 200 women ages 26–43) to obtain the provisional scale. Then internal consistency statistics were used to eliminate items that were not highly correlated with the total score. This procedure resulted in a final scale with high internal consistency and a clear relationship with the first factor (anxiety) of the MMPI. Even though the clinical diagnosis of psychasthenia does not exist in today's psychiatric nomenclature, the features central to the syndrome (anxiety, ruminations, feelings of insecurity, and so on) are very much apparent in most clinical settings. Scale composition for Pt did not change in the MMPI-2 and MMPI-A.

Item Content

There are no specific content subscales for Pt because the items on this scale are homogeneous, measuring a single dimension. As noted previously, this scale was developed, in part, by internal consistency procedures (i.e., only items with a high correlation with the total score were included on the scale). Consequently, scale 7 contains items that assess anxiety or general maladjustment.

Illustrative Empirical Research

Research on scale 7 has shown it to be associated with severe and debilitating anxiety. For example, Schofield (1956) found Pt to be the peak score among neurotic outpatients diagnosed as having anxiety-state or obsessive-compulsive disorders. In inpatient psychiatric settings with a large percentage of severe affective disorders and schizophrenics, the behavioral correlates for the MMPI-2 Pt scale suggest disabling psychological symptoms. Graham and Butcher (1988) found that the MMPI-2 Pt scale had several significant correlates in inpatient psychiatric settings, including severe guilt, low energy, depressed mood, and hallucinations.

Scale 7 has been shown to have clear behavioral correlates in the normal range of subjects as well. In the MMPI-2 normative study, Pt received substantial empirical support from the couples' rating comparisons (Butcher et al., 1989). Normal men and women with high Pt scores were rated by their spouses as having many fears, being nervous and jittery, being indecisive, lacking in self-confidence, and having sleeping problems.

Descriptors

People who score high on Pt tend to be anxious, tense, and agitated. They report great discomfort, worry, and feelings of apprehension. They are considered to be high-strung, depressed, and jumpy and have concentration difficulties. They report being introspective, ruminative, indecisive, obsessive, and compulsive. They feel insecure and inferior, lack self-confidence, are plagued by self-doubt, and are self-critical, self-conscious, and self-derogatory. They are viewed as rigid and moralistic because they profess high standards for themselves and others, are overly perfectionistic, conscientious, and are guilt prone. They lack ingenuity and originality in problem solving, are dull and formal, and are vacillating. They tend to

Table 4-7. Scale 7 Interpretive Guidelines for the MMPI-2

☐ High elevations on scale 7 are T scores ≥ 65. The probability that the descriptors listed below apply to a given individual increases with higher scale elevations.

☐ Moderate elevations on scale 7 are T scores of 60 to 64, inclusive. Elevations in this range may be associated with some of the descriptors listed below.

☐ Descriptors for elevated scores:
- Anxious, tense, and agitated
- Discomfort, worry, and apprehension
- High-strung and jumpy
- Difficulties in concentrating
- Introspective, ruminative, obsessive, and compulsive
- Feels insecure and inferior
- Lacks self-confidence, has great self-doubts
- Self-critical, self-conscious, and self-derogatory
- Rigid and moralistic
- High standards for self and others
- Overly perfectionistic and conscientious
- Tends to be guilty and depressed
- Often orderly and meticulous
- Persistent and performs tasks in a stereotyped manner
- Often constricted in action and lacks ingenuity and originality in problem solving
- Indecisive
- Overreacts to minor problems
- Shy and does not interact well socially
- Hard to get to know but worries about popularity and acceptance
- Reports physical complaints—particularly heart palpitations
- Often feels fatigued
- May show some insight into problems
- Intellectualizes and rationalizes
- Resistant to interpretations in therapy
- Remains in therapy longer than most patients
- Makes slow but steady progress in therapy

---

distort the importance of problems and overreact to minor situational problems. They usually are shy and do not interact well socially. They are hard to get to know, yet they worry about their popularity and acceptance. They are sensitive, show insight into problems, and tend to intellectualize and rationalize. They are often described as neat, orderly, organized, meticulous, persistent, and reliable. They are somewhat resistant to interpretations in therapy, express hostility toward their therapist, remain in therapy longer than most patients, and usually make slow, gradual progress in therapy. Interpretive guidelines for scale 7 are provided in Table 4-7.

Scale 8: Schizophrenia (Sc)

Scale Development

The development of the Schizophrenia (Sc) scale differed somewhat from the development of the other MMPI standard scales. Hathaway (1956) indicated that he and McKinley attempted to develop several separate scales for the four recognized subtypes of schizophrenia identified at the time (i.e., catatonic, paranoid, simple, and hebephrenic) using two partly overlapping groups of 50 patients who had been diagnosed as having schizophrenia. However, because they could not effectively differentiate between the subtypes of schizophrenia, Hathaway and McKinley simply merged all the items into a single scale for schizophrenia. Consequently, the resulting Sc scale is quite long and complex. It contains the same items in the MMPI-2 as in the original MMPI, although one item was dropped from the MMPI-A.

Item Content

As indicated previously, the procedures used in the development of scale 8 produced a rather long and heterogeneous scale. A high score on this scale reflects a number of diagnostic possibilities because individuals with many disorders can receive high elevations, including schizophrenics, chronic psychiatric patients with affective disorders, persons with organic brain disorders or severe personality disorders, normal individuals with severe sensory impairment, and unconventional, rebellious, and counterculture people (e.g., the hippies of the 1960s).

Interpretation of Sc can be facilitated by examining the relative contributions of the different content subgroups to the total score. Harris and Lingoes (1955), in their rational categorization of the item content for scale 8, suggest the following subcategories:

Sc_1—*Social Alienation* (21 items)
High scorers endorse items that suggest feelings of being misunderstood and mistreated. They report that their family situation is lacking in love and support, and they feel hostility and hatred toward their family members. They feel lonely and empty, having never experienced a love relationship. They feel that they are being plotted against.

Sc_2—*Emotional Alienation* (11 items)
High scorers report feelings of depression and despair. They may wish they were dead and are frightened and apathetic.

Sc_3—*Lack of Ego Mastery, Cognitive* (10 items)
High scorers fear losing their mind. They report having strange thought processes, feelings of unreality, and problems with concentration and attention.

Sc_4—*Lack of Ego Mastery, Conative* (14 items)
High scorers feel that life is a strain. They report having depression, despair, and worry. They have problems coping with everyday life. Life is not interesting or rewarding for them. They seem to have given up hope and may wish they were dead.

Sc_5—*Lack of Ego Mastery, Defective Inhibition* (11 items)
High scorers report feeling out of emotional control. They are impulsive, restless, hyperactive, and irritable. They may have laughing or crying spells and may not remember previously performed activities.

Sc$_6$—*Bizarre Sensory Experiences* (20 items)
High scorers feel their body is changing in unusual ways. They may have
   blank spells, hallucinations, unusual thoughts, or external reference. They
   report skin sensitivity, weakness, and ringing in the ears. They report having peculiar and strange experiences.

Illustrative Empirical Research

The Sc scale has been shown to be empirically related to a number of extreme
personality characteristics and symptomatic behaviors, including the diagnosis of
schizophrenia (Lewinson, 1968; Moldin, Gottesman, Rice & Erlenmeyer-Kimling,
1991; Rosen, 1958; Wauck, 1950). Shaffer, Ota, and Hanlon (1964) found that Sc was
associated with the severity of the disorder. More recently, with the MMPI-2,
Graham and Butcher (1988) found that psychiatric inpatients obtaining high Sc
scores were rated by clinicians as having suspiciousness and unusual thought content. Penk, Rierdan, Knight, and Mesheda (1996) found the Sc scale to be the most
prominent elevation among severely mentally ill patients. In addition, Sc was significantly elevated in a sample of the homeless mentally ill.

Descriptors

Given this scale's complexity and the large number of personality and symptomatic behaviors it assesses, interpretation may change somewhat, depending on
scale elevation. It is possible, for example, for an individual to obtain a moderate
elevation (e.g., 60–65) on the scale if he or she has a sensory impairment or lives a
rather unconventional life. Possible interpretation of scale elevations in this range
should be verified with reference to demographic or admitting complaint information. However, marked elevation on the scale (T > 70) suggests significant personality problems and symptoms.

   Individuals who score 65 to 69 on Sc tend to have an unconventional lifestyle
and feel somewhat alienated from others. They feel distant and different from others and may tend toward reclusiveness. They tend to feel inferior and socially different from others and may appear aloof and uninterested. They tend to employ
fantasy as a defense against unpleasant situations and may daydream a great deal.
High Sc scorers are somewhat immature and self-preoccupied. They may be nonconforming and reluctant to go along with conventions. Some high scale 8 individuals are impulsive, aggressive, or anxious.

   Very high scorers (70–79) tend to have a schizoid lifestyle, do not feel a part of
the social environment, or are isolated, alienated, and misunderstood. They report
feeling unaccepted by peers and are often seen as withdrawn, reclusive, secretive,
and inaccessible. They avoid dealing with people and new situations and are seen
as shy, aloof, and uninvolved. These individuals are anxious, resentful, hostile,
and aggressive. They are unable to express their feelings and tend to react to stress
by withdrawing into fantasy and daydreaming. They have difficulty separating
reality and fantasy, have great self-doubts, and feel inferior, incompetent, and dissatisfied. They may manifest sexual preoccupation and experience gender-role

confusion. They are nonconforming, unusual, unconventional, and eccentric. Others view them as stubborn, moody, opinionated, immature, and impulsive. Some high-scoring Sc persons are also reported to be imaginative, to be abstract, and to have vague goals. They often appear to lack basic information for problem solving, have a poor prognosis for therapy, and are reluctant to relate in a meaningful way to a therapist. They may stay in therapy longer than most patients and may eventually come to trust their therapist. Extremely high scorers (T > 80) may show blatantly psychotic behavior, confusion, disorganization, and disorientation. They typically report unusual thoughts or attitudes, delusions, hallucinations, and poor judgment. Table 4-8 summarizes the interpretive guidelines for scale 8.

Scale 9: Hypomania (Ma)

Scale Development

McKinley and Hathaway (1944) were interested in developing a measure of manic or hypomanic behavior, that is, the tendency to act in euphoric, aggressive, and hyperactive ways. The Ma scale was developed initially by contrasting a group of 24 individuals who were experiencing manic (usually less intense hypomanic) episodes of euphoria. All the patients were in an inpatient facility and had been clearly diagnosed as having manic or hypomanic behaviors. A total of 46 items were found to significantly discriminate the clinical cases from normals. All the original 46 items appear in the MMPI-2 and MMPI-A.

Item Content

Harris and Lingoes found four rational categories summarizing the item content on Ma:

Ma_1—*Amorality* (6 items)
High scorers may see others as selfish and dishonest, which provides justification for their behaving this way as well. They derive vicarious satisfaction from the manipulative exploits of others.

Ma_2—*Psychomotor Acceleration* (11 items)
High scorers show accelerated speech, overactive thought processes, and excessive motor activity. They may be tense, restless, excited, and elated without cause. They are easily bored and tend to seek out excitement. They can be impulsive and do harmful or shocking things.

Ma_3—*Imperturbability* (8 items)
High scorers deny social anxiety. They are not especially sensitive about what others think. They are often impatient and irritable toward others.

Ma_4—*Ego Inflation* (9 items)
High scorers appraise themselves unrealistically. They are resentful of demands made by others.

Table 4-8. Scale 8 Interpretive Guidelines for the MMPI-2

☐ Extremely high elevations on scale 8 are T scores ≥ 80. Very high elevations on scale 8 are scores of 70 to 79, inclusive. High elevations are 65 to 69, inclusive. Different descriptors are associated with these differing levels.

☐ Descriptors for extremely high scale 8 scores:
- Blatantly psychotic behavior
- Confused, disorganized, and disoriented
- Unusual thoughts or attitudes, delusions, hallucinations
- Shows poor judgment

☐ Descriptors for very high scale 8 scores:
- Possibility of a psychotic disorder
- Disorganized, confused
- Possible presence of delusional beliefs
- Schizoid lifestyle
- Does not feel a part of social environment; feels isolated, alienated, and misunderstood
- Unaccepted by peers, withdrawn, seclusive, and secretive
- Emotionally inaccessible
- Avoids dealing with people and new situations
- Shy, aloof, and uninvolved
- Experiences generalized anxiety
- Resentful, hostile, and aggressive
- Unable to express feelings; reacts to stress by withdrawing into fantasy and daydreaming
- Difficulty separating reality and fantasy
- Many self-doubts; feels inferior, incompetent, and dissatisfied
- Shows considerable sexual preoccupation and sex-role confusion
- Nonconforming, unusual, unconventional, and eccentric
- May present long-standing physical complaints
- Often seen as stubborn, moody, and opinionated
- Immature and impulsive
- Lacks basic information for problem-solving
- Shows a poor prognosis for therapy but may stay in therapy longer than most patients

☐ Descriptors for high elevations:
- Unconventional lifestyle
- Nonconforming
- Somewhat alienated from others
- Distant and feels different from others
- Feelings of inferiority
- Aloof and uninterested
- Uses fantasy as a defensive mechanism
- Daydreams frequently
- Immature and self-preoccupied
- May be impulsive, aggressive, or anxious

☐ Elevations on scale 8 can be more fully understood by examining the item content, as assessed by the Harris-Lingoes subscales, contributing to the scale elevation. The Harris-Lingoes subscales for scale 8 are:
- Social Alienation
- Emotional Alienation
- Lack of Ego Mastery, Cognitive
- Lack of Ego Mastery, Conative
- Lack of Ego Mastery, Defective Inhibition
- Bizarre Sensory Experiences

Illustrative Empirical Research

Research on scale 9 has shown it to be related to pathological behavioral and symptomatic correlates. Gilberstadt and Duker (1965) found that patients with high Ma elevation were hyperactive, alcoholic, grandiose, and talkative. They were most frequently diagnosed as manic-depressive or manic type and tended to have work adjustment problems. Graham and Butcher (1988) found that psychiatric inpatients with high scores on the MMPI-2 Ma scale were rated by clinicians as having an elevated mood, being hostile, and having conceptual disorganization.

Normal individuals with elevations on this scale have been shown to be ebullient, overactive, and guileful (Gough, McKee & Yandell, 1955). The traditional correlates for Ma scores for normal individuals received considerable empirical support from the couples rating study in the MMPI Restandardization Project (Butcher et al., 1989). High Ma wives were rated by their husbands as wearing strange or unusual clothes, talking too much, making big plans, getting very excited or happy for little reason, stirring up excitement, taking many risks, and telling people off. High Ma men were viewed by their wives as acting bossy, talking back to others without thinking, talking too much, whining and demanding attention, and taking drugs other than those prescribed by a doctor.

Descriptors

Since many individuals in normal samples obtain high scores on this scale and some patients with affective disorder do not, it is important to keep the level of elevation in mind when interpreting this scale. Very high scorers (T ≥ 75) are viewed as hyperactive, have accelerated speech, and may have hallucinations or delusions of grandeur. They may express a wide range of interests but do not use energy wisely and tend not to complete projects. They may be viewed as somewhat disorganized. Many individuals with very high Ma elevations are viewed as creative, enterprising, and ingenious; however, they show little interest in routine or detail. They become easily bored and restless, have a low frustration tolerance, and may have difficulty in inhibiting expression of impulses. Episodes of irritability, hostility, and aggressive outbursts may occur. They are usually viewed as unrealistic, possessing unqualified optimism, having grandiose aspirations, and exaggerating self-worth and self-importance. Individuals who score very high on Ma are unable to see their own limitations. They are viewed by others as outgoing, sociable, and gregarious. They like to be around other people and may create a good first impression because they are friendly, pleasant, and enthusiastic. Their relationships tend to be superficial. They tend to be highly manipulative, deceptive, and unreliable, and they experience relationship problems as a result. They may have periods of agitation and periodic episodes of depression. Difficulties at school or work are common. They tend to be resistant to interpretations. They attend therapy sessions irregularly and may terminate therapy prematurely.

Individuals who score high on scale 9 (T scores of 65–74, inclusive) are viewed as energetic, active, and talkative and as having a broad range of interests. They seem to prefer action to thought but may not use their energies wisely or see projects through to completion. Individuals with elevated Ma scores are usually sociable, manipulative, persuasive, glib, and somewhat impulsive.

Although some normals score in this range of Ma, most high scorers on this scale encounter interpersonal problems as a result of their manipulativeness and lack of follow-through. They tend to experience mood problems, such as elation or euphoria without cause, extreme self-orientation, or impulsivity.

Low scorers (T $\leq$ 35) report having low energy and activity levels, lethargy, listlessness, and apathy and are difficult to motivate. They report chronic fatigue, physical exhaustion, depression, anxiety, and tension. Low scorers approach problems in conventional, practical ways. They tend to lack self-confidence and are sincere, quiet, modest, withdrawn, seclusive, unpopular, and overcontrolled. Interpretive guidelines for scale 9 are provided in Table 4-9.

Scale 0: Social Introversion (Si)

Scale Development

The Si scale was originally published as a separate measure of social introversion-extroversion by Drake (1946). The scale was developed by contrasting groups of college students who scored high and low on another measure of introversion-extroversion. The original scale 0 contained 70 items dealing with social discomfort, inferiority, low affiliation, interpersonal sensitivity, lack of trust, and physical complaints. One item was deleted in the MMPI restandardization owing to its objectionable content, leaving a total of 69 items on the MMPI-2. A total of 8 items was deleted from this long scale to shorten the MMPI-A.

Item Content

The items on the Si scale have been classified into three subscales using a combined statistical-rational scale construction strategy (Ben-Porath, Hostetler, Butcher & Graham, 1989). The subscales were developed to provide high internal consistencies and were validated against external criteria. These subscales can be used to clarify elevations on Si. The Si subscales are as follows:

Si_1—*Shyness* (14 items)
High scorers are shy in interpersonal situations. They show discomfort around others and are reluctant to begin relationships. They deny being sociable.

Si_2—*Social Avoidance* (8 items)
High scorers tend to avoid groups, are unfriendly and socially withdrawn, and eschew participation with others. They dislike parties and dances.

Si_3—*Self-Other Alienation* (17 items)
High scorers report feeling alienated from others and from themselves. They feel estranged from people and are apprehensive and mistrustful of others and at the same time possess a very poor self-image. They feel disappointed by others.

Table 4-9. Scale 9 Interpretive Guidelines for the MMPI-2

☐ There are four levels of elevation on scale 9: very high (T scores ≥ 75), high (T scores of 65 to 74, inclusive), moderate (T scores of 60 to 64, inclusive), and low (T scores ≤ 35). Interpretive statements vary for each of these levels.

☐ Descriptors for very high scale 9 scores (T ≥ 75):
- Possible manic behavior may be shown
- Overactive and may have accelerated speech
- May have hallucinations or delusions of grandeur
- May be experiencing a mood disorder
- Energetic and talkative
- May be extremely narcissistic
- Prefers action to reflection
- Shows a wide range of interests and activities
- Does not utilize energy wisely; does not see projects through to completion
- Has little interest in routine or detail
- Becomes easily bored and restless
- Low frustration tolerance
- Difficulty in inhibiting expression of impulses
- Episodes of irritability, hostility, and aggressive outbursts
- Often has unrealistic, unqualified optimism
- Has grandiose aspirations
- Exaggerates self-worth and self-importance
- Unable to see own limitations
- Outgoing, sociable, and gregarious
- May have periods of agitation
- May have periodic episodes of depression
- Resistant to interpretations in therapy
- Attends therapy irregularly; may terminate therapy prematurely

☐ Descriptors for high scale 9 scores:
- Overactive
- Exaggerated sense of self-worth, narcissistic
- Energetic, talkative, prefers action to reflection
- Shows a wide range of interests
- Does not utilize energy wisely and does not complete projects
- May be viewed as enterprising and ingenious
- Shows inattention to routine matters
- Becomes bored and restless easily
- Low frustration tolerance
- May be impulsive
- May have episodes of irritability, hostility, and aggressive outbursts
- May be overly optimistic at times
- May show some grandiosity and be unable to see own limitations
- Outgoing, sociable, and gregarious
- Socially manipulative
- Repeat problems
- Usually considers therapy unnecessary and is resistant to interpretations in therapy
- Attends sessions irregularly and may terminate therapy prematurely

☐ Many individuals without psychological problems score in the moderate range on scale 9. Elevations in this range suggest several positive attributes, such as energetic, enthusiastic, outgoing, and high activity level.

☐ Low scores (T ≤ 35) are associated with having a low energy level, apathy, fatigue, depression, and chronic problems of low self-esteem, lack of confidence, and withdrawal.

Table 4-9. Scale 9 Interpretive Guidelines for the MMPI-2, continued

☐ Elevations on scale 9 can be more fully understood by examining the item content, as assessed by the Harris-Lingoes subscales, contributing to the scale elevation. The Harris-Lingoes subscales for scale 9 are:
  • Amorality
  • Psychomotor Acceleration
  • Imperturbability
  • Ego Inflation

Illustrative Empirical Research

Gough et al. (1955) provided a clear picture of high-scoring Si individuals as slow paced, lacking in originality, insecure, indecisive, inflexible, and socially overcontrolled and inhibited. Low-scoring Si subjects were viewed by Hathaway and Meehl (1952) as outgoing, sociable, talkative, assertive, and adventurous. The interpretation of elevated Si scale scores for nonclinical subjects received substantial empirical support from the couples rating study in the MMPI Restandardization Project (Butcher et al., 1989). Spouses indicated that high-scoring subjects act very shy, lack self-confidence, avoid contact with people, are unwilling to try new things, and put themselves down a lot.

Sieber and Meyers (1992) conducted a cross-validation study of the MMPI-2 Social Introversion subscales on a sample of 410 college students. They found that persons with elevations on Si_1 were more socially anxious, were less social, and had lower self-esteem. Those with elevations on Si_2 were viewed as more shy and less social. Persons with elevated Si_3 showed less self-esteem and had an external locus of control.

Descriptors

The Si scale measures a bipolar personality dimension in which high scores assess social introversion and low scores reflect social extroversion. Unlike other MMPI-2 standard scales, low as well as high Si scale elevations can be clinically interpreted.

High scorers (T $\geq$ 65) are socially introverted, more comfortable alone or with a few close friends, and reserved, shy, and retiring. They tend to be uncomfortable around members of the opposite gender, are hard to get to know, and are sensitive to what others think. However, they are troubled by lack of involvement with other people. They tend to be overcontrolled and are not likely to display feelings openly. They are typically submissive and compliant in relationships and are overly accepting of authority. Others see high Si individuals as serious, slow paced, reliable, dependable, cautious, conventional, unoriginal in approach to problems, rigid, inflexible in attitudes and opinions, and indecisive. High Si scorers tend to worry a great deal; are irritable and anxious, moody, and guilt prone; and have episodes of depression or low mood.

Low Si scorers (T $\leq$ 45) are sociable, extroverted, outgoing, gregarious, friendly, and talkative. They have a strong need to be around other people. They are usually expressive, verbally fluent, active, energetic, and vigorous; are interested in status, power, and recognition; and seek out competitive situations. Many low Si individuals have problems with impulse control and may act without considering the consequences of their actions. They may be immature, self-indulgent, superficial, insincere in relationships, manipulative, and opportunistic and arouse resentment and hostility in others. Table 4-10 provides interpretive guidelines for scale 0.

Case Example of the Standard Scales and Their Subscales

As we have seen, several possible descriptors can be associated with elevated scores on the standard scales. The interpretation of a standard scale can sometimes be complicated by the scale's heterogeneous content. On some standard scales, an individual can obtain an elevated score by endorsing a smaller grouping of more homogeneous items. This has relevance for the selection of potential descriptors for the elevated standard scale score. The Harris-Lingoes subscales and the Si subscales are valuable for selecting the most relevant standard scale descriptors from the large pool of potential descriptors.

The most effective approach to incorporating the Harris-Lingoes MMPI-2 subscales into clinical profile interpretation is to use them to clarify or substantiate particular interpretations of the parent scale. That is, they should be used to clarify or refine the scale correlates relevant for the interpretation of the scale on which they are contained. This approach is illustrated with a case, Ann, shown in Figure 4-4.

Ann's MMPI-2 profile would generate a considerable number of possible descriptors or correlates from her elevations on scales 2 and 4. However, by examining the relative elevations on the Harris-Lingoes subscales for scales 2 and 4, we can narrow down this large list of potential descriptors. Table 4-11 shows that the elevation on Pd comes predominantly from responses to items in the Pd_1 (Familial Discord) cluster, suggesting an unpleasant home situation that is viewed as lacking in love, support, and understanding. Ann feels that her family is very critical and controlling. She reports little of the authority problems, social alienation, or self-alienation item content measured by the other Pd subscales. Her elevation on the D scale comes predominantly from the D_1 (Subjective Depression) subscale, suggesting that she feels depressed, unhappy, and nervous. She lacks energy and interest and is not coping well. She has problems in concentration and attention. She reports feeling inferior, lacks self-confidence, and is shy and uneasy in social situations. Response to the content on other subscales of the D scale is negligible. Consequently, we can surmise that Ann's elevations on the Pd and D scales were produced largely by her family problems and depression over them. We would thus minimize the other possible scale 4 correlates suggesting more severe character pathology.

Limitations of the Harris-Lingoes Content Interpretation Approach

As valuable as they are for understanding the correlates for particular MMPI-2 standard scales, the Harris-Lingoes subscales have clear limitations as content

Table 4-10. Scale 0 Interpretive Guidelines for the MMPI-2

☐ Scale 0 assesses a bipolar personality dimension that includes introversion at the high end and extroversion at the low end of the continuum. Both high and low scale 0 scores are considered to have valuable personality information.

☐ High elevations on scale 0 are T scores ≥ 65. The probability that the descriptors listed below for high elevations apply to a given individual increases with higher scale elevations.

☐ Moderate elevations on scale 0 are T scores of 60 to 64, inclusive. Elevations in this range may be associated with many of the descriptors listed for elevated scores.

☐ Low elevations on scale 0 are T scores ≤ 45.

☐ Descriptors for elevated Si scores:
- Socially introverted
- More comfortable alone or with a few close friends
- Reserved, shy, and retiring
- Uncomfortable around members of opposite gender
- Hard to get to know
- Sensitive to what others think of them
- Troubled by lack of involvement with other people
- Overcontrolled and inhibited
- Not likely to display feelings openly
- Tends to be submissive and compliant
- Compliant toward authority
- Serious, reliable, dependable, cautious, conventional
- Slow personal tempo
- Rigid, inflexible in attitudes and opinions
- Having difficulty making even minor decisions
- Tends to worry and feels guilty easily

☐ Descriptors for low Si scores:
- Sociable and extroverted
- Outgoing, gregarious, friendly, and talkative
- Strong need to be around other people
- Mixes well in groups
- Socially expressive, verbally fluent, active, energetic
- Interested in status, power, and recognition
- Seeks out competitive situations
- May have problems with impulse control
- May act without considering the consequences of actions
- May be immature and self-indulgent
- May be superficial and insincere in relationships
- May be manipulative and opportunistic in relationships

☐ Elevations on scale 0 can be more fully understood by examining the item content, as assessed by the scale 0 subscales, contributing to scale elevation. The content subscales for scale 0 are:
- Shyness
- Social Avoidance
- Self-Other Alienation

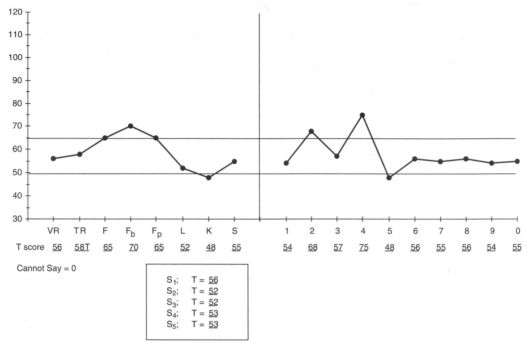

Cannot Say = 0

S_1;	T = 56
S_2;	T = 52
S_3;	T = 52
S_4;	T = 53
S_5;	T = 53

Figure 4-4. Ann's MMPI-2 basic scales profile.

Table 4-11. Harris-Lingoes D and Pd Subscale Scores for Ann

Scale 2	(Depression)	
	D_1—Subjective Depression	85 T
	D_2—Psychomotor Retardation	60 T
	D_3—Physical Malfunctioning	55 T
	D_4—Mental Dullness	45 T
	D_5—Brooding	55 T
Scale 4	(Psychopathic Deviate)	
	Pd_1—Familial Discord	80 T
	Pd_2—Authority Problems	55 T
	Pd_3—Social Imperturbability	56 T
	Pd_4—Social Alienation	50 T
	Pd_5—Self-Alienation	55 T

measures. First, they assess content factors only on a particular MMPI-2 scale. Consequently, they do not sufficiently assess the full range of content in the MMPI-2. They do not, for example, incorporate any of the new MMPI-2 content dimensions because they are limited to the original MMPI scales. Second, many of the Harris-Lingoes subscales are very short, some with as few as six items. The reliability of a scale depends, in part, on its length. Thus, many of the Harris-Lingoes subscales have low reliabilities and should not be relied on as independent psychometric measures.

The Harris-Lingoes subscales provide a basis for understanding the items that comprise a particular elevation on a standard scale. That is, the relative contribution of the subscales to the total score can help the clinician order the empirical correlates for the scale better by suggesting what scale content best summarizes the individual's problems. Broader content coverage is assessed by the MMPI-2 content scales (Chapter 5) and the MMPI-A content scales (Chapter 12).

Highlight Summary: Alice's Standard Scale Profile

In interpreting the MMPI-2 standard scales, a client's scores are compared with those of people in the normative sample using the T-score distribution on the MMPI-2 profile sheet. Interpretation of the standard scales involves assessing the elevation of the highest scales and applying the appropriate scale descriptors. In our continuing case analysis of Alice's MMPI-2 profile, we refer to her standard scale elevations to obtain information about her current symptomatic behavior and personality functioning (Figure 4-5).

Alice's elevated Pt score indicates that she is likely to be experiencing considerable anxiety, tension, and perhaps agitation. She has reported a great deal of discomfort, worry, and feelings of apprehension. She would likely be considered high-strung, depressed, and jumpy and may show concentration difficulties. Personality features associated with scale 7 elevations include being introspective, ruminative, indecisive, obsessive, and compulsive. She responds to MMPI-2 items in

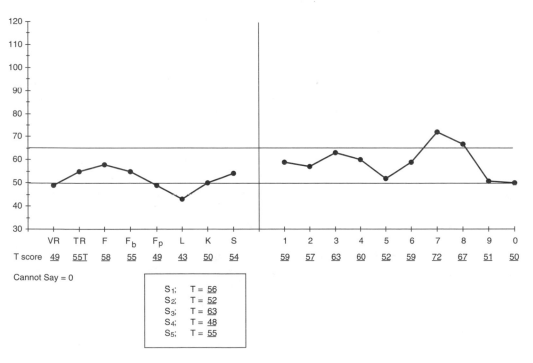

Figure 4-5. Alice's MMPI-2 basic scales profile.

a manner suggesting that she feels insecure and inferior and lacks self-confidence. She is likely to be overly self-conscious and self-derogatory. Many individuals with this prominent pattern are viewed as rigid, moralistic, overly perfectionistic, conscientious, and guilt prone. She is likely to be interested in entering therapy because she is probably experiencing considerable discomfort.

Her moderate elevation on scale 8 is likely to reflect feelings of alienation and distance from others. Individuals with elevated Sc tend to feel inferior and socially different from others. They may appear aloof and uninterested in others. They tend to employ fantasy as a defense against unpleasant situations and may daydream a great deal. High Sc individuals such as Alice are somewhat immature and self-preoccupied. They may be nonconforming and reluctant to go along with the majority. Some high Sc individuals are impulsive, aggressive, or anxious. Alice's Harris-Lingoes subscales for the Sc scale are useful to the interpreter in deciding what her Sc scale elevation represents. The two most prominent subscale elevations were on Lack of Ego Mastery, Cognitive (Sc_3, T = 74), and Lack of Ego Mastery, Conative (Sc_4, T = 70), indicating that she fears losing her mind and feels unable to cope with her problems. She endorses less content dealing with feelings of social and emotional alienation, indicating that she is less likely to be withdrawn and isolated from others. This is confirmed by her average score on Si. Alice probably does not have extreme problems with interpersonal relationships, which is a strength that can be used during therapy.

Analyzing MMPI-2 profiles by examining the correlates of prominent scale elevations a scale at a time can provide valuable clues to the individual's problems and personality. However, a scale-by-scale analysis can also be somewhat problematic in that numerous, sometimes even contradictory, correlates may be obtained if several scales are elevated. As we will soon see, scale relationships are also viewed as important considerations in profile interpretation. For example, analysis of scales 8 and 7 together or in configuration provides additional information. The relationship between scales 8 and 7 provides clues to whether the individual's problems are acute or chronic. If scale 7 is higher in elevation than scale 8 (as is the case with Alice), the individual's problems are likely to be acute. If scale 8 is higher in elevation than scale 7, the problems are considered to be chronic.

In the next chapter, we consider interpretation of MMPI-2 profiles from a somewhat different perspective—by considering all the prominently elevated scores as a single index or profile code (often referred to as a code type). The profile configuration or code-type approach is often considered to be the most efficient, systematic way of analyzing the multiple scale elevations that are commonly found in MMPI-2 standard scales profiles. However, as we will see in Chapter 9, this code-type approach has not been validated for adolescents.

Chapter 5

Interpreting MMPI-2 Profile Types (Code Types)

This chapter explains the definition, structure, and use of MMPI-2 profile types, often referred to as code types. Code types are MMPI-2 clinical scale summary indexes that include the most prominent scale elevations in a configuration of the standard MMPI-2 scales. Code-type interpretation was developed early in the MMPI's history when it was recognized that, in many cases, more than one standard scale was usually elevated. Psychologists observed that scale patterns occurred with great frequency in some settings and began to develop empirical descriptions of individuals who matched these MMPI patterns. In this chapter, we examine factors important to understanding and using MMPI-2 code types and summarize the well-established behavioral correlates for the most frequently occurring MMPI-2 profile codes. We also explore the congruence of MMPI-2 and MMPI codes. In Chapter 9, we explain why the code-type approach is not recommended for interpretation of the MMPI-A. Keep in mind that unlike other chapters, the material in this chapter relates only to MMPI-2 use with adults.

A code type is defined by the highest elevated scale or scales in the standard profile and their rank order in terms of elevation. Most of the empirical research on MMPI code types has included only scales Hs, D, Hy, Pd, Pa, Pt, Sc, and Ma. However, some research on special populations (e.g., college students) has included other scales, such as Mf and Si (Kelly & King, 1978). As was true of the standard scales, it is important to have a high degree of familiarity with the behavioral correlates for each of the frequently occurring code types. The behavioral descriptions associated with code types can be confidently applied to individuals whose profile matches the code type.

Several code types have been described in the empirical literature. The single-point code, or "profile spike," occurs when a single standard scale is elevated in the critical range. The two-point code type, one of the more frequently researched profile codes, occurs when two clinical scales, such as scales 2 and 7, are elevated in the critical range, that is, greater than or equal to T of 65. This code type would be defined as a two-point code of 2-7/7-2. The three-point code, prominent in several research populations, occurs when three clinical scales are elevated in the profile. For example, clinical elevations on scales 2, 4, and 7 produce a three-point code of 2-4-7, a profile type often found in drug- and alcohol-treatment programs. The four-point code is somewhat rare, though several have been researched extensively, for example, the 1-2-3-4 code type in medical settings. No research exists on profile codes having greater than four-point elevations.

When and Why to Use Code Types

There are two general rules for determining when to use the MMPI-2 code-type approach instead of the scale-by-scale approach described in Chapter 4:

1. The profile should be clearly defined (i.e., two or more scales reach interpretive significance using the definitions discussed in the following). Recent research has confirmed that more well-defined code types provide better matches with the correlate literature than profiles that are less well-defined (Graham, Ben-Porath & McNulty, 2000).

2. There has been sufficient research on behavioral descriptions for the code. For some code types, such as the 2-6-9, there are too few empirical descriptors to provide much information about the client. If a code type is an infrequent one, the scale-by-scale interpretation strategy should be followed.

Why use a simple technique such as code-type analysis when more sophisticated statistical approaches to profile analysis (such as cluster analysis, discriminant analysis, and other profile similarity measures) are available? In general, these multivariate research strategies, although providing a statistical means of evaluating research data for stringently classifying diverse subjects, have not provided a practical means of grouping MMPI profiles for clinical practice. They are somewhat cumbersome to use in applied settings, and research has not demonstrated that they provide a more accurate classification schema than simple code types.

Code types are more practical, easier to apply, and seemingly no less valid than more complex statistical analyses in most settings. In general, the code type not only may be more efficient to use than multivariate techniques but also may actually better summarize the most important elements of a given profile.

Code-Type Definitions and Stability

Much of the early literature on the established behavioral correlates of code types used research designs producing codes that were less refined than they might have been. Typically, a large number of cases is required to obtain a sufficient number of subjects with a particular code. For example, from a sample of 556 women and 270 men, Marks and Seeman (1963) found only 20 patients who met the criteria for the 1-3 code type. To have a large enough sample, most researchers studying code types have followed the practice of combining similar code groups, for example, 2-7 and 7-2, ignoring the score level and relative elevation of scales within a code type. However, both elevation level and rank order of elevated scales in the code type have been found to have important differentiating characteristics.

The order of the scales within the code type might make an important difference regarding the relative importance of empirical descriptors that applied to a case. For example, the 3-4 code type has been found to have rather different behavioral features than the 4-3 code type (Persons & Marks, 1971). If scale 4 is higher than scale 3, the individual is considered to act out rather than control emotions. In general, it is best to emphasize the correlates of the higher elevated scale of the code type. Similarly, the elevation range of the code type might also make an important difference in the type, quality, and number of symptoms or descriptions that are applied to the case. The ordering of scales within the code suggests the relative saliency of the empirical correlates and gives clues to the interpreter about which should be given most prominence in the report. The elevation of the scales in the code type provides a confidence estimate of the likelihood that the empirical correlates apply in the case. The higher the scale elevation, the more confident one can be that the prototype pattern matches the client.

As a general rule, MMPI scales have high test-retest stability (Dahlstrom, Welsh & Dahlstrom, 1975). Test-retest correlations for various groups have been reported to range from moderate to high, depending upon the population studied and the retest interval (Dahlstrom et al., 1975). However, the stability of code types depends on how well the code type is defined. Graham, Smith, and Schwartz (1986) reported that the percentages of people with the same high-point, low-point, and two-point code showed only modest congruence on retest (43%, 44%, and 28%, respectively). They noted, however, that code types with more extreme scores (i.e., those that were well-defined by a substantial point separation between the scale scores in the code type and those not included in the code) tended to be similar at retest. The greatest code-type agreement at retest was obtained for profiles having a 10-point T-score spread between the code type and the rest of the profile code. However, high congruence was obtained at retest if the code type was even 5 points higher than the next scale in the profile.

Several rules of thumb have been suggested by Graham et al. (1986) for assessing the stability of a profile code:

1. Profile code types that are 10 points or more above the next highest score are very likely to be found on retest.

2. Profile code types that are 5 to 9 points above the next score are likely to remain constant on retest.

3. Profile code types that are 4 or fewer points higher than the next score may shift on later retest, but future profiles will probably maintain some elements (and correlates) of the initial code types.

In general, Graham et al. (1986) recommend exercising caution in applying traditional MMPI behavioral correlates for a given code type if the profile does not possess clear code-type definition, a clear elevation above the next scale in the profile.

Similarity of the Traditional MMPI and MMPI-2 Code Types

The standard scale scores are quite consistent between the MMPI and MMPI-2 despite the T-score distributions being based on responses of different subjects. However, the need to make the T scores fall at equivalent percentile values across scales has affected some code types slightly, especially those cases with less clear profile definition. For example, in a three-point code, if the three scale scores are

Hs at 77, D at 76, and Hy at 75, the profile will be more likely to shift (i.e., change from a 1-2/2-1 to a 1-3/3-1 or 2-3/3-2) than if the first three scale scores are Hs at 77, Hy at 76, and D at 71. Actually, in this example it would be better to use the three-point code (1-2-3). Graham, Timbrook, Ben-Porath, and Butcher (1991) demonstrated that MMPI-2 code types were quite congruent with MMPI code types when code-type definition was maintained. Over 90% of the profiles with a five-point profile code definition will have the same code type on MMPI-2 as on the original MMPI. In a recent evaluation of the MMPI-2, Vincent (1990) concluded that "we can be reasonably confident that its compatibility with the original is as good as the original to itself and the well-known adaptations" (p. 802). Thus, if the profile code is at least 5 points greater than the next scale in the profile, the code type is likely to be the same on MMPI or MMPI-2 norms.

There are several limitations to using MMPI-2 code types that the clinician needs to keep in mind when using the empirical research literature on code types to interpret profiles. First, although the MMPI Restandardization Committee maintained continuity between the MMPI-2 and the original MMPI standard scales, there may be some shifting of scales within the profile code between the two forms because different standardization samples and T-score transformation procedures were used. This requires some adaptation on the part of the test interpreter. However, Graham et al. (1991) found that when code types differed (completely different profile codes are rare), the MMPI-2 code type had an external validity equal to or greater than the MMPI code type.

Recent studies have confirmed the traditional correlates for many of the code types (Archer, Griffin & Aiduk, 1995; Butcher, Rouse & Perry, 2000). Graham et al. (1999), in an extensive study of the behavioral correlates of MMPI-2 profile codes in an outpatient sample, found that many of the established correlates are the same in MMPI-2 codes as in the earlier studies by Gilberstadt and Duker (1965) and Marks and Seeman (1963).

With the MMPI-2, as with the original MMPI, empirical descriptors are scarce for some code types. Not enough code types have been empirically studied and described to classify the range of profiles that clinicians obtain. In addition, some settings in which the MMPI-2 is widely used are underrepresented in the research literature defining and describing MMPI-2 code types.

Although code types have been valuable in interpreting the MMPI and MMPI-2, a considerable amount of additional valuable information can be found in the MMPI-2 profile, for example, from Si, MAC-R, APS, or the MMPI-2 content scales. Consequently, rather than limiting interpretation to information from the MMPI code-type literature, one might wish to use the available code-type descriptions as an "outline" to which other MMPI-2–based information can be added. This interpretive strategy for MMPI-2 profiles are discussed more fully in Chapter 8.

Research on MMPI/MMPI-2 Code Types

Interpreting MMPI profiles using actuarial tables was initially shown by Meehl (1954) to be a more powerful strategy than clinical interpretation. He convincingly demonstrated that clinical predictions based on automatic combination of actuarial data for MMPI code types were more accurate than those based on "clinical" or intuitive interpretation of psychological test data. A number of empirical studies followed Meehl's recommendations for developing an actuarial "cookbook" as an aid to stringent test interpretation. One of Meehl's students, Halbower (1955), empirically demonstrated that behavioral correlates for test scores could be accurately and objectively applied to new cases meeting the established test criteria. More recently, Grove, Zald, Lebow, Snitz, and Nelson (2000), conducting a meta-analysis of studies comparing actuarial and clinical prediction, found that actuarial prediction methods were significantly more effective at prediction (about 10% greater) than clinical strategies. Meehl's compelling argument on the strength of the actuarial method and the empirical demonstration that such mechanically generated predictions were highly accurate (Halbower, 1955) influenced a number of investigators to develop "actuarial tables" for personality description using MMPI scales and profile codes (e.g., Altman, Gynther, Warbin & Sletten, 1973; Archer, Griffin & Aiduk, 1995; Arnold, 1970; Boerger, Graham & Lilly, 1974; Drake & Oetting, 1959; Fowler & Athey, 1971; Gilberstadt & Duker, 1965; Graham, 1973; Graham et al., 2000; Gynther, 1972a; Gynther, Altman & Sletten, 1973; Gynther, Altman & Warbin, 1972, 1973a, 1973b, 1973c; Gynther, Altman, Warbin & Sletten, 1972; Halbower, 1955; Kelly & King, 1978; Lewandowski & Graham, 1972; Marks & Seeman, 1963; Marks, Seeman & Haller, 1974; Meikle & Gerritse, 1970; Persons & Marks, 1971; Sines, 1966; Warbin, Altman, Gynther & Sletten, 1972).

Empirical research on MMPI profile patterns established a broad interpretive base for many of the common MMPI code types found in clinical settings. The MMPI code-type research literature is widely scattered and not conveniently organized for clinical use. Clinicians might find it helpful to develop a format for their particular setting and catalog appropriate personality and symptomatic descriptors for the various code types. The outline that we follow in this chapter illustrates one approach to organizing code-type information by putting correlate data into three categories:

Symptoms and Behaviors

Symptomatic behaviors the client reports along with an estimate, if available, of the severity of the individual's problems or behaviors are included in this section.

Personality Characteristics

Information related to the individual's personality adjustment or personality characteristics is provided.

Predictions or Dispositions

Hypotheses or predictions about the individual's behavior, such as diagnoses, likely outcomes, treatment amenability, and so on, are indicated.

Other approaches to organizing correlates have been published. Most MMPI computer interpretation systems incorporate descriptive and diagnostic information into client reports by organizing the narratives into categories or problem considerations. For example, Butcher (1987, 1989b, 1998b) developed the computer interpretation system published by the University of Minnesota, The Minnesota Report™, which organizes empirical correlate information pertinent to different settings and profile codes according to a number of hypothesized clinically meaningful topics: Profile Validity, Symptomatic Behavior, Interpersonal Relationships, Behavior Stability, Diagnostic Considerations, and Treatment Considerations. Chapter 12 provides a more detailed description of The Minnesota Report™ Computer Interpretation System.

Two-Point Code-Type Descriptors

Correlates for the two-point code types described in this section typically were obtained by collecting groups of patients who had similar code types and studying their behavioral characteristics by the use of Q-sort ratings, history, or other assessment methods. These empirical descriptions can be applied to other cases who meet the code-type classification rules. The remainder of this chapter highlights empirical correlates for many of the two- and three-point code types. Table 5-1 provides the general defining characteristics for code types. For a more extensive discussion of MMPI-2 code types, see Graham, Ben-Porath, and McNulty (1999).

1-2/2-1 Code Type

Symptoms and Behaviors

Patients are likely to present with extreme somatic problems or chronic pain and to complain of being physically ill although there may not be an organic basis to their problem. They become overly concerned about health and bodily functions and overreact to minor physical dysfunction. Somatic symptoms in the digestive system are common, as are reports of weakness, fatigue, and dizziness. They appear anxious, tense, nervous, restless, irritable, dysphoric, brooding, and unhappy. They show loss of initiative. They may report depressed mood, withdrawal, and reclusiveness. These individuals may be very self-conscious in talking with others. Doubts about their own ability are common, as is vacillation and indecision about even minor matters. They are likely to be hypersensitive.

Table 5-1. General Guidelines for Code-Type Interpretation

☐ The MMPI-2 code type is defined by the highest two, three, or four scale elevations in the profile code. All scales comprising the code are elevated at a T score ≥ 65.
☐ The descriptors for the code types are most applicable when the code type is well defined, that is, when the scales making up the code type are elevated more than 5 T-score points above the next elevated scale(s).
☐ Less well-defined code types, those in which several scales are near the same level of elevation (i.e., less than 4 T-score points among them), should be interpreted more cautiously because they tend not to be as stable at retest as the more well defined code types.

Table 5-2. Descriptors for the 1-2/2-1 Code Type

☐ Extreme somatic problems or chronic pain

☐ Complaints of being physically ill (may occur in the absence of organic findings)

☐ Overly concerned about health and bodily functions

☐ Overreacts to minor physical dysfunction

☐ Weakness, fatigue, and dizziness

☐ Anxious, tense, nervous, restless

☐ Irritable, dysphoric, brooding, unhappy

☐ Low initiative

☐ Depressed mood, withdrawn, and reclusive

☐ Doubts about ability

☐ Vacillation and indecision about even minor matters

☐ Hypersensitive

☐ Self-conscious in social situations

☐ Introverted and shy

☐ Passive-dependent in relationships

☐ Hostile toward others

☐ Uses repression as a defense

☐ May use alcohol or prescription drugs to reduce tension

☐ Resists psychological interpretations of symptoms

☐ Lacks insight and self-understanding

Personality Characteristics

Individuals with this profile code are viewed as self-conscious, introverted, and shy in social situations. They may be passive-dependent and harbor hostility toward those who are perceived as not offering enough attention and emotional support.

Predictions or Dispositions

Excessive use of alcohol or prescription drugs may occur as a tension-reduction mechanism. Individuals with this profile type are usually diagnosed as neurotic (hypochondriacal, anxious, or depressive). They are thought to have a poor prognosis for traditional psychotherapy. They usually can tolerate high levels of discomfort before becoming motivated to change. They resist psychological interpretations of symptoms. They tend to use repression and somatization. They lack insight and self-understanding and resist accepting responsibility for their own behavior. Treatment gains, if they occur, are typically short-lived symptomatic changes. Table 5-2 summarizes the characteristics associated with the 1-2/2-1 code type.

1-3/3-1 Code Type

Symptoms and Behaviors

Individuals with this pattern tend to report vague physical complaints that might increase under stress and often disappear when stress subsides. Severe anxiety and depression are usually absent. Clients are likely to function at a reduced level of efficiency. They prefer medical explanations of symptoms and tend to resist psychological interpretations. They tend to deny and rationalize, and they are seen as uninsightful. They view themselves as normal, responsible, and without fault. They lack appropriate concern about their symptoms and problems and are overly optimistic and Pollyannaish in manner.

Personality Characteristics

Clients with this code type tend to be seen as immature, egocentric, and selfish. They may be viewed as passive and dependent and may become insecure when their strong needs for attention, affection, and sympathy are not met. They are viewed as outgoing and socially extroverted, but their relationships are typically superficial. They appear to be self-preoccupied and lack genuine involvement with people. They are manipulative in social relationships, lack skills in dealing with the opposite gender, and tend to be low in heterosexual drive.

Individuals with this clinical profile may show resentment and hostility toward those who are viewed as not offering enough attention and support. They are seen as overcontrolled and passive-aggressive in relationships. They may have occasional angry outbursts. They are usually conventional and conforming in attitudes and beliefs.

Predictions or Dispositions

Clients with this pattern are usually diagnosed as having a psychophysiologic disorder or anxiety disorder, such as conversion or psychogenic pain disorders. They are not likely to be motivated for psychotherapy. They usually expect definite or simple answers and solutions to problems. They may terminate therapy prematurely when the therapist fails to respond to their demands. Interpretive guidelines for the 1-3/3-1 code type are highlighted in Table 5-3.

1-4/4-1 Code Type

Symptoms and Behaviors

Severe hypochondriacal symptoms are probably present with this profile type, especially nonspecific headaches and stomach distress. Individuals fitting this pattern are viewed as indecisive and anxious. They may be socially extroverted but lack skills with the opposite gender. They may be rebellious toward home and parents but do not express these feelings openly. They are likely to be dissatisfied, pessimistic, demanding, and grouchy. Many persons with this profile type show

Table 5-3. Descriptors for the 1-3/3-1 Code Type

☐ Vague physical complaints (often without an organic basis)
☐ Reacts to stress with physical symptoms
☐ Anxiety and depression are usually absent
☐ Functions at reduced level of efficiency
☐ Prefers medical explanations of symptoms
☐ Resists psychological interpretations
☐ Denies and rationalizes faults
☐ Lacks appropriate concern about their symptoms
☐ Overly optimistic and Pollyanna-like in manner
☐ Immature, egocentric, and selfish
☐ Passive-dependent
☐ Becomes insecure when their strong needs for attention, affection, and sympathy are not met
☐ Viewed as outgoing and socially extroverted
☐ Superficial relationships
☐ Self-preoccupied and lacks genuine involvement with others
☐ Manipulative in social relationships
☐ Coquettish, flirtatious
☐ Lacks skills in dealing with opposite gender and tends to be low in heterosexual drive
☐ Shows resentment and hostility toward those who are viewed as not offering enough attention and support
☐ Overcontrolled and passive-aggressive in relationships
☐ Occasional angry outbursts
☐ Usually conventional and conforming in attitudes and beliefs
☐ Uninsightful and unmotivated for therapy

a pattern of acting out behavior leading up to or contributing to their somatic distress.

Personality Characteristics

Personality problems are likely to be central in his or her problem expression. Acting-out behavior and poor judgment are likely to be factors in his or her maladjustment.

Predictions or Dispositions

Excessive use of alcohol is likely. Individuals with this clinical profile are likely to lack drive and may encounter problems in sustaining work or productive

Table 5-4. Descriptors for the 1-4/4-1 Code Type

☐ Hypochondriacal symptoms
☐ Indecisive and anxious
☐ Socially extroverted
☐ Lacks skills with the opposite gender
☐ Rebellious toward home and parents but does not express these feelings openly
☐ Dissatisfied, pessimistic, demanding, and grouchy
☐ Personality problems are likely
☐ Acting-out behaviors and poor judgment are possible
☐ Excessive use of alcohol is likely
☐ Lacks drive and may encounter problems in sustaining work
☐ Poorly defined goals and motivations
☐ Resistant to traditional psychotherapy

activity. They often have poorly defined goals and motivations. They are often seen as resistant to traditional psychotherapy. The descriptors for the 1-4/4-1 code type are provided in Table 5-4.

1-8/8-1 Code Type

Symptoms and Behaviors

Individuals with the 1-8/8-1 code type tend to have long-term psychological problems. They tend to harbor feelings of hostility and aggression but cannot express them in a modulated, adaptive manner. They are often either inhibited and "bottled up" or overly belligerent and abrasive. They are characterized by feeling unhappy, depressed, confused, and distractible. Many individuals with this profile configuration show flat affect. They tend to feel socially inadequate and have difficulty relating to the opposite gender.

Personality Characteristics

Long-term personality characteristics are likely to be a factor in the present symptom pattern for these individuals. They report feeling socially inadequate and lack trust in other people. They are isolated and alienated and may report having a nomadic lifestyle.

Predictions or Dispositions

Some individuals with this pattern are diagnosed as schizophrenic. Bizarre somatic complaints may make treatment difficult. Some medical patients with this profile are not schizophrenic but present with severe, chronic, unusual, intractable symptoms. Table 5-5 summarizes the 1-8/8-1 descriptors.

Table 5-5. Descriptors for the 1-8/8-1 Code Type

☐ Long-term psychological problems
☐ Feelings of hostility and aggression
☐ Either inhibited or overly belligerent and abrasive
☐ Unhappy, depressed, confused, and distractible
☐ Flat affect
☐ Long-standing adjustment problems
☐ Feels socially inadequate
☐ Lacks trust in other people
☐ Isolated and alienated
☐ Bizarre somatic complaints or long-term and intractable symptoms

1-9/9-1 Code Type

Symptoms and Behaviors

Extreme distress is usually present in individuals with this profile. They are likely to be anxious, tense, and restless and to have somatic complaints. They may be aggressive and belligerent if their somatic problems are minimized. Some individuals with this pattern can be ambitious and have high drive level, but they tend to lack clear goals, becoming frustrated by an inability to achieve at a high level.

Personality Characteristics

There is some indication that these clients have a passive-dependent personality style but try to deny personality problems.

Predictions or Dispositions

Individuals with this code type are likely to be reluctant to accept psychological explanations for their perceived medical problems. This code type can be found in brain-damaged persons who are experiencing difficulty in coping with organic deficits. Table 5-6 provides a summary of the descriptors for the 1-9/9-1 code type.

2-3/3-2 Code Type

Symptoms and Behaviors

Individuals with the 2-3/3-2 code type do not usually experience disabling anxiety but report feeling nervous, tense, worried, sad, and depressed. They usually express somatic symptoms such as fatigue, exhaustion, physical weakness, or gastrointestinal complaints. Individuals with this pattern tend to lack interest and involvement in life. They report being unable to "get started." They show decreased physical activity and lethargy.

Table 5-6. Descriptors for the 1-9/9-1 Code Type

☐ Extreme somatic distress and psychological turmoil
☐ Anxious, tense, restless
☐ Aggressive and belligerent if somatic problems are minimized
☐ Frustrated by an inability to achieve
☐ Passive-dependent or passive-aggressive personality style
☐ Denies personality problems
☐ Reluctant to accept psychological explanations for problems
☐ Determine whether a neuropsychological assessment is appropriate

Personality Characteristics

Individuals with this pattern appear passive, docile, and dependent. They have a history of self-doubt, inadequacy, insecurity, and helplessness. They engage in behavior that elicits nurturance from others but do not get what they consider adequate recognition for accomplishments. They are hurt by even minor criticism. They tend to be overcontrolled and unable to express feelings, are "bottled up," deny unacceptable impulses, avoid social involvement, and feel especially uncomfortable around the opposite gender. Sexual maladjustment, including frigidity and impotence, may be present.

Predictions or Dispositions

Individuals with this code type are usually diagnosed as having a depressive disorder. They tend not to be very responsive to psychotherapy and seem to lack introspective ability. They lack insight and resist psychological formulations of problems. Such people tend to function at a lower level of efficiency for long periods and appear to tolerate a great deal of unhappiness without seeking behavior change. They may seem driven to succeed but are afraid to place themselves in directly competitive situations. They feel the need to increase their responsibility in life but dread the pressure associated with this. Descriptors associated with the 2-3/3-2 code type are summarized in Table 5-7.

2-4/4-2 Code Type

Symptoms and Behaviors

Clients with the 2-4/4-2 code type often have a history of legal problems and an impulsive behavioral history. They tend to be unable to delay gratification of impulses, and they get into difficulty with others. They show little respect for social standards and values and tend to act out, perhaps by excessive drinking. They may appear to be frustrated by their lack of accomplishments and may be resentful of demands placed by others. After acting out, they may express guilt and remorse but are not sincere about changing.

Table 5-7. Descriptors for the 2-3/3-2 Code Type

☐ Feels nervous, tense, worried, sad, and depressed

☐ Expresses somatic symptoms, such as fatigue, exhaustion, or physical weakness

☐ Gastrointestinal complaints

☐ Lacks interest and involvement in life situations

☐ Has difficulty getting started on things

☐ Shows decreased physical activity and lethargy

☐ Appears passive, docile, and dependent

☐ Has a history of self-doubt, inadequacy, insecurity, and helplessness

☐ Seeks excessive nurturance and sympathy from others

☐ Feels that accomplishments are not adequately recognized

☐ Feels hurt by even minor criticism

☐ Appears overcontrolled

☐ Denies unacceptable impulses

☐ Functions at lower level of efficiency for long periods

☐ Avoids social involvement and feels especially uncomfortable around the opposite gender

☐ Sexual maladjustment, including frigidity and/or impotence, may be present

☐ Depressive disorder likely

☐ Not very responsive to traditional psychotherapy

☐ Lacks introspective ability

☐ Resists psychological formulations of problems

Personality Characteristics

Individuals with this code type may appear sociable and outgoing and may make a favorable first impression. They tend to manipulate others and show some long-term maladaptive personality characteristics. They cause resentment in long-term relationships. Beneath a facade of competence and self-assurance, these individuals may actually be overly self-conscious and dissatisfied with themselves. Characteristically, they are passive-dependent persons.

Predictions or Dispositions

Suicidal ideation and attempts are possible (especially if both scales are grossly elevated). Individuals with this clinical profile may express the need for help and desire to change, but prognosis for psychotherapeutic change is poor. They are likely to terminate therapy prematurely when the outside stress subsides or when their environmental pressures or legal difficulties subside. Table 5-8 highlights the descriptors for the 2-4/4-2 code type.

Table 5-8. Descriptors for the 2-4/4-2 Code Type

☐ History of impulsive behaviors
☐ May have legal or family difficulties
☐ Unable to delay gratification of impulses
☐ Interpersonal difficulties
☐ Shows little respect for social standards and values
☐ Acts out, perhaps accompanied by excessive drinking
☐ Frustrated with lack of accomplishments
☐ Resentful of demands placed by others
☐ After episodes of acting out, may express guilt and remorse but is not sincere about changing
☐ Appears sociable and outgoing and may make a favorable first impression
☐ Manipulates others
☐ Possesses long-term maladaptive personality characteristics
☐ Depressed
☐ Causes resentment in long-term relationships
☐ Appears competent and self-assured but may be overly self-conscious and self-dissatisfied
☐ Passive-dependent
☐ Suicidal thinking and attempts may be present
☐ Expresses the need for help and desire to change, but prognosis for psychotherapeutic change is poor
☐ May terminate therapy prematurely when stress subsides

2-7/7-2 Code Type

Symptoms and Behaviors

Individuals with this code type appear anxious, tense, nervous, and depressed. They report feeling unhappy and sad and tend to worry excessively. They feel vulnerable to real and imagined threats and typically anticipate problems before they occur—often overreacting to minor stress as though it is a major catastrophe. They usually report somatic complaints, fatigue, exhaustion, tiredness, weight loss, slow personal tempo, slowed speech, and retarded thought processes. They tend to brood and ruminate a great deal.

These persons may show a strong need for achievement and recognition and have high expectations for themselves and others. They may feel guilty when their goals are not met. These individuals typically have perfectionistic attitudes and a history of being conscientious. They may be excessively religious and extremely moralistic.

Personality Characteristics

Individuals with this pattern appear docile and passive-dependent in relationships. They report problems in being assertive. They usually show a capacity for forming deep, emotional ties and tend to lean on people to an excessive degree. They tend to solicit nurturance from others. Feelings of inadequacy, insecurity, and inferiority are long-term issues. They tend to be intropunitive in dealing with feelings of aggression.

Predictions or Dispositions

Individuals with the 2-7/7-2 code type are usually diagnosed as depressive, obsessive-compulsive, or anxiety disordered. They are usually motivated for psychotherapy and tend to remain in therapy longer than other patients. They tend to be somewhat pessimistic about overcoming problems and are indecisive and rigid in their thinking. This negative mind-set is likely to interfere with their problem-solving ability. However, they usually improve in treatment (Meresman, 1992). Table 5-9 summarizes the descriptors for the 2-7/7-2 code type.

2-8/8-2 Code Type

Symptoms and Behaviors

Individuals with this pattern appear anxious, agitated, tense, and jumpy. They often report having a sleep disturbance and are unable to concentrate. Disturbed affect and somatic symptoms usually characterize their clinical picture. They are often seen as clinically depressed and have soft and slowed speech and thought. In interviews they may be tearful and emotional, yet they are more characteristically viewed as apathetic and indifferent. Problems with anger and interpersonal relationships are usually noted. They indicate that they are often forgetful, confused, and inefficient in carrying out responsibilities. Others may view them as unoriginal and stereotyped in their thinking and problem solving. They tend to underestimate the seriousness of problems and engage in unrealistic self-appraisal. They are overly sensitive to the reactions of others and suspicious of others' motivations and may have a history of being hurt emotionally. They fear being hurt more and avoid close interpersonal relationships. Feelings of despair and worthlessness are common.

Personality Characteristics

Personality features include being dependent, unassertive, irritable, and resentful. They often fear losing control over their emotions. They may deny impulses, but dissociative periods of acting out may occur. Chronic, incapacitating symptoms are usually present. They tend to be guilt ridden and self-punitive.

Predictions or Dispositions

Serious maladjustment is likely to be present among individuals with this profile code, and they tend to underevaluate the seriousness of their problems. The

Table 5-9. Descriptors for the 2-7/7-2 Code Type

☐ Anxious, tense, nervous, and depressed
☐ Unhappy and sad and tends to worry excessively
☐ Feels vulnerable to real and imagined threats
☐ Anticipates problems before they occur and may overreact to minor stress
☐ Reports somatic symptoms such as fatigue, exhaustion, weight loss, slowed speech, and retarded thinking
☐ Broods and ruminates a great deal
☐ Shows great indecisiveness
☐ Sleep disturbance reported
☐ Feels guilty when personal goals are not met
☐ Perfectionistic and conscientious
☐ Excessively religious or extremely moralistic
☐ Appears docile and passive-dependent in relationships
☐ Nonassertive
☐ Shows a capacity for forming deep emotional ties but tends to lean on people to an excessive degree
☐ Seeks excessive nurturance from others
☐ Feelings of inadequacy, insecurity, and inferiority
☐ Intropunitive
☐ May be diagnosed as depressive, obsessive-compulsive, or anxiety disordered
☐ Pessimistic about overcoming problems and indecisive and rigid in their thinking
☐ Usually motivated for symptom relief in psychotherapy

most common diagnoses are manic-depressive psychosis, schizophrenia, schizo-affective type, or severe personality disorder. They are often preoccupied with suicidal thoughts and may have specific plans for doing away with themselves. Interpretive guidelines for the 2-8/8-2 code type are provided in Table 5-10.

2-9/9-2 Code Type

Symptoms and Behaviors

Patients are likely to be self-centered and narcissistic and tend to ruminate a great deal about their self-worth. They are likely to express concern about achieving at a high level but appear to set themselves up for failure. Younger persons with this pattern may be experiencing an identity crisis. Symptomatically, clients may be anxious and tense and have somatic complaints, particularly concerning

Table 5-10. Descriptors for the 2-8/8-2 Code Type

☐ Anxious, agitated, tense, and jumpy
☐ Sleeping disturbance
☐ Unable to concentrate
☐ Somatic symptoms, such as dizziness, blackouts, and nausea
☐ Clinically depressed
☐ Tearful and emotional yet viewed as apathetic and indifferent
☐ Anger problems
☐ Relationship problems are usually noted
☐ Forgetful, confused, and inefficient
☐ Engages in unrealistic self-appraisal
☐ Oversensitive to reactions of others
☐ Suspicious of others' motivations and may have a history of being hurt emotionally
☐ Fearful of being hurt
☐ Avoids close relationships
☐ Feelings of despair and worthlessness
☐ Dependent and unassertive
☐ Irritable and resentful of others
☐ Fears losing control over emotions
☐ Has chronic, incapacitating symptoms
☐ Guilt ridden and self-punitive
☐ Serious maladjustment is likely to be present
☐ Preoccupied with suicidal thoughts

the gastrointestinal tract. Some individuals with this pattern are not currently depressed but may have a history of serious depression.

Personality Characteristics

A pattern of denial may cover feelings of inadequacy and worthlessness. Some individuals with this profile tend to be defending against depression through excessive activity.

Predictions or Dispositions

Alternating periods of increased activity and fatigue are possible. The most common diagnosis is bipolar disorder. This profile is sometimes found among brain-damaged patients who have lost control or who are trying to cope with

Table 5-11. Descriptors for the 2-9/9-2 Code Type

☐ Self-centered and narcissistic
☐ Ruminates a great deal about self-worth
☐ Concerned about achieving at a high level
☐ Sets self up for failure
☐ Experiencing an identity crisis
☐ Anxious and tense
☐ Somatic complaints
☐ May not appear depressed but has a history of serious depression
☐ May cover up feelings of inadequacy and worthlessness by denial
☐ May be defending against depression through excessive activity
☐ May have alternating periods of increased activity and fatigue
☐ May have a history of a bipolar disorder
☐ May have a history of brain damage
☐ May use alcohol as an escape from stress and pressure

deficits through excessive activity. Many individuals with this profile use alcohol as an escape from stress and pressure. The 2-9/9-2 descriptors are highlighted in Table 5-11.

3-4/4-3 Code Type

Symptoms and Behaviors

Chronic and intense anger may be present. Individuals with this clinical profile may harbor hostile and aggressive impulses but cannot express them appropriately. Individuals with this pattern of MMPI-2 scores have problems of self-control. Usually somewhat overcontrolled, they tend to experience occasional brief episodes of assaultive, violent acting out. They tend to lack insight into the origins and consequences of their aggressive behavior. They tend to be extrapunitive but do not see their own behavior as problematic.

Individuals with this clinical profile are likely to be free of disabling anxiety and depression but may have somatic complaints. Occasional upset does not seem to be related directly to external stress. Sexual maladjustment and promiscuity are common among clients with this pattern.

Personality Characteristics

Individuals with this code type show long-term and ingrained feelings of hostility toward family members. They tend to demand attention and approval from others. They are overly sensitive to rejection and are usually hostile when criticized. They may be outwardly conforming but inwardly rebellious.

Table 5-12. Descriptors for the 3-4/4-3 Code Type

☐ Chronic and intense anger-control problems
☐ Hostile and aggressive
☐ Correctional inmates with this pattern have a history of violent crime
☐ Experiences occasional brief episodes of assaultive, violent acting out
☐ Lacks insight into the origins and consequences of aggressive behavior
☐ Tends to be extrapunitive but does not see own behavior as problematic
☐ Free of disabling anxiety and depression but may have somatic complaints
☐ Frustration does not seem to be related directly to external stress
☐ Sexual maladjustment and promiscuity are common
☐ Shows long-term and ingrained feelings of hostility toward family members
☐ Demands attention and approval from others
☐ May have somatic symptoms that have a manipulative quality to them
☐ Overly sensitive to rejection and usually hostile when criticized
☐ May be outwardly conforming but is inwardly rebellious

Predictions or Dispositions

Suicidal thoughts and attempts may follow acting-out episodes. The most common diagnoses for this code type are passive-aggressive personality or emotionally unstable personality. Table 5-12 summarizes the correlates for the 3-4/4-3 code type.

3-6/6-3 Code Type

Symptoms and Behaviors

Presenting problems may not seem incapacitating, though moderate tension, anxiety, and physical complaints may occur. Individuals with a 3-6/6-3 code type may not recognize their hostile feelings, but they may appear defiant, uncooperative, and hard to get along with. They appear suspicious and resentful at times. Clients with this pattern may be self-centered and narcissistic. They tend to deny serious psychological problems.

Personality Characteristics

These individuals tend to harbor deep and chronic feelings of hostility toward family members and others close to them. They are not likely to express negative feelings directly.

Predictions or Dispositions

Individuals with this profile configuration tend to have naive attitudes toward others and may be gullible at times. Descriptors for the 3-6/6-3 code type are listed in Table 5-13.

Table 5-13. Descriptors for the 3-6/6-3 Code Type

☐ Experiences moderate tension, anxiety, and physical complaints
☐ May not recognize his or her own hostile feelings but may appear defiant and uncooperative
☐ Hard to get along with, suspicious and resentful at times
☐ Self-centered and narcissistic
☐ Denies serious psychological problems
☐ Chronic feelings of hostility toward family members and others close to him or her
☐ Not likely to express negative feelings directly
☐ Naive attitudes toward others and may be gullible at times

3-8/8-3 Code Type

Symptoms and Behaviors

Individuals with this code typically show intense psychological turmoil, including anxiousness, tension, nervousness, and fearfulness. Disturbed thinking is likely to be present, perhaps involving somatic delusions. Phobias may be present. Some symptomatic depression and feelings of hopelessness may occur behind a smiling facade. Indecisiveness, even with regard to minor decisions, is characteristic. A wide variety of physical complaints may occur. Individuals may be vague and evasive when talking about complaints and difficulties. They may show disturbed thinking, concentration problems, lapses of memory, unusual or unconventional ideas, loose ideational associations and obsessive ruminations, delusions, hallucinations, and irrelevant and incoherent speech.

Personality Characteristics

Individuals with this pattern are likely to be immature and dependent. They may show strong needs for attention and affection. They may show intropunitive interpersonal behavior.

Predictions or Dispositions

Persons fitting this pattern may be seen as apathetic, pessimistic, and not very actively involved or interested in life activities. This apathy tends to limit rehabilitation efforts. Insight-oriented therapy may not be very effective. They may seem unoriginal and stereotyped in their approach to problems. The most common diagnosis is schizophrenia. They tend to be responsive to supportive therapy. Table 5-14 describes the correlates for this code type.

4-6/6-4 Code Type

Symptoms and Behaviors

Individuals with this code type are likely to be narcissistic, immature, and self-indulgent. They typically make excessive and unrealistic demands on relation-

Table 5-14. Descriptors for the 3-8/8-3 Code Type

☐ Shows intense psychological turmoil, including anxiousness, tension, nervousness, and fearfulness

☐ Phobias may be present

☐ Depression and hopelessness may occur behind a smiling facade

☐ Indecisive, even over minor decisions

☐ Vague physical complaints

☐ Disturbed thinking possible (e.g., concentration problems, lapses of memory, unusual or unconventional ideas, loose ideational associations, obsessive ruminations, delusions, hallucinations, and irrelevant or incoherent speech)

☐ Immature and dependent

☐ May show strong needs for attention and affection

☐ May show intropunitive interpersonal behavior

☐ Apathetic, pessimistic, and not very actively involved or interested in life

☐ Insight-oriented therapy may not be very effective

ships. Individuals with this pattern are attention and sympathy seekers. They are usually suspicious of others and resentful of demands made on them. Relationship problems are characteristic of their psychological conflicts, especially those involving members of the opposite gender. They are mistrustful of the motives of others and tend to avoid deep emotional involvement. Persons with this profile pattern are often viewed as irritable, sullen, argumentative, generally obnoxious, and resentful of authority.

In an interesting study of imprisoned Palestinian and Israeli terrorists, using the Arabic and Hebrew translations of the MMPI-2, Gottschalk (1999) found that their overall mean profile was a 4-6/6-4 pattern. However, there were some notable differences between the terrorists, particularly between those he defined as "religious fundamentalist" and revolutionary. He reported that the more "religious fundamentalist" terrorists produced higher scale elevations on scale 8 in addition to the 4-6/6-4 profile pattern.

Personality Characteristics

Personality adjustment problems are common among individuals with this profile type. Some individuals with this pattern are viewed as passive-dependent. They are often characterized by hostility and anger.

Predictions or Dispositions

Individuals with this profile configuration probably deny serious psychological problems through rationalization and transfer of blame to others. They cannot accept responsibility for their own behavior and are unrealistic and grandiose in their self-appraisals. They are viewed as unreceptive to psychotherapy. The typical personality disorder diagnosis for individuals with this personality pattern is

Table 5-15. Descriptors for the 4-6/6-4 Code Type

☐ Immature, narcissistic, and self-indulgent
☐ Makes excessive and unrealistic demands on relationships
☐ Seeks attention and sympathy to excess
☐ Suspicious of others and resentful of demands made by others
☐ Relationship problems
☐ Mistrustful of the motivation of others and tends to avoid deep emotional involvement
☐ Irritable, sullen, argumentative, and obnoxious
☐ Resentful of authority
☐ Personality adjustment problems
☐ Hostile and angry behavior likely
☐ Denies serious psychological problems through rationalization and transfer of blame to others
☐ Does not accept responsibility for own behavior
☐ Unrealistic and grandiose in self-appraisals
☐ Unreceptive to psychotherapy
☐ Tend to act out their problems rather than reflect on them

passive-aggressive or paranoid personality. They may also receive a diagnosis of paranoid schizophrenia. The descriptors for the 4-6/6-4 code type are provided in Table 5-15.

4-7/7-4 Code Type

Symptoms and Behaviors

Individuals with this code type may alternate between periods of gross insensitivity to the consequences of their own actions and excessive concern about the effects of their behavior. They engage in episodes of acting out followed by temporary guilt and self-condemnation. Vague somatic complaints, tension, and fatigue are also common. They often report feeling exhausted and being unable to face their pressing environmental problems.

Personality Characteristics

Pervasive feelings of dependency and personal insecurity plague their adjustment.

Predictions or Dispositions

In therapy, these individuals may respond to support and reassurance, but permanent personality changes are difficult for them to make. These individuals are typically so insecure that they require frequent reassurance of their self-worth. Table 5-16 lists the descriptors for the 4-7/7-4 code type.

Table 5-16. Descriptors for the 4-7/7-4 Code Type

☐ Alternates between periods of acting out and excessive concern about the effects of his or her behavior

☐ Temporary guilt and self-condemnation possible

☐ Vague somatic complaints, tension, and fatigue

☐ Frequently reports being exhausted and unable to face pressing environmental demands

☐ Feelings of dependency and insecurity plague adjustment

☐ Permanent personality changes are difficult to make

☐ Typically very insecure, requiring frequent reassurances of self-worth

4-8/8-4 Code Type

Symptoms and Behaviors

Serious psychological problems are characteristic of individuals with this code type. They do not seem to fit into society very well. They are viewed as odd, peculiar, nonconforming, and resentful of authority. They may espouse unusual religious or political views and behave in erratic, unpredictable ways. Some individuals with this pattern withdraw into fantasy or strike out in anger as a defense against being hurt. Problems with impulse control are likely. They are viewed as angry, irritable, and resentful. They typically act out in asocial ways. Delinquency, criminal acts, or sexual deviation may be present. Excessive drinking and drug abuse are characteristic. Many individuals with this profile type are obsessed with sexual thoughts. They may be afraid of being unable to perform sexually or may indulge in antisocial sexual acts in an attempt to demonstrate sexual adequacy. This is one of the most frequent profile patterns among rapists.

They may be withdrawn and isolated socially. Some individuals with this pattern have periods of suicidal obsessions. They are often distrustful of others and avoid close relationships. They are seen as being impaired in empathic ability and as lacking in basic social skills.

Personality Characteristics

A poor self-concept is central to the problems of these individuals. They set themselves up for rejection and failure and have deep feelings of insecurity. They tend to have exaggerated needs for attention and affection.

Predictions or Dispositions

Usually, individuals with this profile have a history of underachievement and marginal adjustment. The most common diagnoses are severe personality disorders such as antisocial, paranoid, schizoid, or even schizophrenic disorder.

Because these individuals accept little responsibility for their own behavior, they tend not to respond well to psychological treatment. They tend to rationalize and blame others for their own difficulties. They typically see the world as

Table 5-17. Descriptors for the 4-8/8-4 Code Type

- ☐ Serious psychological problems likely
- ☐ May not fit into society very well
- ☐ Viewed as odd, peculiar, and nonconforming
- ☐ Resentful of authority
- ☐ Espouses unusual religious or political views and behaves in erratic and unpredictable ways
- ☐ Withdraws into fantasy or strikes out in anger as a defense against being hurt
- ☐ Impulse-control problems
- ☐ Angry, irritable, and resentful
- ☐ Acts out in asocial ways, sometimes bizarre ways
- ☐ Delinquency, criminal acts, or sexual deviation possible
- ☐ Excessive drinking and drug abuse possible
- ☐ Obsessed with sexual thoughts
- ☐ May indulge in antisocial sexual acts
- ☐ Withdrawn and socially isolated
- ☐ Suicidal obsessions
- ☐ Distrustful of others
- ☐ Avoids close relationships
- ☐ Impaired in empathic ability and lacking in basic social skills
- ☐ Poor self-concept is central
- ☐ Prone to rejection and failure
- ☐ Deep feelings of insecurity
- ☐ Sees the world as threatening and rejecting place
- ☐ Accepts little responsibility for own behavior
- ☐ May not to respond well to psychological treatment

threatening and rejecting and thus may encounter some problems in developing a treatment relationship. Table 5-17 presents 4-8/8-4 descriptors.

4-9/9-4 Code Type

Symptoms and Behaviors

Individuals with the 4-9/9-4 code type show a marked disregard for social standards and values, exhibit antisocial behavior, have poorly developed consciences, and demonstrate loose morals and fluctuating ethical values. A wide array of antisocial acts (e.g., alcoholism, fighting, stealing, and sexual acting out) may be characteristic. They are seen as selfish, self-indulgent, and impulsive. They typically cannot delay gratification of impulses. They show poor judgment and may act without considering the consequences of their actions. They seemingly fail to learn from punishing experiences. They typically manifest low frustration tolerance, moodiness, irritability, and a caustic manner. They show intense feelings of anger and hostility, which are expressed in negative emotional outbursts.

They may be viewed as energetic, restless, overactive, and needing to seek out emotional stimulation and excitement. They are seen as uninhibited, extroverted, and talkative. They tend to create a good first impression, but their relationships are superficial and tend to wear thin over time.

Personality Characteristics

Individuals with this profile configuration are likely to be narcissistic and incapable of deep emotional ties. They tend to keep others at a distance emotionally. Their social facade may hide a lack of self-confidence and security. Features of an immature, insecure, and dependent personality structure may be present. The typical diagnosis is antisocial personality disorder.

Predictions or Dispositions

Individuals with the 4-9/9-4 code type typically do not accept responsibility for own behavior and tend not to seek treatment unless others pressure them to do so. They rationalize their own shortcomings and failures and blame their difficulties on others. Their legal, work, or relationship problems tend to persist over time. Table 5-18 lists the descriptors for the 4-9/9-4 code type.

6-8/8-6 Code Type

Symptoms and Behaviors

Feelings of inferiority and insecurity, low self-confidence, and poor self-esteem are prominent. Individuals with this profile configuration may feel guilty about their perceived failures. Withdrawal from activity and emotional apathy are likely. They are not usually very involved with other people. They are viewed as suspicious and distrustful of others. They tend to avoid deep emotional ties and are thought to be deficient in social skills. These people tend to be most comfortable when alone. They resent demands placed on them. They are moody, irritable, unfriendly, and negativistic. Clearly psychotic behavior may be present. Their thinking is likely to be autistic, fragmented, tangential, and circumstantial. They manifest bizarre thought content, difficulties in concentrating, attention deficit, and memory problems. They are likely to have poor judgment. They may exhibit severe confusion, delusions of persecution and/or grandeur, feelings of unreality, and preoccupation with abstract or obscure matters. Blunted affect may be present. In addition, they may show rapid and incoherent speech, withdrawal into fantasy and daydreaming, and may have difficulty differentiating fantasy from reality.

Table 5-18. Descriptors for the 4-9/9-4 Code Type

☐ Marked disregard for social standards and values
☐ Exhibits antisocial behavior, has poorly developed conscience, and demonstrates loose morals and fluctuating ethical values
☐ Alcoholism possible
☐ Fighting and sexual acting out possible
☐ Selfish, self-indulgent, and impulsive
☐ Cannot delay gratification of impulses
☐ Poor judgment
☐ Fails to learn from punishing experiences
☐ Manifests low frustration tolerance, moodiness, irritability, and a caustic manner
☐ Shows intense feelings of anger and hostility, which are expressed in negative emotional outbursts
☐ Energetic, restless, overactive, and needing emotional stimulation and excitement
☐ Uninhibited, extroverted, and talkative
☐ May create a good first impression but relationships are superficial
☐ Narcissistic and incapable of deep emotional ties
☐ Keeps others at emotional distance
☐ Immature, insecure, and dependent
☐ Rationalizes own shortcomings and failures and blames difficulties on others
☐ Has legal, work, or relationship problems
☐ Does not accept responsibility for own behavior
☐ Tends not to seek treatment unless by external pressure

They seemingly lack effective defenses and tend to react to stress and pressure by regressing.

Personality Characteristics

Severe long-term psychological problems are indicated. A schizoid lifestyle is likely to be present.

Predictions or Dispositions

Individuals with the 6-8/8-6 code type are usually diagnosed as schizophrenic. This is the most frequent profile type for schizophrenics in other countries as well (Butcher, 1996; Lucio, Palacios, Duran & Butcher, 1999). Treatment often involves psychotropic medication and placement in a supportive, structured environment if they are viewed as being dangerous to themselves or others. Table 5-19 lists the correlates for the 6-8/8-6 code type.

Table 5-19. Descriptors for the 6-8/8-6 Code Type

☐ Feelings of inferiority and insecurity

☐ Low self-confidence and poor self-esteem

☐ Feels guilty about perceived failures

☐ Withdraws from activity

☐ Emotional apathy

☐ Not usually very involved with others

☐ Suspicious and distrustful of others

☐ Avoids deep emotional ties

☐ Deficient in social skills

☐ Feels most comfortable when alone

☐ Resents demands placed by others

☐ Moody, irritable, unfriendly, and negativistic

☐ Psychotic behavior may be present

☐ Thinking is likely to be autistic, fragmented, tangential, and circumstantial

☐ Manifests bizarre thought content, difficulties in concentrating, attention deficit, and memory problems

☐ Has poor judgment

☐ Exhibits severe confusion, delusions of persecution and/or grandeur, feelings of unreality

☐ Preoccupied with abstract or obscure matters

☐ Blunted affect may be present

☐ Shows rapid and incoherent speech, withdraws into fantasy and daydreaming

☐ Has difficulty differentiating between fantasy and reality

☐ Lacks effective defenses and tends to react to stress and pressure by regressing

☐ Severe long-term psychological problems

☐ Schizoid lifestyle

☐ Schizophrenic diagnosis possible

☐ Treatment often involves psychotropic medication and placement in a supportive, structured environment

6-9/9-6 Code Type

Symptoms and Behaviors

Individuals with this profile configuration are likely to be overly sensitive and mistrustful. They are likely to feel vulnerable to real or imagined threat or to feel anxious much of the time and may be tearful and trembling. They tend to

Table 5-20. Descriptors for the 6-9/9-6 Code Type

☐ Overly sensitive and mistrustful
☐ Feels vulnerable to real or imagined threats
☐ Anxious much of the time
☐ Tearful and trembling
☐ Overreacts to minor stress and may respond to severe setbacks by withdrawing into fantasy
☐ May show a strong need for affection but passive-dependent in relationships
☐ Has problems expressing emotions in adaptive, modulated ways
☐ May alternate between overcontrol and direct, uncontrolled emotional outbursts
☐ Complains of difficulties in thinking and concentration problems
☐ May show signs of thought disorder
☐ May have delusions and hallucinations and irrelevant or incoherent speech and appears disoriented and perplexed
☐ Psychological treatment may be difficult to implement because patients may be plagued by disorganized, unproductive, and ruminative thinking

overreact to minor stress and may respond to severe setbacks by withdrawing into fantasy.

Individuals with this profile type may show signs of thought disorder, complain of difficulties in thinking, and have concentration problems. They may have delusions and hallucinations, have irrelevant and incoherent speech, and appear disoriented and perplexed.

Personality Characteristics

Individuals with this profile pattern may show a strong need for affection and are passive-dependent in relationships.

Predictions or Dispositions

Psychiatric inpatients with the 6-9/9-6 code type may be diagnosed as schizophrenic (paranoid type) or as having a mood disorder. Psychological treatment may be difficult to implement because patients may be plagued by being disorganized and unproductive, and have ruminative thinking. Implementation of behavior change programs may be hampered by their tendency to be overideational and obsessional. They tend to have problems expressing emotions in adaptive, modulated ways. They may alternate between overcontrol and more direct, uncontrolled emotional outbursts. The descriptors for individuals with the 6-9/9-6 code type are listed in Table 5-20.

7-8/8-7 Code Type

Symptoms and Behaviors

Patients with this profile code typically show a great deal of turmoil. They are not usually hesitant to admit to psychological problems. They tend to lack defenses to keep themselves comfortable or anxiety free. They report feeling depressed, worried, tense, and nervous. They may be confused and in a state of panic and show indecisiveness and poor judgment. They do not seem to profit from experience. They tend to be overly introspective, ruminative, and ideational.

Personality Characteristics

Chronic feelings of insecurity, inadequacy, inferiority, and indecisiveness are likely. Individuals with this profile are not socially poised or confident and tend to withdraw from social interactions. They are passive-dependent and cannot take a dominant role in relationships. They tend to have difficulties with mature heterosexual relationships and tend to feel inadequate in traditional gender roles. They tend to engage in extreme or unusual sexual fantasies.

Predictions or Dispositions

Patients with this profile may be diagnosed as anxiety disordered; however, the likelihood of psychotic and personality disorder diagnoses increases with elevation on Sc. Even when diagnosed as psychotic, individuals with this pattern may not show blatant psychotic symptoms. Medications to control intense anxiety and thinking problems are likely to be considered. Table 5-21 summarizes the descriptors for the 7-8/8-7 code type.

8-9/9-8 Code Type

Symptoms and Behaviors

Serious psychological disturbance is likely with this profile. Individuals may show social withdrawal and isolation. They may be especially uncomfortable in heterosexual relationships and show poor sexual adjustment. They often are seen as hyperactive, emotionally labile, agitated, and excited. They may be loud and excessively talkative. They typically are unrealistic in their self-appraisals, grandiose, boastful, and fickle. Their behavior is characterized by denial of problems. They may be vague and circumstantial. They report feeling inferior and inadequate, having low self-esteem and limited involvement in competitive or achievement-oriented situations.

Personality Characteristics

Individuals with this profile code are viewed as self-centered and infantile in their expectations of others. They tend to demand much attention and become resentful and hostile when their demands are not met. They appear to resist and even fear close emotional involvement. They avoid close relationships. They are

Table 5-21. Descriptors for the 7-8/8-7 Code Type

☐ Shows a great deal of turmoil
☐ Admits to psychological problems
☐ Lacks defenses to feel comfortable or anxiety free
☐ Feels depressed, worried, tense, and nervous
☐ Confused and in a state of panic
☐ Shows indecisiveness and poor judgment
☐ Does not seem to learn from experience
☐ Tends to be overly introspective, ruminative, and ideational
☐ Chronic feelings of insecurity, inadequacy, inferiority, indecisiveness are likely
☐ Not socially poised or confident and tends to withdraw from social interactions
☐ Passive-dependent
☐ Nondominant in relationships
☐ Has difficulties with mature heterosexual relationships
☐ Feels inadequate in traditional gender roles
☐ Engages in extreme or unusual sexual fantasies
☐ May be diagnosed as anxiety disordered; however, the likelihood of psychotic and personality disorder diagnoses increases with elevations on scale 8
☐ Intense anxiety and thinking problems need to be considered in treatment

typically unable to focus on issues and are viewed as odd, unusual, and autistic. Circumstantial thinking, bizarre speech (clang associations, neologisms, and echolalia), delusions, and hallucinations are sometimes present.

Predictions or Dispositions

The most common diagnosis is schizophrenic disorder or severe personality disorder. A severe thought disturbance may be present, for example, and they may be confused, perplexed, and disoriented; show feelings of unreality; and have difficulty in thinking and concentrating. Individuals with this profile code may state no need for professional help and may not enter willingly into psychological treatment. Although some need to achieve and feel pressure to perform, their actual performance tends to be mediocre. Table 5-22 lists the 8-9/9-8 descriptors.

Three-Point Code-Type Descriptors

1-2-3 Code Type

Symptoms and Behaviors

Individuals with this clinical profile report much physiological distress and difficulty adjusting psychologically. They seem to lack stamina and may feel weak,

Table 5-22. Descriptors for the 8-9/9-8 Code Type

☐ Serious psychological disturbance is likely
☐ May show social withdrawal and isolation
☐ Uncomfortable in heterosexual relationships and has poor sexual adjustment
☐ Hyperactive, emotionally labile, agitated, and excited
☐ Loud and excessively talkative
☐ Unrealistic in self-appraisal, grandiose, boastful, and fickle
☐ Characterized by denying problems
☐ Vague and circumstantial speech
☐ Feels inferior and inadequate
☐ Has low self-esteem
☐ Limited involvement in competitive or achievement-oriented situations
☐ Self-centered and infantile in expectations of others
☐ Demands much attention and becomes resentful and hostile when the demands are not met
☐ Resists and even fears close emotional involvement
☐ Confused, perplexed, disoriented
☐ Shows feelings of unreality and difficulties in thinking and concentrating
☐ Unable to focus on issues and viewed as odd, unusual, and autistic
☐ Circumstantial thinking, bizarre speech (clang associations, neologisms, echolalia), delusion and hallucinations are sometimes found
☐ Severe thought disturbance may be present
☐ Possible schizophrenic disorder or severe personality disorder

fatigued, tense, and nervous much of the time. They tend to react to stress by developing physical symptoms. They often overreact to minor or even normal physical changes with extreme concern and complaints. Although physical symptoms may be the primary problems reported, the individual also feels dysphoric and worried. Many individuals with this profile type develop physical symptoms centered around abdominal pain or headaches.

Personality Characteristics

Clients with this code type are rather passive in interpersonal relationships and may interact with others by whining and complaining. Individuals with this profile configuration are usually somewhat dependent and often feel the need to be taken care of. They are likely to become irritable and hostile if their needs are not met.

Predictions or Dispositions

These individuals are likely to experience low sexual drive and may have problems in heterosexual adjustment because of this. There are likely to be

Table 5-23. Descriptors for the 1-2-3 Code Type

☐ Physiological distress and difficulty in adjusting psychologically

☐ Lacks stamina and may feel weak, fatigued, tense, and nervous much of the time

☐ Reacts to stress by developing physical symptoms and frequently overreacts to minor or normal physical changes with extreme concern and complaints

☐ Feels dysphoric and worried

☐ Physical symptoms often center around abdominal pain or headaches

☐ Passive in interpersonal relationships and may interact with others by whining and complaining

☐ Dependent and often feels the need to be taken care of

☐ Becomes irritable and hostile if needs are frustrated

☐ Experiences low sexual drive and may have problems in heterosexual adjustment

☐ Long-standing personality characteristics that predispose to development of physical symptoms under stress

☐ Viewed as having psychophysiological disorders

☐ Sees problems as physical and probably does not recognize that psychological factors contribute to the symptoms

☐ Tends to be uninsightful and not likely to feel any control over symptoms

long-standing personality factors predisposing them to develop physical symptoms under stress. Individuals with this profile are often viewed as having psychophysiological disorders. The diagnosis of somatoform disorder in a passive-aggressive or dependent personality is probable. These individuals may view their problems as physical and probably do not recognize that psychological factors contribute to their symptoms. They tend to be uninsightful and are not likely to feel that they have any control over their symptoms. Thus, they are poor candidates for insight-oriented psychotherapy. However, they might need to be confronted with the possible psychological origin of their symptoms. Stress management approaches might help them develop more effective problem-solving skills to better cope with stressful situations. Individuals with this clinical profile often have a hostile manner of interacting with others, which might carry over into the treatment situation, reducing the likelihood of therapeutic gain. Individuals with this personality style are not very receptive to suggestions from others. Descriptors for the 1-2-3 code type are provided in Table 5-23.

2-4-7/2-7-4 Code Type

Symptoms and Behaviors

Individuals with this code type are likely to have alcohol or drug abuse problems that require intervention. These individuals may alternate between periods of gross insensitivity to the consequences of their own actions and excessive concern about the effects of their behavior. They may engage in episodes of acting out

Table 5-24. Descriptors for the 2-7-4/2-4-7 Code Type

☐ Chronic psychological maladjustment
☐ Impulse control problems
☐ Tends to be angry, hostile, and immature
☐ Feels like other people take advantage of them
☐ Associated with substance abuse problems
☐ Frequently diagnosed as passive-aggressive personality disorder
☐ Shows conflict over dependency
☐ Feels depressed and pessimistic about current life situation
☐ May experience suicidal ideation
☐ Strong unfulfilled needs for attention
☐ Functions at a very low level of efficiency
☐ Tends not to do well in traditional psychotherapy
☐ Poor work and achievement history
☐ Has problematic interpersonal relationships
☐ Tends not to do well in insight-oriented therapy and may actually return to prior behavior problems after treatment

followed by temporary guilt and self-condemnation. Vague somatic complaints, tension, and fatigue are also common. They often report feeling exhausted and being unable to face their pressing environmental problems. Individuals with this pattern tend to be depressed and experience extensive life problems as a result of their hedonistic behavior. Marital or work problems are quite common among individuals with this pattern.

Personality Characteristics

Feelings of dependency and personal insecurity plague their adjustment. Individuals with this pattern tend to be viewed as having severe personality problems. Self-oriented and hedonistic behavior is common.

Predictions or Dispositions

Permanent personality changes are difficult for them to make. These individuals may act out rather than deal with conflict. Table 5-24 lists the descriptors for the 2-7-4/2-4-7 code type.

2-7-8 Code Type

Symptoms and Behaviors

A pattern of chronic psychological maladjustment characterizes individuals with this MMPI-2 profile. Individuals with this clinical profile are probably feeling overwhelmed by anxiety, tension, and depression. Individuals with this code type feel helpless, alone, inadequate, and insecure and believe that life is hopeless and that nothing is working out. They attempt to control their worries through intellectualization and unproductive self-analysis, but they have difficulty concentrating and making decisions. They are functioning at a very low level of efficiency. They tend to overreact to even minor stress and may show rapid behavioral deterioration. They also tend to blame themselves for problems. Their lifestyle is typically chaotic and disorganized, and they have a history of poor work and achievement. They may be preoccupied with obscure religious ideas.

Personality Characteristics

Problematic interpersonal relationships are also characteristic of such clients. Individuals with this profile configuration seem to lack basic social skills and are often behaviorally withdrawn. They may relate to others ambivalently, never fully trusting or loving anyone. Many 2-7-8 individuals never establish lasting, intimate relationships. Their interpersonal relationships are likely to be unrewarding and impoverished owing, in part, to their feelings of inadequacy and insecurity.

Predictions or Dispositions

This is a rather chronic behavioral pattern. Individuals with this profile usually live a disorganized and pervasively unhappy existence. They may have episodes of more intense and disturbed behavior resulting from an elevated stress level. Individuals with this profile show a severe psychological disorder and would probably be diagnosed as severely neurotic with an anxiety disorder or dysthymic disorder in a schizoid personality. However, the possibility of a more severe psychotic disorder, such as schizophrenic disorder, should also be considered. Many individuals with this profile seek and require psychological treatment for their problems. Because many of their problems tend to be chronic, an intensive therapeutic effort might be required to bring about any significant change. Patients with this profile typically have many psychological and situational concerns; thus, it is often difficult to maintain a focus in treatment. They probably need a great deal of emotional support at this time.

Individuals with this profile configuration usually have low self-esteem and feelings of inadequacy, which make it difficult for them to get energized toward therapeutic action. Their expectation for positive change in therapy may be low. Therapists need to promote a positive, optimistic attitude if treatment is to be successful.

These individuals tend to be overideational and given to unproductive rumination. They tend not to do well in unstructured, insight-oriented therapy and may actually deteriorate in functioning if they are asked to be introspective. They might respond more to supportive treatment of a directive, goal-oriented type. Individuals with this profile present a clear suicide risk, and precautions should be taken. Table 5-25 summarizes the 2-7-8 code-type correlates.

Table 5-25. Descriptors for the 2-7-8 Code Type

☐ Chronic psychological maladjustment

☐ Overwhelmed by anxiety, tension, and depression

☐ Feels helpless, alone, inadequate, and insecure

☐ Believes that life is hopeless and that nothing is working out right

☐ Uses intellectualization as a defense

☐ Engages in unproductive self-analyses but has difficulty concentrating and making decisions

☐ Functions at a very low level of efficiency

☐ Overreacts to even minor stress and may show rapid behavioral deterioration

☐ Blames self for problems

☐ Has low self-esteem and feelings of inadequacy

☐ Tends to be overideational and given to unproductive rumination

☐ Chaotic and disorganized, with a history of poor work and achievement

☐ May be preoccupied with obscure religious ideas

☐ Has problematic interpersonal relationships

☐ Lacks basic social skills and is often withdrawn

☐ Relates to others ambivalently, never fully trusting or loving anyone

☐ Never establishes lasting, intimate relationships

☐ Interpersonal relationships are likely to be unrewarding and impoverished

☐ Feels inadequate and insecure

☐ Chronic behavioral problems

☐ Lives a disorganized and pervasively unhappy existence

☐ Has episodes of more intense and disturbed behavior

☐ Has a severe psychological disorder

☐ Possibly diagnosed as a severe anxiety disorder or dysthymic disorder in a schizoid personality

☐ Possibility of a more severe psychotic disorder, such as schizophrenic disorder

☐ Tends not to do well in unstructured, insight-oriented therapy and may actually deteriorate in functioning if encouraged to be introspective

Highlight Summary: Analysis of Alice's Code Type

Following the interpretive procedures suggested in this chapter, we examine the possible descriptive information from the MMPI code-type literature for Alice's profile that was presented in Chapter 4. We organize the potential behavioral descriptions of Alice's case into the same three categories used throughout this chapter: Symptoms and Behaviors, Personality Characteristics, and Predictions or Dispositions.

Alice's MMPI-2 code type is not a well-defined 7-8/8-7. The code-type definition tells us how confident we can be that the available code-type descriptors apply to her and increases the likelihood that her pattern will remain stable over time. Alice's scale elevations indicate that she has two standard scales with elevations greater than a T score of 65: scale 7 (T = 72) and scale 8 (T = 67). Because the next closest scale, scale 3, is 4 T-score points below, at a T score of 63, we can be somewhat assured that this code type may be similar on retest, although it does not reach the recommended five-point level.

Symptoms and Behaviors

How would Alice be described on the basis of the MMPI-2 profile code? Patients with the 7-8/8-7 code type usually show a great deal of emotional turmoil and an essentially psychoneurotic pattern. They openly report many psychological problems. They tend to lack defenses to keep themselves comfortable or anxiety free. They report feeling depressed, worried, tense, and nervous. They may be confused, be in a state of panic, show indecisiveness, and have poor judgment. They do not seem to learn from experience. They tend to be overly introspective and ruminative and overideational.

Personality Characteristics

Chronic feelings of insecurity, inadequacy, inferiority, and indecisiveness are likely. Individuals with this code type are not socially poised or confident and tend to withdraw from social interactions. Alice is likely to be passive-dependent and unable to take a dominant role in relationships. She probably has difficulties with mature heterosexual relationships and tends to feel inadequate in her gender-role attitudes. She may engage in excessive sexual fantasies.

Predictions or Dispositions

Patients with this profile may be diagnosed as anxiety disordered. Medications or behavioral interventions to control intense anxiety can be considered as treatment options.

The descriptive information obtained from Alice's MMPI-2 code type resembles the information we obtained in the scale-by-scale review described in the last chapter. In Alice's case, the code-type interpretation (i.e., taking both scales into consideration simultaneously) provides a diagnostic picture that emphasizes the central role of acute anxiety and a psychoneurotic, rather than a schizophrenic, process. A psychotic process might have been considered more likely in a scale-by-scale analysis that placed equal emphasis on scales 7 and 8.

Chapter 6

Interpreting the MMPI-2 Content Scales

If people respond to personality items in a cooperative manner, what they say about themselves in a clinical situation should be given considerable weight in the assessment process. The traditional approach to interpreting the empirically derived clinical scales of the MMPI-2 does not directly consider item responses as personal information. Rather, it assumes that answers to MMPI-2 items are simply signs of problem types without regard to specific response content. What matters is the way an item is endorsed, not its content. The meaning of an empirical scale is based not on the makeup of the constituent items but on the empirical relationships that have been established for the scale. Interpretation of the traditional clinical scales and code types thus requires that an extensive network of empirical correlates be established for each scale or index before meaning can be attached to particular scores.

Content interpretation, on the other hand, is based on the view that responses to items are communications about one's feelings, personality style, and past or current problems. A major assumption of content interpretation is that the subject wishes to reveal his or her ideas, attitudes, beliefs, and problems and then cooperates with the testing by truthfully acknowledging them. Most people taking the MMPI-2 under clinical conditions provide accurate personality information. However, subjects taking the MMPI-2 under pressure, under court order, or in employment-selection situations may distort their responses to create a particular impression. In these cases, the scores on the content scales may be suppressed somewhat, reflecting a problem-free picture, and thus may not be as accurate as the scale scores of a cooperative subject.

Several approaches to assessing content themes have been explored with the MMPI instruments. In Chapter 4, we discussed one important way in which item content, through the use of subscales, is used to refine interpretation of the standard scales. These rationally derived subscales provide a very useful, though somewhat limited, view of what an individual is communicating through item endorsement.

A more comprehensive and psychometrically sound approach to assessing item content dimensions in the original MMPI was developed by Wiggins (1966, 1969), who published a set of content homogeneous scales that represented the major dimensions in the item pool. Each dimension had high internal consistency and strong predictive validity. Because a number of the Wiggins content scales contained items with objectionable content and were deleted in the revision of the MMPI and a number of new items were added to the MMPI-2 to address additional content areas, a new set of MMPI-2 content scales was developed (Butcher, Graham, Williams & Ben-Porath, 1990). Similarly, as described in Chapter 12, a new set of content scales was developed for the MMPI-A (Williams, Butcher, Ben-Porath & Graham, 1992).

MMPI-2 Content Scale Development

The MMPI-2 content scales were developed following a multistage, multimethod scale-construction strategy. Initially, content dimensions were derived from the 704-item experimental booklet, Form AX. These item groups were then purified statistically using item-scale correlations on normal (college students and military personnel) and clinical samples. The MMPI-2 restandardization sample (N = 2,600) was employed only for developing norms in the final stages of scale development. The item dimensions were purified by eliminating items that were uncorrelated with the total score of the scale. Additional items were obtained by evaluating item-scale correlations of the 704 items with the total score of the defined dimensions. The revised dimensions (content scales) were then rationally reviewed to ensure that the additional items met the criterion of content homogeneity. Alpha coefficients were computed to ensure that all the items on a particular scale actually added to the scale homogeneity, that is, that they increased the scale's alpha level. The last psychometric stage involved reducing and, in most cases, eliminating item overlap by dropping items from the scales on which their correlation was lower. In other words, an item was kept on a scale only if it was most highly correlated with that scale. Some item overlap was allowed on scales that measured general problems such as WRK and TRT. Finally, norms were constructed using the MMPI-2 community normative sample. The uniform-T-score method adopted in the MMPI-2 restandardization was also employed in the development of T scores for the content scales so that the two types of scales would be comparable.

Psychometric Properties of the MMPI-2 Content Scales

Internal Consistency

The MMPI-2 content scales, having been developed in part following an internal consistency strategy, have internal consistency coefficients ranging from .68 to .86 in the normative sample (Butcher, Graham, Dahlstrom & Bowman, 1990). These internal consistency coefficients compare quite favorably to the Wiggins content scales for the original MMPI. The internally consistent scale properties allow the interpreter to consider the scale as having a single dimension that is readily interpretable by rational or intuitive strategies.

Validity

Although the MMPI-2 content scales were derived rationally and refined by item-scale statistical analyses, the empirically based descriptors have proven to be an important characteristic of the scales as well. Butcher et al. (1990) report acceptable external correlates for many of the scales based on the behavior ratings of the couples in the MMPI-2 restandardization study. In particular, the ANX, DEP, HEA,

ANG, ASP, LSE, SOD, and TPA scales showed strong external relationships to behavior as rated by the individual's spouse. The TPA scale for men also showed strong external correlates. The validity coefficients for the MMPI-2 content scales obtained in the normative study were equal to or higher than those obtained for the MMPI-2 clinical scales using the same external correlate ratings.

Several more recent studies have found strong external correlates for some of the content scales, particularly FAM and ASP. In a study of marital couples in distress, Hjemboe and Butcher (1991) found that the FAM scale was associated with marital and family problems. ASP has been found to predict antisocial personality characteristics and behavior. Lilienfeld (1991, 1996) reported that scores on the MMPI-2 ASP scale were significantly related to *DSM III-R*–based antisocial personality. Moreover, Lilienfeld (1996) found that the ASP scale was a better predictor of antisocial behavior than was the Pd scale of the MMPI-2. Egeland, Erickson, Butcher, and Ben-Porath (1991) found that scores on the ASP scale differentiated mothers who had been identified as being at high risk for abusing their children from other women taking the test. Bosquet and Egeland (2000) also found the ASP scale to be associated with negative parenting behavior such as harshness, hostility, and low understanding.

The content scales provide the clinician with as valid a psychometric comparison of the client as other MMPI-2 scales do. A study by Keller and Butcher (1991) showed that chronic pain patients can be empirically distinguished from the MMPI-2 normative sample by using the HEA scale. Schill and Wang (1990) found that the ANG scale correlated significantly with other measures of anger. The role of the MMPI-2 content scales in discriminant diagnosis has been evaluated in two recent investigations. Two studies using inpatient psychiatric profiles (Ben-Porath, Butcher & Graham, 1991; Munley, Busby & Jaynes, 1997) showed that the BIZ and DEP scales separated inpatient depressed patients from schizophrenic patients more effectively than did MMPI-2 clinical scales D and Sc. Faull and Meyer (1993) conducted a construct validity study of the DEP scale and found that it had higher internal consistency and greater convergent validity with other depression measures than did scale 2 of the MMPI-2.

In another study, Walsh et al. (1991) found that the MMPI-2 content scales outperformed the clinical scales in differentiating between alcohol-abusing groups. Boone (1994) reported that the DEP content scale was significantly intercorrelated with other measures, including those for depression, hopelessness, low self-esteem, and suicidal ideation. He also found that the DEP scale significantly differentiated depressed patients from nondepressed patients.

Recent studies have examined how the special-problems content scales—WRK, TPA, and TRT—assess relevant behavior. Quereshi and Kleman (1996) found that the WRK scale was associated with lowered productivity as assessed by a Productive Persistence Measure. They also found that the TPA scale was correlated with assertiveness. In a treatment outcome study, Chisolm, Crowther, and Ben-Porath (1997) examined the MMPI-2 content scales DEP, ASP, ANX, and TRT and the MMPI-2 clinical scales in a treatment continuation outcome study. They found that the content scales emerged as better predictors of outcome than the clinical scales. Finally, Brems and Lloyd (1995) found that the LSE scale showed high internal consistency and strong assessment of a global self-esteem assessment.

An Interpretive Strategy for the MMPI-2 Content Scales

Clinical interpretation of the MMPI-2 content scales, unlike interpretation of the empirically derived clinical scales, is relatively straightforward and requires few assumptions. Endorsement of the items comprising a particular scale indicates admission of symptoms and attitudes contained in the items—assuming, of course, that the protocol is valid. The content scales are interpretable as summaries of the extent to which clients admit to particular problem areas. As noted earlier, they provide psychometric comparisons that are as reliable and valid as those of other MMPI-2 scales. However, interpreting these scales is not limited to predicting membership in a clinical group. More important, because the content scales contain homogeneous item content, the clinician is able to employ the descriptive qualitative characteristics reflected in the scale's items to describe the behavioral features the client acknowledges. For example, a client with an elevated score on HEA (T = 65) could accurately be described as endorsing excessive somatic complaints across several body systems, including gastrointestinal symptoms (e.g., constipation, nausea and vomiting, stomach trouble), neurological problems (e.g., convulsions, dizzy and fainting spells, paralysis), sensory problems such as poor hearing or eyesight, cardiovascular symptoms (e.g., heart or chest pains), and respiratory troubles (e.g., coughs, hay fever, asthma). Such a client is likely to worry about his or her health, report feeling sicker more often than the average person, report experiencing a great deal of pain (e.g., headaches, neck pains), and seek attention for his or her complaints.

The interpreter should be aware of several ways in which the MMPI-2 content scales can add to interpretation. First, the content scales can often help clinicians understand clinical scale elevations by allowing them to confirm or eliminate certain behavioral features represented in the scale. For example, if an individual has a high Pd score but a low ASP score and a high elevation on FAM, the elevation on scale 4 is likely due to family problems rather than antisocial features. Or, if the individual has a high elevation on the Pt scale but a low elevation on OBS, then one would conclude that the client does not appear to be plagued with excessive rumination and obsessive behavior but may be experiencing more generalized anxiety without obsessive features.

The MMPI-2 content scales can also provide information that is not available through the clinical scales because they contain new items in the MMPI-2 item pool. Several recent studies have shown that the content scales add incremental validity to the clinical scales in clinical prediction studies (Archer, Aiduk, Griffin & Elkins, 1996; Ben-Porath, McCully & Almagor, 1993; Ben-Porath et al., 1991; Lilienfeld, 1996; Munley et al., 1997). The MMPI-2 content scales are grouped to provide information in several areas.

The Internal Symptom Cluster

The six scales constituting this group (ANX, FRS, OBS, DEP, HEA, and BIZ) address symptoms and maladaptive cognitions the individual might be experiencing. Clues to internal symptomatic behavior, maladaptive cognitive beliefs, and disabling thoughts are found in elevations on this cluster.

Table 6-1. ANX Interpretive Guidelines for the MMPI-2

☐ High elevations on ANX are T scores ≥ 65. High scores indicate the endorsement of many of the anxiety symptoms included in the scale.

☐ Moderate elevations on ANX are T scores of 60 to 64, inclusive. Elevations in this range suggest that the individual has endorsed several symptoms of anxiety.

☐ High scorers on ANX report:
  • Symptoms of anxiety, worry, and tension
  • Somatic problems, such as heart pounding and shortness of breath
  • Sleep difficulties
  • Decision-making difficulties
  • Poor concentration
  • Being fearful of losing their mind
  • Indecision
  • Finding life a strain
  • An awareness of these symptoms and problems
  • A willingness to admit to anxiety-related symptoms

Table 6-2. FRS Interpretive Guidelines for the MMPI-2

☐ High elevations on FRS are T scores ≥ 65. High scores indicate the endorsement of many of the fears included in the scale.

☐ Moderate elevations on FRS are T scores of 60 to 64, inclusive. Elevations in this range suggest that the subject has endorsed several different fears.

☐ High scorers on FRS report:
  • Having many specific fears (e.g., blood, high places, money, animals, leaving home, fire, storms, natural disasters, water, the dark, being indoors, and dirt)

Anxiety

The ANX scale of 23 items addresses problems of generalized anxiety. Individuals who score high on ANX report symptoms including tension, somatic problems such as heart pounding and shortness of breath, sleep difficulties, excessive worries, and concentration problems. High scorers fear that they are losing their minds, find life a strain, and have difficulties making decisions, even minor ones. They appear to be very aware of these symptoms and problems and are willing to admit to them. Table 6-1 summarizes the ANX interpretive guidelines.

Fears

The FRS scale, containing 23 items, focuses on specific fears or phobias. Individuals who score high on FRS report an inordinate number of fears or phobias of many different situations or things. These include blood, high places, money, animals (such as snakes, mice, or spiders), leaving home, fire, storms and natural disasters, water, the dark, being indoors, and dirt. This scale does not contain general symptoms of anxiety, which are addressed by the ANX scale. Interpretive guidelines for FRS are included in Table 6-2.

Table 6-3. OBS Interpretive Guidelines for the MMPI-2

☐ High elevations on OBS are T scores ≥ 65. High scores indicate the endorsement of many obsessional behaviors assessed by the scale.

☐ Moderate elevations on OBS are T scores of 60 to 64, inclusive. Elevations in this range suggest that several of the obsessive behaviors are endorsed.

☐ High scorers on OBS report:
  - Tremendous difficulties making decisions
  - Being likely to ruminate excessively about issues and problems
  - Fearing that they cause others to become impatient with them
  - Being distressed by having to make changes
  - Compulsive behaviors, such as counting or saving unimportant things
  - Worrying excessively
  - Feeling overwhelmed by their own thoughts

Obsessiveness

The OBS scale of 16 items addresses the cognitive processes of maladaptive rumination and obsessive thinking. Individuals who score high on OBS have tremendous difficulties making decisions and are likely to ruminate excessively about issues and problems, causing others to become impatient. Having to make changes distresses them, and they may report some compulsive behaviors, such as counting or saving unimportant things. They are excessive worriers who frequently become overwhelmed by their own thoughts and appear unable to function in a practical manner. The interpretation of OBS is summarized in Table 6-3.

Depression

The DEP scale, containing 33 items, assesses symptomatic depression. Individuals who score high on this scale are characterized as having significant depressive thoughts. They report feeling blue and uncertain about their future and seem uninterested in their lives. They are likely to brood, be unhappy, cry easily, and feel hopeless about the future. They report feeling empty and may have thoughts of suicide or wish they were dead. They may believe that they are condemned or have committed unpardonable sins. They tend to consider other people unsupportive. Table 6-4 summarizes the DEP interpretive statements.

Health Concerns

The HEA scale of 36 items addresses health symptoms and concerns. Individuals with high scores on HEA report many physical symptoms across several body systems, including gastrointestinal symptoms (e.g., constipation, nausea and vomiting, stomach trouble), neurological problems (e.g., convulsions, dizzy and fainting spells, paralysis), sensory problems (e.g., poor hearing or eyesight), cardiovascular symptoms (e.g., heart or chest pains), skin problems, pain (e.g., headaches, neck pains), and respiratory troubles (e.g., coughs, hay fever, asthma). Individuals who score high on HEA tend to worry about their health and report feeling sick more often than does the average person. HEA interpretive guidelines can be found in Table 6-5.

Table 6-4. DEP Interpretive Guidelines for the MMPI-2

☐ High elevations on DEP are T scores ≥ 65. High scores indicate the endorsement of many of the mood problems included in the scale.

☐ Moderate elevations on DEP are T scores of 60 to 64, inclusive. Elevations in this range suggest that several of the depressive symptoms are endorsed.

☐ High scorers on DEP report:
  • Significant depressive thoughts
  • Feeling blue and uncertain about their future
  • Being uninterested in their life
  • Being likely to brood, being unhappy, and crying easily
  • Feeling hopeless and empty much of the time
  • Possible thoughts of suicide or wishes that they were dead
  • Beliefs that they are condemned or have committed unpardonable sins
  • Feeling that other people are not supportive

Table 6-5. HEA Interpretive Guidelines for the MMPI-2

☐ High elevations on HEA are T scores ≥ 65. High scores indicate the endorsement of many of the health concerns included in the scale.

☐ Moderate elevations on HEA are T scores of 60 to 64, inclusive. Elevations in this range suggest that several somatic symptoms are endorsed.

☐ High scorers on HEA report:
  • Many physical symptoms across several body systems, including gastrointestinal symptoms, neurological problems, sensory problems, cardiovascular symptoms, skin problems, pain, and respiratory troubles
  • Worries about their health
  • Feeling sicker than the average person

Bizarre Mentation

The BIZ scale, containing 24 items, addresses severe symptoms of thought disorder. Individuals who respond to items on this scale are likely to manifest psychotic thought processes. They may report auditory, visual, or olfactory hallucinations and may recognize that their thoughts are strange and peculiar. Paranoid ideation (e.g., the belief that they are being plotted against or that someone is trying to poison them) may be reported as well. These individuals may feel that they have a special mission or powers. Elevations greater than 65 on this scale suggest severe and unusual thinking problems. Table 6-6 has the BIZ interpretive guidelines.

The External Aggressive Tendencies Cluster

The four scales in this cluster (ANG, CYN, ASP, and TPA) center around behavior control, negative attitudes toward others, and outward expression of emotions. Scores on these scales indicate how the individual is dealing with others—high elevations on these scales suggest that the individual has maladaptive behaviors

Table 6-6. BIZ Interpretive Guidelines for the MMPI-2

☐ High elevations on BIZ are T scores ≥ 65. High scores indicate the endorsement of many of the unusual thinking problems included in the scale.

☐ Moderate elevations on BIZ are T scores of 60 to 64, inclusive. Elevations in this range suggest that several of the problem behaviors are endorsed.

☐ High scorers on BIZ report:
  • Possible auditory, visual, or olfactory hallucinations
  • Recognizing that their thoughts are strange and peculiar
  • Paranoid ideations (e.g., being plotted against or someone trying to poison them)
  • Unrealistic feelings that they have a special mission or powers in life

---

Table 6-7. ANG Interpretive Guidelines for the MMPI-2

☐ High elevations on ANG are T scores ≥ 65. High scores indicate the endorsement of many of the anger-control problems included in the scale.

☐ Moderate elevations on ANG are T scores of 60 to 64, inclusive. Elevations in this range suggest that several of the anger behaviors are endorsed.

☐ High scorers on the ANG scale report:
  • Anger-control problems
  • Feeling irritable, grouchy, and impatient
  • Being hotheaded, annoyed, and stubborn
  • Sometimes feeling like swearing or smashing things
  • Concern over losing self-control
  • Having been physically abusive toward people and objects

---

or attitudes about the way he or she attempts to deal with demands of their life situation.

Anger

The ANG scale of 16 items assesses loss of control while angry. Individuals who score high on ANG are likely to have anger control problems. These individuals report being irritable, grouchy, impatient, hotheaded, annoyed, and stubborn. They feel like swearing or smashing things at times. They may lose self-control and report having been physically abusive of people and objects. Interpretive guidelines are in Table 6-7.

Cynicism

The CYN scale, measuring cynical beliefs and misanthropic attitudes, contains 23 items, 20 of which were initially developed through item factor analysis of the MMPI in a study by Johnson, Butcher, Null, and Johnson (1984). Three new MMPI-2 items were added to the scale through item analysis procedures. Individuals who score high on this scale have negative attitudes toward others and seem to expect hidden, negative motives behind the actions of others. For example, they believe that most people are honest simply because they fear being caught, that other people are to be distrusted, or that other people use each other and are

Table 6-8. CYN Interpretive Guidelines for the MMPI-2

☐ High elevations on CYN are T scores ≥ 65. High scores indicate extensive endorsement of the cynical attitudes and behaviors included in the scale.

☐ Moderate elevations on CYN are T scores of 60 to 64, inclusive. Elevations in this range suggest that many of the cynical attitudes and behaviors are endorsed.

☐ High scorers on the CYN scale report:
- Many misanthropic beliefs
- Expecting hidden, negative motives behind the actions of others
- Believing that most people are honest simply because they fear being caught
- Distrusting other people
- Believing that people use others and are friendly only for selfish reasons
- Negative attitudes about those close to them, including fellow workers, family, and friends

Table 6-9. ASP Interpretive Guidelines for the MMPI-2

☐ High elevations on ASP are T scores ≥ 65. High scores indicate extensive endorsement of the antisocial problems included in the scale.

☐ Moderate elevations on ASP are T scores of 60 to 64, inclusive. Elevations in this range suggest that many of the antisocial behaviors are endorsed.

☐ High scorers on the ASP scale report:
- Misanthropic attitudes similar to high CYN scorers
- Problem behaviors during their school years
- Antisocial practices, such as being in trouble with the law, stealing, or shoplifting
- Enjoying the antics of criminals
- Believing that it is all right to get around the law as long as it is not broken

friendly only for selfish reasons. High scorers are likely to hold negative attitudes about those close to them, including fellow workers, family, and friends. Table 6-8 provides the CYN interpretive statements.

Antisocial Practices

The ASP scale of 22 items addresses antisocial personality characteristics. High scorers, in addition to holding misanthropic attitudes similar to high scorers on the CYN scale, are likely to report problem behaviors during their school years and other antisocial practices, such as being in trouble with the law, stealing, or shoplifting. They admit to enjoying the antics of criminals and believe that it is all right to get around the law, as long as it is not broken. Table 6-9 summarizes the ASP interpretive statements.

Type A

The 19 items of the TPA scale, most of them new with the MMPI-2, address a driven, competitive, and hostile personality style. High scorers on TPA are hard-driving, fast-moving, and work-oriented individuals who frequently become impatient, irritable, and annoyed when they are interrupted. They do not like to wait or be delayed in tasks they are attempting. They report that there is never

Table 6-10. TPA Interpretive Guidelines for the MMPI-2

☐ High elevations on TPA are T scores ≥ 65. High scores indicate extensive endorsement of the behaviors found in Type A personalities.

☐ Moderate elevations on TPA are T scores of 60 to 64, inclusive. Elevations in this range suggest that many of the Type A behaviors are endorsed.

☐ High scorers on TPA report:
   • Being hard driving, fast moving, and work oriented
   • Frequently becoming impatient, irritable, and annoyed
   • Not liking to wait or being interrupted at a task
   • Never having enough time in a day to complete their tasks
   • Being direct and overbearing in their relationships with others

---

enough time in a day for them to complete their tasks. They tend to be direct, blunt, and overbearing in their relationships with others. Others view them as aggressive, overbearing, and petty about minor details. Table 6-10 provides the TPA interpretations.

Negative Self-View

The LSE scale provides clues to how the individual views him- or herself. This scale measures feelings of self-efficacy and of security about being able to function in life—it provides information about how confidently the individual deals with the demands of his or her life.

Low Self-Esteem

The LSE scale of 24 items addresses negative self-views. It was developed to provide a relatively "symptom-free" measure of negative attitudes toward the self. That is, an effort was made to exclude items related to depression and anxiousness. Individuals who score high on LSE tend to characterize themselves in negative terms and have low opinions of themselves. They do not believe that they are liked by others or that they are important. They hold many negative attitudes about themselves, including beliefs that they are unattractive, awkward, clumsy, useless, and a burden to others. They report that they lack self-confidence and find it hard to accept compliments. They tend to feel overwhelmed by all the faults they see in themselves. Others view them as too hard on themselves. LSE interpretations are summarized in Table 6-11.

General Problem Areas Cluster

The scales included in this interpretive cluster (SOD, FAM, WRK, and TRT) are more complex problem areas, not simply symptoms, personality traits, attitudinal dispositions, or specific behaviors, as in the previous three groups of scales. These scales summarize problems in social relationships, perceptions and concerns over family problems, maladaptive attitudes and activities related to work adjustment,

Table 6-11. LSE Interpretive Guidelines for the MMPI-2

☐ High elevations on LSE are T scores ≥ 65. High scores indicate extensive endorsement of low self-esteem problems.

☐ Moderate elevations on LSE are T scores of 60 to 64, inclusive. Elevations in this range suggest that many of the negative self-views are endorsed.

☐ High scorers on LSE report:
- Low opinions of themselves
- Not believing that they are liked by others
- Feeling that they are unimportant
- Holding many negative attitudes about themselves, including beliefs that they are unattractive, awkward and clumsy, useless, and a burden to others
- Lacking self-confidence
- Finding it hard to accept compliments from others
- Feeling overwhelmed by all the faults they see in themselves

Table 6-12. SOD Interpretive Guidelines for the MMPI-2

☐ High elevations on SOD are T scores ≥ 65. High scores indicate extensive endorsement of social discomfort behaviors.

☐ Moderate elevations on SOD are T scores of 60 to 64, inclusive. Elevations in this range suggest that many of the social discomfort items are endorsed.

☐ High scorers on SOD are:
- Very introverted and distant from others
- Very uneasy around others, preferring to be by themselves
- Likely to sit alone rather than joining in the group
- Shy and disliking parties and other group events

and clues as to whether the individual holds negative views about the change process that would interfere with a psychological intervention.

Social Discomfort

The SOD scale, containing 24 items, assesses uneasiness in social situations. Individuals who score high on SOD tend to be very uneasy around others and prefer to be by themselves. In social situations, they are likely to sit alone rather than join in the group. They view themselves as shy and dislike parties and other group events. Interpretive statements for SOD are summarized in Table 6-12.

Family Problems

The FAM scale of 25 items centers around family relationship problems. Individuals who score high on FAM experience considerable family discord. Their families are described as lacking in love and being quarrelsome and unpleasant. High scorers may report hating members of their families. Their childhoods are usually portrayed as abusive, and their marriages may be seen as unhappy and lacking in affection. Individuals in marital distress have significantly more elevation on FAM than the normative MMPI-2 sample (Hjemboe & Butcher, 1991). FAM interpretive guidelines are summarized in Table 6-13.

Table 6-13. FAM Interpretive Guidelines for the MMPI-2

☐ High elevations on FAM are T scores ≥ 65. High scores indicate extensive endorsement of family problems included in the scale.

☐ Moderate elevations on FAM are T scores of 60 to 64, inclusive. Elevations in this range suggest that the individual has endorsed many problems centering around family relationships.

☐ High scorers on FAM report:
  • Considerable family discord
  • Their families are lacking in love and are quarrelsome and unpleasant
  • Hatred of members of their families
  • Their childhoods may have been abusive
  • Their marriages are unhappy and lacking in affection

Table 6-14. WRK Interpretive Guidelines for the MMPI-2

☐ High elevations on WRK are T scores ≥ 65. High scores indicate extensive endorsement of the problems likely to interfere with job performance.

☐ Moderate elevations on WRK are T scores of 60 to 64, inclusive. Elevations in this range suggest that many negative work items are endorsed.

☐ High scorers on WRK report:
  • Behaviors or attitudes that are likely to contribute to poor work performance
  • Low self-confidence
  • Concentration difficulties, obsessiveness, tension, and pressure
  • Difficulty getting started on things
  • Giving up quickly when difficulties mount
  • Decision-making problems
  • Lack of family support for their career choice
  • Personal questioning of career choice
  • Negative attitudes toward co-workers and supervisors

Work Interference

The WRK scale, containing 33 items, addresses problems and negative attitudes related to work or achievement. Individuals who score high on WRK are likely to possess negative work attitudes or personal problems that contribute to poor work performance. Some of the problems relate to low self-confidence, concentration difficulties, obsessiveness, tension and pressure, and indecision. Others suggest lack of family support for their career choice, their own questioning of career choice, and negative attitudes toward co-workers. Table 6-14 has the WRK interpretations.

Negative Treatment Indicators

The TRT scale of 26 items focuses on attitudes or problems in accepting help or in changing behavior. Individuals who score high on TRT possess negative attitudes toward doctors and mental health treatment. High-scoring individuals do not believe that anyone can understand or help them with their problems. They acknowledge that they have problems they are not comfortable discussing with

Table 6-15. TRT Interpretive Guidelines for the MMPI-2

☐ High elevations on TRT are T scores ≥ 65. High scores indicate extensive endorsement of the negative attitudes toward mental health treatment.

☐ Moderate elevations on TRT are T scores of 60 to 64, inclusive. Elevations in this range suggest that many of the negative treatment indicators are endorsed.

☐ High scorers on TRT report:
- Having negative attitudes toward physicians and mental health treatment professionals
- Feeling that no one can understand or help them
- Having issues or problems that they are not comfortable discussing with anyone
- Not wanting to change anything in their lives
- Not believing that change is possible
- Preferring to give up rather than face a crisis or difficulty

anyone. They may not want to change anything in their lives, and they feel that changing their present situation is not possible. They prefer giving up rather than facing a crisis or difficulty. Table 6-15 summarizes TRT interpretive guidelines.

MMPI-2 Content Component Scales

The MMPI-2 content scales were developed according to strategies that would maximize the psychometric and semantic internal consistency of each scale, as described earlier. These developmental strategies did yield a set of homogeneous scales. For example, all the items on the MMPI-2 Depression (DEP) content scale incorporate symptoms, behaviors, attitudes, and complaints that are typically associated with the clinical syndromes of depression. However, a closer examination of these items indicates that, at least on a conceptual level, it is possible to identify clusters of items *within* the content scales. Some of the items on the DEP scale, for example, reflect dysphoric affect, whereas others show self-deprecatory cognitions that are commonly associated with depression. In clinical situations, it is relatively common to find two individuals both suffering from depression but manifesting a *different* symptomatic pattern, for example, one focusing on the dysphoric affective aspect of the disorder and the other showing more of the negative-self views and self-deprecatory behavior.

Recently, Ben-Porath and Sherwood (1996) conducted a project that was aimed at further refinement of the content components of the MMPI-2 content scales. Their goals were (a) to determine whether it was possible to identify meaningful subgroups of items within the content scales and (b) to explore whether item subclusters could be detected that would result in useful subscales in a manner similar to the Harris-Lingoes subscales for some of the MMPI-2 clinical scales. These investigators, using both empirical and rational approaches, identified several clusters of items on various scales that tend to covary semantically and psychometrically. In each case, the items needed also to demonstrate a sufficient degree of independence from other clusters of items within the same scale.

These investigators determined that 27 subscales for 12 of the MMPI-2 content

Table 6-16. The MMPI-2 Content Component Scales

Fears (23 items in full scale)
  FRS1: Generalized Fearfulness (12 items)
  FRS2: Multiple Fears (10 items)

Depression (33 items in full scale)
  DEP1: Lack of Drive (12 items)
  DEP2: Dysphoria (6 items)
  DEP3: Self-Deprecation (7 items)
  DEP4: Suicidal Ideation (5 items)

Health Concerns (36 items in full scale)
  HEA1: Gastrointestinal Symptoms (5 items)
  HEA2: Neurological Symptoms (12 items)
  HEA3: General Health Concerns (6 items)

Bizarre Mentation (23 items in full scale)
  BIZ1: Psychotic Symptomatology (11 items)
  BIZ2: Schizotypal Characteristics (9 items)

Anger (16 items in full scale)
  ANG1: Explosive Behavior (7 items)
  ANG2: Irritability (7 items)

Cynicism (23 items in full scale)
  CYN1: Misanthropic Beliefs (15 items)
  CYN2: Interpersonal Suspiciousness
    (8 items)

Antisocial Practices (22 items in full scale)
  ASP1: Antisocial Attitudes (16 items)
  ASP2: Antisocial Behavior (5 items)

Type A Behavior (19 items in full scale)
  TPA1: Impatience (6 items)
  TPA2: Competitive Drive (9 items)

Low Self-Esteem (24 items in full scale)
  LSE1: Self-Doubt (11 items)
  LSE2: Submissiveness (6 items)

Social Discomfort (24 items in full scale)
  SOD1: Introversion (16 items)
  SOD2: Shyness (7 items)

Family Problems (25 items in full scale)
  FAM1: Family Discord (12 items)
  FAM2: Familial Alienation (5 items)

Negative Treatment Indicators (26 items in full scale)
  TRT1: Low Motivation (11 items)
  TRT2: Inability to Disclose (5 items)

Source. Ben-Porath and Sherwood (1996).

scales would likely be valuable clinical subscales. (There were no usable item component clusters for the ANX [Anxiety], OBS [Obsessiveness], and WRK [Work Interference] scales.) The 27 component scales for the MMPI-2 content scales are listed in Table 6-16.

The content component subscales are used in ways similar to the Harris-Lingoes subscales to refine interpretation when its content scale is elevated. For example, if the TPA scale is elevated, it may be helpful to know whether the Competitive Drive subscale is the most elevated of the subscales.

Case Example of the Utility of the Content Scales

The case shown in Figures 6-1 and 6-2 provides a clear example of how the MMPI-2 content scales can aid in understanding clinical scale elevations as well as providing useful hypotheses about how the client has described herself through MMPI-2 content. This woman, who is quite emotionally unstable, sought psychological treatment for depression, relationship problems, and an eating disorder. She has had a substantial and lengthy history of psychological treatment over the past 5 years. This history, along with her MMPI-2 performance, was valuable in obtaining an appropriate referral for her.

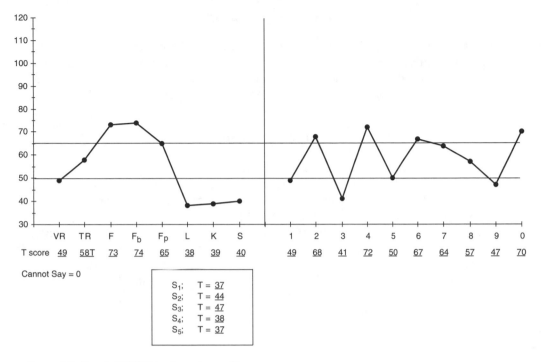

Cannot Say = 0

S_1;	T = 37
S_2;	T = 44
S_3;	T = 47
S_4;	T = 38
S_5;	T = 37

Figure 6-1. Rena's MMPI-2 basic scales profile.

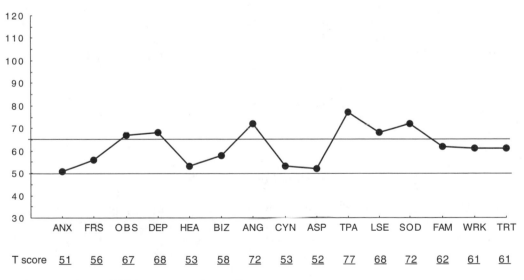

Figure 6-2. Rena's MMPI-2 content scales profile.

Presenting Problems

Rena, an overweight, single 37-year-old woman, had a long history of psychological problems involving intense anger conflicts and relationship problems. She was seen in an outpatient private practice and reported severe depression, intense mood fluctuation, work difficulties, and continued eating problems.

Treatment History

The client had a substantial history of mental health treatment:

She reportedly had a psychiatric breakdown (depression) and could not function at work. She was hospitalized and received treatment in an open psychiatric unit. She left the hospital, after only a short time, against medical advice.

In the fall of the same year, she was hospitalized in an inpatient eating disorders facility for severe bulimia for about 3 weeks. She reportedly was always overweight and tended to binge eat. Before being hospitalized, she was eating about $25 worth of candy at a sitting. She binged mostly in the evenings and used laxatives (often as many as 100 daily). During her initial period in the program, she alienated most of the staff and other patients. She was very verbally aggressive toward others and did not cooperate fully with the treatment. She remained for the course of the treatment and participated in the group treatment, although it was traumatic for her and for others. Her intense anger toward her parents and toward men was the focus of many sessions. She was discharged "improved." Her discharge diagnoses were bulimia and borderline personality.

A year later, Rena entered outpatient treatment but became angry with the therapist and terminated after only two sessions. The following year, after an intense argument with her mother, she entered therapy again. She remained in treatment for five sessions before leaving "disappointed" with the results. Her persistent problems continued, and a few months later, after experiencing a breakup in a relationship, having an abortion, and making a serious suicide attempt, she entered treatment again. She became angry over the therapist's questioning and stormed out of the initial session. In the next year, she was treated by a psychiatrist for her depression and was placed on antidepressant medication. She has been taking medication regularly over the past year. The present referral (a year after her last mental health contact) for depression and eating problems was self-initiated.

Family and Personal History

Rena lived alone but spent most of her time with her mother, age 60, who was somewhat dominating. Rena worked as a lower-level manager with a large corporation but had been having considerable difficulty getting along with others. Her position was recently "downgraded" (because of her interpersonal problems), and she was no longer supervising other employees.

Rena's personal relationships were quite estranged in recent years. She did not have any stable relationships. She broke up with her fiancé about 4 years ago and was not dating anyone on a regular basis. She had had a number of "one-night stands" over the past few years. She viewed herself as sexually promiscuous; she usually met men in bars and had sex with them, but they seldom saw each other after that.

MMPI-2 Basic Scales Interpretation

Rena's validity scale configuration suggested that she approached the MMPI-2 items in a frank, open manner, producing a valid clinical profile. She cooperated fully with the evaluation, endorsing a number of psychological problems that she appeared concerned about. Her MMPI-2 clinical profile (elevations on scales 2, 4, 6, and 0) showed a high degree of psychological distress. She appeared to have a mixed pattern of symptoms, including tension, depression, and agitation over problems she had in her life situation. She appeared to be socially alienated and distant from others and was likely to be overly sensitive to rejection. She was likely to be very suspicious of other people's motives and may have great difficulty trusting anyone.

Long-standing personality problems are likely to be central to her clinical picture. She appears to be angry over her present situation and feels that others are responsible for her problems. She tends to show poor impulse control and appears not to accept societal values. She may be seeking a temporary respite from the intense situational problems she is encountering. Drug use or alcohol abuse are probably central to her problem situation, given her elevations on D and Pd.

Rena's interpersonal relationships appear to be strained. She is likely to be a manipulative individual who views others as a means to her own gratification. She appears to be somewhat hedonistic and may attempt to control people. She is likely to view her home life as very unpleasant and feels that she is being dominated by her family.

Individuals with this MMPI-2 pattern may express a great need for treatment, but they tend to be marginal candidates for psychological treatment because their difficulty in forming positive personal relationships could impair the development of a treatment alliance. Her long-standing personality problems are probably resistant to behavioral change. Individuals with this profile tend to have problems with anger control and often become enraged and aggressive toward others. Many individuals with this clinical pattern tend to be experiencing extensive family problems that need to be addressed in treatment.

MMPI-2 Content Scale Interpretation

Rena's MMPI-2 content scale performance is very useful in clarifying her clinical scale elevations as well as in providing information not available through the clinical scale scores. Her high elevation on the Pd scale raises the possibility that she has an antisocial personality disorder. However, the ASP content scale is not elevated, suggesting that her Pd elevation does not represent purely antisocial features but rather self- and social-alienation, anger, and family relationship problems. Consequently, our interpretation of her clinical profile should minimize discussion of antisocial personality features or criminal behavior and instead stress her negative alienation, lack of anger control, and family problems.

The aggressiveness suggested by her Pd scale elevation is further clarified by her high scores on ANG. People who score high on ANG, as she does, are likely to have anger-control problems. These individuals report being irritable, grouchy, impatient, hotheaded, annoyed, and stubborn. They feel like swearing or smashing things at times. Rena acknowledges that she loses self-control in interactions with others and may be abusive toward people. Rena's scores on the content component scales provide further insight into her symptoms. She scored a 76 T score on the A1 (Explosive Behavior) subscale and a 70 on the TPA1 (Impatience) subscale.

She appears to be feeling quite depressed at this time, as reflected in her high score on the DEP scale. She reports feeling blue and uncertain about her future. She broods a lot, is unhappy, and feels hopeless about the future. She feels empty and may have thoughts of suicide. She reports feeling that she has committed unpardonable sins. She feels that other people are not supportive of her. Perhaps central to her problems is her indication of low self-esteem as measured by the LSE scale. People who have elevations on this scale tend to characterize themselves in negative terms and have low opinions of themselves. Apparently, Rena has many negative attitudes about herself, including beliefs that she is unattractive, useless, and a burden to others. She lacks self-confidence. She seems to be overwhelmed by all the faults she sees in herself.

The difficulties that she encounters in relationships and in continuing in therapy may be explained somewhat by her high score on OBS. She appears to have tremendous difficulties making decisions and is likely to ruminate excessively about issues and problems, causing others to become impatient with her. She apparently has difficulty making changes in her life and is distressed by change. She seems to be an excessive worrier who frequently becomes overwhelmed by her own thoughts and is at times unable to function in a practical manner.

Treatment Referral

Because of Rena's extensive interpersonal relationship problems and her history of having been moderately successful in group treatment in the past, it was recommended that she enter a group-therapy treatment program to work on her interpersonal problems. In addition, she was seen in individual psychological treatment for a period of time.

Any treatment program should consider the following features of Rena's personality and address them early in treatment if progress (including her remaining in treatment) is to occur:

She tends to mistrust others and overreacts to minor problems as though great injustices have been done to her.

She tends to obsess and ruminate over minor irritations to the point that she makes great problems of them.

She manifests low self-esteem and is likely to be prone to feeling rejected.

She has many personality features of aggressiveness, alienation, and interpersonal hostility.

She has a low tolerance for frustration and is likely to react to minor problems with considerable rage.

She is socially ineffective and withdrawn from others.

Treatment Progress

Rena's individual sessions were described as usually stormy and somewhat unproductive because she tended to focus blame for her problems on others and was not open to viewing her own contribution to them. Her experiences in group treatment were initially quite traumatic for her. She reportedly began to attack others in the group in a highly aggressive manner. In one very dramatic session, the group retaliated against her persistent attacks by providing her extensive feedback on her behavior without rejecting her. Although she was hurt by their criticisms, she remained in the group, participating in a less aggressive manner.

Highlight Summary: Alice's Content Scale Performance

The MMPI-2 standard scales are based on the assumption that they are diagnostic signs without regard to specific item content. Thus, the traditional clinical scales and code types require an extensive network of empirical correlates for interpretation. Content interpretation, on the other hand, is based on the view that responses to items are communications between the client and the clinician.

The MMPI-2 content scales provide a summary, in a psychometric framework, of the major content themes as viewed by the client. Through these measures, the specific problems or characteristics in the client's themes are compared with others in a standardized manner.

The interpretive hypotheses derived from Alice's content scale elevations provide information about her that was not available through the standard scales. As noted in Chapter 3, Alice's approach to the validity scales suggests that her content endorsement is likely to be an accurate reflection of her view of her problems. Figure 6-3 presents her Content Scale profile.

In Alice's case, we are able to learn more about the focus of her anxiety by evaluating the elevations on the three MMPI-2 content scales that assess anxiety (ANX), fears (FRS), and obsessiveness (OBS). Her anxiety appears to be quite generalized, as shown by the high score she obtained on ANX, rather than emphasizing specific fears or phobias, as shown by her lower score on FRS. She appears to have some obsessive qualities as well, as shown by the score on OBS. The general rather than

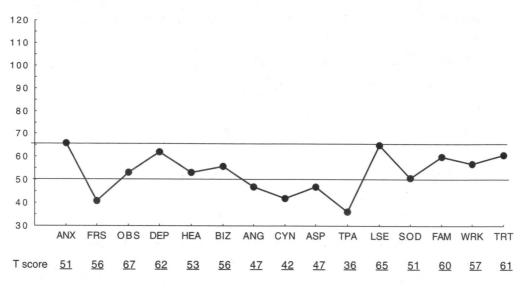

T score	51	56	67	62	53	56	47	42	47	36	65	51	60	57	61
	ANX	FRS	OBS	DEP	HEA	BIZ	ANG	CYN	ASP	TPA	LSE	SOD	FAM	WRK	TRT

Figure 6-3. Alice's MMPI-2 content scales profile.

specific forms of her anxiousness can assist us in pretreatment planning, as we will see in Chapter 8.

Her elevation on the LSE scale warrants particular attention. Perhaps basic to her tendency to become anxious are her low self-confidence and feelings of ineffectiveness. She appears to be very uncertain about her ability to function. Her high score on LSE indicates an extremely negative self-appraisal. Her negative self-views might create a vulnerability to self-defeating behavior, which could, of course, trigger further experience of anxiety.

Chapter 7

Interpreting the MMPI-2 Supplementary Measures

The standard scales, with their focus on psychopathology, do not address all personality characteristics or problems of interest to practitioners and researchers. A number of additional scales, often referred to as supplementary or special scales, can be used to augment the standard MMPI-2 measures. Their application is usually more narrow and more limited in scope than the standard scales or the MMPI-2 content scales.

We find the most clinically useful supplementary scales available on the MMPI-2 to be the MacAndrew Alcoholism Scale (MAC-R), the Addiction Potential Scale (APS), the Addiction Admission Scale (AAS), the Marital Distress Scale (MDS), and the Hostility (Ho) scale. Our discussion of each of these is followed by illustrative cases. Several other special scales, including Dominance (Do), Responsibility (Re), Posttraumatic Disorder (PK), Anxiety (A), and Repression (R), are discussed. We also include a discussion of the PSY-5 scales, newly developed experimental scales based on the five-factor model. The PSY-5 scales were derived by factor analysis of the MMPI-2 item content. Several indexes or combinations of scales are briefly described, for example, the Megargee Classification System for Criminals and the Chronic Pain Classification System (PAIN). Finally, the use of MMPI-2 critical items to provide clues to a patient's symptoms and behavior is described. Similar information is presented in Chapter 13 for the MMPI-A.

MacAndrew Alcoholism Scale

The MacAndrew Alcoholism Scale (MAC) was originally developed to assess alcohol abuse problems in clinical settings (MacAndrew, 1965). It was constructed by selecting items that statistically differentiated individuals with alcohol abuse problems from individuals experiencing psychiatric problems that were not alcohol related. The MAC scale originally contained 51 items, but MacAndrew recommended using a 49-item version that eliminated two items with obvious alcohol abuse content: "I have used alcohol excessively" and "I have used alcohol moderately or not at all." MacAndrew surmised that many alcoholics would not admit to abusing alcohol, and he viewed these two items as nonproductive in many assessments because alcoholics would recognize their content and distort their responses to them.

MacAndrew originally recommended employing a raw-score cutoff of 24 for men and 22 for women as suggestive of alcohol abuse potential. However, practitioners typically find a raw-score cutoff of 26 for men and 24 for women (about one standard deviation above the mean) more effective. Empirical research with the MAC scale has generally been supportive of its use in the assessment of addiction problems (Graham & Strenger, 1988). As noted, the scale is likely to be less effective when the lower cutoff scores (i.e., 24 for men and 22 for women) are used (Gottesman & Prescott, 1989). In contemporary use a T score of 60 is considered suggestive of substance-abuse problems.

Research suggests that a high MacAndrew score is associated with addiction problems such as drug abuse and pathological gambling (Graham & Strenger, 1988) but is not useful for differentiating between alcohol abuse and abuse of other drugs. The MAC scale is best thought of as a measure of addiction proneness rather than as an alcohol use or abuse scale.

In the revision of the MMPI, several MAC items containing objectionable content, particularly of a religious nature, were deleted from the booklet. Because many practitioners use raw scores rather than T scores, these deleted items were replaced with four items from the new MMPI-2 item pool on the MAC-R. The criteria for selecting replacement items on MAC-R were essentially the same as those used by MacAndrew (1965) in his original scale development. That is, items were selected that significantly separated alcoholics from non–alcohol-abusing psychiatric patients (McKenna & Butcher, 1987).

The MAC-R appears to perform in the MMPI-2 much as it did in the original instrument. Babcock (1995) and Legan and Craig (1996) reported that the MAC-R was equivalent to the original MAC scale in its power to differentiate alcoholics in a Veterans Administration population. Several studies of the MAC-R for detecting possible substance abuse problems have been reported. Levenson et al. (1990) studied alcohol abuse and other problem behaviors in a large normal population (1,117 men in the Normative Aging Study) and found support for MacAndrew's interpretation of the meaning of the MAC scale. They found that heavy drinkers and problem drinkers had higher MAC-R scores than did lighter drinkers or non–problem drinkers. Moreover, men who had higher arrest records (possibly related to substance use or abuse) had MAC-R scores nearly identical to those of men who were problem drinkers. In another study, Graham (1989) reported that MAC-R scores were significantly associated with the following problems as rated by spouses in the MMPI-2 restandardization study:

> For men: According to their wives, the high MAC-R husband has been arrested or in trouble with the law, swears and curses, drinks alcohol to excess (gets sick and passes out), has temper tantrums, takes drugs other than those prescribed by a doctor, does not show sound judgment, drives fast and recklessly, takes too many risks, laughs and jokes with people, and tells lies for no apparent reason.

> For women: Wives with high MAC-R scores were rated by their husbands as drinking alcohol excessively (gets sick and passes out), taking too many risks, extroverted, giving advice too freely, having been arrested or in trouble with the law, and not seeming to care about other people's feelings.

Two recent studies have found the MAC-R scale to be an effective screening device in detecting potential substance-abuse problems in outpatient samples. Rouse, Butcher, and Miller (1999) compared 68 substance-abusing therapy patients with 392 psychotherapy patients without alcohol or drug abuse problems. The

Table 7-1. MAC-R Interpretive Guidelines for the MMPI-2

☐ T scores on MAC-R are linear, not uniform, because the scale is usually interpreted alone, not as part of a configuration with other scales.
☐ T scores ≥ 65 on MAC-R strongly suggest the presence of lifestyle characteristics associated with developing an addictive disorder.
☐ T scores of 60 to 64, inclusive, on MAC-R suggest that characteristics of the individual's lifestyle could lead to an alcohol or drug abuse problem.
☐ Current use or abuse of addictive substances is not assessed by MAC-R; rather, the potential for developing an alcohol or drug abuse problem is suggested by elevations on MAC-R.
☐ Use or abuse of particular substances, such as alcohol or drugs, cannot be determined by scores on the MAC-R scale.
☐ Low MAC-R T scores (≤ 59) in a known alcohol or drug abuser can be valuable information for treatment planning. This suggests the possibility that the substance abuse is based more on psychological maladjustment than the typical behavior pattern.

MAC-R significantly discriminated these groups, showing both sensitivity and specificity in differentiating the two groups of treatment cases. Stein, Graham, Ben-Porath, and McNulty (1999) found that the MAC-R scale significantly differentiated outpatient clients who had been identified as having substance abuse problems in an outpatient sample.

These behavioral correlates suggest that the MAC-R scale, for both men and women, assesses behaviors that are relevant to determining alcohol or drug abuse problems. Interpretive guidelines for elevations on MAC-R are included in Table 7-1. Because the scale is widely used in clinical assessment and research, we have included an illustrative case (Figure 7-1).

Case Example of Use of MAC-R

Background Information

For the past two years, Mr. Gabriel has been employed as a security guard in a nuclear power facility, where he has had free access to the nuclear control room. Previously, for about 10 years, he had been employed by the same corporation in a fossil fuel plant and had been a loyal, effective employee. Since transferring to the corporation's nuclear division, he has had some difficulty with his immediate supervisor and has complained to fellow workers about his supervisor's "lack of knowledge." About 3 months before the referral, Mr. Gabriel began writing letters to the corporate vice president in charge of personnel. He wrote three different letters about 2 weeks apart. They were extremely difficult to read; contained unusual, obscure references; and appeared to become increasingly hostile and aggressive. Fearing that Mr. Gabriel was deteriorating and potentially dangerous to the plant's operation, the vice president recommended a psychological evaluation to determine his fitness for duty.

When Mr. Gabriel came to the psychological evaluation, he was very friendly, extroverted, articulate, and outgoing. He cooperated with the evaluation in a

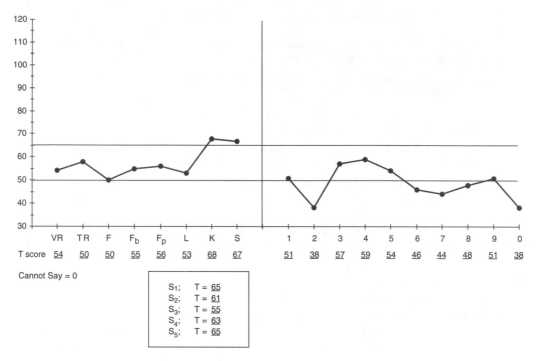

Figure 7-1. Mr. Gabriel's MMPI-2 basic scales profile.

generally nondefensive manner. He voiced some pleasure over the attention that his complaints had received. During the 3-hour interview, he showed no bitterness or anger toward the company, although he acknowledged having some problems with his supervisor. In the 2 weeks before the evaluation, he was especially pleased that the supervisor was drawing a great deal of negative attention from his own superior for some problems he had created a few days before. During the evaluation, Mr. Gabriel showed no signs of depression, anxiety, antisocial features, or psychotic thinking.

Interpretation of the MMPI-2 Basic and Content Scales Profiles

Mr. Gabriel's performance on the validity scales of the MMPI-2 indicated that his approach to the items was generally open and valid. Scores on the MMPI-2 L, F, and K scales were within the normal range, suggesting that he cooperated sufficiently with the evaluation to produce an interpretable profile. The range of elevations on the standard scales and the content scales (not shown) indicates that Mr. Gabriel is not reporting any symptoms of psychological distress, such as depression, anxiety, or thought disorder. The generally low scores suggest that he has no extreme symptoms of psychological disturbance at this time.

Interpretation of MAC-R

Mr. Gabriel's score of 26 on MAC-R is much more revealing of problems than is his basic scale profile. It suggests the possibility that alcohol or other drug abuse might be related to his difficulties at work. His elevation on MAC-R can be used as a beginning point for further assessment in this area.

Follow-Up Interview and Referral

Mr. Gabriel was seen in a follow-up session in which behavior leading to the referral, his MMPI-2 profiles, and his possible substance abuse were discussed. He was generally open and cooperative in the interview although somewhat concerned about having been referred. He explained that he had written the letters to the vice president because he had considered the vice president to be open, considerate, and interested in the company's problems. Mr. Gabriel recalled meeting the vice president at an employee orientation during which the vice president, in a somewhat casual manner, had seemingly promoted the idea of letter writing by inviting any employee to "let him know if problems occur."

Although Mr. Gabriel's motivation for the letters was explained, their unusual content and somewhat disconnected quality needed further exploration. Mr. Gabriel confessed that the letters were written during drinking episodes that usually followed an altercation with his supervisor. He acknowledged, after considerable probing (which included discussion of MAC-R and his score), that he was drinking too much and at times things "got out of hand." The remainder of the session was devoted to exploring an alcohol treatment program to help him deal with his alcohol-control problems.

Addiction Potential Scale

The Addiction Potential Scale (APS) was designed as a measure of the personality factors underlying the development of addictive disorders (Weed, Butcher & Ben-Porath, 1995; Weed, Butcher, Ben-Porath & McKenna, 1992). The scale was empirically derived by selecting items that differentiated alcoholics and drug abusers from psychiatric patients and normals. Scale development procedures followed those used by MacAndrew (1965) in developing the MAC scale, except that the MMPI-2 item pool, which incorporated additional relevant item content, was used. The APS contains 39 items, 9 of which overlap with MAC.

Weed et al. (1992) and Greene, Weed, Butcher, Arredondo, and Davis (1992) found that APS outperformed the MAC-R scale and another MMPI addiction scale, the Substance Abuse Proneness Scale (MacAndrew, 1986) in discriminating groups of substance abusers from psychiatric patients and normals. Table 7-2 presents interpretive guidelines for the APS. Rouse et al. (1999) found that APS significantly discriminated substance-abusing psychotherapy clients from those who did not abuse drugs or alcohol.

Addiction Acknowledgment Scale

The Addiction Acknowledgment Scale (AAS) was developed as a measure of willingness to acknowledge problems with alcohol or drugs (Weed et al., 1992). The scale provides a psychometric comparison of acknowledged alcohol or drug

Table 7-2. APS Interpretive Guidelines for the MMPI-2

☐ Individuals with T scores ≥ 65 on APS possess a great many of the lifestyle characteristics associated with developing an addictive disorder.

☐ T scores of 60 to 64, inclusive, on APS suggest that the individual endorses many lifestyle characteristics found among individuals with an alcohol or drug abuse problem.

☐ Current use or abuse of addictive substances is not assessed by APS; rather, the potential for developing an alcohol or drug abuse problem is suggested by high scores on APS.

☐ Use or abuse of particular substances, such as alcohol or drugs, cannot be determined by scores on APS.

☐ Low APS T scores (≤ 59) in a known alcohol or drug abuser can be valuable information for treatment planning. This situation reflects the possibility that the substance abuse disorder is based more on psychological maladjustment than the typical addictive behavior pattern.

Table 7-3. AAS Interpretive Guidelines for the MMPI-2

☐ T scores ≥ 65 on AAS indicate that the individual has acknowledged many serious alcohol or drug abuse problems.

☐ T scores of 60 to 64, inclusive, on AAS suggest that the individual has acknowledged several alcohol or drug abuse problems.

☐ Elevations on AAS suggest that the individual is aware of and willing to share personal information about his or her past substance abuse problems.

☐ Low scores on AAS (T scores ≤ 59) do not indicate the absence of alcohol or drug problems. Low scores signify only that the person did not acknowledge these problems.

---

problems. This 13-item scale was developed using a combined rational-statistical scale construction strategy. Initially, items that clearly addressed substance abuse problems were selected from the MMPI-2 item pool. This provisional scale was then correlated with the other MMPI-2 items to determine whether any other items in the pool were significantly associated with it. Then the scale was purified by examining the alpha coefficients, keeping items that improved scale homogeneity. The AAS assesses the extent to which the individual has acknowledged having problems in using or abusing drugs or alcohol.

The AAS has been cross-validated in several recent studies. Weed et al. (1992) and Greene et al. (1992) reported that the AAS significantly discriminated individuals in alcohol or drug treatment from normals and psychiatric patients better than either the MAC scale or the Substance Abuse Proneness Scale. Interpretive guidelines for AAS are provided in Table 7-3. Rouse et al. (1999) found the AAS to be the most powerful discriminator (over MAC-R and APS) of substance-abusing clients in an outpatient psychotherapy study. Stein et al. (1999) found that the AAS added significant incremental validity over the MAC-R in assessing substance-abusing clients in an outpatient sample.

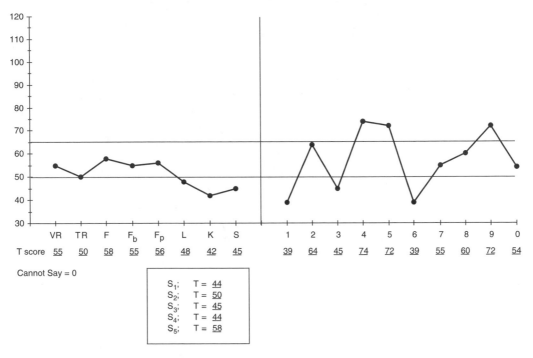

Figure 7-2. Mr. Jenkins's MMPI-2 basic scales profile.

Case Example of Use of the APS and AAS Scales

The case presented in Figures 7-2 and 7-3 illustrates the joint use of APS and AAS in evaluating drug or alcohol problems. Mr. Jenkins, a 42-year-old salesman, had been experiencing substantial life problems in recent years. Along with his marital problems, financial difficulties, and work problems, he was arrested recently for driving under the influence of alcohol (a charge that was reduced to careless and reckless operation of a motor vehicle). Following an incident in which a bottle of bourbon was found in his office, his employer referred him for a substance abuse evaluation as a condition of further employment. Initially quite incensed about being asked to undergo psychological evaluation, he finally agreed, although he denied having a problem with alcohol. Mr. Jenkins's MMPI-2 basic profile is given in Figure 7-2, and his supplementary scale profile is given in Figure 7-3. His relative performance on the APS and the AAS is informative. He obtained a very high score (T = 74) on the APS, suggesting that he possesses many of the lifestyle characteristics associated with developing a drug or alcohol problem. However, his relatively low score on the AAS (T = 32) indicates that he has not been willing to directly endorse having a substance abuse problem. His reluctance to admit having alcohol or drug problems suggests that any effort to confront him with his abuse may be met with great resistance. In addition, his seemingly high potential for abuse along with his unwillingness or lack of recognition of problems with

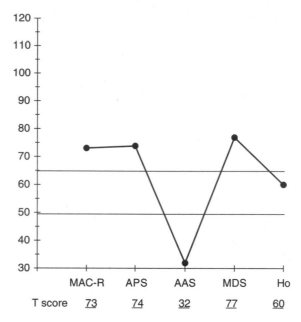

Figure 7-3. Mr. Jenkins's MMPI-2 selected supplementary scales profile.

substance abuse suggests that he may not be willing to cooperate in a treatment program if one is proposed. This case is discussed further with a computerized MMPI-2 report in Chapter 15.

Marital Distress Scale

Many marital therapists have sought to understand marital maladjustment by examining the personality profiles of husbands and wives. Early studies of MMPI profiles of couples in marital distress focused on clinical scale and profile differences between distressed and "normal" couples (Arnold, 1970; Barrett, 1973; Snyder & Regts, 1990). The Pd scale typically has been found to be associated with marital disturbance. More recently, Hjemboe and Butcher (1991) also found the MMPI-2 FAM content scale to be significantly related to marital distress. Neither of these scales was developed for or specifically related to marital distress. They tend to be associated with family problems in general.

Hjemboe, Almagor, and Butcher (1992) developed a specific scale for assessing marital distress, a 14-item empirically derived scale called the Marital Distress Scale (MDS). The MDS was developed by selecting items that were strongly associated with a measure of marital distress, the Spanier Dyadic Adjustment Scale. The scale contains items with content related to marital problems or relationship difficulties. The MDS shows a higher degree of association with measured marital distress than does either the Pd or the FAM scale (Hjemboe et al., 1992). The MDS interpretive guidelines are presented in Table 7-4.

Table 7-4. MDS Interpretive Guidelines for the MMPI-2

☐ The MDS is interpreted only for clients who are married, separated, or (if relevant) divorced.
☐ Some indication of marital relationship problems is noted for MDS T scores of 60 to 64, inclusive.
☐ Strong indication of marital distress is found with clients who obtain T scores ≥ 65 on MDS.

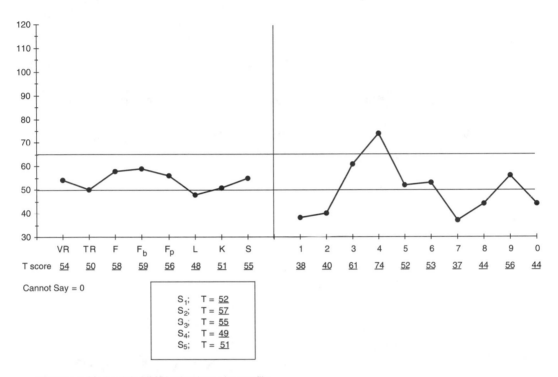

Figure 7-4. Mr. Levin's MMPI-2 basic scales profile.

Case Example of Use of MDS Scale

Figures 7-4 to 7-7 present the MMPI-2 profiles from a couple with elevated scores on the MDS (Mr. Levin had a T score of 71, Ms. Levin a T score of 73) illustrating the potential usefulness of the MDS in detecting marital relationship problems. Both Mr. and Ms. Levin reported a substantial degree of marital distress on the MMPI-2 MDS. We examine their history and MMPI-2 profiles to highlight the usefulness of the MMPI-2 in the assessment of marital distress. Their marital problems are likely to be a central concern in their psychological evaluation.

Referral Problems

The Levins have known each other for 11 years. Mr. Levin is a 43-year-old Jewish self-employed professional. Ms. Levin is a 39-year-old Catholic who works part time. The Levins have one child, a boy of 9. Ms. Levin has a 19-year-old child from

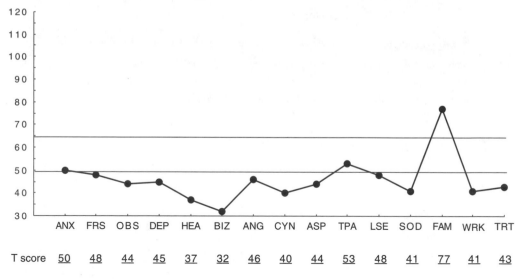

T score	ANX	FRS	OBS	DEP	HEA	BIZ	ANG	CYN	ASP	TPA	LSE	SOD	FAM	WRK	TRT
	50	48	44	45	37	32	46	40	44	53	48	41	77	41	43

Figure 7-5. Mr. Levin's MMPI-2 content scales profile.

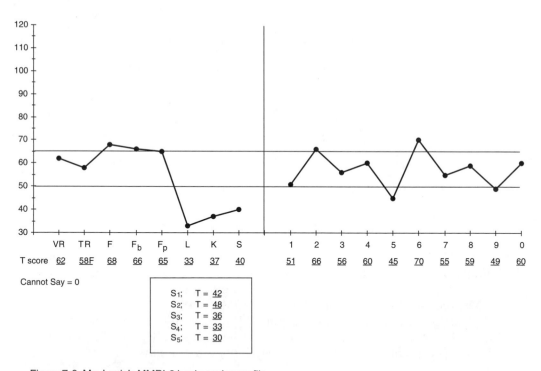

T score	VR	TR	F	F_b	F_p	L	K	S		1	2	3	4	5	6	7	8	9	0
	62	58F	68	66	65	33	37	40		51	66	56	60	45	70	55	59	49	60

Cannot Say = 0

S_1;	T = 42
S_2;	T = 48
S_3;	T = 36
S_4;	T = 33
S_5;	T = 30

Figure 7-6. Ms. Levin's MMPI-2 basic scales profile.

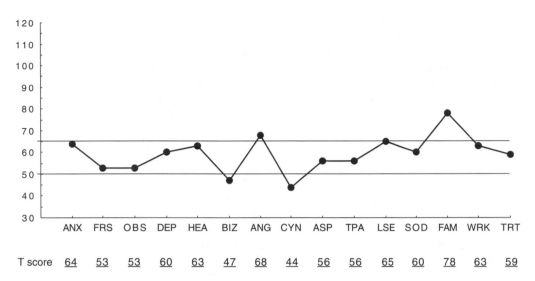

T score	ANX	FRS	OBS	DEP	HEA	BIZ	ANG	CYN	ASP	TPA	LSE	SOD	FAM	WRK	TRT
	64	53	53	60	63	47	68	44	56	56	65	60	78	63	59

Figure 7-7. Ms. Levin's MMPI-2 content scales profile.

a previous marriage who is presently in college. Although the Levins currently live together, Mr. Levin has been threatening to move out, claiming that he can no longer tolerate living with her severe drinking episodes.

Ms. Levin reports serious problems, both personal and marital. She acknowledges that she has a severe drinking problem but feels that she is now getting it under control. She reportedly is quite anxious and depressed over recent financial setbacks, problems with her older son, and the deterioration in her marital relationship. She is having problems sleeping at night and reports problems in concentration. She considers her marital problems to be quite significant, including lack of communication, absence of love, her failure in family roles, and her work responsibilities. She has recently reduced her work to half time in order to solve some of her personal problems.

Mr. Levin also reports significant problems in the marriage but attributes most of them to Ms. Levin. He considers her addiction one of the more serious problems but also believes their verbal abuse of each other and their poor money management contribute substantially to their marital problems. He reports that he sometimes drinks to the point of feeling high but does not consider himself a problem drinker. He has one brother, who has been treated for emotional problems.

Interpretation of Ms. Levin's MMPI-2

Ms. Levin's performance on the MMPI-2 suggests that she approached the test openly and acknowledged a considerable number of psychological problems. Her standard profile reveals a number of psychological maladjustment problems, including a tendency to feel mistreated or picked on, to feel anger and resentment toward others, to harbor grudges, to be overly sensitive to interpersonal relationships, to bear hostility and resentment toward others and to express this in an argumentative manner, and to having difficulty in establishing rapport with others. Ms. Levin tends to use projection as a defense mechanism by attributing negative qualities to other people when she feels stressed. She tends to be rather suspicious and guarded in interpersonal situations and overly self-protective. Ms. Levin appears at this time to be somewhat depressed, tense, and angry and hostile toward other people around her. Her score on the MDS confirms that her marital relationship is a major focus of her problems.

On the MMPI-2 content scales, Ms. Levin reports a considerable number of family problems. She indicates that her family situation is lacking in love and is unpleasant. Quarrelsome relationships and abusive interactions are likely to be characteristic of her marriage at this point. In addition, Ms. Levin's high score on the ANG suggests that she is having a great deal of difficulty with anger control. She reports being quite irritable, grouchy, impatient with others, hotheaded, and annoyed. She indicates that she sometimes swears and curses and feels like smashing things or being abusive toward members of her family. She often loses self-control. Ms. Levin also has considerable problems with self-esteem, as shown by a high score on the LSE. She has a low opinion of herself, does not believe that she is liked by others, and does not feel that she is very important to other people. She holds many negative attitudes about herself, including feelings that she is unattractive, awkward, and useless. She at times feels that she is a burden to others and expresses a great deal of self-pity. She is lacking in self-confidence and at times feels overwhelmed by the faults she sees in herself.

Interpretation of Mr. Levin's MMPI-2

On the validity scales, Mr. Levin performed well within the normal range. His performance indicates that his MMPI-2 profile is valid, interpretable, and probably a good indication of his present personality functioning. The only prominent clinical scale elevation is on scale 4. This high elevation is usually interpreted as reflecting problems incorporating the values and standards of society. Individuals with Pd elevations engage in somewhat antisocial acts, are rebellious toward authority figures, and have other antisocial personality characteristics.

However, on closer evaluation, and especially considering Mr. Levin's performance on the MDS and MMPI-2 content scales, we would want to modify our interpretation of these antisocial attributes of the Pd elevation. The only significant content theme he presents throughout the entire MMPI-2 protocol is that of intense family and marital problems. He reported no other antisocial features or emotional problems. Consequently, our interpretation of his MMPI-2 performance would focus more clearly on stormy relationships within his family, his tendency to blame other family members for his difficulties, his experience of extreme marital problems at this time, his anger and frustration over his family situation, and reports of his immaturity and childishness and poor judgment. We might also consider the possibility that he is not feeling emotionally responsive toward his wife, tends to be resentful and aggressive toward her, and is unable to maintain a warm attachment to her and that his relationships in general tend to be somewhat shallow and superficial. He seems insensitive to the needs and feelings of others at this time and seems interested in others only in terms of how they can be used.

The Levins's MDS scores showed a clear problem with marital distress, which they both reported in interviews. In this case, the MDS was confirmatory and did not provide new information. However, the MDS may serve a discovery role in other cases—for example, where the major complaint is a mental health problem such as depression, not relationship problems. A high MDS score might serve as a screening aid or as a clue to an unexpressed problem for the clinician to follow up in the clinical interview.

Hostility Scale

The Hostility (Ho) scale was developed by Cook and Medley (1954) to identify individuals who could work harmoniously within a group, could establish rapport with others, and could maintain group morale. They developed the scale by comparing samples of schoolteachers that were formed on the basis of their ability to get along with others. Those persons scoring high on the Ho scale appeared to have difficulty with anger and judged other people in a negative light (for example, considered them untrustworthy, lazy, or insincere). People who score high on the Ho scale (T $\geq$ 60) tend be viewed as overtly hostile in interpersonal situations and generally negative in their approach to others.

One interesting set of correlates for the Ho scale that emerged during a longitudinal study of personality factors and health behavior was that the scale was associated with the development of arteriosclerosis (Barefoot, Dahlstrom & Williams, 1983). Men in the study who later developed coronary disease were found (on an earlier testing with the MMPI) to be more aggressive, competitive, and hostile in their interpersonal interactions than those who did not develop the disease. The Ho scale has been widely used in health psychology research as a means for studying the relationship between hostility and health behavior. Specifically, the Ho scale has been shown to assess the personality factors in Type A personalities that appear to be associated with the development of coronary heart disease in some clients (Barefoot, Dodge, Peterson, Dahlstrom & Williams, 1989; Williams, Barefoot & Shekelle, 1985).

The items on the MMPI-2 version of Ho are the same as those on the original MMPI except that nine of the items were edited slightly during the MMPI restandardization to make them more readable. The Ho scale for the MMPI-2 was refined in a recent project by Han, Weed, Calhoun, and Butcher (1995). These investigators conducted a study in which the Ho scale was renormed and validated on data that had been accumulated on the MMPI restandardization project. The Ho scale can be quite valuable to a clinician in appraising personality factors central to a hostile, competitive lifestyle. The guidelines for interpreting Ho are summarized in Table 7-5.

Table 7-5. Ho Interpretive Guidelines for the MMPI-2

☐ Elevated Ho scores are T scores $\geq$ 60. Elevated Ho scores are associated with negative personality characteristics, such as hostility, cynical attitudes toward other people, hypersensitivity in social relations, and avoidance of others.

☐ The Ho scale is valuable as a personality measure of hostile, irritable personality characteristics.

☐ The Ho scale has been associated with the development of aggressive, competitive, and hostile personality factors that lead to the development of coronary disease in some individuals.

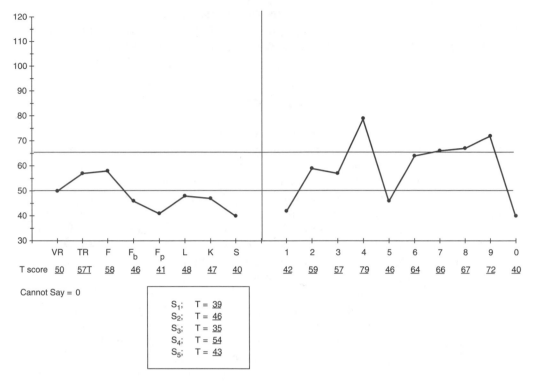

Figure 7-8. Mr. Kevin E.'s MMPI-2 basic scales profile.

Case Example of Use of the Ho Scale

Figures 7-8 and 7-9 present the profiles of a 26-year-old man who was single and had been evaluated in a pre-sentencing assessment following his conviction for a violent crime. Mr. E. had been charged (and convicted) of a felony, and the psychological evaluation was ordered to aid the court in sentencing. The main question being addressed in the assessment centered on whether the defendant could serve his time in a minimum-security prison (a jail without bars) or whether his conduct required a maximum-security incarceration. This was his second violent offense.

Validity Pattern

Mr. E.'s MMPI-2 profiles were valid and interpretable. He was cooperative in describing his personality and problems in the assessment. The MMPI-2 profiles are probably a good indication of his current personality functioning.

Standard Profile and Content Scales

The MMPI-2 clinical scales suggested that he was an extroverted, enthusiastic, and verbal person who was generally uninhibited in his behavior. He tends to seek stimulation and engages in many activities of a hedonistic nature. He is viewed as self-indulgent, manipulative, and aggressive in his actions toward others. He

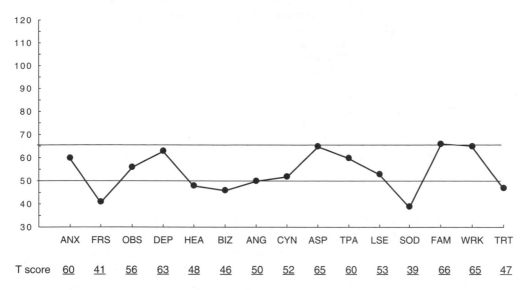

| T score | 60 | 41 | 56 | 63 | 48 | 46 | 50 | 52 | 65 | 60 | 53 | 39 | 66 | 65 | 47 |

Figure 7-9. Mr. Kevin E.'s MMPI-2 content scales profile.

tends to become easily bored and may engage in impulsive behavior at times. His content scale scores suggested that he endorses antisocial content and behavior and admits to rule violations. He appears to have an overinflated view of himself and seems to resent it when others make demands on him. He seems to have had much past conflict with authority and is quite resentful of societal standards of conduct.

Ho Scale

His elevated score on the Ho scale (T > 70) indicates further that he shows a highly competitive and aggressive personality pattern. He appears to interact with others in a negative and aggressive manner and tends to view others in a negative light.

Case Conclusions

Mr. E.'s MMPI-2 performance suggests that he is typically an impulsive and irresponsible individual who tends to manipulate other people to satisfy his own inclinations. He tends to have a low tolerance for frustration and an animosity toward rules. It is likely that he would not be able to function effectively in a minimum-security environment given his proclivity toward aggression and disagreeable relations with others.

Other Scales

Dominance Scale

The Dominance (Do) scale was developed by Gough, McClosky, and Meehl (1951) to assess personality characteristics of social dominance. The authors defined high

Table 7-6. Do Interpretive Guidelines for the MMPI-2

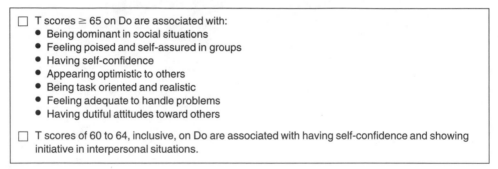

☐ T scores ≥ 65 on Do are associated with:
- Being dominant in social situations
- Feeling poised and self-assured in groups
- Having self-confidence
- Appearing optimistic to others
- Being task oriented and realistic
- Feeling adequate to handle problems
- Having dutiful attitudes toward others

☐ T scores of 60 to 64, inclusive, on Do are associated with having self-confidence and showing initiative in interpersonal situations.

and low dominant individuals by asking their peers to identify the subjects as either passive or dominant in social relationships. The authors then performed an item analysis using the MMPI to separate the two groups. The Do scale measures personality attributes such as comfort in social relationships, self-confidence, possessing strong opinions, persevering at tasks, and having the ability to concentrate. Individuals who score high on the Do scale are generally viewed as dominant in social situations. This scale is widely used in personnel-screening applications, such as police officer selection, to assess whether the individual might have personality characteristics, such as passivity, that could interfere with job performance. The Do interpretive guidelines are provided in Table 7-6.

Social Responsibility Scale

The Social Responsibility (Re) scale was developed by Gough, McClosky, and Meehl (1952) as an assessment of an individual's sense of responsibility toward others. Individuals who were high and low "responsible," as identified by peer nominations or teacher ratings, served as criterion groups. Originally, 32 MMPI items that separated individuals into the two groups constituted the Re scale. High scores on this scale suggest that an individual is dependable and willing to accept the consequences of his or her behavior. High scorers (T score > 60) are thought to have a strong sense of justice and high standards; to be self-confident, trustworthy, and dependable; and to possess a sense of social obligation. Low scorers (T score > 40) are thought to be unwilling to assume responsibility and may not have accepted societal values or conduct. This scale has been widely used as an index of positive personality characteristics in personnel screening. The Re scale contains 30 items on the MMPI-2; two items were deleted in the revision. The Re interpretive guidelines are provided in Table 7-7.

Posttraumatic Stress Disorder Scale

The Posttraumatic Stress Disorder (PK) scale was developed by Keane, Malloy, and Fairbank (1984) to assess the presence of posttraumatic stress disorder (PTSD) symptoms in military veterans. The authors employed a group of 100 veterans who had been diagnosed as having PTSD and contrasted their MMPI responses with

Table 7-7. Re Interpretive Guidelines for the MMPI-2

☐ T scores ≥ 65 on Re are associated with:
- Rigidly accepting and maintaining values
- Having a strong sense of justice and propriety
- Setting high standards to follow
- Being responsible toward others
- Having self-confidence

☐ T scores of 60 to 64, inclusive, on Re suggest that the individual may be willing to accept the consequences of his or her behavior.

Table 7-8. PK Interpretive Guidelines for the MMPI-2

☐ T scores ≥ 65 on PK are associated with:
- Feelings of intense emotional distress
- Experiencing anxiety and sleep disturbances
- Feeling guilty
- Depression
- Having disturbed, intrusive thoughts
- Experiencing loss of control over thinking
- Believing that they are misunderstood or mistreated

☐ High scores on PK do not indicate the experience of recent trauma. Trauma must be established by other assessment procedures before a diagnosis of posttraumatic stress disorder is indicated.

those of 100 veterans having other psychiatric problems. The PK scale contains 49 items with a broad range of somatic and psychological symptoms. The scale was found to have an 82% rate in classifying the disorder among veterans.

The PK scale was developed on the original MMPI and has been continued for the MMPI-2 (Keane, Weathers & Kaloupek, 1992). Research by Litz et al. (1991) has shown the scale to operate in the same manner in the MMPI-2 as it did in the original MMPI because most of the items on the scale are also found in MMPI-2. The PK scale appears to be highly related to other MMPI indices of anxiety, such as the Pt and A scales.

Combat veterans and others who have experienced a catastrophic event who score high on this scale are likely to have PTSD symptoms, including anxiety, depression, emotional turmoil, sleep disturbance, intrusive thoughts, and feelings of being misunderstood or mistreated (Kubany, Gino, Denny & Torigoe, 1994; Munley, Bains, Bloem & Busby 1995; Scotti, Sturges, Veltum & Lyons, 1996). Table 7-8 summarizes the interpretive guidelines for the PK scale.

Ego Strength Scale

The Ego Strength (Es) scale was developed as a potential measure of the ability to benefit from a psychotherapeutic experience (Barron, 1953). The scale was developed by contrasting groups of successful and unsuccessful patients in psychotherapy. Much of the research on Es suggests that it actually measures "ability to

Table 7-9. Es Interpretive Guidelines for the MMPI-2

☐ T scores ≥ 65 on the Es scale suggest:
- Ability to withstand stress
- Absence of chronic psychological problems
- Being emotionally stable
- Having tolerance and lack of prejudice
- Possessing self-confidence
- Having intelligence and resourcefulness
- Being accepted by others
- Having well-developed interests
- Being determined and persistent
- Responding well to verbal psychotherapy
- Tolerance of confrontation in therapy

withstand stress" more than potential for therapeutic success. The scale originally contained 68 items; however, 12 were deleted during the MMPI revision. The extent to which the MMPI-2 version of the Es scale assesses the characteristics measured by the original scale has not been determined. Consequently, the use of the scale in the MMPI-2 should be considered experimental until empirical research has further documented its predictive power. Table 7-9 summarizes the Es interpretive guidelines.

Anxiety Scale

The Anxiety (A) scale was developed as a measure of the first, and largest, factor dimension in the original MMPI (Welsh, 1956), which also defines the first factor of the MMPI-2 (Butcher, Dahlstrom, Graham, Tellegen & Kaemmer, 1989). All but one of the 39 items on the scale are endorsed True. The scale contains items that assess general maladjustment or emotional upset, for example, "I wish I could be as happy as others seem to be" and "Criticism or scolding hurts me terribly." The A scale and the second factor, R, are not widely used as clinical assessment measures, but they are valuable in research as marker variables of the first two MMPI factors. The information provided by the A scale is available through other MMPI-2 measures, especially the Pt scale, which is highly correlated with A (.75).

Researchers and practitioners can evaluate proposed new measures by determining their relationship to the A factor. Many scales that have been developed for the MMPI in the past have turned out to be simply redundant measures or markers of the Anxiety factor (i.e., they correlated highly enough with the A scale to be considered an alternative measure of the first MMPI factor). For example, Stein (1968) proposed that several cluster scales (the Tryon, Stein, and Chu, or TSC, scales) represented the MMPI item domain. However, all seven of the TSC scales were found to be highly correlated with the A and Pt scales. Thus, they actually provided little additional information beyond their association with anxiousness. Individuals who score high on the A scale are endorsing symptoms of anxiety, tension, inability to function, and lack of efficiency in managing everyday affairs and admitting numerous psychological symptoms. These features are summarized in Table 7-10.

Table 7-10. A Interpretive Guidelines for the MMPI-2

☐ The A scale is a marker of the first factor dimension (Anxiety) of the MMPI-2. The scale is highly correlated with scales 7 and 8.

☐ T scores ≥ 65 are elevated and are associated with individuals who are:
- Anxious
- Disorganized and maladaptive under stress
- Lacking in self-confidence
- Pessimistic
- Shy and retiring
- Insecure
- Slow in personal tempo

Table 7-11. R Interpretive Guidelines for the MMPI-2

☐ The R scale is a marker of the second major factor of the MMPI-2, often referred to as Repression or overcontrol. This scale is correlated with scales 2, L, and K.

☐ T scores ≥ 65 on R are elevated and associated with individuals who are viewed as:
- Overcontrolled
- Having a tendency to deny and rationalize
- Submissive
- Conventional and formal
- Exhibiting caution in their approach to life

Repression Scale

Like the A scale, the Repression (R) scale was derived through factor analysis and marks the second major factor in the MMPI item pool: overcontrol or denial of conflict. The R scale is composed of 37 items that assess the tendency to deny problems, such as "I believe my sins are unpardonable—False." However, the scale also measures the general tendency of some subjects to respond False to everything, even to somewhat neutral items, such as "I think I would like the work of a forest ranger" or "I like science." The scale content addresses overcontrol and defensive reliance on denial and repression (Welsh, 1956).

Individuals who score high on R appear to be uninsightful, overcontrolled, and socially inhibited. High scorers are considered emotionally constricted, bland, and nonspontaneous. They tend to deal with conflict by avoidance rather than direct action. Others view them as overly conservative in actions and behavior. People who score high on the R scale generally report few psychological problems, tending rather to view themselves as problem free compared to other people. They tend to see themselves as conventional and reserved in relationships. These features are summarized in Table 7-11.

The Personality Psychopathology 5 (PSY-5) Scales

In recent years, personality researchers have been intrigued with the idea that personality can be understood by a limited number of characteristics or traits, in fact,

Table 7-12. The Item-Scale Membership and Scoring Direction of the PSY-5 Scales

Scale	Item
Aggressiveness	27 50 (70) 85 134 239 323 324 346 350 358 414, 423 (446) 452 (503) 521 548
Psychoticism	24 42 48 72 96 99 138 144 (184) 198 241 259 315 319 336 355 361 374 (427) 448 466 490 508 549 551
Disconstraint	(34) 35 84 88 (100) 103 105 (121) 123 (126) (154) 209, 222 250 (263) (266) 284 (309) 344 (351) 362 385 (402) 412 417 418 431 477 (497)
Negative Emotionality	37 52 (63) 82 93 116 166 196 213 (223) 290 301 305 329 (372) 375 389 390 395 397 (405) 407 409 415 435 442 444 451 (496) 513 542 556 (564)
Introversion	(9) 38 (49) 56 (61) (75) (78) (86) (95) (109) (131) (174) (188) (189) (207) (226) (231) 233 (244) (267) (318) (330) (340) (342) (343) (353) (356) (359) (370) (460) 515 517 (531) (534)

Note: Provided by McNulty (personal communication, 1999) and reprinted with permission. Items in parentheses are scored if False; all others are scored if True.

only five. This view has been referred to as the *Five Factor Model* or the "Big Five" (Goldberg, 1990). The proponents of this view culled dictionaries to obtain a universe of item content (adjectives) by which people can be described (Costa & McCrae, 1988; Norman, 1963) that was reduced (through factor analysis) to five dimensions that are thought to sufficiently describe personality: surgency or extraversion, agreeableness, conscientiousness, emotional stability versus neuroticism, and openness to experience. The items developed to mark the five factors were composed of "normal" range personality characteristics rather than psychopathology. Other investigators took issue with the adequacy of five-factor tests such as the NEO to describe personality (Loevinger, 1994) and psychopathy (Waller & Ben-Porath, 1992).

Harkness and McNulty (1994) developed a model that had content validity for assessing psychopathology. They obtained their descriptive statements through examination of *DSM-III* rather than through common adjectives. Next they used the MMPI-2 item pool to select items that matched the five-factor psychopathological content model (Harkness, McNulty & Ben-Porath, 1995) and found a sufficient number of items to serve as test stimuli for the PSY-5 model. The dimensions were described by Harkness and colleagues (1995). Subsequently, the names of two of the scales were modified ("Constraint" to "Disconstraint" and "Positive Emotionality/Extroversion" to "Introversion") so that scale elevations reflect the expression of problems, as do the other MMPI-2 scales (McNulty, personal communication, 1999). The items remained the same, but the scoring direction was reversed. The item-scale membership of the PSY-5 scales is provided in Table 7.12. The PSY-5 scales are as follows:

1. *Aggressiveness* assesses the potential for offensive and instrumental aggression. The scale also addresses cognitive systems for promoting or inhibiting aggression, such as grandiosity versus egalitarianism. The desire for power and domination over others is also central in the con-

struct. Aggressiveness is thought to have links to "behavioral facilitation" or "behavioral activation" systems or acting-out potential.

2. *Psychoticism* measures reality contact or distorted views of the social and object world. Items on this dimension address unusual sensory and perceptual experiences or impaired reality contact. There are a number of suspiciousness items on this scale. These items reflect unusual beliefs and attitudes.

3. *Disconstraint* is adapted from the "Constraint" construct, introduced by Tellegen (1982) and elaborated by Watson and Clark (1993). It measures elements of risk aversiveness, desire for plans and order rather than impulsive action, and traditional morality. The items address rule-following versus rule-breaking and criminal behavior.

4. *Negative Emotionality/Neuroticism* is a broad affective disposition of unpleasant emotions, particularly anxiety, nervousness, and guilt, leading to internal suffering.

5. *Introversion (Lack of Positive Emotionality)* is a broad affective disposition related to the difficulty of experiencing positive affect, the desire to avoid social experiences, and the lack of energy to pursue goals and be engaged in life's tasks (Harkness et al., 1995; McNulty, personal communication, 1999).

Several studies have been published on the PSY-5 scales since they were introduced. Trull, Useda, Costa, and McCrae (1995) found that the PSY-5 scales showed cross-measure consistency with the NEO-PI scales. Despite these methodological differences, strikingly similar results were found. PSY-5 Positive Emotionality and Negative Emotionality strongly resembled the NEO-PI dimensions of Extraversion and Neuroticism, respectively. The other PSY-5 scales did not show a one-to-one correspondence with NEO-PI dimensions, but they were related to specific NEO-PI facet scales; Aggressiveness appears to combine some aspects of low Agreeableness and high Extraversion, Constraint may be characterized by high Agreeableness and high Conscientiousness, and Psychoticism was positively related to openness. It appears that these two instruments—one representing personality pathology constructs and the other measuring general dimensions of personality—assess overlapping but not identical sets of constructs (Trull et al., 1995, p. 514).

Rouse and colleagues (1999) found that the constraint scores were lower in a sample of substance-abusing psychotherapy clients compared with their nonalcoholic controls. At this point in time, the PSY-5 scales have not been used much in clinical interpretation of the MMPI-2 but are promising new measures warranting further study. To foster research, they are being made available in the MMPI-2 product line as experimental scales.

Useful Indexes for the MMPI-2

A number of indexes that combine MMPI scales have been developed for special interpretive purposes. These indexes are either clinically or actuarially devised measures and serve to give the interpreter a valuable perspective on scale relationships. Among the more useful indexes are the Megargee Classification System for Criminal Offenders and the Chronic Pain Classification System (PAIN).

Megargee Classification System for Criminal Offenders

Megargee and Bohn (1977) identified 10 types of criminal offenders in the Florida State Correctional System by using their MMPI test patterns and related a number of demographic variables and prison behaviors to these profile groupings. The Megargee system has been widely used since it was first published. A number of articles have provided empirical tests of the system (Bohn, 1979; Booth & Howell, 1980; Dahlstrom, Panton, Bain & Dahlstrom, 1986; Edinger, 1979; Edinger, Reuterfors & Logue, 1982; Hanson, Moss, Hosford & Johnson, 1983; Johnson, Simmons & Gordon, 1983; Louscher, Hosford & Moss, 1983; Megargee, 1984; Moss, Johnson & Hosford, 1984; Motiuk, Bonta & Andrews, 1986; Mrad, Kabacoff & Duckro, 1983; Simmons, Johnson, Gouvier & Muzyczka, 1981; Walters, 1986; Zager, 1983). For an informative review, see Kennedy (1986).

The 10 Megargee types appear to replicate across different inmate samples. For example, the same types are found in similar proportions in maximum-security prisons, medium-security facilities, and halfway houses (Dahlstrom et al., 1986; Edinger, 1979; Edinger et al., 1982; Johnson et al., 1983; Mrad et al., 1983; Walters, 1986). No well-defined demographic characteristics are typically associated with the different types.

Although the Megargee classification types can be found across many settings, correlates of the types have not been consistently found to generalize across settings. Several studies reported no history, psychiatric, demographic, prison adjustment, or outcome variables to be differentially associated with any of the types. However, two exceptions may be the CHARLIE and HOW types. The CHARLIE type seems to be the class of inmate that has most consistently been associated with psychological maladjustment and poor adjustment to prison. The HOW type also seems to be fairly consistently related to adjustment problems.

Research to date does not support the stability of the types over time. Some studies have questioned the stability of any of the Megargee types, finding that 60% to 90% change after as little as 4 months (Dahlstrom et al., 1986; Johnson et al., 1983; Simmons et al., 1981). However, whether these changes reflect unreliable typology or actual changes in inmate personality, coping style, behavior, and so on remains an open question (Zager, 1983). One study reported that a sample of death-row inmates who had their sentences commuted shifted away from the pathological types of CHARLIE and HOW into less pathological ITEM, EASY, or GEORGE types (Dahlstrom et al., 1986). This finding might reflect a valid change in mental state after the sentence change. In general, caution should be exercised in making administrative or clinical decisions based on the Megargee typology; however, the system could provide useful hypotheses when supplemented with other information. The Megargee classification system has been revised to accommodate MMPI-2 scale scores. Megargee (1994) reported that the modified classification rules classified 82% of men in his prison sample and 87% of the women (Megargee, 1997).

The Chronic Pain Typology

The MMPI has been the most widely used personality measure for investigating the personality characteristics and symptomatic behaviors of chronic pain patients (Armentrout, Moore, Parker, Hewett & Feltz 1982; Bernstein & Garbin, 1983; Bradley, Prokop, Margolis & Gentry, 1978; Bradley & Van der Heide, 1984; Fordyce, 1987; Hart, 1984; McCreary, 1985; McGill, Lawlis, Selby, Mooney & McCoy, 1983; Prokop, Bradley, Margolis & Gentry, 1980). To systematize the MMPI factors associated with chronic pain, Costello, Hulsey, Schoenfeld, and Ramamurthy (1987) summarized the extensive MMPI chronic pain research literature, demonstrating that four main clusters of MMPI types account for a significant percentage of pain patients. They found that pain patients from a wide variety of treatment settings appeared to fall into the four groups, which they referred to as P, A, I, or N subtypes (i.e., the PAIN typology). Preliminary research has supported the view that these profile types represent distinctly different problem and personality types in terms of symptoms, treatment amenability, and outcome.

Keller and Butcher (1991), using the MMPI-2, found the Costello et al. (1987) PAIN subtypes in a large sample of chronic pain patients. Their study demonstrated that the chronic pain typology can be useful in assessing individuals in pain treatment programs. However, the PAIN classification rules identified only about half of their total sample, suggesting that the guidelines are overly conservative in assigning patients to a cluster type.

Critical Items

The critical item approach involves using individual MMPI items as signs or pathognomic indicators of pathology, specific content themes, or special problems the patient is experiencing. This approach has a long history in personality assessment. The first formal personality inventory, the Personal Data Sheet (Woodworth, 1920), incorporated critical items or pathognomic indicators to highlight special problems the individual might be experiencing.

For the MMPI, early critical item approaches, such as the Grayson (1951) critical items, were developed largely through purely rational means by simply selecting those items believed to reflect particular problems of interest to the clinician. The first effort to develop an empirically valid MMPI critical set was conducted by Koss and colleagues (Koss, 1979; Koss & Butcher, 1973; Koss, Butcher & Hoffmann, 1976). They developed and validated a set of critical items by differentiating patients who were experiencing a crisis requiring hospitalization from other patients not experiencing that particular crisis. The items that empirically differentiated the crisis groups from other patients or crisis groups were shown to have both empirical and content validity (i.e., they directly assessed symptoms, themes, and attitudes related to the actual crisis and reported them accurately through the MMPI booklet). These critical items were shown to have considerable clinical utility when used as clues to special problems. They have been maintained with some revisions in the MMPI-2 booklet. Four items each were added to the alcohol-drug crisis set and to the depressed-suicidal item set through further empirical analysis with MMPI-2 research groups (Butcher et al., 1989).

Another critical item set was published by Lachar and Wrobel (1979) to address several different crisis-problem areas. About two-thirds of the Koss-Butcher items were replicated in the Lachar-Wrobel study. However, several additional item groups were constructed to focus on different areas of concern. Both the Koss-Butcher critical items and items from the Lachar-Wrobel set that are not redundant with the Koss-Butcher are listed in Table 7-13.

How Are Critical Items Used in Clinical Assessment?

Critical items are used clinically or impressionistically to suggest possible interpretive hypotheses about the individual's current problems, beliefs, or attitudes. For example, the clinician assessing an individual who is depressed might examine the client's responses to the following items to determine what the individual reported their thoughts about suicide to be:

506.   I have recently considered killing myself. (T)

520.   Lately I have thought a lot about killing myself. (T)

524.   No one knows it but I have tried to kill myself. (T)

Critical items should not be used as psychometric indicators or scales because single-item responses tend to be much less reliable as psychometric predictors than are groups of items or scales. The critical item has its greatest value as a suggested hypothesis to follow up in clinical interview or in further scrutiny of the assessment data.

Cautions about Other Supplementary Measures

Over the first 50 years of the MMPI's development, many scales were published for particular applications and special populations. In fact, there were actually more scales available for the MMPI than there were items on the inventory. Scales proliferated, in part, because empirical scale-construction methodology encouraged the development of new scales, and any number of scales is possible, limited only by the imagination of the researcher. A new empirical scale could be developed by simply compiling cases fitting an interesting group and then performing an item analysis between that group and another group, such as normal subjects. Consequently, "blind empiricism," as this approach is usually called, promoted the development of hundreds of scales, many based on samples of convenience that had little underlying conceptual rationale. Many, if not the majority, of these scales were not sufficiently cross-validated (or even initially validated) before being used.

Some experimental MMPI scales, developed to study particular problems and

Table 7-13. MMPI-2 Critical Item Sets

Koss-Butcher Critical Items, Revised

Acute Anxiety State

2. I have a good appetite. (F)
3. I wake up fresh and rested most mornings. (F)
5. I am easily awakened by noise. (T)
10. I am about as able to work as I ever was. (F)
15. I work under a great deal of tension. (T)
28. I am bothered by an upset stomach several times a week. (T)
39. My sleep is fitful and disturbed. (T)
59. I am troubled by discomfort in the pit of my stomach every few days or oftener. (T)
140. Most nights I go to sleep without thoughts or ideas bothering me. (F)
172. I frequently notice my hand shakes when I try to do something. (T)
208. I hardly ever notice my heart pounding and I am seldom short of breath. (F)
218. I have periods of such great restlessness that I cannot sit long in a chair. (T)
223. I believe I am no more nervous than most others. (F)
301. I feel anxiety about something or someone almost all the time. (T)
444. I am a high-strung person. (T)
463. Several times a week I feel as if something dreadful is about to happen. (T)
469. I sometimes feel that I am about to go to pieces. (T)

Depressed Suicidal Ideation

9. My daily life is full of things that keep me interested. (F)
38. I have had periods of days, weeks, or months when I couldn't take care of things because I couldn't "get going." (T)
65. Most of the time I feel blue. (T)
71. These days I find it hard not to give up hope of amounting to something. (T)
75. I usually feel that life is worthwhile. (F)
92. I don't seem to care what happens to me. (T)
95. I am happy most of the time. (F)
130. I certainly feel useless at times. (T)
146. I cry easily. (T)
215. I brood a great deal. (T)
233. I have difficulty in starting to do things. (T)
273. Life is a strain for me much of the time. (T)
303. Most of the time I wish I were dead. (T)
306. No one cares much what happens to you. (T)
388. I very seldom have spells of the blues. (F)
411. At times I think I am no good at all. (T)
454. The future seems hopeless to me. (T)
485. I often feel that I'm not as good as other people. (T)
506. I have recently considered killing myself. (T)
518. I have made lots of bad mistakes in my life. (T)
520. Lately I have thought a lot about killing myself. (T)
524. No one knows it but I have tried to kill myself. (T)

Threatened Assault

37. At times I feel like smashing things. (T)
85. At times I have a strong urge to do something harmful or shocking. (T)
134. At times I feel like picking a fist fight with someone. (T)
213. I get mad easily and then get over it soon. (T)
389. I am often said to be hotheaded. (T)

Table 7-13. MMPI-2 Critical Item Sets, continued

Situational Stress Due to Alcoholism

125. I believe that my home life is as pleasant as that of most people I know. (F)
264. I have used alcohol excessively. (T)
487. I have enjoyed using marijuana. (T)
489. I have a drug or alcohol problem. (T)
502. I have some habits that are really harmful. (T)
511. Once a week or more I get high or drunk. (T)
518. I have made lots of bad mistakes in my life. (T)

Mental Confusion

24. Evil spirits possess me at times. (T)
31. I find it hard to keep my mind on a task or a job. (T)
32. I have had very peculiar and strange experiences. (T)
72. My soul sometimes leaves my body. (T)
96. I see things or animals or people around me that others do not see. (T)
180. There is something wrong with my mind. (T)
198. I often hear voices without knowing where they come from. (T)
299. I cannot keep my mind on one thing. (T)
311. I often feel as if things are not real. (T)
316. I have strange and peculiar thoughts. (T)
325. I have more trouble concentrating than others seem to have. (T)

Persecutory Ideas

17. I am sure I get a raw deal from life. (T)
42. If people had not had it in for me, I would have been much more successful. (T)
99. Someone has it in for me. (T)
124. I often wonder what hidden reason another person may have for doing something nice for me. (T)
138. I believe I am being plotted against. (T)
144. I believe I am being followed. (T)
145. I feel that I have often been punished without cause. (T)
162. Someone has been trying to poison me. (T)
216. Someone has been trying to rob me. (T)
228. There are persons who are trying to steal my thoughts and ideas. (T)
241. It is safer to trust to nobody. (T)
251. I have often felt that strangers were looking at me critically. (T)
259. I am sure I am being talked about. (T)
314. I have no enemies who really wish to harm me. (F)
333. People say insulting and vulgar things about me. (T)
361. Someone has been trying to influence my mind. (T)

Lachar-Wrobel Critical Items

Characterological Adjustment (Antisocial Attitude)

27. When people do me a wrong I feel I should pay them back if I can, just for the principle of the thing. (T)
35. Sometimes when I was young I stole things. (T)
84. I was suspended from school one or more times for bad behavior. (T)

Table 7-13. MMPI-2 Critical Item Sets, continued

105. In school I was sometimes sent to the principal for bad behavior. (T)
227. I don't blame people for trying to grab everything they can get in this world. (T)
240. At times it has been impossible for me to keep from stealing or shoplifting something. (T)
254. Most people make friends because friends are likely to be useful to them. (T)
266. I have never been in trouble with the law. (F)
324. I can easily make other people afraid of me, and sometimes do for the fun of it. (T)

Characterological Adjustment (Family Conflict)

21. At times I have very much wanted to leave home. (T)
83. I have very few quarrels with members of my family. (F)
125. I believe that my home life is as pleasant as that of most people I know. (F)
288. My parents and family find more fault with me than they should. (T)

Somatic Symptoms

18. I am troubled by attacks of nausea and vomiting. (T)
28. I am bothered by an upset stomach several times a week. (T)
33. I seldom worry about my health. (F)
40. Much of the time my head seems to hurt all over. (T)
44. Once a week or oftener I feel suddenly hot all over, for no real reason. (T)
47. I am almost never bothered by pains over the heart or in my chest. (F)
53. Parts of my body often have feelings like burning, tingling, crawling, or like "going to sleep." (T)
57. I hardly ever feel pain in the back of my neck. (F)
59. I am troubled by discomfort in the pit of my stomach every few days or oftener. (T)
101. Often I feel as if there is a tight band around my head. (T)
111. I have a great deal of stomach trouble. (T)
142. I have never had a fit or convulsion. (F)
159. I have never had a fainting spell. (F)
164. I seldom or never have dizzy spells. (F)
175. I feel weak all over much of the time. (T)
176. I have very few headaches. (F)
182. I have had attacks in which I could not control my movements or speech but in which I knew what was going on around me. (T)
224. I have few or no pains. (F)
229. I have had blank spells in which my activities were interrupted and I did not know what was going on around me. (T)
247. I have numbness in one or more places on my skin. (T)
255. I do not often notice my ears ringing or buzzing. (F)
295. I have never been paralyzed or had any unusual weakness of any of my muscles. (F)
464. I feel tired a good deal of the time. (T)

Sexual Concern and Deviation

12. My sex life is satisfactory. (F)
34. I have never been in trouble because of my sex behavior. (F)
62. I have often wished I were a girl. (or if you are a girl) I have never been sorry that I am a girl. (T—males, F—females)
121. I have never indulged in any unusual sex practices. (F)
166. I am worried about sex. (T-males, F-females)
268. I wish I were not bothered by thoughts about sex. (T)

meant for somewhat limited application, have been expanded and used for purposes very different from those their originators intended. In all fairness, it should be pointed out that the scale originators often had little to do with the scale after its initial development. For example, when Hal Williams, who developed the Ca scale for his doctoral dissertation (Williams, 1952), was told that many people were using his scale to assess organic damage and were widely disseminating the scores in computerized reports, he exclaimed in embarrassment, "That's ridiculous, that was only my doctoral research. . . . [It was] not intended to be used for any practical purposes!" Another example is the scale called "Success in Baseball" (LaPlace, 1952). The original author was attempting to appraise cooperative teamwork, yet some mistakenly thought it assessed the ability or mind-set to succeed in baseball!

This section is not intended to discourage the development of new empirical scales but to caution users that the development and naming of a scale does not necessarily imply that it satisfactorily assesses the behaviors it purports to measure. Many MMPI scales have been developed that do not consistently perform as proposed, and they are probably quite misleading. We caution users of the MMPI-2 and MMPI-A to be wary consumers before using any new scale to make predictions about an individual.

The "Subtle Keys"

One of the most widespread misconceptions about the MMPI is that several clinical scales contain "subtle" items that allow the clinician to assess individuals without their being consciously aware that they are providing important personal information in the assessment. Wiener (1948) believed that all items on a scale were equally valid as predictors of the characteristics involved. Because some of the items are not obviously related to the criterion characteristics (e.g., "I am happy most of the time" is not obviously related to paranoid thinking on the Pa scale), these items are "subtle" predictors and have special properties. Wiener and Harmon developed subtle and obvious subscales for several scales: D, Hy, Pd, Pa, and Ma (see Wiener, 1948).

There are several points to consider when evaluating the utility of subtle items as predictors of psychopathology and as validity indicators. One likely explanation for the lack of content relevance in the subtle items is that they are imperfectly related to the criterion and were actually selected by chance as a result of incomplete validation procedures. As we saw in Chapter 4, Hathaway and McKinley (1940) used relatively small samples in their original scale development and in some cases no cross-validation procedures. In developing a scale to assess characteristic "x" using 550 items, chance alone would place 27 items on the scale. We assume that cross-validation would have eliminated the chance items, leaving only those items that are valid indicators of the characteristic being assessed. A second major point to consider in evaluating the subtle subscales is that they have not been shown to be valid measures of the types of psychopathology they purportedly measure. Several studies have shown that the subtle scales do not predict behaviors as clearly as the obvious items on the scales do (Grossman, Haywood, Ostrov, Wasyliw & Cavanaugh, 1990; Herkov, Archer & Gordon, 1991; Nelson, 1987; Nelson & Cicchetti, 1991; Osberg & Harrigan, 1999; Timbrook, Graham, Keiller & Watts, 1991). In fact, Weed, Ben-Porath, and Butcher (1990) found that the subtle items actually lower the validities of the full scale score. Greene (1991) suggests that the subtle items give the interpreter a way to evaluate invalid or unusual response attitudes. In his view, the differences in responses to obvious, as opposed to subtle, items on a scale can be used as an indicator of test invalidity. However, empirical support for this view is lacking (Timbrook et al., 1991). The subtle items are not able to correct for intentional deception on the part of the test taker. The MMPI-2, like the original MMPI, is an instrument for people who want to be and are cooperative with the psychological evaluation. The MMPI-2 obvious-subtle keys have been discontinued by the test publisher and are not available either in computer-scoring programs or for hand scoring.

Developing and Evaluating New Scales
for the MMPI-2 and MMPI-A

It is likely that new scales will be developed for the MMPI-2 and MMPI-A, as they were for the original instrument. New scales and improved versions of the original scales are desirable because both the MMPI-2 and the MMPI-A contain some new items that would allow for an expanded assessment and could improve the existing clinical scales. The following guidelines are suggested for appraising the value and suitability of proposed new measures.

A scale should be used because it performs a particular assessment better or more efficiently than other scales or provides valuable information not accessible through another assessment approach. For example, to determine an individual's "social facility," one could observe the subject in several situations and record his or her behavior or, perhaps more efficiently, have someone who knows the person well observe him or her and rate the person's social facility. Another way of obtaining social skills information is to ask the person to rate him- or herself. The MMPI-2 and MMPI-A Si scale does just that, and it does it quite well. The Si scale performs as well as behavioral ratings in predicting sociability (Williams, 1981).

It seems desirable that standards be established for the construction of MMPI-2 and MMPI-A scales to aid both scale developers and scale users in evaluating psychometric characteristics and clinical utility. Following are some suggested guidelines that could serve as a "checklist" for the practitioner and researcher in evaluating potential MMPI-2 and MMPI-A scales:

1. *The construct under study is well defined.* The variable in question should not simply be the result of interesting group differences in convenience samples. The construct should be related to personality or symptomatic variables. The dimension or set of characteristics should be a personality variable and not factors such as abilities, intellectual qualities, and so on, which are better assessed with other instruments.

2. *The item pool is relevant for the construct being assessed.* The MMPI-2 and MMPI-A item pools have limitations. It is not possible, for example, to develop a scale measuring language ability or successful performance

as a business manager. Scale developers should ascertain whether the item content of the MMPI-2 or MMPI-A is relevant to the question studied.

3.   *The research design includes cross-validation.* This is most necessary for empirically derived scales to eliminate items that would be selected on the basis of chance or specific sample characteristics. The sample sizes for both the developmental and the cross-validated samples should be sufficient to provide stable test scores and to reduce error.

4.   *The scale has appropriate statistical properties, including the following:*

   a.   Adequate internal consistency (e.g., an alpha coefficient of .70 or greater), if the scale is desirable as a measure of a single dimension.

   b.   A meaningful factor structure, if the scale is multifaceted and made up of several discrete content groups. The scale's factor structure should be reported.

   c.   If the proposed measure is an empirical scale, it is not required that the scale possess split-half reliability. However, it should possess other relevant psychometric properties, such as test-retest reliability.

5.   *All scales, even those developed by rational or internal consistency methods, should have demonstrable validity.* It is important for any scale to measure what it is supposed to measure regardless of the method of scale construction. That is, all personality measures should predict, describe, or detect the psychological characteristics that they purport to measure.

6.   *Uses are explored and demonstrated.* Does the scale possess sensitivity and specificity in predicting the quality that it is supposed to assess? How well the scale classifies relevant cases should be reported.

7.   *Correlations between the proposed scale and other, well-established MMPI-2 and MMPI-A measures are presented.* This will enable users to compare the new measures with existing ones. For example, the correlations between the proposed scale and the factor dimensions A and R are important to establish the new scale's independence.

Highlight Summary: Alice's Supplementary Measures

As described in Chapters 4 to 6, Alice's high elevations on scales 7 and 8 and the MMPI-2 content scales focus attention on her extreme anxiousness, insecurity, lack of self-confidence, and low cognitive problem-solving skills. The special or supplementary measures that have been developed for the MMPI-2 provide some elaboration for Alice's problems or personality. Several of her supplementary scale scores support the results of the standard scales. Other scales, such as the MDS, are not relevant to her case. Her relatively high score on the A (T = 61) and the PK (T = 61) scales indicate that she has some tendency to become anxious under stressful conditions. However, she does not have a history of a recent catastrophic stressor to support a PTSD diagnostic hypothesis. Her relatively low score on Es (T = 35) supports the interpretation that Alice has little ability to withstand stress and meet challenges in her life situation.

Alice's low score on the Dominance (Do) scale adds further support to the interpretation, based on her standard scale scores, that she is lacking in self-confidence and is not assertive in relationships. Her low Re score also suggests a lack of self-confidence and an unwillingness to assume responsibility.

Alice's low scores on the MAC-R (T = 42) and the APS (T = 50) suggest that she is not likely to develop addiction problems, and her low score on the AAS (40) indicates that she has not reported problems with drugs or alcohol. This suggests that if psychotropic medication is considered, medications abuse is less likely to become a problem. Given Alice's willingness to admit to other problems, addiction proneness is unlikely.

Chapter 8

Integrating MMPI-2 Inferences
into an Interpretive Report

Thus far, we have discussed a number of diverse sources of information available in the MMPI-2. These measures range from indicators of response attitudes to empirically derived symptom scales to content-based descriptions to specially focused problem scales. As we have seen, these measures differ in their purpose, their value as predictors, and their psychometric basis. In interpreting a client's MMPI-2, the practitioner faces a wide array of inferences about personality and symptomatic characteristics from varying sources that may, at first examination, appear difficult to integrate.

In this chapter, we consider an approach to organizing MMPI-2–based inferences into an integrated interpretation. We provide a framework for establishing interpretive priorities and for incorporating hypotheses into an internally consistent report. The interpretive approach in this chapter is organized by formulating particular questions or issues that a clinician might encounter in interpreting a profile and then examining the elements in the MMPI-2 profile that can provide clues to help resolve the questions. We point to MMPI-2–based information that might confirm the existence of a problem or elucidate a behavior pattern. We explore the information that might help the clinician set priorities for the diverse inferences and integrate them into a meaningful, organized report. Finally, Alice's case is again used to illustrate the process by which information can be integrated into a personality study. A similar process is covered in Chapter 14 for the MMPI-A.

A Strategy for Integrating MMPI-2 Information

A purposeful strategy for organizing psychological test information can most effectively follow from a structured inquiry into what is needed to resolve particular questions that bear on the dispositions of a case. The shape of our conclusions and the form that the clinical report will take depend as much on how well we are able to formulate questions as on the data available in the clinical evaluation. The strategy we suggest for interpreting the MMPI-2 is much the same, whether it is the only instrument being employed or whether it is used as part of a test battery.

In initially approaching an MMPI-2 interpretation, it is desirable to pose a series of questions or issues that can be addressed regardless of the reason for referral. Several general issues that are pertinent to most MMPI-2 interpretations are listed in Table 8-1. In seeking answers to these questions, the interpreter is likely to obtain a fairly good picture of the client's personality and problem situation from the

Table 8-1. Questions for MMPI-2 Interpretations

1. Are there any extratest factors that can possibly influence the MMPI-2 results?
2. What are the individual's attitudes toward the test?
3. What are the individual's reported symptoms and behaviors? Is the client experiencing any acute mood states?
4. Is the individual experiencing problems in self-control? If so, how might they be manifested?
5. Are there any trait-based hypotheses about the individual's personality characteristics?
6. Does the individual show a potential for developing a problem with alcohol or other drugs? Has he or she acknowledged excessive alcohol or other drug use?
7. What are the individual's interpersonal relationships like? Is he or she able to deal effectively with others?
8. How frequent or rare is this pattern?
9. How stable is the individual's profile likely to be over time?
10. How severely disturbed is the individual compared to others?
11. What are the diagnostic considerations in the case?

Table 8-2. MMPI-2 Treatment Planning Questions

1. Is the individual in need of psychological treatment at this time?
2. How aware is the individual of his or her problems?
3. How credible is the individual's self-report?
4. Is the individual willing to disclose personal information to the therapist?
5. How motivated is the individual for treatment?
6. Is the individual capable of gaining insight into his or her problems?
7. Is he or she amenable to treatment? Is the individual willing to change his or her behavior?
8. Are there specific treatment needs suggested by the MMPI-2?
9. Are there any strengths or assets that can be built on in treatment?
10. Are there negative personality features that could interfere with the treatment relationship?

perspective of the MMPI-2. We provide a similar strategy and list of questions in Chapter 14 (Table 14-1) for the MMPI-A.

We address several general issues pertaining to demographic and cultural influences on personality tests that might affect the interpretive process. We also explore a number of additional questions that can influence our interpretation of the MMPI-2, for example, "Is this client in need of psychological treatment at this time?," "Is he or she able to form a treatment relationship?," "Is he or she amenable to change?," and "Are there negative personality characteristics that could interfere with treatment?" These specific treatment-oriented questions are listed in Table 8-2. Similar issues are addressed in Chapter 14 (Table 14-1) for the MMPI-A.

Extratest Information

Basic demographic and setting characteristics are important considerations because they set the stage for test interpretation by providing clear expectations by which to judge the client's MMPI-2. One can gauge the believability of a personality study by considering the individual's performance in light of the background factors. For example, consider the background features in the following cases:

A 37-year-old middle-class client with a high school education took the MMPI-2 in the context of a psychological evaluation. She is being evaluated for outpatient psychotherapy.

An 81-year-old former mechanic with a sixth-grade reading level is being evaluated to determine his competency at a commitment hearing.

The 19-year-old son of a Somali refugee is being assessed for an insanity defense in a pretrial investigation for a capital crime that he allegedly committed.

In the case of the 37-year-old woman, we would not expect reading problems, cultural factors, or an uncooperative attitude toward testing to interfere with the information-gathering process. With the 81-year-old man, we would need to consider the possibility that reading skills, comprehension difficulties, fatigue, or sensory impairment might interfere with his responses to MMPI-2 items. In assessing the 19-year-old Somali man, we would wish to consider further the possibility of cultural or language problems influencing the evaluation. Additionally, we might consider the possibility that the evaluation's setting, as part of an insanity defense, could compromise profile validity.

Although much can be said about an MMPI-2 or MMPI-A profile without information about the client, the more one knows about the individual's life circumstances, the more specific the test interpretation can be. Several demographic or situational variables might influence an individual's performance on personality scales. Some that should be taken into account in MMPI-2 and MMPI-A interpretations are described in the following sections.

Setting

The setting in which the MMPI-2 or MMPI-A is administered is an important determinant of responses to test items. The MMPI-2 or MMPI-A interpreter should be aware of factors that might distort responses in a particular setting and attempt to either alleviate their influence or compensate for them in the interpretation. Settings that can produce distortion include personnel screening and domestic court (child-custody) assessments, in which subjects may try to present an overly favorable view of themselves. Other settings can produce an opposite but equally troublesome distortion: the exaggeration or feigning of mental illness. Exaggerated profiles of this type typically are produced in settings such as court referrals involving personal injury litigation or an insanity defense following a capital crime. In these cases, the individual attempts to claim a severe mental disorder needing attention or special services.

The MMPI-2 validity scales are important interpretive elements when considering the possibility that individuals in some settings may be trying to create a certain image. Psychologists working in settings that tend to elicit distorted profiles should be aware of the typical or base-rate validity pattern for that setting. For example, clients being seen in child-custody evaluations typically produce profiles with high elevations on L (T $\geq$ 58), low elevations on F (T $<$ 50), and high elevations on K (T $\geq$ 58) (Butcher, 1997). The absence of profile elevations in settings that generate defensive profiles does not necessarily indicate that the individual is psychologically healthy. On the other hand, when elevated profiles are obtained in these settings and validity scores are acceptable, the profile is likely to be interpretable.

Gender

It has been held traditionally that gender influences responses to personality inventory items. Consequently, most personality scales, including scales on the MMPI-2 and the MMPI-A, incorporate separate norms for men and women, as was true of the original MMPI. Thus, it is important that the appropriate norms (T-score tables) are used for the two genders. Most of the descriptors for the MMPI-2 standard and content scales appear to work equally well for men and women. However, some adjustment might be needed for certain scales. As we have seen, for example, interpretive rules differ by gender for the Mf scale. Another example is the MMPI-2 content scale TPA, which appears to be a better scale (and construct) for men than for women.

Keep in mind that there are ungendered norms available for special applications of the MMPI-2 (e.g., in personnel screening) should you wish to examine an individual's MMPI-2 responses with T scores derived from a combined sample of men and women rather than from the gender-specific norms (Tellegen, Butcher & Hoegliund, 1993).

Age

Age can influence responses to personality items. Research with the MMPI indicated that people below age 18 responded to the MMPI items differently than did adults (see Chapter 9). This influenced the decision to develop a different version of the instrument for adolescents, which included new item content and age-specific adolescent norms. Individuals younger than 18 years should be tested with the MMPI-A.

Research with the original MMPI also suggested that some older individuals respond somewhat differently to MMPI items than do younger adults. For example, older persons tend to endorse more frequently items dealing with somatic changes, low mood, reduced risk taking, and introverted thinking. These differences influence scoring on several standard scales, such as D, Pd, and Si. Although some mean scale score differences between older individuals and the normative populations on the MMPI and MMPI-2 have been noted (Butcher et al., 1991), these group differences are typically small and not powerful enough to be used for individual prediction. In fact, the general conclusion from most MMPI/MMPI-2 aging research is that there are few differences between individuals at various age or cohort levels. Separate norms for older adults are not provided (Butcher, Dahlstrom, Graham & Tellegen, 1989), nor do they appear to be needed (Butcher et al., 1991).

Social Class

Social class factors, except in the case of very low socioeconomic level on two of the standard scales, have not proven to be of much importance in interpreting MMPI profiles—at least not sufficiently important to recommend the development of special norms for various socioeconomic groups. On the original MMPI, lower social status individuals showed some tendency to report more symptoms than higher social class individuals. On the original norms, higher social class individuals are viewed as more "defensive," at least as measured by higher scores on K (Dahlstrom, Welsh & Dahlstrom, 1975). These individuals also tended to score higher on Mf. These scale relationships probably reflect the higher education level usually accompanying higher social class. The original MMPI normative sample was relatively uneducated compared to most people today, which perhaps accounts for elevations on K and Mf in more contemporary samples using the older norms.

As we saw in Chapter 1, the new MMPI-2 norms are based on a more representative sample of middle- and higher-SES subjects. Interpretive adjustments do not appear to be needed for MMPI-2 profiles from most socioeconomic strata. However, the K and Mf scores from very low SES individuals, who often have a lower education level, should be interpreted with care, as noted in the next section. These socioeconomic differences have not been studied with adolescents, so their relevance for those younger is unknown at present.

Education

In the original MMPI, educational factors were considered to influence, to some extent, performance on two MMPI basic scales: K and Mf. Interpretive adjustments had to be made when interpreting profiles of more educated individuals (college education) because the original MMPI normative group had only a ninth-grade education on average. This contrasts with the projected average education for the United States in the 1990s as more than two years of college (Bogue, 1985).

The MMPI-2 normative sample has an average education level that is closer to the contemporary subjects taking the test (15.0 years for men and 14.4 for women). All educational levels except the lowest produce mean profiles that match the full MMPI-2 normative sample, indicating that for most people the new norms can be applied without adjustments.

For individuals with very low education levels (6th through 11th grades) some adjustment might be needed because the new MMPI-2 norms contain somewhat fewer subjects with this level of education. Some scales, such as K and Mf, may need to be cautiously interpreted for individuals of lower education levels. Reading comprehension is also an issue. The examiner should ensure that the individual's F and VRIN scores are within the interpretable range (below a T score of 90 for F and 80 for VRIN) before interpretive statements are applied to the profile.

Ethnic and Cultural Factors

The criticism that the original MMPI needed special norms for blacks and other minorities (Gynther, 1972b) arose from the absence of minority subjects in the original MMPI normative sample. The possible influence of ethnic background on

Table 8-3. Means and Standard Deviations by Ethnic Origin for 1,138 Community Adult Men

Scale	White (N = 933)		Black (N = 126)		Native American (N = 38)		Hispanic (N = 35)		Asian (N = 6)	
	Mean	S.D.	Mean	S.D.	Mean	S.D.	Mean	S.D.	Mean	S.D.
L	3.36	2.13	4.26	2.77	4.26	2.78	4.51	2.63	4.50	3.27
F	4.29	2.98	5.18	3.76	6.42	4.46	6.17	4.07	7.33	5.61
K	15.45	4.74	15.08	4.88	13.55	4.64	14.29	4.50	13.83	5.08
Hs	4.69	3.78	5.58	3.91	6.92	4.48	6.17	4.11	6.50	5.28
D	18.16	4.59	19.02	4.24	19.08	4.98	19.06	5.00	16.83	3.97
Hy	21.06	4.60	20.03	5.06	20.42	5.49	19.77	5.56	17.50	4.89
Pd	16.25	4.49	17.57	4.40	19.50	5.23	18.29	5.62	16.67	4.13
Mf	26.21	5.13	25.84	4.20	23.39	6.07	24.43	4.60	24.17	6.18
Pa	10.09	2.82	9.87	3.09	10.70	3.21	10.51	3.07	10.33	2.16
Pt	11.04	6.53	11.60	6.75	12.79	7.34	13.00	6.81	14.33	7.15
Sc	10.75	6.86	12.79	7.38	13.82	9.01	13.89	8.20	16.50	10.05
Ma	16.58	4.46	18.33	4.31	17.84	4.59	18.77	4.88	15.83	5.98
Si	25.80	8.70	25.56	7.43	28.32	8.63	24.77	8.26	32.17	9.45

MMPI scores was the subject of considerable empirical research and debate. A major question was whether separate norms for minorities were needed. Dahlstrom, Lachar, and Dahlstrom (1986), after reviewing the extensive empirical research, concluded the following:

> When all the background factors introduced in these analyses are considered, it is apparent that they do not account for the major portion of the variance in the component scales of the MMPI. (p. 202)
>
> At this stage in the development of the knowledge of how to use the MMPI in personnel and psychiatric assessments with various minority subjects or clients, the best procedure would seem to be to accept the pattern of results generated by the standard scales on the basic MMPI Profile. (p. 204)

The MMPI-2 is less controversial to use with members of ethnic minority groups than the original MMPI because approximately representative samples of minority subjects were included in the new norms. The ethnic group membership of the MMPI-2 normative samples is shown in Tables 8-3 for men and Table 8-4 for women. All the ethnic group samples fall very near the general normative sample mean on the MMPI-2 validity and standard scales. These data indicate that the MMPI-2 norms apply equally well regardless of ethnic group background and that no special interpretive considerations need to be made with regard to race.

Subsequent research has confirmed the appropriateness and utility of the MMPI-2 with clients from diverse ethnic settings. Two recent reviews of the impact of ethnic status on MMPI and MMPI-2 scores have been published. Although their approach to the topic was somewhat different—Hall, Bansal, and Lopez (1999) conducted a meta-analysis of studies comparing the differences among ethnic minority samples, and Waller, Thompson, and Wenk (in press) studied MMPI item-response differences using Item Response Theory—their conclusions reinforced

Table 8-4. Means and Standard Deviations by Ethnic Origin for 1,462 Community Adult Women

Scale	White (N = 1,184)		Black (N = 188)		Native American (N = 39)		Hispanic (N = 38)		Asian (N = 13)	
	Mean	S.D.	Mean	S.D.	Mean	S.D.	Mean	S.D.	Mean	S.D.
L	3.47	1.98	3.95	2.32	4.64	2.68	2.92	2.16	4.85	3.31
F	3.89	2.64	4.43	3.38	5.69	3.99	6.32	4.35	3.54	2.07
K	15.34	4.47	14.13	4.56	12.41	5.67	12.37	4.88	14.85	4.04
Hs	5.49	4.24	7.50	5.16	8.74	4.63	8.92	5.50	6.38	2.84
D	19.93	4.97	21.00	4.99	21.33	4.84	21.55	4.69	19.23	4.28
Hy	22.05	4.55	22.17	5.38	22.59	5.39	22.53	6.00	20.62	4.09
Pd	15.68	4.48	18.30	4.42	19.08	4.74	19.89	5.34	14.31	4.89
Mf	36.31	3.91	34.60	4.22	33.23	4.85	34.05	4.76	35.62	4.39
Pa	10.13	2.91	10.40	3.11	11.51	3.62	11.34	3.15	9.54	2.88
Pt	12.27	6.89	13.55	7.68	17.64	8.76	17.21	8.92	10.00	5.03
Sc	10.39	6.88	14.10	8.63	17.00	9.93	18.42	10.63	8.92	4.01
Ma	15.61	4.29	17.85	4.62	17.90	5.29	20.00	4.91	15.31	3.84
Si	27.78	9.36	28.37	8.54	32.26	7.25	27.45	7.79	28.77	7.67

the view that minority differences on MMPI-2 responding have little practical difference. Recent empirical studies illustrate these findings. Ben-Porath, Shondrick, and Stafford (1994) found that African American and Caucasian American clients who were being evaluated in a court setting produced essentially identical clinical scores (a 4-6 profile). Tinius and Ben-Porath (1993) compared Caucasian and American Indian alcoholics being evaluated in a substance abuse treatment program and found highly similar MMPI-2 patterns (4-2 profiles) in both groups. Keefe, Sue, Enomoto, Durvasula, and Chao (1996) studied Asian American and Caucasian American college students. They found that Asian Americans who had acculturated to the United States were highly similar to Caucasian Americans. However, Asian Americans who were unacculturated to the United States showed many profile elevations. Finally, Stein, Graham, Ben-Porath, and McNulty (1995) found that the correlations for MMPI-2 scales were essentially the same for African Americans as for Caucasian Americans. Ethnic minorities with defined clinical problems tend to show the same clinical patterns on the MMPI-2 as Caucasian Americans.

Psychologists in the United States may find the need to assess a client who does not speak English. For example, a client who was originally from Laos, Iran, or Italy may now be living in the United States and require psychological evaluation. If they are unable to read English at the sixth-grade level, then the psychologist might find that an appropriate foreign language version is available. The MMPI-2 and MMPI-A have been widely translated and adapted for international use (Butcher, 1996).

Can a test such as the MMPI-2 measure the same constructs in other languages and cultures? Yes, if careful adaptation procedures have been followed. Psychological disorders, at least the major ones, have been shown to be comparable across cultures (Tsai, Butcher, Munoz & Vitusek, in press). If the MMPI-2 items are carefully translated into another language, they tend to assess problems in the new culture in an equivalent manner (Butcher, Lim & Nezami, 1998; Kwan, 1999). Studies using the MMPI-2 with psychiatric patients show that the test assesses abnormal behavior in other countries as it does in the United States (Lucio & Reyes-Lagunes, 1996; Pancheri, Sirigatti & Biondi, 1996; Rissetti, Himmel & Gonzales-Moreno, 1996). Recent research has shown that computer-based MMPI-2 reports show a high degree of accuracy across cultures (Butcher et al., 1998).

In some countries (e.g., Norway and Iceland) the American norms appear to serve as a comparable normative population (Ellertsen, Havik & Skavhellen, 1996; Konraos, 1996). In other countries, such as Holland (Sloore, Derksen, de Mey & Hellenbosch, 1996) and France (Gillet et al., 1996), indigenous norms were developed, although research on normals indicated that the American norms were quite close to these normal populations.

Response Attitudes

As noted in Chapters 3 and 10, it is extremely important to assess the individual's view of the test situation and how he or she deals with its demands. The MMPI-2 and MMPI-A validity scale patterns provide important clues to the subject's cooperativeness, ability to understand the items, literacy level, and willingness to follow instructions. The Cannot Say score, for example, indicates whether the individual has answered all or most of the items. The TRIN and VRIN scales provide information about response inconsistency. The F scale indicates whether the individual is responding in a frank and open manner or is exaggerating symptoms to convince the examiner that he or she is more disturbed than is actually the case. Other validity scales, such as L and K, indicate whether the individual is willing to admit relevant problems. L and K scores below a T of 65, for example, show a nondefensive symptom pattern. It is important to assess the individual's approach to the test situation to determine how credible his or her scores are when interpreting the standard and content scale profiles.

Assessing Symptoms and Behaviors

The MMPI-2 standard scales and profile configurations described in Chapters 4 and 5 have been related to descriptions of presenting problems, typical symptoms, unusual beliefs, and characteristic problems that patients with similar scores have. Evaluation of a client's personality and behavioral problems should proceed from appraising the most significantly elevated scale scores or profile configurations. In profile interpretation, we must first decide which of the prototype (scale or code-type) MMPI-2 descriptors to use as the empirical structure of the report, that is, which scale or code-type correlates would most likely apply to a particular case. For example, if the individual has a T score of 75 on D and 68 on Pd, we would consider this profile a 2-4 and search through the relevant code-type descriptors and organize the correlates as they apply to our case and the referral problem. With a profile that has a significant elevation on Pt (T = 69) and no other scales elevated above a T score of 64, we would use correlate literature on scale 7.

With many profiles it is relatively easy to choose the proper correlate data set to use in the interpretation. We simply take the highest clinical profile point, two-point pair, or three- or four-point code type as our prototype. However, in some cases, several scales will be elevated above a T score of 65, and it may be difficult to determine what scale or code type should be used as the correlate prototype. In these more complicated cases, it is best to determine the prototype that includes the greatest number of scales in the profile code. For example, if scales 1, 2, 3, 4, and 7 are elevated, the 1-2-3-4 code type is employed. Because scale 7 is also elevated above a T score of 65, we will want to incorporate major features of the Pt scale (i.e., indications the individual is anxious, tense, ruminative, perfectionistic, and so on) into our report. The interpreter should keep profile definition (discussed in Chapter 5) in mind when determining the extent to which the traditional scale correlates fit the client.

Once we have determined the most suitable profile prototype to follow and have chosen the correlates to serve as the empirical outline of our report, we can search other scale elevations (e.g., the Harris-Lingoes subscales or the supplementary scales) for additional hypotheses about the individual's problems and behavior. Next, we would consult scores on the MMPI-2 content scales to confirm previously generated hypotheses or to develop new ones. In evaluating other scales, a T score of 65 will yield the likely correlate to incorporate in the evaluation; however, for many scales a T score of 60 might be used for hypotheses about the client's behavior.

In using correlates or personality descriptions from many scales or code types, it is possible that contradictory hypotheses will be suggested. To use an extreme example, if an individual obtained an elevated D score, we would consider the scale correlate "fatigued and low energy." If this same individual had a high elevation on Ma, a possible correlate would be "energetic, talkative, preferring action to reflection." How does the interpreter resolve the apparent contradiction to prevent the report from appearing internally inconsistent? Actually, internal contradictions in the test data can provide the interpreter with more interesting and fruitful assessment data. Resolving apparent internal inconsistencies may provide important clues to understanding the patient. The case of the individual with elevations on both D and Ma is quite unusual and raises the question of a bipolar disorder, which would require additional assessment to confirm. The Harris-Lingoes subscales should be consulted to see whether they can resolve the discrepancy. For example, if the elevated D score was accompanied by elevations on D_1 (Subjective Depression) and D_5 (Brooding) but not with elevations on D_2 (Psychomotor Retardation) or D_4 (Mental Dullness), fatigue and lack of energy might not be highlighted as a prominent descriptor for the individual. Similarly, if Ma_1 (Amorality) and Ma_3 (Imperturbability) were the only elevated Ma subscales, then a high energy level would not be highlighted. We provide other examples of resolving conflicting descriptors in Chapter 14 on the MMPI-A.

As Table 8-1 indicates, assessing the presence of an acute mood state is an important question in the interpretive process. These acute states, such as periods of anxiousness or depressed mood, are reflected in MMPI-2 profile elevations. The presence of several scale elevations or profile relationships should alert the interpreter to the possibility that the individual is experiencing acute mood states. Several clinical states have been recognized in MMPI-2 profiles:

Anxiety:	Pt 65–79; Pt greater than Sc (Moderate) Pt 80–89; Pt greater than Sc (Marked) Pt 90+; Pt greater than Sc (Severe)
Depressive state:	D 65–79; Ma less than 40 (Moderate) D 80–89; Ma less than 40 (Marked) D 90+; Ma less than 40 (Severe)
Manic state:	Ma greater than 80; Ma highest score; D less than 55
Psychosis:	Sc greater than 80; Sc the highest score; Sc greater than Pt by 10 points
Suspicion-mistrust:	Pa greater than 70; Pa the highest score
Acting out:	Pd greater than 65 or Ma greater than 70 and Si lower than 40 or ANG greater than 65
Confused, disoriented:	F greater than 80 Sc greater than 80 or Pt greater than 80 or Mean Profile Elevation greater than 70
Crisis states:	Koss-Butcher and Lachar-Wrobel critical items serve as clues to significant problems

Assessing Self-Control or Acting Out

There are a number of indicators of self-control and acting-out potential in the MMPI-2 to answer the fourth set of questions in Table 8-1. These indicators should be evaluated to appraise the possibility of control problems or disabling overcontrol. The following factors are assessed by MMPI-2 scales:

Inhibition (constriction):	Indicated by scores greater than 65 on the Si scale
Overcontrol (repression):	Suggested by scores greater than 65 on the Hy scale
Acting out (impulsivity):	Suggested by scores greater than 65 on the Pd and Ma scales or low Si scores (below a T score of 40)
Anger (loss of control):	Suggested by scores greater than 65 on the ANG or Ho scale

Generating Trait-Based Hypotheses

The MMPI-2, like its predecessor, contains several indicators that address long-term personality characteristics or traits. Various MMPI-2 scales are trait-based measures that contain many items that assess personality characteristics. Some of these measures and the traits they reflect are as follows:

Impulsivity:	Indicated by Pd greater than 65 or Ma greater than 70 with Si below 40
Introversion:	Si greater than 65
Obsessiveness:	Pt greater than 65; Pt highest point in the profile; OBS greater than 65
Dominance:	Do greater than 65
Cynicism:	CYN greater than 65

Problems with Alcohol or Other Drugs

Several MMPI-2 scales provide useful information about possible difficulties with alcohol or drug abuse. Substantial research on MMPI-2 clinical scales Pd, D, and Pt in the assessment of substance abuse problems has shown these scales are prominent in individuals with addictive disorders. In addition, the APS and MAC-R scales, described in Chapter 6, have been developed to assess alcohol and drug problem potential. The AAS scale addresses the individual's willingness to acknowledge problems with alcohol or drug use.

The MMPI-2 scale patterns most commonly associated with disorders of substance use or abuse are as follows:

High elevations (T > 65) on Pd

High elevations (T > 65) on D and Pd

High elevations (T > 65) on D, Pd, and Pt

Moderate to high elevations (T > 60) on MAC-R, APS, or AAS

Assessing Quality of Interpersonal Relations

The MMPI-2 can provide hypotheses about how an individual interacts with others and whether social factors might influence the individual's psychological adjustment in order to answer the seventh set of interpretive questions in Table 8-1. Information about the client's social skills and interpersonal problems is available from several sources in the MMPI-2. Most directly, the Si scale addresses social introversion and social maladjustment. The Si scale provides a reliable evaluation of the individual's basic sociability and comfort in social situations. Moreover, the Si subscales allow the interpreter to determine the relative contribution of the subscale components (shyness, avoidance, or self-alienation) to the individual's self-reported interpersonal attitudes. However, there are other social adjustment and relationship indicators in the MMPI-2; the scale and code-type descriptors provide additional clues about how the individual interacts with others. Following are examples:

High scorers on scale 1 are viewed by others as passive, self-preoccupied, dissatisfied, and unhappy. They tend to make others feel miserable with their complaining, whining, demanding, and critical behavior, but they may express hostility indirectly.

High scorers on scale 4 tend to have considerable social adjustment problems. Although they may be seen as extroverted, outgoing, talkative, active, energetic, spontaneous, and self-confident, they are also viewed as ostentatious, exhibitionistic, insensitive, and manipulative. They tend to be interested in others only in terms of how they can be used to satisfy their own needs. Although they tend to make good first impressions, their relationships tend to be shallow and superficial. They seem unable to form lasting, warm attachments. Their interpersonal and family relationships tend to be stormy.

High scores on Dominance (Do) suggest that individuals tend to view themselves as the dominant person in interpersonal interaction. They are quite assertive in interpersonal situations.

High scorers on scale 6 appear to others as hypersensitive, moralistic, and overly responsive to reactions of others. They feel they are picked on and become resentful and angry. They typically harbor grudges against others and are often suspicious and guarded in relationships.

High scorers on scale 8 typically do not feel a part of the social environment. They are isolated and alienated from other people and feel misunderstood. They are unaccepted by their peers and are often seen as withdrawn, seclusive, secretive, and emotionally inaccessible. They usually avoid dealing with people and new situations.

High scores on MDS for married or separated clients indicate the possibility of marital distress.

High scores on the MMPI-2 content scale SOD can provide clues about how the individual feels in interpersonal situations.

Base-Rate Information

It is often useful when interpreting a profile to know the relative frequency of the prominent scores or profile codes in the population from which the test was obtained. The "base rates" of the population can be important to understanding the case. The term *base rate* refers to the relative frequency of a particular problem in a given population (see Finn & Kamphuis, 1995). For example, the following information was developed about a profile of a person being assessed in a pretrial criminal investigation according to The Minnesota Report™ for forensic settings (Butcher, 1998b).

Profile interpretation can be greatly facilitated by examining the relative frequency of clinical scale patterns in various settings. The client's high-point clinical scale score (Sc) is the least frequent MMPI-2 peak score in the MMPI-2 normative sample of men, occurring in only 4.7% of the cases. Only 2.6% of the sample have Sc as the peak score at or above a T score of 65, and less than 1% have well-defined Sc spikes. His elevated MMPI-2 two-point profile configuration (4-8/8-4) is very rare in samples of normals, occurring in less than 1% of the MMPI-2 normative sample of men.

This profile is relatively frequent in various inpatient settings. In the Graham and Butcher (1988) sample of psychiatric inpatients, the Sc high-point score occurs in 13.8% of the males, with 13.2% scoring at or above a T score of 65 (3.8% are well defined in that high range). In the NCS inpatient sample, 9.1% of the males have this high-point clinical scale score. Moreover, 8.5% of the males in the inpatient sample have the Sc scale spike at or over a T score of 65, and 4.4% produce well-defined Sc spike scores in that range.

The male inpatients in a Veterans Administration sample (Arbisi & Ben-Porath, 1997) produce this high-point peak score with 13.8% frequency. In addition, 5.8% are elevated at or above a T score of 65 and are well-defined profiles.

This MMPI-2 clinical scale spike on Sc was one of the more frequent high-point configurations for general psychiatric inpatients in the study conducted by Arbisi, Ben-Porath, Marshall, Boyd, and Strauman (1997). They found this high-point score occurred in 8.6% of the high-point codes (3.2% were well-defined high-point profiles).

This elevated MMPI-2 two-point profile configuration (4-8/8-4) is found in 6.9% of the males in the Graham and Butcher (1988) sample and in 2.9% of the males in the NCS inpatient sample. As the highest scale pair, this code type is found in 3.9% of the men in a Veterans Administration inpatient sample (Arbisi & Ben-Porath, 1997), and it is elevated at or above a T of 65 in less than 1% of the cases. The 4-8/8-4 code type occurred with relatively high frequency (5.9%) in the general psychiatric inpatient study conducted by Arbisi et al. (1997). They reported that this high-point pattern occurred with 1.6% frequency as a well-defined high-point profile.

Ben-Porath and Stafford (1997) conducted a study of high-point and code-type frequencies for men and women undergoing competency evaluations. The high-point score on Sc that the client received occurred with 9.1% frequency in that sample. Additionally, it occurred with relatively low frequency (4.8%) in terms of well-defined profiles at or above a T score of 65. This high-point MMPI-2 code (4-8/8-4) can best be understood in the context of cases reported by Ben-Porath and Stafford (1997) in their study of individuals undergoing competency evaluations. This profile configuration occurred in 3.4% of the cases, and 1.7% were well-defined scores at or above a T of 65.

This type of frequency information can also be obtained from several published sources in addition to The Minnesota Report™, for example, normative samples, psychiatric inpatients, chronic pain patients (Keller & Butcher, 1991), prison inmates (Megaragee, 1995, 1997), custody cases (Bathurst, Gottfried, & Gottfried, 1997); and personal injury litigants (Lees-Haley, 1997).

Stability of the Profile

The stability of MMPI-2 profiles over time is an important interpretive question (Table 8-1). Clinicians need to be able to appraise whether a client's behavior will likely change over time or persist regardless of treatment. The MMPI-2 profile can aid in assessing whether change is likely. Some MMPI-2 indicators have quite stable test-retest characteristics. For example, Spiro, Butcher, Levenson, Aldwin, and Bosse (2000) and Leon et al. (1979) found the test-retest correlation for the Si scale to be .73 over 30 years with a sample of normals. The Si scale measures personality characteristics that are not likely to change very much. Other scales, such as D and Pt, are likely to reflect a situational problem that could alter with a change in circumstances.

As noted earlier, an important factor in assessing profile stability is determining how well defined the profile is. For example, if the two highest scales are 10 T-score points above the next scale in the code, the profile is considered to have very high profile definition. These profiles tend to be quite stable over time. Profiles with a 5 to 9 T-score gap between them and the next highest scale or code type (high profile definition) also tend to be very stable. Those profiles with fewer T scores separating the code from the next scale or code type (low profile definition) tend to be relatively unstable over time (Graham, Smith & Schwartz, 1986).

Severity of Disorder

Level of psychological adjustment and a disorder's severity are other questions that can be addressed by an individual's scores on MMPI-2 scales and patterns (Table 8-1). An evaluation of the individual's standard and content scale profiles and performance on the supplementary scales provides some general guidelines to how severely disturbed the individual is. For example, an individual having a profile within normal limits, with all scales and indicators below a T score of 60, would be viewed as well adjusted, provided that his or her validity scales did not indicate a defensive response attitude. Similarly, if an individual has several clinical and content scale scores ranging in the 80+ T-score range, severe psychological maladjustment is suggested. A number of indexes and configural patterns, described in Chapter 6, have been developed to aid the interpreter in appraising adjustment.

Diagnostic Considerations

Although the MMPI was originally constructed with the idea that clinical scale elevations would correspond to diagnostic groups, clinical diagnosis has not been the primary focus in using the instrument. The MMPI is used most extensively for descriptive diagnosis, that is, providing behavioral and personality descriptions of an individual based on the empirical scale and code-type literature. In descriptive diagnosis of clients with the MMPI-2, several sources of information are used:

Standard scale elevations

Slope of profile

Code-type information

Content scale scores

Many MMPI scales and code types have been shown to have good correspondence with clinical diagnostic groups, especially with the latest categories provided in the American Psychiatric Association's *Diagnostic and Statistical Manual*, that are based on clearer diagnostic criteria than were earlier versions (Moldin, Gottesman, Rice & Erlenmeyer-Kimling, 1991; Savacir & Erol, 1990; Thatte, Manos & Butcher, 1987). The MMPI-2 content scales have recently been found to make a contribution to differential diagnosis (Ben-Porath, Butcher & Graham, 1991; Ben-Porath, McCulley & Almagor, 1993; Lilienfeld, 1996; Walsh et al., 1991) as well as providing content-based assessment information. When preparing a clinical report, the interpreter may find the correspondence between scale information and clinical diagnosis useful, although it should not be the primary consideration in reaching a clinical diagnosis.

Treatment Considerations

An important use of the MMPI-2 in clinical assessment involves evaluation of relevant personal characteristics in treatment planning (see Butcher [1990a] for an extended discussion of the use of the MMPI-2 in treatment planning). The MMPI-2 profiles and supplementary scores provide several sources of information that assist in treatment planning by addressing the questions listed in Table 8-2. For example, response attitudes provide clues about the individual's willingness to share personal information, awareness of problems, and ability to understand his or her problems. The clinical scales provide clues about the extent of problems and motivation for treatment. The MMPI-2 content scales provide information about the nature of the individual's problems, attitudes, self-views, or behaviors that might interfere with treatment progress.

Highlight Summary: Alice's MMPI-2 Interpretation

At several points in earlier chapters, we discussed specific aspects of Alice's MMPI-2 profile to illustrate how the various scales are interpreted. We now turn to a fuller exploration of her MMPI-2 profiles and will provide an integrated presentation of her important test responses. The case of 18-year-old Alice, being evaluated in a pretreatment planning assessment, illustrates how the MMPI-2 variables can provide descriptive and predictive information about her before treatment is initiated. Her standard and content scale profiles are repeated in Figures 8-1 and 8-2 for convenience. Relevant extratest information to assist with her MMPI-2 interpretation is presented in the following summary of her past history, symptomatic problems, and life-situation demands. Alice's MMPI-2 profile is interpreted by answering the questions pertinent to understanding her case.

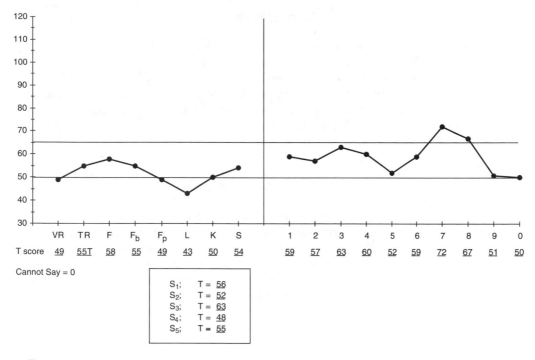

	VR	TR	F	F_b	F_p	L	K	S		1	2	3	4	5	6	7	8	9	0
T score	49	55T	58	55	49	43	50	54		59	57	63	60	52	59	72	67	51	50

Cannot Say = 0

S_1;	T =	56
S_2;	T =	52
S_3;	T =	63
S_4;	T =	48
S_5;	T =	55

Figure 8-1. Alice's MMPI-2 basic scales profile.

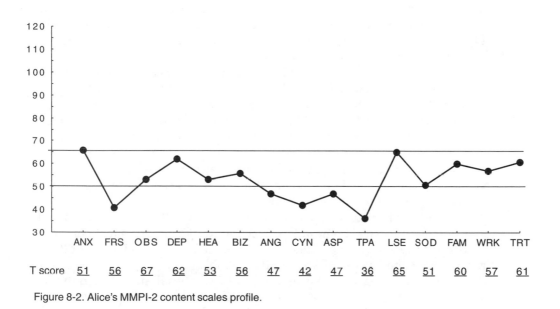

	ANX	FRS	OBS	DEP	HEA	BIZ	ANG	CYN	ASP	TPA	LSE	SOD	FAM	WRK	TRT
T score	51	56	67	62	53	56	47	42	47	36	65	51	60	57	61

Figure 8-2. Alice's MMPI-2 content scales profile.

Referral Problem

Alice is an 18-year-old unemployed Caucasian woman who was referred to an outpatient mental health center by her parents following an intense episode of extreme anxiety and panic. Alice was accompanied on all clinic visits by her mother. She had been seen by her family physician for physical complaints (nausea, chest pains, shortness of breath, and sweating), but the physician felt that a psychological referral was more appropriate. Alice reportedly had been feeling quite insecure and inadequate, that she let her family down in not being able to keep a job.

Behavioral Observations

In the initial interview, Alice appeared to be quite tense and under considerable strain. She had difficulty sitting still in the waiting room and walked about talking with her mother. Alice was a rather plain woman who was mildly overweight and had a very informal, almost unkempt appearance. She appeared rather disorganized and carried a handbag from which numerous papers were sticking out. She had a very serious manner and appeared preoccupied. She smiled very little, even when it would have been appropriate to do so.

History

Alice completed high school about 8 months earlier and had difficulty finding stable employment. Recently, she took a job as a cashier in an all-night convenience store. However, after only a few days of work, she felt that she was not learning the job well, and she quit. She reportedly felt that she was making too many mistakes and was embarrassed to continue working.

Alice presently lived at home with her mother, who was 58 years old, and her father, who was 55 years old. She was born when her mother was almost 40 years old, and her three older siblings, all girls, were 15 or more years older than she. All her siblings were married and living elsewhere in the state. Alice's mother had been a general office worker for an insurance company for the past 8 years. Alice's father had not worked since he had a stroke about 8 years ago, forcing his early retirement. He spent most of his time at home watching television. None of her sisters was employed outside the home, although one sister completed business school and worked in business for a while.

Alice considered her home situation unpleasant, but felt that she was not able to move out of her parents' home at the present time. She reported that her family relationships were not close and that she felt somewhat distant from both her mother and her father ever since she could remember.

Alice reportedly was quite sickly as a child. She was hospitalized when she was 4 years old for a period of about 4 days with high fever of unknown origin. Alice missed a great deal of school during first and second grades as a result of sickness and had a great deal of difficulty learning how to read. Her parents obtained special tutors during her third and fourth grades to enable her to keep up with her classmates.

Alice's academic work during high school was marginal and her motivation for school quite low. She reportedly "couldn't wait 'til graduation." Her grades during high school were mostly Ds and Cs. Alice had very little involvement with extra-curricular activities and reportedly did not feel that she was very close to many people at school. Alice reported that she had two close girlfriends with whom she liked to spend time.

Alice dated only occasionally in high school, considering herself not to be very popular. She reportedly stayed at home during school activity nights, such as proms, dances, and so on. Alice reported that she had had three sexual experiences during the past year. Her first experience occurred with a young man in the neigh-borhood who was home on leave from the Navy. This was a difficult experience for her, in part because the situation was interrupted by her parents coming home. Her second sexual experience was with a divorced man for whom she was baby-sitting. This experience, which she reportedly did not initiate or want, left her "feeling dumb and used." About 6 months ago, shortly after her high school graduation, she reported that she had sexual intercourse with one of her former classmates, after which she developed a great concern over AIDS. In the weeks that followed, she was fearful that she had contracted AIDS and eventually went to see a physician to be tested. The medical examination was negative.

Clinical Symptoms

In the initial interview, Alice reported feeling quite anxious and tense much of the time and reported that she was having difficulties concentrating and making de-cisions. She had been experiencing shortness of breath, heart palpitations, and chest pains. Alice indicated that she was having a great deal of difficulty falling asleep at night and tended to lie awake much of the night worrying about what she was going to do next. She indicated that she had a tightness in her chest most of the time and had difficulty breathing. She felt that these problems interfered at work, and she was very slow at learning to work the cash register, which caused her embarrassment.

Alice viewed herself as a very passive person who cannot "stick up for herself." She felt as though she never thought of the right thing to say, particularly when someone made unrealistic demands on her. She became frustrated and angry when people tried to take advantage of her. However, she reported being unable to tell them what she thought or to stand up for herself. Alice was quite self-critical during the interview and stated that she had not lived up to the standards that her mother had set for her. She thought that she had let her mother down and felt quite guilty about this.

Goals

At the end of the initial session, Alice indicated that she would like to get relief from the tension and anxiety she was currently experiencing. She also reported that she would like to obtain medication so that she might be able to sleep better. Further, she felt that she needed to talk over her feelings of failure and inability to make decisions with a therapist so that she might conquer her concerns about working in public.

MMPI-2 Interpretation

We begin Alice's MMPI-2 interpretation by considering possible extraneous demographic factors that might influence her responses to the MMPI-2. Although Alice still lived at home, the clinician chose to administer the MMPI-2 rather than the MMPI-A. Either instrument can be used with 18-year-olds, but the content of the MMPI-2 related to work rather than school was thought to be more relevant to Alice's life circumstances. Alice did not appear to present any problematic demographic or status factors that were likely to adversely affect her MMPI-2 performance. She was a high school graduate from a lower-middle-class background. No known environmental or cultural factors required consideration. It is, of course, important to determine whether the appropriate norms for women were used to plot her profiles.

Because Alice was being administered the MMPI-2 in an outpatient treatment setting in which she was seeking psychological treatment, it is unlikely that she would be uncooperative or defensive in responding to test items. Thus, we would expect that her validity configuration would be problem oriented and open.

Validity Appraisal

Alice's MMPI-2 validity pattern is clearly in the interpretable range. Her scores on VRIN and TRIN show that she has responded to the MMPI-2 items in a consistent manner throughout the booklet. The slight elevation on F indicates that she has endorsed some psychological problems but has not exaggerated her symptom picture. Her low score on L and average score on K demonstrate that she responded to the MMPI-2 items in an open and nondefensive manner. Overall, Alice's approach to the MMPI-2 items was open and cooperative. Her MMPI-2 profile is a valid indication of her present personality functioning and problems.

Symptoms and Behavior

Alice's clinical profile suggests that she is experiencing intense anxiety, considerable ruminations, and self-critical behavior, as reflected in her Pt score. She apparently has great self-doubt and feels that she is unworthy. Individuals with high Pt scores such as Alice's are prone to worry and are indecisive even when minor decisions need to be made. She is likely experiencing an acute anxiety state of moderate severity. More information about Alice's anxiousness is available by evaluating the relative elevations on the three MMPI-2 content scales that assess anxiousness: Anxiety (ANX), Fears (FRS), and Obsessiveness (OBS). We see that her anxiety is generalized, as shown by the high score on ANX, rather than related to specific fears or phobias, as shown by her lower score on FRS. She does appear to have some obsessive qualities as well, as shown by the score on OBS.

Perhaps basic to her tendency to worry and feel uncertain about her ability to function is her very low self-esteem. The feelings of low self-worth are reflected in several MMPI-2 measures. Her high score on the Low Self-Esteem (LSE) scale shows an extremely negative self-appraisal. These negative self-views might create in her a vulnerability to self-defeating behavior that could, of course, trigger further experience of anxiety.

Assessing Alice's Self-Control

On the MMPI-2, Alice appears to be a generally constricted individual who tends to intellectualize and ruminate a great deal. This is suggested by her high elevation on the Pt scale. In addition, she probably overrelies on denial as a defense mechanism, as noted by her slight Hy and high R elevations; however, at this time she appears to be experiencing more stress than she can manage through her normal defenses. Again, central to her management of conflict appears to be her low self-esteem; she may be nonassertive in interpersonal contexts because of her own feelings of uncertainty and inferiority.

Assessing Problems with Alcohol or Other Drugs

Addiction problems or addiction potential in Alice's case would be considered relatively low. She appears to possess few of the personality factors or "lifestyle" features, measured by Pd, MAC-R, and APS scale scores, that appear to predispose people to abusing addictive substances. Although she has a prominent elevation on Pt, a scale that appears elevated among some severe alcohol and drug abusers, this does not present a problem in her case. The role of Pt in the manifestation of alcohol and drug abuse problems requires further clarification. The Pt scale alone does not reflect alcohol or drug abuse problems; it seldom appears as the single prominent scale in alcohol treatment populations. When the Pt scale is elevated in alcohol- or drug-abusing cases, it indicates the presence of acute anxiety, perhaps associated with the situational problems that the individual has caused for him- or herself. The Pt scale also can be associated with compulsive characteristics that appear to add an element of extreme urgency to the use of addictive substances. For example, correlates for the 4-7 profile type discussed in Chapter 5 reflect a cyclical pattern of acting-out behavior involving alcohol or drugs. The individual experiences periods of seemingly compulsive excess alternating with periods of guilt and superficial remorse over his or her actions.

Alice appears to be seeking relief for her anxiety and may benefit from anti-anxiety medication for symptom relief. No contraindicating factors (such as high MAC-R, high Pd, or AAS) appear in her personality profile.

Interpersonal Behavior

The MMPI-2 provides useful information about Alice's interpersonal behavior. Her score on Si suggests that she has average social skills, although her relatively higher score on the Si subscale Si_1 suggests some degree of self-consciousness. Individuals with her Si score can, however, function well in interpersonal situations, and she appears not to have any extreme problems interpersonally.

However, individuals with her clinical profile (7-8) typically are somewhat overideational, perfectionistic, and nonassertive in relationships. Her nonassertiveness with regard to her own wishes and rights could create frustration if others take advantage of her. Alice's low score on Do, discussed in Chapter 7, also supports the interpretation of passivity in interpersonal situations.

Assessing the Frequency of Alice's Profile

It is usually valuable in MMPI-2 clinical profile interpretation to consider the relative frequency of a given profile pattern in various settings. The client's MMPI-2 high-point clinical scale score (Pt) is found in only 5.1% of the MMPI-2 normative sample of women. Only 2.1% of the women have Pt as the peak score at or above a T score of 65, and only 1% have well-defined Pt spikes. Her elevated MMPI-2 two-point profile configuration (7-8/8-7) is rare in samples of normals, occurring in only 1.4% of the MMPI-2 normative sample of women.

Assessing Alice's MMPI-2 Profile Stability

The major elements in her clinical profile, particularly the high Pt elevation, may have a strong situational component. It is likely that the manifest anxiety that this profile reflects could be reduced by treatment or more adaptive efforts on her part. Thus, if retested at a later date or after treatment, her profile is likely to shift somewhat if her ability to deal with anxiety improves.

However, some aspects of her profile are likely not to change much over time, even with intervention. Her generally effective social orientation and ability to deal with others in social situations is not likely to change much. On the positive side, after successful treatment she is not likely to be viewed as extremely introverted or extremely extroverted.

Assessing the Severity of Alice's Disorder

Although she is experiencing troublesome psychological symptoms and anxiety-based physical discomfort, Alice's MMPI-2 profiles suggest that her disorder is mild to moderate in severity. Her problems appear to be somewhat disabling yet not severe enough to require hospitalization. First, her profile elevations are in the range associated with moderate psychological problems. Moreover, the relative scale elevations suggest that her problems are acute rather than chronic because her Pt elevation is greater than her Sc elevation.

Diagnostic Considerations

Any clinical diagnosis in Alice's case should take into consideration the anxiety-based nature of the problems she is experiencing. Panic disorder is a likely diagnosis because her score on the Pt scale reflects considerable anxiety. The clinical diagnosis can be further refined by using the MMPI-2 content scale scores. Alice produced a high score on the ANX content scale but a relatively low score on FRS, suggesting that she is generally anxious but does not report extensive fears or phobias. This possibly rules out agoraphobia in the clinical diagnosis. Thus, the diagnosis of panic disorder without agoraphobia is supported by her performance on the MMPI-2.

Potential Factors in Alice's Response to Treatment

To illustrate the information available to the practitioner in treatment planning, we evaluate Alice's MMPI-2 profiles and scale scores to determine possible recommendations for treatment and to address the referral questions the clinician encounters in her case. To organize the MMPI-2 information in this case, we address the questions from Table 8-2 about Alice:

—*Does she need to be in psychological treatment at this time?*

According to Alice's MMPI-2 profile, she appears to be a very unhappy individual who is experiencing considerable emotional turmoil at present. In addition, she appears to have strong feelings of insecurity, inferiority, and low self-esteem that make her vulnerable to anxiety states.

—*How aware is Alice of the problems she is experiencing?*

Alice appears to be intensely aware of her present anxious state, as noted by her willingness to report problems through the MMPI-2. She has endorsed a large number of symptoms related to anxiety and general maladjustment, as shown by her high score on Pt. The intensity of her awareness is shown by her seeming inability to act effectively to resolve her problems at this time.

—*How credible is her personality appraisal?*

Alice is presenting a valid symptom pattern according to her performance on the F scale. She is not exaggerating her symptoms. Rather, she is selectively responding to the item content. This suggests that she would probably enter into treatment sessions with a problem-oriented approach.

—*How willing is Alice to disclose personal information to the therapist?*

Alice's approach to the MMPI-2 items, as reflected in her validity scale pattern, shows her openness to evaluation and her willingness to disclose personal information. She is not defensive and presents an open self-appraisal, which is also reflected in her elevations on the MMPI-A scales.

—*How motivated is Alice to become engaged in therapy?*

Alice's symptom expression and need for relief of her intense anxiety are likely to be strong motivating factors for psychological treatment.

—*Is she capable of gaining insight into her problems?*

Individuals with her validity profile configuration appear to have a problem-oriented approach to life's difficulties. Moreover, individuals with high Pt scores tend to be introspective and conscientious.

—*Is she amenable to treatment? Will she be able to change her behavior?*

With her motivation to get help and her willingness to enter treatment, she is likely to benefit from psychological treatment.

—*Are there any specific treatment needs suggested by the MMPI-2?*

Anxiety reduction would be an important component in any treatment program with Alice. Whether it be anti-anxiety medication or behavior therapy, her intense anxiety and her tendency to have panic episodes should be primary treatment focuses.

In addition, she appears to have a very poor self-concept and low self-esteem, which might make her prone to further problems. Insight-oriented treatment to reduce her negative self-views and improve her morale would be valuable.

A third factor that might be addressed is her tendency toward passivity in relationships. Alice appears to have little self-confidence and assertiveness. She might benefit from having assertiveness training in order to learn to stand up for herself more effectively.

— *Are there any personality strengths that can be used as assets in therapy?*

Alice has several areas that can be considered assets in therapy. Her intense discomfort and emotional distress are strong motivating factors for behavioral change. She is responsible and organized and shows a willingness to discuss her problem areas.

— *Are there any persistent personality problems that could interfere with the treatment relationship?*

One caution that the therapist should keep in mind is that many individuals with elevated Pt scores may ruminate and obsess about their inadequacy and may be unable to put into practice any behavioral changes. Any treatment program involving high-Pt clients should have a clear behavioral component, that is, it should require the client to take practical steps to implement behavioral changes.

Closing Comments

This chapter illustrated the importance of organizing MMPI-2–based inferences into an integrated and internally consistent personality appraisal. In considering information from the various MMPI-2 sources, clinicians need to establish clear interpretive priorities and incorporate hypotheses into an internally consistent, accurate interpretation. By using the suggested interpretive outline, evaluators can organize MMPI-2 inferences from several sources into a cohesive picture. This strategy provides a number of questions to assist the interpreter in formulating a personality evaluation. A number of MMPI-2–based variables help the clinician set priorities within the various inferences and integrate them into a meaningful, organized picture. As we saw in the case of Alice, considered incrementally in previous chapters, this integrated approach using the many information sources available provides the most comprehensive picture of the client and his or her problems to address in psychological treatment. This approach is modified for the MMPI-A in Chapter 14. The next chapter turns to a discussion of the MMPI-A.

Chapter 9

The MMPI-A: Extending the
Use of the MMPI to Adolescents

The MMPI has been used with adolescents to meet the same practical needs for an assessment device that was the reason Hathaway and McKinley developed the original instrument for adults. Much of the early MMPI research with adolescents concentrated on identifying youth prone to juvenile delinquency. This work had a public health focus, growing out of the mental hygiene movement that began in 1908 and the subsequent child-guidance-clinic movement that started during the 1920s. Unlike the development of the MMPI for adults, work with adolescents was not limited to improving psychiatric diagnosis within clinical or personnel settings.

Starke Hathaway and his collaborator, Elio Monachesi, recognized that underlying many aspects of primary prevention efforts, such as the child-guidance movement, was the assumption that therapeutic work with individual children would decrease the likelihood of later development of delinquency or mental illness. Hathaway and Monachesi (1953a) suggested that there was little experimental evidence supporting this basic assumption:

> But even if we did know that special therapeutic efforts would decrease the later incidence of maladjustment, we have no established, practical, reliable, and valid survey method for identifying the various subgroups of children that are more likely than others to have trouble. We must either blindly do general preventive work on whole populations or wait for children to become deviant in behavior and then offer treatment, depending on the unhappy fact that a person already in trouble is more likely than others to have additional trouble. (p. 3)

The earliest studies using the MMPI with adolescents sought to determine whether the instrument could reliably and validly identify subgroups of youth predisposed to delinquency. Although Hathaway and Monachesi (1953a) recognized the etiological significance of the social environment, they also observed that not all children living in stressful environments became delinquent. Rather, they theorized, some personality characteristics might predispose youth toward deviant behavior. More than 50 years after Hathaway and Monachesi's (1953a) efforts to provide better measures for primary prevention research, several MMPI-A scales proved useful in evaluating the effectiveness and outcomes of a multiyear, multicomponent community-wide program for young adolescents designed to reduce alcohol-related problems and delay the age for the onset of drinking

(Williams, Perry, Dudovitz, Veblen-Mortenson & Anstine, 1995; Williams, Perry, Farbakhsh & Veblen-Mortenson, 1999).

The first extension of MMPI research to adolescents was attributed to Dora Capwell (1945a, 1945b, 1953). She began her work even before the completed instrument was available, using a card-box form that did not include items for scales K, 5, and 0. Capwell sought to determine whether the MMPI would provide useful information about 101 delinquent girls from the Minnesota Home School for Girls in the small town of Sauk Centre. Because she speculated that adult normative comparisons might not be the most appropriate for adolescents, Capwell included a comparison group of 85 nondelinquents from the Sauk Centre public schools. Her design was longitudinal, with a retesting from 4 to 15 months after the first examination, and included the MMPI and several other personality tests as well as intelligence and academic achievement tests. She found that of all the personality measures studied, the MMPI most clearly differentiated the two groups. The delinquent girls had reliably greater mean adult T scores on all the validity and clinical scales, except for L and scale 3. She further demonstrated that this difference in mean scores on the scales did not seem to be related to intelligence.

Shortly after Capwell's pioneering efforts, Elio Monachesi began studies to extend her findings to boys using the published version of the instrument that included scales K, 5, and 0 (Monachesi, 1948, 1950a, 1950b, 1953). Monachesi was able to confirm Capwell's original findings. The scales on which delinquent boys and girls most clearly exceeded control group means were scales 4, 6, 7, 8, and 9. Scale 4 was the most different. In keeping with expectations, scales 1, 2, and 3 were not consistently elevated among the delinquent boys or girls. These studies also presented important differences between the genders. Delinquent girls seemed to have more tendencies toward sensitivity and feelings that they were unduly controlled, indicated by their elevations on scale 6. A subsequent follow-up of Capwell's samples (Hathaway, Hastings, Capwell & Bell, 1953) found that slight elevations on scale 6 seemed to be a positive factor in girls' adjustment. The interpersonal sensitivity indicated by scale 6 elevations proved to be beneficial later on.

These earlier studies led to a landmark 15-year prospective study, funded by the National Institute of Mental Health (NIMH) and the University of Minnesota Graduate School (Hathaway & Monachesi, 1963). A total of 15,300 ninth-graders from throughout Minnesota was assessed with the MMPI. In addition to MMPIs on each of these subjects, information was collected about them from schools, law enforcement agencies, and social service agencies. Subjects included 3,971 Minneapolis public school ninth-graders from the 1947–1948 school year, representing 89% of the total ninth-grade enrollment for that year. The rest of the sample, 11,329 subjects, was collected outside Minneapolis from 92 schools in 86 Minnesota communities during the spring of 1954. This extensive database was used to investigate the prediction of delinquency and other acting-out behaviors as well as to describe differences in adult and adolescent personality as measured by the MMPI. In their studies predicting delinquency and other behavior problems, Hathaway and Monachesi demonstrated the utility and validity of the MMPI with adolescents. The studies on adult-adolescent differences helped in understanding how to use the MMPI with adolescents. Williams (1986) summarized their findings about adult-adolescent differences into three main areas: (1) item endorsements, (2) code types, and (3) elevation. Over the years, other researchers documented these differences, including our work on the development of the MMPI-A (e.g., Butcher et al., 1992; Williams, Butcher, Ben-Porath & Graham, 1992).

Adult-Adolescent Differences on the MMPI

Item Endorsements

Item-level differences are perhaps the most basic distinction between adult and adolescent MMPI responding. These item differences are understandable when viewed from a developmental perspective (Williams, 1986; Williams et al., 1992). The first four items found by Hathaway and Monachesi (1963) to most differentiate boys from men illustrate this:

> I am neither gaining nor losing weight.
> My relatives are nearly all in sympathy with me.
> Sometimes at elections I vote for men about whom I know very little.
> I would like to hunt lions in Africa.

Ninth-grade boys, unlike men, are in the adolescent growth spurt, which accounts for their greater likelihood of reporting fluctuations in weight. Adolescents' increasing needs for autonomy, along with their proclivity for excitement and adventure (illustrated by their greater desire to hunt lions), can account for some increasing tension with family members. Because the elections in which they participate are usually within school settings, they are much more likely to know all the candidates. This contrasts with the dilemma faced by adults in a typical election.

It is interesting that both Hathaway and Monachesi's (1963) data set and the data from the MMPI Restandardization Project reveal that girls differ more from women than boys do from men (Williams et al., 1992). Girls and women have a far greater number of item-endorsement differences than do boys and men. Some of the differences in the earlier samples are related to gender roles, with girls endorsing more stereotypically feminine vocation items and preferring to flirt more than did women. For example, over half the girls but only 6% of the women report a preference to work with women in the Hathaway and Monachesi (1963) data set. However, the restandardization samples of girls and women do not differ in expressed preferences for being a nurse, dressmaker, or private secretary, as did the earlier samples (Williams et al., 1992).

Williams et al. (1992) summarized many of these adult-adolescent item differences. Adolescents tended to express greater interest in excitement and loud fun (e.g., "When I get bored I like to stir up some excitement"—True), coupled with greater dislike of intellectual pursuits (e.g., "I like to read about history"—False) relative to adults. Adolescents were more likely to endorse emotionality (e.g., "At times I feel like picking a fist fight with someone"—True; "At times I have fits of laughing and crying that I cannot control"—True).

Some of the items assessing more pathological problems in adults also demonstrated adult-adolescent response differences. For example, 45% of the normative boys and 46% of the normative girls admitted to having "strange and peculiar thoughts," compared with only 15% of normative men and 10% of normative women (Williams et al., 1992). Adolescents were more likely to report urges to do harmful or shocking things, ideas of reference, feelings of unreality, and peculiar and strange experiences. These items appeared on several of the validity and standard scales originally developed with adult samples. These item-level differences indicate that the items are not psychometrically equivalent with adults and adolescents. This may contribute to differential validity of these scales with adults and adolescents.

Code Types

A "no-high-point" profile type (i.e., one with no scales with a T score greater than 54) was used in early research on the MMPI. Hathaway and Monachesi (1963) were struck by the greater number of no-high-point profiles occurring in adults compared with adolescents. They wondered whether this profile type was indicative of normal personality. If so, their results suggested that normal personality was much more frequent among adults than among adolescents. However, subsequent studies did not support this definition of normal personality.

Hathaway and Monachesi's (1963) comparative data showed several other code-type differences as well. Adults, especially women, had more profiles suggestive of neuroses (i.e., elevations on scales 1, 2, and 3). Adolescents, even those in school populations, more often had sociopathic or psychotic profile types (i.e., elevations on scales 4, 8, and 9). The 4-9/9-4 code type was the most frequently occurring code type among adolescents in clinical settings (Marks, Seeman & Haller, 1974; Williams & Butcher, 1989b) as well as in delinquent (e.g., Peña, Megargee & Brody, 1996) and normative (e.g., Butcher et al., 1992) samples.

Code types have been the basis of MMPI interpretation for both adults and adolescents (Marks et al., 1974). Surprisingly, however, we were able to demonstrate only limited validity for the code-type approach with adolescents (Williams & Butcher, 1989b). In this study only the 4-6/6-4 code type had adequate empirical validity. Adolescents elevated on this code type seemed to have the most serious psychopathology. It is important to note that sample differences between ours and the Marks et al. (1974) study cannot account for our inability to support the validity of code types with adolescents. When using the earlier rules for defining code types, we demonstrated remarkable similarities in the two samples. Although there was good congruence between code types based on the earlier adolescent norms and the new MMPI-A norms, the MMPI-A manual advises clinicians to use caution in following the code-type approach with MMPI-A interpretations, suggesting that further research is needed (Butcher et al., 1992).

Peña and colleagues (1996), after finding few two-point code types in their sample of 162 delinquent boys that met minimal requirements for elevation (both coded scales ≥ 65) and definition (i.e., two-point code types in which the second-ranked scale is at least 5 T higher than the third), recommended continued caution in using MMPI-A code types with adolescents until there is adequate research on their empirical correlates. Such research requires the participation of several thousand adolescents to permit reliable observations of the characteristics of individuals with varying code types, which is not predicted to happen in the foreseeable future (Archer, 1997a).

Scale Elevations

Hathaway and Monachesi (1963) found that scale elevation is another important dimension differentiating adult and adolescent MMPI responding. This finding has been replicated many times subsequently, including in the large study reported by Marks et al. (1974) and the MMPI Restandardization Project (Butcher et al., 1992; Williams et al., 1992). Figures 9-1 and 9-2 illustrate the scale-elevation differences between adults and adolescents for MMPI-A normative sample boys and girls, respectively. These figures present the normative adolescents' mean scores on two adult norm sets (i.e., original MMPI and MMPI-2) and the adolescent norms presented by Marks et al. (1974). Normal adolescents score at least one standard deviation higher than adults on the original F, Pd, Pa, Pt, Sc, and Ma scales when using the original adult norms (Williams, Butcher & Graham, 1986). Elevation differences, although somewhat reduced, remain meaningful with the new MMPI-2 adult norms. Scale-elevation differences between adults and adolescents are most directly related to interpretation and led to the development of adolescent norms for the MMPI. However, the adolescent norms presented by Marks et al. (1974) do not yield mean scale T scores of 50 for normal adolescents, as is true for normal adults. Figures 9-1 and 9-2 illustrate that most adolescent mean scale scores are elevated at T scores of 55 to 60 on the Marks et al. (1974) norms. On the other hand, the MMPI-A norms produce mean scale scores of 50, which is consistent with the adult MMPI-2 mean scale scores.

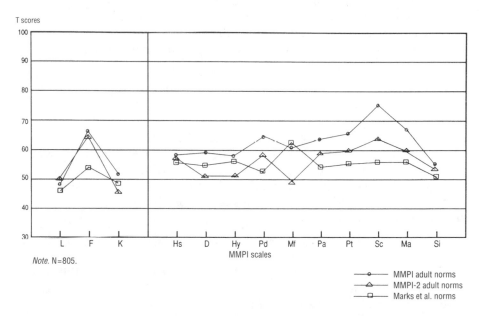

Figure 9-1. Boys' normative sample plotted on three different norms (N = 805).

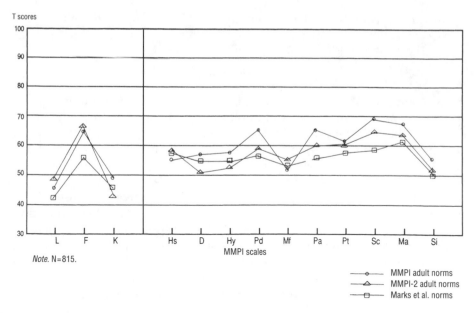

Figure 9-2. Girls' normative sample plotted on three different norms (N = 815).

The Norm Issue and Adolescents

Elevation differences between adults and adolescents led to the development of a separate norm set for adolescents. This was done despite opposition from Starke Hathaway and Elio Monachesi. They questioned whether it would be fairer to compare adolescents to other young people rather than to the average adult. Hathaway and Monachesi (1953a) argued that even though differences are recognized in adolescents and adults, society still judges the appropriateness of behavior using an adult standard:

> In light of this attitude, the application of adult norms to young people is proper and adjustment of the norms would obscure the very real fact that there is a significant, almost universal, quality in young people that makes them prone to socially unacceptable behavior. We want our scales to show behavior differences that are significant to society even if the implied personalities are "normal" for the age level. Since the core of society is the early adult and middle aged pattern of mores, the use of MMPI norms based chiefly on middle aged married persons can be justified even for young people. (p. 25)

Because of emphatic statements such as this from the test author, some argued for the exclusive use of adult norms in interpreting adolescents' profiles. Hathaway and Monachesi's (1961) *Atlas of Juvenile MMPI Profiles* used the adult norms to present information for over 1,000 profiles of adolescents from their extensive sample. However, the atlas approach to MMPI interpretation proved unwieldy and was never widely used.

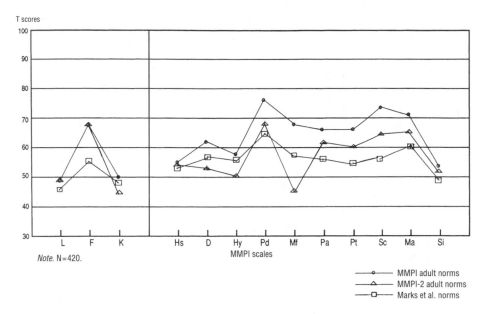

Figure 9-3. Boys' clinical sample plotted on three different norms (N = 420).

The first interpretative manual to extend the instrument's use to boys and girls as young as 12 or 13 was presented by Philip Marks and his colleagues (1974). This volume included an adolescent norm set to be used with their actuarial system. These norms were based on the Minnesota data collected by Hathaway and Monachesi (1963), combined with data from six other states. Peter Briggs worked with Marks et al. (1974) to develop these adolescent norms. Although Marks et al. (1974) developed and presented the most widely used adolescent norm set, they did not advocate its exclusive use. Rather, they indicated that there might be times, particularly for 17- and 18-year-olds, when the adult norm set would produce a more valid profile. Others, however, argued for the exclusive use of these adolescent-derived norms when interpreting MMPIs in this age range (e.g., Archer, 1984, 1987).

Unfortunately, use of the adolescent norms in clinical settings frequently produced false negative results (i.e., normal-limits profiles). Studies of adolescents in treatment for emotional and behavioral problems frequently yielded mean scores within normal limits (e.g., Ehrenworth & Archer, 1985; Klinge, Culbert & Piggott, 1982; Klinge, Lachar, Grisell & Berman, 1978; Lachar, Klinge & Grisell, 1976), a concern that lingers with the MMPI-A (Archer, 1997a; Janus, Tolbert, Calestro & Toepfer, 1996). Figure 9-3, mean scores of boys in clinical settings, and Figure 9-4, mean scores of girls in clinical settings, highlight this problem. Boys in the clinical sample used in the development of the MMPI-A produced a normal-limits profile on the Marks et al. (1974) adolescent norms (Figure 9-3). A similar pattern is evident for the clinical girls plotted on the adolescent norms, although the elevation on scale 4 approaches the T-score cutoff of 70 (Figure 9-4). By contrast, both sets of adult norms (i.e., MMPI and MMPI-2) produced clinically significant elevations on several scales.

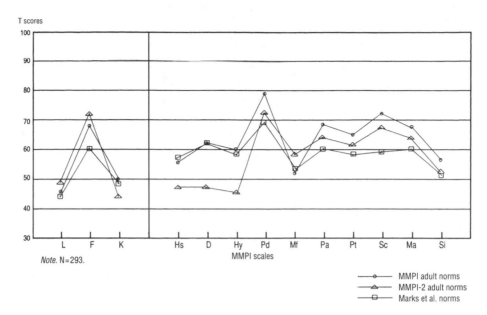

Figure 9-4. Girls' clinical sample plotted on three different norms (N = 293).

Two recommendations for interpretation evolved to handle the problem of fewer clinically meaningful elevations with the Marks et al. (1974) norms. Some suggested that profiles from both the adult and the adolescent norm sets be plotted for each adolescent (Graham, 1987; Williams, 1986). Interpretations would incorporate information from both norm sets. Another suggestion was to use an adolescent T-score cutoff of 65 rather than the traditional T-score cutoff of 70 for adults (Archer, 1987; Ehrenworth & Archer, 1985). However, a T-score cutoff of 65 was used in the code-type study described earlier and yielded only limited evidence of validity for code-type interpretations for adolescents.

In the 1980s, two additional adolescent norm sets were introduced as potential replacements for the Marks et al. (1974) adolescent norms (i.e., Colligan & Offord, 1989; Gottesman, Hanson, Kroeker & Briggs, 1987). These norm sets were included as appendices in Archer (1987). Both norm sets were limited for clinical use. Neither had been studied to determine the validity of MMPI interpretations based on its scores, and one study suggested that each of these potential replacements was roughly equivalent to the Marks et al. (1974) norms in discriminating among adolescents in outpatient, inpatient, and normal settings (Klinefelter, Pancoast, Archer & Pruitt, 1990). The Gottesman et al. (1987) adolescent norms were actually based on a reanalysis of the original Hathaway and Monachesi data set collected in the 1940s and 1950s.

The norms offered by Colligan and Offord (1989) had limited clinical applications for several reasons. Their MMPI profiles were collected from adolescents in three midwestern states near Rochester, Minnesota (Minnesota, Iowa, and Wisconsin), raising questions about the norms' generalizability to youth from other areas. Their design included mailing the instrument to the subjects' homes, which did not ensure the required supervised administration. Another important limitation was the use of a procedure to generate T scores that yielded results not comparable to traditional MMPI T scores. Rather than using linear T scores, as Hathaway and McKinley (1940) did with the original MMPI norms for adults and as Marks et al. (1974) did with the adolescent norms, Colligan and Offord used a normalized T-score approach. Normalizing procedures result in T-score distributions that are artificially restricted in range. The normalizing procedure thus resulted in considerable attenuation of T scores at clinically meaningful levels of scale elevation.

After clinicians using the original MMPI decided on norms, they next faced the issue of which descriptors to use to derive interpretive statements. Until 1989 there were two primary sources of MMPI descriptors: the adult code-type and scale literature (e.g., Graham, 1977, 1987) and the Marks et al. (1974) adolescent code-type correlates. In 1989 we provided additional information in the form of scale descriptors (Williams & Butcher, 1989a). Table 9-1 summarizes the different interpretive strategies that evolved for interpreting adolescents' MMPI profiles based on the use of various combinations of norms and descriptors. We look briefly at the adult interpretive approach, adolescent interpretive approach, mixed interpretive approach, combined interpretive approach, and scale descriptor interpretive approach.

Strategies for Interpreting Adolescents' MMPI Profiles

The interpretive strategies described in Table 9-1 evolved over the years as research accumulated on the use of the MMPI with adolescents. As we have seen, one of the test authors, Starke Hathaway, did not believe that special norms were required in interpreting the instrument for adolescents. Instead, he suggested that adolescents' mean scores and two standard deviations above the mean be plotted on any individual adolescent's profile. Hathaway probably agreed with the theory that adolescence was a time of "storm and stress" (Hall, 1904) and preferred not to disguise what he believed to be an essential feature of adolescence. However, the first comprehensive approach to interpreting MMPI profiles for adolescents provided age-appropriate norms and code-type descriptors from samples of adolescents as a source of interpretive statements (Marks et al., 1974). When clinicians discovered problems with the accuracy of interpretations based on either the adult or the adolescent interpretive approaches, the next strategy emerged (i.e., the mixed interpretive approach). This approach drew on both previous methods with its recommendation to use the adolescent norm set (Marks et al., 1974) along with adult descriptors (e.g., Graham, 1987).

Only one empirical study examined the accuracy of these three primary adolescent interpretive strategies (Ehrenworth & Archer, 1985). In it, clinicians rated the accuracy of narrative reports based on the three approaches. Both the adult and the mixed interpretive strategies were rated more accurate than the adolescent interpretive approach. A partial replication of this study demonstrated higher accuracy ratings for two sets of adolescent norms, (i.e., the ones developed by Marks and Briggs and the new MMPI-A norms) when compared with the original MMPI adult K-corrected norms (Janus et al., 1996).

Table 9-1. Examples of the Differing Interpretive Strategies Developed for Use of the Original MMPI with Adolescents

---

ADULT INTERPRETIVE APPROACH

This approach was essentially the same as used when deriving interpretations from adults' MMPI profiles. It was based on the adult norms and adult scale and code-type descriptors. It assumed that no special procedures were required for interpreting adolescents' profiles.

ADOLESCENT INTERPRETIVE APPROACH

The Marks, Seeman, and Haller (1974) book was the basis for this strategy. Their age-appropriate norms and code-type descriptors were used to derive interpretive statements. However, Marks et al. suggested that this approach be used in combination with the adult interpretive approach, particularly with older adolescents.

MIXED INTERPRETIVE APPROACH

This strategy used the adolescent norms (Marks et al., 1974) in combination with the adult MMPI code-type descriptors available in interpretive manuals such as Graham's (1987). It evolved because of problems with the accuracy of interpretations based on the two previous approaches (i.e., the adult and adolescent interpretive strategies).

COMBINED INTERPRETIVE APPROACH

This strategy was developed by Archer (1987) after a review of the literature. He combined adolescent descriptors found in Marks et al. (1974) with the adult-derived descriptors available in Graham (1977), Greene (1980), and Lachar (1974), providing narrative descriptions for 29 different code types. These descriptors began with statements found to be common in the adolescent and adult sources and concluded with information found in one but not the other. Subsequently, Archer (1992, 1997b) recommended this strategy for the MMPI-A.

SCALE DESCRIPTOR INTERPRETIVE APPROACH

We suggested a scale descriptor interpretive approach based on empirical findings as an interim strategy to be used until the MMPI-A became available (i.e., Williams & Butcher, 1989a, 1989b).

The last two approaches in Table 9-1 were developed in the 1980s as interim procedures until the MMPI-A became available. The combined interpretive approach was presented by Archer (1987) based on descriptors found in the literature until 1986. Archer (1992, 1997b) continued to recommend this strategy for the MMPI-A. After our studies on the MMPI standard scales and code types (Williams & Butcher, 1989a, 1989b), we recommended the scale descriptor interpretive approach. Given our findings, it seemed more prudent to rely on scale descriptors rather than code-type descriptors (Greene, 1991). Because of problems that had earlier been identified with the adolescent norm set described previously, raw-score cutoffs rather than T scores were provided for generating interpretations as an interim strategy to be used until the MMPI-A became available. As described in the following chapters, interpretations based on the MMPI-A use a variation of the scale elevation approach (Ben-Porath & Davis, 1996; Butcher et al., 1992; Peña et al., 1996). However, age-appropriate T scores rather than raw scores were provided for the MMPI-A.

Problems with Using the Original MMPI with Adolescents

Although almost from its inception the MMPI was used with young people for both research and clinical purposes, its use in this age range was controversial in spite of positive findings about its reliability and validity. Despite its wide use and research with adolescents, the test did not have the same extensive research base with this population that it did with adults. Even after Dora Capwell's and Elio Monachesi's careful preliminary studies, Hathaway and Monachesi (1953b) noted concerns about the possible inappropriateness of some of the MMPI items for younger adolescents. Because of this, Hathaway and Monachesi speculated that it might be best to use the instrument only at upper grade levels. However, because their research focused on the development of juvenile delinquency, the MMPI was used with younger adolescents.

Hathaway and Monachesi (1953b) recognized an abrupt rise in the incidence of juvenile delinquency at approximately age 14. Thus, they felt compelled to begin their large prospective study with comparatively younger children in the ninth grade. Because of the possibility that parents or others might object to MMPI item content, Hathaway and Monachesi (1953b) designed a pilot study to determine whether there would be adverse reactions to testing school children with the MMPI. They selected a school with a ninth-grade enrollment of 192 students and solicited the cooperation of the principal, counselors, and teachers. These staff members became actively interested in the project. Two-hour periods were set aside for the testing, and boys and girls were segregated during the testing sessions. (Such segregation did not prove feasible, or particularly necessary, during their later data collection.)

Test instructions addressed the possibility of inappropriate or objectionable item content and advised use of the Cannot Say response category when necessary. Instructions used with adolescents were as follows:

> This is a test to study personality. The study is being made by the University and your records will be kept by them. No one will look at your answers to individual questions because the grades depend on counting up the marks only. The test has a great many statements about people, what they are like, and what they think. It is used to aid in advising men and women about jobs and other problems. We want to see if it will be a help when taken by persons who are younger. So we arc asking you to do it. You may find that some of the statements don't fit you at all, or they won't fit you until you are older. If you find any of these answer them the best you can or leave them blank, but try to answer every statement. Work quickly, but don't be careless. Some statements will be in the past tense, for example: 'My father was.' Answer as though in the present if your father is still living and you are with him. (Hathaway & Monachesi, 1953b, p. 88)

The boys and girls were instructed to read the directions printed on the Hankes answer sheet and to feel free to ask for any other information they needed. Teachers and other supervisors were available to answer questions. Furthermore, the test administrators wandered about the room unobtrusively, watching for children who appeared to be "in any way bewildered by the MMPI." It was common for students to inquire about the meaning of a word or whether he or she should answer it in a particular way. The examiners were instructed to evade direct responses.

Hathaway and Monachesi (1953b) indicated that these test instructions and administration procedures resulted in very few problems during the testing. Following the pilot test, the teachers and counselors were instructed to be alert to any discussion among the children or others that might be related to the MMPI. Four months were allowed to elapse before large-scale testing proceeded in other schools. No disturbing events or adverse reactions were reported during this 4-month period. Researchers were gratified by this because the trial school was more culturally, economically, and socially diverse than most other schools in their sample.

Thus, Hathaway and Monachesi (1953a, 1953b) set the precedent for using the MMPI with adolescents. No attempts were made to change the item content, and very few attempts were made to improve the scales for adolescents (Williams et al., 1992). An instrument written and developed for adults was simply adopted for use with adolescents. No structural changes were made. It became widely used with adolescents despite recognized problems and criticism of this practice.

Table 9-2 summarizes the problems with using the original MMPI with adolescents. These problems occur at several levels, including item, scale, norm, interpretation, and general criticisms. Many may be related to failure to adapt the instrument for adolescents. The most general problem is the more limited research base on the use of the MMPI with adolescents. As we have seen, this has contributed to the employment of the many idiosyncratic procedures for interpreting MMPI profiles for adolescents described in Table 9-1.

Many of the item-level problems noted in Table 9-2 apply equally as well to adults, although adolescents seem to be even more distracted when encountering them. The out-of-date phrases and awkward wording characteristic of the original instrument, written during the 1930s and not updated until the MMPI Restandardization Project, tended to annoy and confuse adolescents. These stylistic problems exacerbated the comprehension difficulties of younger adolescents, who had more limited reading abilities. Early on, Hathaway and Monachesi (1953b) noted that the sexual behavior items were not as relevant for adolescents as adults yet were surprised that they did not pose a major problem during testing sessions. However, as people became more familiar with the MMPI and its content, the sexual behavior items became more associated with the instrument, which sometimes led to difficulties in administering the instrument in school settings, particularly those serving younger adolescents (Butcher et al., 1992; Crewe & Crewe, 1973). It is interesting that Hathaway and Monachesi (1953b) recognized that a shorter version of the MMPI might be better for use with adolescents.

In one normative data collection site for the MMPI Restandardization Project, Regis High School in New York City, we used a brief follow-up questionnaire to survey students' reactions to the MMPI (Williams, Ben-Porath & Hevern, 1994). The items that bothered the young people most were of a fairly consistent type. These were items without face validity, including questions about "fixing door latches" and "liking mannish women" and items about bowel and bladder functioning. This offensive content was eliminated from the MMPI-A.

Table 9-2. Problems in Using the Original MMPI with Adolescents

ITEM PROBLEMS	SCALE AND NORM PROBLEMS	INTERPRETATION PROBLEMS	GENERAL CRITICISMS
• The MMPI's content was sometimes confusing to today's adolescents owing to out-of-date phrases, awkward wording, and other stylistic problems.	• Scales developed specifically for adolescent populations were not available.	• Predictive and descriptive accuracy for adolescents was lower than for adults.	• There was not one widely used method of interpreting MMPI profiles from adolescents, resulting in several idiosyncratic procedures being used.
• Some items were not appropriate for young adolescents.	• No research data were available from adolescents for the potentially useful content scales, subscales, or other special scales. No adolescent norms were available for these scales. (The one notable exception was the MacAndrew Alcoholism Scale).	• Many interpretive statements were available only from research on adult populations.	• Much less research was available about the use of the MMPI with adolescents.
• The limited item pool did not have themes specific to adolescents and their problems.		• Code types, and thus the resulting interpretations, would change dramatically when going from adult to adolescent norms.	
• Items did not directly assess important problems that occurred more frequently with today's adolescents (e.g., eating problems, suicide, marijuana and other drug use).	• Scale norms were out-of-date, based on responses from adolescents in the 1940s to 1960s.	• Often the interpretations based on the adolescent code-type descriptors provided by Marks et al. (1974) differed from interpretations based on the adult code-type descriptors.	
• The limited item pool did not measure other important areas: personal strengths, motivations for treatment, or change potential.	• Results of available research studies were equivocal about which norms (i.e., adolescent or adult) were most appropriate to use with an adolescent patient, although some studies suggested that the adolescent norms might be more appropriate.	• Use of potentially valid content measures was hampered because of limited research with adolescents.	
• There were too many items for an adolescent to answer, and some adolescents in clinical settings did not have an adequate reading level or the necessary attention and concentration skills to successfully complete the test.	• Mean profiles of adolescents in clinical settings scored on adolescent norms were in the normal range.	• Williams and Butcher (1989a) was the only source of MMPI standard-scale descriptors from a large adolescent clinical sample.	
	• Practice dictated adding a K correction to scales 1, 4, 7, 8, and 9 when using adult norms. The K correction was not used with adolescent norms, which further contributed to the differences between the two sets of norms.	• Williams and Butcher (1989b) found only limited validity for the code-type approach in their large adolescent clinical study.	
	• Other adolescent norms were proposed during the 1980s, but none were derived from a contemporary, nationwide, representative sample of adolescents.		

Very little scale development for adolescents was done using the original MMPI. For example, no age-appropriate norms were ever provided for the Wiggins content scales, Harris-Lingoes subscales, and other supplementary MMPI scales. Although the MacAndrew Alcoholism Scale (MAC-R) was an exception to this generalization, this lack of scale development hampered the interpretation process. Until the development of the MMPI-A, the use of content measures to enhance interpretation had limited research support, including the lack of a set of adolescent norms.

The different strategies described in Table 9-1 highlighted many of the interpretation problems with the original instrument. A basic issue was that predictive and descriptive accuracy for adolescents appeared to be lower than for adults, perhaps because many interpretive statements were available only from research on adult populations. The code-type approach was shown to have limited validity with adolescents, and code types would change dramatically when going from adult to adolescent norms. When the code type changed, the resulting interpretation also changed (Williams, 1986). Despite all these problems, there were clear advantages in using the MMPI with adolescents and even greater advantages associated with the MMPI-A.

Highlight Summary: Advantages of Using the MMPI-A

From its inception, the MMPI had been used with both adults and adolescents. It was essentially an adult-derived instrument, adopted without modifications of its basic structure (i.e., item content or scales) for younger test takers. Problems in using the MMPI with adolescents had been apparent over the years, leading to different interpretive strategies. However, even given these problems, the MMPI's reliability, validity, and utility in assessing psychopathology in adolescents had been demonstrated. Many of the difficulties in using the instrument with adolescents were addressed during the restandardization of the MMPI. In addition to collecting contemporary normative and clinical data for determining norms and descriptors, improvements were made in the items and scales to make the MMPI-A more relevant for younger people and easier to interpret.

Table 9-3 describes the advantages of the MMPI-A. The general advantages apply equally well to the original instrument and its newest version, the MMPI-A (see also Chapter 1, Table 1-1, for other advantages). Practitioners and researchers choose the MMPI-A or MMPI-2 over other personality measures because of its cost-effectiveness or ability to provide a large amount of clinically relevant information using limited professional time (Ben-Porath & Davis, 1996; Klump & Butcher, 1997).

Adolescents, even those who are reluctant to admit to problems in clinical interviews, frequently are willing to disclose psychological problems with their responses to MMPI items. One of the 16 case studies described by Ben-Porath and Davis (1996) provided a dramatic illustration of the MMPI-A's ability to alert clinicians to issues that have yet to surface. Kyle (case 11 in Ben-Porath & Davis, 1996), who initially was quiet and withdrawn on admission to an acute care center, was put under close supervision after his MMPI-A profile suggested poor impulse

Table 9-3. Advantages of Using the MMPI-A

GENERAL	ITEM	SCALE	NORM/ DESCRIPTOR	INTERPRETATION
• A wide variety of psychological problems is assessed with the MMPI-A, which requires little professional time for administration.	• 70 items with problematic wording were rewritten for the MMPI-A booklet.	• Continuity between the original MMPI and the MMPI-A was maintained for several validity scales, the clinical scales, and MAC, A, and R.	• MMPI-A scale norms were based on a contemporary sample, selected from several regions of the United States, and included minority youth.	• The MMPI-A manual presents one norm set to use with adolescents. This eliminates the need for multiple interpretive strategies, based on different norms, for adolescents.
• Many adolescents who are reluctant to admit to problems in clinical interviews will respond less defensively to the MMPI-A.	• Offensive items that were eliminated from the MMPI-2 booklet were also deleted from the MMPI-A. In addition, some items assuming sexual activities were eliminated because they were objectionable for youth and did not necessarily have the same psychological meaning.	• Scales 5 and 0, two rather long scales on the MMPI and MMPI-2, were shortened on the MMPI-A without significant psychometric cost.	• MMPI-A norms, like the MMPI-2 norms, were based on a uniform T-score transformation that ensured percentile equivalence across the different MMPI scale scores.	• The same cutoff for clinical interpretations (i.e., T score of 65) is recommended for the MMPI-A and MMPI-2. However, for adolescents, clinicians are advised to consider scales elevated in the 60 to 64 T-score range as yielding potentially useful descriptors.
• Most adolescents like the true-false format of the MMPI-A.	• Unique items with adolescent-specific themes, including peer-group influences, family relations, and issues about school and teachers, were added to MMPI-A.	• MMPI-2 scales were not simply assumed to work with adolescents. Rather, statistical analyses using adolescent samples and rational procedures that included a developmental perspective were used in refining or developing the F scale (including F_1 and F_2), VRIN, TRIN, the MMPI-A content scales, and two scales assessing alcohol and other drug problems.	• Both the MMPI-A and the MMPI-2 norms were developed using the same target distribution, ensuring percentile equivalence across the two forms. Thus, as a person ages, his or her MMPI-A and MMPI-2 T scores can be compared directly.	• Interpretation can be based on scales and descriptors derived from studies of adolescents.
• The MMPI-A can be scored quickly and accurately by computer. A number of content scales, subscales, and special scales are available through computer scoring. The test can be adapted for computer administration, a format that many adolescents prefer.	• Items were added to assess problems more commonly seen in contemporary treatment settings serving adolescents, including eating problems, suicidal behavior, and alcohol and other drug problems.		• Descriptors were derived from the normative sample and a large clinical sample of boys and girls. Thus, with the MMPI-A, scale descriptors based on adolescent responding (not adult responding) were presented separately by gender and by normative or treatment settings.	• Code-type congruence between the MMPI-A and original adolescent norms is substantial, allowing for use of the original Marks, Seeman, and Haller (1974) adolescent code-type descriptors. However, the contemporary MMPI-A samples do not provide evidence for the validity of the code-type descriptors. Future studies are needed to demonstrate the validity of code-type descriptors.
• The MMPI-2 can be used with parents and the MMPI-A with adolescent siblings of clients, thus reducing the tendency to single out the referred adolescent as the only family member with problems.	• MMPI-2 items used to develop the Negative Treatment Indicators content scale were also included in the MMPI-A.	• Some of the MMPI-A content scales were developed from the adolescent-specific items and thus are unique on the MMPI-A. Other MMPI-A content scales, such as A-fam, were revised with the addition of adolescent-specific content.	• A Spanish version of the MMPI-A is available with Hispanic norms.	
• A feedback session with the adolescent can be used for relationship building and gathering further information.				

control, substantial risk of suicidal gestures, and possible initial symptoms of a psychotic disorder. One day after the MMPI-A was administered, Kyle became floridly psychotic and extremely combative. Because the staff had been alerted to this possibility by the MMPI-A, they responded quickly and supportively, thus preventing harm to Kyle and those around him.

Ease of scoring the MMPI increased with the advent of computer scoring. This scoring method allowed many different scales, including content scales, subscales, and special scales, to be scored quickly and accurately. The computer-administered adaptation of the test seemed to be preferred by adolescents. Young people also liked the true-false style of the questions, and its objective nature makes it easy to administer in settings such as schools.

A clear advantage of the MMPI-A and MMPI-2 is that they can be used with other family members, including parents and adolescent siblings. This reduces the frequently occurring tendency in treatment settings to single out the referred adolescent as the only family member with problems. Adolescent clients are more willing to complete the MMPI-A knowing that their parents and/or siblings will be completing a similar instrument. The therapeutic use of feedback sessions for adolescents is described in Chapter 14.

Although many of the general advantages listed in Table 9-3 were relevant for using both the MMPI and the MMPI-A with adolescents, the item, scale, norm/ descriptor, and interpretation advantages apply only to the MMPI-A. These advantages resulted from changes made in the original instrument. As indicated previously, the item-level problems were originally handled through instructions given to the subjects. However, the MMPI Restandardization Committee actually changed the item content to make the instrument more appropriate for young people. Some of the item-level changes were common to both the MMPI-2 and the MMPI-A (i.e., rewording awkward items, eliminating offensive items, and including items to assess amenability to treatment). Other item-level changes were implemented to make the instrument more appropriate for adolescents. Items with adolescent-specific themes, including peer-group influences, family relations, and school issues, were added to the MMPI-A. Items that are objectionable for youth and that do not have the same psychological meaning as they have for adults were eliminated. Hathaway and Monachesi's (1953b) suggestion to shorten the instrument for adolescents was accomplished with the 478-item MMPI-A booklet (in contrast to the 567-item MMPI-2 booklet).

Most of the previous work on the original instrument with adolescents focused on the norm and descriptor levels. The new instrument offers improvements in these areas as well (Table 9-3). MMPI-A scale norms are based on a contemporary sample of adolescents selected from schools in several regions of the United States and include minority youth (Butcher et al., 1992). The uniform T-score transformation (Tellegen & Ben-Porath, 1992), which ensured percentile equivalence across the different MMPI scale scores, was used on the MMPI-A norms, as it was for the MMPI-2. Both the MMPI-A and MMPI-2 norms were developed using the same target distribution, which ensured percentile equivalence across the two forms. This means that as a person ages, his or her MMPI-A and MMPI-2 T scores can be compared directly. In addition, a Spanish-language version of MMPI-A is available from National Computer Systems. Butcher et al. (1998) collected a large sample of Spanish-speaking adolescents from Puerto Rico, Florida, California, and Mexico and developed separate Hispanic norms for the MMPI-A.

Several scale-level advantages are apparent on the MMPI-A. As for the MMPI-2, continuity between the original instrument and the MMPI-A was maintained for the original L and K validity scales, the standard scales, MAC-R, and supplementary scales Anxiety (A) and Repression (R). Scales 5 and 0, which were quite long on the original instrument and on the MMPI-2, were shortened on the MMPI-A without significant psychometric cost. Whereas continuity was maintained with the original scales of the MMPI, the new features of the MMPI-2 were not simply assumed to work with adolescents. More specifically, the MMPI-2 content scales were reexamined to determine their appropriateness for adolescents and then submitted to similar rational and statistical procedures using adolescent samples (Williams et al., 1992). Similarly, the MMPI-A contains VRIN and TRIN scales that were developed specifically for adolescents by Tellegen and his colleagues. Finally, the F validity scale was revised significantly for the MMPI-A.

Descriptors for the MMPI-A scales are based on data from adolescent normative and clinical samples (e.g., Butcher et al., 1992; Williams et al., 1992). These descriptors are presented separately by gender because, like Hathaway and Monachesi (1963), we found some differences between the genders. Clinicians, for the first time, have clinically relevant scale descriptors based on adolescent responding (not adult responding) presented separately by gender and by normative and clinical settings. Several new studies provide additional sources for scale descriptors (e.g., Basham, 1992; Cashel, Rogers, Sewell & Holliman, 1998; Gallucci, 1994; Kopper, Osman, Osman & Hoffman, 1998; Wrobel & Lachar, 1992).

The MMPI-A has several other substantive interpretation advantages, as indicated in Table 9-3. One norm set is provided, which will greatly reduce the number of idiosyncratic strategies for adolescents. The same cutoff score for clinical interpretations (i.e., T score of 65) is recommended for the MMPI-A and MMPI-2. Clinicians with expertise in MMPI-2 interpretation will be able to use their skills with the new instrument. Clinicians are also advised to consider moderately elevated scales in the 60 to 64 T-score range on the MMPI-A as possibly yielding significant descriptors. More precise interpretive guidelines are presented in the following chapters.

Chapters 10 and 11 focus on the MMPI-A validity and standard scales, which have the most overlap with the original MMPI and its successor, the MMPI-2. Chapter 12 presents the MMPI-A content scales. Chapter 13 describes relatively newer measures for the MMPI-A: the supplementary scales, the PSY-5 scales, and a set of critical items developed especially for the MMPI-A. The MMPI-A content scales, the PSY-5 scales, and the MMPI-A critical item set contributed to the improvement of the MMPI-A over its predecessor, the MMPI. These measures represented the first time that adolescent samples and item content relevant to adolescence were used rather than just assuming that adult-derived measures would work the same with adolescents as with adults or that adolescents should be judged using the same standards as adults. Chapter 14 integrates information from across the MMPI-A, providing an interpretive strategy to use. Chapter 15 concludes with a description of computerized scoring and interpretation for the MMPI-A and MMPI-2.

Chapter 10

Interpreting the MMPI-A Validity Measures

One of the most effective ways to identify malingering and deception in psychological assessment is to use standardized tests such as the MMPI-A and MMPI-2 with their validity scales and indicators (McCann, 1998). Because the MMPI-A and MMPI-2 are based on self-report, it is crucial to first know the attitude of the person completing these inventories before interpreting his or her other scores. The accuracy of an MMPI-A interpretation is dependent on the degree to which the individual responds honestly to the MMPI-A item pool in providing a self-description. If an individual distorts his or her answers to MMPI-A items, the precision of the interpretation can be compromised.

Although many see a person's willingness to be honest as imperative in interpreting content-based measures, individuals who distort their answers also constrain the validity of the empirically derived standard scales. Because of this, Hathaway and his colleagues included validity indicators in the original instrument that were maintained in the MMPI-A and MMPI-2. These indicators address whether the individual responds inconsistently, misunderstands items, or exaggerates psychological symptoms and problems.

Proper administration and instructions are effective in reducing response sets that can compromise the accuracy of an MMPI-A interpretation (see Chapter 2). However, even after ensuring that a young person has the necessary reading level for the instrument (sixth grade), understands the purpose of the testing, and knows that he or she will be given feedback about the MMPI-A interpretation, there are times when adolescents distort their responses (Ben-Porath & Davis, 1996; McCann, 1998). Thus, the first step in interpreting an adolescent's MMPI-A is to determine whether he or she responded to the items openly and honestly and produced a valid test profile (Ben-Porath & Davis, 1996; McCann, 1998). Note that profile validity refers to the quality of information contained in a set of scores produced by a given individual; it is distinguished from test validity, which is a psychometric concept referring to an instrument's ability to measure what it is intended to measure (Ben-Porath & Davis, 1996). Even though the test validity of the MMPI-A has been established through psychometric studies, an individual adolescent may produce an invalid MMPI-A profile for a number of reasons.

Ben-Porath and Davis (1996) described two broad classes of threats to MMPI-A profile validity: random and nonrandom responding. Random responding occurs when an adolescent provides indiscriminant and nonsystematic responses, which can result in inconsistent responses to MMPI-A items with similar content. For example, a True response to the item "I am bothered by an upset stomach several times a week" is inconsistent with a False response to a similar item: "I have a great deal of stomach trouble." To complicate matters further, random responding may not be due only to dissimulation; it may result also from poor reading skills, verbal comprehension difficulties, or clinical conditions, such as psychosis or extreme mental confusion (McCann, 1998).

At least one random response to the 478 items of the MMPI-A is probably not unusual, given that 73% of a general population sample of adolescents reported doing so on a feedback form completed immediately after a testing session (Baer, Ballenger, Berry & Wetter, 1997). When asked about three possible explanations for their random responses, these adolescents were more likely to acknowledge difficulty understanding items and difficulty deciding on a response, rather than lapses in concentration, as reasons for random responses. Participants also reported that their random answers tended to be scattered throughout the booklet, not in any particular location. However, lapses in concentration (likely to occur more frequently at the end of the booklet) may be more common in clinical samples.

The average number of random responses by adolescents in the study by Baer et al. (1997) was almost 14 items. This level of random responding did not appear to compromise the validity of the adolescents' MMPI-A profiles. Also reassuring was that although adolescents reported difficulty in deciding on a response, this was not significantly related to their scores on the MMPI-A validity measures of inconsistent responding, suggesting that they were able to respond consistently even when they reported some difficulty in selecting the appropriate response (Baer et al., 1997).

Two types of nonrandom responding can compromise profile validity: fixed responding and misleading responding (Ben-Porath & Davis, 1996). Fixed responding is also referred to as "yea-saying" or "nay-saying" (i.e., giving either True or False responses without considering the item's content). In contrast, when an adolescent gives a misleading response, he or she has understood the item but is not giving an accurate self-description with his or her answer. The MMPI literature classifies misleading responses into two broad categories,: "fake good" (i.e., defensiveness) and "fake bad" (i.e., malingering or exaggerated responding). Ben-Porath and Davis (1996) suggest that although adolescents' misleading responses are usually intentional, that is not always the case. For example, some young people may be in such a crisis state that they unintentionally exaggerate their symptoms, whereas others may have been raised with such rigid moral standards that they claim many unusually virtuous behaviors that unintentionally misrepresent their actual behaviors.

Overview of the MMPI-A Validity Measures

The MMPI-A provides six primary measures for determining whether an adolescent's response style may be compromising the validity of his or her self-report. The six measures, as well as the two subscales of the F scale, can be grouped into two categories: (1) measures of defensiveness and fixed responding (i.e., yea- or nay-saying) and (2) measures of random and exaggerated responding. In some

Table 10-1. The MMPI, MMPI-A, and MMPI-2 Validity Indicators

Category and name	Abbreviation	Number of items		
		MMPI	MMPI-A	MMPI-2
Defensiveness and fixed responding				
Cannot Say indicator	? or Cs	Varies	Varies	Varies
Lie scale	L	15	14	a
Defensiveness scale	K	30	a	a
Inconsistency scale	TRIN	NA	21 item pairs	20 item pairs
Exaggerated and random responding				
Infrequency scale	F	64[b]	66[b]	60[b]
Infrequency subscale 1	F_1	NA	33	NA
Infrequency subscale 2	F_2	NA	33	NA
Variable Response Inconsistency scale	VRIN	NA	42 item pairs	45 item pairs

Notes: NA = not available on this version of the instrument.
[a] Indicates item content identical with original MMPI.
[b] The item content for the MMPI-A and MMPI-2 F scales differs substantially. The MMPI-A item overlap with the original MMPI F scale is 58% (only 37 of the 64 original MMPI F scale items are on the MMPI-A), compared to a 94% item overlap between the MMPI-2 and MMPI versions of the F scale (i.e., only 4 items were deleted from the original 64 items for the MMPI-2 F scale).

cases, as in obviously fixed responding throughout the booklet—for example, an all-True pattern or an all-False pattern (see the section "Case Examples Highlighting Extreme Fixed Responding" in this chapter)—the response style is so problematic that the entire profile is invalidated. The individual simply did not comply with the test instructions by providing an accurate self-description using the MMPI-A items. In other, less extreme cases, the profile can be interpreted with adjustments, taking into consideration the response style used by the young person.

Table 10-1 lists the MMPI-A validity indicators and notes the differences in content and number of items in the MMPI, MMPI-A, and MMPI-2. Scales L, F, and K and the Cannot Say validity indicator were included on the original instrument. They were developed in studies using adult subjects and were used without any change when the original MMPI was administered to adolescents. On the MMPI-A, some revisions were made, most notably in the F scale. As shown in Table 10-1, the item content of the MMPI-A F scale is substantially different from the MMPI and MMPI-2 versions of F, with only 58% of its items (compared to 94% for the MMPI-2) overlapping with the original MMPI F scale. In addition, the MMPI-A F scale was divided into two subscales so that the validity of the entire booklet could be assessed. Two other measures of MMPI profile validity introduced in the MMPI-2 (Chapter 3) were included on the MMPI-A: the inconsistency measures VRIN and TRIN. The MMPI-2 has two validity scales that do not have counterparts in the MMPI-A: the Psychopathology Infrequency (F_p) scale and the Superlative Self-Presentation (S) scale.

As we noted in Chapter 3, there really is no right or wrong starting point for considering MMPI-2 or MMPI-A validity scales. Thus, this chapter follows a slightly different organizational structure from the structure used for the MMPI-2 in Chapter 3 (see Table 10-1). We describe Cs, L, K, and TRIN, followed by F, F_1, F_2, the F − K index, and VRIN. Case examples of problematic validity patterns are provided throughout the chapter, which concludes with Tony's case. First, however, we begin with some cautionary comments about using cutoff scores.

Cautions about Cutoff Scores

Cutoff scores are used to interpret the MMPI-A, including the validity indicators and scales. Cutoffs are usually provided using T scores, although sometimes raw scores are used. However, MMPI-A validity indicators and their cutoff scores should not be used to make simple categorical decisions (e.g., valid or invalid); a more sophisticated view treats profile validity as a continuous dimension with gradations between the extremes of valid and invalid (Ben-Porath & Davis, 1996). Furthermore, the accuracy of the cutoff scores is very much dependent on the base rate of the various threats to MMPI-A profile validity in a given setting.

Rates of honest responding, malingering, denial, and random responding or some other response style are likely to vary across settings (e.g., inpatient treatment units, school-based clinics, juvenile detention facilities), reasons for the testing (e.g., anonymous research participants, child-custody evaluations), and perhaps even how adolescents are treated during the test administration (e.g., informed about the purpose of the testing, given frequent breaks and encouragement). Unfortunately, there is very limited research on the prevalence of the various forms of invalid responding in the self-report of adolescents (Baer, Ballenger & Kroll, 1998; Baer et al., 1997; McCann, 1998; Rogers, Hinds & Sewell, 1996; Stein, Graham & Williams, 1995). For these reasons, we agree with Ben-Porath and Davis's (1996) recommendation of using cutoff scores, including those suggested in this book, as general interpretive guidelines, not as absolute indicators of a dichotomous outcome of valid versus invalid.

Measures of Defensiveness and Fixed Responding

Cannot Say (? or Cs) Score

As with the MMPI-2, the Cannot Say score (abbreviated by either ? or Cs) is not a scale but simply a count of items either left unanswered or marked both True and False by the young person. Because Cs items are not scored (i.e., they are omitted from the test), a large number of them can lead to lower scores on the MMPI-A scales. Cs raw scores of 30 or more raise concerns about the profile's validity.

The number of Cs items can be decreased by encouraging the individual to answer previously omitted items. If it is not possible to have the young person complete the omitted items, the psychologist should determine where on the answer sheet the items were omitted. If the omissions occurred after the first 350 items on the MMPI-A, the original validity (L, F, and K) and standard scales (Chapter 11) can be interpreted because all their items appear in items 1 to 350. However, VRIN, TRIN, the content scales (Chapter 12), and the supplementary measures (Chapter 13) should not be interpreted.

Computerized reports, such as The Minnesota Report™: Adolescent Interpretive System (Butcher & Williams, 1992), provide information that can make profile interpretation possible when 30 or more items have been omitted. The Minnesota Report™ includes a list of all omitted items, allowing the clinician to determine whether a pattern exists for the nonresponding (e.g., whether the adolescent refused items relating to family problems or psychotic symptoms). In addition, the percentage of items completed on each MMPI-A scale is printed on the profile sheets, allowing the clinician to determine whether the adolescent answered enough of a given scale's items to produce an accurate score. Scores on scales with 95% or more of their items answered can be interpreted because this is the equivalent of what is required for interpreting the full MMPI-A (i.e., ≤ 30 item omissions out of the 478 items). Clinically significant elevations on scales with more than 5% missing items can also be interpreted because omitted items tend to produce lower, not more elevated, scores. However, scales that are not clinically elevated and are missing more than 5% of their items should not be interpreted as indicating the absence of problems.

A young person may have a number of reasons for omitting items on the MMPI-A. The test interpreter should attempt to evaluate which reasons are likely to apply to the particular individual. One of the best ways to determine this is in an interview with the young person about his or her opinion of the MMPI-A and how he or she responded to the items. Some adolescents will indicate that they omitted a few items because they did not understand the meaning or because they considered them irrelevant to their life experiences. Carelessness, poor reading skills, or indecision also account for omitted items. Very depressed individuals may not have the energy to complete an MMPI-A. An overly defensive test-taking attitude is also related to high Cs responding. The interpretive report should address which of these reasons likely accounts for the individual's score. Guidelines for Cs interpretations are provided in Table 10-2.

Lie (L) Scale

Hathaway and Monachesi (1953a) indicated that the 15 items on the MMPI Lie (L) scale detected any naive attempt by a young person to put him- or herself in a favorable light, particularly with reference to personal ethics and social behavior. Individuals with high L scores were thought to be trying, sometimes unconsciously, to answer all the MMPI items in ways that denied even relatively minor flaws or weaknesses. One L item, about voting in elections, was dropped from the MMPI-A because it did not function as intended with adolescents.

As noted, the L scale was developed to detect a naive and virtuous presentation of self, alerting the interpreter to the possible presence of this response set. However, adolescents who come from very traditional or conservative backgrounds may produce higher-than-average scores on L because of their upbringing rather than because of a defensive response set (Ben-Porath & Davis, 1996). This alterna-

Table 10-2. Cs Interpretive Guidelines for the MMPI-A

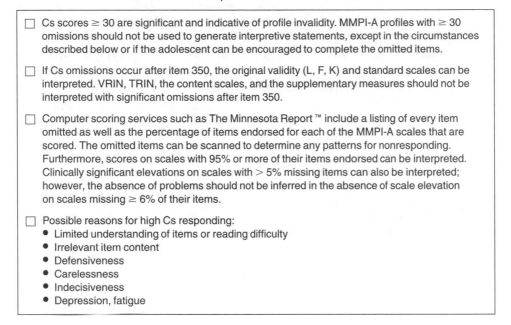

☐ Cs scores ≥ 30 are significant and indicative of profile invalidity. MMPI-A profiles with ≥ 30 omissions should not be used to generate interpretive statements, except in the circumstances described below or if the adolescent can be encouraged to complete the omitted items.

☐ If Cs omissions occur after item 350, the original validity (L, F, K) and standard scales can be interpreted. VRIN, TRIN, the content scales, and the supplementary measures should not be interpreted with significant omissions after item 350.

☐ Computer scoring services such as The Minnesota Report ™ include a listing of every item omitted as well as the percentage of items endorsed for each of the MMPI-A scales that are scored. The omitted items can be scanned to determine any patterns for nonresponding. Furthermore, scores on scales with 95% or more of their items endorsed can be interpreted. Clinically significant elevations on scales with > 5% missing items can also be interpreted; however, the absence of problems should not be inferred in the absence of scale elevation on scales missing ≥ 6% of their items.

☐ Possible reasons for high Cs responding:
  • Limited understanding of items or reading difficulty
  • Irrelevant item content
  • Defensiveness
  • Carelessness
  • Indecisiveness
  • Depression, fatigue

tive explanation for an L scale elevation can be ruled out by interviewing the adolescent or his or her parents.

Because the scored direction of all L scale items is False, adolescents who indiscriminately respond False (i.e., nay-sayers) are more likely to have elevated L scores. The converse is true: Adolescents who respond indiscriminately True (i.e., yea-sayers) are more likely to have lower-than-average L scores. The MMPI-A TRIN scale (see the following discussion) can be used to rule out nay-saying as an explanation for an elevated L score (Ben-Porath & Davis, 1996).

A T-score elevation in the shaded area on the profile (60–64) suggests a moderate elevation on L, requiring a cautionary statement in the interpretive report. Greater certainty of a problematic response set is indicated with higher elevations (i.e., T scores ≥ 65). An MMPI-A L score in these ranges, coupled with a flat MMPI-A profile on the standard, content, and supplementary scales (no T scores ≥ 60) should be interpreted as a defensive profile, not as the absence of significant psychopathology. However, when adolescents with this defensive test-taking attitude also achieve clinical elevations on the standard, content, or supplementary scales, problems are presented.

Support for the validity of the MMPI-A L scale in both community and clinical settings was provided in a study demonstrating that the scale was effective in distinguishing adolescents instructed to complete the MMPI-A as if they were trying to demonstrate excellent psychological adjustment from adolescents who received the standard instructions for completing the MMPI-A (Baer et al., 1998). The validity data presented in the MMPI-A manual (Butcher et al., 1992) support interpreting the L scale as a measure of naive defensiveness in adolescents. The higher their L score, the less likely the MMPI-A normative subjects were to be doing well

Table 10-3. L Interpretive Guidelines for the MMPI-A

☐ T scores ≥ 65 signify a high elevation on L indicative of a potentially problematic and defensive response set.
☐ T scores of 60 to 64, inclusive, on L are moderately elevated, suggestive of a possibly defensive response set.
☐ Absence of psychological problems should not be assumed with an elevated L score and normal-limits scale scores.
☐ Elevated MMPI-A scales should be interpreted in the presence of elevated L scores. The TRIN scale can be used to determine whether indiscriminate "nay-saying" accounts for the elevated L score.
☐ Clinical interviews or other methods can be used to indicate whether a very traditional or conservative upbringing may contribute to an elevated L score.
☐ Descriptive statements: • Naive and virtuous presentation of self   • Unwilling to admit to relatively minor flaws   • Claiming high moral and ethical code   • Somewhat unlikely to act out   • Possible "nay-saying" response set (use TRIN to rule out)

in school. High L adolescents in clinical samples were less likely to act out, in keeping with responses indicating a high moral or ethical code. Table 10-3 provides the interpretive rules for L scale elevations.

Defensiveness (K) Scale

The Defensiveness (K) scale was also developed to identify attempts to deny psychopathology and present an overly favorable picture by individuals with non-test evidence of significant psychopathology (i.e., those in clinical settings). It is similar to L in its purpose of identifying individuals who are defensive and not candid and in its ability to detect adolescents feigning excellent psychological health from those who were instructed to respond honestly (Baer et al., 1998). Hathaway and Monachesi (1953a) indicated that K was developed for adults in clinical settings as a correction for scores on five of the clinical scales (1, 4, 7, 8, and 9). However, the K correction was not routinely employed when the test was used with adolescents because its use as a correction factor had not been validated in this age range. The original adolescent norms presented by Marks, Seeman, and Haller (1974) did not include the K correction, nor is the K correction included in the new MMPI-A norms. A subsequent attempt to develop a K-correction procedure failed to produce systematic improvements in interpreting MMPI-A profiles (Alperin, Archer & Coates, 1996).

Few descriptors for the K scale were found for the adolescent normative or clinical restandardization samples (Butcher et al., 1992). Elevated T scores (i.e., in the shaded range of the profile or those ≥ 65) should include a cautionary statement about the possibility of a defensive test-taking attitude. The TRIN scale should be used to clarify elevations on K because all but one of the 30 K items are keyed False

Table 10-4. K Interpretive Guidelines for the MMPI-A

☐ T scores ≥ 65 signify a high elevation on K indicative of the presence of a potentially problematic defensive response set.
☐ T scores of 60 to 64, inclusive, on K are moderately elevated, suggestive of a possible defensive response set.
☐ The TRIN scale can be used to determine whether indiscriminate "nay-saying," or False responding, accounts for the elevated K score or, alternatively, whether indiscriminate "yea-saying," or True responding, accounts for a very low K score.
☐ MMPI-A profiles should not be declared uninterpretable based solely on elevated K scores.
☐ The K correction is not used for any MMPI-A scale.
☐ Absence of psychological problems should not be assumed with an elevated K score and normal-limits scale scores.

(see the following discussion). However, an adolescent's MMPI-A profile should not be invalidated solely on the basis of K. Table 10-4 summarizes the interpretive guidelines for K.

True Response Inconsistency (TRIN) Scale

The True Response Inconsistency (TRIN) scale is a measure of inconsistent responding developed by Tellegen (1988) for the MMPI-2 and adapted for the MMPI-A. Like its companion VRIN, the MMPI-A TRIN was developed from the MMPI-A item pool and with adolescent samples (Tellegen, 1991). The MMPI-2 TRIN scale was not simply incorporated in the MMPI-A, although the scales have some items in common. The MMPI-A TRIN scale is made up of 24 item-response pairs for which the same response is inconsistent. For example, answering True to both "I have no close friends" and "I have a close friend whom I can share secrets with" is inconsistent.

TRIN assesses the tendencies toward indiscriminate yea-saying (True-response inconsistency) or nay-saying (False-response inconsistency). All TRIN T scores are equal to or greater than 50. T scores above 50 are followed by a T or F (e.g., 61T, 72F), indicating a True or False pattern of inconsistency. Elevations on TRIN distinguish indiscriminate yea- or nay-saying from the patterns obtained by adolescents seen in clinical settings. For example, a TRIN score of 120T indicates that at least 21 (raw score for girls) or 22 (raw score for boys) of its 24 item pairs were endorsed as True regardless of their content, which could signal the extreme "all-True" response set (see the section "Case Examples Highlighting Extreme Fixed Responding" in this chapter). Similarly, with zero items endorsed as True (i.e., all were endorsed as False) the TRIN T score for boys is 101F and for girls 110F, raising the possibility of the extreme "all-False" response set (see the section "Case Examples Highlighting Extreme Fixed Responding").

Tellegen (1991) indicated that MMPI-A TRIN elevations greater than or equal to a T score of 75 were more common among randomly generated True- or False-response biased protocols than in a sample of adolescents tested in clinical settings, leading to the recommendation in the MMPI-A manual that TRIN scores of 75 or higher could be used to identify profiles with significant inconsistency (Butcher et al., 1992). However, as a general guideline for most settings, we now recommend the more conservative cutoff score suggested by Ben-Porath and Davis (1996) of a T score of 100 or higher (in either the True or the False direction) for declaring profile invalidity owing to indiscriminant yea- or nay-saying and T scores from 75 to 99 for including cautionary statements in the MMPI-A interpretation. These cautionary statements should indicate that the adolescent had more inconsistently True or False responses than most adolescents, which may decrease the accuracy of his or her MMPI-A interpretation. Our recommended cutoff scores should not be used as invariant standards. For example, psychologists may use the lower cutoff scores (T of 75 or higher) to determine profile invalidity, depending on several factors, such as the purpose of the testing, knowledge about base rates for invalid responding in their setting, or in situations (e.g., some forensic evaluations) where there is greater harm in interpreting an invalid profile than there is in declaring a valid profile invalid. In research studies, it may be best to use the lower cutoff scores for profile invalidity to reduce error associated with including profiles in the data set that have significant inconsistent responding.

TRIN can also be helpful in refining the interpretation of elevations ($\geq$ 65) on L or K. Because all the L items and all but one K item are keyed False, a tendency toward nay-saying may cause elevations on L and K that do not reflect a defensive test-taking attitude. Instead, elevations on L and K coupled with an elevation on TRIN ($\geq$ 75) indicate an inconsistent False-response pattern, not necessarily defensiveness.

Traditionally, low scores ($\leq$ 40) on L and K are interpreted as indicating openness and a willingness to admit to problems or difficulties. For example, low K scores are seen as similar to high F scores, indicating a degree of frankness and self-criticalness. We did not include these descriptors of low scores in the interpretive rules for the MMPI-A L and K scales because the meaning of low scores on these scales for adolescents has not been adequately investigated. We recommend that clinicians whose interpretation of low L and K scores on the MMPI-A follows the traditional interpretations used with adults rule out indiscriminate yea-saying on the basis of the TRIN score before interpreting a low score on L or K as indicative of openness and a self-critical attitude. Likewise, indiscriminate True responding (yea-saying) may cause a lowering of scores on L and K. Table 10-5 summarizes the interpretive guidelines for TRIN.

Case Examples Highlighting Defensiveness and Fixed Responding

Russ, a 15-year-old white adolescent, produced the MMPI-A validity and standard scale profile seen in Figure 10-1, illustrating the validity indicators covered to this point. His Cs raw score was 0, indicating that he omitted no items (thus raising no concerns about profile validity from this measure). L and K are quite low, possibly indicating a willingness to describe problems, which is reflected in high elevations on several standard scales. If one looks only at the original MMPI validity scales (Cs, L, K, as well as F, which is described in the next section), no validity problems

Table 10-5. TRIN Interpretive Guidelines for the MMPI-A

☐ TRIN scores ≥ 100 are significant and indicative of profile invalidity because of indiscriminate "yea-saying" (indicated by a "T" following the T score; e.g., 100T) or "nay-saying" (indicated by an "F" following the T score; e.g., 100F). No other MMPI-A scores should be interpreted in the presence of this response set.

☐ A TRIN score of 120T is invalid and suggests that an all-True extreme response pattern may have been used. The answer sheet should be examined.

☐ TRIN scores of 101F for boys and 110F for girls are invalid and suggest that an all-False extreme response pattern may have been used. The answer sheet should be examined.

☐ TRIN scores of 75 to 99, inclusive, are suspect, possibly indicative of profile invalidity. Other MMPI-A scores should be interpreted with cautionary statements about possible invalidity.

☐ Elevations on L and K (≥ 65 T score) combined with an elevation on TRIN (≥ 75) indicate an invalidating inconsistent "nay-saying" response set, not defensiveness. Other MMPI-A scores should not be interpreted.

☐ Low scores on L and K (≤ 40) combined with an elevation on TRIN (≥ 100) indicate an invalidating inconsistent "yea-saying" response set, not frankness. Other MMPI-A scores should not be interpreted.

☐ These recommended cutoff scores to declare profile invalidity based on TRIN are not invariant standards. The lower cutoff score (≥ 75) may be more appropriate to use for some clinical decisions (e.g., forensic evaluations) and in research studies.

are indicated. The rest of Russ's MMPI-A could be interpreted according to the original validity scales. However, Russ's very high score on TRIN (T score = 99T) raises the possibility of an invalid response pattern of inconsistent yea-saying. Even though this TRIN score was 1 point below the cutoff of 100 recommended in Table 10-5, the psychologist working with Russ used a feedback session to rule out inconsistent yea-saying. The psychologist began the feedback session in the following manner:

"Do you remember the MMPI-A? What did you think of it?"

"How could I forget? Where did you get all those dumb questions? I didn't think I'd ever finish it!" [Suggests boredom or impatience as possible contributors to his elevated TRIN score.]

"We ask so many questions to be sure to cover all the areas where kids may be having trouble. Did you have any problems understanding the questions?"

"Nope." [Suggests his inconsistent yea-saying was not due to reading comprehension problems.]

After explaining a little background about the MMPI-A validity and standard scales, the psychologist continued the interview:

"So, we use these scales on this side of the profile to tell whether there are any problems with how you responded to the items. On your profile, all these scales look pretty good, no problems, except this one [pointing to TRIN]. Do you have any idea what problem this scale might be measuring?"

"Not a clue."

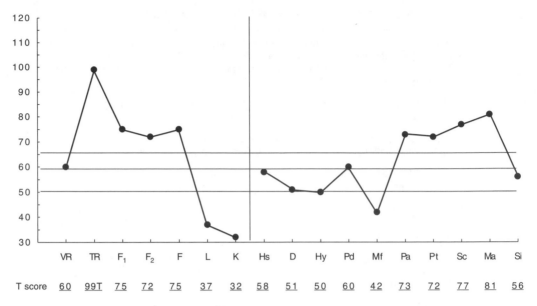

T score   60   99T   75   72   75   37   32   58   51   50   60   42   73   72   77   81   56

Figure 10-1. Russ's MMPI-A basic scales profile.

"Well, sometimes people get a little bored with the test and begin answering the items True without even reading them. That's what this high
score says might have happened to you."

"Wow! How did it do that? How do you know that?"

Russ's MMPI-A TRIN score illustrates how psychologists should recognize that
a TRIN T-score in the 75 to 99 range may indicate an inconsistent response set that
invalidates the profile. A feedback session with the adolescent may help determine
whether the profile should be declared invalid and not interpreted. During the
feedback session, it is important to maintain respect for the young person and
present the information in a nonaccusatory fashion. In the previous example, although Russ is asked about an invalid response style, he is not demeaned for responding inconsistently. Instead, the psychologist appears to be trying to understand him using an instrument that has several features that interest Russ. Now
that he has a greater understanding of the MMPI-A, Russ may agree to a retest and
respond more consistently.

Figure 10-2, 16-year-old Lisa's MMPI-A profile, illustrates how TRIN can confirm the interpretation of elevated L and K scores as indicative of a defensive testing attitude. Although Lisa had zero Cs responses, her L score of 64 is a moderately
high elevation, along with a very high elevation on K at 78. However, before calling
her profile defensive, inconsistent nay-saying should be ruled out. Her TRIN score
of 54T indicates that she did not inconsistently endorse items as False. Her interpretation should include statements about her unwillingness to admit to even
minor flaws, that she responded to MMPI-A items somewhat naively, and that she
presented herself as highly virtuous. She subscribes to a high moral standard or

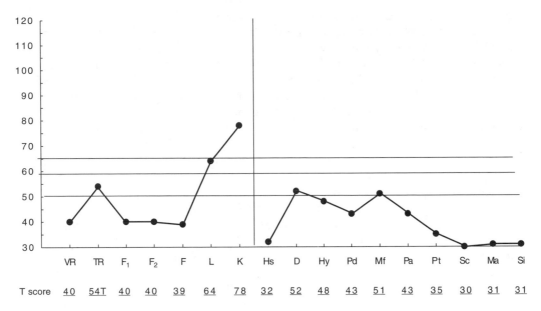

T score	40	54T	40	40	39	64	78	32	52	48	43	51	43	35	30	31	31
	VR	TR	F₁	F₂	F	L	K	Hs	D	Hy	Pd	Mf	Pa	Pt	Sc	Ma	Si

Figure 10-2. Lisa's MMPI-A basic scales profile.

ethical code and may, in fact, be less likely than other adolescents to act out, although this cannot be assumed. Her defensive test-taking attitude is evident in what is an unusually submerged standard-scale profile for an adolescent. Because of her defensive test-taking attitude, this submerged profile should not be interpreted as "normal." Lisa did not produce elevations on any of the other MMPI-A supplementary or content scales. This is a result of her defensiveness, not an indication of psychological health.

Measures of Random and Exaggerated Responding

Infrequency (F) Scale

The Infrequency (F) scale was described by Hathaway and Monachesi (1953a) as somewhat the opposite of the L scale. Unlike high L scores with their suggestion of faking good, persons with high F scores seem to be attempting to present themselves in a bad light or "faking bad" (perhaps unconsciously). As with high L scores, there could be several reasons for elevated F scores. Hathaway and Monachesi (1953a) suggested that some adolescents simply could be overly candid. The F score could also be elevated if the young person, for any reason, failed to answer carefully or consistently, as for those who cannot read well enough. Reading comprehension problems were particularly relevant in using the inventory with adolescents. The F score could also be high if the young person answered carelessly or made random or facetious responses to the items. A final hypothesis for elevated F scores was general maladjustment of a severe nature.

Interpretation of the F scale with adolescents has been difficult over the years. It consistently appeared as one of the more elevated scales in adolescent clinical settings. Archer (1987) reports that using the conservative adult standard to define MMPI profile invalidity (i.e., F ≥ 16 raw score) seemed unwarranted with adolescents, given the large number of cases that would be defined as invalid (i.e., between 34% and 44% in clinical settings) and the meaningful descriptors found associated with high F responding in adolescents (e.g., acting-out behaviors, psychotic symptoms). Gallucci (1987) suggested that the F scale did not measure motivation to exaggerate symptoms or a "plea for help" in adolescents; rather, elevated F scores were a feature of the modal adolescent MMPI profile.

Williams, Butcher, Ben-Porath, and Graham (1992) noted that despite the straightforward development of F (i.e., items were selected on the basis of endorsement frequencies; see Chapter 3), no attempts were made before the MMPI Restandardization Project to refine the F scale for adolescents. When the endorsement percentages of F scale items were examined for the adolescent normative sample (Butcher et al., 1992), many of the items did not act as infrequency indicators with adolescents. Because of this, a new version of the F scale was developed for the MMPI-A.

F is the only basic scale with items substantially different on the MMPI-A from those on the MMPI and MMPI-2. Items were selected for the adolescent version of F if they were endorsed in the deviant direction by no more than 20% of the adolescent normative sample. As with adults, high F responding in adolescents can be due to inconsistent responding, reading problems, faking bad, exaggeration, or serious psychopathology. Its external correlates from both normative and clinical samples and across genders, reported in the MMPI-A manual, provide support for this interpretation (Butcher et al., 1992).

Two studies examined the validity of the MMPI-A version of the F scale by instructing adolescents to feign symptoms of psychopathology in their responses to the MMPI-A item pool and then determining whether the F scale was able to correctly classify subjects as having received standard instructions or "fake bad" instructions (Rogers et al., 1996; Stein et al., 1995). These studies provided general support for the validity of the MMPI-A F scale by demonstrating that it distinguished a community sample of adolescents instructed to "respond to the items to give the impression that you have very serious emotional problems" from clinical and community samples given standard instructions (Stein et al., 1995). The study by Rogers et al. (1996) showed that the F scale differentiated a clinical sample of adolescents residing in a state hospital tested under two conditions: once with standard instructions and once with instructions to feign schizophrenia, major depression, or generalized anxiety disorder (simple descriptions and typical symptoms were included in the instructions given to the adolescents). The results of these two studies demonstrated that adolescents instructed to "fake bad" produced very different MMPI-A profiles than those receiving standard instructions. Subjects from the state hospital with the "fake bad" instructions had significantly elevated profiles on the clinical scales that were 16 points higher than when they took the MMPI-A in the honest condition (Rogers et al., 1996). Similarly, in the study comparing community adolescents with either "fake bad" or standard instructions to actual clinical cases, the F scale mean scores were significantly highest in the "fake bad" community adolescents (mean T score = 99.7), followed by the clinical adolescents (mean T score = 52.6) and the community adolescents with standard instructions (mean T score = 46.3; Stein et al., 1995).

Although these studies support the validity of the MMPI-A version of the F scale, they also highlight the difficulties in determining general cutoff scores for the F scale when little is known about the prevalence of malingering or adolescents' motivation for feigning across different settings (McCann, 1998; Rogers et al., 1996; Stein et al., 1995). Furthermore, because the accuracy of a cutoff score is determined in part by the base rate of the characteristic being assessed, findings from studies with base rates of "faking bad" set by the investigators at 33% (Stein et al., 1995) or 50% (Rogers et al., 1996) may not generalize to real-world settings with perhaps much lower base rates of malingering. Clinicians also have to weigh which is the greater error when using cutoff scores for an adolescent in their setting (i.e., classifying an MMPI-A profile as malingering, thus not interpretable, or interpreting a "faked" MMPI-A profile). As mentioned earlier, this suggests that the interpretation of MMPI-A validity scales should be viewed on a continuum rather than as a dichotomous decision (Ben-Porath & Davis, 1996).

The optimal cutoff score on the F scale for classifying subjects into the "fake bad" condition in the study by Stein et al. (1995) was a raw score of 23 (this represents a T score of 66 for boys and 71 for girls). This suggests that suspicions about a problematic response pattern are raised with elevations in the 66-to-89 range for F and its subscales, F_1 and F_2. Greater likelihood of a problematic response set occurs with elevations between 90 and 109. Only the most extremely elevated profiles above 110 on F should be declared invalid.

The test interpreter must determine which of several possible reasons for elevations on F apply for a given adolescent. Careless or inconsistent responding should be ruled out as an explanation of an elevated F score using the VRIN scale described shortly. Again, an MMPI-A feedback session can assist, along with a review of the adolescent's records or information from school about potential reading problems. Reasons for exaggeration of symptoms or malingering can also be examined by interview with the young person and parents. Extratest evidence of severe psychopathology (e.g., observations of hallucinations) would suggest that severe symptoms likely account for the elevated F.

The Structured Interview of Reported Symptoms (SIRS) is a 172-item structured interview booklet (Rogers, Bagby & Dickens, 1992) that has promise as a corroborative measure to assist in determining whether malingering likely accounts for an adolescent's elevated F score (McCann, 1998; Rogers et al., 1996). Although originally developed for adults, Rogers et al. (1996) demonstrate its validity with adolescents. The SIRS is designed to measure self-report tendencies associated with feigning and distortion. Administration and scoring are highly structured and straightforward. The SIRS primary scales include Rare Symptoms, Symptom Combination (i.e., genuine symptoms that rarely occur together), Improbable or Absurd Symptoms, Blatant Symptoms (overendorsement of obvious signs of mental disorders), Subtle Symptoms (overendorsement of everyday problems not always associated with mental disorders), Severity of Symptoms (tendency to rate symptoms as unbearable), Selectivity of Symptoms (indiscriminant endorsement of psychiatric symptoms), and Reported versus Observed Symptoms. The SIRS supplementary scales include Direct Appraisal of Honesty, Defensive Symptoms (tendency to deny everyday problems), and Symptom Onset (symptoms with uncharacteristically abrupt onset). McCann (1998) provides useful suggestions of how to use the SIRS to corroborate (i.e., by ruling in or ruling out malingering) an elevated F score on the MMPI-A.

Infrequency 1 and 2 (F_1 and F_2) Subscales

The F scale is divided into two subscales on the MMPI-A. F_1 assesses responding on the first half of the booklet up to item 236. F_2 assesses the second half of the booklet, beginning with item 242, and is comparable to the F Back (F_b) scale on the MMPI-2 (see Chapter 3). The F subscales can be used to determine whether a problematic response pattern occurred in only one half of the booklet or throughout it. This is important because the original validity and standard scales are included within the first 350 items, whereas items for VRIN, TRIN, the content scales, and the supplementary scales are located throughout the booklet. Support for the validity of the F_1 and F_2 subscales was provided by Stein et al. (1995).

An elevation on F_2, but not F_1, suggests that boredom may have occurred during the administration of the second half of the booklet, perhaps resulting in random responding. If only F_2 is elevated, even with an elevation on the full F scale, the standard scales, but not the supplementary measures or content scales, may be interpreted.

Marked discrepancies in the F_1 and F_2 subscales (i.e., more than 20 T-score points) indicate that a substantial change in response style occurred over the course of the test administration (Ben-Porath & Davis, 1996). Higher F_2 scores are more easy to interpret, suggesting boredom, loss of concentration, or loss of motivation as the testing continued. Elevations on F_2 may be prevented by administering the MMPI-A in two shorter sessions or giving frequent breaks. Because F_1 and F_2 are made up of items solely from the F scale, and they are used in conjunction with F to determine where in the booklet the random response style may have occurred, the same cutoff scores are recommended for their interpretation. VRIN cannot be used to resolve score discrepancies between F_1 and F_2.

The Dissimulation (F – K) Index

The F – K index (see Chapter 3), a measure of dissimulation scored by subtracting the raw score of the K scale from the raw score of the F scale, was not recommended for use with adolescents with the original MMPI. Nor was its use recommended at the time of the release of the MMPI-A, given that no research existed supporting its use, coupled with the substantive changes made to the MMPI-A version of the F scale. However, both Rogers et al. (1996) and Stein et al. (1995) found support for the validity of this index, along with very similar cutoff scores (raw scores $\geq$ 20 and $\geq$ 19, respectively). These cutoff scores recommended for adolescents are much higher than those suggested in Chapter 3 for adults. Similar to the recommendations we provided in Chapter 3 for adults, the F – K index may be best used for adolescents as corroboration of malingering as an explanation for elevated F scores. However, no research currently exists supporting the use of the

Table 10-6. F, F$_1$, F$_2$, and F − K Interpretive Guidelines for the MMPI-A

☐ T scores ≥ 110 indicate an invalid MMPI-A that should not be interpreted.

☐ T scores ≥ 90 on F, F$_1$, or F$_2$ signify very high elevations indicative of a potentially problematic response set. Possible reasons for this elevation have to be determined using the list of interpretive statements provided below. VRIN T scores < 70 can be used to rule out inconsistent responding, and VRIN T scores ≥ 75 indicate inconsistent responding.

☐ T scores of 66 to 89, inclusive, on F, F$_1$, and F$_2$ indicate high elevations suggestive of a potentially problematic response set. The interpreter should determine the probable reasons for this high elevation. VRIN T scores < 70 can be used to rule out inconsistent responding, and VRIN T scores ≥ 75 indicate inconsistent responding.

☐ T scores of 65 to 79, inclusive, on F, F$_1$, or F$_2$ indicate moderate elevations reflecting endorsement of a variety of symptoms. VRIN T scores < 70 can be used to rule out inconsistent responding, and VRIN T scores ≥ 75 indicate inconsistent responding.

☐ Elevations on F$_2$, but not F$_1$, indicate that the potentially problematic response set occurred in the second half of the booklet, not the first. In this instance, the content scales and supplementary measures will be affected more than the standard scales.

☐ An F − K index ≥ 19 (raw score on K subtracted from raw score on F) suggests the possibility of malingering.

☐ Interpretive statements for elevated F scores:
- Possible random responding (use VRIN to rule out)
- Possible confusion or reading problems
- Possible faking bad or malingering
- Possible exaggeration of symptoms
- Possible serious psychopathology

---

corollary index K − F (used when the raw score of K is higher than the raw score of F) as a measure of defensiveness. Interpretive rules for F, its subscales, and the F − K index are summarized in Table 10-6.

Variable Response Inconsistency (VRIN) Scale

The Variable Response Inconsistency (VRIN) scale was developed for the MMPI-2 and the MMPI-A (Tellegen, 1988) to assess inconsistent responding. Inconsistency occurs if an adolescent responds carelessly or randomly. The VRIN scale, unlike F, is not confounded with severe psychopathology; it is elevated only by inconsistent responding.

The MMPI-A VRIN scale was developed from the MMPI-A item content and with adolescent samples using the same procedures that were used to develop the MMPI-2 VRIN scale (see Chapter 3 for further discussion of its development). Although there is item overlap, the MMPI-2 and MMPI-A VRIN scales are not identical. MMPI-A VRIN T-score elevations equal to or greater than 80 are highly suspect and far more common in a sample of randomly generated records than in adolescent clinical samples. VRIN T-score elevations of 70 to 79 are also quite unusual in clinical adolescents and may indicate random inconsistent responding. In the absence of elevations on the F scale, we recommend using a VRIN elevation of 80 to declare a profile invalid because of inconsistent responding. A VRIN score

Table 10-7. VRIN Interpretive Guidelines for the MMPI-A

☐ In the absence of elevations on the F scale, VRIN scores ≥ 80 are significant and indicative of profile invalidity because of marked inconsistency. No other MMPI-A scales should be interpreted in the presence of this response set.

☐ VRIN scores of 70 to 79, inclusive, are suspect, possibly indicative of profile invalidity. Other MMPI-A scores should be interpreted with cautionary statements about the possibility of significant response inconsistency.

☐ Interpretation of moderate to very high elevations on F can be refined by using VRIN scores to rule in (VRIN ≥ 75) or rule out (VRIN < 70) inconsistent responding.

---

between 70 and 79 is suspect, and its interpretation should include a cautionary statement about potentially invalidating inconsistency.

VRIN can also be used to refine the interpretation of elevated F scores (Table 10-6). An elevated F score paired with a VRIN score of lower than 74 T rules out inconsistent responding as the explanation for the F elevation. Other reasons for the elevation on F have to be explored (e.g., serious psychopathology, exaggeration of symptoms, malingering). VRIN guidelines are provided in Table 10-7.

Case Examples Highlighting Random and Exaggerated Responding

Jodi's MMPI-A profile presented in Figure 10-3 illustrates the use of VRIN to detect inconsistent responding. Jodi, a 14-year-old white girl, had no significant elevations on F, F_1, and F_2. This level of elevation on F in a clinical setting is not at all unusual and would not invalidate the protocol under the guidelines for interpreting the MMPI for adolescents. However, her extremely elevated VRIN score of 93 indicates that she responded highly inconsistently to the MMPI-A item content. Her scores on the MMPI-A scales would not provide an accurate interpretation of her problems.

On the other hand, 16-year-old Elizabeth's profile (Figure 10-4) does not provide evidence of inconsistency, even in the presence of fairly extreme elevations on F and its subscales (i.e., F of 82, F_1 of 95, F_2 of 90). With a VRIN score of 40, the test interpreter can rule out inconsistency as contributing to the F elevations. Likewise, her low scores on L (38) and K (33) cannot be attributed to inconsistent yea-saying with her average TRIN score. Her F – K index score is very high at 27 (F raw score 31 – K raw score 4), raising the possibility of some exaggeration of symptoms or malingering. Her MMPI-A profile also suggests the possibility of severe psychopathology.

Case Examples Highlighting Extreme Fixed Responding

All-True Response Set

Figure 10-5 shows the pattern of MMPI-A validity and standard scale scores that is obtained when an individual endorses all the items on the MMPI-A True. Note that the all-True response set produces an average VRIN score. However,

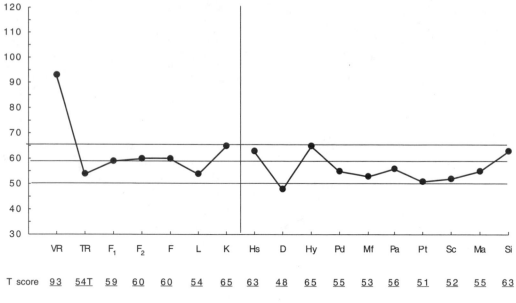

Figure 10-3. Jodi's MMPI-A basic scales profile.

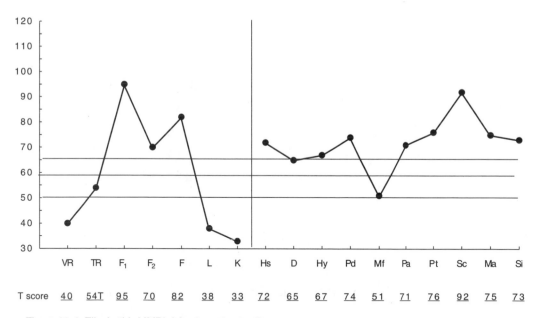

Figure 10-4. Elizabeth's MMPI-A basic scales profile.

TRIN, F, F_1, and F_2 are extremely elevated under this condition. The TRIN T score of 120T and raw score of 24 indicate that all the TRIN items were endorsed as True regardless of their content. Because many of the items on the F scale and its sub-scales (F_1, F_2) are keyed in the True direction, these scores are also highly elevated. L and K produce very low scores in this condition because all L items are keyed

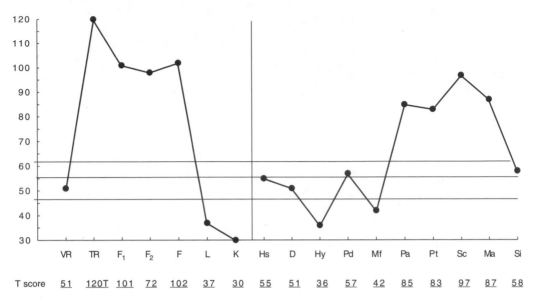

T score	51	120T	101	72	102	37	30	55	51	36	57	42	85	83	97	87	58

Figure 10-5. All-True response set: MMPI-A basic scales profile.

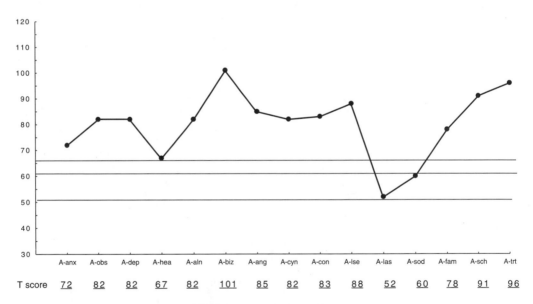

T score	72	82	82	67	82	101	85	82	83	88	52	60	78	91	96

Figure 10-6. All-True response set: MMPI-A content scales profile.

False, as are all but one K item. The standard scale profile does show some variation in scale scores. Only scales on the right side of the profile (i.e., those measuring more psychotic-like disturbances) are extremely elevated. Scales on the left side of the profile (i.e., the neurotic and acting-out scales) are not elevated under this response condition. The profile in Figure 10-6 provides an all-True response pattern to the MMPI-A Content Scales.

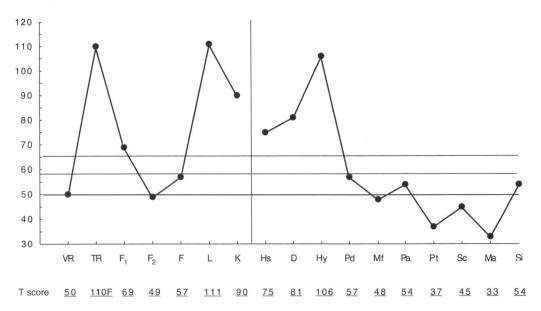

Figure 10-7. All-False response set: MMPI-A basic scales profile.

All-False Response Set

Figure 10-7 presents the validity and standard scale profile that would emerge if an individual endorses all MMPI-A items False. Again, the VRIN score produced under this condition is average. However, the TRIN score is highly elevated, as are L and K. The F scores themselves do not suggest a problematic response set. The opposite pattern occurs for the standard scales compared with the all-True response seen in Figure 10-5. Here, the neurotic scales (1, 2, and 3) are extremely elevated, with all other scales below a T score of 60. Figure 10-8 provides an all-False response pattern to the MMPI-A content scales.

Highlight Summary: Tony, an Adolescent Case

In concluding this chapter, we turn our attention from Alice. At 18 years of age, Alice could have been administered the MMPI-A, but her psychologist felt that her life circumstances would be better assessed with the MMPI-2 item content. However, the MMPI-A is the appropriate instrument for our new case, Tony, a 14-year-old black Hispanic eighth-grader being evaluated at a special public school for youth with emotional and behavioral problems. Tony's school provided a more structured, therapeutic environment than is available in mainstream schools. The problems leading to Tony's referral included theft (resulting in court-ordered probation), fighting, truancy, and oppositional behavior. He had previously been treated for similar problems in an outpatient mental health clinic.

Tony's Hispanic ethnicity raises the possibility that English may not be his primary language. Furthermore, his special education placement suggests a greater likelihood of reading comprehension problems. Before administering an MMPI-A

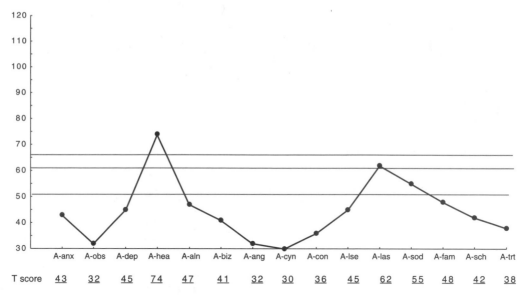

T score	A-anx	A-obs	A-dep	A-hea	A-aln	A-biz	A-ang	A-cyn	A-con	A-lse	A-las	A-sod	A-fam	A-sch	A-trt
	43	32	45	74	47	41	32	30	36	45	62	55	48	42	38

Figure 10-8. All-False response set: MMPI-A content scales profile.

in these circumstances, it is important to determine whether the young person has the necessary sixth-grade reading level in English required for the instrument. In Tony's case, his educational testing records revealed no potential reading difficulties that would preclude administration of the MMPI-A or the need to administer the Spanish version of the MMPI-A.

MMPI-A interpretations should be made using available diagnostic information, along with any other information known about the young person. However, psychiatric diagnoses were not routinely made for students at Tony's school. Because Tony was part of the MMPI-A clinical sample, he was administered a computerized version of the Diagnostic Interview for Children and Adolescents (DICA; Herjanic & Campbell, 1977). His DICA diagnostic report was consistent with the referral concerns and included the following *DSM-III*–based diagnoses: conduct disorder, socialized, aggressive; oppositional disorder; and marijuana use.

Tony was a bright student, capable of above-average work when he applied himself. He reported enjoying his participation in sports and band and was hoping to participate in a work-study program. However, he had a number of problems in school, including suspension and course and grade failures. His teacher indicated that he frequently did not apply himself and was somewhat inattentive and distractible. He did not like school and was argumentative, disobedient, and disruptive in class. School officials reported that he had a history of gang involvement and assaultive behavior. There were also problems in his family, including heavy drinking by his stepfather and possible wife abuse. Tony reported being worried about his mother's safety along with the safety of himself and his younger sister. Other members of the family also experienced difficulties with the law.

Tony produced an interpretable MMPI-A profile, with no evidence of an overly defensive response style, indicated by the L and K scales (Figure 10-9) and his zero

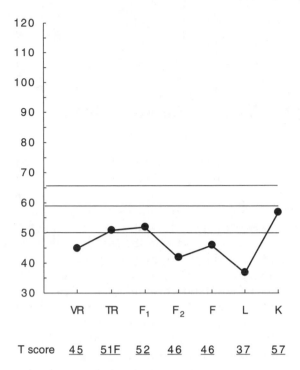

Figure 10-9. Tony's MMPI-A validity scales profile.

Cannot Say responses. He was careful and attentive to the task of completing the MMPI-A as revealed by his F and VRIN scores. His F_1 and F_2 scores showed that this cooperative response style was maintained throughout the booklet. His TRIN score provided further support of the validity of his self-report, revealing no tendencies toward inconsistent yea- or nay-saying. This validity pattern indicated that other MMPI-A scores could be used to provide inferences about his behavior and problems. The following chapters cover the rest of Tony's MMPI-A interpretation.

Chapter 11

Interpreting the MMPI-A Standard Scales

For almost 50 years, the MMPI standard scales have been the basis of interpretations for both adults and adolescents. These scales were empirically developed using samples of adult psychiatric patients contrasted with adult control subjects who were visitors to the University of Minnesota hospitals (see Chapter 4). The scales were never adapted or adjusted when used with adolescents. For the most part, the standard scales were included in the MMPI-A without substantial revisions to maintain continuity with the original instrument.

There were a few exceptions to the general rule of maintaining continuity between the MMPI and MMPI-A standard scales, including some item deletions and wording improvements. (Table 11-1 summarizes the item-level differences on the MMPI, MMPI-A, and MMPI-2 for the standard scales.) Changes in the MMPI-A include deletion of items dropped from the original MMPI in developing the MMPI-2 because of their objectionable content, 70 items rewritten in the MMPI-2, as well as item/scale changes unique to the MMPI-A (phrasing youthful activities and behaviors in the present tense, shortening the instrument by deleting items from longer scales, and deleting developmentally inappropriate or objectionable content).

Even with these changes, most of the MMPI-A standard scales have either very minor or no changes. Scales 3, 6, 7, and 9 have the same item content on all three versions of the instrument. Two MMPI-A standard scales have the same content as the MMPI-2 (scales 1 and 2). Scale 1 lost one objectionable item, "I have no difficulty in starting or holding my bowel movements," on the newer versions of the instrument. Scale 2 lost three items about religious practices and beliefs on the restandardized versions. Two MMPI-A standard scales (4 and 8) differ from the MMPI-2 standard scales by only one item. "My sex life is satisfactory" was dropped from both scale 4 and scale 8 because of its objectionable content for adolescents and because it did not necessarily have the same psychological meaning for adults and adolescents.

Only two of the MMPI-A basic scales (5 and 0) had more than one or two items deleted. The original scales were rather long (60 items for Mf and 70 items for Si) and were shortened without reducing their reliability and validity. Scale 5 item deletions included those with limited face or content validity (e.g., "I used to like drop-the-handkerchief," "I liked 'Alice in Wonderland' by Lewis Carroll"), objectionable content (e.g., "I believe there is a Devil and a Hell in afterlife"), developmentally inappropriate content (e.g., "I have never had any breaking out on my skin that has worried me"), and developmentally objectionable content (e.g., "I am strongly attracted by members of my own sex," "I have never indulged in any unusual sex practices"). Scale 0 item deletions included those with limited face or

Table 11-1. The MMPI, MMPI-A, and MMPI-2 Standard Scales

Scale	Name	Abbreviation	Number of items		
			MMPI	MMPI-A	MMPI-2
1	Hypochondriasis	Hs	33	32	a
2	Depression	D	60	57	a
3	Hysteria	Hy	60	b	b
4	Psychopathic Deviate	Pd	50	49	b
5	Masculinity-Femininity	Mf	60	44	56
6	Paranoia	Pa	40	b	b
7	Psychasthenia	Pt	48	b	b
8	Schizophrenia	Sc	78	77	b
9	Hypomania	Ma	46	b	b
0	Social Introversion	Si	70	62	69

[a] Items identical with the MMPI-A.
[b] Items identical with the original MMPI.

content validity (e.g., "I would like to be a singer," "I am embarrassed by dirty stories") and those with objectionable content (e.g., "I have had no difficulty starting or holding my urine").

General Interpretive Guidelines for the MMPI-A Standard Scales

Eight of the MMPI-A standard scales—Hs, D, Hy, Pd, Pa, Pt, Sc, and Ma—are interpreted using uniform T scores generated from the adolescent normative sample (Butcher et al., 1992), similar to the process described in Chapter 4 for interpretations of the MMPI-2. It is important to note that MMPI-2 uniform T scores generated from the adult normative sample are never used with MMPI-A interpretations (see Chapter 2, "Selecting the Proper Form"). The MMPI-A Mf and Si scales, like their MMPI-2 counterparts, use linear T scores, which, for the MMPI-A, are generated from the adolescent normative samples. MMPI-A interpretation is much more straightforward than interpretation of the original instrument, which required integrating information from both adult and adolescent norm sets (see Chapter 9). The MMPI-A profile has a shaded area between T scores of 60 and 64 to indicate moderate elevations. Interpretations can be made for scale scores in this range, although less confidence is placed in interpretations of scores in these lower ranges. A T score of 65 is the cutoff for determining clinically significant elevations. Standard scale scores at or above a T score of 65 indicate a greater probability that the scale descriptors apply to the individual.

Elevations on the standard scales vary across scales, settings, and gender. Table 11-2 highlights this variability using the MMPI-A normative and clinical samples. The MMPI-A normative sample was selected from school settings, and the percentages in Table 11-2 for the normative boys and girls estimate the frequency of the standard scale elevations in general population school settings. The MMPI-A clinical samples were drawn from alcohol and other drug problem treatment units (65% of the sample), psychiatric inpatient units (23%), a special school for emotionally or behaviorally disturbed adolescents (7%), and a day treatment

Table 11-2. Percentages of Elevated Standard Scale Scores in the MMPI-A Normative and Clinical Samples

		1	2	3	Scales 4	5	6	7	8	9	0
Normative	Boys	9.4	10.2	7.2	11.3	6.0	9.4	8.8	8.4	10.1	6.8
	Girls	9.3	9.7	10.3	8.0	7.4	10.7	10.1	9.4	7.2	7.5
Clinical	Boys	5.2	8.8	3.8	33.8	3.1	11.4	14.0	11.0	18.3	5.7
	Girls	11.9	19.8	19.5	33.8	4.8	18.8	19.1	15.0	10.2	9.9

Note: Elevations are defined as T scores $\geq$ 65. Normative boys = 805 subjects, normative girls = 815 subjects; clinical boys = 420 subjects, clinical girls = 293 subjects.

center (5%). The percentages in Table 11-2 estimate the frequency of standard scale elevations in these types of treatment facilities for boys and girls.

A further illustration of the variability of elevations on the standard scales in different settings can be seen in a sample of 93 boys and 84 girls receiving inpatient treatment for mental disorders at a private psychiatric hospital (Gallucci, 1994). Similar to the elevations for the MMPI-A normative and clinical samples in Table 11-2, scale 4 was the most highly elevated, with 48% of this psychiatric inpatient sample scoring at or above 65 T. The next highest scale was 2 with 37% of the sample with elevated scores, followed by scale 9 (31% of the sample), scale 8 (29%), scale 7 (27%), scale 3 (25%), scale 1 (21%), scale 6 (21%), scale 5 (13%), and scale 0 (9%). In general, the combined gender sample of psychiatric inpatients (Gallucci, 1994) had higher elevations than either boys or girls in the MMPI-A clinical sample (Butcher et al., 1992) in Table 11-2. This may be due to the differences in a psychiatric inpatient sample (Gallucci, 1994) compared with a sample of adolescents from predominantly alcohol and other drug treatment inpatient units (Butcher et al., 1992).

The percentages in Table 11-2 from Butcher et al. (1992) and those described previously from Gallucci (1994) provide estimates of the frequency of standard scale elevation in various treatment facilities for adolescents. These percentages can be used to determine how unusual a given adolescent's standard scale elevations are. For example, a boy seen in an alcohol or drug treatment setting with elevations on scales 1, 3, and 0 would be unlike most boys in these facilities and might not respond to the standard treatment protocol designed for boys with elevations on the more frequently occurring scales 4 and 9.

As we indicated in Chapter 4, because the standard scales are empirically derived, their scores do not indicate whether a given individual has more or less of the construct being assessed. For example, a higher elevation on scale 8 does not indicate that the person is more "schizophrenic" than those with lower scores. Rather, an elevated score indicates a higher probability that the given individual is more like the criterion group of schizophrenic adult patients than those with lower scores. Over the years, descriptors have been found to be associated with the various scale elevations. Again, an elevated T score on these scales indicates the greater

probability that an individual has the characteristics associated with scale elevations. This meaning of scale elevation should be kept in mind when writing interpretive statements based on the elevations of the standard scales. As we will see in
Chapter 12, elevations on the MMPI-A content scales have somewhat different
meanings.

Because the MMPI-A standard scales parallel the MMPI-2 standard scales, the
reader is referred to Chapter 4 for information about scale-development procedures and the content of each scale. The Harris-Lingoes subscales described in
Chapter 4 for the MMPI-2 are relevant for interpreting the MMPI-A standard
scales. The MMPI-A manual presents T scores based on the adolescent normative
sample to facilitate use of the Harris-Lingoes subscales. In the original MMPI,
adolescent-based T scores were not available for subscales. Another set of useful
subscales, developed by Ben-Porath, Hostetler, Butcher, and Graham (1989), facilitate interpretation of Si elevations and are also described in Chapter 4.

The Harris-Lingoes and Si subscales are used to refine interpretations on the
standard scales. Because many of the standard scales have quite heterogeneous
item content, these subscales can be used to determine which of the many possible
descriptors to emphasize in the interpretation (see the description of Ann's interpretation in Chapter 4 for an example). As indicated in Chapter 4, item overlap in
the Harris-Lingoes subscales can detract from their usefulness, and because they
are short, they are less reliable measures than the standard scales.

Until recently, no studies assessed the validity of the Harris-Lingoes subscales,
particularly for adolescents. Thus, interpretations are based primarily on the content of the items rather than empirically derived descriptors. In the absence of
demonstrated validity, a cautious interpretive strategy is used. A difference of only
1 or 2 raw score points can make a substantial T-score difference that seems clinically significant (Peña, Megargee & Brody, 1996). For these reasons, the Harris-
Lingoes subscales are interpreted only when its standard scale is elevated (T scores
$\geq$ 60) and the Harris-Lingoes subscale is elevated at or above 65 T. Some exceptions
to this general interpretive strategy can be made because recent studies provide
empirical descriptors for several Harris-Lingoes subscales. For example, Gallucci
(1994) provided descriptors for five of the Harris-Lingoes subscales (Hy_2, Hy_5, Pa_3,
Ma_1, and Ma_3) that supported their validity, as did Basham (1992) for three scale 4
subscales (Pd_1, Pd_2, and Pd_5). These descriptors are included in the interpretations
provided in the next sections of this chapter. The validity of the Harris-Lingoes
subscales for scales 2, 4, and 9 as predictors of suicidal risk also has empirical support (Kopper, Osman, Osman & Hoffman, 1998), and descriptors are included for them. Table 11-3 summarizes the general guidelines for interpreting the
MMPI-A standard scales.

Although the development and content are similar on the standard scales for
the MMPI, MMPI-2, and MMPI-A, new empirical descriptors are available for
these scales derived from adolescent samples (Butcher et al., 1992). This information, taken from the MMPI-A manual and combined with correlates derived from
earlier studies of adolescents, particularly those of Hathaway and Monachesi, is
used to develop the following interpretive guidelines for use of the standard scales
with adolescents. New research with adolescents in several settings, including
psychiatric inpatient units (Gallucci, 1994; Kopper et al., 1998), combined inpatient

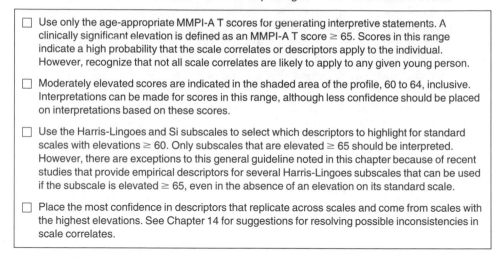

Table 11-3. General Guidelines for Interpreting the MMPI-A Standard Scales

☐ Use only the age-appropriate MMPI-A T scores for generating interpretive statements. A clinically significant elevation is defined as an MMPI-A T score ≥ 65. Scores in this range indicate a high probability that the scale correlates or descriptors apply to the individual. However, recognize that not all scale correlates are likely to apply to any given young person.

☐ Moderately elevated scores are indicated in the shaded area of the profile, 60 to 64, inclusive. Interpretations can be made for scores in this range, although less confidence should be placed on interpretations based on these scores.

☐ Use the Harris-Lingoes and Si subscales to select which descriptors to highlight for standard scales with elevations ≥ 60. Only subscales that are elevated ≥ 65 should be interpreted. However, there are exceptions to this general guideline noted in this chapter because of recent studies that provide empirical descriptors for several Harris-Lingoes subscales that can be used if the subscale is elevated ≥ 65, even in the absence of an elevation on its standard scale.

☐ Place the most confidence in descriptors that replicate across scales and come from scales with the highest elevations. See Chapter 14 for suggestions for resolving possible inconsistencies in scale correlates.

and outpatient psychiatric facilities (Wrobel & Lachar, 1992), a substance abuse inpatient facility (Basham, 1992), and a correctional facility (Cashel, Rogers, Sewell & Holliman, 1998), are also used to supplement the interpretations for the standard scales.

Scale 1: Hypochondriasis (Hs)

Consistent with research on the original MMPI (e.g., Wrobel & Lachar, 1992), moderate to high adolescent scorers on Hs have a wide variety of physical complaints across several body systems. Because Hs is a very homogeneous scale, no subscales were needed to facilitate its interpretation. Although moderate scores could occur in individuals with known physical illness, more extreme scores suggest a greater preoccupation with health than occurred in patients with known illnesses. In addition to its association with numerous physical complaints, several personality and behavioral descriptors are associated with elevations on scale 1. Boys and girls in school settings who scored high on scale 1 were unlikely to be doing well in school and reported increasing problems, particularly academic. Girls were also likely to report more family problems, including parental marital disagreements and financial difficulties. It was an unusual elevation for boys in clinical settings. Although also somewhat uncommon in girls, scale 1 elevations were more likely for girls than for boys (see Table 11-2). Girls seen in clinical settings might have eating problems along with their numerous physical complaints. Parents of high-scoring boys seen in clinical settings described their sons as having many internalizing problems in addition to their physical complaints, including being fearful, guilt prone, withdrawn, perfectionistic, clinging, and worrying. Incarcerated delinquent boys with high scores on scale 1 had fears of dying or losing control, had difficulty concentrating, and showed cruelty toward others (Cashel et al., 1998). Interpretive guidelines are summarized in Table 11-4.

Table 11-4. Scale 1 Interpretive Guidelines for the MMPI-A

☐ Elevated Hs scores suggest a greater preoccupation with health than occurs in patients with known illnesses. However, adolescents with chronic illnesses sometimes score in the moderately elevated range.
☐ Elevations are unusual for boys in clinical settings and although also somewhat uncommon for girls, they are more likely than for boys. Because these young people are unlike others in treatment settings, program modifications may be necessary to accommodate their differences.
☐ Boys and girls in school settings with elevated scores are unlikely to be doing well and may report increasing problems, particularly academic. Girls are also likely to report more family problems, including marital discord and financial difficulties.
☐ Parents of clinical boys describe their sons as having many internalizing problems in addition to their physical complaints, including being fearful, guilt prone, withdrawn, perfectionistic, clinging, and worrying.
☐ Clinical girls may have eating problems in addition to their numerous physical complaints.
☐ Incarcerated delinquent boys may have fears of dying or losing control, have concentration difficulties, and show cruelty to others.

Scale 2: Depression (D)

Scale 2 is a measure of depression for both adolescents and adults. Hathaway and Monachesi (1953a) reported that high scorers were likely to feel unsure of themselves and the future, often saying that they were sad and blue. They suggested that high scores normally occurred when individuals were in trouble, so that the absence of a higher score from someone in trouble was an unexpected sign indicating that the person was not responding in the modal way. Because high D scores indicated personal unhappiness and dissatisfaction, elevations on D were seen to be a good prognostic indicator for psychotherapy and their absence indicative of a person not particularly motivated for change. Archer, Gordon, Giannetti, and Singles (1988) replicated the prognostic significance of elevated D scores in adolescents (i.e., therapists rated high D adolescents as being more willing to seek advice, open in discussing feelings, and more motivated to make change than other adolescents).

The validity of scale 2 as a measure of depression on the MMPI-A was confirmed; its correlates included an association with suicidal ideations and gestures (Butcher et al., 1992; Kopper et al., 1998) and indications of depression in hospital records (Butcher et al., 1992). More significant correlates were found for girls on scale 2 than for boys (Butcher et al., 1992; Wrobel & Lachar, 1992). However, a study of boys in a correctional facility found several significant descriptors, including depressed mood, restlessness, anorexia, self-pity, obsessions and compulsions, need for reassurance, nightmares, concentration difficulties, and cruelty toward others (Cashel et al., 1998).

Girls in school settings with high scale 2 scores are unlikely to be doing well in school and more likely to report that their parents' arguments have worsened. The parents of clinical boys described their sons as guilt prone, fearful, withdrawn, perfectionistic, clinging, and worrying (Butcher et al., 1992). Similar correlates were found by Archer et al. (1988) with a combined gender sample using the original MMPI D scale. High-scoring girls in clinical settings were less likely to engage in acting-out behaviors, including sexual promiscuity, and much more likely to be socially withdrawn, with few or no friends, and to have eating problems, somatic concerns, and low self-esteem (Butcher et al., 1992). Social withdrawal and limited friendships were also characteristic of girls (Gallucci, 1994; Wrobel & Lachar, 1992). Earlier research established D as an inhibitory scale in both boys and girls (Hathaway & Monachesi, 1963). Adolescents in Archer et al's (1988) combined gender samples were likely to have low self-esteem, eating problems, somatic complaints, and sleep difficulties. Both boys and girls were found to be self-critical and had difficulty making up their minds (Gallucci, 1994).

The Harris-Lingoes subscales can be used to clarify scale 2 elevated scores in adolescents. The MMPI-A provides age-appropriate T scores for D_1 (Subjective Depression), D_2 (Psychomotor Retardation), D_3 (Physical Malfunction), D_4 (Mental Dullness) and D_5 (Brooding). Only those Harris-Lingoes scores greater than or equal to 65 should be interpreted in the presence of an elevated D score. However, scores on D_1 (Subjective Depression) have been found to make an independent contribution to the assessment of suicidal risk, even when considering scores on scale 2 (Kopper et al., 1998). Thus, an elevation at 65 or higher on D_1 signals a potential risk for suicidal behaviors, even in the absence of an elevation on scale 2. Table 11-5 summarizes the interpretive guidelines for scale 2.

Scale 3: Hysteria (Hy)

The validity of scale 3 was more limited than the validity of some of the other standard scales in the MMPI-A clinical sample (Butcher et al., 1992). Hathaway and Monachesi (1963), in their general population sample, found that adolescents with scale 3 as the highest point were more likely to come from an upper socioeconomic level and more likely to be above average in intelligence. Their study did not include somatic complaints as possible correlates. Only elevated Hy scores for girls were shown to be associated with somatic complaints in the MMPI-A clinical sample, again perhaps owing to the low prevalence of elevated Hy scores for boys (Table 11-2). Normative boys were more likely to have problems in school, and boys in the clinical sample were likely to have a history of suicidal ideas and/or gestures, a descriptor also found in the study of incarcerated boys (Cashel et al., 1998). However, in a smaller, combined-gender clinical sample tested with the original MMPI, Archer et al. (1988) found evidence that elevated Hy adolescents were likely to react to stress with somatic complaints, to be seen as passive-dependent, to be unpredictable, and to have limited friendships. Wrobel and Lachar (1992) found parent-reported paralysis associated with high scores in outpatient boys. Other descriptors for delinquent boys included concentration difficulties, restlessness, anorexia, cruelty toward others, and greater feelings of depression in the afternoon (Cashel et al., 1998).

The Harris-Lingoes subscales—Hy_1 (Denial of Social Anxiety), Hy_2 (Need for Affection), Hy_3 (Lassitude-Malaise), Hy_4 (Somatic Complaints), and Hy_5 (Inhibition of Aggression)—can refine interpretations of elevated scores on scale 3.

Table 11-5. Scale 2 Interpretive Guidelines for the MMPI-A

☐ Elevations on D (and its subscale, D_1 [Subjective Depression]) indicate depression and possible suicidal ideations and gestures in both boys and girls in clinical settings. High scorers tend to be self-critical and have difficulty making up their minds.

☐ Girls in school settings with elevated scores are unlikely to be doing well in school and are more likely to report a worsening in parents' arguments.

☐ Parents of clinical boys describe their sons as guilt prone, fearful, withdrawn, perfectionistic, clinging, and worrying.

☐ High-scoring clinical girls are less likely to engage in acting-out behaviors (including sexual promiscuity) and much more likely to be socially withdrawn, with few or no friends, and to have eating problems, somatic concerns, and low self-esteem.

☐ Incarcerated boys may show depressed mood, restlessness, anorexia, self-pity, obsessions and compulsions, need for reassurance, nightmares, concentration difficulties, and cruelty toward others.

☐ Somatic complaints and sleep difficulties are possible correlates, based on research from the original MMPI.

☐ Because high scale 2 scores indicate personal unhappiness and dissatisfaction, they are seen to be a good prognostic indicator for psychotherapy and their absence indicative of a person not particularly motivated for change. Research on the original MMPI suggests that high D adolescents may be more willing to seek advice, more open in discussing feelings, and more motivated for change.

☐ An elevation ≥ 65 on Harris-Lingoes subscale D_1 (Subjective Depression) is associated with increased suicidal risk.

☐ Several Harris-Lingoes subscales can be used to clarify elevated scale 2 scores. Only Harris-Lingoes T scores ≥ 65 should be interpreted. The following are content-based hypotheses for each of the D subscales:

D_1—Subjective Depression (29 items)

- Worried, nervous, brooding
- Feelings of inadequacy, low self-esteem
- Lassitude, listlessness, fatigue
- Dysphoric, unhappy
- Sleep difficulties
- Concentration problems
- Social withdrawal
- Apathetic
- Denial of feeling contentment
- Other symptoms of depression, such as crying spells and poor appetite

D_2—Psychomotor Retardation (14 items)

- Denial of strong affect
- Apathetic
- Lassitude, listlessness, low energy
- Social withdrawal
- Fear of losing his or her mind
- Denial of persistence on a task

Table 11-5. Scale 2 Interpretive Guidelines for the MMPI-A, continued

D_3—Physical Malfunction (11 items)

- Denial of good health
- Multiple somatic complaints like nausea, vomiting, hay fever, convulsions
- Weakness
- Poor appetite, fluctuating weight

D_4—Mental Dullness (15 items)

- Concentration, memory problems
- Limited self-confidence
- Lassitude, listlessness
- Apathetic
- Denial of ability to work as well as before
- Feels tension

D_5—Brooding (10 items)

- Desires to be as happy as others, denies feeling happy
- Denial of concern about what happens to him or her
- Denies that life is worthwhile
- Broods, is hurt by criticisms
- Fears losing mind
- Crying spells
- Feels useless

Empirical correlates, consistent with the subscales' content interpretation, were found for two of the Harris-Lingoes scale 3 subscales with a sample of inpatient adolescents (Gallucci, 1994). Adolescents with high scores on Hy_2 (Need for Affection) were unlikely to like new and exciting experiences or feelings, did not have angry arguments with adults, and were unlikely to abuse cocaine or other stimulants. Hy_5 (Inhibition of Aggression) was associated with youth who were perfectionistic and planful, who were unlikely to act impulsively, who talk before thinking, or who engage in verbal arguments with adults or other adolescents. These young people did not like to do frightening things, nor did they seem to experience guilt after doing something wrong. Table 11-6 provides a summary of scale 3 interpretive rules.

Scale 4: Psychopathic Deviate (Pd)

Scale 4 is one of the more prominent scales on adolescents' profiles (e.g., Archer, 1987; Cashel et al., 1998; Gallucci, 1994; Marks, Seeman & Haller, 1974; Moore, Thompson-Pope & Whited, 1996; Williams & Butcher, 1989b). It is by far the most frequently elevated scale in the MMPI-A clinical sample, with over one-third of the boys and girls scoring greater than or equal to a T score of 65 (Table 11-2). Hathaway and Monachesi (1953a) indicated that high scorers are often young, delinquent, affected little by remorse, and not particularly responsive to censure or punishment. They are more likely to commit asocial acts, be in conflict with their families, and have more extensive social problems.

Table 11-6. Scale 3 Interpretive Guidelines for the MMPI-A

☐ Elevations on Hy may be associated with somatic complaints.

☐ Boys in school settings are more likely to have problems in school; clinical boys, including delinquents, could be assessed for a history of suicidal ideation and/or gestures.

☐ Previous research on the MMPI with adolescents suggests that elevations may be associated with the tendency to develop physical problems as a reaction to stress or paralysis in outpatient boys.

☐ Incarcerated delinquent boys may have concentration difficulties, restlessness, anorexia, cruelty toward others, and depressive feelings, particularly in the afternoon.

☐ Psychiatric inpatients with elevations $\geq$ 65 on Harris-Lingoes subscale Hy_2 (Need for Affection) are unlikely to show anger toward adults, probably would not like new and exciting experiences or feelings, or use cocaine or other stimulants.

☐ Psychiatric inpatients with elevations $\geq$ 65 on Harris-Lingoes subscale Hy_5 (Inhibition of Aggression) may be perfectionistic and planful as well as unlikely to engage in verbal disagreements with adults or peers, talk before thinking, or act impulsively.

☐ The content of the Harris-Lingoes subscales with elevations $\geq$ 65 can be consulted to refine interpretations of scale 3 elevations ($\geq$ 60). The following are content-based interpretive statements:

Hy_1—Denial of Social Anxiety (6 items)

- Denies concerns about shyness
- Denies difficulties in meeting or talking to others
- Denies that his or her behavior is influenced by others
- Denies not speaking unless spoken to

Hy_2—Need for Affection (12 items)

- Denies negative feelings or thoughts about others or concerns about his or her motivations
- Denies that others exaggerate problems to elicit sympathy or use unfair means
- Denies that others lie or that it is best to trust no one
- Denies getting mad easily or engaging in oppositional behavior
- Indicates being friendly with others even if they do things considered wrong

Hy_3—Lassitude-Malaise (15 items)

- Denies good health
- Denies feeling fresh and rested in mornings, reports tiring quickly and having fitful and disturbed sleep
- Reports sadness, denies happiness
- Weak
- Restless
- Apathetic
- Poor appetite
- Problems with staying on task
- Denies that home life is pleasant

Table 11-6. Scale 3 Interpretive Guidelines for the MMPI-A, continued

Hy$_4$—Somatic Complaints (17 items)

- Headaches or tight band around head
- Fainting or dizzy spells, balance problems
- Hand shaking or twitching muscles
- Eye problems
- Cardiovascular symptoms, such as chest pains, heart pounding, shortness of breath
- Other symptoms, such as a lump in the throat, nausea, hot flashes, general pains

Hy$_5$—Inhibition of Aggression (7 items)

- Dislikes crime articles, mystery or detective stories
- Denies irritability or feeling like swearing
- Denies that what others think does not bother him or her
- Denies that seeing blood does not bother him or her
- Denies problems with indecisiveness

Numerous descriptors have been found to be associated with high scale 4 responding in adolescents. Even in general population samples (e.g., Hathaway & Monachesi, 1963), many behavior problems are associated with high Pd responding (e.g., family problems, poor school adjustment, poor school conduct, school dropout, teacher-predicted delinquency, and emotional problems). More recent studies demonstrate that high scale 4 adolescents are more likely to be involved with the use of alcohol or other drugs (e.g., Archer et al., 1988; Basham, 1992; Butcher et al., 1992). The problems become more severe when one is sampling from clinical settings where elevated Pd responding is also associated with school, family, and legal problems (Butcher et al., 1992; Wrobel & Lachar, 1992). Adolescents with elevations on scale 4 who are being treated in inpatient psychiatric settings are at risk for suicidal behaviors (Kopper et al., 1998).

Parents of these young people describe numerous externalizing behavior problems, including lying, cheating, stealing, temper outbursts, and aggression. In the MMPI-A clinical samples, high scale 4 responding also is associated with having been physically abused and a runaway (boys) or sexually abused and active (girls). Runaway behavior was found for high-scoring outpatient girls by Wrobel and Lachar (1992). High scoring boys and girls liked wild parties and doing new and exciting things, even if they were frightening, unusual, or illegal (Gallucci, 1994). In addition to disturbances of conduct, boys incarcerated for a number of offenses also reported disturbances in mood, sleep, and concentration and symptoms of anxiety (Cashel et al., 1998). Therapists rated adolescents with elevated Pd scores as less motivated and open in therapy sessions (Archer et al., 1988).

A major problem in interpreting high scale 4 responding is determining which of the many possible descriptors apply to a given adolescent. Inspection of the Harris-Lingoes subscales is one way to resolve these questions. The Harris-Lingoes subscales are Pd$_1$ (Family Discord), Pd$_2$ (Authority Problems), Pd$_3$ (Social Imperturbability), Pd$_4$ (Social Alienation), and Pd$_5$ (Self-Alienation). Pd$_5$ made an independent contribution to assessing suicide risk for both boys and girls, and Pd$_4$ made an additional contribution to assessing suicide risk in boys (Kopper et al.,

Table 11-7. Scale 4 Interpretive Guidelines for the MMPI-A

☐ In both school and clinical settings, elevations on scale 4 are associated with numerous behavior problems, including family difficulties, poor school adjustment, poor school conduct, school dropout, suspensions, and failures.

☐ Use of alcohol or other drugs is likely in those with elevated scores. These problems become more extreme in young people seen in clinical settings.

☐ Difficulties with the law and juvenile authorities increase in clinical settings. High-scoring boys and girls enjoy wild parties and new and exciting experiences, even if they are frightening, unusual, or illegal.

☐ Parents of clinical adolescents report many externalizing behavior problems, including lying; cheating; disobedience; impulsivity; stealing; swearing; associating with a bad peer group; poor school work; alcohol and other drug use; being remorseless, secretive, threatening, cruel, argumentative, jealous, moody, and demanding of attention; and having temper outbursts and feelings of persecution.

☐ Therapists of clinical boys also report similar, very problematic acting-out behaviors as well as moodiness, attention seeking, resentfulness, clinging to adults, and beliefs that they are evil or deserving of severe punishment. In addition to conduct problems, incarcerated delinquent boys may show disturbances in mood, sleep, and concentration and have anxiety symptoms.

☐ Boys are more likely to have a history of running away from home and could be evaluated for a history of being physically abused. Previous MMPI research suggests that clinical girls may also run away.

☐ Clinical girls could be evaluated for having a history of sexual abuse and are likely to be sexually active.

☐ Based on the original MMPI, adolescents with high Pd may be less motivated and open in therapy sessions.

☐ Adolescents who are being treated in inpatient psychiatric settings and have elevations on scale 4 are at risk for suicidal behaviors. Alienation appears to be a factor, with increasing risk in both boys and girls if Harris-Lingoes subscale Pd_5 (Self-Alienation) is elevated ≥ 65. An elevation ≥ 65 on Pd_4 (Social Alienation) for boys is another indicator for the risk of suicidal gestures.

☐ Elevations ≥ 65 on Harris-Lingoes subscales Pd_1, Pd_2, and Pd_5 are associated with the following descriptors for inpatients:
- Pd_1—Family Discord: Clinicians seeing boys are more likely to report family conflict.
- Pd_2—Authority Problems: Greater likelihood of legal system involvement and increased acting out and aggressiveness.
- Pd_5—Self-Alienation: Greater substance abuse problems for both genders treated in an inpatient substance abuse facility and more acting-out problems for girls.

☐ The content of Harris-Lingoes subscales ≥ 65 can be used to resolve which of the many descriptors to emphasize for an elevated Pd score (≥ 60):

Pd_1—Family Discord (9 items)

- Quarrelsome, unpleasant family life
- Fault-finding family members
- Little love and companionship
- Desire to leave home
- Parental disapproval of peer group
- Parental disapproval of future career choice

Table 11-7. Scale 4 Interpretive Guidelines for the MMPI-A, continued

---

Pd_2— Authority Problems (8 items)
- Admits stealing, problematic sexual behavior, or being in trouble with the law
- Dislikes school or reports school behavior problems
- Denies being influenced by others or giving up easily in arguments
- Denies being disgusted when criminals are freed by smart lawyers

Pd_3— Social Imperturbability (6 items)
- Denies concerns about shyness or difficulties meeting or talking to others
- Denies being easily downed in arguments or that his or her behavior is influenced by others

Pd_4— Social Alienation (12 items)

- Feels misunderstood by others
- Feels mistreated by others
- Projects blame onto others
- May have been disappointed by love
- Frequently is regretful about his or her behavior
- Denies that his or her behavior is influenced by others
- Denies not being bothered by what others think of him or her

Pd_5— Self-Alienation (12 items)

- Self-critical, regretful
- Desires being as happy as others, denies feeling happy
- Hopeless and apathetic
- Problems with concentrating on a task or job
- Admits peculiar and strange experiences
- May report excessive alcohol use

1998). Pd_5 was also related to clinicians' ratings of chemical dependency problems for both boys and girls in an inpatient substance abuse treatment facility and ratings of total acting-out problems in girls (Basham, 1992). Basham (1992) found support for the empirical validity of Pd_2, with associations with clinicians' ratings of legal system involvement, total acting out, and aggressiveness for both boys and girls. Pd_1 was related to clinicians' ratings of family conflict in boys only (Basham, 1992). As we will discover in Chapter 12, use of the MMPI-A content scales is also very helpful in further interpreting high Pd responses. Table 11-7 provides a summary of interpretive guidelines for Pd.

Scale 5: Masculinity/Femininity (Mf)

Hathaway and Monachesi (1953a) described scale 5 as a measure of masculinity or femininity of interests. They suggested that high scores in boys or men were indicative of general feminine interests as they appeared in contrast to the average man. According to Hathaway and Monachesi (1953a), high scores in girls and women indicated masculine interests. In Chapter 4, we described several conceptual and methodological problems in the development of the Mf scale that suggest that caution be used in deriving interpretive statements for elevations on Mf. The interpretation of scale 5 is less straightforward than the interpretation of most of the other MMPI-A scales. We suggested that Mf could be dropped from the MMPI-A without a significant loss of information (Williams & Butcher, 1989a). Perhaps studies will be done that will indicate its usefulness in clinical assessment. Until that time, scale 5 is best considered a general personality measure, not an indicator of psychopathology. Correlates for high-scoring boys and girls differ and are described separately. Mf elevations are rare in the MMPI-A clinical sample, with only 3% of the clinical boys and 4.8% of the clinical girls having elevations at or above a T score of 65 (T scores for Mf are linear, not uniform). Scale 5 elevations are also relatively uncommon in a psychiatric inpatient sample (Gallucci, 1994). It is surprising, as indicated in Table 11-2, that elevated scores (T scores $\geq$ 65) are slightly more common, although still unusual, in the MMPI-A normative sample (6% boys, 7% girls).

Boys

High-scoring boys endorse an unusual pattern of stereotypically feminine interests. Hathaway and Monachesi (1963) suggested that high-scoring scale 5 boys were more intelligent, had higher grades, and had better school adjustment than those who had lower scores. They also demonstrated scale 5 as an inhibitory scale for acting-out behaviors in both boys and girls. High scale 5 boys were less likely to be engaged in delinquent behavior or to receive predicted delinquency and emotional problem ratings from teachers. This inhibitory effect of scale 5, although not found in our first descriptor study using contrasting high- and low-scoring groups (Williams & Butcher, 1989a), was weakly demonstrated in the correlation analyses presented in the MMPI-A manual (Butcher et al., 1992). However, given the relatively weak negative association with acting-out behaviors, along with Hathaway and Monachesi's caveat that the inhibitory scales were less salient than the excitatory scales, an inhibitory effect for scale 5 should not be overinterpreted in an adolescent's profile. No descriptors for scale 5 scores were found for boys in a correctional facility (Cashel et al., 1998).

Girls

High-scoring girls endorse many unusual stereotypically masculine-oriented, or "macho," interests. According to Hathaway and Monachesi's (1963) findings, these girls were less likely to be highly intelligent and more likely to have lower grades in school. High-scoring scale 5 girls were also less likely to have poor school conduct or receive teacher-predicted delinquency and emotional problem ratings. Elevated scores in the MMPI-A normative girls were also related to poor grades but, inconsistent with Hathaway and Monachesi's (1963) findings, were associated with behavior problems and suspensions from school. Behavior problems were also apparent in the clinical girls, including suspensions, history of learning disabilities, and therapists' ratings of acting-out behaviors. The therapists were likely to describe these girls as oppositional, resentful, having poor anger control, easily upset, moody, lying, stealing, and having other problem behaviors. Wrobel and Lachar (1992) reported that scale 5 scores in outpatient girls were related to parents' report of being in trouble for attacking others and having behavior that is different and makes others angry.

Table 11-8. Scale 5 Interpretive Guidelines for the MMPI-A

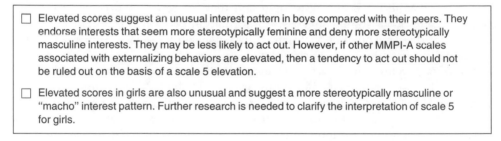

☐ Elevated scores suggest an unusual interest pattern in boys compared with their peers. They endorse interests that seem more stereotypically feminine and deny more stereotypically masculine interests. They may be less likely to act out. However, if other MMPI-A scales associated with externalizing behaviors are elevated, then a tendency to act out should not be ruled out on the basis of a scale 5 elevation.

☐ Elevated scores in girls are also unusual and suggest a more stereotypically masculine or "macho" interest pattern. Further research is needed to clarify the interpretation of scale 5 for girls.

The inconsistencies in the descriptors from Hathaway and Monachesi (1963) and more contemporary studies (Butcher et al., 1992; Wrobel & Lachar, 1992) indicate problems with interpreting this scale for adolescent girls. The inconsistencies could be due to differences in the samples and analyses used by each (i.e., the earlier descriptors are derived for normative girls when scale 5 is the highest point in the profile, whereas the MMPI-A descriptors are based on correlational analyses of raw scores across the entire range of elevations from both normative and clinical samples of girls). Unless further research clarifies its interpretation for girls, we recommend making only the cautious interpretive statements provided in Table 11-8.

Scale 6: Paranoia (Pa)

Hathaway and Monachesi (1953a) reported an interesting gender difference in the interpretation of scale 6 elevations. Moderate elevations from girls in juvenile delinquency facilities were seen to be a personality asset in that, perhaps because of their greater tendency for interpersonal sensitivity, delinquent girls with Pa elevations made special efforts to be liked and appreciated. On the other hand, Hathaway and Monachesi (1953a) noted that boys with high scores on scale 6 dropped out of school early. In Gallucci's (1994) psychiatric inpatient sample, high scale 6 adolescents were perfectionistic, were planful, and felt guilt after wrongdoing. Scale 6 scores in boys were associated with difficulties making up one's mind, liking to do frightening things, and being emotionally involved with others. High scoring girls were able to anticipate the consequences of their actions, were self-critical and doubtful, and thought about how their behavior would affect others.

The MMPI-A manual reported a number of school-related problems (behavioral and academic) for both boys and girls in the normative sample with elevations on scale 6 (Butcher et al., 1992). In addition, clinical boys were also described by their parents as being more hostile and withdrawn (i.e., unliked and having poor peer relations and feelings of persecution, immature, destructive, argumentative, and fighting). Their treatment counselors were also likely to describe them as overly dependent, clinging to adults, attention seeking, resentful, anxious, worried or obsessed, and believing that they were bad and deserving of punishment. High scale 6 scores in boys in a juvenile delinquency setting were associated with suicidal ideation and gestures, cruelty to others, blaming others, panic symptoms, fears of dying or losing control, restlessness, problems completing tasks, hopelessness/

helplessness, anorexia, sleep disturbance, and depressed mood (Cashel et al., 1998). The only significant descriptor for clinical girls was a self-reported increase in disagreements with parents (Butcher et al., 1992).

Pancoast and Archer (1988) found that normal adolescents endorsed more scale 6 items than did normal adults, particularly for Harris-Lingoes Pa$_1$ (Persecutory Ideas). The other Harris-Lingoes subscales for refining interpretations of Pa elevations are Pa$_2$ (Poignancy) and Pa$_3$ (Naïveté). Gallucci (1994) examined the empirical validity of only one Harris-Lingoes subscale for scale 6 (Naïveté), finding high scores related to concern for the welfare of others, not acting impulsively, and having at least one enduring friendship. High-scoring boys were planful and perfectionist, and high-scoring girls were self-critical and had self-doubts. These guidelines are summarized in Table 11-9.

Scale 7: Psychasthenia (Pt)

Although scale 7 as a high point was relatively frequent in Hathaway and Monachesi's (1963) adolescent normative samples, few descriptors were found for Pt elevations, perhaps because their correlates did not include anxiety-based measures. Cashel et al. (1998) provide the strongest support for the validity of scale 7 for adolescents in her study of incarcerated boys. Scale 7 descriptors from those boys included depressed mood, concentration difficulties, restlessness, pacing, excessive running or climbing, generalized anxiety, fears of dying or losing control, fear of public speaking, obsessions and compulsions, problems completing activities, and bullying and teasing.

Wrobel and Lachar (1992) indicated that elevated scores for outpatient boys were related to limited self-confidence and for girls to suicidal threats and stealing. High scores were related to self-criticism and doubt, difficulties making up one's mind, and guilt feelings after wrongdoing among inpatient adolescents (Gallucci, 1994). Many of the items on scale 7 deal with uncontrollable or obsessive thoughts, feelings of fear and/or anxiety, self-doubts, physical complaints, and concentration difficulties. No Harris-Lingoes subscales were developed for scale 7. The MMPI-A manual indicated that Pt elevations were related to depression and increasing discord with parents for clinical girls and to a history of sexual abuse for clinical boys (Butcher et al., 1992). Additional verification of its validity with adolescents would prove useful. Hathaway and Monachesi (1963) speculated that Pt might reflect a rigid personality style that does not become problematic until adulthood, an issue for longitudinal study. Interpretive guidelines are summarized in Table 11-10 for scale 7.

Scale 8: Schizophrenia (Sc)

Hathaway and Monachesi (1963) found several problems associated with high Sc responding in their general population sample. High scorers on scale 8 were more likely to have low intelligence and few achievements in school. They became school dropouts and had family problems. Similar findings are reported in the MMPI-A manual (Butcher et al., 1992). High 8 normative boys and girls were more

Table 11-9. Scale 6 Interpretive Guidelines for the MMPI-A

☐ Pa elevations are related to both behavioral and academic problems for boys and girls in school settings. They are likely to report more problems than the average young person, including school suspensions and poor grades. Girls may report school failures as well.

☐ Clinical girls are likely to report more disagreements with their parent(s), and they also are able to anticipate consequences of their actions, may consider how their behavior affects others, and may be self-critical and doubtful.

☐ Parents of clinical boys describe them as hostile and withdrawn (e.g., being unliked and having poor peer relationships; having feelings of persecution; being immature, destructive, and argumentative; and fighting).

☐ Clinical boys' treatment counselors are also likely to describe them as overly dependent, clinging to adults, attention seeking, resentful, anxious, and worried or obsessed and believing that they are bad and deserving of punishment. Inpatient boys may have difficulties making up their minds, like to do frightening activities, and may be involved emotionally with others.

☐ Psychiatric inpatients with Pa elevations may be perfectionistic, planful, and guilt prone after wrongdoing.

☐ Earlier research with girls in correctional facilities suggests that an elevated Pa may mark a personality asset whereby these girls may have greater interpersonal sensitivity that makes them more likely to make special efforts to be liked and appreciated.

☐ Incarcerated delinquent boys may have suicidal ideations and gestures; show cruelty to others; have panic symptoms and fears of dying or losing control, restlessness, problems completing tasks, hopelessness/helplessness, anorexia, sleep disturbance, and depressed mood; and may blame others.

☐ Elevations $\geq$ 65 on the Harris-Lingoes subscale Pa_3 (Naïveté) may suggest concern for others, having at least one enduring friend, and being unlikely to act impulsively. High-scoring inpatient boys may be planful and perfectionistic, whereas girls are more likely to be self-critical and have self-doubts.

☐ The content of Harris-Lingoes subscales $\geq$ 65 can be used to refine elevated Pa ($\geq$ 60) interpretations:

Pa_1—Persecutory Ideas (17 items)

- Feels misunderstood by others or punished without cause
- Projects blame onto others
- Feels talked about or that others are trying to control him or her
- Has identified someone who is responsible for his or her problems
- Feels threatened
- May indicate being followed, plotted against, poisoned, or hypnotized

Pa_2—Poignancy (9 items)

- Intensely sensitive
- Feels lonely or misunderstood
- Feels uneasy indoors
- Cries easily
- Denies never having participated in a dangerous, thrill-seeking activity
- Denies that excitement can alleviate "down" feelings

Pa_3—Naïveté (9 items)

- Denies negative feelings or thoughts about others or concerns about their motivations
- Denies that others lie or are honest only because they fear being caught
- Denies oppositional behavior
- May report occasionally thinking about something too bad to discuss

Table 11-10. Scale 7 Interpretive Guidelines for the MMPI-A

☐ Correlates have yet to be found for adolescents in school settings with elevated Pt scores.

☐ Clinical girls are likely to be depressed and report more disagreements with parents.

☐ Clinical boys could be evaluated for a history of being sexually abused.

☐ Incarcerated delinquent boys may have depressed mood, concentration difficulties, restlessness, pacing, excessive running or climbing, generalized anxiety, fears of dying or losing control, fear of public speaking, obsessions and compulsions, and problems completing tasks and may bully or tease others.

☐ Previous research with the original MMPI suggests that high Pt clinical boys may have limited self-confidence and that clinical girls may make suicide threats or steal.

---

likely to have behavior problems in school and lower grades. Normative boys reported school suspensions. Normative girls with high scale 8 scores were less likely to report outstanding personal achievement, and they reported weight gain.

In the MMPI-A clinical samples, elevated Sc scores in both genders were associated with a history of having been sexually abused. Adolescents with elevations on scale 8 could be assessed for the possibility of abuse. Girls, regardless of setting, were quite likely to report an increase in disagreements with parents. The clinical boys had more correlates than the girls. Their therapists were likely to describe them as exhibiting psychotic behaviors (e.g., hallucinations, delusions, ideas of reference, peculiar speech and mannerisms, and grandiose beliefs). Their parents reported many internalizing behavior problems, including fears, withdrawal, being guilt prone, perfectionism, worries, and clinging behaviors. The parents also reported several somatic complaints (e.g., stomachaches and nausea, headaches, and dizziness) in these high 8 boys. Finally, their hospital records were likely to note low self-esteem as a problem.

Archer et al. (1988) found similar correlates in combined gender samples for the original MMPI Sc scale. In addition, high 8 adolescents were rated as having a poor prognosis for psychotherapy because they were distrustful of their therapists, less motivated for therapy, reluctant to discuss feelings, and had a poor relationship with their therapist. They were also slow to adjust to treatment routines and expectations. Wrobel and Lachar (1992) reported that both genders were seen as different from their peers; outpatient boys were shy, were withdrawn, and had low self-confidence; outpatient girls were very aggressive, had temper outbursts, acted out, and threatened suicide. Cashel et al. (1998) found that scale 8 descriptors for incarcerated boys included depressed mood, suicidal ideation and attempts, concentration difficulties, self-pity, fear of dying or losing control, obsessions and compulsions, blaming others, problems completing tasks, impulsivity, excessive running or climbing, and cruelty to people. The six Harris-Lingoes subscales for Sc are Sc_1 (Social Alienation), Sc_2 (Emotional Alienation), Sc_3 (Lack of Ego Mastery, Cognitive), Sc_4 (Lack of Ego Mastery, Conative), Sc_5 (Lack of Ego Mastery, Defective Inhibition), and Sc_6 (Bizarre Sensory Experiences). A summary of the Sc interpretive guidelines is provided in Table 11-11.

Table 11-11. Scale 8 Interpretive Guidelines for the MMPI-A

☐ Both boys and girls in school settings with elevated Sc scores are more likely to have several behavior problems in school and lower grades. Normative boys may also be suspended from school. Normative girls are less likely to have an outstanding personal achievement and more likely to report weight gain.

☐ Elevated Sc scores in clinical settings are associated with a history of having been sexually abused. Adolescents with Sc elevations could be assessed for the possibility of abuse.

☐ Girls, regardless of setting, are quite likely to report an increase in disagreements with parents.

☐ Clinical boys are likely to exhibit psychotic behaviors, which may include hallucinations, delusions, ideas of reference, peculiar speech and mannerisms, or grandiose beliefs.

☐ Parents of boys in clinical settings report many internalizing behavior problems, including fears and withdrawal; being guilt prone, perfectionistic, and worried; and exhibiting clinging behaviors. Parents also report several somatic complaints, including stomachaches, nausea, headaches, and dizziness.

☐ Low self-esteem is likely to be a problem in clinical boys.

☐ Incarcerated delinquent boys may have depressed mood, suicidal ideation and attempts, concentration difficulties, self-pity, fear of dying or losing control, obsessions and compulsions, problems completing tasks, impulsivity, excessive running or climbing, and cruelty to others and may blame others.

☐ Previous MMPI research suggests that clinical boys may be shy and withdrawn and have low self-confidence. Clinical girls may be aggressive, have temper outbursts, act out, and threaten suicide.

☐ Research with the original MMPI suggests that adolescents with high Sc elevations may have a poor prognosis for psychotherapy because of being distrustful of their therapists, less motivated for therapy, reluctant to discuss feelings, and have a poor relationship with their therapists. They may also be slow to adapt to treatment unit routines and expectations.

☐ The six Harris-Lingoes subscales can be interpreted if elevated ≥ 65 and if the Sc scores are ≥ 60). Their content-based hypotheses are:

Sc_1—Social Alienation (21 items)

- Family discord, very negative feelings toward family
- Withdrawal, relationship problems
- Feels mistreated, punished without cause
- Feels misunderstood
- Loneliness
- Fearfulness
- Indicates being plotted against

Sc_2—Emotional Alienation (11 items)

- Unhappy, apathetic
- Feels condemned, life is a strain
- Enjoys hurting others, being hurt by others
- Has a death wish
- Fearfulness

Table 11-11. Scale 8 Interpretive Guidelines for the MMPI-A, continued

Sc$_3$— Lack of Ego Mastery, Cognitive (10 items)

- Concentration difficulties, memory problems
- Fears losing mind
- Peculiar and strange experiences or thoughts
- Feels things are not real

Sc$_4$— Lack of Ego Mastery, Conative (14 items)

- Apathetic, difficulty staying on task
- Concentration difficulties
- Unhappy
- Feels condemned, life is a strain
- Withdraws into daydreams
- Has a death wish

Sc$_5$— Lack of Ego Mastery, Defective Inhibition (11 items)

- Uncontrollable urges
- Blank spells
- Emotional outbursts
- Restlessness, excitement
- Fearfulness
- Being touchy

Sc$_6$— Bizarre Sensory Experiences (20 items)

- Blank spells
- Auditory or olfactory hallucinations
- Speech problems
- Twitching muscles, clumsiness, balance problems
- Paralysis
- Emotional outbursts
- Peculiar and strange experiences
- Hot flashes
- Feeling unreal or that others are hypnotizing him or her

Scale 9: Mania (Ma)

Hathaway and Monachesi (1953a) indicated that scale 9 was related to enthusiasm and energy. High scorers were quite interested in many things and approached problems with animation. When this became abnormal, the person's activity level could lead to antisocial acts or irrational manic behavior. Hathaway and Monachesi (1953a) indicated that young people were normally characterized by a considerable amount of the construct that this scale measures, also confirmed later by Pancoast and Archer (1988). However, when adolescents had too much Ma, they became restless and frequently stirred up excitement for excitement's sake.

The study by Cashel et al. (1998) provided support for the validity of scale 9 with delinquent boys, finding the following descriptors: manic behavior; elevated or expansive mood; shouting and complaining; irritability and anger; unusually active, oppositional behavior; blaming others; and cruelty to animals. Scale 9 elevations in these boys were also associated with more lethal suicidal acts. Inpatient adolescents scoring high on scale 9 enjoyed wild parties and getting high with a variety of drugs and alcohol (Gallucci, 1994). Boys liked to do frightening things and often got into arguments with peers; girls often said things without thinking and got into arguments with adults.

High scale 9 scorers are reported in the MMPI-A manual to be associated with both school and home problems in normal girls. School behavior problems were apparent in the clinical girls, as was less likelihood of participating in social organizations. Academic underachievement was also found to be a descriptor. The only correlate for clinical boys was a notation in their records of having previous experience with amphetamines, although Kopper et al. (1998) found an association with suicidal behaviors for both boys and girls. Elevations on the original MMPI Ma were also associated with experience with drugs (Archer et al., 1998; Gallucci, 1994), and these adolescents were also described as having poor motivation for therapy, being less willing to explore feelings, and being insensitive to criticism (Archer et al., 1988).

Harris-Lingoes identified four subscales for elevated Ma scores: Ma_1 (Amorality), Ma_2 (Psychomotor Acceleration), Ma_3 (Imperturbability), and Ma_4 (Ego Inflation). Gallucci (1994) determined empirical correlates for two Harris-Lingoes subscales for scale 9: Ma_1 (Amorality) and Ma_3 (Imperturbability). High scorers on Ma_1 do not have self-doubts, nor do they seem to care for or be emotionally involved with others. They enjoy new and exciting experiences and feelings, even if they are frightening, unusual, or illegal. Abuse of cocaine or other drugs may be possible. For boys, an elevation on Ma_1 was associated with increased risk for suicidal behaviors. High scorers on Ma_3 prefer new experiences that may be unusual, frightening, or even illegal; wild parties; and the company of others who like to party and are exciting and unpredictable. High Ma_3 boys have no difficulty making up their minds, nor do they seem to be attached to or emotionally involved with others. Elevations on Ma_3, for both boys and girls, were associated with increased risk for suicidal behaviors (Kopper et al., 1998). In addition, an elevation on Ma_2 (Psychomotor Acceleration) in girls was associated with suicidal behaviors (Kopper et al., 1998). Table 11-12 summarizes the Ma interpretive guidelines.

Scale 0: Social Introversion (Si)

Si is a very strong measure of problems in social relationships for clinical boys and girls (Butcher et al., 1992; Wrobel & Lachar, 1992). Elevated Si scores are associated with social withdrawal and low self-esteem in both genders. More correlates have been found for girls in clinical settings than for boys (Butcher et al., 1992; Gallucci, 1994), possibly a result of the slightly higher prevalence of elevated Si responding in girls compared with boys in the MMPI-A clinical sample (Table 11-12). It is interesting that the opposite pattern of significant correlates by gender was reported by Wrobel and Lachar (1992). Clinical girls with high scale 0 scores were likely to have eating problems and reported weight gain, depression, suicidal ideations and/or gestures, and a history of few or no friends. Their therapists were likely to describe them as withdrawn, timid, shy, physically weak and uncoordinated, fearful, and depressed. Therapists saw these girls as unlikely to have interests in heterosexual relationships or to act sexually provocatively. Scale 0 appeared to be an

Table 11-12. Scale 9 Interpretive Guidelines for the MMPI-A

☐ Elevated Ma scores are associated with both school and home problems in girls from school settings. School behavior problems are also apparent in clinical girls, as is less likelihood of participating in social organizations at school. Academic underachievement can also be seen in boys.

☐ Experience with a variety of drugs, including alcohol and amphetamines is possible, particularly if the individual is an inpatient or a boy.

☐ Inpatient adolescents likely enjoy wild parties. Inpatient boys like to do frightening things and often get into arguments with peers. Girls are also argumentative, particularly with adults, and frequently say things without thinking.

☐ Suicidal behaviors are possible. Incarcerated boys may use more lethal methods.

☐ Incarcerated delinquent boys may show manic behaviors, elevated or expansive mood, shouting and complaining, irritability and anger, excess activity, oppositional behavior, and cruelty to animals and may blame others.

☐ Elevation > 65 on Ma_1 (Amorality), Ma_2 (Psychomotor Acceleration), and Ma_3 (Imperturbability) are associated with the following descriptors for psychiatric inpatients:
  • Ma_1—Unlikely to have self-doubts or care for or be involved emotionally with others; likely to enjoy new and exciting experiences, even if they are frightening, unusual, or illegal. Abuse of cocaine or other drugs is possible. Boys are at an increased risk for suicidal behaviors.
  • Ma_2—Girls with elevated scores are at an increased risk for suicidal behaviors.
  • Ma_3—May be at increased risk for suicidal behaviors; likely to prefer wild parties and new experiences that may be unusual, frightening, or even illegal; and enjoy the company of others with similar interests. Boys show no difficulty making up their minds, nor do they seem emotionally attached to others.

☐ Work with the original MMPI suggests that scale 9 elevations may be related to enthusiasm, interest in many things, and an animated approach to problems. These descriptors frequently characterize the adolescent years although in extremes may be associated with antisocial acts or irrational, manic behaviors.

☐ Ma elevations for adolescents using the original MMPI suggest a poor motivation for therapy, little willingness to explore feelings, and insensitivity to criticisms.

☐ The content-based interpretations for the four Harris-Lingoes subscales with elevations ≥ 65 for evaluating elevated Ma scores ≥ 60 are:

Ma_1—Amorality (6 items)

  • Believes in taking advantage of others
  • Identifies with a peer group, indicates that peers should agree on a single story in times of trouble
  • Enjoys antics of criminals or having criminals freed by smart lawyers

Ma_2—Psychomotor Acceleration (11 items)

  • Enjoys excitement
  • Restlessness
  • Racing thoughts
  • Harmful or shocking urges
  • Denies ever having participated in a dangerous, thrill-seeking activity
  • Feels tension

Table 11-12. Scale 9 Interpretive Guidelines for the MMPI-A, continued

Ma$_3$— Imperturbability (8 items)

- Denies social anxiety or discomfort around others
- Denies being irritable even when ill
- Denies being impatient

Ma$_4$— Ego Inflation (9 items)

- Believes that authority figures often do not know as much as he or she does and that they punish without cause
- Intentionally oppositional at times
- Self-confident
- Others get impatient with him or her

inhibitory scale for girls (i.e., there is a negative association with alcohol or other drug use, delinquent behaviors as reported by parents, and other indicators of acting out). Clinical boys were very unlikely to participate in school activities. Three subscales, developed by Ben-Porath et al. (1989), refine Si interpretations: Si$_1$ (Shyness/Self-Consciousness), Si$_2$ (Social Avoidance), and Si$_3$ (Alienation—Self and Others). Table 11-13 provides the Si interpretive guidelines.

Highlight Summary: Interpretation of Tony's MMPI-A Standard Scales

Tony's Ma, at a T score of 62, was the only standard scale reaching an interpretable level (Figure 11-1). Thus, only limited inferences about Tony's behavior can be made on the basis of the standard scales. His moderate Ma elevation was not unusual for an adolescent, suggesting enthusiasm and possibly higher-than-average activity level with some tendencies toward acting out. Academic underachievement and drug use are possible problems, as are suicidal ideations and gestures. However, the severity of Tony's acting-out problems noted at referral were not reflected in his scores on the standard scales, particularly his low score on scale 4 (53) and moderate scale 9 elevation. Tony is not likely to be a good candidate for psychotherapy given his moderate Ma score and lack of other indicators of personal distress. Tony's low score on Si suggests facility in social relationships, with no indication of social anxiety or withdrawal, which is consistent with his moderate elevation on Ma$_3$.

An examination of Tony's scale 9 Harris-Lingoes subscale scores (Ma$_1$ = 66, Ma$_2$ = 57, Ma$_3$ = 62, Ma$_4$ = 48) provided another source of inferences about his moderately elevated scale 9 score. This pattern of subscale scores suggests that Tony may take advantage of others and identify with an acting-out peer group that believes it is better to cover for one another rather than admitting wrongdoing. His elevated Ma$_1$ and moderately elevated Ma$_3$ scores increase concerns about suicide potential. Given his Ma$_1$ elevation, he is unlikely to express self-doubts, is unlikely to be emotionally involved with others (although he may like wild

Table 11-13. Scale 0 Interpretive Guidelines for the MMPI-A

☐ Si elevations are a strong indicator of problems in social relationships in clinical boys and girls. They are associated with social withdrawal and low self-esteem.

☐ Clinical girls with elevated Si scores are likely to have eating problems and report weight gain, depression, suicidal ideations and/or gestures, and a history of few or no friends.

☐ Therapists of clinical girls are likely to see them as withdrawn, timid, shy, physically weak and uncoordinated, fearful, and depressed. These girls are unlikely to be seen as having an interest in heterosexual relationships or to act sexually provocative.

☐ Elevated scale 0 scores appear to have an inhibitory effect on girls in that they are unlikely to use alcohol or other drugs or to have delinquent behaviors reported by their parents or other acting-out behaviors.

☐ Clinical boys are unlikely to participate in school activities.

☐ The content of three subscales, developed by Ben-Porath, Hostetler, Butcher, and Graham (1989), when elevated ≥ 65, can refine elevated Si interpretations (≥ 60):

Si_1—Shyness/Self-Consciousness (14 items)

- Difficulties meeting or talking to others
- Shy, bashful
- Social anxiety
- Uncomfortable at parties
- Denies being sociable

Si_2—Social Avoidance (8 items)

- Dislikes parties, socials, or dances
- Dislikes and avoids crowds

Si_3—Alienation—Self and Others (17 items)

- Lacks self-confidence
- Distrusts others' motivation
- Easily overwhelmed by difficulties
- Concentration or memory problems
- Disappointed by others
- Impatient with others
- Ruminates
- Desires to be as happy as others

---

parties), and probably enjoys new, exciting, and possibly frightening, unusual, or even illegal activities.

The only other elevated Harris-Lingoes subscale on Tony's MMPI-A was Pd_2 (Authority Problems) (T = 67). Tony endorsed six of its eight items. Although an elevation on Pd_2 is associated with greater likelihood of legal system involvement, increased acting out, and aggressiveness, our confidence in these descriptors is reduced because of the absence of a scale 4 elevation.

Tony's limited elevations on the MMPI-A standard scales was somewhat surprising given the intensity of his behavior problems and the setting in which he was seen. If his MMPI-A interpretation was limited to the scales covered in this

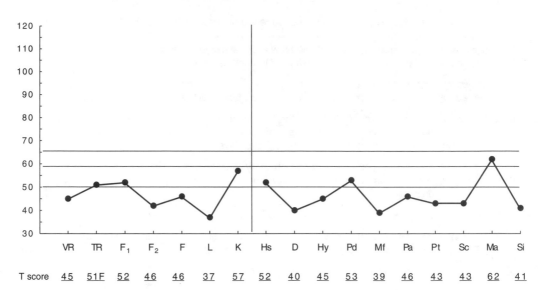

| T score | 45 | 51F | 52 | 46 | 46 | 37 | 57 | 52 | 40 | 45 | 53 | 39 | 46 | 43 | 43 | 62 | 41 |

Figure 11-1. Tony's MMPI-A basic scales profile.

chapter, Tony's problems would not be attributed to significant psychopathology. There was only very marginal support for the conduct disorder that was identified by the diagnostic interview and was probable given his behavioral problems in school, history of assaultive behavior, and difficulties with the law. However, as we will see in the following chapters, the new features of the MMPI-A add greatly to Tony's MMPI-A interpretation.

Chapter 12

Using the MMPI-A Content Scales

The development of the MMPI-A content scales represented a refinement of the instrument for use with adolescents. These scales were created using the multi-stage, multistep scale-development procedures from our work with the MMPI-2 content scales described in Chapter 6. However, for the first time in the use of MMPI scales with adolescents, content scales were constructed using adolescent samples combined with rational procedures that ensured consideration of the unique developmental features of this age range. In addition, item content new to the MMPI-A and specifically related to adolescence was used. Williams, Butcher, Ben-Porath, and Graham (1992) described the details of the development of these scales. We begin this chapter with a synopsis of the development of the content scales, compare them with the MMPI-2 content scales, summarize the scale descriptions used for interpretations, and conclude with a discussion of Tony's MMPI-A content scales profile and his content component scale scores.

Development of the MMPI-A Content Scales

The first stage in the development of the MMPI-A content scales was rational and involved an examination of the appropriateness of the MMPI-2 content scales for adolescents. Step 1 within this stage was to determine whether any of the constructs measured by the MMPI-2 content scales seemed developmentally inappropriate for adolescents. The Work Interference scale was identified as less relevant for adolescents. Furthermore, its items had not been included in the Form TX experimental booklet. However, many school-related items took the place of the Work Interference items and allowed for the development of a School Problems scale. We next determined how many items from the other 14 MMPI-2 content scales were retained on Form TX. All the items for some of the MMPI-2 content scales were included in Form TX (e.g., Anxiety, Antisocial Practices), whereas other scales lost several items (e.g., Obsessiveness, Type A Behavior). The new adolescent-specific content was examined to determine whether any items could be added to the 14 basic MMPI-2 content scales. We then went through the provisional content scales to identify any items that seemed developmentally inappropriate as measures of personality or psychopathology in adolescents. There were only a few items that we rationally deleted at this stage. Some examples included a Health Concerns item, "I have never had any breaking out on my skin that has worried me," and another example from the Anxiety Scale, "I worry over money and business."

By the last step in the first rational stage, we had a list of provisional content scales derived from the MMPI-2 list. However, we also had a substantial number of adolescent-specific items that were not appropriate for any of the MMPI-2 content scales. Thus, we took the next step of having independent raters identify a list of potential adolescent-specific content scales. Three of these provisional scales were developed for the MMPI-A (Adolescent-School Problems, Adolescent-Alienation, and Adolescent-Low Aspirations).

The last step in stage 1 was the elimination of most item overlap. We were aware of the problems of the high prevalence of scale 4 responding in adolescents, which has been a source of difficulty in interpreting adolescent MMPIs, described in the previous two chapters. Scale 4 had quite heterogeneous content, and it was difficult to know which of its many descriptors applied in any individual's case. For the content scales that assess acting-out problems, we developed separate scales with no item overlap: Adolescent-Conduct Problems (A-con), Adolescent-School Problems (A-sch), Adolescent-Family Problems (A-fam), and Adolescent-Alienation (A-aln).

Stage 2 in the development of the MMPI-A content scales was very similar to the second stage in the development of the MMPI-2 content scales. It involved statistical verification of the provisional content scales. Item/scale correlations were run to determine whether the items rationally selected actually belonged on the scales. The internal consistency of these scales was examined, and the validity coefficients of those with low reliability were studied further.

Both the MMPI-2 Type A and the Adolescent-Low Aspirations (A-las) scales had reliability coefficients in the .55 to .65 range. We examined the validity coefficients of these scales before making a decision about whether to drop or retain them. The Type A scale was dropped from the MMPI-A because of both low reliability and low validity. There were just too few items on Form TX to develop a reliable and valid Type A measure for adolescents. On the other hand, because A-las demonstrated good validity with measures of poor school performance, it was retained on the MMPI-A.

Stage 3, like the analogous stage in the development of the MMPI-2 content scales, was the final rational review of the provisional scales. One of the most significant outcomes of this stage was the development of an alternative Antisocial Practices scale. The Adolescent-Conduct Problems scale (A-con) scale was developed during stage 3 because of the relatively poor validity for the Antisocial Practices scale in our adolescent samples.

The final statistical refinement occurred at stage 4. Items that were more highly correlated with other scales were eliminated from the provisional scales. The final reliability and validity coefficients were calculated, as were uniform T scores. The validity coefficients from stage 4 indicated that nine of the scales had strong support of their validity (A-hea, A-biz, A-ang, A-con, A-lse, A-las, A-sod, A-fam, and A-sch). Several other scales showed adequate validity (A-anx, A-dep, and A-aln). Additional validity work is needed for the A-cyn and A-trt scales. Studies using more adequate criterion measures are needed, as are treatment-outcome studies.

The final stage 5 was rational and involved writing descriptions of the scales. These descriptions, along with the validity coefficients from stage 4, were the basis of the descriptors presented in the next section. One of the MMPI-2 content scales, Fears, survived through stage 5 but was dropped from the MMPI-A. It contained approximately 13 items that were unique to it; by dropping the Fears scale, the MMPI-A could be further shortened. Because there were several other anxiety-related measures on the MMPI-A, the decision was made to drop it. All the procedures described in this summary are detailed in Williams et al. (1992).

Comparison of the MMPI-A and MMPI-2 Content Scales

The MMPI-A and MMPI-2 content scales were developed using similar procedures and theoretical perspectives, although with different age-appropriate samples. They have many similarities but do not overlap exactly. Table 12-1 compares the two sets of content scales. Some of these scales differ by very few items (A-anx and ANX, A-hea and HEA, and A-cyn and CYN), whereas others have much less overlapping content (A-fam and FAM). As mentioned previously, one MMPI-2 scale changed substantially on the MMPI-A and was renamed (ASP became A-con).

There are three content scales unique to the MMPI-A because their content is not developmentally appropriate for adults (A-las, A-sch, and A-aln). Likewise, three MMPI-2 content scales were not included on the MMPI-A (FRS, WRK, and TPA). The MMPI-A and MMPI-2 content scales contribute to the uniqueness of the revised instruments. This is particularly true of the adolescent scales because this is the first time a full set of scales has been developed and normed for adolescents.

Interpretation of the MMPI-A Content Scales

The two primary sources for interpretive statements for the MMPI-A content scales are the item content of the scales and the empirically derived descriptors or correlates of the scales (Williams et al., 1992). The addition of content-based statements in the interpretive process differs from the guidelines for interpreting the empirical or standard scales. Although the Harris-Lingoes and Si subscales allow for some content-based interpretive statements for the standard scales, their interpretation, as we saw in Chapters 4 and 11, relies primarily on empirically established correlates and much less on their heterogeneous content.

Elevations on the MMPI-A content scales (T scores of 60–64, inclusive, are moderate elevations; T scores $\geq$ 65 are high elevations) mean that the young person has endorsed more of a particular group of symptoms (e.g., anxiety, bizarre mentation, or school problems) than individuals in the normative sample. The higher the score, the more symptoms endorsed. Average and low scores indicate the converse (i.e., the individual does not acknowledge problems in the area being assessed). Average and low scores indicate that the individual does not say that the scale's content is descriptive of him- or herself. This may be an accurate characterization, or it may indicate an unwillingness to admit to the problems or even an unawareness of the problems. In any event, item content has direct meaning for interpretation.

In addition to item content, Williams et al. (1992) presented empirically derived

Table 12-1. Comparison of the MMPI-A and MMPI-2 Content Scales

MMPI-A scale	MMPI-A abbreviation	MMPI-2 scale	MMPI-2 abbreviation	Number of items		
				MMPI-A	MMPI-2	Overlap
Adolescent-Anxiety	A-anx	Anxiety	ANX	21	23	20
Adolescent-Obsessiveness	A-obs	Obsessiveness	OBS	15	16	12
Adolescent-Depression	A-dep	Depression	DEP	26	33	25
Adolescent-Health Concerns	A-hea	Health Concerns	HEA	37	36	34
Adolescent-Alienation	A-aln	NA	NA	20	NA	NA
Adolescent-Bizarre Mentation	A-biz	Bizarre Mentation	BIZ	19	23	17
Adolescent-Anger	A-ang	Anger	ANG	17	16	11
Adolescent-Cynicism	A-cyn	Cynicism	CYN	22	23	21
Adolescent-Conduct Problems	A-con	Anti-Social Practices	ASP	23	22	7
Adolescent-Low Self-Esteem	A-lse	Low Self-Esteem	LSE	18	24	18
Adolescent-Low Aspirations	A-las	NA	NA	16	NA	NA
Adolescent-Social Discomfort	A-sod	Social Discomfort	SOD	24	24	21
Adolescent-Family Problems	A-fam	Family Problems	FAM	35	25	15
Adolescent-School Problems	A-sch	NA	NA	20	NA	NA
Adolescent-Negative Treatment Indicators	A-trt	Negative Treatment Indicators	TRT	26	26	21
NA	NA	Fears	FRS	NA	23	NA
NA	NA	Type A	TPA	NA	19	NA
NA	NA	Work Interference	WRK	NA	33	NA

Note: NA indicates the scale is not available on this version.

Table 12-2. General Interpretive Guidelines for the MMPI-A Content Scales

☐ High scores on MMPI-A content scales are T scores ≥ 65. High elevations indicate that the adolescent endorses many of the items on the scale. These items usually are symptoms or behaviors related to the construct assessed by the particular scale (e.g., anger, bizarre mentation, school problems). Thus, higher scores indicate more symptoms or problems endorsed as well as a greater likelihood of the scale descriptors applying to the individual.

☐ Moderate elevations on the MMPI-A content scales are T scores of 60 to 64, inclusive. Adolescents with moderate elevations endorse fewer symptoms or problem behaviors than those with higher elevations. Less confidence should be placed in interpretive statements based on moderate elevations, although young people with scores in this range are somewhat more likely than the average adolescent to have some of the symptoms and problem behaviors assessed by the particular content scale.

☐ Average to low elevations on MMPI-A content scales are T scores ≤ 50. These lower elevations suggest that the adolescent did not endorse the scale's symptoms or problems as relevant in their self-descriptions. This may be an accurate characterization, or it may indicate an unwillingness to admit to the problems or even an unawareness of the problems.

descriptors based on correlations between the content scales and external data (i.e., parent and treatment-staff ratings, record reviews) for the MMPI-A content scales. More recent studies provided further empirically based descriptors for the content scales from other samples, including psychiatric inpatients (Arita & Baer, 1998; Kopper, Osman, Osman & Hoffman, 1998) and incarcerated delinquent boys (Cashel, Rogers, Sewell & Holliman, 1998). For each of the 15 MMPI-A content scales, we provide interpretations of elevated scores, first based on content and then on their associated descriptors. In most cases, the empirical descriptors provide validation for the content-based interpretations, as we will see in the following sections. The more general interpretive guidelines for the MMPI-A content scales are summarized in Table 12-2.

Adolescent-Anxiety

Content-Based Interpretive Statements

Adolescents who score high on A-anx report many symptoms of anxiety, including tension, frequent worrying, nervousness, and difficulties sleeping (e.g., nightmares, disturbed sleep, difficulty falling asleep). They report problems with concentration, confusion, and inability to stay on task. Life is a strain for them, their difficulties are insurmountable, and they are under much stress. High scorers worry about losing their minds or going to pieces. They may feel that something dreadful is about to happen. They appear aware of their problems and how they differ from others.

Empirically Based Interpretive Statements

The empirical validity of the Anxiety scale was supported in a combined gender sample of psychiatric inpatients (Arita & Baer, 1998) and in a sample of incarcer-

Table 12-3. A-anx Descriptors for the MMPI-A

☐ Adolescents with moderate to high elevations on A-anx report:
  • Many symptoms of anxiety, including nervousness, tension, and worrying
  • Sleep difficulties (e.g., nightmares, disturbed sleep, problems falling asleep)
  • Concentration problems, confusion, inability to stay on task
  • Life is a strain, their problems are insurmountable
  • Considerable stress
  • Worries about losing their mind, going to pieces
  • Fears about something dreadful happening
  • Awareness of their problems and how they differ from others

☐ High scorers are likely to experience increasing family discord.

☐ High-scoring adolescents in psychiatric or delinquent residential facilities are more likely to report feelings of anxiety, including physiological symptoms, low energy, depressive symptoms, somatic complaints, and social withdrawal and introversion but not externalizing symptoms, such as anger or aggression.

☐ Delinquent boys may also have suicidal ideation, concentration difficulties, restlessness and agitation, self-pity, fears of dying or losing control, and obsessions and compulsions and a need to be reassured.

☐ Inpatient boys with elevated A-anx scores may have a higher risk of suicide.

☐ High-scoring girls in clinical settings are likely to be depressed and have somatic complaints.

ated delinquent boys (Cashel et al., 1998). High scorers are more likely to report feelings of anxiety, including physiological symptoms, low energy, depressive symptoms, somatic complaints, and social withdrawal and introversion, but not externalizing symptoms, such as anger and aggression (Arita & Baer, 1998; Cashel et al., 1998). Delinquent boys may also have suicidal ideation, concentration difficulties, restlessness and agitation, self-pity, fears of dying or losing control, obsessions and compulsions, and a need to be reassured (Cashel et al., 1998). Inpatient boys with elevated A-anx scores had a higher risk of suicide (Kopper et al., 1998). High-scoring adolescents are likely to be experiencing increasing family discord, and girls in clinical settings are likely to be depressed and have somatic complaints (Williams et al., 1992). Table 12-3 summarizes these descriptive statements.

Adolescent-Obsessiveness

Content-Based Interpretive Statements

Adolescent high scorers on A-obs report worrying excessively, often over trivial matters. They report great difficulty making decisions and frequently dread having to make changes in their lives. They have times when they are unable to sleep because of their worries. They are often regretful about things they may have said or done. They may ruminate about "bad words" or may count unimportant items. Others sometimes lose patience with them because of these behaviors.

Table 12-4. A-obs Descriptors for the MMPI-A

☐ Adolescents with moderate to high elevations on A-obs report:
- Worrying excessively, often over trivial matters
- Decision-making difficulties
- Dread of making changes in their lives
- Sleep difficulties because of worrying
- Regrets about things they may have said or done
- Ruminations about "bad words" or counting unimportant items
- Others sometimes losing patience with them because of these behaviors

☐ High-scoring girls are likely experiencing increasing family discord.

☐ High-scoring girls in clinical settings are likely to have suicidal thoughts among their obsessions and/or possible suicidal gestures. Incarcerated delinquent boys with high A-obs scores may use more lethal methods in suicide attempts.

☐ High-scoring boys in clinical settings are described by treatment staff as:
- Overly dependent and clinging to adults
- Anxious and overly concerned about the future
- Resentful, obsessed, worried, or preoccupied
- Having feelings of being bad or deserving punishment

☐ Incarcerated delinquent boys may be agitated and restless but also have slowed speech and psychomotor retardation at other times.

Empirically Based Interpretive Statements

High-scoring girls are likely to have increasing disagreements with their parents. Girls in clinical settings may have suicidal thoughts among their obsessions or possible suicidal gestures. However, more serious suicide attempts were not associated with high A-obs scores in girls (Williams et al., 1992), although Cashel and colleagues (1998) found an association with greater lethality of suicidal acts for delinquent boys with high A-obs scores. Clinical boys with elevated A-obs scores are seen by treatment staff as overly dependent and clinging to adults, anxious and overly concerned about the future, resentful, obsessed, worried, and preoccupied, often with feelings of being bad or deserving of punishment (Williams et al., 1992). Delinquent boys may be agitated and restless but also may have slowed speech and psychomotor retardation at other times (Cashel et al., 1998). Table 12-4 provides the A-obs interpretive guidelines.

Adolescent-Depression

Content-Based Interpretive Statements

Adolescents who score high on A-dep report many symptoms of depression. Frequent crying spells and fatigue are problems. They have many self-deprecative thoughts, including believing that they have not lived the right kind of life, they are condemned, and their sins are unpardonable. Their future seems hopeless, and life is neither worthwhile nor interesting. Most of the time they report feeling blue or wishing they were dead. Sometimes they may think of killing themselves. They report loneliness, even when with other people, and feeling useless or that no one seems to care about them. Their future seems too uncertain for them to make serious plans, and they have periods when they are unable to "get going." Others are seen as much happier. A sense of hopelessness, not caring what happens, and an inclination to take things hard are other characteristics. They are dissatisfied with their lives.

Empirically Based Interpretive Statements

Support for the empirical validity of A-dep was provided in a combined gender sample of adolescent inpatients (Arita & Baer, 1998) and with delinquent boys (Cashel et al., 1998). Psychiatric inpatients with high A-dep scores reported feelings of depression, low energy, somatic complaints, anxiety (including physiological symptoms), and social withdrawal and problems (Arita & Baer, 1998). Delinquent boys reported multiple symptoms, including depression, irritability, excessive guilt, fatigue, restlessness and agitation, concentration difficulties, periods of psychomotor retardation, insomnia, anorexia, self-pity, fears of dying and losing control, panic symptoms, and a need for reassurance. They also had chronic rule violations and often acted before thinking. Their potential for suicide was high, with multiple, serious, and more lethal methods (Cashel et al., 1998). It is interesting that Kopper et al. (1998) did not find that elevated A-dep scores made an independent contribution to suicide risk over and above elevations on scale 2 for boys, although they did find an independent contribution for girls. However, suicidal ideations and/or gestures were associated with high-scoring boys and girls in the MMPI-A clinical sample (Williams et al., 1992). Boys with high A-dep scores in clinical settings could be evaluated for a history of sexual abuse. Clinical girls are likely to have low self-esteem and depression noted as problems in their records. Girls in normative settings with elevated A-dep scores are less likely to have good grades or to be recognized for outstanding personal achievement. They are also more likely to be concerned with significant weight gain (Williams et al., 1992). The A-dep descriptors are included in Table 12-5.

Adolescent-Health Concerns

Content-Based Interpretive Statements

Adolescents with high scores on A-hea report numerous physical problems that interfere with their enjoyment of after-school activities and that contribute to significant school absence. They may report that their physical health is worse than that of their friends. Their physical complaints cross several body systems. Included are gastrointestinal problems (e.g., constipation, nausea and vomiting, stomach trouble), neurological problems (e.g., numbness, convulsions, paralysis, fainting and dizzy spells), sensory problems (e.g., hearing difficulty, poor eyesight), cardiovascular symptoms (e.g., heart or chest pain), skin problems, pain (e.g., headaches, neck pain), and respiratory problems. High scorers report worrying about their health and feeling that their problems would disappear if only their health would improve.

Table 12-5. A-dep Descriptors for the MMPI-A

☐ Adolescents with moderate to high elevations on A-dep report:
- Many symptoms of depression
- Frequent crying spells and fatigue
- Several self-deprecative thoughts (e.g., beliefs that they have not lived the right kind of life, they are condemned, their sins are unpardonable)
- Their future seems hopeless
- Life is neither worthwhile nor interesting
- Feeling blue
- Sometimes thinking of killing themselves and/or wishing they were dead
- Loneliness even when with other people
- Feelings of uselessness or that no one seems to care about them
- Their future seems very uncertain
- Periods when they are unable to "get going"
- Other people are much happier than they
- Hopelessness, not caring what happens, inclination to take things hard
- Dissatisfaction with their lives

☐ Psychiatric inpatients with high A-dep scores report feelings of depression; low energy; somatic complaints; anxiety, including physiological symptoms; and social withdrawal and problems.

☐ High scorers in clinical settings are likely to have suicidal ideations and/or gestures. The potential for suicide may be especially high among incarcerated delinquent boys, who may have multiple and serious attempts using more lethal methods.

☐ High-scoring girls in clinical settings have noticeably low self-esteem and depression.

☐ High-scoring girls in school settings are the following:
- Less likely to have good grades
- Less likely to be recognized for an outstanding personal achievement
- More likely to be concerned with significant weight gain

☐ High-scoring boys in clinical settings could be evaluated for a history of sexual abuse.

☐ Delinquent boys report multiple symptoms, including depression, irritability, excessive guilt, fatigue, restlessness and agitation, concentration difficulties, periods of psychomotor retardation, insomnia, anorexia, self-pity, fears of dying and losing control, panic symptoms, and need for reassurance. They also may have chronic rule violations and often act before thinking.

Empirically Based Interpretive Statements

Somatic complaints are verified as empirical descriptors of high-scoring adolescents (Arita & Baer, 1998; Williams et al., 1992). In addition, young people in normative settings are more likely to have both academic and behavioral problems in school, including poor grades, course failures, and suspensions (Williams et al., 1992). Parents of adolescents in clinical settings are likely to report numerous physical problems in their offspring, including nausea and vomiting, pains, headaches, dizziness, rashes, and eye problems. Their parents may see them as fearful of school. Clinical girls are likely to report increasing disagreements with parents. Many other problems are associated with elevated A-hea scores in clinical boys. Their parents see them as very worried and anxious, accident and guilt prone, clinging, fearful, and perfectionist. High-scoring boys may be less bright than

Table 12-6. A-hea Descriptors for the MMPI-A

☐ Adolescents with moderate to high elevations on A-hea report:
  • Numerous physical problems that interfere with their enjoyment of after-school activities and contribute to significant school absence
  • That their physical health is worse than their friends'
  • Physical complaints across several body systems
  • Gastrointestinal problems (e.g., constipation, nausea and vomiting, stomach trouble)
  • Neurological problems (e.g., numbness, convulsions, paralysis, fainting, dizzy spells)
  • Sensory problems (e.g., hearing difficulty, poor eyesight)
  • Cardiovascular symptoms (e.g., heart or chest pain)
  • Skin problems
  • Pain (e.g., headaches, neck pain)
  • Respiratory problems
  • Worries about their health
  • Feelings that their problems would be solved if only their health would improve

☐ High scorers in school settings are more likely to have both academic and behavioral problems in school, including poor grades, course failures, and suspensions.

☐ High-scoring boys may be less bright than others and are more likely to have lost weight.

☐ Parents of adolescents seen in clinical settings are likely to describe their offspring as:
  • Having numerous physical problems (e.g., nausea and vomiting, pains, headaches, dizziness, rashes, and eye problems)
  • Being fearful of school

☐ Clinical girls are likely to report increasing disagreements with parents.

☐ Clinical boys' parents also describe them as very worried and anxious, accident prone, guilt prone, clinging, fearful, and perfectionistic.

☐ Delinquent boys may report feeling depressed about the incident leading to their incarceration, try to resist feelings of irritability, are restless, and may show cruelty toward others.

others and are more likely to have lost weight (Williams et al., 1992). Delinquent boys may report feeling depressed about the incident leading to their incarceration, try to resist feelings of irritability, are restless, and may show cruelty toward others (Cashel et al., 1998). The A-hea descriptive statements are summarized in Table 12-6.

Adolescent-Alienation

Content-Based Interpretive Statements

High scorers on A-aln report considerable emotional distance from others. They believe that they are getting a raw deal from life and that no one cares about or understands them. They feel unliked by others and report an inability to get along with others. They report having no one, including parents or close friends, who understands them. They feel that others are out to get them and are unkind to

Table 12-7. A-aln Descriptors for the MMPI-A

☐ Adolescents with moderate to high elevations on A-aln report:
  • Considerable emotional distance from others
  • Beliefs that they are getting a raw deal from life and that no one cares about or understands them
  • Feeling unliked by others
  • An inability to get along with others
  • Having no one, including parents and close friends, who understands them
  • Feelings that others are out to get them and are unkind to them
  • That they do not have as much fun as other adolescents
  • They would prefer living all alone in a cabin in the woods
  • Having difficulty self-disclosing
  • Feeling awkward when having to talk in a group
  • Not appreciative when others give their opinions
  • Seeing others as blocking their attempts at success

☐ High scorers are less likely to report having good grades in school.

☐ High-scoring girls in school settings are likely to report a weight gain.

☐ High scores on A-aln are associated with feelings of depression, hopelessness and helplessness, and low energy in psychiatric and delinquent residential settings.

☐ Elevations on A-aln are associated with suicide risk for boys, but not girls, in psychiatric settings.

☐ Social problems (e.g., few or no friends, social skills deficits) are possible in clinical populations.

☐ Delinquent boys may show sleep problems, aches and pains, panic symptoms, difficulties concentrating, pacing, restlessness, and cruelty toward others.

them. They do not believe that they have as much fun as other adolescents and would prefer living all alone in a cabin in the woods. They have difficulty self-disclosing and report feeling awkward when having to talk in a group. They may not appreciate hearing others give their opinions. Other people are seen as blocking their attempts at success.

Empirically Based Interpretive Statements

High scores on A-aln are associated with feelings of depression, hopelessness and helplessness, and low energy (Arita & Baer, 1998; Cashel et al., 1998). Kopper et al. (1998) found that elevations on A-aln made an independent contribution beyond that made by scale 2 in the assessment of suicide risk for boys but not girls. Social problems are possible in clinical populations (Arita & Baer, 1998; Williams et al., 1992). Adolescents with high scores on A-aln are less likely to report having good grades in school, and normative girls with high scores may have a problem with weight gain (Williams et al., 1992). Delinquent boys may show sleep problems, aches and pains, panic symptoms, difficulties concentrating, pacing, restlessness, and cruelty toward others (Cashel et al., 1998). These interpretive statements are included in Table 12-7.

Table 12-8. A-biz Descriptors for the MMPI-A

☐ Adolescents with moderate to high elevations on A-biz report:
  - Very strange thoughts and experiences, including possible auditory, visual, and olfactory hallucinations
  - Strange and unusual experiences
  - Beliefs that there is something wrong with their minds
  - Paranoid ideations (i.e., beliefs that they are being plotted against or someone is trying to poison them)
  - Beliefs that others are trying to steal their thoughts and ideas or control their minds
  - Evil spirits or ghosts possess or influence them

☐ High scorers in school settings report many serious behavior and academic problems, including poor grades, course failures, and suspensions.

☐ Adolescents in clinical settings are likely to show bizarre or psychotic behaviors.

☐ Clinical girls are likely to come from disruptive families characterized by parents or siblings with arrest records.

☐ Clinical boys may have had a child-protection worker assigned to them in the past, and the treatment staff is likely to observe them exhibiting strange behaviors and mannerisms.

☐ Delinquent boys showed depression associated with the event leading to their incarceration; had concentration difficulties, anorexia, or suicidal ideation; blamed others; were cruel to others; and reported childhood perceptual phenomena.

Adolescent-Bizarre Mentation

Content-Based Interpretive Statements

Adolescents scoring high on A-biz report very strange thoughts and experiences, including possible auditory, visual, or olfactory hallucinations. They characterize their experiences as strange and unusual and believe that there is something wrong with their minds. Paranoid ideations (i.e., beliefs that they are being plotted against or someone is trying to poison them) may also be reported. They may believe that others are trying to steal their thoughts and ideas or control their minds. They may believe that evil spirits or ghosts possess or influence them.

Empirically Based Interpretive Statements

Boys and girls with elevated A-biz scores in the MMPI-A normative sample experience numerous behavior and academic problems in school, including poor grades, course failures, and suspensions (Williams et al., 1992). Adolescents in the MMPI-A clinical settings were likely to show bizarre or psychotic behaviors. Clinical girls came from disruptive families characterized by parents or siblings with arrest records. Clinical boys had a child-protection worker assigned to them. Treatment staff were likely to observe strange behaviors and mannerisms in boys with elevated A-biz scores (Williams et al., 1992). Delinquent boys showed depression associated with the event leading to their incarceration; had concentration difficulties, anorexia, or suicidal ideation; blamed others; were cruel to others; and reported childhood perceptual phenomena (Cashel et al., 1998). The A-biz interpretive descriptors are available in Table 12-8.

Adolescent-Anger

Content-Based Interpretive Statements

Adolescents with high scores on A-ang report considerable anger-control problems. They often feel like swearing, smashing things, or starting a fistfight. Not surprisingly, they frequently get into trouble for breaking or destroying things. They report having considerable problems with irritability and impatience with others. They have been told that they throw temper tantrums to get their way. They especially do not like others to hurry them or to get ahead of them in a line. They indicate that they are hotheaded and often have to yell in order to make a point. Occasionally they report getting into fights, especially when drinking.

Empirically Based Interpretive Statements

Adolescents with elevated A-ang scores are very likely to act out in school or at home (Arita & Baer, 1998; Cashel et al., 1998; Williams et al., 1992). It is not unexpected that the intensity of acting-out behaviors increases in clinical settings. Both boys and girls in these settings are likely to have histories of assaultive behaviors. Both parents and treatment staff observe numerous instances of anger-control problems, resentfulness, impulsivity, impatience, variable moods, and other externalizing behaviors. These young people may be overly interested in violence and aggression (Williams et al., 1992).

Clinical boys with high A-ang scores may need reassurance (Cashel et al., 1998) or may be seen as overly clinging and dependent by treatment staff (Williams et al., 1992). Although resentful, they are also attention seeking, self-condemning, and anxious about the future. They may feel deserving of punishment. Clinical boys could be evaluated for a possible history of sexual abuse (Williams et al., 1992). Incarcerated delinquent boys may present a mixed picture with complaints of depression associated with the event leading to incarceration, attempts to resist irritability, fatigue, shouting, complaining, agitation, insomnia, grandiosity, racing thoughts, impulsivity, difficulty playing quietly, blaming others, and cruelty toward animals and people (Cashel et al., 1998).

High-scoring clinical girls are likely to have had court appearances. Their parents describe them as aggressive and delinquent, which is also confirmed by treatment staff. They may act out sexually with promiscuity and provocative clothing and behaviors. Treatment staff are likely to report a need to supervise these girls around boys (Williams et al., 1992). The A-ang descriptive statements are summarized in Table 12-9.

Adolescent-Cynicism

Misanthropic attitudes are held by adolescents scoring high on A-cyn. They believe that others are out to get them and will use unfair means to gain an advantage. They look for hidden motives whenever someone does something nice for them. They believe that it is safer to trust no one because people make friends in order to use them. Others are seen as inwardly disliking to help another person, and they are on guard when people seem more friendly than they expect. They

Table 12-9. A-ang Descriptors for the MMPI-A

☐ Adolescents with moderate to high elevations on A-ang report:
  • Considerable anger-control problems
  • Feeling like swearing, smashing things, or starting a fistfight
  • Getting into trouble for breaking or destroying things
  • Considerable problems with irritability and impatience
  • Throwing temper tantrums to get their way
  • Not liking others to hurry them or get ahead of them in a line
  • Being hotheaded and having to yell in order to make a point
  • Getting into fights, especially when drinking

☐ Adolescents with elevated A-ang are very likely to act out in school or at home, and, not unexpectedly, the intensity of the acting-out behaviors increases in clinical settings.

☐ High-scoring adolescents in clinical settings:
  • Have histories of assaultive behaviors
  • Are likely to be described by both parents and treatment staff as having anger-control problems, resentfulness, impulsivity, impatience, variable moods, and other externalizing behaviors
  • Are overly interested in violence and aggression

☐ High-scoring clinical girls:
  • Have had court appearances
  • Are likely to be described as aggressive and delinquent by parents and treatment staff
  • Act out sexually with promiscuity, wearing provocative clothing, and behaving flirtatiously
  • Need supervision around boys

☐ High-scoring clinical boys:
  • May be seen as overly clinging and dependent or needing reassurance by treatment staff
  • Although resentful, they are also attention seeking, self-condemning, and anxious about the future
  • May feel deserving of punishment
  • May have a history of sexual abuse

☐ Delinquent boys may present with a mixed picture:
  • Complaints of depression associated with the event leading to incarceration
  • Attempts to resist irritability
  • Fatigue
  • Shouting and complaining
  • Agitation
  • Insomnia
  • Grandiosity
  • Racing thoughts
  • Impulsivity
  • Difficulty playing quietly
  • Blaming others
  • Cruelty toward animals and people

feel misunderstood by others and see others as very jealous of them. Only two empirical descriptors have been presented in the literature for high A-cyn scores. Cashel et al. (1998) indicated that high-scoring delinquent boys were likely to be argumentative and unusually energetic or active. Interpretive descriptors for A-cyn are summarized in Table 12-10.

Table 12-10. A-cyn Descriptors for the MMPI-A

☐ Adolescents with moderate to high elevations on A-cyn report:
- Beliefs that others are out to get them and will use unfair means to gain an advantage
- Looking for hidden motives whenever someone does something nice for them
- Beliefs that it is safer to trust no one because people make friends in order to use them
- Seeing others as inwardly disliking helping another person
- Being on guard when people seem more friendly than they expect
- Feeling misunderstood by others
- Seeing others as being very jealous of them

☐ High-scoring delinquent boys are likely to be argumentative and unusually energetic or active.

Adolescent-Conduct Problems

Content-Based Interpretive Statements

Adolescents scoring high on A-con report many different behavioral problems, including stealing, shoplifting, lying, swearing, breaking or destroying property, and being disrespectful and oppositional. They may report having legal difficulties and see no problems in trying to get around the law. Their peer group is often in trouble and can talk them into doing things they know they should not do. At times they may try to make other people afraid of them, just for the fun of it. They are entertained by another's criminal behavior and do not blame people for taking advantage of others. They may admit to doing bad things in the past that they cannot tell anyone about.

Empirically Based Interpretive Statements

Elevated scores on A-con are related to the many very serious acting-out behaviors described previously in its item content (Arita & Baer, 1998; Cashel et al., 1998; Williams et al., 1992). High-scoring boys and girls, even from general-population school settings, are likely to have many behavior problems in school and are less likely to be doing well academically (Williams et al., 1992). There is a tendency for these problems to be acknowledged more readily by high-scoring girls compared with boys. Descriptors found for the normative girls included self-reported disciplinary and probation problems, suspension, course failures, and cheating or lying in school. This does not mean that high-scoring girls have more of these problems than boys because even though the boys admit to fewer problems, their parents indicate otherwise (see the following discussion).

Adolescent high scorers on A-con are likely to use alcohol and other drugs. More problematic alcohol and drug use is evident in high scorers seen in clinical settings. In fact, high-scoring girls in clinical settings are likely to have had records indicating previous treatment for substance abuse problems (Williams et al., 1992).

Adolescents in clinical settings show more extreme behaviors than the normative sample when A-con is elevated. Parents of both genders report many delinquent behaviors in their offspring, including lying, cheating, stealing, running away, and truancy. In addition, they describe high scorers as disobedient, impulsive, and swearing. Girls are more likely to report increasing family discord. Parents of high-scoring boys report even more behavior problems and less social competence at school than do parents of girls (Williams et al., 1992).

There is empirical evidence that high-scoring adolescents have court involvement for problems such as stealing (girls), status offenses (girls), being placed on probation (girls), and violent nonstatus offenses (boys). Boys have a greater likelihood of having a child-protection worker assigned to them (Williams et al., 1992).

Treatment staff of high-scoring girls report numerous behavior problems, including anger-control problems, lying, cheating, unpredictability, volatility, and being moody, bossy, and easily upset. These girls are seen as sexually active, provocative, and requiring supervision when around the opposite gender. They are likely to be impatient, resentful, persistent, and impulsive. They are unlikely to be seen as depressed (Williams et al., 1992). The A-con interpretive statements are summarized in Table 12-11.

Adolescent-Low Self-Esteem

Content-Based Interpretive Statements

Adolescents with high A-lse scores have very negative opinions of themselves, including being unattractive, lacking self-confidence, feeling useless, having little ability and several faults, and not being able to do anything well. They are likely to yield to pressure from others, changing their minds or giving up in arguments. They tend to let other people take charge when problems have to be solved and do not feel that they are capable of planning for their own future. They have difficulty accepting or believing compliments from others. They may get confused and forgetful.

Empirically Based Interpretive Statements

Girls in the MMPI-A normative sample who scored high on A-lse were more likely to report having poor grades and significant weight gain. They were less likely to report having a recent outstanding personal achievement. No correlates were found for the normative boys, which may be more related to the relative infrequency of low scores in boys than to differential validity for the genders (Williams et al., 1992).

Clinical boys, as well as girls in these settings, were likely to have low self-esteem noted as a problem in their treatment records. Boys were also seen as having poor social skills. High-scoring boys could be evaluated further for the possibility of a history of sexual abuse. Clinical girls were likely to be seen as depressed, with the possibility of suicidal thoughts and/or gestures. They were likely to have a history of learning disabilities and to report increasing disagreements with parents (Williams et al., 1992). Incarcerated delinquent boys were likely to report excessive guilt, self-pity, concentration difficulties, and excessive

Table 12-11. A-con Descriptors for the MMPI-A

☐ Adolescents with moderate to high elevations on A-con report:
  - Many different behavior problems, including stealing, shoplifting, lying, swearing, and breaking or destroying property
  - Being disrespectful and oppositional
  - Legal difficulties
  - Having a peer group that is often in trouble and who talk them into doing things they know they should not
  - At times trying to make other people afraid of them, just for the fun of it
  - Being entertained by another's criminal behavior
  - Not blaming people for taking advantage of others
  - Admitting to doing bad things in the past they can tell no one

☐ Adolescent high scorers are likely to use alcohol and other drugs, with even more problematic alcohol and drug use evident in the high scorers seen in clinical settings. In fact, girls in clinical settings are likely to have had previous treatment for alcohol and drug problems.

☐ High-scoring adolescents are likely to have court involvement for problems like stealing (girls), status offenses (girls), being placed on probation (girls), violent nonstatus offenses (boys), and having a child-protection worker assigned to them (boys).

☐ High scorers are likely to have:
  - The many serious acting-out behaviors described in A-con item content
  - Many behavior problems in school and less likely to be doing well academically
  - A tendency to acknowledge these problems more readily if a girl
  - Self-reported disciplinary and probation problems, suspension, course failures, and being caught cheating or lying in school (particularly if a girl)

☐ High scorers in clinical settings:
  - Show more extreme behaviors than the normative sample
  - Have parents who report many delinquent behaviors including lying, cheating, stealing, running away, and truancy. Their offspring are seen as disobedient, impulsive, and swearing

☐ Parents of high-scoring boys report even more behavior problems and less social confidence at school than the parents of girls.

☐ Treatment staff of high-scoring girls report numerous behavior problems, including anger control, lying, unpredictable behavior, volatility, moodiness, cheating, being bossy, and becoming easily upset. These girls are likely to be sexually active, be provocative, and require supervision when around boys. They are likely to be impatient, resentful, persistent, and impulsive but are unlikely to be seen as depressed.

---

shifts in activities (Cashel et al., 1998). The A-lse descriptors are summarized in Table 12-12.

Adolescent-Low Aspirations

Content-Based Interpretive Statements

High scorers on A-las are disinterested in being successful, particularly academically. They do not like to study or read about things, and they dislike science and lectures on serious topics. They may prefer work that allows them to be care-

Table 12-12. A-lse Descriptors for the MMPI-A

☐ Adolescents with moderate to high elevations on A-lse report:
  • Very negative attitudes of themselves, including being unattractive, lacking self-confidence, feeling useless, having little ability, having several faults, and not being able to do anything well
  • Being likely to yield to pressure from others
  • Frequently changing their minds or giving up in arguments
  • Tendencies to let other people take charge when problems have to be solved
  • Feeling that they are not capable of planning their own future
  • Difficulties accepting or believing compliments from others
  • Confusion and forgetfulness

☐ Girls in normative settings with elevated scores are likely to report having poor grades and having significant weight gain. They are less likely to have had an outstanding personal achievement.

☐ High scorers in clinical settings are likely to be seen as having low self-esteem among their problems.

☐ Clinical girls are likely to be seen as depressed, with the possibility of suicidal thoughts and/or gestures. They are likely to have a history of learning disabilities and report increasing disagreements with parents.

☐ Clinical boys are seen as having poor social skills.

☐ High-scoring boys could be evaluated further for the possibility of a history of sexual abuse.

☐ Incarcerated delinquent boys may report excessive guilt, self-pity, concentration difficulties, and excessive shifts in activities.

less. Their expectations of success are low. They avoid reading editorials, believing that the comic strips are the only interesting part of a newspaper. They report difficulty starting things and quickly give up when things go wrong. They let other people solve problems and avoid facing difficulties. They believe that others block their success. Others also tell them that they are lazy. They probably do not want to go to college.

Empirically Based Interpretive Statements

As would be expected, given the item content of A-las, high scorers, regardless of setting, were more likely to have poor grades in school and less likely to participate in school activities (Williams et al., 1992). There is some possibility that high-scoring boys may also have more school-related problems. Boys in clinical settings are more likely to be truant or avoid school. They are also more likely to run away from home. Girls in clinical settings are more likely to be seen as engaging in sexual acting out and less likely to report winning an outstanding prize or award (Williams et al., 1992). Delinquent boys with high A-las scores likely have depressive and irritable feelings associated with the event that led to their incarceration; problems with insomnia, anorexia, hopelessness, and helplessness; fears of dying, losing control, heights or depths; and panic symptoms. They should be evaluated

Table 12-13. A-las Descriptors for the MMPI-A

☐ Adolescents with moderate to high elevations on A-las report:
  • Disinterest in being successful, particularly in academics
  • Dislike of studying or reading about things
  • Dislike of science and lectures on serious topics
  • Preference for work that allows them to be careless
  • Low expectations of success
  • Avoidance of reading editorials and preference for the comic strips
  • Difficulty starting things
  • Quickly giving up when things go wrong
  • Letting other people solve problems
  • Avoiding facing difficulties
  • Beliefs that others block their attempts for success
  • Others tell them that they are lazy
  • A disinterest in going to college

☐ High scorers, as expected from the item content, are more likely to:
  • Have poor grades in school
  • Be less willing to participate in school activities
  • Perhaps have more school-related problems, particularly if a boy

☐ Girls in clinical settings are:
  • More likely to be seen as acting out sexually
  • Less likely to report winning an outstanding prize or award

☐ Boys in clinical settings are more likely:
  • To be truant or avoid school
  • To run away from home

☐ Delinquent boys with high A-las scores likely have depressive and irritable feelings associated with the event that led to their incarceration; problems with insomnia; anorexia; hopelessness and helplessness; fears of dying, losing control, heights or depths; and panic symptoms.

☐ Incarcerated delinquent boys should be evaluated for suicide potential, with attention paid to the seriousness of any past attempts and the lethality of methods available to them.

for suicide potential, with attention paid to the seriousness of any past attempts and the lethality of methods available to them (Cashel et al., 1998). Table 12-13 summarizes the A-las interpretive guidelines.

Adolescent-Social Discomfort

Content-Based Interpretive Statements

Adolescents with high scores on A-sod find it very difficult to be around others. They report being shy and much prefer to be alone. They dislike having people around them and actively avoid others. They do not like parties, crowds, dances, or other social gatherings. They avoid initiating conversations. They report embarrassment when having to give an opinion to a group. Others indicate that it is hard to get to know them. They report having difficulty making friends and do not like to meet strangers.

Empirically Based interpretive Statements

Boys and girls in an inpatient psychiatric unit with high A-sod scores were introverted, withdrawn, and had social problems, low energy, and symptoms of depression (Arita & Baer, 1998). Inpatient girls were at increased risk for suicidal behaviors (Kopper et al., 1998). High A-sod boys from the MMPI-A normative sample were more likely to avoid participation in school activities. They were less likely to report using alcohol or other drugs, perhaps because of the strong role that peer groups have in influencing such use. There were no descriptors for the MMPI-A clinical boys, again possibly because of the low frequency of high A-sod scorers among boys in the treatment centers (Williams et al., 1992). However, Cashel and colleagues found the following descriptors in their sample of delinquent boys: frequent and more lethal suicide attempts; irritability, particularly in the afternoon; and need for reassurance.

High-scoring MMPI-A normative girls are also unlikely to report using alcohol or other drugs. In clinical settings high A-sod scores in girls have an inhibitory effect on acting-out behaviors. Both parents and treatment staff are unlikely to describe high-scoring girls as having behavior problems, including alcohol and drug use, sexual acting out, or irresponsibility. They are likely to be seen as withdrawn, timid, fearful, physically weak, and a fringe participant in peer activities. They show little interest in the opposite gender. They have few or no friends, are likely to be depressed, and have eating problems (Williams et al., 1992). Table 12-14 provides interpretive statements for A-sod.

Adolescent-Family Problems

Content-Based Interpretive Statements

Adolescents with high A-fam scores report considerable problems with their parents and other family members. Family discord, jealousy, fault finding, anger, serious disagreements, lack of love and understanding, and limited communication characterize these families. These adolescents do not believe that they can count on their families in times of trouble. They may wish for the day when they are able to leave their homes. They feel that their parents frequently punish them without cause and treat them more like children. They report that their parents dislike their peer group. They do not accept responsibilities around the home and may have run away. They may report having many beatings.

Empirically Based Interpretive Statements

As expected, elevated A-fam scores are associated with many problems in the family and reported increases in family discord. Some of these adolescents' problems spill over into the school setting. However, high A-fam scorers do not show the same asocial behaviors as do high scorers on A-con. Elevations on A-fam are not associated with problems with the courts and police, as are A-con elevations (Williams et al., 1992).

Normative adolescents who score high on A-fam reveal that in addition to overall family discord, there may be increases in parental marital problems. These adolescents report poor grades and more school problems, including suspensions.

Table 12-14. A-sod Descriptors for the MMPI-A

☐ Adolescents with moderate to high elevations on A-sod report:
- Difficulty being around others and making friends
- Shyness and preferring to be alone
- Disliking having others around them and actively avoiding others
- Disliking parties, crowds, dances, or other social gatherings
- Avoidance of initiating conversations
- Embarrassment in having to give an opinion in a group
- Others find it hard to get to know them
- Dislike of meeting others

☐ High-scoring adolescents in school settings are unlikely to report use of alcohol and other drugs, perhaps owing to the strong role that peer groups have in influencing such use.

☐ High-scoring boys are:
- More likely to avoid participation in school activities
- Very unusual in treatment settings

☐ Boys and girls in inpatient psychiatric units with high A-sod scores are likely introverted and withdrawn and have social problems, low energy, and symptoms of depression.

☐ High-scoring clinical girls are:
- At increased risk for suicidal behaviors
- Very unlikely to be in treatment for acting-out behavior problems
- Likely to have parents and treatment staff indicating that they do not engage in behavior problems, including alcohol and drug use, sexual acting out, or irresponsibility
- Instead seen as withdrawn, timid, fearful, physically weak, and a fringe participant in peer activities
- Uninterested in the opposite gender
- Have few or no friends
- Likely to be depressed
- May have eating problems

☐ Incarcerated delinquent boys may have frequent and more lethal suicide attempts; irritability, particularly in the afternoon; and need for reassurance.

Normative girls high on A-fam are more likely to report weight gain, job loss, and failure on a major exam (Williams et al., 1992).

Parents of adolescents in clinical settings report numerous behavior problems in their offspring. Their reports are not limited to externalizing behaviors, as was true with elevations on A-con and A-ang. In addition to lying, cheating, stealing, and other externalizing behaviors, parents of high A-fam youth report somatic complaints, guilt, fearfulness, worrying, crying, clinging, timidity, and withdrawal as characteristic. Boys are seen by their parents as uncommunicative, secretive, sad, self-conscious, unloved, disliked, and lonely. Girls, in addition to being seen by parents as cruel, destructive, prone to fight, immature, and hyperactive, are also reported to be sad, secretive, and self-conscious (Williams et al., 1992).

Treatment staff are also less likely to describe these adolescents' problems solely with acting-out descriptors. Rather, high-scoring boys are seen as overly dependent and clinging, resentful, attention seeking, anxious about the future, preoccupied, and having feelings of self-condemnation and blame. Girls, on the other hand, were seen as likely to act out sexually by being promiscuous, provocative, and preoccupied by sex (Williams et al., 1992).

Hospital records indicated significant family-related problems in high scorers, including running away (boys), physical abuse (boys), and sexual abuse (girls). Risk of serious and potentially lethal suicide attempts were related to high A-fam scores in delinquent boys (Cashel et al., 1998), and increased suicide risk was found for inpatient girls (Kopper et al., 1998). Recommendations for further assessment of these very serious problem areas are indicated for high scorers. Interpretive guidelines for A-fam are provided in Table 12-15.

Adolescent-School Problems

Content-Based Interpretive Statements

Numerous difficulties in school characterize adolescents scoring high on A-sch. They often may be upset by things that happen at school. Poor grades, suspension, truancy, learning problems, negative attitudes toward teachers, and dislike of school are characteristic of high scorers. The only pleasant aspect of school for youth high on A-sch is their friends. They avoid participation in school activities or sports. School is a waste of time in their opinion. Others may consider them lazy. They report frequent boredom and sleepiness at school. Some of these individuals may report being afraid to go to school or missing school because of illness.

Empirically Based Interpretive Statements

Like A-fam, described previously, elevations on A-sch indicate problems in primarily one setting, in this case the school. High scorers are quite likely to have both academic and behavior problems. Interestingly, the A-sch correlates are pretty much limited to school and do not include the asocial activities covered by A-con, the anger-control problems associated with A-ang, or the family discord assessed by A-fam (Williams et al., 1992).

As its item content implies, A-sch elevations are associated with a wide range of school problems, including poor grades, course failures, repeating a grade, disciplinary actions and probation, and suspensions. Parents of high scorers are unlikely to report that their offspring are socially competent in school. They report several school problems that can include poor school work, truancy, lying and cheating, impulsivity, disobedience at school and home, and concentration difficulties. They may also report more general behavior problems, including associating with a bad peer group, running away, alcohol and other drug use, stealing, swearing, and secretiveness (Williams et al., 1992).

Their hospital records revealed many school-related problems as well. Truancy and school avoidance were characteristic responses of both boys and girls. Boys were more likely to run away, act irresponsibly, and have a history of drug use, particularly amphetamines. They could be further evaluated for a history of sexual abuse. Clinical girls were characterized by histories of academic underachievement and/or learning disabilities (Williams et al., 1992). Delinquent boys had problems with generalized depressive feelings as well as depression associated

Table 12-15. A-fam Descriptors for the MMPI-A

☐ Adolescents with moderate to high elevations on A-fam report:
- Considerable problems with their parents and other family members
- Family discord, jealousy, fault finding, anger, serious disagreements, lack of love and understanding, and limited communication
- Beliefs that they cannot count on their family in times of trouble
- Wishes for the day when they are able to leave home for good
- Feeling that their parents punish them without cause
- Beliefs that their parents treat them more like children
- Their parents dislike their peer group
- They do not accept responsibilities around the home
- Possible runaway
- Possible beatings

☐ High scores on A-fam are associated with many of the problems reflected in the item content. Some of these problems do spill over into the school setting. However, elevated scorers on A-fam do not show the same asocial behaviors as do elevated scorers on A-con. Elevations on A-fam are not associated with problems with the courts and police as are elevations on A-con.

☐ Adolescents in school settings with elevated A-fam scores:
- Reveal possible increases in parental marital problems in addition to overall family discord
- Report poor grades and more school problems, including suspensions

☐ Girls in school settings are more likely to report weight gain, job loss, and failure on a major exam.

☐ Parents of adolescents in clinical settings report numerous behavior problems:
- Not limited to the externalizing behaviors associated with elevations on A-con and A-ang. In addition to the lying, cheating, stealing, and other externalizing behaviors, parents also report somatic complaints, guilt, fearfulness, worrying, crying, clinging, timidity, and withdrawal
- Boys especially are seen as uncommunicative, secretive, sad, self-conscious, unloved, disliked, and lonely.
- Girls are likely to be seen as cruel, destructive, prone to fight, immature, and hyperactive but also sad, secretive, and self-conscious.

☐ Treatment staff are also less likely to describe these adolescents' problems solely with acting-out descriptors:
- High-scoring boys are seen as overly dependent and clinging, resentful, attention seeking, anxious about the future, preoccupied, and feeling self-condemnation and blame.
- Girls are seen to act out sexually by being promiscuous, provocative, and preoccupied by sex.

☐ Boys are likely to have a history of running away.

☐ Interpretive reports should include recommendations of further assessment of the possibility of physical abuse, particularly for boys, and sexual abuse, particularly for girls.

☐ Risk of serious and more lethal suicide attempts are related to high A-fam scores in delinquent boys and increased suicide risk for inpatient girls.

Table 12-16. A-sch Descriptors for the MMPI-A

☐ Adolescents with moderate to high elevations on A-sch report:
  • Numerous difficulties in school
  • Being easily upset by things that happen at school
  • Poor grades, suspension, truancy, learning problems, negative attitudes toward teachers, and dislike of school
  • Only pleasant aspect of school is their friends
  • Avoidance of participation in school activities or sports
  • School is a waste of time
  • Others may consider them lazy
  • Frequent boredom and sleepiness in school
  • Possible fears of going to school or missing school because of illness

☐ Elevations on A-sch indicate problems in primarily one setting, in this case the school. High scorers are quite likely to have both academic and behavior problems. As was the case with A-fam, the A-sch correlates are setting specific and do not include the asocial activities covered by A-con, the anger-control problems associated with A-ang, or the family discord assessed by A-fam.

☐ Similar to the item content described above, A-sch elevations are also associated with:
  • A wide range of school problems
  • Poor grades, course failures, repeating a grade, disciplinary actions and probation, and suspensions

☐ Parents of high scorers seen in clinical settings:
  • Are unlikely to report that their offspring are socially competent in school
  • Describe many school behavior problems (e.g., poor school work, truancy, lying and cheating, impulsivity, disobedience at school and home, and concentration difficulties)
  • May also report more general behavior problems, including associating with a bad peer group, running away, alcohol and other drug use, stealing, swearing, and secretiveness

☐ School-related problems, including truancy and school avoidance, were confirmed in the treatment records of these young people.

☐ Clinical boys are more likely to run away or act irresponsibly and may have a history of drug use, particularly amphetamines.

☐ Clinical boys could be further evaluated for a history of sexual abuse.

☐ Delinquent boys may have problems with generalized depressive feelings, depression associated with the event leading to their incarceration, and concentration difficulties.

☐ Clinical girls are characterized by histories of academic underachievement and/or learning disabilities.

---

with the event leading to their incarceration and concentration difficulties (Cashel et al., 1998). The A-sch interpretive guidelines are provided in Table 12-16.

Adolescent-Negative Treatment Indicators

High scorers on A-trt describe several attitudes and behaviors that are unlikely to be conducive to psychotherapy. High scores indicate very negative attitudes toward physicians or mental health professionals. They do not believe that others are capable of understanding them or care much about what happens to them.

Table 12-17. A-trt Descriptors for the MMPI-A

☐ Adolescents with moderate to high elevations on A-trt describe several attitudes and behaviors that are unlikely to be conducive to psychotherapy:
   • Very negative attitudes toward physicians or mental health professionals
   • Others are incapable of understanding them
   • Others do not care what happens to them
   • Great unwillingness to discuss problems with others
   • Indications that they will not be able to share some issues with anyone
   • Reports of nervousness when others ask them personal questions
   • Reports of many secrets best kept to themselves
   • Unwillingness to take charge and face their problems or difficulties
   • Several faults and bad habits that are insurmountable
   • An inability to plan their own future
   • An unwillingness to assume responsibility for the negative things in their lives

☐ Treatment outcome studies are needed to verify whether the negative attitudes toward mental health professionals, ability to change, and desire to change affects the course of psychotherapy. Until these studies are completed, high scores can be interpreted as indicating attitudes that may be lead to difficulties in psychotherapy outcome. Low scores on A-trt should not be interpreted as indicating a potential for psychotherapy, unless future studies indicate such an association.

They also report great unwillingness to discuss their problems with others and indicate that there are some issues that they would never be able to share with anyone. They report being nervous when others ask them personal questions and have many secrets that they feel are best kept to themselves. They are unwilling to take charge and face their problems or difficulties. They report several faults and bad habits that they feel are insurmountable. They do not feel that they can plan their own future. They will not assume responsibility for the negative things in their lives.

Treatment outcome studies are needed to verify whether the negative attitudes toward mental health professionals, ability to change, and desire to change affect the course of psychotherapy. Until these studies are completed, high scores can be interpreted as reflecting attitudes that may contribute to difficulties in psycho-therapy outcome. Williams et al. (1992) note that this scale is not simply a measure of general maladjustment. Table 12-17 provides descriptors for A-trt.

The MMPI-A Content Component Scales

Similar to the development of the MMPI-2 content scales (see Chapter 7), the MMPI-A content scales were developed with a process designed to maximize psychometric and content internal consistency. However, even though the content scales were designed to measure homogeneous constructs, it is possible to identify clusters of items within several of the scales (Sherwood, Ben-Porath & Williams, 1997). For example, the Adolescent-Health Concerns scale includes items that are somatic complaints. However, one set of A-hea items can be identified that assess gastrointestinal complaints, whereas another includes neurological symptoms. Adolescents may present with differing symptomatic patterns and the MMPI-A content component scales can be used to further refine the interpretation of elevations on the MMPI-A content scales.

Sherwood et al. (1997) described a similar rational and empirical process for developing content component scales for the MMPI-A as was done for the MMPI-2. Their process resulted in a total of 31 subscales for 13 of the 15 MMPI-A content scales. The Adolescent-Anxiety and Adolescent-Obsessiveness content scales were the only ones that did not include item clusters that met the rational or statistical criteria used in the study.

Table 12-18 lists each of the MMPI-A content scales with their component scales. As described in Chapter 7, the content component scales can be used in ways similar to how the Harris-Lingoes subscales are used with the standard scales. They are most helpful when used to clarify elevations on a parent content scale. Additional research on their validity would be helpful.

Highlight Summary: Tony's MMPI-A Content Scales Profile

We ended Chapter 11 with 14-year-old Tony, a black Hispanic eighth-grader being assessed with the MMPI-A to help the staff in his special school plan for his psychological and educational needs. Tony was placed in the special school because of numerous behavior problems, including theft (for which he was on court-ordered probation), fighting, truancy, and oppositional behavior. It was surprising that Tony's MMPI-A standard scale scores did not correspond to the severity of his already identified behavior problems.

Figure 12-1 presents Tony's MMPI-A content scales profile, which can be used for further elaboration of his problems in the MMPI-A interpretive report. Tony's scores on the MMPI-A content scales provide several sources of inferences. Tony is well above the T-score cutoff of 65 on two content scales: A-con and A-ang (Figure 12-1) and the three content component scales for A-con and the two content component scales for A-ang (Table 12-19). As Tables 12-9 and 12-11 reveal, A-ang and A-con are associated with very serious behavior problems. Accordingly, Tony is much more likely to experience problems such as stealing, shoplifting, lying, destroying property, and being disrespectful and oppositional. He is quite likely to be part of a peer group that frequently talks him into doing things that he knows he should not. Poor academic performance and school behavior problems are also quite likely. His A-con score also indicates alcohol and drug problems.

Tony may also have a history of running away from home, and his parents would likely confirm many behavior problems, including lying, cheating, stealing, disobedience, impulsivity, and swearing. His parents likely are aware of his school behavior problems and see him as less socially competent than other boys, given his elevation on A-con.

Anger control is a significant issue for Tony with his elevated A-ang score. He is likely to lose control, swear, smash things, or start a fight. He is prone to be impatient and irritable with others. Temper tantrums may be a frequent response to get his way. He may have a history of aggressive or assaultive acts and be overly interested in violence and aggression. On the other hand, he may also be dependent and clinging in relationships with adults, frequently needing reassurance.

Table 12-18. The Content Component Scales for the MMPI-A

Adolescent—Depression (full scale = 26 items)
- A-dep$_1$: Dysphoria (5 items)
- A-dep$_2$: Self-Deprecation (5 items)
- A-dep$_3$: Lack of Drive (7 items)
- A-dep$_4$: Suicidal Ideation (4 items)

Adolescent—Health Concerns (full scale = 37 items)
- A-hea$_1$: Gastrointestinal Complaints (4 items)
- A-hea$_2$: Neurological Symptoms (18 items)
- A-hea$_3$: General Health Concerns (8 items)

Adolescent—Alienation (full scale = 20 items)
- A-aln$_1$: Misunderstood (5 items)
- A-aln$_2$: Social Isolation (5 items)
- A-aln$_3$: Interpersonal Skepticism (5 items)

Adolescent—Bizarre Mentation (full scale = 19 items)
- A-biz$_1$: Psychotic Symptomatology (11 items)
- A-biz$_2$: Paranoid Ideation (5 items)

Adolescent—Anger (full scale = 17 items)
- A-ang$_1$: Explosive Behavior (8 items)
- A-ang$_2$: Irritability (8 items)

Adolescent—Cynicism (full scale = 22 items)
- A-cyn$_1$: Misanthropic Beliefs (13 items)
- A-cyn$_2$: Interpersonal Suspiciousness (9 items)

Adolescent—Conduct Problems (full scale = 23 items)
- A-con$_1$: Acting-Out Behaviors (10 items)
- A-con$_2$: Antisocial Attitudes (8 items)
- A-con$_3$: Negative Peer Group Influences (3 items)

Adolescent—Low Self-Esteem (full scale = 18 items)
- A-lse$_1$: Self-Doubt (13 items)
- A-lse$_2$: Interpersonal Submissiveness (5 items)

Adolescent—Low Aspirations (full scale = 16 items)
- A-las$_1$: Low Achievement Orientation (8 items)
- A-las$_2$: Lack of Initiative (7 items)

Adolescent—Social Discomfort (full scale = 24 items)
- A-sod$_1$: Introversion (14 items)
- A-sod$_2$: Shyness (10 items)

Adolescent—Family Problems (full scale = 35 items)
- A-fam$_1$: Familial Discord (21 items)
- A-fam$_2$: Familial Alienation (11 items)

Adolescent—School Problems (full scale = 20 items)
- A-sch$_1$: School Conduct Problems (4 items)
- A-sch$_2$: Negative Attitudes (8 items)

Adolescent—Negative Treatment Indicators (full scale = 26 items)
- A-trt$_1$: Low Motivation (11 items)
- A-trt$_2$: Inability to Disclose (8 items)

Source: Sherwood, Ben-Porath, and Williams (1997).

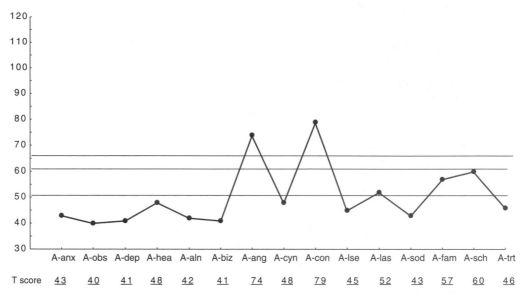

Figure 12-1. Tony's MMPI-A content scales profile.

Although he can be resentful, he is also attention seeking, self-condemning, and anxious about the future.

The possibility of abuse should be assessed, given the association of scores on A-ang and sexual abuse in boys. However, his profile should not be cited as providing evidence of sexual abuse. Rather, it would be much more consistent with available research to include a statement in his report calling for further assessment of the possibility of abuse. Given the description of Tony's concerns for his mother's and other family members' safety (including his own) during episodes of heavy drinking by his father, a call for an assessment of possible abuse (not just limited to sexual abuse) is warranted.

Tony's A-fam score did not reach an interpretable level (T score = 57), although he endorsed 13 of the 21 items of A-fam$_1$ (Familial Discord), a moderate (T score = 63) elevation (Table 12-19). A-fam$_2$ (Familial Alienation) was not elevated (Table 12-19), suggesting that Tony still has an emotional bond with his family, even given possible high levels of conflict, arguments, and anger in his family. Tony's other MMPI-A elevations suggest that his home life is highly unlikely to be problem free, given the family problems associated with elevations on A-con and A-ang.

Notably, given his current placement, the A-sch scale was only moderately elevated at a T score of 60. Most of the elevation on A-sch may be due to his reports of acting-out problems in school, given his high elevation (T score = 69) on the A-sch$_1$ content component scale but not on A-sch$_2$ (Negative Attitudes) (Table 12-19). School-related problems should be part of Tony's MMPI-A interpretation, which would also be consistent with his scores on A-con and A-ang. His average A-las score is interesting with his history and the MMPI-A indications of a significant conduct disorder (i.e., his score on A-con). Tony's A-las score suggests that he has

Table 12-19. Tony's Content Component Scores

	Raw score	Linear T score
Adolescent—Depression		
A-dep$_1$: Dysphoria	0	39
A-dep$_2$: Self-Deprecation	0	38
A-dep$_3$: Lack of Drive	2	47
A-dep$_4$: Suicidal Ideation	0	42
Adolescent—Health Concerns		
A-hea$_1$: Gastrointestinal Complaints	0	46
A-hea$_2$: Neurological Symptoms	4	50
A-hea$_3$: General Health Concerns	0	38
Adolescent—Alienation		
A-aln$_1$: Misunderstood	1	43
A-aln$_2$: Social Isolation	2	54
A-aln$_3$: Interpersonal Skepticism	0	38
Adolescent—Bizarre Mentation		
A-biz$_1$: Psychotic Symptomatology	0	38
A-biz$_2$: Paranoid Ideation	0	42
Adolescent—Anger		
A-ang$_1$: Explosive Behavior	6	66
A-ang$_2$: Irritability	7	64
Adolescent—Cynicism		
A-cyn$_1$: Misanthropic Beliefs	9	54
A-cyn$_2$: Interpersonal Suspiciousness	4	48
Adolescent—Conduct Problems		
A-con$_1$: Acting Out Behaviors	8	70
A-con$_2$: Antisocial Attitudes	7	68
A-con$_3$: Negative Peer Group Influences	2	62
Adolescent—Low Self-Esteem		
A-lse$_1$: Self-Doubt	2	44
A-lse$_2$: Interpersonal Submissiveness	1	46
Adolescent—Low Aspirations		
A-las$_1$: Low Achievement Orientation	5	58
A-las$_2$: Lack of Initiative	2	49
Adolescent—Social Discomfort		
A-sod$_1$: Introversion	3	41
A-sod$_2$: Shyness	4	51
Adolescent—Family Problems		
A-fam$_1$: Familial Discord	13	63
A-fam$_2$: Familial Alienation	3	52
Adolescent—School Problems		
A-sch$_1$: School Conduct Problems	3	69
A-sch$_2$: Negative Attitudes	4	57
Adolescent—Negative Treatment Indicators		
A-trt$_1$: Low Motivation	3	49
A-trt$_2$: Inability to Disclose	3	47

not given up on achievement in school and that he has some interest in academic topics. This is something that his school environment may use as a resource. His average A-las score is consistent with his reported interest in school extracurricular activities, such as band and sports, and his teacher's reports that he does excel when he chooses to do so. His moderate elevation on A-sch and average scores on A-sch$_2$ and A-las, along with his above-average performance in some subjects and enjoyment of sports and band, suggest the possibility of structuring his school environment to increase his motivation and performance.

Chapter 13

Interpreting MMPI-A Supplementary Measures

Over the years a number of additional measures were developed for the MMPI. Very few of these supplementary scales were studied adequately to recommend their use in interpreting adolescents' profiles. In fact, only three of the original supplementary scales were among the "protected scales" when the MMPI Adolescent Project Committee took on the task of reducing the Form TX booklet from 704 items to the 478-item MMPI-A booklet (Butcher et al., 1992). Those three scales included a revised version of the MacAndrew Alcoholism Scale (MAC-R) and the Anxiety (A) and Repression (R) factor scales. Many of the other MMPI scales and indexes have not been adequately studied with adolescent samples to recommend their use for adolescent clinical interpretations.

This chapter describes the development and use of the supplementary measures that may be most helpful for generating clinical interpretations of adolescents' MMPI-A profiles. These include two alcohol and drug problem scales developed using the MMPI-A item pool, the Alcohol/Drug Problem Acknowledgment (ACK) and Alcohol/Drug Problem Proneness (PRO) scales (Weed, Butcher & Williams, 1994); MAC-R; Anxiety (A) and Repression (R); and the Immaturity (Imm) scale, introduced in the MMPI-A (Archer, Pancoast & Gordon, 1994; Imhof & Archer, 1997). An experimental set of PSY-5 scales has also been developed for the MMPI-A (McNulty, Harkness, Ben-Porath & Williams, 1997), as has the first critical item set for use with adolescents (Forbey & Ben-Porath, 1998).

Alcohol and Drug Problem Scales

MacAndrew Alcoholism Scale—Revised

The MacAndrew Alcoholism Scale was developed from the original MMPI item pool using adult subjects (see Chapter 7). It was revised for both the MMPI-2 and the MMPI-A, with four of the original items deleted because of objectionable content. Because normative scores were unavailable for the MacAndrew scale on the original MMPI and the scale was interpreted using raw scores, the same number of items was included on MAC-R. In each version, the four omitted items were replaced with other items that empirically separated individuals in clinical settings with alcohol and other drug problems from those without a history of such problems. The revised version of the MacAndrew is referred to as the MAC-R.

The MacAndrew scale is one of the few original MMPI scales to be studied using adolescent samples. Wolfson and Erbaugh (1984) recommended raw-score cutoffs on the original MacAndrew of 24 for girls and 26 for boys as best distinguishing adolescents in treatment for substance abuse from psychiatric patients

Table 13-1. MAC-R Interpretive Guidelines for the MMPI-A

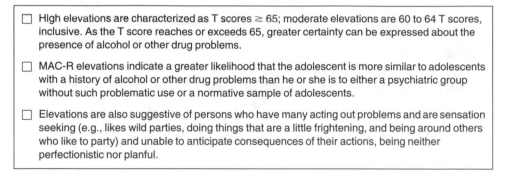

☐ High elevations are characterized as T scores ≥ 65; moderate elevations are 60 to 64 T scores, inclusive. As the T score reaches or exceeds 65, greater certainty can be expressed about the presence of alcohol or other drug problems.

☐ MAC-R elevations indicate a greater likelihood that the adolescent is more similar to adolescents with a history of alcohol or other drug problems than he or she is to either a psychiatric group without such problematic use or a normative sample of adolescents.

☐ Elevations are also suggestive of persons who have many acting out problems and are sensation seeking (e.g., likes wild parties, doing things that are a little frightening, and being around others who like to party) and unable to anticipate consequences of their actions, being neither perfectionistic nor planful.

and from high school students. A raw score of 24 for girls equals a linear T score of 60 on the MMPI-A norms, which is the beginning of the shaded area on the profile characterizing a moderately elevated profile. A raw score of 26 for males is the equivalent of a linear T score of 61 on the MMPI-A norms, again indicative of moderate elevation. Both these raw scores are consistent with the interpretation of the possibility of an alcohol or other drug problem. Higher raw-score cutoffs of 27 for girls (T-score equivalent of 68) and 28 for boys (T-score equivalent of 66) were recommended in a study by Gantner, Graham, and Archer (1992). We recommend that clinicians switch to linear T scores rather than raw scores with the MMPI-A, similar to the interpretive guidelines for the standard scales. If the T scores exceed 65, greater certainty can be expressed in the interpretive report about the presence of alcohol or other drug problems. T scores of 60 might be suggestive of drug or alcohol problems.

Elevations on MAC-R indicate a greater likelihood that the young person is more similar to adolescents with a history of alcohol or other drug problems than either a psychiatric sample without such problematic use or a normative sample of adolescents (e.g., Gantner et al., 1992; Weed et al., 1994). Over the years, elevations of MAC have been refined to indicate an association with a general tendency toward alcohol or other drug problems rather than alcoholic tendencies alone. In addition, elevations are suggestive of persons who are sensation seeking, including enjoying wild parties, being around those who party, and doing frightening, unusual, or even illegal things (Gallucci, 1994, 1997; Gantner et al., 1992); have many acting-out problems (Basham, 1992; Gallucci, 1997; Gantner et al., 1992); and are unable to anticipate consequences of their actions, being neither perfectionistic nor planful (Gallucci, 1994, 1997). The interpretive guidelines for MAC-R are presented in Table 13-1.

Alcohol and Drug Problem Acknowledgment Scale

The Alcohol and Drug Problem Acknowledgment (ACK) scale is a newly developed measure for the MMPI-A (Weed et al., 1994). It is similar to the adult AAS on the MMPI-2 (see Chapter 7). ACK assesses an adolescent's willingness to acknowledge having problematic alcohol or drug use, with its associated symptoms.

The scale was developed using a combined rational-empirical scale-construction strategy. Initially, items that contained obvious references to alcohol or other drug problems were selected for potential membership. Next, these provisional items were correlated with the remaining MMPI-A items to uncover any other items that, when combined with the provisional problem acknowledgment items, improved discrimination of individuals with known alcohol-drug problem use from those without these problems.

Elevations on ACK indicate the extent to which the adolescent has admitted having alcohol or drug problems. Interpretation should begin in the shaded range of the profile (T scores of 60–64); increased confidence can be placed on elevations at or above a T score of 65. These high scores indicate that the young person openly acknowledges having alcohol and drug problems. Gallucci (1997) demonstrated that ACK was related to therapists' ratings of alcohol and drug use problems but not to other measures of behavioral undercontrol or therapists' ratings of impulsivity, sensation seeking, or aggression. Adolescent patients seemed to be more open in acknowledging alcohol and drug problems on the MMPI-A than to their therapists (Gallucci, 1997). ACK appeared to be a somewhat specific measure of a young person's willingness to acknowledge problematic use, as its developers intended (Gallucci, 1997; Weed et al., 1994). However, Cashel, Rogers, Sewell, and Holliman (1998) found a number of descriptors for high ACK scores in their sample of incarcerated delinquent boys, including depression, irritability, and anger associated with the incident leading to their incarceration; attempts to resist depression and irritability; fatigue and lack of energy; restlessness and excessive running and climbing; psychomotor retardation and slowed movements; hopelessness and helplessness; suicidal ideation, including greater lethality of methods; grandiosity; aches and pains; obsessions and compulsions; blaming of others; temper tantrums; oppositional behaviors; cruelty toward people and animals; fire setting; and acting before thinking. Table 13-2 summarizes these interpretive guidelines.

Alcohol and Drug Problem Proneness Scale

The Alcohol and Drug Problem Proneness (PRO) scale is an empirically derived measure to assess the likelihood of a young person developing an alcohol or drug problem (Weed et al., 1994). It is similar in construct to the MMPI-2 APS (see Chapter 7). PRO was developed by identifying items that significantly differentiated adolescent boys and girls in alcohol and drug inpatient treatment units from adolescents without alcohol or other drug problems who were in psychiatric inpatient treatment or those in the normative sample. The items selected for the final PRO scale were those cross-validating without significant shrinkage. It is interesting that many of the new adolescent-specific items about negative peer-group influences, unavailable on the original MMPI, were related to this construct and are included on PRO. Behavior problems at home and school are also included in PRO's item content. The shaded area (T ≥ 60 and ≤ 64) indicates moderate elevations, and T scores greater than or equal to 65 indicate high scorers.

Elevations suggest a proneness to develop problematic alcohol or drug use.

Table 13-2. ACK Interpretive Guidelines for the MMPI-A

☐ High elevations on ACK are T scores ≥ 65; moderate elevations are in the 60 to 64 T-score range. Elevations on ACK indicate the extent to which the adolescent has admitted to having alcohol or drug problems.

☐ High scores indicate that the young person openly acknowledges using alcohol, marijuana, or other drugs. High scorers report problem use, having harmful habits, and relying on alcohol or other drug use to express true feelings or as a coping strategy. Others may tell them that they have a problem with alcohol use, and they may get into fights when drinking.

☐ Incarcerated delinquent boys with high ACK scores may show both internalizing and externalizing problems, including feelings of depression, irritability, and anger associated with the incident leading to their incarceration; attempts to resist depression and irritability; fatigue and lack of energy; restlessness and excessive running and climbing; psychomotor retardation and slowed movements; hopelessness and helplessness; suicidal ideation, including greater lethality of methods; grandiosity; aches and pains; obsessions and compulsions; blaming of others; temper tantrums; oppositional behaviors; cruelty toward people and animals; fire setting; and acting before thinking.

High scores on PRO were related to therapists' ratings of substance abuse problems, aggression (physical fights and angry, verbal disagreements with peers and adults), and sensation seeking (liking wild parties; doing frightening, unusual, or even illegal things; and liking to be around people with those interests). In addition, those with high PRO scores were unlikely to be planful, perfectionistic, or able to anticipate the consequences of their actions (Gallucci, 1997). High PRO scores in incarcerated delinquent boys were related to restlessness, shouting and complaining, insomnia, self-pity, poor judgment, blaming others, and breaking and entering (Cashel et al., 1998). The interpretive guidelines for PRO can be found in Table 13-3.

Factor Scales

Two scales were derived from a factor analysis of the basic MMPI-A scales. As indicated in Chapter 7, these are the Anxiety (A) and Repression (R) scales. The A scale is based on the first factor that emerges when the MMPI basic scales are factor analyzed. Its 35 items (the original A scale had 39 items) are best characterized as a measure of general maladjustment. Individuals with moderately and highly elevated scores are likely to be in distress and report anxiety, discomfort, and greater emotional upset based on studies of adults. Incarcerated delinquent boys with high scores on A are likely to feel depressed about the incident leading to their incarceration; have excessive guilt; and experience generalized anxiety, fatigue and lack of energy, restlessness and excessive running and climbing, pacing and agitation, and suicidal ideation with very serious, more lethal attempts (Cashel et al., 1998).

Repression (R) is the second factor when the basic MMPI scales are factor analyzed. The MMPI-A version of R has 33 items (the original R had 40 items). Adult high scorers on R are characterized as being conventional and submissive and striving to avoid unpleasantness or disagreeable situations. Additional research

Table 13-3. PRO Interpretive Guidelines for the MMPI-A

☐ High elevations on PRO are T scores ≥ 65; moderate elevations are 60 to 64, inclusive.

☐ Elevations suggest a proneness to develop problematic alcohol or drug use.

☐ Item content includes negative peer-group influences as well as behavior problems at home and school. No obvious items about problematic alcohol or other drug use are included in PRO's content.

☐ Elevations indicate a greater likelihood of belonging to the criterion group of adolescents in alcohol and drug treatment evaluation units than to those in psychiatric inpatient treatment or school settings.

☐ Incarcerated delinquent boys with high PRO scores are likely to be restless; shout and complain; have insomnia, self-pity, and poor judgment; and blame others. They may have a history of breaking and entering.

with adolescent samples is needed to determine whether these descriptors generalize to those younger.

Immaturity Scale

The Immaturity (Imm) scale was added to the supplementary MMPI-A scales to provide an objective measure of ego development based on Loevinger's (1976) work (Archer, Belevich & Elkins, 1994; Imhof & Archer, 1997). Its multistage development process has been described by Archer and his colleagues (Archer, 1997b; Archer et al., 1994). Its item content included lack of self-confidence, externalization of blame, lack of insight and introspection, interpersonal and social discomfort, alienation, limited future orientation, hostile and antisocial attitudes, and egocentricity and self-centeredness (Archer, 1997b). Correlates in a sample of psychiatric inpatients included poor reading ability, possible limited capacity to think in abstract terms, being less likely to identify with the values and beliefs of their social group, having poorer perspective taking, and being less likely to have completed or be engaged in the process of identity formation (Imhof & Archer, 1997). Descriptors for incarcerated delinquent boys included depression, irritability, and anger about the incident leading to their incarceration; attempts to resist irritability; shouting and complaining with temper tantrums; psychomotor retardation and slowed speech; anorexia; self-pity; suicidal ideation; aches and pains; concentration difficulties; acting impulsively; frequent shifts in activities; cruelty toward people; and elaborate fantasies (Cashel et al., 1998). Additional research would be helpful in establishing this scale's clinical utility.

Personality Psychopathology 5 (PSY-5) Scales

Since the publication of the MMPI-A, researchers have begun to explore whether its item pool can be used to develop measures that provide information in addition to the scales included in the test manual. The Personality Psychopathology 5 (PSY-5) scales (Harkness & McNulty, 1994; McNulty et al., 1997) are examples of

Table 13-4. Item Composition of the MMPI-A—Based PSY-5 Scales

Scale	Items
Aggressiveness	**24**, 34, **47, 81, 128**, 200, 201, 282, **303, 325, 334, 354**, (355), 367, 378, **382**, 453, 458, 461, (465)
Psychoticism	12, **22**, 29, **39, 45, 92, 95, 132, 136, 225, 250, 286, 295**, 296, **299, 315, 332, 337**, (**387**), 417, 439
Disconstraint (originally named Constraint)	**32**, 69, **80**, (**96**), **99, 101, 117**, (**120**), 144, **197, 234**, (**246**), (**249**), **323, 338, 361, 380, 389**, 440, 456, (457), (**460**), 462, 467
Negative Emotionality/ Neuroticism	**49**, (**60**), **78, 89, 111**, (**134**), 139, **159, 185**, (**209**), **271, 281, 285, 357**, 364, **368**, (**375**), **383, 392, 394**, 412, (**424**)
Introversion (originally named Positive Emotionality/ Extraversion)	(**9**), (**46**), (**58**), (**71**), (**74**), (**82**), (**91**), (**105**), (**125**), (**170**), (**179**), (**180**), (**228**), (262), (**289**), (**292**), (**298**), (**319**), (**322**), (329), (**331**), (**335**), (436), (**447**), (450), 463, 473, (476)

Note: Items in parentheses are scored if False; all others are scored if True. Items in boldface type also appear on the corresponding MMPI-2—based PSY-5 scale (see Table E-1 in Butcher et al., 1992, for item number conversions).
Source: Taken from McNulty, Harkness, Ben-Porath, and Williams (1997) with permission.

recent work using both the MMPI-2 and the MMPI-A item pools (see Chapter 7 for a description of the rationale for the PSY-5 scales). The PSY-5 MMPI-A scales measure the constructs of Aggressiveness, Psychoticism, Disconstraint (originally presented as Constraint, but its scoring was reversed and its name changed to ease scoring and interpretation; see Chapter 7 for more information), Negative Emotionality/Neuroticism, and Introversion (originally presented as Positive Emotionality/Extraversion, but its scoring was reversed and its name changed to ease scoring and interpretation). Because scoring keys and computerized scoring for the PSY-5 scales are not yet available commercially, the MMPI-A PSY-5 item content, scoring direction, and overlap with the MMPI-2 PSY-5 scales are described in Table 13-4.

The PSY-5 scales differ from other MMPI-A scales with their emphasis on specific traits or dispositional differences, rather than major psychopathological classes (McNulty et al., 1997). The Aggressiveness scale was strongly correlated with assaultive, aggressive, and delinquent behaviors in both girls and boys. Although the Psychoticism scale was related to therapists' ratings of psychotic behaviors, additional research on its validity would be useful. Disconstraint scores were related to acting out, drug use, sexual activity, and delinquent behavior, consistent with the scale's construct. Negative Emotionality/Neuroticism was related to symptoms of anxiety, worry, guilt, and excessive reliance on adults. Introversion was related to social withdrawal, shyness, and few friends but not to anxious or worried behaviors. These correlates suggest the potential usefulness of these scales for clinical interpretation (McNulty et al., 1997).

MMPI-A Critical Items

The first exploration of the potential usefulness of critical items for the MMPI-A (see Chapter 7 for an overview of the use of critical items with the MMPI-2)

Table 13-5. MMPI-A Critical Items Presented by Item Grouping

MMPI-A item number	Critical item	Scored response
Aggression		
303.	Sometimes I enjoying hurting persons I love.	True
453.	Others say I throw temper tantrums to get my way.	True
465.	I don't like having to get "rough" with people.	False
Anxiety		
36.	My sleep is fitful and disturbed.	True
163.	I am afraid of losing my mind.	True
173.	There is something wrong with my mind.	True
297.	I get anxious and upset when I have to make a short trip away from home.	True
309.	Almost everyday something happens to frighten me.	True
353.	I have nightmares every few nights.	True
Cognitive Problems		
141.	I cannot understand what I read as well I used to.	True
158.	My memory seems to be all right.	False
288.	I forget right away what people say to me.	True
Conduct Problems		
224.	At times it has been impossible for me to keep from stealing or shoplifting something.	True
249.	I have never been in trouble with the law.	False
345.	My friends are often in trouble.	True
354.	I can easily make other people afraid of me, and sometimes do so for the fun of it.	True
440.	I have spent nights away from home when my parents did not know where I was.	True
445.	I often get into trouble for breaking or destroying things.	True
460.	I have never run away from home.	False
Depression/Suicidal Ideation		
62.	Most of the time I feel blue.	True
71.	I usually feel that life is worthwhile.	False
88.	I don't seem to care what happens to me.	True
177.	I sometimes think about killing myself.	True
242.	No one cares what happens to you.	True
283.	Most of the time I wish I were dead.	True
399.	The future seems hopeless to me.	True
Eating Problems		
30.	Sometimes I use laxatives so I won't gain weight.	True
108.	Sometimes I make myself throw up after eating so I won't gain weight.	True
Family Problems		
365.	When things get really bad, I know I can count on my family for help.	False
366.	I have gotten many beatings.	True
405.	I hate my whole family.	True

Hallucinatory Experiences

92.	I see things or animals or people around me that others do not see.	True
278.	Peculiar odors come to me at times.	True
299.	I hear strange things when I am alone.	True
433.	When I am with people, I am bothered by hearing very strange things.	True
439.	I often hear voices without knowing where they come from.	True

Paranoid Ideation

95.	Someone has it in for me.	True
132.	I believe I am being plotted against.	True
136.	I believe I am being followed.	True
155.	Someone had been trying to poison me.	True
294.	I have no enemies who really wish to harm me.	False
315.	Someone has control over my mind.	True
332.	At one or more times in my life I felt that someone was making me do things by hypnotizing me.	True
337.	Someone has been trying to influence my mind.	True
428.	There are persons who are trying to steal my thoughts and ideas.	True

School Problems

33.	I'm afraid to go to school.	True
80.	I have been suspended from school one or more times for bad behavior.	True
101.	In school I have sometimes been sent to the principal for bad behavior.	True
380.	Often I have not gone to school even when I should have.	True
389.	In school my grades in classroom behavior (conduct) are quite regularly bad.	True

Self-Denigration

90.	Much of the time I feel as if I have done something wrong or evil.	True
219.	I believe I am a condemned person.	True
230.	I believe my sins are unpardonable.	True
321.	At times I have enjoyed being hurt by someone I loved.	True
392.	I deserve severe punishment for my sins.	True

Sexual Concerns

31.	I have never been in trouble because of my sex behavior.	False	
59.	I have often wished I were a girl. (Or if you are a girl) I have never been sorry that I am a girl.	True	(M)
		False	(F)
159.	I am worried about sex.	True	
251.	I wish I were not bothered by thoughts about sex.	True	

Somatic Complaints

113.	I have never vomited or coughed up blood.	False
138.	I have never had a fit or convulsion.	False
165.	I frequently notice my hands shake when I try to do something.	True
169.	My hands have not become clumsy or awkward.	False
172.	I have had no difficulty in keeping my balance in walking.	False
175.	I have had attacks in which I could not control my movements or speech but in which I knew what was going on around me.	True

Table 13-5. MMPI-A Critical Items Presented by Item Grouping, continued

214.	I have had blank spells in which my activities were interrupted and I did not know what was going on around me.	True
231.	I have numbness in one or more places on my skin.	True
275.	I have never been paralyzed or had any unusual weakness of any of my muscles.	False

Substance Use/Abuse

144.	I have a problem with alcohol or drugs.	True
161.	I have had periods in which I carried on activities without knowing later what I had been doing.	True
247.	I have used alcohol excessively.	True
342.	I can express my true feelings only when I drink.	True
429.	I have some habits that are really harmful.	True
431.	Talking over problems and worries with someone is often more helpful than taking drugs or medicines.	False
458.	I sometimes get into fights when drinking.	True
467.	I enjoy using marijuana.	True
474.	People often tell me I have a problem with drinking too much.	True

Unusual Thinking

22.	Evil spirits possess me at times.	True
250.	My soul sometimes leaves my body.	True
291.	I often feel as if things are not real.	True
296.	I have strange and peculiar thoughts.	True
417.	Ghosts or spirits can influence people for good or bad.	True

Source: Adapted from Forbey and Ben-Porath (1998) with permission.

concluded that the commonly used MMPI-2 critical item sets developed for adults may not be useful with the MMPI-A and that adolescents in clinical settings may not endorse critical items more frequently than normal adolescents, thus making it difficult to construct critical item lists for adolescents (Archer & Jacobson, 1993). However, the development of a critical item set for the MMPI-A was completed by Forbey and Ben-Porath (1998) with a combination of statistical steps using the MMPI-A normative sample and a new clinical sample, along with rational procedures with 11 doctoral-level clinicians familiar with the MMPI-A or adolescent development serving as judges. Their clinical sample of 404 adolescents was subdivided into two groups, one consisting of residents of the locked intensive care facility and the other of residents of an open facility and an outpatient program. Forbey and Ben-Porath (1998) developed 15 critical item groups: Aggression, Anxiety, Cognitive Problems, Conduct Problems, Depression/Suicidal Ideation, Eating Problems, Family Problems, Hallucinatory Experiences, Paranoid Ideation, School Problems, Self Denigration, Sexual Concerns, Somatic Complaints, Substance Use/Abuse, and Unusual Thinking. Table 13-5 lists the critical items by group, including their item number in the MMPI-A booklet and scored response.

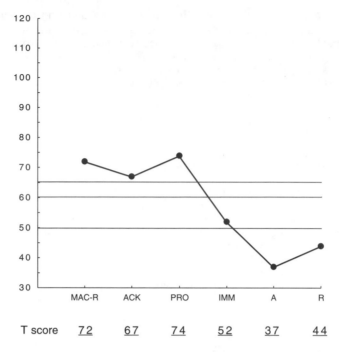

Figure 13-1. Tony's MMPI-A supplementary scales profile.

Similar to what was suggested in Chapter 7 for adults, the MMPI-A critical items can be used for generating hypotheses about an adolescent's behavior that can be followed up in a clinical interview. For example, if a young person endorses the eating problems items "Sometimes I use laxatives so I won't gain weight" and "Sometimes I make myself throw up after eating so I won't gain weight," a more detailed evaluation of his or her eating behaviors is indicated. Young people may endorse the MMPI-A critical items about problems that they initially are reluctant to admit in an interview. Clinicians can use the young person's MMPI-A responses to open discussions about difficult topics.

Highlight Summary: Tony's MMPI-A Supplementary Measures

Interpretation of Alcohol and Drug Problem Scales

Tony's scores on the three scales measuring alcohol and drug problems identified severe difficulties in this area (see his supplementary scales profile in Figure 13-1). Tony readily acknowledged problems associated with the use of alcohol and other drugs, given his ACK elevation. He recognized this as a problem area. His MAC-R and PRO scores suggested a personality style consistent with alcohol and other drug problems. He likely enjoys wild parties, being around others who party, and doing frightening, unusual, or even illegal activities. He probably does not consider the consequences of his actions, nor is he planful or perfectionistic. Although Tony is in a special school for students with serious behavioral problems and not

Table 13-6. Tony's Critical Items

Critical item group	Critical items endorsed by Tony
Aggressiveness (2 of 3 items)	453. Others say I throw temper tantrums to get my way. (T)
	465. I don't like having to get rough with people. (F)
Anxiety (0 of 6 items)	None
Cognitive Problems (0 of 3 items)	None
Conduct Problems (6 of 7 items)	224. At times it has been impossible for me to keep from stealing or shoplifting something. (T)
	249. I have never been in trouble with the law. (F)
	345. My friends are often in trouble. (T)
	440. I have spent nights away from home when my parents did not know where I was. (T)
	460. I have never run away from home. (F)
Depression/Suicidal Ideation (0 of 7 items)	None
Eating Problems (0 of 2 items)	None
Family Problems (0 of 3 items)	None
Hallucinatory Experience (0 of 5 items)	None
Paranoid Ideation (1 of 9 items)	294. I have no enemies who really wish to harm me. (F)
School Problems (3 of 5 items)	80. I have been suspended from school one or more times for bad behavior. (T)
	101. In school I have sometimes been sent to the principal for bad behavior. (T)
	380. Often I have not gone to school even when I should have. (T)
Self-Denigration (0 of 5 items)	None
Sexual Concerns (0 of 4 items)	None
Somatic Complaints (2 of 9 items)	113. I have never vomited or coughed up blood. (F)
	138. I have never had a fit or convulsion. (F)
Substance Use/Abuse (4 of 9 items)	161. I have had periods in which I carried on activities without knowing later what I had been doing. (T)
	429. I have some habits that are really harmful. (T)
	458. I sometimes get into fights when drinking. (T)
	467. I enjoy using marijuana. (T)
Unusual Thinking (0 of 5 items)	None

Note: The "T" in parentheses indicates a True endorsement, and the "F" indicates a False endorsement.

in a residential juvenile delinquency facility, many of the descriptors for incarcerated boys with an elevated ACK score are more consistent with Tony's history and the MMPI-A content scales profile described in Chapter 12 than with what we learned from his standard scales profile in Chapter 11. His ACK score also raises the question of suicide potential.

Interpretation of Other Supplementary Scales

Tony produced very low scores on A and R, which was not surprising given his standard and validity scale scores. (The A and R scales were derived from a factor analysis of these scales.) No interpretive statements should be made for such low scores on these scales. That Tony did not evidence significant maladjustment (A) was also inconsistent with the significant problems observed at referral. Tony also produced an average score on the Immaturity scale (T score − 52), which provides no descriptors for his MMPI-A interpretation.

Tony's scores on the PSY-5 scales were as follows: Aggressiveness, T score of 70 (raw score = 15); Psychoticism, T score of 46 (raw score = 3); Disconstraint, T score of 79 (raw score = 18); Negative Emotionality, T score of 45 (raw score = 8); and Introversion, T score of 45 (raw score = 5). Tony's elevated Aggressiveness score is consistent with his elevations on the MMPI-A content scales and the descriptors associated with his elevated ACK score. Descriptors associated with elevated Aggressiveness scores include numerous acting-out behavior problems, including a history of assaultive behavior. Tony should be evaluated for a history of sexual abuse, and he may act out sexually. He may show some internalizing behaviors, such as excessive dependency or clinging. His elevated Disconstraint score also suggests a broad range of rule-breaking behaviors, being sexually active, possible history of sexual abuse, delinquent and aggressive behaviors, and internalizing symptoms.

Table 13-6 presents the critical items that Tony endorsed. They indicate his willingness to admit to a number of conduct problems, aggressive behaviors, and behaviors associated with drug use. He denied internalizing symptoms such as depression, anxiety, and self-denigration, although his PSY-5 scores suggest some problems in those areas. Although he denied all the Depression/Suicidal Ideation items, a follow-up evaluation would be helpful because suicidal behaviors are correlates for some of his scale elevations.

Chapter 14

Guidelines for MMPI-A Interpretation

Chapters 10 to 13 describe the numerous scale descriptors associated with elevations on the MMPI-A validity, standard, content, and supplementary scales. The task of incorporating all these potential descriptors into an integrated report may at first seem daunting. However, much of the information presented in Chapter 8 about the integration of MMPI-2 inferences into interpretive reports applies equally well to the MMPI-A. This chapter adapts for the MMPI-A the basic strategy for writing MMPI-2 reports.

The interpretive strategy recommended for the MMPI-A is based on the scale descriptor interpretive approach described in Chapter 9. An important change made possible by the MMPI-A is the use of T scores derived from adolescent samples rather than raw scores used in the interim scale descriptor strategy. The MMPI-A scale descriptor approach is recommended because of the poor validity for adolescents associated with code-type interpretations of the MMPI and the greater validity of scale descriptors in empirical studies with adolescents (Cashel, Rogers, Sewell & Holliman, 1998; Gumbiner, 1997; Peña, Megargee & Brody, 1996; Williams & Butcher, 1989a, 1989b). Fortunately, as Chapters 11 to 13 indicate, there are sufficient descriptors for MMPI-A scales, based on studies with adolescents, not adults, to generate interpretive statements without having to resort to extrapolations from the adult code-type literature based primarily on studies using the original MMPI. Ben-Porath and Davis (1996) illustrate the use of a scale descriptor interpretive strategy with 16 adolescent cases from a broad range of settings covering a wide variety of referral issues.

Our interpretive strategy differs substantially from a recently suggested structural summary that was designed to integrate and interpret information from 69 MMPI-A scales and subscales (Archer, 1997a, 1997b; Archer & Krishnamurthy, 1994). Before detailing the interpretive strategy we recommend, we describe this structural summary and the reasons we do not recommend it for clinical interpretations. The structural summary was based on a scale-level factor analysis of 69 MMPI-A scales and subscales using the MMPI-A normative sample (combining the genders) of 1,620 adolescents (Archer, Belevich & Elkins, 1994; Archer & Krishnamurthy, 1994). It consists of eight factor groupings (General Maladjustment, Immaturity, Disinhibition/Excitatory Potential, Social Discomfort, Health Concerns, Naïveté, Familial Alienation, and Psychoticism) that are made up of the validity scales, standard scales, Harris-Lingoes subscales, content scales, and supplementary scales. For example, the Immaturity factor grouping is scored by listing, in the following order, T-score values for the Immaturity supplementary scale; F validity scale; standard scales 8 and 6; ACK and MAC-R alcohol and drug scales;

Harris-Lingoes subscales Pa$_1$ (Persecutory Beliefs), Sc$_2$ (Emotional Alienation), and Sc$_6$ (Bizarre Sensory Experiences); the content scales A-sch, A-biz, A-aln, A-con, A-fam, and A-trt; and then counting the number with elevations greater than or equal to 60 (Archer, 1997a, 1997b; Archer & Krishnamurthy, 1994).

Scores on these eight factor groupings were designed to identify salient dimensions for describing adolescents' personality functioning (Archer 1997a). Empirical correlates for each of the eight factor groupings were presented from the MMPI-A normative sample and a sample of 122 adolescent psychiatric inpatients (Archer 1997a; Archer & Krishnamurthy, 1994). However, this structural summary is based on some faulty assumptions, including that there are "largely arbitrary distinctions between the MMPI-A basic, content, and supplementary scales" (Archer & Krishnamurthy, 1994, p. 556). No theoretical rationale is presented to explain how the eight factor groupings reflect "the basic dimensions of overall importance in describing adolescents' functioning" (Archer, 1997a, p. 268). In fact, its development is atheoretical, derived solely from factor analytic techniques "without reliance on an a priori theoretical model" (Archer & Krishnamurthy, 1994, p. 557).

The reduction of 69 MMPI-A measures with differing rationales, purposes, and underlying psychometric characteristics into eight factor groupings is problematic because it obscures important information from the MMPI-A. For example, combining two of the three alcohol and drug problem scales with the others listed in the Immaturity factor grouping conceals interpretation of a major concern for clinicians evaluating adolescents. Alcohol and drug use problems are not among the descriptors for the Immaturity factor grouping, although they are included in the descriptors for the Disinhibition/Excitatory Potential factor grouping (which also has MAC-R among its 12 scales or subscales but not ACK).

The structural summary was designed to address the redundancy of information from scales with overlapping items or constructs. It is hard to see how problems with redundant information have been addressed when considering, for example, the content of the Immaturity factor grouping, which includes scales 8 and 6, along with several of their subscales, and the A-biz content scale. The Psychoticism factor grouping is made up of scale 6, A-biz, and two Harris-Lingoes subscales, Pa$_1$ and Sc$_6$, all of which are on the Immaturity factor grouping as well. For these conceptual reasons, as well as methodological issues (e.g., the use of a combined gender sample and the relatively small numbers of adolescents from clinical settings, especially alcohol and other drug treatment programs), we do not recommend its use in clinical settings or suggest it as a promising technique for further research.

As noted, the MMPI-A interpretive strategy presented in this chapter is very similar to the strategy described in Chapter 8 for the MMPI-2. A series of eight groups of questions guides the process of integrating descriptors from the various MMPI-A scales and indicators. An outline for an MMPI-A interpretive report is included to facilitate the process of interpretation. Finally, 14-year-old Tony's MMPI-A interpretation is used at the conclusion of this chapter to highlight the interpretive procedures.

Table 14-1. Questions for MMPI-A Interpretations

1. Are there any extratest factors that can explain the MMPI-A results?
2. What are the individual's response attitudes?
3. What are the individual's symptoms and behaviors? What is the likelihood of acting-out behaviors? If present, are acting-out problems likely to be seen across settings or in specific settings? How severe is the acting out likely to be? Does the MMPI-A suggest a need for evaluation of possible physical or sexual abuse? Are there any indications of suicidal ideation or behaviors?
4. Do problems in school play a significant role in the adolescent's clinical picture? What, if any, are they likely to be?
5. Does the adolescent admit to having a problem with alcohol or other drugs? Does she or he have the potential for developing such a problem?
6. What are the individual's interpersonal relationships like? Are there negative peer-group influences? Are family problems significant? How does he or she respond to authority? Are alienation, cynicism, or isolation a factor?
7. What strengths or assets are apparent in the individual?
8. What are the diagnostic implications of the MMPI-A profile?
9. What treatment implications or recommendations are suggested from the MMPI-A including:
   - Is this individual in need of psychological treatment at this time?
   - How aware is the individual of his or her problems?
   - How credible is the individual's self-report?
   - Is the individual willing to disclose personal information to the therapist?
   - How motivated is the individual for treatment?
   - Is the individual capable of gaining insight into his or her problems?
   - Is he or she amenable to treatment? Is the individual willing to change his or her behavior?
   - Are there specific treatment needs suggested by the MMPI-A?
   - Are there negative personality features that could interfere with the treatment relationship?

Interpretive Questions and Report Outline

Although some of the questions for the MMPI-A are identical to those suggested for the MMPI-2, others are unique to the MMPI-A, highlighting developmental issues and characteristics (e.g., the importance of school adjustment, the prevalence of acting-out problems during adolescence, and negative peer-group influences). Because less research is available on the use of the MMPI with adolescents, we are more limited in making some of the inferences that have been established for adults (e.g., the interpretive guidelines appearing in Chapter 8 about the likelihood of an acute mood state or those about dominance as a personality characteristic). These MMPI-2 inferences have not been validated for adolescents. Furthermore, adolescence is a time of tremendous growth and change, which makes us more cautious in making long-term predictions about adjustment, severity of the disorder, or trait-based personality characteristics. Perhaps longitudinal studies using the MMPI-A will allow us to make these long-term predictions at a future time.

Table 14-1 presents an outline of questions to address during an MMPI-A interpretation. Answers to these questions come primarily from the descriptors associated with the various MMPI-A indicators, scales, and subscales that are elevated in an individual's profile. These questions and their answers can be

grouped into sections of an MMPI-A interpretive report, including validity considerations, symptoms and behaviors, school problems, alcohol and other drug problems, interpersonal relationships, strengths, diagnostic hypotheses, and treatment
recommendations. Figure 14-1 provides this suggested outline for an MMPI-A interpretive report. In the following sections, we describe further the interpretive
questions and their place in an MMPI-A report.

Extratest Information

Consideration of demographic and setting characteristics is as important in interpreting the MMPI-A as it is for the MMPI-2 (e.g., Cashel et al., 1998; Cheung & Ho,
1997; Gallucci, 1994; Kopper, Osman, Osman & Hoffman, 1998; Negy, Leal-Puente,
Trainor & Carlson, 1997; Schinka, Elkins & Archer, 1998; Williams & Butcher,
1989a; Williams, Butcher, Ben-Porath & Graham, 1992; Wrobel & Lachar, 1992,
1995). The accuracy of an MMPI-A interpretation is enhanced by knowledge of
these important extratest characteristics. For example, in presenting Tony's case in
Chapter 10, we noted that his Hispanic ethnicity raises the possibility that English
may not be his primary language. If he has substantially better skills in Spanish,
his responses to an MMPI-A administered in English might not give as accurate
a description of his problems as would the Spanish version of the instrument
(Butcher et al., 1998). Before we proceeded with our MMPI-A interpretation, we
verified that Tony had the sixth-grade reading level in English required for the test.

Chapter 8 describes several demographic and setting characteristics for the
MMPI-2 that also apply to the MMPI-A. The importance of gender and setting
for MMPI-A interpretations is highlighted in many of the guidelines for the various MMPI-A scales presented in this chapter and the previous ones. Slightly different descriptors apply, depending on the adolescent's gender or setting (i.e., a
school population or treatment facility). The tables summarizing the interpretive
guidelines for each scale indicate how the descriptors may differ, depending on
gender and setting (Gallucci, 1994; Kopper et al., 1998; Williams & Butcher, 1989a;
Wrobel & Lachar, 1992).

Any unusual extratest characteristic or circumstance that might influence the
individual's responses to the MMPI-A items should be noted at the beginning of
the interpretive report, perhaps in the section on validity considerations. For example, if the interpreter is uncertain about the young person's ability to read or
comprehend the items, this should be noted and followed up with an examination
of the validity indicators, particularly the VRIN and TRIN scales.

There are several other important extratest variables that we illustrate with two
examples. Extreme responding to the MMPI-A content may occur if the individual
recently experienced a catastrophic life event (e.g., a sexual assault or witnessing
the violent death of a parent). In this case, it would be important to discuss this
extratest information in the diagnostic considerations section of the report. An individual with a history of alcohol or drug problems may respond affirmatively to
the items indicating hallucinations because of experiences while intoxicated. This
may cause elevations on the scales associated with psychotic processes (e.g., Sc,
A-biz) that should not necessarily be interpreted as indicating the presence of a

Name _____ Age and Grade _____

Setting _____ Gender _____

Validity Considerations

_____

_____

Symptoms and Behaviors

_____

_____

School Problems

_____

_____

Alcohol and Other Drug Problems

_____

_____

Interpersonal Relationships

_____

_____

Strengths

_____

_____

Diagnostic Hypotheses

_____

_____

Treatment Recommendations

_____

_____

Figure 14-1. Form of an MMPI-A interpretive report.

psychotic disorder. Again, this and similar information should be noted in relevant sections of the interpretive report.

Validity Considerations

The first step in any MMPI interpretation is an examination of the validity of the individual's self-report. As we saw in Chapters 3 and 10, some response styles are so problematic (e.g., inconsistent responding, an all-False pattern) that no MMPI-2 or MMPI-A scale should be interpreted. With other response attitudes (e.g., defensiveness), the profile can be interpreted by including cautionary statements about potentially compromising validity. In other cases, the validity pattern reveals an honest and open response style. The first section of an MMPI-A interpretive report should begin with a description of the individual's response attitudes as revealed by his or her scores on the validity scales and indicators.

Assessing Symptoms and Behaviors

Answers to the third set of questions in Table 14-1 about the individual's symptoms and behaviors form a major section in an MMPI-A interpretation. Descriptors associated with high and moderate scale elevations provide the sources for this section of the report. MMPI-A interpretations rely on these scale elevations and not on the code-type approach described in Chapter 8 for the MMPI-2. Test interpretation begins with a review of the descriptors associated with any MMPI-A scale that is elevated (generally defined as T scores greater than or equal to 65 for high elevations and T scores of 60–64, inclusive, for moderate elevations) in the individual's MMPI-A profiles. Confidence that a descriptor applies to the individual is greatest for those descriptors coming from highly elevated scales, scales with the strongest evidence for their validity, scales rather than subscales, and those descriptors that replicate across MMPI-A scales.

As is true with the MMPI-2, there may be times when an individual's scale elevations on the MMPI-A produce conflicting descriptors. For example, 15-year-old Mandy obtained elevations over 80 on Si and A-sod, along with a highly elevated A-fam score of 75 and a Pd score of 64. None of the other content scales associated with acting-out problems were elevated. Descriptors for Si and A-sod are similar and, in addition to withdrawal, shyness, and timidity, include less likelihood of engaging in acting-out behaviors and of having parents report delinquent behaviors. On the other hand, A-fam elevations are associated with numerous behavior problems, including parental reports of lying, cheating, stealing, and other acting-out behaviors. Her moderate elevation on Pd provides replication of these acting-out behaviors as well. It is noteworthy that A-fam elevations are also associated with withdrawal and timidity, which provides additional verification for the Si and A-sod descriptors.

The general guidelines described previously for resolving discrepancies are not very helpful for interpreting Mandy's MMPI-A scores because Si, A-sod, and A-fam are all scales evidencing strong validity, and Mandy's scores on all three scales are highly elevated. Si and A-sod descriptors suggesting less likelihood of acting out provide replication across scales, although the item overlap between these two scales is high and likely contributes to this descriptor overlap. Should the acting-out descriptors from A-fam and Pd be discounted in her interpretation?

Although Mandy's significant problems in social relationships should be prominently highlighted in her MMPI-A interpretation, her potential for acting out should not be dismissed because of her Si and A-sod elevations. Earlier data from Hathaway and Monachesi (1963) suggested that when both "excitatory" (i.e., scales positively associated with delinquency, such as Pd) and "inhibitory" (i.e., scales with a negative association with delinquency, such as Si) scales are elevated, the acting-out descriptors are more likely to apply than the inhibitory ones. However, Mandy's potential for acting out is less than if she had elevations on the other scales associated with acting out, such as A-con, and may be limited to the family setting. She does not fit the personality profile of individuals belonging to a destructive peer group, and this should be noted in her MMPI-A interpretation. She would likely have difficulty relating to other adolescents in treatment for more typical delinquency problems.

As is true with the MMPI-2, interpretation of Mandy's scores on Si, A-sod, A-fam, and Pd demonstrates how seemingly conflicting MMPI-A correlates can result in useful personality descriptions. In cases in which differing correlates cannot be resolved, they should be noted in the report. (See the following section on alcohol and other drug problems for another example.)

Sexual or Physical Abuse

Data collected during the MMPI Restandardization Project revealed that elevations on several MMPI-A scales were associated with sexual or physical abuse in clinical boys and girls (Butcher et al., 1992; Williams et al., 1992). The base rate for physical abuse in the clinical sample was 34% (30% boys, 40% girls). Likewise, the base rate for sexual abuse was 29% (16% boys, 48% girls). These base rates were determined from the 696 adolescents (N = 412 boys, N = 284 girls) in the clinical sample whose hospital or school records were summarized by research assistants using a record review form. Rates of abuse were determined by this review of records, not from self-report.

The associations between abuse and the MMPI-A scales were included as descriptors in the interpretive guidelines of the relevant scales for adolescents in clinical settings. Like all other MMPI-A correlates, the abuse descriptors will apply to some, but certainly not all, individuals with elevated scores. In general, the higher the T score, the greater likelihood of any descriptor applying. However, the abuse correlates should never be interpreted as confirmation that a given individual has been abused. Rather, elevations on these scales suggest that a careful evaluation is needed in this area. Furthermore, these descriptors should be limited to adolescents in clinical settings with similar base rates of abuse. Recommendations for further evaluation of possible abuse could be included in the treatment recommendations section of the MMPI-A report.

Boys with histories of sexual abuse noted in their treatment records are more likely to have elevations on Pt, Sc, A-dep, A-ang, A-lse, A-fam, and A-sch. It is interesting that several of these scales measure internalizing symptoms (e.g., anxiety, depression, low self-esteem) that are relatively uncommon in boys in treatment settings. However, only between 21% and 28% of boys with elevations of 60 or above on these scales have histories of sexual abuse recorded in their charts. Although this is above the base rate for boys for sexual abuse (16%), one cannot use this scale correlate to accurately predict sexual abuse. Similarly, sexual abuse in girls is related to three MMPI-A scales (Pd, Sc, and A-fam). The rate of sexual abuse in girls with elevations of 60 or higher on these scales varies between 56% and 59%. Again, although this is higher than the base rate of 48% for girls, it does not accurately predict sexual abuse for individual girls. Only one MMPI-A scale, Pd, was associated with a history of physical abuse, and only in boys.

Perhaps the most appropriate use of the abuse descriptors is simply to facilitate a discussion with the young person about whether any abuse has occurred. An MMPI-A feedback session may be helpful to begin this discussion. In the feedback session, the young person could be told that some adolescents with scale scores similar to his or hers have been abused and the clinician would like to help if he or she has a similar problem. Of course, in settings with high base rates of abuse, assessment of abuse should not be limited to the MMPI-A but should include other techniques as well. The MMPI-A may prove to be a useful tool for research into the psychological aftermath of abuse.

Suicidal Behaviors

Many of the MMPI-A scales include suicidal ideation or attempts among their descriptors based on studies from the original MMPI with adolescents (e.g., Wrobel & Lachar, 1992) as well as the clinical sample used in the Restandardization Project (Butcher et al., 1992; Williams & Butcher, 1989a; Williams et al., 1992) and studies since the publication of the MMPI-A (e.g., Cashel et al., 1998; Kopper et al., 1998). Scale descriptors can range from suicidal ideation to serious attempts with more lethal methods. Forbey and Ben-Porath (1998) also present a set of seven MMPI-A critical items called Depression/Suicidal Ideation that can indicate which, if any, MMPI-A items suggesting suicidal risk have been endorsed by a given adolescent.

Kopper et al. (1998) investigated the clinical utility of the MMPI-A in assessing suicidal risk factors by examining the unique contribution of the content scales and the Harris-Lingoes subscales, beyond that provided by the standard scales, separately for boys and girls. They found that both boys and girls with elevations on standard scales 2, 4, and 9 and the Harris-Lingoes D_1, Pd_5, and Ma_3 subscales had increased risk of suicidal behaviors. For boys, elevations on the A-aln and A-anx content scales and the Pd_4 Harris-Lingoes subscale were also predictive of suicidal risk. For girls, elevations on the A-fam, A-dep, and A-sod content scales made independent contributions to the prediction of suicide risk.

A study of incarcerated delinquent boys provided further information about suicidal behaviors. Cashel et al. (1998) used a semistructured diagnostic interview for children that included questions about suicidal ideation, number of suicidal acts, seriousness of suicidal acts, and lethality of suicidal acts and found that the MMPI-A scales were differentially associated with these items. These descriptors are included in the tables highlighting the interpretive guidelines for the various scales.

Descriptors for suicidal ideation and behaviors should be used in a similar fashion to that suggested previously for the descriptors related to physical or sexual abuse. That is, an elevation on a scale with suicidal behaviors as a descriptor cannot be used as a definitive indicator of the presence of the problem for an individual adolescent (nor can the absence of elevations on scales associated with suicidal risk definitively rule out the problem). Rather, elevations on scales associated with higher probability of suicidal risk suggest that a careful evaluation is needed. Recommendations for such an evaluation should be included in the treatment recommendations section of the MMPI-A report.

School Problems

The MMPI-A provides a more direct assessment of school-related problems than did the original instrument. Two scales deal directly with school: A-sch and A-las. Both academic and behavior problems are covered. Because these two scales are content based, they will be elevated only if the young person describes problems in these areas. Some young people may not view school as problematic even though they are quite troubling to teachers and school officials. Elevations on other scales (e.g., Pd, A-con) include school problems that should be interpreted even in the presence of low scores on A-sch or A-las. School problems can be included in the symptoms and behaviors section of the interpretive report or in a separate section, as we suggest in Figure 14-1.

Problems with Alcohol and Other Drugs

One of the advantages in using the MMPI-A to assess psychopathology during adolescence is its alcohol and other drug problem scales. There are three separate scales developed to discriminate adolescents with alcohol or other drug problems from those with different types of psychopathology. In addition, elevations on several clinical and content scales are associated with alcohol or other drug use. Scores on the MAC-R, ACK, and PRO scales should be examined to determine whether they are elevated. The ACK scale indicates whether the young person openly acknowledges having problematic alcohol or other drug use, and the other two scales indicate a personality style associated with a proneness for developing such problems.

There is a great likelihood of the individual having and acknowledging alcohol and drug problems if all three scales are elevated. If MAC-R and PRO are elevated but ACK is not, then the likelihood of a problem in this area is high, but the young person is unwilling to admit to it. If an ACK elevation is present in the absence of MAC-R or PRO elevations as well as in the absence of exaggeration or malingering, then the adolescent is showing an atypical problem in this area.

A more equivocal pattern of scores occurs with elevations on only MAC-R or PRO. Until future research suggests otherwise, it may be best in this case to indicate in the interpretive report that the evidence is equivocal about the presence of an alcohol or other drug problem. Scores from 17-year-old Stan's MMPI-A are used to illustrate this. Stan scored low on both ACK and PRO (50 and 43, respectively) but was very high on MAC-R at a T score of 70. There was no evidence of defensiveness in his profile; in fact, to the contrary, he had high elevations on three of the standard scales and six content scales. Two of his highest elevations were on Si and A-sod, which suggest less likelihood of problem use. Given this, the alcohol and other drug problem section in his interpretive report reads as follows:

> Stan's scores on the alcohol and other drug problem scales suggested a mixed picture of his potential for developing serious problems in this area. He had some of the personality features associated with individuals who have problems in this area (e.g., risk taking), yet he did not acknowledge having problematic alcohol and drug use, nor is it likely he belonged to a peer group who used drugs or alcohol. Given his willingness to admit to many other problem areas and his openness in his approach to the MMPI-A, problematic alcohol and other drug use may be less relevant in his current circumstances than the many other problem areas described in this report.

Interpersonal Relationships

Si, its subscales, and A-sod are the primary sources for information about the in-dividual's interpersonal behavior. However, as we saw in Chapter 8 about the MMPI-2, other scales have descriptors related to interpersonal relationships that can be included in this section. In addition, several of the content scales describe characteristics that are relevant to an individual's relationships with others (e.g., A-aln, A-ang, A-cyn, and A-fam). The content of PRO suggests that an elevation on it raises the possibility of belonging to a negative peer group. These descriptors should be highlighted in a section of the interpretive report about interpersonal relationships (Figure 14-1).

Strengths

Although the MMPI and its successors are measures primarily of psychopathol-ogy and not indicators of personality strengths, there are some MMPI-A descrip-tors that can be categorized in this area. It is useful to have such a section in an MMPI-A report, particularly when giving feedback to the young person, his or her parents, or school staff. Some of the Harris-Lingoes subscales offer examples of possible strengths (e.g., Hy_1 [Denial of Social Anxiety], comfortable around others, finds it easy to talk with others; Pd_3 [Social Imperturbability], confident in social situations, willing to defend his or her strong opinions). In some cases, extreme emotional distress can be interpreted as an asset for treatment because the young person will be more motivated to make difficult changes in his or her life.

Diagnostic Considerations

The last two sets of questions in Table 14-1 and the corresponding last two sections of an interpretive report (Figure 14-1) rely on information from the MMPI-A as well as on other sources of information about the individual. In arriving at a pos-sible diagnosis, the clinician integrates information from the MMPI-A to form an impression of the individual's overall symptoms, behaviors, likelihood of alcohol or other drug problems, interpersonal relationships, and strengths. From this, the clinician can consult the current diagnostic manual to see whether the MMPI-A description of the adolescent coincides with any of the current diagnostic categories. Unfortunately, less research is available in relating the MMPI-A to diagnostic categories common during adolescence than was described in Chapter 8 for the MMPI-2.

Treatment Implications or Recommendations

Similar treatment-related questions presented in Chapter 8 for the MMPI-2 are relevant to the MMPI-A and are included in Table 14-1. Some of the answers to these questions can come from an elevation on the A-trt scale, which should be interpreted as an indication of the presence of negative attitudes toward mental health treatment that may interfere with building a therapeutic relationship. However, treatment-outcome studies are needed to determine whether these negative attitudes predict poor prognosis for psychotherapy. Low scores on A-trt should not be interpreted.

Other MMPI-A descriptors can provide answers to the treatment-relevant questions in Table 14-1. Noncompliance with the MMPI-A instructions indicated by the validity scales suggests an unwillingness to reveal problems or even an unawareness of problems that does not bode well for psychotherapy. The types of problems revealed by elevated scale scores suggest problem areas to concentrate on in treatment and give an indication of the need for treatment.

An MMPI-A Feedback Session

A major advantage in using the MMPI with adolescents (and adults as well) is the use of a feedback session (Finn, 1996; Finn & Tonsager, 1992; Williams, 1982, 1986). In a feedback session, the clinician provides interpretive statements based on MMPI-A scale elevations. However, these are not presented to the young person as the "absolute truth." Rather, the young person can be encouraged by the therapist to begin problem solving by deciding whether the interpretation applies to him or her. The MMPI-A interpretation is presented as a series of hypotheses or guesses that the patient and therapist explore for accuracy. This strategy can be used at the beginning of therapy to build a relationship with the young person (e.g., Williams, 1982, 1986). Adolescents enjoy MMPI feedback sessions, perhaps partly because of the process of identity formation.

The feedback session can be extended to other family members as well. After providing individual interpretations for each family member, the therapist can meet with the family as a group. It is important in the individual interpretation sessions to determine whether there is anything that the adolescent or parent would prefer not be discussed in the general family session. Some areas, such as possible marital problems or the sexual behavior of the adolescent (or parent), are probably best not interpreted in a family feedback session held relatively early in the therapeutic process. However, a number of MMPI-2 and MMPI-A correlates describe personality features of importance to other family members. For example, one could describe potential conflicts between individuals who are high on Si and those low on Si. The Family Problems content scale would be another interesting source for discussions.

Often the feedback session provides even richer information for the clinician to use in formulating a treatment plan. Some clinicians use information from the MMPI throughout the course of treatment when examples of personality descriptors occur. For example, an overly sensitive person, indicated by a high Pa elevation, may, in the process of therapy, report interpersonal difficulties stemming from suspicion of other people's behavior. Going back to the MMPI interpretation may be a less threatening way to introduce the individual's possible contribution to these problems.

Highlight Summary: Integrating Tony's MMPI-A Responses

Tony's MMPI-A profiles demonstrate how some features of the instrument can be used to provide rich inferences about a troubled adolescent's symptoms and behavior. The original validity scales, combined with information from the new indicators (F_1, F_2, VRIN, TRIN), increase our confidence that he has an interpretable profile (Figure 14-2). Tony's MMPI-A standard scales profile provides only limited inferences about his behavior, given that only one standard scale, Ma, is moderately elevated (Chapter 11). This is not consistent with the severity of his acting-out problems noted at referral. His moderate scale 9 elevation (Figure 14-1) suggests the following symptoms and behaviors: possible arguments with peers, academic underachievement, alcohol or other drug use, participation in wild parties, and liking to do frightening activities. He may be enthusiastic and have a

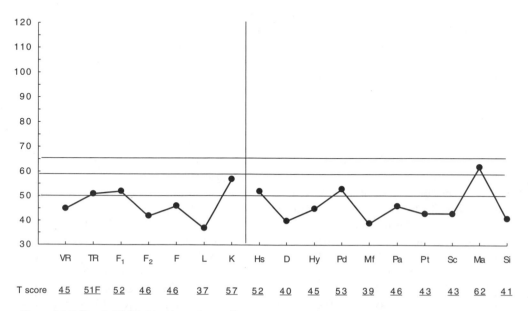

Figure 14-2. Tony's MMPI-A basic scales profile.

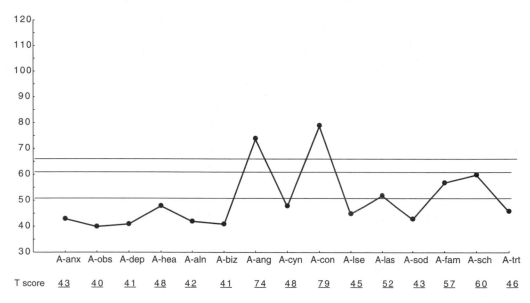

Figure 14-3. Tony's MMPI-A content scales profile.

higher-than-average activity level, which could be noted in the section on strengths in his interpretive report. However, he is unlikely to be motivated for therapy, is not likely to be willing to explore feelings, and may be insensitive to criticism—important issues to note in the treatment recommendations section. Suicidal behaviors are possible. His high elevation on Ma_1 and moderate elevation on Ma_3 increase the possibility of suicidal behaviors.

Other inferences that can be made from his Harris-Lingoes subscale scores include information about interpersonal relationships. His subscale scores indicate that Tony may take advantage of others and probably belongs to a peer group whose members are likely to agree on a single story in times of trouble. He likely denies being impatient or irritable as well as having social anxiety or discomfort. Tony's low score on Si suggests facility in social relationships, with no indication of social withdrawal.

Tony's MMPI-A content scale profile (Figure 14-3) and content component scale scores (Table 14-2) provide much richer inferences about his problems and behaviors (Chapter 12). The severity of his behavior problems and anger-control issues, including assaultive behaviors, are noted, as is the presence of internalizing problems, such as dependency and clinging in relationships with adults, having a frequent need of reassurance, being self-condemning, and having anxiety about the future. The possibility of sexual abuse is raised, given his elevation on A-ang.

Tony's average score on A-fam suggests that he maintains an emotional bond with his family, although the moderate elevation on the A-fam$_1$ content component scale (Table 14-2) indicates high levels of conflict, which is consistent with descriptors from the A-con and A-ang elevated scores. Given his current school placement, it is notable that his A-sch score is only moderately elevated and that much of the elevation may be due to acting-out problems, given his content component

Table 14-2. Tony's Content Component Scores

	Raw score	Linear T score
Adolescent—Depression		
A-dep$_1$: Dysphoria	0	39
A-dep$_2$: Self-Deprecation	0	38
A-dep$_3$: Lack of Drive	2	47
A-dep$_4$: Suicidal Ideation	0	42
Adolescent—Health Concerns		
A-hea$_1$: Gastrointestinal Complaints	0	46
A-hea$_2$: Neurological Symptoms	4	50
A-hea$_3$: General Health Concerns	0	38
Adolescent—Alienation		
A-aln$_1$: Misunderstood	1	43
A-aln$_2$: Social Isolation	2	54
A-aln$_3$: Interpersonal Skepticism	0	38
Adolescent—Bizarre Mentation		
A-biz$_1$: Psychotic Symptomatology	0	38
A-biz$_2$: Paranoid Ideation	0	42
Adolescent—Anger		
A-ang$_1$: Explosive Behavior	6	66
A-ang$_2$: Irritability	7	64
Adolescent—Cynicism		
A-cyn$_1$: Misanthropic Beliefs	9	54
A-cyn$_2$: Interpersonal Suspiciousness	4	48
Adolescent—Conduct Problems		
A-con$_1$: Acting-Out Behaviors	8	70
A-con$_2$: Antisocial Attitudes	7	68
A-con$_3$: Self-Doubt	2	62
Adolescent—Low Self-Esteem		
A-lse$_1$: Self-Doubt	2	44
A-lse$_2$: Interpersonal Submissiveness	1	46
Adolescent—Low Aspirations		
A-las$_1$: Low Achievement Orientation	5	58
A-las$_2$: Lack of Initiative	2	49
Adolescent—Social Discomfort		
A-sod$_1$: Introversion	3	41
A-sod$_2$: Shyness	4	51
Adolescent—Family Problems		
A-fam$_1$: Familial Discord	13	63
A-fam$_2$: Familial Alienation	3	52
Adolescent—School Problems		
A-sch$_1$: School Conduct Problems	3	69
A-sch$_2$: Negative Attitudes	4	57
Adolescent—Negative Treatment Indicators		
A-trt$_1$: Low Motivation	3	49
A-trt$_2$: Inability to Disclose	3	47

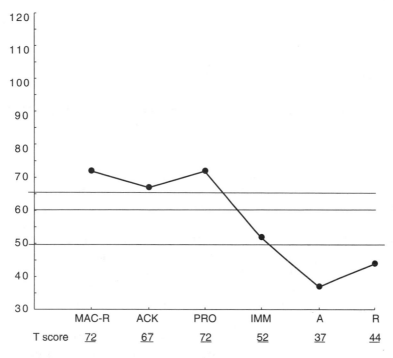

Figure 14-4. Tony's MMPI-A supplementary scales profile.

scores. Tony's average A-las score suggests that he has not given up on achievement in school, which should be noted in his interpretive report.

Tony's scores on the three alcohol and drug problem scales (Figure 14-4) indicated severe problems in this area (Chapter 13), and the PSY-5 scale elevations on Aggressiveness (T score = 70) and Disconstraint (T score = 79) provided corroboration for the descriptors from his content scale elevations. Although the critical items revealed Tony's willingness to admit to a number of conduct problems, aggressive behaviors, and behaviors associated with drug use, he denied internalizing symptoms, such as depression, anxiety, and self-denigration. He also denied all the Depression/Suicidal Ideation items, although a follow-up evaluation is still indicated because of the association of suicidal behaviors with some of his scale elevations.

A treatment plan for Tony's acting-out behaviors would emphasize externalizing problems perhaps best controlled with clear expectations and behavioral contracting. Tony's abuse of drugs and alcohol must be addressed in any therapeutic approach. An evaluation of possible abuse and attention to family issues are suggested by his profile. Tony has some academic interests that can be used in his school planning. He may respond to a strong, nurturing adult role model who frequently verbalizes expectations and fairly applies the stated contingencies. If he is able to establish a relationship with a supportive adult, perhaps he will be able to address some of his troubling feelings, dependency needs, and anxiety.

Chapter 15

Computerized MMPI-2 and MMPI-A Interpretive Reports

In years past, it often took several days to have an MMPI administered, scored, and interpreted and a report of the test results generated that could be used to provide personality feedback to the individual. Today computers play an important role in mental health services and have all but eliminated the lag time between test administration and reporting. A recent survey of the membership of the Society for Personality Assessment and members of the Clinical Psychology Division of the American Psychological Association found that almost two-thirds of the respondents indicated that they use computers to assist with psychological testing (Ball, Archer & Imhof, 1994). A more recent survey of independent-practice psychologists (McMinn, Buchanan, Ellens & Ryan, 1999) found that "computer software has become widely accepted as a way to administer, score, and interpret psychological tests" (p. 171), and "little controversy surrounding the use of computerized test administration, scoring, and interpretation software was reported, with most respondents viewing these computer applications as ethical" (p. 168). The following situation illustrates a relatively common type of clinical test application:

> A woman enters a community mental health center for an initial appointment to see a psychologist about the problems she has been having. In an initial session with an intake professional, she is asked to discuss her reason for referral and is given a briefing on the clinical evaluation procedures used in the clinic. Then she is ushered into a private room and seated at a computer console.
>
> In the testing room, she receives instructions on how to respond to the questions that are presented on the TV screen and begins to respond to them by pressing the proper key on the keyboard. After completing the computerized test, she is given a few minutes' break while the computerized narrative report is generated by the computer and given to the psychologist.
>
> Shortly thereafter, the client is introduced to the psychologist, who has now had an opportunity to review the computer-based MMPI-2 report and already has an understanding of the patient's symptoms, possible diagnostic issues to address, possible long-standing personality characteristics, the client's openness to sharing personal information with the clinician, the likely need for therapy, and probable prognosis for treatment if that is the recommendation.

Many practitioners in contemporary clinical settings find that computers are indispensable tools for collecting, processing, and interpreting psychologist test data. Computer processing of test protocols provides clinicians with immediate results on the MMPI-2 or MMPI-A. Rapid access to MMPI-2/MMPI-A information facilitates assessment and enhances treatment planning early in the intervention, even in the initial session. Computer-based interpretation usually provides the clinician with more extensive personality information than is typically available to practitioners using traditional test-scoring and interpretation approaches. Because of the amount of time it takes to hand score MMPI-2 and MMPI-A scales, the tendency is to use as few measures as possible. If computer scoring is used, a larger number of test indexes can be more efficiently incorporated.

Most contemporary clients are accustomed to seeing computer-based information, such as bank statements, grade reports, and so on, and usually accept or even prefer information processed through a computer. Computerized MMPI-2 and MMPI-A reports can be used to provide test feedback to clients, which enhances and facilitates the clinical interaction (Butcher, 1990a; Finn & Tonsager, 1992; Newman & Greenway, 1997).

In this chapter, we describe computer-based MMPI-2 and MMPI-A scoring and interpretation and explain how computerized (often referred to as automated) interpretation works. Examples of computer-generated MMPI-2 and MMPI-A reports illustrate the kind of information that is provided through this service. Later in the chapter, we examine several important issues in computer-based interpretation.

Automated Interpretation of Personality Tests

Meehl (1954) reviewed the literature on clinical prediction and evaluated the relative effectiveness of clinical and actuarial (use of objectively derived rules and information) methods at predicting and describing behavior. He found that assessment approaches using objective classification rules consistently outperformed those based on intuitive or clinical strategies. More recently, Grove, Zald, Lebow, Snitz, and Nelson (2000), using a meta-analysis of all studies to date, found that actuarial prediction outperformed clinical prediction by about 10%. One of Meehl's students (Halbower, 1955) demonstrated that objectively derived correlate information for particular test indexes (i.e., MMPI profiles) could be automatically applied to new cases with a high degree of accuracy. This objective assessment approach (see the discussion in Chapter 5) spawned the development of a number of MMPI "cookbooks," or codebooks, that served as the interpretive base for computer assessment systems.

The use of computers for the interpretation of MMPI profiles has a long history. Computers became widely available in the 1960s, prompting several psychologists to develop automated test interpretation systems by simply programming a computer to apply predetermined test correlates for specific test scores or combinations of MMPI scores. A recent review of the validity and utility of computer-based assessment techniques (Butcher, Perry & Atlis, 2000) concluded that computer-based test analytic strategies provided accurate interpretations of the MMPI-2.

The first computer-based interpretation system for the MMPI was developed by Pearson and Swenson in 1961 at the Mayo Clinic in Rochester, Minnesota (Rome et al., 1962). This program demonstrated that Meehl's actuarial approach to test interpretation could be implemented effectively by computer. A library of over 100 personality and symptomatic behaviors, which had been associated with certain test scores, was stored in the computer and programmed to print when the specified test scores were in the interpretable range. The computer output included an MMPI profile along with a listing of up to six of the relevant descriptors from the statement library. This computer interpretation system, though limited in scope, was readily accepted by the psychology and medical staffs at the Mayo Clinic (Pearson & Swenson, 1967; Pearson, Swenson, Rome, Mataya & Brannick, 1965).

In subsequent years, several other more comprehensive and sophisticated MMPI interpretation programs were developed. The computer program developed by Fowler (1969) for Roche Laboratories was particularly impressive because it provided personality and symptomatic information about clients in a highly objective format. More recent computer-based MMPI programs have become even more elaborate in that they typically provide extensive information in a readable, narrative report format (Fowler, 1987).

Three general types of computer-based MMPI or MMPI-2 interpretation programs have been developed, differing largely in terms of complexity. The first and simplest type of program was the "cookbook," or codebook, approach; the second type is the automated clinician; and the third type is the complex decision model. These different approaches are described in the following sections in more detail.

The Automated Cookbook

In this approach, the psychologist simply programs the test correlates to be automatically listed when certain test scores are obtained. This approach was exemplified by the innovative Mayo Clinic study developed by Pearson et al. (1965).

The Automated Clinician

The second approach to computer-generated psychological reports has been referred to as the automated clinician (Fowler, 1969). Most of the commercially available computerized psychological test reporting programs are of this variety. They are computerized lists of statements or paragraphs that can be associated with particular test scores or profile types. The computer is programmed to look up the stored information for a particular set of test scores or indexes. It is important to realize that most such systems are not strictly actuarial because they incorporate clinical inferences and hypotheses that may or may not have been validated against external criteria.

The Complex Decision Model

The third approach to computer-based test interpretation involves a somewhat greater use of the rapid combinatory powers of the computer than simply a lookup or listing function. In this approach, the computer is programmed to combine data and make more complex decisions following more elaborate decision rules. This approach is somewhat more complicated than the other approaches because of the procedures making specific higher-level decisions more closely simulate a clinician's judgment processes; numerous possible scale combinations are specified in order for relatively detailed decisions to be made (Butcher, 1989b). The complex decision model is an "expert system," encapsulating specialist knowledge about a particular domain and making intelligent decisions within that area of expertise (Forsyth & Naylor, 1986). For example, an individual's "Potential for Addiction" might be classified into several categories, such as highly likely, likely, problems possible, or not likely. The following illustrate a set of MMPI-2 complex decision rules that could be used to define these categories:

If any of the following conditions are present, classify the profile as "Addictive Problems are highly likely":
    If the T score for MAC-R is greater than or equal to a T score of 70
    If the T score for APS is greater than or equal to a T score of 70
    If the T score for AAS is greater than or equal to a T score of 70
    If the T scores for D, Pd, and Pt are greater than or equal to a T score of 80
    If the profile fails to meet any of the prior conditions then go to the next set

If any of the following conditions are present, classify the profile as "Addictive Problems likely":
    If the T score for MAC-R is greater than or equal to a T score of 65
    If the T score for APS is greater than or equal to a T score of 65
    If the T score for AAS is greater than or equal to a T score of 65
    If the T scores for D, Pd, and Pt are greater than or equal to a T score of 70
    If the profile fails to meet any of the prior conditions then go to the next set

If any of the following conditions are present, classify the profile as "Addictive Problems possible":
    If the T score for MAC-R is greater than or equal to a T score of 60
    If the T score for APS is greater than or equal to a T score of 60
    If the T score for AAS is greater than or equal to a T score of 60
    If the T scores for D, Pd, and Pt are greater than or equal to a T score of 65
    If the profile fails to meet any of the prior conditions then go to the next set

If all of the following conditions are present, classify the profile as "Addictive Problems are not likely":
    If the T score for MAC-R is less than a T score of 59
    If the T score for APS is less than a T score of 59
    If the T score for AAS is less than a T score of 59
    If the T scores for D, Pd, and Pt are less than a T score of 59

Options for Obtaining Computer-Based MMPI-2 and MMPI-A Reports

There are several options for administering and processing MMPI-2 and MMPI-A protocols to obtain computer-based MMPI-2/MMPI-A reports. Many of these options were briefly described in Chapter 2. This chapter provides more detail about the MMPI-2 and MMPI-A scoring and interpretation services provided by National Computer Systems (NCS; P.O. Box 1416, Minneapolis, MN 55440; phone: 1-800-627-7271).

Mail-in Service

Clinicians using the mail-in service administer the booklet versions of the MMPI-2 or MMPI-A to the client and mail or express mail the answer sheets to NCS for processing. The completed report is sent to the clinician by return mail within 24 hours of receipt. Practitioners with a low volume of patients and ample time to process the MMPI-2 (e.g., if the therapist sees the patient on a weekly basis) can use this option. This is probably the most cost-effective test-processing option if time is not a factor and there is a low volume of clients assessed.

In-Office Processing by Computer

Practitioners with access to a computer can immediately process the MMPI-2 or MMPI-A in their office with or without using a booklet and answer sheet. Clients can actually be given the MMPI on-line (see Chapter 2), and their responses can be immediately scored and used to generate a complete interpretive report. Another option, if the practitioner does not wish to dedicate a computer for test administration purposes, is to administer the MMPI-2 or MMPI-A by booklet and answer sheet and then have a clerk key enter the item responses onto a computer file. The computer file can then be used to score and interpret the profiles. This is a relatively cost-efficient approach because it requires only about 8 minutes for an individual to key enter an entire answer sheet and even less with practice. There are problems with this procedure, the most evident being human error in entering the client's responses.

Optical Scanning of Answer Sheets

Practitioners or clinics with a high volume of tests to process, say five or six per day, may find that on-line administration or key entry of test responses by clerical staff is cumbersome and inefficient. An attractive and relatively cost-effective option is to use an optical scanner to read and process the item responses. The optical scanner, which is directly wired to the computer, records the answers into a data file that can be processed by the computer. The MMPI-2 and MMPI-A scores can then be generated and the protocol processed by the computer. The answer sheet is fed into the scanner, and within seconds the computer processes the scores and begins to print out the report.

Computer-Based MMPI-2/MMPI-A Narrative Reports

In this section, we describe how a computer can construct a narrative report from the information available on the MMPI-2 or MMPI-A scales. Before doing so, several misconceptions about computer-based interpretation should be dealt with. We begin by describing what a computerized report is *not:*

1. An MMPI-2/MMPI-A computerized report is not a purely scientific or actuarially based personality description. The necessary information for a complete actuary is not yet available; thus, most computer interpretation systems incorporate some clinically derived hypotheses as well as actuarially combined data.

2. An MMPI-2/MMPI-A computerized personality report is not designed for use by individuals who are not trained in working with the MMPI-2 or MMPI-A. Computerized reports provide interpretive hypotheses to be used in conjunction with other clinical or test information by trained interpreters.

3. A computerized report is not an independent or "stand-alone" psychological evaluation. It should be considered an aid to psychological interpretation, not an end in itself.

Computerized personality reports are "electronic reference sources" that contain the most likely interpretations for test scores and indices. They provide summaries of hypothesized characteristics, symptomatic behavior, or other descriptions that are generated by a computer using specified test indexes that have been related empirically or theoretically to the behavior in question. Computerized reports are best considered as professional-to-professional consultations. Automated interpretation systems are analogous to reference books that serve as a convenient source of information for consultation as needed. These systems are ethical to use when following the Computerized Testing Guidelines of the American Psychological Association (American Psychological Association, 1986). They provide summaries of behavior-test relations and clinically derived or postulated relationships. The practitioner must decide how well the computerized prototype actually fits the patient in question.

The database for MMPI-2/MMPI-A interpretations can come from several sources: the established empirical literature for MMPI-2/MMPI-A scales and indexes; predictive decisions or personality descriptions based on scale relationships or indexes (e.g., the Megargee Rules for adult correctional settings); problems or themes reflected through the MMPI-2/MMPI-A content scales, the Harris-Lingoes subscales, and the MMPI-2 critical items; and, finally, the clinical experience of the system developer. These reports or automated clinicians vary in their comprehensiveness and accuracy in describing and predicting behavior, depending in part on how closely they follow validated test correlates.

A number of computerized interpretive reports are available for the MMPI-2, including the Caldwell Report, developed by Alex Caldwell; Roger Greene's MMPI Adult Interpretive System; and The Minnesota Report™, described in the following section. The Minnesota Report™, by Butcher and Williams, is also available for the MMPI-A. Robert Archer developed an MMPI-A report as well.

The Minnesota Report™

The Minnesota Report™, a series of computerized interpretation systems for the MMPI, was developed to aid clinicians in their clinical assessment (Butcher, 1987,

1989, 1998b; Butcher & Williams, 1992). The Minnesota Report™ was developed with several goals in mind. The information included in the statement library of the various interpretive systems was based as closely as possible on established, replicable research data with the goal of providing highly generalizable and accurate descriptions. These systems take into account differences in MMPI-2/MMPI-A profiles across settings (i.e., the base rates of the population under consideration).

The MMPI-2/MMPI-A Minnesota Reports™ usually follow a plan that allows for the following operations:

1. The first step in computerized interpretation involves processing the raw answers by scoring relevant scales, compiling appropriate indexes, and storing the information in accessible disk reference files.

2. The next step involves determining profile validity, eliminating invalid records, drawing profiles, and printing out a summary of the client's validity scale pattern.

3. Next, the stored data files are searched for relevant scale scores and indexes to determine the appropriate prototypal information to apply to the case. The computer is programmed to search the stored database (reference files or lookup tables) to locate the relevant personality and symptom information for particular scale scores in the protocol, that is, for the highest clinical scales or code type for the MMPI-2. The prototype information for the clinical scale or code type is supplemented with information from the content scales and the supplementary scales, such as APS or AAS in the MMPI-2 or ACK and PRO in the MMPI-A.

4. Finally, the computer prints out a narrative report that addresses the validity of the self-report, summarizes the individual's symptomatic status, and describes personality characteristics and significant problems. The interpretive programs also generate hypotheses about diagnostic possibilities and suggest treatment plans.

Several systems are available for The Minnesota Report™:

1. The Minnesota Report™: Adult Clinical System provides MMPI-2 reports developed for a number of specific clinical settings, including adult inpatient, adult outpatient, college counseling, correctional, medical settings, and chronic pain programs.

2. The Minnesota Report™: Personnel Selection System was developed to provide reports for job applicants in occupations for which the MMPI-2 is used (i.e., those in which there is great public responsibility or high stress). The specific occupations include nuclear power plant employees, police officers, airline pilots, fire department personnel, medical and psychological personnel, and ministerial candidates.

3. The Minnesota Report™: Alcohol and Drug Treatment Program was developed specifically for use with clients who have or are thought to have substance abuse problems. Information on profile type frequency, likelihood of substance abuse as measured by APS and MAC-R, and

whether the individual has acknowledged problems with alcohol or drugs is included.

4. The Minnesota Report™ for Forensic Settings was developed for use with clients being assessed in court cases. Several settings are available: family custody, personal injury, personal injury (neurological), pretrial criminal, correctional, and competency evaluations. Extensive setting-specific information, such as base rates for profiles, is included.

5. The Minnesota Report™ for Adolescents (MMPI-A) was developed for the following settings: outpatient mental health, inpatient mental health, correctional, drug and alcohol treatment, medical, and school.

The interpretive reports were written in a format that would meet the clinician's needs for information on symptom description, diagnostic hypotheses, and treatment considerations. The interpretive system was designed to allow for easy modification as new research findings on the MMPI-2 and MMPI-A emerge.

Case Illustration of The Minnesota Report™: Adult Clinical System

For our illustration of the Adult Clinical System of The Minnesota Report™, we use the case of Alice, with which you have already obtained a high degree of familiarity, repeating her basic scale and content scale profiles here (Figures 15-1 and

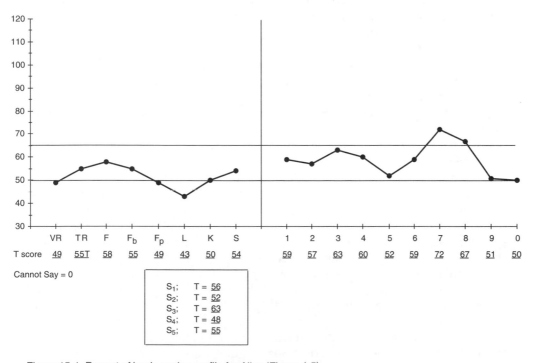

Figure 15-1. Repeat of basic scales profile for Alice (Figure 4-5).

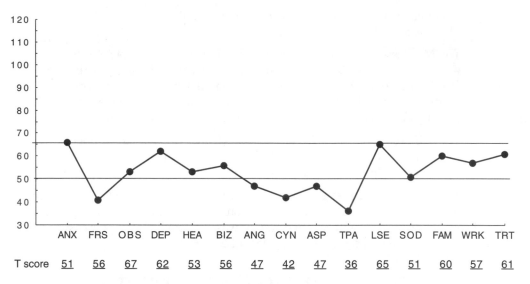

Figure 15-2. Repeat of content scales profile for Alice (Figure 6-3).

15-2) and providing the computer-generated narrative in Figure 15-3. Her narrative indicates that many of the elements from the basic profile, the content profile, and the supplementary profile that were explored in earlier chapters have been incorporated in the computer narrative report.

The computer report based on Alice's validity scale pattern notes that her MMPI-2 profile is interpretable and is likely to be a good indication of her present personality functioning. The computer report also indicates that her cooperative approach toward the testing was likely to suggest a favorable treatment prognosis. Individuals with this pattern are likely to be willing to share personal information in therapy.

Alice's MMPI-2 standard scale profile pattern, with the high-point scale 7 and prominent elevation on scale 8, was employed in the narrative report. Thus, her high anxiety, insecurity, concentration problems, and inability to function were highlighted in the symptomatic pattern. These are essentially the same personality features and problems that were addressed in the interpretive section in Chapter 8. The computer-based report incorporated high-likelihood descriptors in the symptom section of the report. As the clinical interpretation of Alice's profile showed in Chapter 8, the computerized report considered the general problem area of anxiety disorder to be important in her clinical diagnosis.

The computer-based report concluded that psychological treatment was indicated in Alice's case and that she is likely to be motivated to become involved because of her feelings of discomfort. The report also noted a number of problems that would likely become central in her treatment, including her family conflicts and her nonassertiveness in interpersonal relationships.

Profile Validity

This client's approach to the MMPI-2 was open and cooperative. The resulting MMPI-2 profile is valid and probably a good indication of her present level of personality functioning. This may be viewed as a positive indication of her involvement with the evaluation.

Symptomatic Pattern

The client appears to be anxious and tense, and is having difficulty concentrating or making routine decisions. She ruminates a great deal and feels worried, guilty, and depressed.

She seems insecure, and she is experiencing generalized fears that are difficult for her to control. She feels that her life is failing apart. She may be feeling panicky as well as worried about possible health problems. She reports no significant sex-role conflicts.

Interpersonal Relations

She is somewhat shy and insecure, nonassertive in social situations, and apparently ineffective and often covertly hostile in dealing with others. She also seems quite guilt-prone and ruminates excessively about personal and interpersonal failings. Furthermore, her perfectionistic standards and rather moralistic attitudes are likely to create relationship problems for her. Her feelings of inadequacy may impair close intimate relationships.

The content of this client's MMPI-2 responses suggests the following additional information concerning her interpersonal relations. She feels a moderate degree of family conflict at this time, and reported some troublesome family issues. She feels that her family life is not as pleasant as that of other people she knows.

Behavioral Stability

She is apparently highly distressed, and this might have a situational component. This appears to be an acute state which may subside as stress dissipates, or as treatment produces symptom relief. Her interpersonal style is not likely to change significantly if retested at a later date.

Diagnostic Considerations

Psychiatric patients with this profile are often diagnosed as having an anxiety disorder or a compulsive personality disorder. Phobic or obsessive-compulsive behavior is likely to be present.

Treatment Considerations

Since they desire symptom relief for anxiety and tension, individuals with this profile tend to be quite motivated for help and tend to remain in treatment for a long time. However, they are likely to rationalize, intellectualize, and ruminate at great length in psychotherapy, and may find it difficult to focus on specific topics. They may also be somewhat hostile or sarcastic toward the therapist.

Some individuals with this profile respond to relaxation or desensitization therapy for their fears. Since these clients are passive and nonassertive and have difficulty openly expressing their anger, they might benefit from assertiveness training or stress inoculation training.

If psychological treatment is being considered, it may be profitable for the therapist to explore the client's treatment motivation early in therapy. The item content she endorsed includes some feelings and attitudes that could be unproductive in psychological treatment and in implementing self-change.

Note: This MMPI-2 interpretation can serve as a useful source of hypotheses about clients. This report is based on objectively derived scale indexes and scale interpretations that have been developed in diverse groups of patients. The personality descriptions, inferences, and recommendations contained herein need to be verified by other sources of clinical information since individual clients may not fully match the prototype. The information in this report is most appropriately used by a trained, qualified test interpreter, and should be considered confidential.

Figure 15-3. Computer-based interpretation of the MMPI-2 for Alice.

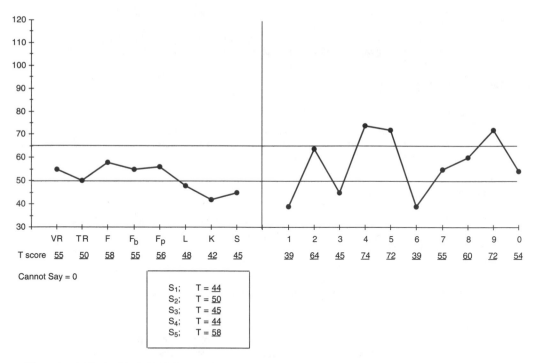

Figure 15-4. Mr. Jenkins's MMPI-2 basic scales profile.

Case Illustration of The Minnesota Report™
for Alcohol and Drug Treatment Settings

The Minnesota Report™ for Alcohol and Drug Treatment Settings is illustrated with the case of Mr. Jenkins. The patient, a 42-year-old salesman (see the case description in Chapter 7), was being evaluated for admission to an inpatient alcohol treatment program at the insistence of his employer after a series of work problems related to alcohol use. His wife also refused to continue in their marriage unless he sought treatment for his alcoholism. She reported that he had been very irresponsible by drinking all night and frequently missing work the next day. He reportedly physically abused his wife on two occasions while drinking. He carelessly spends money by running up debts on his credit cards and by writing checks when he does not have money in the bank. His wife reported that she has had to borrow money several times to cover his bank overdrafts. His wife has attempted to get him to go into alcohol treatment on several occasions, but he has always refused, saying that he does not have a problem with alcohol. She recently left him after an incident in which he drank excessively, was arrested for drunken driving, and was very abusive toward the family. She took him back only after he agreed to go to the alcohol treatment program.

Mr. Jenkins's MMPI-2 basic profile is given in Figure 15-4, the content scale profile in Figure 15-5, the supplementary scale profile in Figure 15-6, and the narrative report summarizing the profile information in Figure 15-7.

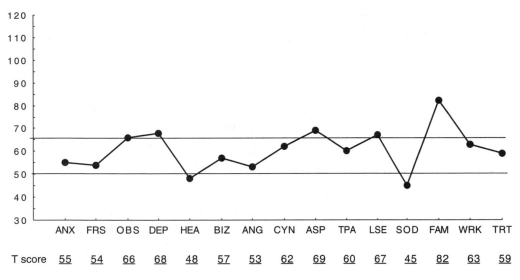

T score															
	ANX	FRS	OBS	DEP	HEA	BIZ	ANG	CYN	ASP	TPA	LSE	SOD	FAM	WRK	TRT
	55	54	66	68	48	57	53	62	69	60	67	45	82	63	59

Figure 15-5. Mr. Jenkins's MMPI-2 content scales profile.

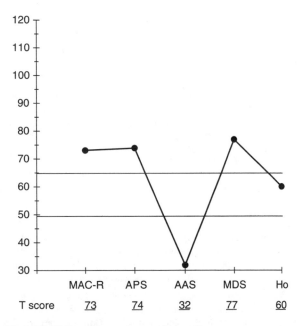

	MAC-R	APS	AAS	MDS	Ho
T score	73	74	32	77	60

Figure 15-6. Mr. Jenkins's MMPI-2 supplementary scales profile.

Profile Validity

This is a valid MMPI-2 profile. The client was quite cooperative with the evaluation and appears to be willing to disclose personal information. There may be some tendency on his part to be overly frank and to exaggerate his symptoms in an effort to obtain help. These hypotheses should be kept in mind when evaluating the clinical patterns reflected in the profile.

Symptomatic Pattern

The client appears to have long-standing impulse-control problems. Extraverted, uninhibited, and rather self-indulgent, he has a low frustration tolerance and a need for constant stimulation that cause him to behave recklessly or irresponsibly at times. Many individuals with this pattern use alcohol or drugs to excess. He apparently has an exaggerated sense of importance and may have grandiose plans. He has a gift for charming others and for appearing self-confident, but he may actually feel quite insecure and inadequate.

He becomes involved in numerous activities, does not follow through sufficiently on commitments, and tends to deny problems and to blame them on moods and overactivity, and he may explode angrily when he becomes frustrated. Many individuals with this profile develop problems of alcohol or drug abuse.

His MMPI-2 profile code, including Pd and Ma, is the most frequent two-point code among men in alcohol- or drug-abusing populations. Over 15.5% of men in substance-abuse treatment programs have this pattern. It should be noted that this high-point code occurs somewhat less frequently in the normative population (7.9%) and at a considerably lower level of elevation than in alcohol- and drug-abusing samples. This MMPI-2 profile configuration contains the most frequent high point, the Pd score, among alcohol- and drug-abusing populations. Over 24% of the men in substance-abuse treatment programs have this pattern, although it is not particularly frequent among men in the normative population (7.9%).

He experiences some conflicts concerning his sex-role identity, appearing somewhat passive and effeminate in his orientation toward life. He may appear somewhat insecure in a male-oriented role, and he may be uncomfortable in relationships with women. His interests, in general, are more characteristic of women than of men. He tends to be quite passive and submissive in interpersonal relationships, and he may make concessions in an effort to avoid confrontation. In addition, he may have a low heterosexual drive.

In addition, the following description is suggested by the content of this client's responses. He has endorsed a number of items suggesting that he is experiencing low morale and a depressed mood. The client's recent thinking is likely to be characterized by obsessiveness and indecision. Although he may be socially assertive and project a positive social image to others, his response content indicates a rather negative self-view that indicates he thinks little of himself. He reports holding some antisocial beliefs and attitudes, admits to rule violations, and acknowledges a history of antisocial behavior in the past. He seems to have an overinflated view of himself, and he seems to resent others making demands on him. He seems to have had much past conflict with authority and is quite resentful of societal standards of conduct.

Interpersonal Relations

A natural ability to charm, persuade, or even con others is usually found in individuals with this profile. They are very sociable and outgoing, but their relationships are usually quite superficial and manipulative. They tend not to be open and honest in relationships. His marriage does not seem to provide him with sufficient pleasure or happiness. He may be experiencing marital discord at this time.

In addition, the following description is suggested by the content of this client's responses. He tends to approach social relationships with some caution and skepticism. He views his home situation as unpleasant and lacking in love and understanding. He feels like leaving home to escape a quarrelsome, critical situation and to be free of family domination.

Figure 15-7. Computer-based interpretation of the MMPI-2 for Mr. Jenkins.

Behavioral Stability

The relative scale elevation of the highest scales in his clinical profile reflects high profile definition. If he is retested at a later date, the peak scores on this test are likely to retain their relative salience in his retest profile pattern.

This pattern of behavior shows a number of long-standing personality characteristics. Some individuals with this profile tend to "burn out" in later life and act out less, in which case a different pattern of symptoms might occur, including somatic distress, anxiety, and depression.

Diagnostic Considerations

Individuals with this profile are usually diagnosed as having a personality disorder. The possibility of a cyclothymic disorder should be evaluated, however. Excessive alcohol or drug use could be a central part of his clinical picture.

The content of his responses underscores the antisocial features in his history. These factors should be taken into consideration in arriving at a clinical diagnosis.

His extremely high score on addiction-proneness indicators suggests great proclivity to the development of an addictive disorder. Further evaluation of substance use or abuse problems is strongly recommended.

Treatment Considerations

Individuals with this profile tend not to seek psychological treatment on their own and are often seen in therapy only at the insistence of others. They may be seen in family therapy, for example. They may appear to be cooperative and to "enjoy" therapy for a time, but they usually resist any demands that they alter their behavior because they are not very introspective and see little reason to change.

Individuals with this profile assume little responsibility for their problems. Their acting-out behavior is likely to be destructive to treatment planning. The fact that he acknowledges having few or no problems with alcohol or drugs should be taken into consideration in treatment planning.

Examination of item content reveals a considerable number of problems with his home life. He feels extremely unhappy and alienated from his family. He related that he feels his home life is unpleasant and feels pessimistic that the situation will improve. Any psychological intervention will need to focus on his negative family feelings if treatment progress is to be made.

Note: This MMPI-2 interpretation can serve as a useful source of hypotheses about clients. This report is based on objectively derived scale indexes and scale interpretations that have been developed in diverse groups of patients with special emphasis on alcohol- and drug-abuse populations. The personality descriptions, inferences, and recommendations contained herein need to be verified by other sources of clinical information since individual clients may not fully match the prototype. The information in this report should most appropriately be used by a trained, qualified test interpreter. The information contained in this report should be considered confidential.

Figure 15-7. Computer-based interpretation of the MMPI-2 for Mr. Jenkins, continued.

The first step in using Mr. Jenkins's Minnesota Report ™ is to determine whether the report is an appropriate match for his current behavior and personality. This can be done by evaluating his validity pattern and appraising whether the pattern of behavior he has been exhibiting is accurately portrayed by the report. The validity paragraph addresses the generally open and cooperative manner in which he was willing to disclose problems. Some symptom exaggeration might be present. The narrative report is considered to be a good indication of his present personality functioning. Second, the major pattern of symptoms he has been experiencing as reported by his wife, that is, his impulsive and irresponsible behavior, appears to be clearly addressed in the report. The two highest scores in the client's MMPI-2 profile, scales 4 and 9, are commonly found in individuals who are in alcohol treatment programs. Over 15% of inpatient treatment cases produce this two-point profile pattern.

The narrative report points to a number of factors that need to be considered in his treatment planning. Although he reports considerable problems with low morale, low self-esteem, and family conflicts, he may have difficulties dealing with these issues in therapy because he tends to have long-standing personality problems that may insulate him from external feedback. His typical behavior appears to involve externalizing blame rather than changing his behavior. His antisocial and acting-out tendencies might frustrate treatment efforts. The narrative report provides a somewhat negative appraisal of his treatment potential, indicating that he might seek therapy, perhaps to appease his wife's demands, but may have difficulty implementing positive behavior change. His lack of acknowledgment of alcohol or drug problems, as noted by the report, will likely be a deterrent to treatment success because he apparently denies that problems exist. Any treatment program aimed at dealing with his alcohol or drug use would need to confront this problem denial in the early sessions if appropriate motivation for change is to be obtained.

Case Illustration of The Minnesota Report™ for Forensic Settings

Joe was evaluated in his jail cell. He was 34 years old at the time and was short and somewhat obese. He was the youngest of nine children from a large Catholic family. During his childhood, his mother was hospitalized for mental illness (schizophrenia) on several occasions. His father was reportedly a "drunk" who was abusive to his wife and children.

Joe described childhood memories of his father's visits when he was separated from Joe's mother. The young boy would, to be close to his father, massage his feet and seemed to enjoy smelling his father's feet. Over the years, he developed a foot fetish and would at times slip into his father's room to sleep near his feet. He started to get sexually excited by his dad's feet and was beaten for this behavior several times, but that did not lessen his urges. This behavior generalized to black socks, and over the years he has asked his male sex partners to put on black socks when having sex.

When Joe was 21 years old, he enrolled in a seminary but had difficulty academically and flunked out. He enlisted in the Navy and, after training, was assigned as a chaplain's assistant. He liked the kind of work that he was doing but ran into difficulty when he "sexually attacked" a chaplain who was wearing black socks. He was given an undesirable discharge from the service after this incident. In the following years, he experienced five psychiatric hospitalizations for depression and substance abuse treatment.

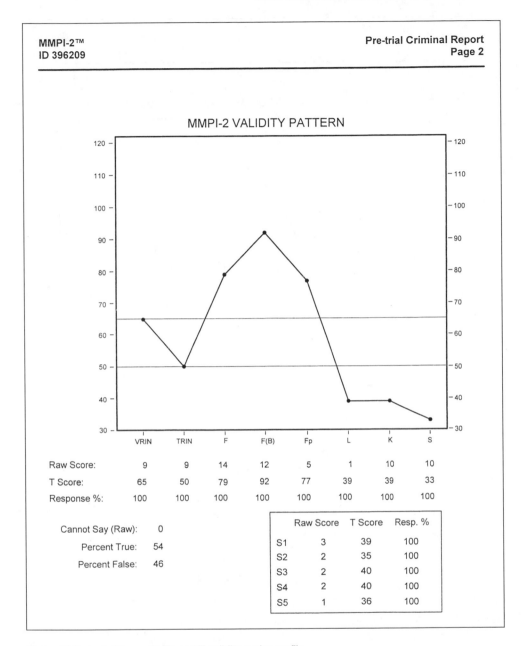

MMPI-2 VALIDITY PATTERN

	VRIN	TRIN	F	F(B)	Fp	L	K	S
Raw Score:	9	9	14	12	5	1	10	10
T Score:	65	50	79	92	77	39	39	33
Response %:	100	100	100	100	100	100	100	100

Cannot Say (Raw):   0

Percent True: 54

Percent False: 46

	Raw Score	T Score	Resp. %
S1	3	39	100
S2	2	35	100
S3	2	40	100
S4	2	40	100
S5	1	36	100

Figure 15-8. Joe's Minnesota Report™ validity scales profile.

Joe described his sexual behavior as homosexual, usually involving black nylon socks, and he reportedly gets erections from smelling his partner's socks. He felt that this behavior was problematic for him and has tried to control it by prayer, but the urges were too powerful. He would often go to bars to pick up men wearing black socks and usually have consensual sex with them. However, he found

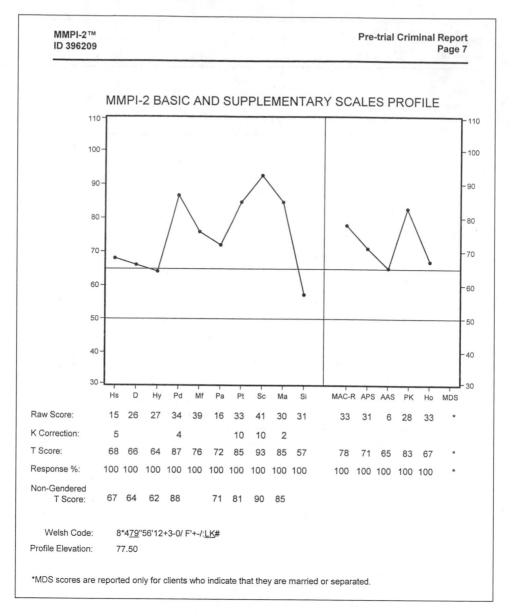

MMPI-2 BASIC AND SUPPLEMENTARY SCALES PROFILE

	Hs	D	Hy	Pd	Mf	Pa	Pt	Sc	Ma	Si		MAC-R	APS	AAS	PK	Ho	MDS
Raw Score:	15	26	27	34	39	16	33	41	30	31		33	31	6	28	33	*
K Correction:	5			4			10	10	2								
T Score:	68	66	64	87	76	72	85	93	85	57		78	71	65	83	67	*
Response %:	100	100	100	100	100	100	100	100	100	100		100	100	100	100	100	*
Non-Gendered T Score:	67	64	62	88		71	81	90	85								

Welsh Code: 8*479"56'12+3-0/ F'+-/:LK#

Profile Elevation: 77.50

*MDS scores are reported only for clients who indicate that they are married or separated.

Figure 15-9. Joe's Minnesota Report™ basic and supplementary scales profile.

himself frequently wanting new partners. At one time, he was arrested for attacking a man on the street who was wearing black socks.

During the time that he committed the crime for which he was being tried, he was living in Hawaii with a man who agreed to help him by offering him a place to stay. His host was an alcoholic, and they began drinking heavily together. After

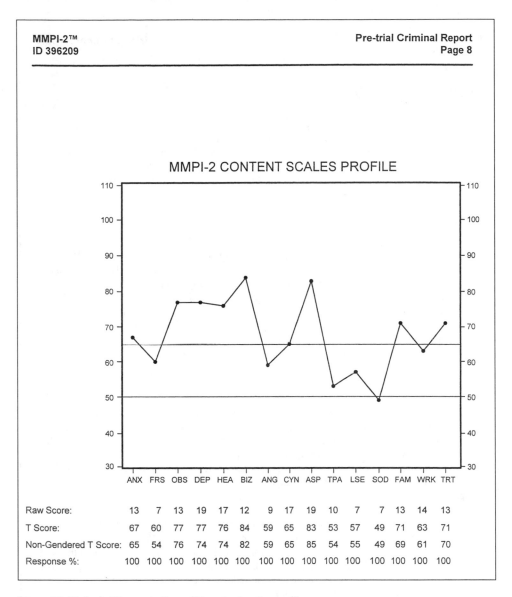

Figure 15-10. Joe's Minnesota Report ™ content scales profile.

a drinking episode, Joe made sexual advances toward his friend but became very frustrated when the friend was not cooperative. Joe, who was very drunk, obtained a hammer and began to beat him over the head until he died, after which he had sex with him. The next day he left town and returned to the mainland but was aware that the police were after him. He later turned himself in to police.

PROFILE VALIDITY

The client's item response pattern suggests that he may have answered items in the latter part of the MMPI-2 in a random or careless manner, thereby invalidating that portion of the test. Although the standard validity and clinical scales are scored from items in the first two-thirds of the test, caution should be used when interpreting the MMPI-2 Content Scales and supplementary scales, which include items found throughout the entire item pool.

SYMPTOMATIC PATTERNS

This report was developed using the *Pd and Sc* scales as the prototype. The client's MMPI-2 clinical profile suggests that he has many psychological problems at this time. He appears to be angry and alienated, and he tends to act out impulsively and unpredictably in antisocial ways. He may engage in dangerous or extremely pleasure-oriented behavior just for the thrill of it, and he has probably had many sexual problems. He is likely to be viewed as immature and irresponsible, and he may have a long history of deviant behavior including poor achievement, poor work history, and problems with authority.

PROFILE FREQUENCY

Profile interpretation can be greatly facilitated by examining the relative frequency of clinical scale patterns in various settings. The client's high-point clinical scale score (Sc) is the least frequent MMPI-2 peak score in the MMPI-2 normative sample of men, occurring in only 4.7% of the cases. Only 2.6% of the sample have Sc as the peak score at or above a T score of 65, and less than 1% have well-defined Sc spikes. His elevated MMPI-2 two-point profile configuration (4-8/8-4) is very rare in samples of normals, occurring in less than 1% of the MMPI-2 normative sample of men.

This profile is relatively frequent in various inpatient settings. In the Graham and Butcher (1988) sample of psychiatric inpatients, the Sc high-point score occurs in 13.8% of the males, with 13.2% scoring at or above a T score of 65 (3.8% are well defined in that high range). In the NCS inpatient sample, 9.1% of the males have this high-point clinical scale score. Moreover, 8.5% of the males in the inpatient sample have the Sc scale spike at or over a T score of 65, and 4.4% produce well-defined Sc spike scores in that range.

The male inpatients in a Veterans Administration sample (Arbisi & Ben-Porath, 1997) produce this high-point peak score with 13.8% frequency. In addition, 5.8% are elevated at or above a T score of 65 and are well-defined profiles.

Figure 15-11. Joe's Minnesota Report™ narrative.

This MMPI-2 clinical scale spike on Sc was one of the more frequent high-point configurations for general psychiatric inpatients in the study conducted by Arbisi, Ben-Porath, Marshall, Boyd, and Strauman (1997). They found this high-point score occurred in 8.6% of the high-point codes (3.2% were well-defined high-point profiles).

This elevated MMPI-2 two-point profile configuration (4-8/8-4) is found in 6.9% of the males in the Graham and Butcher (1988) sample and in 2.9% of the males in the NCS inpatient sample. As the highest scale pair, this code type is found in 3.9% of the men in a Veterans Administration inpatient sample (Arbisi & Ben-Porath, 1997), and it is elevated at or above a T of 65 in less than 1% of the cases. The 4-8/8-4 code type occurred with relatively high frequency (5.9%) in the general psychiatric inpatient study conducted by Arbisi, Ben-Porath, Marshall, Boyd, and Strauman (1997). They reported that this high-point pattern occurred with 1.6% frequency as a well-defined high-point profile.

Ben-Porath and Stafford (1997) conducted a study of high-point and code type frequencies for men and women undergoing competency evaluations. The high-point score on Sc that the client received occurred with 9.1% frequency in that sample. Additionally, it occurred with relatively low frequency (4.8%) in terms of well-defined profiles at or above a T score of 65. This high-point MMPI-2 code (4-8/8-4) can best be understood in the context of cases reported by Ben-Porath and Stafford (1997) in their study of individuals undergoing competency evaluations. This profile configuration occurred in 3.4% of the cases and 1.7% were well-defined scores at or above a T of 65.

PROFILE STABILITY

The relative elevation of his clinical scale scores suggests that his profile is not as well defined as many other profiles. That is, his highest scale or scales are very close to his next scale score elevations. There could be some shifting of the most prominent scale elevations in the profile code if he is retested at a later date. The difference between the profile type used to develop the present report and the next highest scale in the profile code was 2 points. So, for example, if the client is tested at a later date, his profile might involve more behavioral elements related to elevations on Pt. If he is retested, responses related to intensification of anxiety, negative self-image, and unproductive rumination might become more prominent.

INTERPERSONAL RELATIONS

He appears to have poor social skills and, although he is insecure in relationships, he may

Figure 15-11. Joe's Minnesota Report ™ narrative, continued.

manipulate others through aggression and intimidation. He is overly sensitive and frequently misunderstands the motives of others. He seems to have great difficulty relating to the opposite sex. He may use other people for his own gratification with little concern for their needs. His lack of trust may prevent him from developing warm, close relationships. Many individuals with this profile type are unable to develop loving relationships and never trust anyone enough to marry.

MENTAL HEALTH CONSIDERATIONS

Many individuals with this profile receive a diagnosis of severe personality disorder. The possibility of a schizophrenic disorder should also be considered.

His extremely high scores on the addiction proneness indicators suggest the possible development of an addictive disorder. Further evaluation of substance use or abuse problems is strongly recommended. In his responses to the MMPI-2, he acknowledged some problems with excessive use or abuse of addictive substances.

Individuals with this MMPI-2 clinical profile appear to have long-term personality problems that impede psychological treatment. Psychotropic medication is frequently the treatment of choice. Some individuals with these extreme problems require treatment in a controlled setting. Outpatient therapy may be difficult with this individual because of his social alienation and poor ego controls. Insight-oriented psychotherapy tends to be unproductive with individuals of this type because they are likely to act out in unpredictable ways and frequently do not trust the therapist enough to establish a treatment relationship. The client is so emotionally and socially alienated from other people that it would be difficult for a therapist to gain his confidence.

He may respond better to behavioral management therapy than to verbal psychotherapy. Progress is likely to be limited regardless of treatment approach because of his tendency to act out against others. Medication abuse is a possibility because many individuals with this profile develop drug or alcohol problems.

Individuals with this MMPI-2 clinical profile may behave in inappropriately aggressive ways. The client may be antagonistic and abusive toward others. Therapists should be aware of the possibility that he may act aggressively toward other patients or toward individuals in authority.

PRE-TRIAL CRIMINAL CONSIDERATIONS

He responded to the MMPI-2 validity items in a very open manner. He reported many unusual

Figure 15-11. Joe's Minnesota Report™ narrative, continued.

symptoms. This is relatively common in some criminal cases in which the defendant is claiming a broad range of mental health problems. His approach suggests a tendency to exaggerate symptoms. The assessment psychologist should take this into consideration in the evaluation.

Some problems are evident in his MMPI-2 profile. He presented some clear personality and emotional problems that are likely to be important in understanding his day-to-day functioning. His high elevations on the *Pd* and *Sc* scales reflect possible irresponsible, immature, and antisocial behavior. His social relationships are likely to be stormy and trouble-filled at times. His poor self-concept is central to his problems and adds substantial uncertainty to his relationships. His insecurity and tendency to feel rejected may produce an exaggerated need for attention and affection, which can place excessive demands on others. Individuals with this profile pattern are often distrustful of others and avoid close relationships. Their tendency to react to rejection with anger and impulsive behavior can add uncertainty to interpersonal relationships. Problems with impulse control are likely. They are viewed as angry, irritable, and resentful. They typically act out in antisocial ways.

His unconventional behavior seems to make it difficult for him to fit into society. The extent to which his behavior affects his work or social environment should be further evaluated. His tendency to resent and disregard authority might make him vulnerable to legal or work problems.

In addition to the problems indicated by the MMPI-2 clinical scales, he endorsed some items on the Content Scales that could reflect difficulties for him. His numerous family problems should be taken into consideration in the evaluation. His proneness to experience anxiety, depression, obsessive thinking, health problems, and unusual thoughts might make it difficult for him to think clearly or function effectively. The potential impact of his antisocial attitudes and behavior requires further assessment. His likely irresponsible behavior should be assessed to determine if it is affecting his current situation. The possibility that he has a substance abuse or use problem should be evaluated further to determine if this is a possible source of his current problems.

NOTE: This MMPI-2 interpretation can serve as a useful source of hypotheses about clients. This report is based on objectively derived scale indices and scale interpretations that have been developed with diverse groups of people. The personality descriptions, inferences, and recommendations contained herein should be verified by other sources of clinical information because individual clients may not fully match the prototype. The information in this report should be considered confidential and should be used by a trained, qualified test interpreter.

Figure 15-11. Joe's Minnesota Report ™ narrative, continued.

Case Illustration of The Minnesota Report™
for Personnel Screening

The nuclear power company conducting the present evaluation, like most nuclear facilities, typically incorporates a personality screening instrument in its employment program following recommendations of the Nuclear Regulatory Commission (Nuclear Regulatory Commission, 1984). The employment screening program for the nuclear power company involves obtaining several types of information, including a background check, an interview to determine work experience conducted by the operations department, a clinical interview by the psychology staff, and the MMPI-2.

The applicant for one of the technical positions advertised was a 34-year-old woman, Eva, who had previously been employed for 11 months as a technical assistant in a large chemical company. She was terminated from this employment before the end of her probationary period. No reasons were given for her termination. The Minnesota Report™ for Personnel Screening based on her MMPI-2 profile is illustrated in Figures 15-12, 15-13, and 15-14. (Note that the scale order on these profiles represents the unrevised version of this report.)

The applicant's relevant personal history, interview, and psychological test information were evaluated by the psychology staff in making their final employment determination. From the interview and history information, the staff was particularly concerned that the applicant lacked appropriate social skills and tended to interact negatively with others. This hypothesized lack of interpersonal skills might adversely influence her ability to work effectively on a team. In addition, the staff considered that her inability to perform to the satisfaction of her employer in her previous job might reflect both an inability to work in a cooperative team environment and possibly an inability to learn critical elements of the job.

The applicant's qualifications and psychological adjustment were discussed in the employment staffing conference after the evaluation was completed. On the basis of her previous employment difficulties, her lack of experience in a nuclear facility, and the psychological adjustment difficulties that she was likely experiencing (as assessed by the MMPI-2), it was decided to rescind the offer of a position.

Case Illustration of The Minnesota Report™ for the MMPI-A

Computer-based interpretation of the MMPI-A is illustrated by the case of Tony (see Chapters 10 to 14) and analyzed by The Minnesota Report™ for the MMPI-A. Elements of Tony's MMPI-A performance that are incorporated in the narrative report are noted. The MMPI-A validity, basic, and supplementary scales profiles are presented in Figures 15-15 and 15-16, and the content scales profile is given in Figure 15-17. The computer-generated narrative report is presented in Figure 15-18. The Minnesota Report™ is tailored to specific settings. Tony's MMPI-A could have been evaluated for a school setting but was processed to receive an outpatient mental health report because of his referral problem.

The computer-based report addresses several aspects of the client's MMPI-A

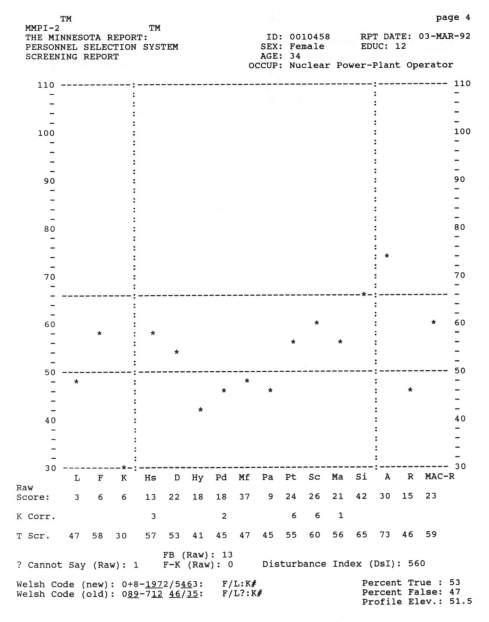

```
        TM
MMPI-2              TM
THE MINNESOTA REPORT:                    ID: 0010458      RPT DATE: 03-MAR-92
PERSONNEL SELECTION SYSTEM               SEX: Female      EDUC: 12
SCREENING REPORT                         AGE: 34
                                         OCCUP: Nuclear Power-Plant Operator
```

Figure 15-12. Eva's Minnesota Report ™ basic and supplementary scales profile.

profile. First, Tony's validity scale performance is described in the Profile Validity section of the report. Because all his validity scales were clearly within the normal range, actually very near the mean score of 50, the computer-generated report accepts the profile as a valid and interpretable performance. No special limitations or interpretive caveats were noted in the Profile Validity section of the report.

Next, the computer narrative report addresses Tony's performance on the

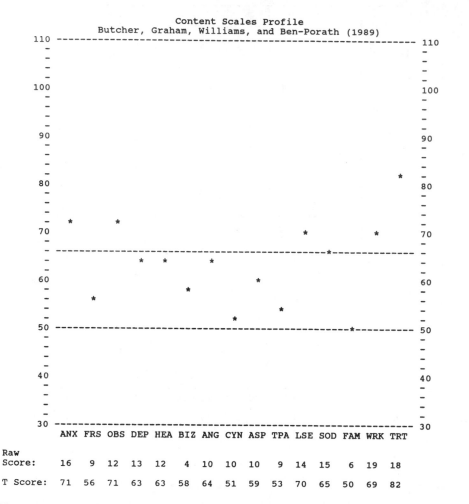

Figure 15-13. Eva's Minnesota Report™ content scales profile.

MMPI-A standard scales. In most cases, this section would incorporate an extended discussion of the empirical correlates of the most salient clinical scales. Because Tony's clinical scales were essentially in the normal range, with only one scale (scale 9) elevated above a T score of 60, the Symptomatic Pattern section is somewhat modest in its behavioral description. Only a few personality characteristics are inferred for individuals with moderate scores on scale 9; these center around overactivity and rebellious behavior. In this computer-based report, Tony's profile is placed in the perspective of other individuals with these peak scores by

```
          TM                                               page 1
MMPI-2                  TM
THE MINNESOTA REPORT:                   ID: 0010458     REPORT DATE: 03-MAR-92
PERSONNEL SELECTION SYSTEM
SCREENING REPORT
```

```
                        _____
                         OPENNESS TO EVALUATION
                        _____


OVERLY     QUITE                   OVERLY
FRANK      OPEN      ADEQUATE       CAUTIOUS      GUARDED      INDETERMINATE

------------X-------------------------------------------------------------


                         _____      _____
                         SOCIAL FACILITY
                        _____


EXCELLENT   GOOD      ADEQUATE      PROBLEMS
                                    POSSIBLE       POOR       INDETERMINATE

---------------------------------------------X----------------------------


                        _____
                         ADDICTION POTENTIAL
                        _____

                           (STANDARD LEVEL)


           NO APPARENT   PROBLEMS
LOW          PROBLEM     POSSIBLE      MODERATE      HIGH      INDETERMINATE

--X-----------------------------------------------------------------------


                        _____
                         STRESS TOLERANCE
                        _____


HIGH         GOOD      ADEQUATE      PROBLEMS
                                     POSSIBLE        LOW      INDETERMINATE

-------------------------------------------------------X------------------


                        _____
                         OVERALL ADJUSTMENT
                        _____


EXCELLENT    GOOD      ADEQUATE      PROBLEMS
                                     POSSIBLE       POOR      INDETERMINATE

----------------------------------------X---------------------------------
```

Her responses to the MMPI-2 items suggests that she may have psychological
problems at this time.

An individual with this level of social introversion is not likely to feel
very comfortable in positions that have many interpersonal demands.

This applicant should be evaluated further to determine if she has
adjustment problems.

NOTE: This MMPI-2 report can serve as a useful guide for employment
decisions in which personality adjustment is considered important for
success on the job. The decision rules on which these classifications are
based were developed through a review of the empirical literature on the
MMPI-2 with "normal-range" individuals (including job applicants) and the
author's practical experience using the test in employment selection. The
report can assist psychologists and physicians involved in personnel
selection by providing an "outside opinion" about the applicant's
adjustment. The MMPI-2 should NOT be used as the SOLE means of determining
the applicant's suitability for employment. The information in this report
should be used by qualified test interpretation specialists ONLY.

Figure 15-14. Eva's Minnesota Report™ personnel selection system screening report.

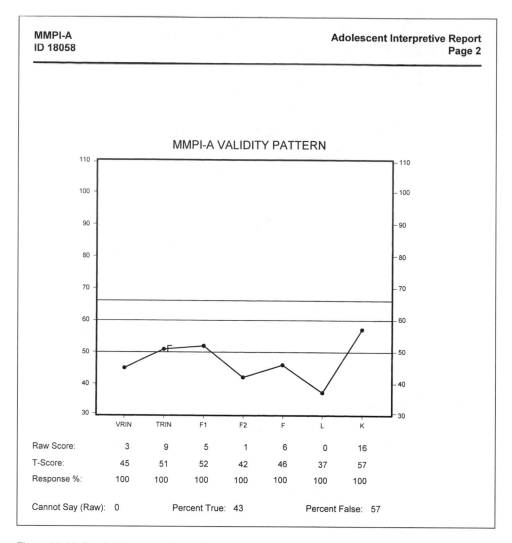

Figure 15-15. Tony's Minnesota Report ™ validity scales profile.

a description of the relative frequency of his profile type in both clinical and normative samples. The report also addresses the adolescent's self-perceptions by analyzing two MMPI-A content scales. His low scores on the A-las and A-lse scales were taken to indicate that he tends to view himself in generally positive ways.

Although few symptoms were noted from the standard profile, the report does take note of several negative symptomatic behaviors through the content of the individual's responses and through the MMPI-A supplementary scales. Specifically, the report addresses the adolescent's high scale elevations on the A-con and A-ang content scales, indicating that these are likely to indicate aggressive acting-out behavior. In addition, the narrative report incorporates a discussion of the adolescent's likelihood of developing drug or alcohol abuse problems and of his willingness to acknowledge that he has had problems with alcohol or drugs. These

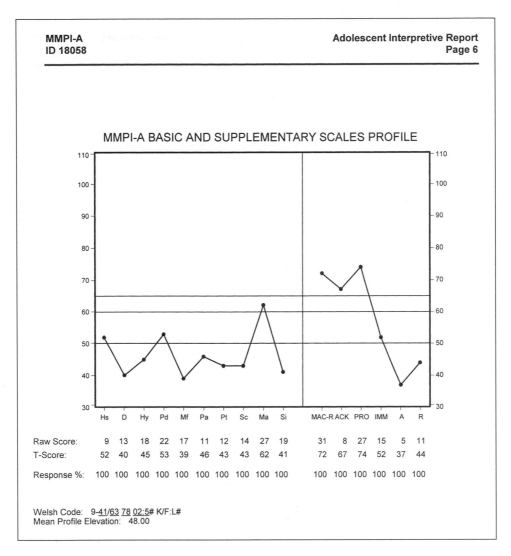

Figure 15-16. Tony's Minnesota Report ™ basic and supplementary scales profile.

severe behavioral problems, highlighted by the report, are important features of Tony's present problem situation that need to be considered in treatment planning. Overall, the computer-based narrative report pointed to several major problem areas in Tony's test performance that could guide the clinician into fruitful areas of exploration.

Evaluation of Computer Interpretation Systems

Research studies comparing the relative accuracy of computer-generated reports with those written by a trained clinician are not available. Most of the computer-

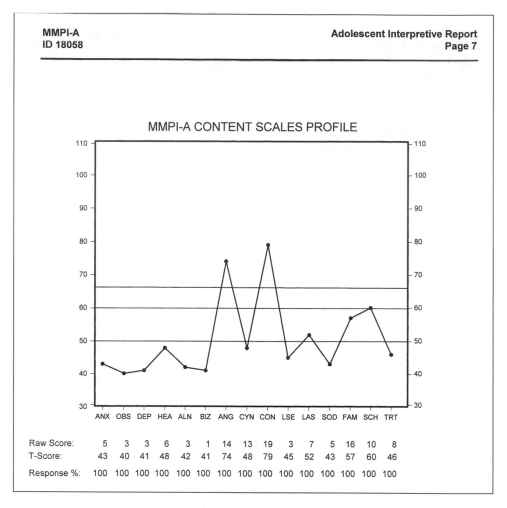

Figure 15-17. Tony's Minnesota Report™ content scales profile.

report evaluation research has employed a research strategy in which a clinician rates acceptability of or satisfaction with the report relative to how it describes the behavior of a client (Moreland, 1987).

Validity of Narrative Reports

Several recent empirical validation studies have been published on computer-based MMPI-2 reports. Shores and Carstairs (1998) recently published a study in which The Minnesota Report™ was shown to detect 94% of fake good records and 100% of fake bad records. Moreland and Onstad (1985) found that computerized psychological reports produced for actual patients were judged by clinicians to be significantly more accurate than random reports. Muller and Bruno (1986) found The Minnesota Report™ for Personnel Screening to be effective in discriminating

VALIDITY CONSIDERATIONS

This adolescent's approach to the MMPI-A was open and cooperative. The resulting MMPI-A is valid and is probably a good indication of his present level of personality functioning. This may be viewed as a positive indication of his involvement with the evaluation.

SYMPTOMATIC BEHAVIOR

His MMPI-A clinical scales profile is only moderately elevated on Ma, which is associated with enthusiasm, wide-ranging interests, and an animated approach to problems. Very limited information is provided on his clinical scales profile about any psychological problems. He may overestimate his capabilities and overextend himself at times. His zeal and intensity may lead to misunderstandings with teachers, parents, or other authority figures.

Adolescent boys with this MMPI-A clinical profile configuration have one of the most frequent high-point scales, the Ma score, found in adolescent treatment units. Over 10% of boys in treatment programs have this well-defined high point in their profile. It should be noted that this high-point score is also the most frequent peak for well-defined profile configurations in the normative sample (over 12%), although it usually has a lower level of elevation than in treatment samples.

His MMPI-A Content Scales profile reveals important areas to consider in his evaluation. He reports many behavioral problems including stealing, shoplifting, lying, breaking or destroying property, being disrespectful, swearing, or being oppositional. He may belong to a peer group that is frequently in trouble and encourages deviant behavior. Poor academic performance and behavioral problems in school are also possible, as are behavior problems at home. Assaultive or aggressive acting-out behavior might be present given his report of considerable problems in controlling his anger. He may appear overly interested in violence and aggression.

INTERPERSONAL RELATIONS

His social behavior might be punctuated with periods of moodiness and open expression of negative feelings.

Some interpersonal issues are suggested by his MMPI-A Content Scales profile. Anger-control problems are significant in his clinical picture. He reports considerable irritability, annoyance, and impatience with others. Temper tantrums and aggressive behavior may characterize his interactions.

Figure 15-18. Computer-based interpretation of Tony's MMPI-A profile.

BEHAVIORAL STABILITY

The relative scale elevation of the highest scale (Ma) in his clinical profile reflects high profile definition. If he is retested at a later date, the peak scores on this test are likely to retain their relative salience in his profile pattern.

DIAGNOSTIC CONSIDERATIONS

The relatively low elevation of his MMPI-A clinical scales does not provide sufficient information to formulate a clinical diagnosis. Additional information from other sources is needed to arrive at a diagnosis. His highly elevated Conduct Problems scale may indicate the presence of an oppositional-defiant disorder or a conduct disorder.

Given his moderate elevation on the School Problems scale, an assessment of possible academic skills deficits and behavior problems could be considered in his diagnostic evaluation.

He obtained extremely high scores on MAC-R and PRO, indicating a high potential for developing alcohol or other drug problems. He probably engages in risk-taking behaviors and tends toward exhibitionism. He probably belongs to a peer group that uses alcohol or other drugs. His involvement in an alcohol- or drug-abusing lifestyle should be further evaluated. Problems at home or school are likely given his problems with alcohol or other drugs.

He has endorsed items that confirm his increasing involvement with alcohol or other drugs. He acknowledges that his use is problematic and reports being criticized for it. He may feel that alcohol or other drugs facilitate social interactions, thus serving as a coping strategy.

TREATMENT CONSIDERATIONS

Adolescents with this clinical scales profile admit to few symptoms that require mental health intervention. Unless problems are revealed in the other MMPI-A profiles or through other sources of assessment, this individual may see no reason to enter therapy at this time.

His very high potential for developing alcohol or drug problems requires attention in therapy if important life changes are to be made. He has acknowledged some problems in this area, which is a valuable first step for intervention.

There are some symptom areas suggested by the Content Scales profile that the therapist may wish to consider in initial treatment sessions. His behavior problems may respond best to behavior management strategies such as contracting.

Figure 15-18. Computer-based interpretation of Tony's MMPI-A profile, continued.

MMPI-A **Adolescent Interpretive Report**
ID 18058 Page 5

Conditions in his environment that may be contributing to his aggressive and hostile behaviors could be explored. Adolescents with anger-control problems may benefit from modelling approaches and rewards for appropriate behaviors. Stress-inoculation training or other cognitive-behavioral interventions could be used to teach self-control. Angry outbursts during therapy sessions can provide opportunities for him to learn about his impulse-control problems and to practice new skills.

He did endorse content suggesting a desire to succeed in life. There may be some positive aspects about school that could be reinforced. This could be an asset to build on during treatment.

NOTE: This MMPI-A interpretation can serve as a useful source of hypotheses about adolescent clients. This report is based on objectively derived scale indexes and scale interpretations that have been developed with diverse groups of clients from adolescent treatment settings. The personality descriptions, inferences, and recommendations contained herein need to be verified by other sources of clinical information because individual clients may not fully match the prototype. The information in this report should most appropriately be used by a trained, qualified test interpreter. The information contained in this report should be considered confidential.

Figure 15-18. Computer-based interpretation of Tony's MMPI-A profile, continued.

problem police applicants from nonproblem applicants. The most comprehensive empirical validation study of computer-based MMPI reports was conducted by Eyde, Kowal, and Fishburne (1987, 1991). These investigators compared the relative accuracy of computerized MMPI reports published by seven commercial scoring and interpretation companies: Behaviordyne, Caldwell, Applied Innovations, Psych Systems, The Minnesota Report™ (NCS), Western, and Tomlinson Report. The investigators submitted MMPI answer sheets for several patients to each computer assessment service. They separated the computer-generated statements, disguised their source, and gave the statements to raters familiar with the actual cases to evaluate for accuracy. Once the ratings were complete, the investigators reassembled the statements into their original context and computed accuracy ratings for each of the seven reports.

Eyde et al. (1991) concluded that "despite the large amount of empirical evidence available for the MMPI and its potential for actuarial prediction, the outputs of CBTI systems for the MMPI for individuals were found to vary significantly in their rated relevance, accuracy, and in their usefulness in case dispositions" (p. 111). In comparison with other available systems, The Minnesota Report™ "received the highest number of accuracy ratings and the lowest number of inaccuracy ratings for the clinical cases" (p. 104).

The accuracy and utility of The Minnesota Report™ for clinical assessments in other countries was shown by Butcher et al. (1998). These investigators explored the usefulness and accuracy of computer-based MMPI-2 test interpretation in Australia, France, Norway, and the United States. In each country, practicing psychologists administered the booklet form of the MMPI-2 to their patients, most of whom were being seen for psychological evaluation before beginning treatment. In France and Norway, translations were used. The patient's answer sheets were scored and interpreted via The Minnesota Report™ using the U.S. norms for the MMPI-2. The Minnesota Report™ narrative was returned to the practitioner, who indicated the percentage of accurate descriptions of the patient. None of the raters reported that the reports were inappropriate or inaccurate. In all four countries, the most useful sections of the report for providing detailed information about the patients were Validity Considerations, Symptomatic Patterns, and Interpersonal Relations. Over two-thirds of the records were judged to be highly accurate (clinicians rated 80% to 100% of the computer-generated narrative statements in them to be appropriate and relevant). Overall, in 87% of the reports, at least 60% of the computer-generated narrative statements were believed to be appropriate and relevant to understanding the client's clinical problems and behavior.

Classification Accuracy of the Computer-Based Decision Rules

To assess whether The Minnesota Report™ Personnel Decision Rules generate credible personality ratings, a study was conducted to compare computer-based ratings with those made by experienced clinicians (Butcher, 1988). The MMPI profiles of 262 airline pilot applicants were rated as to their overall adjustment by three trained clinicians and also processed by computer. The clinicians rated applicants, using their MMPI profiles, on a three-point scale of "Adequate," "Problems Possible," and "Problems Likely." The computer rated adjustment in terms of "Excellent," "Good," "Adequate," "Problems Possible," and "Poor."

Although the computer used a five-point rating scale and the clinicians a three-point scale, we can still evaluate their comparability by adding up the percentages from similar categories. When the expert clinicians rated an applicant as "Adequate," 98.5% of the time the computer also rated the applicant as "Adequate" or better in terms of adjustment (that is, 53.6% were considered "Adequate," 42.5% were "Good," and 2.4% were "Excellent" by the computer). When the clinicians rated the MMPI profile as "Problems likely," the computer agreed 88% of the time. For clear decisions (adequate or poor), agreement was obtained in 89.5% of the cases. A total of 11.5% of the cases were rated by the clinicians as "Problems possible." In these marginal adjustment cases, the computer rules classified 36.7% of them as "Problems possible" or "Poor" in adjustment and 63.3% of the cases as "Adequate" or better. This study suggests that a computer program designed to rate an applicant's MMPI profiles for psychological adjustment could simulate the decisions of clinicians (Butcher, 1988). It did not address external validity because information about the actual adjustment of the applicants was not available.

The personnel decision classification system involves the application of a very complex set of contingency rules to assign "ratings of adjustment." As shown in the study with airline pilot applicants, these ratings have a high degree of comparability with ratings made by expert clinicians evaluating the same MMPI profiles. It is likely that computer-based psychological assessment will be greatly expanded in the future. Future assessments will likely include greater utilization of more complex computerized assessment paradigms to exploit more fully the flexibility and power of the computer in combining assessment information into evaluations.

Issues Concerning Computer-Based MMPI-2 and MMPI-A Interpretation

Computer-based MMPI-2 and MMPI-A reports can be incorporated in a test battery and can provide the practitioner with very valuable information if appropriate cautions are taken and their limitations recognized. There are several caveats to keep in mind when considering the use of computer-generated test reports. First, the practitioner must ensure that the report is appropriate for the case in question and that the information provided in the report matches the test variables produced by the client. Second, care must be taken to employ the most pertinent information and, if necessary, ignore any information of limited relevance. This process, of course, requires that the user have a high degree of familiarity with the test itself. There are other issues with respect to "care and storage" of computerized outputs that require careful consideration. We examine these issues pertinent to using computer-generated information in clinical assessment in more detail.

The Limited Range of Available Test Correlates for the MMPI-2/MMPI-A

Although many studies in the past 25 years have cataloged empirical correlates for the various MMPI scales and indexes, the database for the MMPI, MMPI-2, and MMPI-A does not, at present, provide for interpretation of all possible profile configurations in a strictly actuarial manner. Given that the full range of MMPI code possibilities are not well delineated empirically, the clinical experience of the program developer will determine the makeup of the reports that are generated. Decisions about which components to employ in developing a computer interpretation program clearly influence the accuracy and generalizability of the report. As Fowler (1987) noted, it is thus important, in choosing a computer-based interpretation program, to evaluate carefully the expertise of the system developer. Most of the existing MMPI computer interpretation programs extrapolate from the available research information base to interpret all cases submitted to the service. For example, few actuarial data exist for some codes, such as the 1-9-6 code. The interpretation will likely be based on some combination of the two-point codes or single-scale elevations of the three component scales, depending on the experience of the computer program developer. The approach the program developer chooses will determine the nature of the resulting narrative report.

Determining the Prototypal Match: Does the Computerized Report Actually Fit the Client?

Computer-based test interpretations are best viewed as resource consultations. The computer reporting service provides scoring, indexing, profiling, and listing of relevant test variables along with the narrative statements considered to be most appropriate for the particular test scores. Some of the statements or predictions incorporated in the report may not apply to every patient with a given profile type. It is the responsibility of the test user to determine whether the computer-generated statements are accurate for the particular client. Computer-based MMPI-2 and MMPI-A reports are based on modal or typical descriptions. It is very important for the practitioner to determine whether the computer-based report is appropriate for the patient being assessed. That is, does the information being provided by the report actually apply to the client?

Several factors are important in determining whether the profile and the prototypal descriptions match the individual in question. First, a proper match can be determined only if the clinician is both familiar with the MMPI-2 or MMPI-A measures and associated empirical descriptors and sensitive to the client's actual behaviors and problems. Important to the determination of prototypal match is the clinician's judgment that the behaviors and symptoms obtained from external sources, such as interviews or other test data, are congruent with the hypotheses generated by the computer. The practitioner needs to have a knowledge of the special limiting factors that might influence a particular case, for example, whether the client was blind, had a limited educational background, or was from a different culture.

It is also important for the practitioner to evaluate test validity to ensure that the protocol is interpretable before the personality descriptions and symptoms are attributed to the client. Finally, the issue of profile definition needs to be addressed for the particular client's profile. If the profile is not well defined—that is, if it has many scale scores falling at nearly the same level of elevation—the profile report is less likely to provide specific and reliable information about a client than are those profiles with very high profile definition.

The Role of Computerized Output in the Assessment Report

How is the computerized narrative output used in developing a clinical report? Computer-based outputs are not "stand-alone" clinical reports. Rather, they are best conceptualized as a documented resource or working hypotheses analogous to one's notes obtained from a textbook, actuarial tables, or an informed colleague.

High-probability statements for a particular profile appear in the narrative output as hypotheses about the client. The practitioner determines the congruence and strength of this information in characterizing the client in question. Information that is confirmatory and fits into the clinical picture that is beginning to emerge from other data sources, such as interview, background information, or other test data, may be given a high degree of credence and be included as primary considerations in the evaluation. Many practitioners incorporate the actual wording from the narrative computer output if the information is considered highly relevant for the case.

Some aspects of a particular computerized narrative might appear to the practitioner as relatively unimportant to a case or as not adding particularly useful information to the assessment. For example, a computer-generated statement that "the client shows a lack of impulse control and might act out in an impulsive manner" may not be particularly new or useful information if the client in question is being evaluated in a presentencing investigation after having been convicted of a gruesome murder. The practitioner chooses the information that best fits the case and the purpose of the evaluation.

Where Are Computerized MMPI-2 and MMPI-A Outputs Filed?

As noted earlier, computer-based reports are usually viewed as professional-to-professional consultations analogous to information from a textbook or from a consultation with a specialist in a particular area. The computer scores and narrative reports generated on a particular case can be viewed as the practitioner's working notes from which he or she derives hypotheses or inferences about the client. As working documents in the early stages of a diagnostic evaluation, computerized reports and scores should be kept in the practitioner's working file along with other materials used, and notes should be kept during the assessment process. Computerized narrative outputs are usually not stored in the patient's chart, where they might, perhaps at a later date, be mistaken for the complete report on the case. States have different requirements about the storage of assessment information. Thus, the practitioner should be aware of the legal requirements.

In some settings, computer-based narrative reports are placed in patients' charts, along with other completed reports and pertinent documents, after the psychological evaluation is complete. Practitioners who find this to be the working practice at his or her particular facility should take care to add a summary statement to the output that clarifies the extent to which it entered into the final report on the client.

Limiting Patients' Access to Their
Computerized MMPI-2 and MMPI-A Reports

The computer-based MMPI-2 or MMPI-A report should be viewed as resource material that can provide a number of useful hypotheses, personality descriptions, and test inferences about clients. Clinicians often find that a computerized report is a valuable aid in providing test feedback to clients (Butcher, 1990a; Finn & Tonsager, 1992; Newman & Greenway, 1997). However, care should be taken to limit patient access to reports. Reports should not be provided to clients to keep because there is great potential for misuse and misunderstanding. Computer-generated narrative reports are technical documents developed for professionals and not written for clients' self-use.

Computer-Based Psychological Test
Interpretation: Consumer Qualifications

The American Psychological Association has established guidelines for determining user qualifications to purchase computer-based MMPI-2 reports (American

Psychological Association, 1986). Most computer reporting services follow the user qualification guidelines and determine whether potential subscribers are qualified to use the reports. For example, according to the National Computer Systems user qualifications, Minnesota Reports™ are made available to "fellows, members, and associate members of the American Psychological Association, as well as to psychologists, physicians, and marriage and family therapists licensed by the regulatory board of the state in which they practice."

This chapter has focused on the use of computers to score and interpret the MMPI-2 and MMPI-A. Computer-based interpretive reports can provide the clinician with a convenient "outside opinion" concerning a client's symptoms and behavior based on MMPI-2 or MMPI-A scores. Information based on the most likely empirical descriptors, prominent content themes, and supplementary scales are integrated into a narrative report.

Appendix
MMPI-2 and MMPI-A Translations and Translators

MMPI-2

Arabic:
> Abdalla M. Soliman
> Department of Psychology
> Faculty of Education
> United Arab Emirates University
> AL-AIN, P.O. Box 17771
> United Arab Emirates

Chinese:
> Hong Kong
> > Fanny Cheung
> > Chinese University of Hong Kong
> > Department of Psychology
> > Shatin, N.T. Hong Kong
>
> People's Republic of China
> > Song Wei Zhen
> > Institute of Psychology
> > Chinese Academy of Sciences
> > P.O. Box 1603, Postcode 100012
> > Beijing, China

Dutch/Flemish:
> PEN Test Publishers
> P.O. Box 6537
> 6503 GA Nymegen, Netherlands
>
> Hedwig Sloore
> Free University of Brussels
> Department of Psychology
> Pleinlaan 2
> Brussels, Belgium

French:
> ECPA
> 25 rue de la Plaine
> 75980 Paris, Cedex 20, France

French-Canadian:
> Canadian customers contact:
> > Multi-Health Systems
> > 65 Overlea Blvd., Suite 210
> > Toronto, Ontario M4H 1PI
>
> U.S. customers contact:
> > National Computer Systems
> > P.O. Box 1416
> > Minneapolis, MN 55440

German:
> Jurgen Hogrefe
> Verlag Hans Huber
> Langgass-Strasse 76
> CH-3000
> Bern 9
> Switzerland

Greek:
> Anna Kokkevi
> Dept of Psychiatry
> Athens University Medical School
> Eginition Hospital
> 72-74 Vassilissis Sopphias Ave.
> Athens, 11528 Greece

Hebrew:
> Moshe Almagor
> University of Haifa
> Faculty of Social Sciences
> Mount Carmel, Haifa 31905, Israel

Hmong:
> Customer Service
> National Computer Services
> P.O. Box 1416
> Minneapolis, MN 55440

Icelandic:
> Solvina Konraos
> Hrisholti 7
> 210 Garoabae, Iceland

Italian:
> Roberto Mattei
> Organizzazioni Speciali
> Via Scipione Ammirato 37-50136
> > Firenze, Italy
>
> Saolo Sirigatti
> Dip. Psicologia
> Universita di Firenze
> Via S. Niccolo, 93, Italy
>
> Paolo Pancheri
> CIC Edizioni Internazionali
> 5a Cattedra di clinica Psichiatrica
> 36, Viale Dell= Universita
> 00185 Roma Italia

Japanese:
Noriko Shiota
Department of Psychology
Villanova University
Villanova, PA 19085

Korean:
Kynghee Han
University of Mississippi
Dept of Psychology, 308 Peabody Bldg
P.O. Box 37
University, MS 38677

Norwegian:
Bjorn Ellertsen
University of Bergen
Clinical Neuropsychology
Arstadveien 21
Bergen, Norway N-5009

Russian:
Vladimar Martens
Institute of Biophysics
Zilapistnaya 46
Moscow, 182 Russia

Spanish:
Argentina:
Maria Casullo
University of Buenos Aires
Faculty of Psychology
Tucuman 2162, 8th Floor A
1050 Buenos Aires, Argentina

Chile:
Fernando J. Rissetti
Departmento de Salud Estudiantil
Pontificia Universidad
Catolicia de Chile
JV Lastarria 65
Santiago, Chile SA5

Mexico:
Manuel Moderno
Av Sonora 206
Col. Hipodromo, 06100 Mexico, D.F.

Emilia Lucio G.M. & Isabel Reyes-
Lagunes
Corregidora 30-1
Col. Miguel Hidalgo Tialpan
CP 14410
Mexico, D.F.

Spain:
Alejando Avila-Espade
Universidad de Salamanca
Department of Psychology

United States:
Customer Service
National Computer Services
P.O. Box 1416
Minneapolis, MN 55440

Alex Azan
Florida International University
Student Counseling Services
University Park—GC 211
Miami, FL 33199

Rosa Garcia-Peltoniemi
Center for the Victims of Torture
717 East River Road
Minneapolis, MN 55455

Thai:
La-or Pongpanich
Psychiatric Department
Army General Hospital
Bangkok, Thailand

Turkish:
Merla Culha
%University of Minnesota Press
111 Third Avenue South, Suite 290
Minneapolis, MN 55401-2520

Vietnamese:
Pauline Tran
1258 Capistrano Lane
Vista, CA 92083

MMPI-A

Chinese:
Hong Kong
Fanny Cheung
Chinese University of Hong Kong
Department of Psychology
Shatin, N.T. Hong Kong

French:
ECPA
25 rue de la Plaine
75980 Paris, Cedex 20, France

Greek:
Anna Kokkevi
Dept of Psychiatry
Athens University Medical School
Eginition Hospital
72-74 Vassilissis Sopphias Ave.
Athens, 11528 Greece

Hebrew:
Moshe Almagor
University of Haifa
Faculty of Social Sciences
Mount Carmel, Haifa 31905, Israel

Italian:
Roberto Mattei
Organizzazioni Speciali
Via Scipione Ammirato 37-50136
Firenze, Italy

Korean:
    Jeeyoung Lim
    802-501 Hanjin APT
    Jeongdun-Maul
    193 Jeongja-Dong, Boondang-Gu
    Sungnam-City, Kynuggi-Do
    South Korea

Norwegian:
    Bjorn Ellertsen
    University of Bergen
    Clinical Neuropsychology
    Arstadveien 21
    Bergen, Norway N-5009

Spanish:
    Mexico:
        Manuel Moderno
        Av Sonora 206
        Col. Hipodromo, 06100 Mexico, D.F.

        Emilia Lucio G.M. & Isabel Reyes-
            Lagunes
        Corregidora 30-1
        Col. Miguel Hidalgo Tialpan
        CP 14410
        Mexico, D.F.
    United States:
        Customer Service
        National Computer Services
        P.O. Box 1416
        Minneapolis, MN 55440

Thai:
    La-or Pongpanich
    Psychiatric Department
    Army General Hospital
    Bangkok, Thailand

Glossary

This glossary was designed to provide a quick reference to some of the most frequently used technical terms and abbreviations relating to the MMPI-2 and MMPI-A. It is not a comprehensive psychometric dictionary but simply a handy reference tool. Please note that all content scales unique to the MMPI-A are listed in this glossary—for example, A-aln. Content scales that appear in both the MMPI-2 and the MMPI-A are listed by their MMPI-2 abbreviated and full names—for example, ANX; the MMPI-A scale is A-Anx.

A (Anxiety) Scale (Welsh) A factor analytic scale that defines the first major factor in the MMPI-2 and MMPI-A item pools: anxiety or general maladjustment.

A-aln (Adolescent-Alienation) Scale An MMPI-A content scale measuring the extent to which the adolescent feels distanced from other people.

AAS (Addiction Admission) Scale A rationally derived MMPI-2 scale assessing a client's experience with alcohol or drugs. A high score on this scale indicates that the client has endorsed a significant number of substance abuse problems.

ACK (Alcohol/Drug Problem Acknowledgment) Scale An MMPI-A scale developed to assess whether the adolescent is acknowledging using/abusing alcohol or drugs.

A-con (Adolescent-Conduct Problems) Scale An MMPI-A content scale assessing problems of conduct disorder.

Acting Out A term usually used within a psychoanalytic or psychodynamic framework to denote a defense in which individuals express painful or "unacceptable" emotions through behavior as a way to keep the emotions unconscious (or out of awareness).

Actuarial Prediction The application of probability statistics to human behavior, as in insurance mortality tables.

Acute Posttraumatic Stress Disorder (PTSD) A disorder in which symptoms develop within 6 months of an extremely stressful or traumatic experience.

Adaptive Testing A method of test administration that uses the rapid computational capability of the computer to administer a different set of items for each person, depending on the person's responses to previous items.

Addiction Proneness A theoretical construct concerning the likelihood that an individual will develop substance abuse disorders.

Affect The experience of feelings or emotion.

A-las (Low Aspirations) Scale An MMPI-A content scale assessing poor attitudes toward achievement and being a success in life. Although it is related to the School Problems scale, its content is more general, including dislike of sports and nonschool activities.

ANG (Anger) Scale An MMPI-2 content scale; A-ang is the MMPI-A equivalent.

Antisocial Personality Personality disorder involving a marked lack of ethical or moral development.

ANX (Anxiety) Scale An MMPI-2 content scale; A-anx is the MMPI-A equivalent.

APS (Addiction Potential) Scale An empirically derived MMPI-2 scale assessing the likelihood that an individual has a substance abuse problem.

A-sch (School Problems) Scale An MMPI-A content scale that addresses school-related problems.

ASP (Antisocial Practices) Scale An MMPI-2 content scale. It changed substantially on the MMPI-A and was renamed A-con (Adolescent-Conduct Problems).

Automated Assessment Psychological test interpretation by computer or other mechanical procedure.

Bimodal Distribution   A statistical term indicating a distribution in which two values (or scores) are tied in terms of being most frequent; thus, the distribution has two modes.

BIZ (Bizarre Mentation) Scale   An MMPI-2 content scale; A-biz is the MMPI-A equivalent.

(?) Cannot Say   The total number of unanswered items on the MMPI-2 or MMPI-A, serving as an indicator of test validity.

Central Tendency   A statistical term indicating the average; measures of central tendency include the mean, the median, and the mode (see Mean, Median, Mode).

Clinical Scale   Items that have been grouped into scales according to empirical validation methods; that is, items comprising the scale were found to significantly discriminate a criterion group of patients from a normal reference sample. A particular empirical scale—for example, to measure depression—is interpreted by referring to empirical correlates (extratest behaviors) established through validation research.

Code Type   A summary index of the most prominent MMPI-2 scales. A one-point code, or spike, has one prominent scale; a two-point code type consists of two scales elevated in the interpretable range.

Content Scale   A psychometric measure developed by rational-empirical methods to assess homogeneous content themes in the MMPI-2 and MMPI-A.

Correlation Coefficient   A statistic indicating the degree to which two variables are related (whether they covary or vary together). The coefficient falls somewhere on a continuum from -1 (perfectly negatively correlated) to 0 (no relationship whatsoever) to 1 (perfectly positively correlated).

Criterion Group   A sample of persons, such as depressed clinical patients or persons with a substance abuse disorder, who are assumed to have common characteristics. This group is contrasted with a group of normal individuals to develop empirical scales by selecting items that differentiate the criterion group from normals.

Critical Items   Items that serve as possible indicators of clinical or personality problems—for example, "suicidal ideation" or "anger control problems."

Cutoff Score   A somewhat arbitrary point in an MMPI-2 or MMPI-A scale distribution at which a particular interpretation or decision is made.

CYN (Cynicism) Scale   An MMPI-2 content scale; A-cyn is the MMPI-A equivalent.

D (Depression) Scale (Scale 2)   An MMPI-2 and MMPI-A clinical scale.

Decompensation   A term describing the deterioration of an individual's personality, condition, or functioning.

Defense Mechanisms   A term used to describe a process, usually within a psychoanalytic or psychodynamic framework, by which an individual wards off awareness of unpleasant, frightening, or anxiety-inducing thoughts or experiences; these strategies are carried out on an unconscious level (i.e., the individual is not aware of them).

Delusion   A false belief or one that is not consistent with reality and is rigidly maintained despite strong evidence to the contrary.

Dementia   Substantial loss of mental or cognitive abilities.

DEP (Depression) Scale   An MMPI-2 content scale; A-dep is the MMPI-A equivalent.

Descriptive Statistics   Statistics that apply only to cases that have actually been counted or otherwise measured; no attempt is made to draw inferences about populations beyond what has actually been counted or measured.

Diagnostic and Statistical Manual of Mental Disorders (*DSM*)   A classification system by which mental, emotional, and behavioral disorders have been defined, described, and labeled, published by the American Psychiatric Association, the first edition appearing in 1952. After the second edition in 1968, a multiaxial system of diagnosis was developed (American Psychiatric Association, 1980, 1987): Axis I presents clinical disorders or syndromes (as well as treatment issues that do not concern mental disorders and some supplementary codes), Axis II presents personality and developmental disorders, Axis III presents physical disorders, Axis IV indicates the level of psychosocial stress, and Axis V indicates the best level of functioning the individual has experienced during the past year.

Empirical Correlates   The relationships between MMPI-2 or MMPI-A scores and observed external behavior are described as "empirical correlates" for a given scale. Empirical correlates for the scales are symptoms, behaviors, and attitudes that have been found to be present in patients with prominent elevations on a given scale or scales.

Empirical Scale Construction   A scale construction strategy by which items are selected for a scale if they significantly discriminate two clearly defined groups, such as "depressive patients" and "normals," from each other. Item selection is based on empirical or external validation methods.

F Scale   An MMPI-2 and MMPI-A validity scale measuring "infrequency" or exaggeration of symptoms.

F_b Scale   An MMPI-2 validity scale created to measure exaggeration of symptoms toward the end of the MMPI-2 booklet.

F_p Scale   An MMPI-2 validity scale developed to measure exaggeration of symptoms or infrequent responses within a psychiatric sample.

F_1 Scale   An MMPI-A validity scale measuring infrequent responses or exaggeration of symptoms in the first part of the MMPI-A booklet.

F_2 Scale   An MMPI-A validity scale measuring exaggeration of symptoms or infrequent responses toward the end of the MMPI-A booklet.

Factor Analysis   A statistical technique employed in research to reduce a large array of measurements or data to more concise and fundamental dimensions.

Fake-Bad Profile   A validity scale profile indicating that the test taker has made an effort to distort MMPI-2 results by claiming mental health symptoms that he or she does not have. The "fake-bad" profile usually has an extremely elevated F, F_b, or F_p pattern and relatively low scores on L, K, and S.

Fake-Good Profile   A validity scale profile indicating that the test taker made an effort to distort MMPI-2 results by presenting an overly favorable self-view or a "good impression." The "fake-good" profile usually has an extremely elevated pattern of L, K, and S scales and relatively low scores on F, F_b, and F_p.

False Negative   An error in assessment in which a test falsely indicates that the individual does not have a particular condition (that the test was designed to identify) when in fact the person does have the condition (see False Positive, Sensitivity, Specificity).

False Positive   An assessment error in which a test falsely indicates that an individual has a particular condition (that the test was designed to identify) when in fact the person does not have the condition (see False Negative, Sensitivity, Specificity).

FAM (Family Problems) Scale   An MMPI-2 content scale; A-fam is the MMPI-A equivalent.

Floating Profile   A term indicating that T scores on all 10 standard scales are above 65.

FRS (Fears) Scale   An MMPI-2 content scale; there is no MMPI-A equivalent.

Functional Disorder   A form of psychopathological distress or dysfunction for which a physiological cause is neither known nor presumed.

Functional Psychoses   Severe mental disorders that are attributed primarily to psychological causes, such as stress.

HEA (Health Concerns) Scale   An MMPI-2 content scale; A-hea is the MMPI-A equivalent.

Ho (Hostility) Scale   An MMPI-2 scale assessing interpersonal problems and self-reported hostile, aggressive behavior.

Hs (Hypochondriasis) Scale (Scale 1)   An MMPI-2 and MMPI-A clinical scale measuring somatic concerns (see Chapter 2).

Hy (Hysteria) Scale (Scale 3)   An MMPI-2 and MMPI-A clinical scale measuring physical complaints and denial of problems.

Incidence   The rate at which a phenomenon occurs.

Inferential Statistics   Statistical techniques allowing inferences to be made about a larger population on the basis of a presumably representative sample or subset of that population.

K Correction   Fractions of the K-scale score added to several MMPI-2 clinical scales to correct for defensiveness.

K Scale   An MMPI-2 and MMPI-A validity scale measuring test defensiveness.

Kurtosis   A statistical term describing the degree to which scores or measurements are clustered closely around or are spread far from the mean.

L (Lie) Scale   An MMPI-2 and MMPI-A validity scale measuring the tendency to claim excessive virtue.

Linear T Scores   A statistical term (see T Scores) in which the mean of the distribution is 50 and the standard deviation is 10; the type of score used in the original MMPI. The linear T-distribution formula is defined as follows:

$$T = 50 + [10(X - MEAN)] / SD$$
where

X = each raw score that could potentially be obtained for a given MMPI scale,

MEAN = the mean raw score among subjects for that scale, and

SD = the standard deviation among subjects for that scale.

LSE (Low Self-Esteem) Scale   An MMPI-2 content scale; A-lse is the MMPI-A equivalent.

Ma (Hypomania) Scale (Scale 9)   A clinical scale on the MMPI-2 and MMPI-A measuring behavioral features of manic and manic-depressive episodes (see Chapter 2).

MAC-R (MacAndrew Alcoholism Scale—Revised)   An empirically derived scale assessing addiction potential, revised for inclusion on the MMPI-2 and MMPI-A.

MDS (Marital Distress) Scale   An empirically derived MMPI-2 scale assessing relationship or marital problems.

Mean   An arithmetical average in which the scores (or other numbers) are added and the resulting sum is then divided by the number of scores.

Median   A statistical term indicating the score or measurement that divides all the scores or measurements into two equal groups: those falling below the median and those falling above the median.

Megargee Offender Classification System   A classification system designed to group the MMPI-2 profiles of felons into personality clusters.

Mf (Masculinity-Femininity) Scale (Scale 5)   A scale on the standard MMPI-2 and MMPI-A profiles measuring gender-role reversal or nontraditional sex-role attitudes.

Mode   A statistical term indicating the most frequently occurring score or measurement in a distribution.

Neurotic Triad   The three MMPI-2 and MMPI-A clinical scales: Hs, D, and Hy.

Norm-Referenced Tests   Measures that compare test takers with each other. Grading on a "curve" is an example of norm referencing.

OBS (Obsessiveness) Scale   An MMPI-2 content scale; A-obs is the MMPI-A equivalent.

O-Ho (Overcontrolled Hostility) Scale   A scale that purports to assess overcontrol of hostile, aggressive behavior. It does not predict such behavior but explains it after it has occurred.

Pa (Paranoia) Scale (Scale 6)   An MMPI-2 and MMPI-A clinical scale measuring suspiciousness and paranoid ideation.

Pathognomonic Symptom or Sign   A sufficient indicant for assigning a particular diagnosis or classification (e.g., the use of MMPI-2 items as indicators of pathology, such as suicidal thinking).

Pd (Psychopathic Deviate) Scale (Scale 4)   An MMPI-2 and MMPI-A clinical scale measuring antisocial behavior.

Percentile Rank   The proportion of a group that falls below a particular point.

Percentile Score   The rank from the bottom of a scale expressed as a percentage.

Percentile Value of Elevations   The percentage of cases that obtain scores at the T-score level obtained by the test taker; the percentile values for various T-score levels are slightly different for men and women:

Men:

T = 60   84.4 percentile
T = 65   92.4 percentile
T = 70   96.2 percentile
T = 75   98.2 percentile
T = 80   99.2 percentile
T = 85   99.7 percentile

Women:

T = 60   84.9 percentile
T = 65   91.7 percentile
T = 70   95.8 percentile
T = 75   98.0 percentile
T = 80   99.3 percentile
T = 85   99.8 percentile

Personality Disorder   A group of maladaptive behavioral syndromes originating in the developmental years (usually considered learning-based disorders), not characterized by neurotic or psychotic symptoms.

Prevalence   A statistical term referring to the total number of cases of a particular event or phenomenon within a specified time (see also Incidence).

Profile   A method of displaying test scores that provides a visual comparison of relative performance on scales.

Profile Code   Also referred to as a code type, it is an MMPI-2–based summary of scores that defines the most elevated scores in the profile, either a single scale score or a combination of several scale scores.

Profile Configuration   The shape or pattern of MMPI-2 clinical scale scores on a given profile. For example, the 1-3 configuration is made up of elevations on scale 1 (Hs) and scale 3 (Hy).

Profile Definition   Profile definition refers to how elevated the most elevated clinical scales are above the next highest scales in the profile. For example, if the two highest scales are 10 or more T-score points above the third-ranked scale in the profile, the profile code is said to be well defined or to have very high profile definition; if a profile code is 5 to 9 T-score points higher than the next score, it is said to have high profile definition. Those profiles with 4 or fewer T-score points separating the code from the next score have low profile definition. Profiles with high or very high profile definition tend to be stable over time.

Profile Elevation   Profile elevation of an MMPI-2 or MMPI-A T score is the distance of a given score from the mean score of "normals" expressed in T-score points. For example, a T score of 70 is elevated two full standard deviations above the mean score of the normative sample.

PSY-5 Scales   A set of experimental MMPI-2 scales developed to assess the "five-factor" model of personality.

Psychophysiological (Psychosomatic) Disorders   Physical disorders in which psychological factors are considered to play a major causative role.

Pt (Psychasthenia) Scale (Scale 7)   An MMPI-2 and MMPI-A clinical scale measuring anxiety.

R (Repression) Scale (Welsh)   A factor analytic scale on the MMPI-2 and MMPI-A that defines the second major factor of the item pools: overcontrol.

Random Sample   A subgroup of a larger group (the population) selected in such a way that each member of the larger group has an equal probability of being chosen.

Rational Scale Development   A method of scale construction in which items are selected on the basis of their face validity. This strategy involves "rational" or obvious content item selection procedures.

Reliability   The degree to which a test or other form of measurement is consistent in producing the same result every time it is used to assess or measure a particular person who has not changed significantly between testings (see Chapter 8).

Response Rate   A statistical term for the percentage of those invited to participate in a study who actually participate (e.g., if surveys were mailed to 200 randomly selected individuals, and 150 individuals completed and returned the survey form, the response rate would be 75%).

Sc (Schizophrenia) Scale (Scale 8)   An MMPI-2 and MMPI-A clinical scale measuring bizarre thinking.

Self-Report Questionnaire   A questionnaire or inventory designed to obtain self-descriptions from an individual.

Sensitivity   When a psychological test has been validated to identify a certain condition, sensitivity refers to the proportion of tested individuals who test positive, or who actually have the condition (see False Negative, False Positive, Specificity).

Si (Social Introversion) Scale (Scale 0)   An MMPI-2 and MMPI-A clinical scale measuring introversion.

Skewness   A statistical term indicating the degree to which measurements fall in a symmetrical (i.e., not skewed) or asymmetrical (i.e., skewed) pattern around the mean.

Social Approval or Social Desirability Bias   The tendency for an individual to provide answers that would be perceived as socially approved or socially desirable.

SOD (Social Discomfort) Scale   An MMPI-2 content scale; A-sod is the MMPI-A equivalent.

Somatic   Relating to the body (e.g., headaches and abdominal pain would be characterized as somatic complaints).

Specificity   If a psychological test has been validated to identify a certain condition, specificity refers to the proportion of tested individuals who test negative, or who do not have the condition (see False Negative, False Positive, Sensitivity).

Standard Deviation   A statistical measure of the spread, or dispersion, of scores (or other measures) around the mean; the square root of the variance.

Standard Score   A score (e.g., on a standardized psychological test) that is calculated in terms of standard deviations from the statistical mean of scores.

Submerged Profile   A term describing a profile that has no points at or above a T score of 50.

Syndrome   A group or pattern of symptoms, sequelae, or characteristics of a disorder.

Teleprocessing   A computer-based data processing procedure by which psychological tests are scored and interpreted through telephone linkup with a central processing center.

Test   A standardized procedure for obtaining observations or behaviors and describing them on a numeric scale or in categories.

Test User Qualifications   Guidelines established by a professional organization (e.g., the American Psychological Association) specifying the level of training and experience required for a given test.

TPA (Type A Personality) Scale   An MMPI-2 content scale; there is no MMPI-A equivalent.

TR   Abbreviation for TRIN on MMPI-2 and MMPI-A profile sheets.

TRIN (True Response Inconsistency) Scale   An MMPI-2 and MMPI-A validity scale measuring inconsistency in terms of True responding (yea-saying) and False responding (nay-saying).

TRT (Negative Treatment Indicators) Scale   An MMPI-2 content scale.

T Scores   Scores falling along a distribution in which the mean is 50 and the standard deviation is 10.

Type I Error   A research term indicating that a decision (in interpreting results) was made that there was an actual (i.e., not due to chance) difference or finding when in reality there was no such actual difference or finding; also known as alpha error.

Type II Error   A research term indicating that a decision (in interpreting results) was made that there was no actual (i.e., not due to chance) difference or finding when in reality there was such a difference or finding; also known as beta error.

Uniform T Scores   A statistical term (see T Scores) for the type of scaling used in the MMPI-2 and MMPI-A resulting in comparable percentile values for a given T score across the clinical and content scales.

Validity   The degree to which a test or other form of measurement actually assesses or measures what it is designed to assess or measure.

Variance   A statistical measure of the spread, or dispersion, of scores (or other measures) around the mean; the square of the standard deviation.

VR   Abbreviation for VRIN on MMPI-2 and MMPI-A profile sheets.

VRIN (Variable Response Inconsistency) Scale   An MMPI-2 and MMPI-A validity scale measuring inconsistent responding.

WRK (Work Interference) Scale   An MMPI-2 content scale; there is no MMPI-A equivalent, although A-sch measures a related construct.

Z Scores   Standardized scores falling along a distribution in which the mean is 0 and the standard deviation is 1.

References

Alperin, J. J., Archer, R. P., & Coates, G. D. (1996). Development and effects of an MMPI-A K-correction procedure. *Journal of Personality Assessment, 67*(1), 155–168.

Altman, H., Gynther, M. D., Warbin, R. W., & Sletten, I. W. (1973). Replicated empirical correlates of the MMPI 8-9/9-8 code type. *Journal of Personality Assessment, 37*, 369–371.

American Psychiatric Association (1952). *Diagnostic and statistical manual of mental disorders.* Washington, DC: American Psychiatric Association.

American Psychiatric Association (1968). *Diagnostic and statistical manual of mental disorders* (2nd ed.) (*DSM-II*). Washington, DC: American Psychiatric Association.

American Psychiatric Association (1980). *Diagnostic and statistical manual of mental disorders* (3rd ed.) (*DSM-III*). Washington, DC: American Psychiatric Association.

American Psychiatric Association (1987). *Diagnostic and statistical manual of mental disorders* (3rd ed. revised) (*DSM-III-R*). Washington, DC: American Psychiatric Association.

American Psychological Association (1986). *American Psychological Association guidelines for computer-based tests and interpretations.* Washington, DC: American Psychological Association.

Arbisi, P., & Ben-Porath, Y. S. (1995). An MMPI-2 infrequency scale for use with psychopathological populations: The Infrequency-Psychopathology Scale, F(p). *Psychological Assessment, 7*, 424–431.

Arbisi, P., & Ben-Porath, Y. S. (1997). Characteristics of the MMPI-2 F(p) Scale as a function of diagnosis in an inpatient sample of veterans. *Psychological Assessment, 9*, 102–105.

Archer, R. P. (1984). Use of the MMPI with adolescents: A review of salient issues. *Clinical Psychology Review, 4*, 241–251.

Archer, R. P. (1987). *Using the MMPI with adolescents.* Hillsdale, NJ: Lawrence Erlbaum Associates.

Archer, R. P. (1992). *MMPI-A: Assessing adolescent psychology.* Hillsdale, NJ: Lawrence Erlbaum Associates.

Archer, R. P. (1997a). Future directions for the MMPI-A: Research and clinical issues. *Journal of Personality Assessment, 68*(1): 95–109.

Archer, R. P. (1997b). *MMPI-A: Assessing adolescent psychology* (2nd ed.). Mahwah, NJ: Lawrence Erlbaum Associates.

Archer, R. P., Aiduk, R., Griffin, R., & Elkins, D. E. (1996). Incremental validity of the MMPI-2 content scales in a psychiatric sample. *Assessment, 3*(1), 79–90.

Archer, R. P., Belevich, J. K. S., & Elkins, D. E. (1994). Item-level and scale-level factor structure of the MMPI-A. *Journal of Personality Assessment, 62*(2), 332–345.

Archer, R. P., Gordon, R. A., Giannetti, R. A., & Singles, J. M. (1988). MMPI scale clinical correlates for adolescent inpatients. *Journal of Personality Assessment, 52*, 707–721.

Archer, R. P., Griffin, R., & Aiduk, R. (1995). Clinical correlates for ten common code types. *Journal of Personality Assessment, 65*, 391–408.

Archer, R. P., & Jacobson, J. M. (1993). Are critical items "critical" for the MMPI-A? *Journal of Personality Assessment, 61*(3), 547–556.

Archer, R. P., & Krishnamurthy, R. (1994). A structural summary approach for the MMPI-A: Development and empirical correlates. *Journal of Personality Assessment, 63*(3), 554–573.

Archer, R. P., Pancoast, D. L., & Gordon, R. A. (1994). The development of the MMPI-A Immaturity Scale: Findings for normal and clinical samples. *Journal of Personality Assessment, 62*(1), 145–156.

Arita, A. A., & Baer, R. A. (1998). Validity of selected MMPI-A content scales. *Psychological Assessment, 10*(1), 59–63.

Armentrout, D., Moore, J., Parker, J., Hewett, J., & Feltz, C. (1982). Pain patient subgroups: The psychological dimensions of pain. *Journal of Behavioral Medicine, 5*, 201–211.

Arnold, P. D. (1970). Recurring MMPI two-point codes of marriage counselors and "normal" couples with implications for interpreting marital interaction behavior. Unpublished doctoral dissertation, University of Minnesota.

Babcock, D. J. (1995, March). *Equivalence of the MMPI-2 with the MMPI in alcoholic male veteran samples.* Paper presented at the 30th Annual Symposium on Recent Developments in the Use of the MMPI, MMPI-2, and MMPI-A, St. Petersburg, FL.

Baer, R. A., Ballenger, J., Berry, D. T. R., & Wetter, M. W. (1997). Detection of random responding on the MMPI-A. *Journal of Personality Assessment, 68*(1), 139–151.

Baer, R. A., Ballenger, J., & Kroll, L. S. (1998). Detection of underreporting on the MMPI-A in clinical and community samples. *Journal of Personality Assessment, 71*(1), 98–113.

Baer, R. A., Wetter, M. W., Nichols, D., Greene, R., & Berry, D. T. (1995). Sensitivity of MMPI-2 validity scales to underreporting of symptoms. *Psychological Assessment, 7,* 419–423.

Ball, J. D., Archer, R. P., & Imhof, E. A. (1994). Time requirements of psychological testing: A survey of practitioners. *Journal of Personality Assessment, 63,* 239–249.

Barefoot, J. C., Dahlstrom, W. G., & Williams, R. B. (1983). Hostility, CHD incidence, and total mortality: A 25 year follow-up study of 255 physicians. *Psychosomatic Medicine, 45,* 59–63.

Barefoot, J. C., Dodge, K. A., Peterson, B. L., Dahlstrom, W. G., & Williams, R. B. (1989). The Cook-Medley hostility scale: Item content and ability to predict survival. *Psychosomatic Medicine, 51,* 46–57.

Barrett, R. K. (1973). *Relationship of emotional disorder to marital maladjustment and disruption.* Unpublished doctoral dissertation, Kent State University.

Barron, F. (1953). An ego strength scale which predicts response to psychotherapy. *Journal of Consulting Psychology, 17,* 327–333.

Basham, R. B. (1992). Clinical utility of the MMPI research scales in the assessment of adolescent acting out behaviors. *Psychological Assessment, 4*(4), 483–492.

Bathurst, K., Gottfried, A. W., & Gottfried, A. E. (1997). Normative data for the MMPI-2 in child litigation. *Psychological Assessment, 9,* 205–211.

Beck, E. A., & McIntyre, S. C. (1977). MMPI patterns of shoplifters within a college population. *Psychological Reports, 41,* 1035–1040.

Ben-Porath, Y. S., & Butcher, J. N. (1989a). Psychometric stability of rewritten MMPI items. *Journal of Personality Assessment, 53,* 645–653.

Ben-Porath, Y. S., & Butcher, J. N. (1989b). The comparability of MMPI and MMPI-2 scales and profiles. *Psychological Assessment: A Journal of Consulting and Clinical Psychology, 1,* 345–347.

Ben-Porath, Y. S., Butcher, J. N., & Graham, J. R. (1991). Contribution of the MMPI-2 scales to the differential diagnosis of schizophrenia and major depression. *Psychological Assessment: A Journal of Consulting and Clinical Psychology, 3,* 634–640.

Ben-Porath, Y. S., & Davis, D. L. (1996). *Case studies for interpreting the MMPI-A.* Minneapolis: University of Minnesota Press.

Ben-Porath, Y. S., Hostetler, K., Butcher, J. N., & Graham, J. R. (1989). New subscales for the MMPI-2 Social Introversion (Si) Scale. *Psychological Assessment: A Journal of Consulting and Clinical Psychology, 1,* 169–174.

Ben-Porath, Y. S., McCulley, E., & Almagor, M. (1993). Incremental validity of the MMPI-2 content scales in the assessment of personality and psychopathology by self-report. *Journal of Personality Assessment, 61*(3), 557–575.

Ben-Porath, Y. S., & Sherwood, N. (1996). *The MMPI-2 content component scales.* Minneapolis: University of Minnesota Press.

Ben-Porath, Y. S., Shondrick, D., & Stafford, K. (1994). MMPI-2 and race in a forensic diagnostic sample. *Criminal Justice and Behavior, 22,* 19–32.

Bernstein, I., & Garbin, C. (1983). Hierarchical clustering of pain patients' MMPI profiles: A replication note. *Journal of Personality Assessment, 47,* 171–172.

Berry, D. T. R., Adams, J. J., Smith, G. T., Greene, R. L., Sekirnjak, G. C., Wieland, G., & Tharpe, B. (1997). MMPI-2 clinical scales and 2-point code types: Impact of varying levels of omitted items. *Psychological Assessment, 9,* 158–160.

Berry, D. T., Wetter, M. W., Baer, R. A., Widiger, T. A., Sumpter, J. C., Reynolds, S. K., & Hallam, R. A. (1991). Detection of random responding on the MMPI-2: Utility of F, Back F, and VRIN scales. *Psychological Assessment: A Journal of Consulting and Clinical Psychology, 3,* 418–423.

Boerger, A. R., Graham, J. R., & Lilly, R. S. (1974). Behavioral correlates of single scale MMPI code types. *Journal of Consulting and Clinical Psychology, 42,* 398–402.

Bogue, D. (1985). *The population of the United States: Historical trends and future projections.* New York: The Free Press.

Bohn, M. J. (1979). Management classification for young adult inmates. *Federal Probation, 43,* 53–59.

Boone, D. E. (1994). Validity of the MMPI-2 Depression content scale with psychiatric inpatients. *Psychological Reports, 74*(1), 159–162.

Booth, R. J., & Howell, R. J. (1980). Classification of prison inmates with the MMPI: An extension and validation of the Megargee typology. *Criminal Justice and Behavior, 7,* 407–422.

Bosquet, M., & Egeland, B. (2000). Predicting parent behaviors from Antisocial Practices content scale scores of the MMPI-2 administered during pregnancy. *Journal of Personality Assessment, 74*(1), 146–162.

Bradley, L. A., Prokop, C. K., Margolis, R., & Gentry, W. D. (1978). Multivariate analysis of the MMPI profiles of low back pain patients. *Journal of Behavioral Medicine, 1,* 253–272.

Bradley, L. A., & Van der Heide, L. H. (1984). Pain-related correlates of MMPI profile subgroups among back pain patients. *Health Psychology, 3,* 157–174.

Brems, C., & Lloyd, P. (1995). Validation of the MMPI-2 Low Self-Esteem Scale. *Journal of Personality Assessment, 65*(3), 550–556.

Brown, M. N. (1950). Evaluating and scoring the Minnesota Multiphasic "Cannot Say" items. *Journal of Clinical Psychology, 6,* 180–184.

Brown, P. L., & Berdie, R. F. (1960). Driver behavior and scores on the MMPI. *Journal of Applied Psychology, 44,* 18–21.

Burisch, M. (1984). Approaches to personality inventory construction. *American Psychologist, 39,* 214–227.

Butcher, J. N. (Ed.). (1972). *Objective personality assessment: Changing perspectives.* New York: Academic Press.

Butcher, J. N. (1979). Use of the MMPI in personnel selection. In J. N. Butcher (Ed.), *New developments in the use of the MMPI.* Minneapolis: University of Minnesota Press.

Butcher, J. N. (1985). Current developments in MMPI use: An international perspective. In J. N. Butcher & C. D. Spielberger (Eds.), *Advances in personality assessment* (Vol. 4). Hillsdale, NJ: Lawrence Erlbaum Associates.

Butcher, J. N. (1987). Computerized clinical and personality assessment using the MMPI. In J. N. Butcher (Ed.), *Computerized psychological assessment.* New York: Basic Books.

Butcher, J. N. (1988). *Personality profile of airline pilot applicants.* Unpublished materials, MMPI-2 Workshops, Department of Psychology, University of Minnesota.

Butcher, J. N. (1989a, August). *MMPI-2: Issues of continuity and change.* Paper presented at the 97th annual meeting of the American Psychological Association, New Orleans, LA.

Butcher, J. N. (1989b). *User's guide for the Minnesota Clinical Report.* Minneapolis: National Computer Systems.

Butcher, J. N. (1989c). *User's guide for the Minnesota Personnel Report.* Minneapolis: National Computer Systems.

Butcher, J. N. (1989d). *MMPI-2 profile of depressed inpatients.* Unpublished materials, MMPI-2 Workshops, Department of Psychology, University of Minnesota.

Butcher, J. N. (1990a). *Use of the MMPI-2 in treatment planning.* New York: Oxford University Press.

Butcher, J. N. (1990b). Education level and MMPI-2 measured psychopathology: A case of negligible influence. *MMPI-2 News and Profiles, 1*(2), 2.

Butcher, J. N. (1996). *International adaptations of the MMPI-2: Research and clinical applications.* Minneapolis: University of Minnesota Press.

Butcher, J. N. (1997). Frequency of MMPI-2 scores in forensic evaluation. *MMPI-2 News & Profiles, 8,* 4–5.

Butcher, J. N. (1998a, March). *Analysis of the MMPI-2 subscales to refine interpretation of "good impression."* Paper presented at the 34th Annual conference on Recent Developments in the Use of the MMPI/MMPI-2, Clearwater, FL.

Butcher, J. N. (1998b). *User's guide to the Minnesota Report: Reports for forensic settings.* Minneapolis: National Computer Systems.

Butcher, J. N. (1999). *A beginner's guide to the MMPI-2.* Washington, DC: American Psychological Association.

Butcher, J. N., Aldwin, C., Levenson, M., Ben-Porath, Y. S., Spiro, A., & Bossé, R. (1991). Personality and aging: A study of the MMPI-2 among elderly men. *Psychology of Aging*.

Butcher, J. N., Atlis, M., & Fang, L. (in press). The effects of altered instructions on the MMPI-2 responses of persons who are not motivated to deceive. *Journal of Personality Assessment*.

Butcher, J. N., Berah, E., Ellertsen, B., Miach, P., Lim, J., Nezami, E., Pancheri, P., Derksen, J., & Almagor, M. (1998). Objective personality assessment: Computer-based MMPI-2 interpretation in international clinical settings. In C. Belar (Ed.), *Comprehensive clinical psychology: Sociocultural and individual differences* (pp. 277–312). New York: Elsevier.

Butcher, J. N., Cabiya, J., Lucio, G. M., Peña, L., Reuben, D. L., & Scott, R. (1998). *Manual supplement: Hispanic version of the MMPI-A for the United States*. Minneapolis: University of Minnesota Press.

Butcher, J. N., Dahlstrom, W. G., Graham, J. R., Tellegen, A., & Kaemmer, B. (1989). MMPI-2 (Minnesota Multiphasic Personality Inventory-2): *Manual for administration and scoring*. Minneapolis: University of Minnesota Press.

Butcher, J. N., Graham, J. R., Dahlstrom, W. G., & Bowman, E. (1990). The MMPI-2 with college students. *Journal of Personality Assessment, 54*, 1–15.

Butcher, J. N., Graham, J. R., Williams, C. L., & Ben-Porath, Y. S. (1990). *Development and use of the MMPI-2 Content Scales*. Minneapolis: University of Minnesota Press.

Butcher, J. N., & Han, K. (1995). Development of an MMPI-2 scale to assess the presentation of self in a superlative manner: The S Scale. In J. N. Butcher & C. D. Spielberger (Eds.), *Advances in personality assessment* (Vol. 10, pp. 25–50). Hillsdale, NJ: LEA Press.

Butcher, J. N., & Harlow, T. (1985). Psychological assessment in personal injury cases. In A. Hess & I. Wiener (Eds.), *Handbook of forensic psychology*. New York: John Wiley & Sons.

Butcher, J. N., Jeffrey, T., Cayton, T. G., Colligan, S., DeVore, J., & Minnegawa, R. (1990). A study of active duty military personnel with the MMPI-2. *Military Psychology, 2*, 47–61.

Butcher, J. N., Lim, J., & Nezami, E. (1998). Objective study of abnormal personality in cross-cultural settings: The Minnesota Multiphasic Personality Inventory (MMPI-2). *Journal of Cross-Cultural Psychology, 20*, 189–211.

Butcher, J. N., Morfitt, R., Rouse, S. V., & Holden, R. R. (1997). Reducing MMPI-2 defensiveness: The effect of specialized instructions on retest validity in a job applicant sample. *Journal of Personality Assessment, 68*(2), 385–401.

Butcher, J. N., & Owen, P. (1978). Survey of personality inventories: Recent research developments and contemporary issues. In B. Wolman (Ed.), *Handbook of clinical diagnosis*. New York: Plenum.

Butcher, J. N., & Pancheri, P. (1976). Handbook of cross-national MMPI research. Minneapolis: University of Minnesota Press.

Butcher, J. N., Perry, J., & Atlis, M. (2000). Validity of computerized assessment and interpretation. *Psychological Assessment, 12*, 6–18.

Butcher, J. N., Rouse, S. V., & Perry, J. (in press). *MMPI-2 correlates in an outpatient psychotherapy sample: Basic sources for the MMPI-2*. Minneapolis: University of Minnesota Press.

Butcher, J. N., & Tellegen, A. (1966). Objections to MMPI items. *Journal of Consulting Psychology, 30*, 527–534.

Butcher, J. N., & Williams, C. L. (1992). *User's guide to the Adolescent Interpretive Report for the MMPI-A*. Minneapolis: National Computer Systems.

Butcher, J. N., Williams, C. L., Graham, J. R., Archer, R. P., Tellegen, A., Ben-Porath, Y. S., & Kaemmer, B. (1992). MMPI-A (Minnesota Multiphasic Personality Inventory for Adolescents): *Manual for administration, scoring, and interpretation*. Minneapolis: University of Minnesota Press.

Capwell, D. F. (1945a). Personality patterns of adolescent girls. I. Girls who show improvement in IQ. *Journal of Applied Psychology, 29*, 212–228.

Capwell, D. F. (1945b). Personality patterns of adolescent girls. II. Delinquents and nondelinquents. *Journal of Applied Psychology, 29*, 289–297.

Capwell, D. F. (1953). Personality patterns of adolescent girls: Delinquents and nondelinquents. In S. R. Hathaway & E. D. Monachesi (Eds.), *Analyzing and predicting juvenile delinquency with the MMPI* (pp. 29–37). Minneapolis: University of Minnesota Press.

Cashel, M. L., Rogers, R., Sewell, K. W., & Holliman, N. B. (1998). Preliminary validation of the MMPI-A for a male delinquent sample: An investigation of clinical correlates and discriminate validity. *Journal of Personality Assessment, 71*(1), 49–69.

Cheung, F. M. (1985). Cross-cultural considerations for the translation and adaptation of the Chinese

MMPI in Hong Kong. In J. N. Butcher & C. D. Spielberger (Eds.), *Advances in personality assessment* (Vol. 4, pp. 131–158). Hillsdale, NJ: Lawrence Erlbaum Associates.

Cheung, F. M., & Ho, R. M. (1997). Standardization of the Chinese MMPI-A in Hong Kong: A preliminary study. *Psychological Assessment, 9*(4), 499–502.

Cheung, F. M., & Song, W. Z. (1989). A review on the clinical applications of the Chinese MMPI. *Psychological Assessment: A Journal of Consulting and Clinical Psychology, 1,* 230–237.

Cheung, F. M., Song, W. Z., & Butcher, J. N. (1991). An infrequency scale for the Chinese MMPI. *Psychological Assessment: A Journal of Consulting and Clinical Psychology, 3,* 648–653.

Chisolm, S. M., Crowther, J. H., & Ben-Porath, Y. S. (1997). Selected MMPI-2 scales' ability to predict premature termination and outcome from psychotherapy. *Journal of Personality Assessment, 69*(1), 127–144.

Colby, F. (1989). Usefulness of the K correction in MMPI profiles of patients and nonpatients. *Psychological Assessment: A Journal of Consulting and Clinical Psychology, 1,* 142–145.

Colligan, R. C., & Offord, K. P. (1989). The aging MMPI: Contemporary norms for contemporary teenagers. *Mayo Clinic Proceedings, 64,* 3–27.

Colligan, R. C., Osborne, D., Swenson, W. M., & Offord, K. P. (1983). *The MMPI: A contemporary normative study.* New York: Praeger.

Constantinople, A. (1973). Masculinity-femininity: An exception to a famous dictum? *Psychological Bulletin, 80,* 389–407.

Cook, W. W., & Medley, D. M. (1954). Proposed hostility and pharisaic-virtue scales for the MMPI. *Journal of Applied Psychology, 38,* 414–418.

Costa, P. T., & McCrae, R. R. (1988). From catalog to classification: Murray's needs and the five-factor model. *Journal of Personality and Social Psychology, 55*(2), 258–265.

Costello, R. M., Hulsey, T. L., Schoenfeld, L. S., & Ramamurthy, S. (1987). P-A-I-N: A four-cluster MMPI typology for chronic pain. *Pain, 3,* 199–209.

Crewe, J. C., & Crewe, D. L. (1973). Sex! Who needs it? Not the MMPI! *Pupil Personnel Services, 2,* 13–14.

Cronbach, L. J. (1960). *Essentials of psychological testing.* (2nd ed.). New York: Harper.

Dahlstrom, W. G. (1980). Altered versions of the MMPI. In W. G. Dahlstrom & L. E. Dahlstrom (Eds.), *Basic readings on the MMPI* (pp. 386–393). Minneapolis: University of Minnesota Press.

Dahlstrom, W. G., & Butcher, J. N. (1964). *Comparability of the taped and booklet versions of the MMPI.* Unpublished manuscript.

Dahlstrom, W. G., Lachar, D., & Dahlstrom, L. E. (1986). *MMPI patterns of American minorities.* Minneapolis: University of Minnesota Press.

Dahlstrom, W. G., Panton, J. H., Bain, K. P., & Dahlstrom, L. E. (1986). Utility of the Megargee-Bohn MMPI typological assignments: Study with a sample of death row inmates. *Criminal Justice and Behavior, 13,* 5–17.

Dahlstrom, W. G., & Welsh, G. S. (1960). *An MMPI handbook: A guide to use in clinical practice and research.* Minneapolis: University of Minnesota Press.

Dahlstrom, W. G., Welsh, G. S., & Dahlstrom, L. E. (1975). *An MMPI handbook: Vol. II. Research applications.* Minneapolis: University of Minnesota Press.

Delk, J. (1973). Some personality characteristics of skydivers. *Life-Threatening Behavior, 3,* 51–57.

Drake, L. E. (1946). A social I-E scale for the MMPI. *Journal of Applied Psychology, 30,* 51–54.

Drake, L. E., & Oetting, E. R. (1959). *An MMPI codebook for counselors.* Minneapolis: University of Minnesota Press.

Edinger, J. D. (1979). Cross-validation of the Megargee MMPI typology for prisoners. *Journal of Consulting and Clinical Psychology, 47,* 234–242.

Edinger, J. D., Reuterfors, D., & Logue, P. E. (1982). Cross-validation of the Megargee MMPI typology: A study of specialized inmate populations. *Criminal Justice and Behavior, 9,* 184–203.

Egeland, B., Erickson, M., Butcher, J. N., & Ben-Porath, Y. S. (1991). MMPI-2 profiles of women at risk for child abuse. *Journal of Personality Assessment, 57,* 254–263.

Ehrenworth, N. V., & Archer, R. P. (1985). A comparison of clinical accuracy ratings of interpretive approaches for adolescent MMPI responses. *Journal of Personality Assessment, 49,* 413–421.

Ellertsen, B., Havik, O. E., & Skavhellen, R. R. (1996). The Norwegian MMPI-2. In J. N. Butcher (Ed.), *International adaptations of the MMPI-2: Research and clinical applications* (pp. 350–367). Minneapolis: University of Minnesota Press.

Endicott, N. A., & Jortner, S. (1966). Objective measures of depression. *Archives of General Psychiatry, 15,* 249–255.

Eyde, L., Kowal, D., & Fishburne, F. (1987, August). *Clinical implications of validity research on computer based test interpretations of the MMPI.* Paper presented at the 95th annual meeting of the American Psychological Association, New York, NY.

Eyde, L., Kowal, D., & Fishburne, F. (1991). The validity of computer-based test interpretation of the MMPI. In T. B. Gutkin & S. L. Wise (Eds.), *The computer and the decision making process* (pp. 75–123). Hillsdale, NJ: Lawrence Erlbaum Associates.

Faull, R., & Meyer, G. J. (1993, March 19). *Assessment of depression with the MMPI-2: Distinctions between Scale 2 and DEP.* Paper presented at the annual meeting for the Society for Personality Assessment, San Francisco, CA.

Finger, M., & Ones, D. (1999). Psychometric equivalence of the computer and booklet forms of the MMPI. *Psychological Assessment, 11*(1), 58–66.

Fink, A., & Butcher, J. N. (1972). Reducing objections to personality inventories with special instructions. *Educational and Psychological Measurement, 32,* 631–639.

Finn, S. E. (1996). *Manual for using the MMPI-2 as a therapeutic intervention.* Minneapolis: University of Minnesota Press.

Finn, S., & Kamphuis, J. H. (1995). What a clinician needs to know about base rates. In J. N. Butcher (Ed.), *Clinical personality assessment: Practical approaches* (pp. 214–235). New York: Oxford University Press.

Finn, S. E., & Tonsager, M. E. (1992). Therapeutic effects of providing MMPI-2 test feedback to college students awaiting therapy. *Psychological Assessment, 4*(3), 278–287.

Forbey, J. D., Ben-Porath, Y. S. (1998). *A critical item set for the MMPI-A.* Minneapolis: University of Minnesota Press.

Fordyce, W. (1987). *Use of the MMPI with chronic pain patients.* Paper presented at the Ninth International Conference on Personality Assessment, Brussels, Belgium.

Forsyth, R., & Naylor, C. (1986). *The hitch-hikers guide to artificial intelligence: IBM PC version.* London: Chapman & Hall.

Fowler, R. D. (1969) Automated interpretation of personality test data. In J. N. Butcher (Ed.), *MMPI research developments and clinical applications.* New York: McGraw-Hill.

Fowler, R. D. (1987). Developing a computer based test interpretation system. In J. N. Butcher (Ed.), *Computerized psychological assessment.* New York: Basic Books.

Fowler, R. D., Jr., & Athey, E. B. (1971). A cross-validation of Gilberstadt and Duker's 1-2-3-4 profile type. *Journal of Clinical Psychology, 27,* 238–240.

Gallagher, R. W., & Ben-Porath, Y. S. (1999). *Detection of malingering on the MMPI-2 in a correctional setting.* Manuscript submitted for publication.

Gallucci, N. T. (1987). The influence of elevated F-scales on the validity of adolescent MMPI profiles. *Journal of Personality Assessment, 51,* 133–139.

Gallucci, N. T. (1994). Criteria associated with clinical scales and Harris-Lingoes subscales of the Minnesota Multiphasic Personality Inventory with adolescent inpatients. *Psychological Assessment, 6*(3), 179–187.

Gallucci, N. T. (1997). Correlates of MMPI-A substance abuse scales. *Assessment, 4*(1), 87–94.

Gantner, A. G., Graham, J. R., & Archer, R. A. (1992). Usefulness of the MAC scale in differentiating adolescents in normal, psychiatric, and substance abuse settings. *Psychological Assessment, 4,* 133–137.

Garfinkle, P. E., Bagby, R. M., Waring, E. M., & Dorian, B. (1997). Boundary violations and personality traits among psychiatrists. *Canadian Journal of Psychiatry, 42,* 758–763.

Gilberstadt, H., & Duker, J. (1965). *A handbook for clinical and actuarial MMPI interpretation.* Philadelphia: W. B. Saunders.

Gillet, I., Simon, M., Guelfi, J. D., Brun-Eberentz, A., Monier, C., Seunevel, F., & V-Svarna, L. (1996). The MMPI-2 in France. In J. N. Butcher (Ed.), *International adaptations of the MMPI-2: Research and clinical applications* (pp. 395–415). Minneapolis: University of Minnesota Press.

Goldberg, L. R. (1990). An alternative description of personality: The big-five factor structure. *Journal of Personality and Social Psychology, 59,* 1216–1229.

Goodstein, L. D. (1954). Regional differences in MMPI responses among male college students. *Journal of Consulting Psychology, 18,* 437–441.

Gottesman, I. I., Hanson, D. R., Kroeker, T. A., & Briggs, P. (1987). Appendix C: New MMPI normative data and power-transformed T-score tables for the Hathaway-Monachesi Minnesota cohort of 14,019 15-year-olds and 3,674 18-year-olds. In R. P. Archer (Ed.), *Using the MMPI with adolescents* (pp. 241–297). Hillsdale, NJ: Lawrence Erlbaum Associates.

Gottesman, I. I., & Prescott, C. A. (1989). Abuses of the MacAndrew MMPI Alcoholism Scale: A critical review. *Clinical Psychology Review, 9,* 223–258.

Gottschalk, M. (1999). "Revolutionary" versus religious fundamentalist terrrorism and differential levels of psychopathology. Personal communication, Free University of Brussels.

Gough, H. G. (1950). The F minus K dissimulation index for the MMPI. *Journal of Consulting Psychology, 14,* 408–413.

Gough, H. G., McClosky, H., & Meehl, P. E. (1951). A personality scale for dominance. *Journal of Abnormal and Social Psychology, 46,* 360–366.

Gough, H. G., McClosky, H., & Meehl, P. E. (1952). A personality scale for social responsibility. *Journal of Abnormal and Social Psychology, 47,* 73–80.

Gough, H. G., McKee, M. G., & Yandell, R. J. (1955). *Adjective Check List analyses of a number of selected psychometric and assessment variables* (Technical Memorandum OERL-TM-55-10). Washington, DC: Officer Education Research Laboratory.

Graham, J. R. (1973, March). *Behavioral correlates of simple MMPI code types.* Paper presented at the 8th Annual Symposium on Recent Developments in the Use of the MMPI, New Orleans, LA.

Graham, J. R. (1977). *The MMPI: A practical guide.* New York: Oxford University Press.

Graham, J. R. (1987). *The MMPI: A practical guide* (2nd ed.). New York: Oxford University Press.

Graham, J. R. (1989, August). *The meaning of elevated MacAndrew Alcoholism scale scores for nonclinical subjects.* Paper presented at the 97th annual meeting of the American Psychological Association, New Orleans, LA.

Graham, J. R. (1990). *MMPI-2: Assessing personality and psychopathology.* New York: Oxford University Press.

Graham, J. R., Ben-Porath, Y. S., & McNulty, J. (1999). *MMPI-2 Correlates for outpatient community mental health settings.* Minneapolis: University of Minnesota Press.

Graham, J. R., & Butcher, J. N. (1988, March). *Differentiating schizophrenic and major affective disorders with the revised form of the MMPI.* Paper presented at the 23rd Annual Symposium on Recent Developments in the Use of the MMPI, St. Petersburg, FL.

Graham, J. R., Schroeder, H. E., & Lilly, R. S. (1971). Factor analysis of items on the social introversion and masculinity-femininity scales of the MMPI. *Journal of Clinical Psychology, 27,* 367–370.

Graham, J. R., Smith, R., & Schwartz, G. (1986). Stability of MMPI configurations for psychiatric inpatients. *Journal of Consulting and Clinical Psychology, 54,* 375–380.

Graham, J. R., & Strenger, V. E. (1988). MMPI characteristics of alcoholics: A review. *Journal of Consulting and Clinical Psychology, 56,* 197–205.

Graham, J. R., Timbrook, R., Ben-Porath, Y. S., & Butcher, J. N. (1991). Code-type congruence between MMPI and MMPI-2: Separating fact from artifact. *Journal of Personality Assessment, 57,* 205–215.

Graham, J. R., Watts, D., & Timbrook, R. (1991). Detecting fake-good and fake-bad MMPI-2 profiles. *Journal of Personality Assessment, 57,* 264–277.

Grayson, H. M. (1951). *Psychological admission testing program and manual.* Los Angeles: Veterans Administration Center, Neuropsychiatric Hospital.

Greene, E. B. (1954). Medical reports and selected MMPI items among employed adults. *American Psychologist, 9,* 384.

Greene, R. L. (1982). Some reflections on MMPI short forms: A literature review. *Journal of Personality Assessment, 46,* 486–487.

Greene, R. L. (1991). *The MMPI-2/MMPI: An interpretive manual.* Boston: Allyn and Bacon.

Greene, R. L., Weed, N. C., Butcher, J. N., Arredondo, R., & Davis, H. G. (1992). A cross-validation of MMPI-2 substance abuse scales. *Journal of Personality Assessment, 58,* 405–410.

Grossman, L. S., Haywood, T. W., Ostrov, E., Wasyliw, O., & Cavanaugh, J. L. (1990). Sensitivity of MMPI validity indicators to motivational factors in psychological evaluation of police officers. *Journal of Personality Assessment, 55,* 549–561.

Grove, W., Zald, D. R., Lebow, B. S., Snitz, B. E., & Nelson, C. (2000). Clinical vs. actuarial prediction: A meta analysis. *Psychological Assessment, 12,* 19–30.

Gumbiner, J. (1997). Comparison of scores on the MMPI-A and MMPI-2 for young adults. *Psychological Reports, 81,* 787–794.

Guthrie, G. M. (1952). Common characteristics associated with frequent MMPI profile types. *Journal of Clinical Psychology, 8*, 141–145.

Gynther, M. D. (1961). The clinical utility of "invalid" MMPI F scores. *Journal of Consulting Psychology, 25*, 540–542.

Gynther, M. D. (1972a). *A new replicated actuarial program for interpreting MMPIs of state hospital inpatients.* Paper presented at the 7th Annual Symposium on Recent Developments in the Use of the MMPI, Mexico City.

Gynther, M. D. (1972b). White norms and Black MMPIs: A prescription for discrimination? *Psychological Bulletin, 78*, 386–402.

Gynther, M. D., Altman, H., & Sletten, I. W. (1973). Development of an empirical interpretive system for the MMPI: Some after-the-fact observations. *Journal of Clinical Psychology, 29*, 232–234.

Gynther, M. D., Altman, H., & Warbin, R. W. (1972). A new empirical automated MMPI interpretive program: The 2-4/4-2 code type. *Journal of Clinical Psychology, 28*, 498–501.

Gynther, M. D., Altman, H., & Warbin, R. W. (1973a). A new actuarial-empirical automated MMPI interpretive program: The 4-3/3-4 code type. *Journal of Clinical Psychology, 29*, 229–231.

Gynther, M. D., Altman, H., & Warbin, R. W. (1973b). A new empirical automated MMPI interpretive program: The 2-7/7-2 code type. *Journal of Clinical Psychology, 29*, 58–59.

Gynther, M. D., Altman, H., & Warbin, R. W. (1973c). A new empirical automated MMPI interpretive program: The 6-9/9-6 code type. *Journal of Clinical Psychology, 29*, 60–61.

Gynther, M. D., Altman, H., & Warbin, R. W. (1973d). Interpretation of uninterpretable MMPI profiles. *Journal of Consulting and Clinical Psychology, 40*, 78–83.

Gynther, M. D., Altman, H., Warbin, R. W., & Sletten, I. W. (1972). A new actuarial system for MMPI interpretation: Rationale and methodology. *Journal of Clinical Psychology, 28*, 173–179.

Gynther, M. D., & Petzel, T. P. (1967). Differential endorsement of MMPI F scale items by psychotics and behavior disorders. *Journal of Clinical Psychology, 23*, 185–188.

Gynther, M. D., & Shimunkas, A. M. (1965). More data on MMPI F > 16 scores. *Journal of Clinical Psychology, 21*, 275–277.

Halbower, C. C. (1955). *A comparison of actuarial versus clinical prediction to classes discriminated by MMPI.* Unpublished doctoral dissertation, University of Minnesota.

Hall, G. C. N., Bansal, A., & Lopez, I. R. (1999). Ethnicity and psychopathology: A meta analytic review of 31 years of comparative MMPI/MMPI-2 research. *Psychological Assessment, 11*(2), 186–197.

Hall, G. S. (1904). *Adolescence: Its psychology and its relations to physiology, anthropology, sociology, sex, crime, religion, and education* (Vols. 1 & 2). New York: D. Appleton.

Han, K., Weed, N. C., Calhoun, R. F., & Butcher, J. N. (1995). Psychometric characteristics of the MMPI-2 Cook-Medley Hostility Scale. *Journal of Personality Assessment, 63*(3), 567–583.

Hanson, R. W., Moss, C. S., Hosford, R. E., & Johnson, M. E. (1983). Predicting inmate penitentiary adjustment: An assessment of four classificatory methods. *Criminal Justice and Behavior, 10*, 293–309.

Harkness, A. R., & McNulty, J. L. (1994). The Personality Psychopathology Five (PSY-5): Issues from the pages of a diagnostic manual instead of a dictionary. In N. S. Strack & M. Morr (Eds.), *Differentiating normal and abnormal personality* (pp. 291–315). New York: Springer.

Harkness, A. R., McNulty, J. L., & Ben-Porath, Y. S. (1995). The Personality Psychopathology Five (PSY-5): Constructs and MMPI-2 Scales. *Psychological Assessment, 7*(1), 104–114.

Harris, R. E., & Lingoes, J. C. (1955, 1968). Subscales for the MMPI: An aid to profile interpretation. Mimeographed materials, Department of Psychiatry, University of California.

Hart, R. (1984). Chronic pain: Replicated multivariate clustering of personality profiles. *Journal of Clinical Psychology, 40*, 129–133.

Hart, T. R., McNeill, J. W., Lutz, D. J., & Adkins, T. G. (1986). Clinical comparability of the standard MMPI and the MMPI-168. *Professional Psychology: Research and Practice, 17*, 269–272.

Hathaway, S. R. (1947). A coding system for MMPI profiles. *Journal of Consulting Psychology, 11*, 334–337.

Hathaway, S. R. (1956). Scales 5 (Masculinity-Femininity), 6 (Paranoia), and 8 (Schizophrenia). In W. G. Dahlstrom & L. E. Dahlstrom (Eds.), *Basic readings on the MMPI* (pp. 65–75). Minneapolis: University of Minnesota Press.

Hathaway, S. R. (1965). Personality inventories. In B. Wolman (Ed.), *Handbook of clinical psychology.* New York: McGraw-Hill.

Hathaway, S. R., Hastings, D. W., Capwell, D. F., & Bell, D. M. (1953). The relationship between MMPI profiles and later careers of juvenile delinquent girls. In S. R. Hathaway & E. D. Monachesi (Eds.), *Analyzing and predicting juvenile delinquency with the MMPI* (pp. 70–80). Minneapolis: University of Minnesota Press.

Hathaway, S. R., & McKinley, J. C. (1940). A multiphasic personality schedule (Minnesota): I. Construction of the schedule. *Journal of Psychology, 10,* 249–254.

Hathaway, S. R., & McKinley, J. C. (1942a). A multiphasic personality schedule (Minnesota): III. The measurement of symptomatic depression. *Journal of Psychology, 14,* 73–84.

Hathaway, S. R., & McKinley, J. C. (1942b). *The Minnesota Multiphasic Personality Schedule.* Minneapolis: University of Minnesota Press.

Hathaway, S. R., & Meehl, P. E. (1952). *Adjective check list correlates of MMPI scores.* Unpublished materials.

Hathaway, S. R., & Monachesi, E. D. (Eds.). (1953a). *Analyzing and predicting juvenile delinquency with the MMPI.* Minneapolis: University of Minnesota Press.

Hathaway, S. R., & Monachesi, E. D. (1953b). Personality characteristics of adolescents as related to their later careers: Part I. Introduction and general findings. In S. R. Hathaway & E. D. Monachesi (Eds.), *Analyzing and predicting juvenile delinquency with the MMPI* (pp. 87–108). Minneapolis: University of Minnesota Press.

Hathaway, S. R., & Monachesi, E. D. (1957). The personalities of pre-delinquent boys. *Journal of Criminal Law, Criminology, and Political Science, 48,* 149–153.

Hathaway, S. R., & Monachesi, E. D. (1961). *An atlas of juvenile MMPI profiles.* Minneapolis: University of Minnesota Press.

Hathaway, S. R., & Monachesi, E. D. (1963). *Adolescent personality and behavior: MMPI patterns of normal, delinquent, drop-out, and other outcomes.* Minneapolis: University of Minnesota Press.

Hathaway, S. R., Reynolds, P., & Monachesi, E. D. (1969). Follow-up of the later careers and lives of 1000 boys who dropped out of high school. *Journal of Consulting and Clinical Psychology, 33,* 370–380.

Hedlund, J. L. (1977). MMPI clinical scale correlates. *Journal of Consulting and Clinical Psychology, 43,* 739–750.

Helmes, E., & McLaughlin, J. D. (1983). A comparison of three MMPI short forms: Limited clinical utility in classification. *Journal of Consulting and Clinical Psychology, 51,* 786–787.

Herjanic, B., & Campbell, W. (1977). Differentiating psychiatrically disturbed children on the basis of a structured interview. *Journal of Abnormal Child Psychology, 5,* 127–134.

Herkov, M. J., Archer, R., & Gordon, R. A. (1991). MMPI response sets among adolescents: An evaluation of the limitations of the subtle-obvious subscales. *Psychological Assessment: A Journal of Consulting and Clinical Psychology, 3,* 424–426.

Hill, H. E., Haertzen, C. A., & Glaser, R. (1960). Personality characteristics of narcotic addicts as indicated by the MMPI. *Journal of General Psychology, 62,* 127–129.

Hjemboe, S., Almagor, M., & Butcher, J. N. (1992). Empirical assessment of marital distress: The Marital Distress Scale (MDS) for the MMPI-2. In C. D. Spielberger & J. N. Butcher (Eds.), *Advances in personality assessment* (Vol. 9) (pp. 141–152). Hillsdale, NJ: Lawrence Erlbaum Associates.

Hjemboe, S., & Butcher, J. N. (1991). Couples in marital distress: A study of demographic and personality factors as measured by the MMPI-2. *Journal of Personality Assessment, 57,* 216–237.

Hoffmann, N. G., & Butcher, J. N. (1975). Clinical limitation of three Minnesota Multiphasic Personality Inventory short forms. *Journal of Consulting and Clinical Psychology, 43,* 32–39.

Imhof, E. A., & Archer, R. P. (1997). Correlates of the MMPI-A Immaturity (IMM) Scale in an adolescent psychiatric sample. *Assessment, 4*(2), 169–179.

Iverson, G. L., Franzen, M. D., & Hammond, J. A. (1995). Examination of an inmate's ability to malinger on the MMPI-2. *Psychological Assessment, 7,* 118–121.

Janus, M. D., Tolbert, H., Calestro, K., & Toepfer, S. (1996). Clinical accuracy ratings of MMPI approaches for adolescents: Adding 10 years and the MMPI-A. *Journal of Personality Assessment, 67*(2), 364–383.

Johnson, D. L., Simmons, J. G., & Gordon, B. C. (1983). Temporal consistency of the Meyer-Megargee inmate typology. *Criminal Justice and Behavior, 10,* 263–268.

Johnson, J. H., Butcher, J. N., Null, C., & Johnson, K. N. (1984). Replicated item level factor analysis of the full MMPI. *Journal of Personality and Social Psychology, 47*(1), 105–114.

Katz, M. M. (1968). A phenomenological typology of schizophrenia. In M. M. Katz, J. O. Cole, & W. E.

Barton (Eds.), *The role and methodology of classification in psychiatry and psychopathology*. Washington, DC: Public Health Printing Office.

Keane, T. M., Malloy, P. F., & Fairbank, J. A. (1984). Empirical development of an MMPI subscale for the assessment of combat-related posttraumatic stress disorder. *Journal of Consulting and Clinical Psychology, 52,* 888–891.

Keane, T. M., Weathers, F. W., & Kaloupek, D. G. (1992). Psychological assessment of post-traumatic stress disorder. *PRQ, 3,* 1–3.

Keefe, K., Sue, S., Enomoto, K., Durvasula, R. S., & Chao, R. (1996). Asian American and White college student's performance on the MMPI-2. In J. N. Butcher (Ed.), *International adaptations of the MMPI-2: Research and clinical applications* (pp. 206–220). Minneapolis: University of Minnesota Press.

Keller, L. S., & Butcher, J. N. (1991). *Use of the MMPI-2 with chronic pain patients.* Minneapolis: University of Minnesota Press.

Kelly, C. K., & King, G. D. (1978). Behavioral correlates for within-normal limit MMPI profiles with and without elevated K in students at a university mental health center. *Journal of Clinical Psychology, 34,* 695–699.

Kennedy, T. D. (1986). Trends in inmate classification: A status report of two computerized psychometric approaches. *Criminal Justice and Behavior, 13,* 165–184.

Klinefelter, D., Pancoast, D. L., Archer, R. P., & Pruitt, D. L. (1990). Recent adolescent MMPI norms: T-score elevation comparisons to Marks and Briggs. *Journal of Personality Assessment, 54,* 379–389.

Klinge, V., Culbert, J., & Piggott, L. R. (1982). Efficacy of psychiatric inpatient hospitalization for adolescents as measured by pre- and post-MMPI profiles. *Journal of Youth and Adolescence, 11,* 493–502.

Klinge, V., Lachar, D., Grisell, J., & Berman, W. (1978). The effects of scoring norms on adolescent psychiatric drug users' and non-users' MMPI profiles. *Adolescence, 13,* 1–11.

Klump, K., & Butcher, J. N. (1997). Psychological tests in treatment planning: The importance of objective assessment. In J. N. Butcher (Ed.), *Personality assessment in managed health care: Using the MMPI-2 in treatment planning* (pp. 93–130). New York: Oxford University Press.

Konraos, S. (1996). The Icelandic translation of the MMPI-2: Adaptation and validation. In J. N. Butcher (Ed.), *International adaptations of the MMPI-2: Research and clinical applications* (pp. 368–384). Minneapolis: University of Minnesota Press.

Kopper, B. A., Osman, A., Osman, J. R., & Hoffman, J. (1998). Clinical utility of the MMPI-A Content Scales and Harris-Lingoes subscales in the assessment of suicidal risk factors in psychiatric adolescents. *Journal of Clinical Psychology, 54*(2), 191–200.

Koss, M. P. (1979). MMPI item content: Recurring issues. In J. N. Butcher (Ed.), *New developments in the use of the MMPI* (pp. 3–38). Minneapolis: University of Minnesota Press.

Koss, M. P., & Butcher, J. N. (1973). A comparison of psychiatric patients' self-report with other sources of clinical information. *Journal of Research in Personality, 7,* 225–236.

Koss, M. P., Butcher, J. N., & Hoffmann, N. G. (1976). The MMPI critical items: How well do they work? *Journal of Consulting and Clinical Psychology, 44,* 921–928.

Kubany, E. S., Gino, A., Denny, N. R., & Torigoe, R. Y. (1994). The relationship of cynical hostility and PTSD among Vietnam veterans. *Journal of Traumatic Stress, 7*(1), 21–31.

Kwan, K. L. (1999). MMPI and MMPI-2 performance of the Chinese: Cross-cultural applicability. *Professional Psychology Research and Practice, 30*(3), 260–268.

Lachar, D. (1974). *The MMPI: Clinical assessment and automated interpretation.* Los Angeles: Western Psychological Services.

Lachar, D. (1979). How much of a good thing is enough? A review of T. A. Fashingbauer & C. A. Newmark: Short forms of the MMPI. *Contemporary Psychology, 24,* 116–117.

Lachar, D., Klinge, V., & Grisell, J. L. (1976). Relative accuracy of automated MMPI narratives generated from adult norm and adolescent norm profiles. *Journal of Consulting and Clinical Psychology, 44,* 20–24.

Lachar, D., & Wrobel, T. A. (1979). Validating clinicians' hunches: Construction of a new MMPI critical item set. *Journal of Consulting and Clinical Psychology, 47,* 277–284.

LaPlace, J. P. (1952). An exploratory study of personality and its relationship to success in professional baseball. (Doctoral dissertation, Columbia University, 1952). *Dissertation Abstracts International, 12,* 592.

Lees-Haley, P. R. (1997). MMPI-2 base rates for 492 personal injury plaintiffs: Implications and challenges for forensic assessment. *Journal of Clinical Psychology, 53*(7), 745–756.

Lees-Haley, P. R., Smith, H. H., Williams, C. W., & Dunn, J. T. (1996). Forensic neuropsychological test usage: An empirical survey. *Archives of Clinical Neuropsychology, 11*, 45–51.

Legan, L., & Craig, R. J. (1996). Correspondence of MMPI and MMPI-2 with chemically dependent patients. *Journal of Clinical Psychology, 52*(5), 589–597.

Levenson, M. R., Aldwin, C. M., Butcher, J. N., de Labry, L., Workman-Daniels, K., & Bossé, R. (1990). The MAC scale in a normal population: The meaning of "false positives." *Journal of Studies on Alcohol, 51*, 457–462.

Lewandowski, D., & Graham, J. R. (1972). Empirical correlates of frequently occurring two-point MMPI code types: A replicated study. *Journal of Consulting and Clinical Psychology, 39*, 467–472.

Lewinson, P. M. (1968). Characteristics of patients with hallucinations. *Journal of Clinical Psychology, 24*, 423.

Lichtenberg, P. A., Skehan, M. W., & Swensen, C. O. (1984). The role of personality, recent life stress and arthritic severity in predicting pain. *Journal of Psychosomatic Research, 28*, 231–236.

Lilienfeld, S. O. (1996). The MMPI-2 Antisocial Practices Content Scale: Construct validity and comparison with the Psychopathic Deviate Scale. *Psychological Assessment, 8*, 281–293.

Lim, J., & Butcher, J. N. (1996). Detection of faking on the MMPI-2: Differentiation between faking-bad, denial, and claiming extreme virtue. *Journal of Personality Assessment, 67*, 1–26.

Litz, B. T., Penk, W., Walsh, S., Hyer, L., Blake, D. D., Marx, B., Keane, T. M., & Bitman, D. (1991). Similarities and differences between Minnesota Multiphasic Personality Inventory (MMPI) and MMPI-2 applications to the assessment of post-traumatic stress disorder. *Journal of Personality Assessment, 57*, 238–254.

Loevinger, J. (1994). Has psychology lost its conscience? *Journal of Personality Assessment, 62*, 2–8.

Loevinger, J. (1976). *Ego development: Conceptions and theories.* San Francisco: Jossey-Bass.

Long, K. A., & Graham, J. R. (1991). The Masculinity-Femininity Scale of the MMPI-2: Is it useful with normal men? *Journal of Personality Assessment, 57*, 46–51.

Loper, R., Kammeier, J. M., & Hoffman, H. (1973). MMPI-2 characteristics of college freshman males who later became alcoholics. *Journal of Abnormal Psychology, 82*, 159–162.

Louscher, P. K., Hosford, R. E., & Moss, C. S. (1983). Predicting dangerous behavior in a penitentiary using the Megargee typology. *Criminal Justice and Behavior, 10*, 269–284.

Lubin, B., Larsen, R. M., & Matarazzo, J. (1984). Patterns of psychological test usage in the United States 1935–1982. *American Psychologist, 39*, 451–454.

Lucio, E. M., Palacios, H., Duran, C., & Butcher, J. N. (1999). MMPI-2 with Mexican psychiatric inpatients. *Journal of Clinical Psychology, 55*(12), 1541–1552.

Lucio, E., & Reyes-Lagunes, I. (1996). The Mexican version of the MMPI-2 in Mexico and Nicaragua: Translation, adaptation, and demonstrated equivalency. In J. N. Butcher (Ed.), *International adaptations of the MMPI-2: Research and clinical applications* (pp. 265–283). Minneapolis: University of Minnesota Press.

MacAndrew, C. (1965). The differentiation of male alcoholic outpatients from nonalcoholic psychiatric outpatients by means of the MMPI. *Quarterly Journal of Studies on Alcohol, 26*, 238–246.

MacAndrew, C. (1986). Toward the psychometric detection of substance misuse in young men: The SAP scale. *Journal of Studies on Alcohol, 47*, 161–166.

Marks, P. A., & Seeman, W. (1963). *The actuarial description of abnormal personality.* Baltimore: Williams & Wilkins.

Marks, P. A., Seeman, W., & Haller, D. L. (1974). *The actuarial use of the MMPI with adolescents and adults.* Baltimore: Williams & Wilkins.

McCann, J. T. (1998). *Malingering and deception in adolescence: Assessing credibility in clinical and forensic settings.* Washington, DC: American Psychological Association.

McCreary, C. (1985). Empirically derived MMPI profile clusters and characteristics of low back pain patients. *Journal of Consulting and Clinical Psychology, 53*, 558–560.

McGill, J., Lawlis, G. F., Selby, D., Mooney, V., & McCoy, C. E. (1983). Relationship of MMPI profile clusters to pain behaviors. *Journal of Behavioral Medicine, 6*, 77–92.

McKenna, T., & Butcher, J. N. (1987). *Continuity of the MMPI with alcoholics.* Paper presented at the 23rd Annual Symposium on Recent Developments in the Use of the MMPI, Seattle, WA.

McKinley, J. C., & Hathaway, S. R. (1940). A multiphasic personality schedule (Minnesota): II. A differential study of hypochondriasis. *Journal of Psychology, 10*, 255–268.

McKinley, J. C., & Hathaway, S. R. (1944). The MMPI: V. Hysteria, hypomania, and psychopathic deviate. *Journal of Applied Psychology, 28,* 153–174.

McKinley, J. C., Hathaway, S. R., & Meehl, P. E. (1948). The MMPI: VI. The K scale. *Journal of Consulting Psychology, 12,* 20–31.

McMinn, M. R., Buchanan, T., Ellens, B. M., & Ryan, M. (1999). Technology, professional practice, and ethics: Survey findings and implications. *Professional Psychology: Research and Practice, 30*(2), 165–172.

McNulty, J. L., Harkness, A. R., Ben-Porath, Y. S., & Williams, C. L. (1997). Assessing the Personality Psychopathology Five (PSY-5) in adolescents: New MMPI-A scales. *Psychological Assessment, 9*(3), 250–259.

Meehl, P. E. (1954). *Clinical versus statistical prediction: A theoretical analysis and a review of the evidence.* Minneapolis: University of Minnesota Press.

Meehl, P. E., & Hathaway, S. R. (1946). The K factor as a suppressor variable in the MMPI. *Journal of Applied Psychology, 30,* 525–564.

Megargee, E. I. (1984). A new classification system for criminal offenders: VI. Differences among the types on the Adjective Checklist. *Criminal Justice and Behavior, 11,* 349–376.

Megargee, E. I. (1994). Using the Megargee MMPI-based classification system with the MMPI-2's of male prison inmates. *Psychological Assessment, 6*(4), 337–334.

Megargee, E. I. (1995). Use of the MMPI-2 in correctional settings. In Y. S. Ben-Porath, J. R. Graham, G. C. N. Hall, R. D. Hirschman, & M. S. Zaragoza (Eds.), *Forensic applications of the MMPI-2* (pp. 127–159). Thousand Oaks, CA: Sage.

Megargee, E. I. (1997). Using the Megargee MMPI-based classification system with the MMPI-2s of female prison inmates. *Psychological Assessment, 9,* 75–82.

Megargee, E. I., & Bohn, M. J. (1977). A new classification system for criminal offenders: IV. Empirically determined characteristics of the ten types. *Criminal Justice and Behavior, 4,* 149–210.

Meikle, S., & Gerritse, R. (1970). MMPI "cookbook" pattern frequencies in a psychiatric unit. *Journal of Clinical Psychology, 26,* 82–84.

Meresman, J. F. (1992, May). *The ability of the MMPI-2 to discriminate between responders and non-responders in the treatment of depression.* Paper presented at the 27th Annual Symposium on Recent Developments in the Use of the MMPI (MMPI-2), Minneapolis, MN.

Moldin, S. O., Gottesman, I. I., Rice, J. P., & Erlenmeyer-Kimling, L. (1991). Replicated psychometric correlates of schizophrenia. *American Journal of Psychiatry, 148,* 762–767.

Monachesi, E. D. (1948). Some personality characteristics of delinquents and nondelinquents. *Journal of Criminal Law and Criminology, 38,* 487–500.

Monachesi, E. D. (1950a). Personality characteristics and socioeconomic status of delinquents and nondelinquents. *Journal of Criminal Law and Criminology, 40,* 570–583.

Monachesi, E. D. (1950b). Personality characteristics of institutionalized and noninstitutionalized male delinquents. *Journal of Criminal Law and Criminology, 41,* 167–179.

Monachesi, E. D. (1953). The personality patterns of juvenile delinquents as indicated by the MMPI. In S. R. Hathaway & E. D. Monachesi (Eds.), *Analyzing and predicting juvenile delinquency with the MMPI* (pp. 38–53). Minneapolis: University of Minnesota Press.

Moore, J. M., Thompson-Pope, S. K., & Whited, R. M. (1996). MMPI-A profiles of adolescent boys with a history of firesetting. *Journal of Personality Assessment, 67*(1), 116–126.

Moreland, K. L. (1987). Computerized psychological assessment: What's available. In J. N. Butcher (Ed.), *Computerized psychological assessment.* New York: Basic Books.

Moreland, K. L., & Onstad, J. (1985, March). *Validity of the Minnesota Clinical Report I: Mental health outpatients.* Paper presented at the 20th Annual Symposium on Recent Developments in the Use of the MMPI, Honolulu, HI.

Moss, C. S., Johnson, M. E., & Hosford, R. E. (1984). An assessment of the Megargee typology in lifelong criminal violence. *Criminal Justice and Behavior, 11,* 225–234.

Motiuk, L. L., Bonta, J., & Andrews, D. A. (1986). Classification in correctional halfway houses: The relative and incremental predictive criterion validities of the Megargee-MMPI and LSI systems. *Criminal Justice and Behavior, 13,* 33–46.

Mrad, D. F., Kabacoff, R. I., & Duckro, P. (1983). Validation of the Megargee typology in a halfway house setting. *Criminal Justice and Behavior, 10,* 252–262.

Muller, B., & Bruno, L. (1986). *The MMPI and Inwald Personality Inventory for psychological screening of police candidates*. Paper presented at the 21st Annual Symposium on Recent Developments in the Use of the MMPI, Clearwater Beach, FL.

Munley, P. H., Bains, D. S., Bloem, W. D., & Busby, R. M. 1995). Post-traumatic stress disorder and the MMPI-2. *Journal of Traumatic Stress, 8*(1), 171–178.

Munley, P. H., Busby, R. M., and Jaynes, G. (1997). MMPI-2 findings in schizophrenia and depression. *Psychological Assessment, 9*(4), 508–511.

Murray, J. B. (1963). The Mf scale of the MMPI for college students. *Journal of Clinical Psychology, 19,* 113–115.

Negy, C., Leal-Puente, L., Trainor, D. J., & Carlson, R. (1997). Mexican-American adolescents' performance on the MMPI-A. *Journal of Personality Assessment, 69*(1), 205–214.

Nelson, L. (1987). Measuring depression in a clinical population using the MMPI. *Journal of Consulting and Clinical Psychology, 55*(5) 788–790.

Nelson, L., & Cicchetti, D. (1991). Validity of the MMPI depression scale for outpatients. *Psychological Assessment: A Journal of Consulting and Clinical Psychology, 3,* 55–59.

Newman, M. L., & Greenway, P. (1997). Therapeutic effects of providing MMPI-2 test feedback to clients at a university counseling service: A collaborative approach. *Psychological Assessment, 9,* 122–131.

Nuclear Regulatory Commission (1984). *Guidelines for nuclear power plant access* (NRC 10 CFR Parts 50 & 73). Washington, DC: Nuclear Regulatory Commission.

Osberg, T. M., & Harrigan, P. (1999). Comparative validity of the MMPI-2 Wiener-Harmon-Obvious scales in male prison inmates. *Journal of Personality Assessment, 72*(1), 36–48.

Pancheri, P., Sirigatti, S., & Biondi, M. (1996). Adaptation of the MMPI-2 in Italy. In J. N. Butcher (Ed.), *International adaptations of the MMPI-2: Research and clinical applications* (pp. 416–441). Minneapolis: University of Minnesota Press.

Pancoast, D. L., & Archer, R. P. (1988). MMPI adolescent norms: Patterns and trends across four decades. *Journal of Personality Assessment, 52,* 691–706.

Panton, J. H. (1959). MMPI profile configurations among crime classification groups. *Journal of Clinical Psychology, 15,* 305–308.

Parkison, S., & Fishburne, F. (1984). MMPI normative data for a male active duty Army population. In *Proceedings of the Psychology in the Department of Defense, Ninth Symposium* (USAFA-TR-84-2, pp. 570–574). Colorado Springs, CO: U.S. Air Force Academy, Department of Behavioral Sciences.

Pearson, J. S., & Swenson, W. M. (1967). *A users guide to the Mayo Clinic automated MMPI program.* New York: The Psychological Corporation.

Pearson, J. S., Swenson, W. M., Rome, H. P., Mataya, P., & Brannick, T. L. (1965). Development of a computer system for scoring and interpretation of the Minnesota Multiphasic Personality Inventory in a medical setting. *Annals of the New York Academy of Sciences, 126,* 682–692.

Peña, L. M., Megargee, E. I., & Brody, E. (1996). MMPI-A patterns of male juvenile delinquents. *Psychological Assessment, 8*(4), 388–397.

Penk, W., Rierdan, J., Knight, J., & Mesheda, T. (1996, June). *MMPI-2 profiles of persons with serious mental disorders: The homeless, the unemployed, and the dually diagnosed.* Paper presented at the 31st Annual Symposium on Recent Developments in the Use of the MMPI-2. Minneapolis, MN.

Persons, R. W., & Marks, P. A. (1971). The violent 4-3 MMPI personality type. *Journal of Consulting and Clinical Psychology, 36,* 189–196.

Peterson, C. D. (1989). *Masculinity and femininity as independent dimensions on the MMPI.* Unpublished doctoral dissertation, University of North Carolina, Chapel Hill.

Piotrowski, C., & Keller, J. W. (1992). Psychological testing in applied settings: A literature review from 1982–1992. *Journal of Training & Practice in Professional Psychology, 6*(2), 74–82.

Pope, K. S. (1990). Seven clinical, ethical, and legal pitfalls in using psychological tests. *MMPI-2 News and Profiles, 1,* 2–3.

Pope, K. S., Butcher, J. N., & Seelen, J. (1999). *MMPI/MMPI-2/MMPI-A in court: Assessment, testimony, and cross-examination for expert witnesses and attorneys* (2nd ed.). Washington, DC: American Psychological Association.

Prokop, C. K., Bradley, L. A., Margolis, R., & Gentry, W. D. (1980). Multivariate analyses of the MMPI profiles of low back pain patients. *Journal of Personality Assessment, 44,* 246–252.

Postuma, A. B., & Harper, J. F. (1998). Comparison of MMPI-2 responses of child custody and personal injury litigants. *Professional Psychology: Research and Practice, 29*(5), 437–443.

Quereshi, M. Y., and Kleman, R. (1996). Validation of selected MMPI-2 basic and content scales. *Current Psychology: Developmental, Learning, Personality, Social-Psychology, 15*(3), 249–253.

Reese, P. M., Webb, J. T., & Foulks, J. D. (1968). A comparison of oral and booklet forms of the MMPI for psychiatric inpatients. *Journal of Clinical Psychology, 24,* 436–437.

Rempel, P. P. (1958). The use of multivariate statistical analysis of the Minnesota Multiphasic Personality Inventory in the classification of delinquent and nondelinquent high school boys. *Journal of Consulting Psychology, 22,* 17–23.

Rissetti, F., Himmel, E., & Gonzales-Moreno, F. (1996). Use of the MMPI-2 in Chile: Translation and adaptation. In J. N. Butcher (Ed.), *International adaptations of the MMPI-2: Research and clinical applications* (pp. 221–251). Minneapolis: University of Minnesota Press.

Rogers, R., Bagby, R. M., & Dickens, S. E. (1992). *Structured Interview of Reported Symptoms: Professional manual.* Odessa, FL: Psychological Assessment Resources.

Rogers, R., Hinds, J. D., & Sewell, K. W. (1996). Feigning psychopathology among adolescent offenders: Validation of the SIRS, MMPI-A, and SIMS. *Journal of Personality Assessment, 67*(2), 244–257.

Rogers, R., Sewell, K. W., & Salekin, R. T. (1994). A meta-analysis of malingering on the MMPI-2. *Assessment, 1,* 227–237.

Rome, H. P., Swenson, W. M., Mataya, P., McCarthy, C. E., Pearson, J. S., Keating, F. R., & Hathaway, S. R. (1962). Symposium on automation technics in personality assessment. *Proceedings of the Staff Meetings of the Mayo Clinic, 37,* 61–82.

Roper, B., Ben-Porath, Y. S., & Butcher, J. N. (1991). Comparability of computerized adaptive and conventional testing with the MMPI-2. *Journal of Personality Assessment, 57,* 278–290.

Rosen, A. (1958). Differentiation of diagnostic groups by individual MMPI scales. *Journal of Consulting Psychology, 17,* 217–221.

Rouse, S. V., Butcher, J. N., & Miller, K. (1999). Assessment of substance abuse in psychotherapy clients: The effectiveness of the MMPI-2 substance abuse scales. *Psychological Assessment, 11*(1), 101–107.

Saccuzzo, D. P., Higgins, G., & Lewandowski, D. (1974). Program for psychological assessment of law enforcement officers: Initial evaluation. *Psychological Reports, 35,* 651–654.

Savacir, I., & Erol, N. (1990). The Turkish MMPI. In J. N. Butcher & C. D. Spielberger (Eds.), *Advances in personality assessment* (Vol. 8). Hillsdale, NJ: Lawrence Erlbaum Associates.

Schill, T., & Wang, T. (1990). Correlates of the MMPI-2 Anger Content Scale. *Psychological Reports, 67,* 800–802.

Schinka, J. A., Elkins, D. E., & Archer, R. P. (1998). Effects of psychopathology and demographic characteristics on MMPI-A scale scores. *Journal of Personality Assessment, 71*(3), 295–305.

Schlenger, W. E., & Kulka, R. A. (1987, August). *Performance of the Keane-Fairbank MMPI scale and other self-report measures in identifying post-traumatic stress disorder.* Paper presented at the 95th annual meeting of the American Psychological Association, New York, NY.

Schlenger, W. E., Kulka, R. A., Fairbank, J. A., Hough, R. L., Jordan, B. K., Marmar, C. R., & Weiss, D. S. (1989). *The prevalence of post-traumatic stress disorder in the Vietnam generation: Findings from the National Vietnam Veterans Readjustment Study:* Research report, Research Triangle Institute, Research Triangle Park, NC.

Schofield, W. (1956). Changes following certain therapies as reflected in the MMPI. In G. S. Welsh and W. G. Dahlstrom (Eds.), *Basic readings on the MMPI in psychology and medicine* (pp. 534–547). Minneapolis: University of Minnesota Press.

Schretlen, D. (1988). The use of psychological tests to identify malingered symptoms of mental disorder. *Clinical Psychology Review, 8,* 451–476.

Scotti, J. R., Sturges, L. V., Veltum, L., & Lyons, J. A. (1996). The Keane PTSD scale extracted from the MMPI: sensitivity and specificity with Vietnam veterans. *Journal of Traumatic Stress, 9*(3), 643–650.

Serkownek, K. (1975). *Subscales for Scales 5 and 0 of the Minnesota Multiphasic Personality Inventory.* Unpublished materials.

Shaevel, B., & Archer, R. P. (1996). Effects of the MMPI-2 and MMPI-A norms on T-score elevations for 18 year olds. *Journal of Personality Assessment, 67*(1), 72–78.

Shaffer, J. W., Ota, K. Y., & Hanlon, T. E. (1964). The comparative validity of several MMPI indices of severity of psychopathology. *Journal of Clinical Psychology, 20,* 467–473.

Sherwood, N. E., Ben-Porath, Y. S., & Williams, C. L. (1997). *The MMPI-A Content Component Scales: Development, psychometric characteristics, and clinical applications.* Minneapolis: University of Minnesota Press.

Shores, A., & Carstairs, J. R. (1998). Accuracy of the MMPI-2 computerized Minnesota Report in identifying fake-good and fake-bad response sets. *The Clinical Neuropsychologist, 12,* 101–106.

Sieber, K. O., & Meyers, L. S. (1992). Validation of the MMPI-2 Social Introversion Subscales. *Psychological Assessment: A Journal of Consulting and Clinical Psychology, 4,* 185–189.

Silver, R., & Sines, L. K. (1962). Diagnostic efficiency of the MMPI with and without K correction. *Journal of Clinical Psychology, 18,* 312–314.

Simmons, J. G., Johnson, D. L., Gouvier, W. D., & Muzyczka, M. J. (1981). The Myer-Megargee inmate typology: Dynamic or unstable? *Criminal Justice and Behavior, 8,* 49–54.

Sines, J. O. (1966). Actuarial methods in personality assessment. In B. A. Maher (Ed.), *Progress in experimental personality research* (pp. 133–193). New York: Academic Press.

Sloore, H., Derksen, J., de Mey, H., & Hellenbosch, G. (1996). The Flemish/Dutch version of the MMPI-2: Development and adaptation of the inventory for Belgium and the Netherlands. In J. N. Butcher (Ed.), *International adaptations of the MMPI-2: Research and clinical applications* (pp. 329–349). Minneapolis: University of Minnesota Press.

Snyder, D. K., & Regts, J. M. (1990). Personality correlates of marital satisfaction: A comparison of psychiatric, maritally distressed, and nonclinic samples. *Journal of Sex and Marital Therapy, 16,* 34–43.

Spanier, G. B., & Filsinger, E. E. (1983). The dyadic adjustment scale. In E. E. Filsinger (Ed.), *Marriage and family assessment* (pp. 155–168). Beverly Hills, CA: Sage.

Spiro, A., Butcher, J. N., Levenson, M. R., Aldwin, C., & Bossé, R. (2000). Change and stability in personality: A 5 year study of the MMPI-2 in older men. In J. N. Butcher (Ed.), *Basic sources for the MMPI-2* (pp. 443–462). Minneapolis: University of Minnesota Press.

Stein, K. B. (1968). The TSC Scales: The outcome of a cluster analysis of the 550 MMPI items. In P. McReynolds (Ed.), *Advances in psychological assessment* (Vol. 1, pp. 80–149). Palo Alto, CA: Science & Behavior Books.

Stein, L. A. R., Graham, J. R., Ben-Porath, Y. S., & McNulty, J. (1999). Using the MMPI-2 to detect substance abuse in an outpatient mental health setting. *Psychological Assessment, 11*(1), 94–100.

Stein, L. A. R., Graham, J. R., & Williams, C. L. (1995). Detecting fake-bad MMPI-A profiles. *Journal of Personality Assessment, 65*(3), 415–427.

Streiner, D. L., & Miller, H. R. (1986). Can a good short form of the MMPI ever be developed? *Journal of Clinical Psychology, 42,* 109–113.

Taft, R. (1961). A psychological assessment of professional actors and related professions. *Genetic Psychology Monographs, 64,* 309–383.

Tellegen, A. (1982). *Brief manual for the Differential Personality Questionnaire.* Unpublished manuscript, University of Minnesota, Minneapolis. (Since renamed Multidimensional Personality Questionnaire.)

Tellegen, A. (1988). The analysis of consistency in personality assessment. *Journal of Personality, 56,* 621–663.

Tellegen, A. (1991, August). *Development of consistency measures for the MMPI-A.* Paper presented at the 99th annual meeting of the American Psychological Association, Los Angeles.

Tellegen, A., & Ben-Porath, Y. S. (1992). The new uniform T-scores for the MMPI-2: Rationale, derivation, and appraisal. *Psychological Assessment 4*(2), 145–155.

Tellegen, A., Butcher, J. N., & Hoegliund, T. (1993). Are unisex norms for the MMPI-2 needed? Would they work? *MMPI-2 News & Profiles, 4*(1), 5–6.

Terman, L. M., & Miles, C. (1936). *Sex and personality: Studies in masculinity and femininity.* New York: McGraw-Hill.

Thatte, S., Manos, N., & Butcher, J. N. (1987, July). *Cross-cultural study of abnormal personality in three countries: United States, India, and Greece.* Paper presented at the 10th Annual Conference on Personality Assessment, Brussels, Belgium.

Timbrook, R., Graham, J. R., Keiller, S., & Watts, D. (1991, March). *Failure of the Wiener-Harmon Subscales to discriminate between valid and invalid profiles.* Paper presented at the 26th Annual Symposium on Recent Developments in the Use of the MMPI (MMPI-2), St. Petersburg, FL.

Tinius, T., & Ben-Porath, Y. S. (1993, March). *A comparative study of Native Americans and Caucasian Americans undergoing substance abuse treatment.* Paper presented at the 28th Annual Conference on Recent Developments in the Use of the MMPI/MMPI-2, St. Petersburg, FL.

Trull, T. J., Useda, J. D., Costa, P. T., & McCrae, R. R. (1995). Comparison of the MMPI-2 Personality Psychopathology Five (PSY-5), the NEO-PI, and the NEO-PI-R. *Psychological Assessment, 7*(4), 508–516.

Tsai, J., Butcher, J. N., Munoz, R., & Vitusek, K. (in press). Culture, ethnicity, and psychopathology. In H. E. Adams & P. Sutker (Eds.), *Comprehensive handbook of psychopathology* (3rd ed.). New York: Plenum.

Urmer, A. H., Black, H. O., & Wendland, L. V. (1960). A comparison of taped and booklet forms of the MMPI. *Journal of Clinical Psychology, 16,* 33–34.

Vincent, K. R. (1990). The fragile nature of MMPI codetypes. *Journal of Clinical Psychology, 46,* 800–802.

Waller, N. G., & Ben-Porath, Y. S. (1987). Is it time for clinical psychology to embrace the five-factor model of personality? *American Psychologist, 42*(9), 887–889.

Waller, N. G., Thompson, J., & Wenk, E. (in press). Black-White differences on the MMPI using IRT to separate measurement bias from true group differences. *Psychological Methods.*

Walsh, S., Penk, W., Brett, T., Litz, T., Keane, T. M., Bitman, D., & Marx, B. (1991, August). *Discriminant validity of the new MMPI-2 Content Scales.* Paper presented at the 99th annual meeting of the American Psychological Association, San Francisco, CA.

Walters, G. (1986). Correlates of the Megargee Criminal Classification System: A military correctional system. *Criminal Justice and Behavior, 13,* 19–32.

Warbin, R. W., Altman, H., Gynther, M. D., & Sletten, I. W. (1972). A new empirical automated MMPI interpretive program: 2-8 and 8-2 code types. *Journal of Personality Assessment, 36,* 581–584.

Watson, D., & Clark, L. A. (1993). Behavioral disinhibition versus constraint: A dispositional perspective. In D. M. Wegnar & J. W. Pennebaker (Eds.), *Handbook of mental control* (pp. 506–507). New York: Prentice Hall.

Wauck, L. A. (1950). Schizophrenia and the MMPI. *Journal of Clinical Psychology, 6,* 279–282.

Weed, N., Ben-Porath, Y. S., & Butcher, J. N. (1990). Failure of the Wiener-Harmon MMPI subtle scales as predictors of psychopathology and as validity indicators. *Psychological Assessment: A Journal of Consulting and Clinical Psychology, 2,* 281–283.

Weed, N. C., Butcher, J. N., & Ben-Porath, Y. S. (1995). MMPI-2 measures of substance abuse. In J. N. Butcher & C. D. Spielberger (Eds.), *Advances in personality assessment* (Vol. 10, pp. 121–145). Hillsdale, NJ: Lawrence Erlbaum Associates.

Weed, N. C., Butcher, J. N., Ben-Porath, Y. S., & McKenna, T. (1992). New measures for assessing alcohol and drug abuse with the MMPI-2: The APS and AAS. *Journal of Personality Assessment, 58,* 389–404.

Weed, N. C., Butcher, J. N., & Williams, C. L. (1994). Development of MMPI-A alcohol/drug problem scales. *Journal of Studies on Alcohol, 55*(3), 296–302.

Welsh, G. S. (1948). An extension of Hathaway's MMPI profile coding. *Journal of Consulting Psychology, 12,* 343–344.

Welsh, G. S. (1951). Some practical uses of MMPI profile coding. *Journal of Consulting Psychology, 15,* 82–84.

Welsh, G. S. (1956). Factor dimensions A and R. In G. S. Welsh & W. G. Dahlstrom (Eds.), *Basic readings on the MMPI in psychology and medicine* (pp. 264–281). Minneapolis: University of Minnesota Press.

Wiener, D. N. (1948). Subtle and obvious keys for the MMPI. *Journal of Consulting Psychology, 12,* 164–170.

Wiggins, J. S. (1966). Substantive dimensions of self-report in the MMPI item pool [Special issue]. *Psychological Monographs, 80*(630).

Wiggins, J. S. (1969). Content dimensions in the MMPI. In J. N. Butcher (Ed.), *MMPI: Research developments and clinical applications* (pp. 127–180). New York: McGraw-Hill.

Wilcockson, J. C., Bolton, B., & Dana, R. H. (1983). A comparison of six MMPI short forms: Code type correspondence and indices of psychopathology. *Journal of Clinical Psychology, 39,* 968–969.

Williams, C. L. (1981). Assessment of social behavior: Behavior role play compared with Si scale of the MMPI. *Behavior Therapy, 12,* 578–584.

Williams, C. L. (1982). Can the MMPI be useful to behavior therapists? *The Behavior Therapist, 3,* 83–84.

Williams, C. L. (1986). MMPI profiles from adolescents: Interpretative strategies and treatment considerations. *Journal of Child and Adolescent Psychotherapy, 3,* 179–193.

Williams, C. L., Ben-Porath, Y. S., & Hevern, V. W. (1994). Item level improvements for use of the MMPI with adolescents. *Journal of Personality Assessment, 63*(2), 284–293.

Williams, C. L., & Butcher, J. N. (1989a). An MMPI study of adolescents: I. Empirical validity of the standard scales. *Psychological Assessment: A Journal of Consulting and Clinical Psychology, 1,* 251–259.

Williams, C. L., & Butcher, J. N. (1989b). An MMPI study of adolescents: II. Verification and limitations of code type classifications. *Psychological Assessment: A Journal of Consulting and Clinical Psychology, 1*, 260–265.

Williams, C. L., Butcher, J. N., Ben-Porath, Y. S., & Graham, J. R. (1992). *MMPI-A Content Scales: Assessing psychopathology in adolescents.* Minneapolis: University of Minnesota Press.

Williams, C. L., Butcher, J. N., & Graham, J. R. (1986, March). *Appropriate MMPI norms for adolescents: An old problem revisited.* Paper presented at the 21st Annual Symposium on Recent Developments in the Use of the MMPI, Clearwater, FL.

Williams, C. L., Perry, C. L., Dudovitz, B., Veblen-Mortenson, S., & Anstine, P. (1995). A home-based prevention program for sixth grade alcohol use: Results from Project Northland. *Journal of Primary Prevention, 16*(2), 125–147.

Williams, C. L., Perry, C. L., Farbakhsh, K., & Veblen-Mortenson, S. (1999). Project Northland: Comprehensive alcohol use prevention for young adolescents, their parents, schools, peers, and communities. *Journal of Studies on Alcohol* (Suppl. 13), 112–124.

Williams, H. L. (1952). *Differential effects of focal brain damage on the MMPI.* Unpublished doctoral dissertation, University of Minnesota, Minneapolis.

Williams, R. B., Barefoot, J. C., & Shekelle, R. B. (1985). The health consequences of hostility. In M. A. Chesney & R. H. Rosenman (Eds.), *Anger and hostility in cardiovascular and behavioral disorders* (pp. 173–185). Washington, DC: Hemisphere.

Wolf, S. W., Freinek, W. R., & Shaffer, J. W. (1964). Comparability of complete oral and booklet forms of the MMPI. *Journal of Clinical Psychology, 20*, 375–378.

Wolfson, K. T., & Erbaugh, S. E. (1984). Adolescent responses to MacAndrew Alcoholism scale. *Journal of Consulting and Clinical Psychology, 52*, 625–630.

Woodworth, R. S. (1920). *The Personal Data Sheet.* Chicago: Stoelting.

Wrobel, N. H., & Lachar, D. (1992). Refining adolescent MMPI interpretations: Moderating effects of gender in prediction of descriptions from parents. *Psychological Assessment, 4*(3), 375–381.

Wrobel, N. H., & Lachar, D. (1995). Racial differences in adolescent self-report: A comparative validity study using homogenous MMPI content measures. *Psychological Assessment, 7*(2), 140–147.

Wrobel, T. A. (1992). Validity of Harris and Lingoes MMPI subscale descriptors in an outpatient sample. *Journal of Personality Assessment, 59*(1), 14–21.

Zager, L. D. (1983). Response to Simmons and associates: Conclusions about the MMPI-Based Classification System's stability are premature. *Criminal Justice and Behavior, 10*, 310–315.

Index

Compiled by Celeste Newbrough

Coauthors are listed individually; coauthors in multiple-author studies are listed selectively. Figures and tables are numbered when necessary in order for the reader to locate; otherwise, only the page number is given.

A (Anxiety) supplementary scale, 9, 172, 173*t*7-10, 371, 375

A-aln (Adolescent-Alienation) content scale, 282–83, 283*t*, 371; component scales, 299*t*

A-aln₁ (Misunderstood) component scale, 299*t*

A-aln₂ (Social Isolation) component scale, 299*t*

A-aln₃ (Interpersonal Skepticism) component scale, 299*t*

A-ang (Adolescent-Anger) content scale: component scales, 298, 299*t*; interpretation, 285, 286*t*, 298

A-ang₁ (Explosive Behavior) component scale, 299*t*

A-ang₂ (Irritability) component scale, 299*t*

A-anx (Adolescent-Anxiety) content scale, 277–78, 278*t*, 306, 313

AAS (Addiction Acknowledgment) supplementary scale, 7, 159–60, 160*t*7-3

Abbreviated formats of test measures, 24–25

A-biz (Adolescent-Bizarre Mentation) content scale, 284*t*, 284, 318

A-biz₁ (Psychotic Symptomatology) component scale, 299*t*

A-biz₂ (Paranoid Ideation) component scale, 299*t*

ACK (Alcohol/Drug Problem Acknowledgement) supplementary scale of MMPI-A, 304–5, 306*t*, 312, 323–24, 371

A-con (Adolescent-Conduct Problems) content scale, 298, 299*t*

A-con₁ (Acting-Out Behaviors) component scale, 299*t*

A-con₂ (Antisocial Attitudes) component scale, 299*t*

A-con₃ (Negative Peer Group Influences) component scale, 299*t*; interpretation, 274, 287–88, 289*t*, 298, 328*t*, 371

Acting out: Acon₁ scale and, 299*t*; acute mood state, 195; in adolescence, 258, 260, 270, 287, 290, 308, 314, 329; assessment indicators, 195

Actuarial prediction (Meehl), 102, 331, 371

Acute mood states, 194–95

Acute posttraumatic stress disorder (PTSD), 371; PK scale measuring, 170–71, 171*t*7-8

A-cyn (Adolescent-Cynicism) content scale, 275–86, 287*t*; component scales, 299*t*

A-cyn₁ (Misanthropic Beliefs) component scale, 299*t*

A-cyn₂ (Interpersonal Suspiciousness) component scale, 299*t*

Addiction proneness, 333, 371

A-dep (Adolescent-Depression) content scale, 279–80, 281*t*. *See also* DEP (Depression) content scale

A-dep₁ (Dysphoria) component scale, 299*t*

A-dep₂ (Self-Depreciation) component scale, 299*t*

A-dep₃ (Lack of Drive) component scale, 299*t*

A-dep₄ (Suicidal Ideation) component scale, 299*t*

Administering test measures. *See* Test administration

Adolescent-Alienation (A-aln) content scale, 282–83, 283*t*, 371; component scales, 299*t*

Adolescent-Anger (A-ang) content scale: component scales, 298, 299*t*; interpretation, 285, 286*t*, 298

Adolescent-Bizarre Mentation (A-biz) content scale, 284*t*, 284, 318

Adolescent case illustration: Hispanic adolescent (Tony) content scales, 298–302, 301*t*; Minnesota Report, 337, 356*f*, 358*f*, 359–61*f*, 362–57; supplementary scales, 312*t*, 312–14; test summary, 326, 326–29, 327*f*, 328*t*, 329*f*; validity scales, 237*f*, 245–47, 246*f*

Adolescent-Conduct Problems (A-con) content scale, 298, 299*t*; interpretation, 274, 287–88, 289*t*, 298, 328*t*, 371

Adolescent-Cynicism (A-cyn) content scale, 275–86, 287*t*; component scales, 299*t*

Adolescent-Depression (A-dep) content scale, 279–80, 281t; component scales, 299t

Adolescent-Family Problems (A-fam) content scale, 292–94, 295t; component scales, 299t

Adolescent gender differences on test measures, 219–20, 225, 253t; A-aln scale and, 283; A-ang scale and, 285, 286t, 300; A-con scale and, 287, 288; A-fam scale and, 294; A-lse scale and, 288; Pd₄ scale and, 258; scale 1 (Hs) of MMPI-A and, 252; scale 2 (D) of MMPI-A and, 253–54, 255–56t; scale 4 (Pd) of MMPI-A and, 322; scale 5 (Mf) of MMPI-A and, 261; scale 6 (Pa) of MMPI-A and, 263, 264t; scale 7 (Pt) of MMPI-A and, 263; scale 8 (Sc) of MMPI-A and, 265, 266t; sexual abuse history and, 321–22

Adolescent-Health Concerns (A-hea) content scale, 280–82, 282t; component scales, 299t

Adolescent-Low Aspirations (A-las) content scale: component scales, 299t; interpretation, 289–91, 291t, 300–301, 356, 371

Adolescent-Low Self-Esteem (A-lse) content scale: component scales, 299t; interpretation, 288–89, 290t, 356

Adolescent-Negative Treatment Indicators (A-trt) content scale, 296–97, 297t; component scales, 299t

Adolescent-Obsessiveness (A-obs) content scale, 278–79, 279t

Adolescent-School Problems (A-sch) content scale, 294, 296t, 296, 371; component scales, 299t

Adolescent-Social Discomfort (A-sod) content scale, 291–92, 293t, 324; component scales, 299t

Adolescent substance abuse: case illustrations, 209–10, 260t, 287, 298, 323–24, 329

Adolescent suicide risk assessment, 322–23; A-aln scale, 283; A-dep scale, 280, 279, 281t, 294; A-las scale, 291t, 291; A-lse scale, 288, 290t; A-sod scale, 292; D₁ subscale, 254, 255t, 322; Imm (Immaturity) scale, 307; Kopper et al. study of, 251, 268, 278, 283; Ma₃ subscale, 322; Pd₄ subscale, 258; Pd₅ subscale, 322; scale 2 (D), 322; scale 4 (Pd), 322; scale 7 (Pt), 263; scale 8 (Sc), 265; scale 9 (Ma), 267–68, 269t, 322

Adolescent testing and interpretation, 4, 8, 12–15, 19; debate over adolescent norms and measured differences, 210–20, 221t; differences in item endorsements, 211–12, 220; norms for MMPI-A, 219, 254; original MMPI profile, 217–18, 219–22, 221t. See also Delinquency

Adult Clinical System, Minnesota Report, 336;

case illustration (Alice), 337f, 337–38, 338f, 339f

Adult Interpretive System (computerized), 335

A-fam (Adolescent-Family Problems) content scale, 292–94, 295t; component scales, 299t

A-fam₁ (Familial Discord) component scale, 299t

A-fam₂ (Familial Alienation) component scale, 299t

African Americans: MMPI-2 means and standard deviations for (comparative), 191t, 192t. See also Ethnic and cultural factors

Age-appropriate scores in MMPI-A, 219, 254

Aggression, inhibition of (Hy₅ subscale), 70; adolescent interpretation, 256, 258t

Aggressiveness (Psy 1) scale, 174t, 174–75

Aging studies: age-related elevated scores, 189; study of older men, 6, 156

A-hea (Adolescent-Health Concerns) content scale, 280–82, 282t; component scales, 299t

Ahea₁ (Gastrointestinal Complaints) component scale, 299t

A-hea₂ (Neurological Symptoms) component scale, 299t

A-hea₃ (General Health Concerns) component scale, 299t

Aiduk, R., 102, 103

Airline pilots personnel screening study, 17–18

A-las (Adolescent-Low Aspirations) content scale: component scales, 299t; interpretation, 289–91, 291t, 300–301, 356, 371

A-las₁ (Low Achievement Orientation) component scale, 299t

A-las₂ (Lack of Initiative) component scale, 299t

Alcohol abuse: ACK (Alcohol and Drug Problem Acknowledgement) supplementary scale, 304–5, 306t, 312, 323–24, 371; 1-4/4-1 code type and, 107, 108t; 2-4-7/2-7-4 code type and, 130–31, 131t; in adolescents, 209–10, 260t, 287, 298, 329; critical items for adolescents, 311t; critical items for adults, 180t; treatment setting studies of MMPI correlates, 6, 160. See also Substance abuse

Alcohol abuse case illustrations: MAC-R scale (Mr. Gabriel), 157–59, 158f; Minnesota Report (Mr. Jenkins), 336–37, 340f, 340–44, 341f, 342–43f; MMPI-2 (Mr. Jenkins), 161f, 161, 162f, 163f; substance abuse in adolescents (Stan), 323–24

Alcohol and Drug Problem Proneness (PRO) supplementary scale, 305–6, 307t, 312t, 312, 323–24

Alcohol and Drug Treatment Programs, Minnesota Report, 336–37, 340f, 340–44, 341f, 342–43f

Alienation—Self and Others (Si₃) subscale, 271t

All-False response set, case illustrations of, 245

All-True or all-False pattern, 41–44, 42*f*3-2, 43*t*

All-True response set: case illustrations, 242–44, 244*f*

Almagor, M., 162, 200

Alperin, J. J., 232

A-lse (Adolescent-Low Self Esteem) scale: component scales, 299*t*; interpretation, 288–89, 290*t*, 356

A-lse$_1$ (Self-Doubt) component scale, 299*t*

A-lse$_2$ (Interpersonal Submissiveness) component scale, 299*t*

Altman, H., 45, 103

American Psychological Association (APA): on computerized assessment, 330, 366. *See also DSM (Diagnostic and Statistical Manual of Mental Disorders)*

Amorality (Ma$_1$) subscale, 88

ANG (Anger) content scale: external correlates, 137; interpretation of, 142*t*6-7, 142, 152

ANG$_1$ (Explosive Behavior) component scale, 148*t*

ANG$_2$ (Irritability) component scale, 148*t*

Anger: 3-4/4-3 code type and, 116. *See also* A-ang (Adolescent-Anger) content scale; ANG (Anger) content scale

Anger (ANG) scale: external correlates, 137; interpretation of, 142*t*6-7, 142, 152

Anorexia in adolescents, 254, 290

Antisocial Attitudes (A-con$_2$) component scale, 299*t*

Antisocial Practices (ASP) content scale, 74; content component scales, 148*t*; external correlates, 137; interpretation of, 143–144*t*; scale 4 (Pd) and, 73–74

Antisocial traits, 371; 4-9/9-4 code type and, 122–23, 124*t*, 351*f*; antisocial personality (*DSM III-R* classification), 73; critical items regarding, 180–81*t*. *See also* A-con (Adolescent-Conduct Problems) content scale; ASP (Antisocial Practices) content scale

ANX (Anxiety) content scale, 139*t*6-1, 139, 153

Anxiety: acute mood state, 195; anxiety disorder and 7-8/8-7 code type, 127, 128*t*, 134

Anxiety case illustrations (Alice): clinician's interpretive report, 200–208, 201*f*; code types, 133–34; computerized interpretive report, 337–38, 338*f*, 339*f*; content scales, 153–54, 154*f*; profile validity, 59, 59*f*; standard scales, 97*f*, 97–98; supplementary scales, 184–85

A-obs (Adolescent-Obsessiveness) content scale, 278–79, 279*t*

APS (Addiction Potential) supplementary scale,

159, 160*t*7-2; case illustration (Mr. Jenkins), 161*f*, 161, 162*f*, 163*f*

Arbisi, P.: psychiatric inpatient studies, 344–49, 348*f*; veterans studies, 170–71, 198, 348*f*

Archer, R. P., 14, 232; on adolescent norms, 12, 62, 218, 254, 307, 311; on code types, 102, 103; on computerized interpretive reports, 330; on the MAC-R, 304; structural summary approach to MMPI-A, 315–16

Arita, A. A.: inpatient studies with adolescents, 277–78, 280, 281, 283, 285, 292

A-sch (Adolescent-School Problems) content scale, 294, 296*t*, 296, 371; component scales, 299*t*, 300

A-sch$_1$ (School Conduct Problems) component scale, 299*t*

A-sch$_2$ (Negative Attitudes) component scale, 299*t*

Asian Americans, 191*t*, 192*t*, 192; means and standard deviations for men (comparative), 191*t*; means and standard deviations for women (comparative), 192*t*

A-sod (Adolescent-Social Discomfort) content scale, 291–92, 293*t*, 324; component scales, 299*t*

A-sod$_1$ (Introversion) component scale, 299*t*

A-sod$_2$ (Shyness) component scale, 299*t*

ASP (Antisocial Practices) content scale, 74; ASP$_1$ (Antisocial Attitudes), 148*t*; ASP$_2$ (Antisocial Behavior), 148*t*; external correlates, 137; interpretation of, 143–144*t*; and Scale 4 (Pd), 73–74

Assault-risk critical items, 179–80*t*

Atlis, M., 17, 331

A-trt (Adolescent-Negative Treatment Indicators) content scale, 296–97, 297*t*; component scales, 299*t*

A-trt$_1$ (Low Motivation) component scale, 299*t*

A-trt$_2$ (Inability to Disclose) component scale, 299*t*

Audiocasette versions of test measures, 23

Authority Problems (Pd$_2$) subscale, 72; adolescent interpretation, 260*t*, 260, 271

Automated assessment. *See* Computerized interpretive reports; Computerized testing

Automated clinician, 332

Automated cookbook, 332

Babcock, D. J., 156

Baer, R. A., 52, 229, 231, 277–78, 280, 281, 283, 285, 292

Bagby, R. M., 73

Bains, D. S., 171

Ball, J. D., 330

Ballenger, J., 229

Bansal, A., 191
Barefoot, J. C., 167
Barrett, R. K., 162
Barron, F., 171
Basham, R. B., 251, 258
Bathurst, K., 37
Beck, E. A., 73
Behavior problems, 73–74; 2-4/4-2 code type
    and, 110, 111*t*; content scales and, 141.
    See also Substance abuse; Violent behavior
Ben-Porath, Yossef S., 5, 25; adolescent
    interpretation, 130, 222, 226, 231, 240, 315;
    on code types, 100, 102; on content scales
    of MMPI-2, 7–8, 73, 135; development of
    uniform T scores, 6–7, 30, 224; on empirical
    correlates of content scales, 137, 147–48, 200;
    five-factor models, 174; forensic evaluation
    study, 192, 198, 349*f*; on F scale, 46; MMPI-A
    critical items, 311; psychiatric inpatient
    studies, 6, 67, 137, 200, 344–49, 348*f*; on scale
    0 (Si), 62; veterans studies, 170–71, 198, 348*f*
Berdie, R. F., 73
Berry, D. T. R., 39, 45
Bipolar disorder: 2-9/9-2 code type and, 114–16,
    116*t*
BIZ (Bizarre Mentation) content scale:
    component scales, 148*t*; external correlates,
    137; interpretation of, 141, 142*t6-6*
BIZ₁ (Psychotic Symptomatology) component
    scale, 148*t*
BIZ₂ (Schizotypal Characteristics) component
    scale, 148*t*
Bizarre Mentation. *See* BIZ (Bizarre Mentation)
    content scale
Bizarre Sensory Experiences (Sc₆) subscale, 87;
    adolescent interpretation, 267*t*
Blind empiricism, 178
Bloem, W. D., 171
Bohn, M. J., 45, 176–77
Boone, D. E., 137
Booth, R. J., 176
Bosquet, M., 137
Brems, C., 137
Briggs, P. F., 215
Brooding (D₅) subscale, 67; adolescent
    interpretation, 256*t*
Brown, M. N., 39
Brown, P. L., 73
Bruno, L., 358
Buchanan, T., 330
Busby, R. M., 137
Butcher, James N., 3, 62, 78, 124, 156, 159; on
    adolescent norms, 14, 224–25; on adult norms
    189, 213; chronic pain study (with Keller), 64,
    70, 137, 177; complex decision model, 332–33,

362; on computerized assessment, 25, 331,
    366; critical items (Koss-Butcher) set, 177,
    179–80*t*; cross-cultural studies, 47, 191–92,
    193, 224–25; on inpatient studies, 6, 67, 137,
    200; on litigation cases, 46, 70, 188, 198;
    on marital distress, 6, 74, 137, 145, 162; on
    MMPI-2 content scales, 7–8, 73, 135, 136, 142;
    on MMPI-2 correlates, 62, 102; on personnel
    screening and test defensiveness, 6, 17, 52;
    psychiatric inpatient studies, 64, 67, 70, 82, 87,
    90, 198, 348; on Scale 2 (D), 67–68; on Scale 3
    (Hy), 70; on Scale 5 (Mf), 78, 232; on scales A
    and R, 9; on S scale, 52; on substance abuse
    assessment, 17, 62, 102, 156, 159, 160, 175; on
    validity scales, 51, 53, 238. *See also* Minnesota
    Report

Caldwell, Alex, 335
Calhoun, R. F., 167
Cannot Say Score (?), 39, 40*t*3-1; MMPI-A and,
    228*t*, 229–30, 231*t*
Cashel, M. L.: study of incarcerated adolescent
    boys, 252, 254, 261, 267, 278, 279, 280, 282,
    285, 286, 291, 292, 294, 305, 306, 307, 322
Catastrophic events, 318
Caucasians: means and standard deviations for
    men (comparative), 191*t*; means and standard
    deviations for women (comparative), 192*t*
Cheung, F. M., 47
Child abuse, mothers at risk for, 6, 74
Chisholm, S. M., 137
Chronic pain: HEA content scale and, 137;
    patient studies of, 198
Chronic pain typology (PAIN), 177
Cicchetti, D., 67
Coates, G. D., 232
Codebooks, 376
Code types: adolescent-adult differences on
    MMPI, 212–13; case illustration (Alice),
    133–34; definition and stability of, 100–101;
    empirical research on, 102–4; interpretative
    considerations, 99–100, 194; MMPI/MMPI-2
    similarity, 101–2; well-defined, 100–101, 212–
    13. *See also* Three-point code types; Two-point
    code types
Coding test profiles, 32–35; case illustration,
    35–36
Colby, F., 51
College students, studies of test correlates in, 6
Colligan, R. C., 3–4, 216–17
Competitive Drive (TPA₂) component scale, 148*t*
Complex decision model, 332–33
Computerized interpretive reports based on test
    measures: availability and options, 23–24, 25,
    330–33, 366; case illustration (Alice), 337*f*,

337–38, 338f, 339f; comparative evaluation of, 357–58, 361–66; narrative reports, 334–37; validity and appropriate clinical use of, 363–67

Computerized testing: computer-adaptive short format, 25; scoring and testing services, 333–34, 371

Confusion/disorientation: acute mood state, 195

Constantinople, A., 76–77, 78

Constraint. *See* Disconstraint (Psy 3)

Content component scales: of MMPI-2, 147–48, 148t; of MMPI-A, 297–98, 299t; MMPI-A case illustration (Tony), 298–302, 301t, 328t

Content scales of MMPI-2, 7, 135–36; case illustrations (Rena and Alice), 148–53, 149f, 153–54, 154f; external aggressive tendencies cluster, 141–44; external correlates of, 137; internal consistency of, 136; internal symptoms cluster, 138–41; interpretation of, 138, 151–52; problem areas cluster, 144–47; validity of, 136–37. *See also* ANG (Anger) scale; ANX (Anxiety) scale; BIZ (Bizarre Mentation) scale; CYN (Cynicism) scale; DEP (Depression) scale; FAM (Family Problems) scale; FRS (Fears) scale; HEA (Health Concerns) scale; LSE (Low Self-Esteem) scale; TPA (Type A Behavior) scale; TRT (Negative Treatment Indicators) scale; WRK (Work Interference) scale

Content scales of MMPI-A, 273–75; comparison with MMPI-2 content scales, 275, 276t; interpretation of, 275, 277t, 277

Conversion disorder, 68

Cook, W. W., 167

Cook-Medley Hostility scale (Ho). *See* Hostility scale (Ho)

Coronary disease: Type A personality and, 167

Costa, P. T., 174

Costello, R. M., 177

Couples studies, 90, 156

Craig, R. J., 156

Crewe, D. L., 220

Crewe, J. C., 220

Criminal offenders: classification of, 176–77; forensic assessment case, 337, 344–345f, 346f, 347f, 348–51f; forensic settings, 196

Crisis states. *See* Acute mood states

Criterion group, 372

Critical items: Koss-Butcher set, 179–80t, 195; Lachar-Wrobel set, 180–81t, 195; of MMPI-2, 177–78, 182, 372; of MMPI-A, 308–12, 309–11t, 313t

Cronbach, L. J.: on scale 5 (Mf), 77

Crowther, J. H., 137

Custody evaluations, 188, 198

CYN (Cynicism) content scale, 142–43, 143t6-8; component scales, 148t

CYN₁ (Misanthropic Beliefs) component scale, 148t

CYN₂ (Interpersonal Suspiciousness) component scale, 148t

D (Depression) standard scale, 60, 65; assessment indicators, 195; empirical research on, 67f, 67–68; descriptors and interpretation of, 68, 69t; item content, 66–67; MMPI-A (adolescent) interpretation, 253–54, 254, 255–56t, 266–67t; older subjects' elevated scores in, 189; validity for adolescents, 253

D₁ (Subjective Depression) subscale: adolescent interpretation, 255t, 322

D₂ (Psychomotor Retardation) subscale, 66; adolescent interpretation, 254, 255t

D₃ (Physical Malfunctioning) subscale, 66; adolescent interpretation, 256t

D₄ (Mental Dullness) subscale, 67; adolescent interpretation, 256t

D₅ (Brooding) subscale, 67; adolescent interpretation, 256t

Dahlstrom, L. E., 191; on test-retest reliability, 62, 101

Dahlstrom, W. G., 4, 76, 77, 101, 167, 191; criminal offender studies, 176; on test-retest reliability, 62, 101

Davis, D. L., 222, 226, 231, 240, 315

Defective Inhibition (Sc₅) subscale, 86

Defensiveness scale (K). *See* K scale

Defensive responding, MMPI-A and, 234–36, 235f

Delinquency, 210, 287–88; A-ang scale and, 285; A-dep scale and, 280; incarcerated boys study (Cashel), 252, 254, 261, 267, 278, 279, 280, 282, 285, 286, 291, 292, 294, 305, 306, 307, 322; MMPI-A Pd₂ and, 260t; MMPI-A Scale 7 (Pt) and, 263; MMPI-A Scale 9 (Ma) and, 267; study of (Hathaway), 219, 256, 260. *See also* A-con (Adolescent-Conduct Problems) content scale

Delk, J., 73

Denial of Social Anxiety (Hy₁) subscale, 69; adolescent interpretation, 257t

Denny, N. R., 171

DEP (Depression) content scale: external correlates, 137; interpretation of, 140, 141t6-4, 152. *See also* A-dep (Adolescent-Depression) scale

DEP₁ (Lack of Drive) component scale, 148t

DEP₂ (Dysphoria) component scale, 148t

DEP₃ (Self-Depreciation) component scale, 148t

DEP₄ (Suicidal Ideation) component scale, 148t

Depression: acute mood state, 195; depressive disorder, 110. *See also* A-dep (Adolescent-Depression) scale; DEP (Depression) content scale; D (Depression) standard scale

Disconstraint (Psy 3) scale, 174*t*, 175

Dissimulation index. *See* F–K index (Dissimulation)

Dodge, K. A., 167

Domestic violence history. *See* Marital distress

Dominance (Do) supplementary scale, 169–70, 170*t*

Drake, L. E., 103

Drug abuse. *See* Substance abuse

DSM (Diagnostic and Statistical Manual of Mental Disorders), 3, 200, 372; *DSM-III/III-R*, 73, 174

Duckro, P., 176

Duker, J., 90, 102, 103

Duran, C., 124

Dyadic Adjustment scale (Spanier), 6, 162

Dysphoria component scales: A-dep$_1$ (adolescent), 299*t*; DEP$_2$ (adult), 148*t*

Eating disorders: anorexia in adolescents, 254, 290; overeating (case illustration),148–53, 149*f*

Edinger, J. D., 176

Educational factors, 190

Egeland, B., 137; on mothers at risk for child abuse, 6, 137

Ego Inflation (Ma$_4$) subscale, 88

Ego Mastery: Lack of—Cognitive (Sc$_3$), 86, 267*t*; Lack of—Conative (Sc$_4$), 86, 267*t*

Ego Strength (Es) supplementary scale, 171–72, 172*t*

Ehrenworth, N. V., 217

Elevated scales: intoxication and, 318–20

Ellens, B. M., 330

Emotional Alienation (Sc$_2$) subscale, 86; adolescent interpretation, 266*t*

Endicott, N. A., 67

Erbaugh, S. E., 303

Erickson, M.: on mothers at risk for child abuse, 6, 137

Es (Ego Strength) supplementary scale, 171–72, 172*t*

Ethnic and cultural factors, 190–93; Hispanic adolescent studies, 224–25; minorities in case illustrations, 245–47, 246*f*, 247*f*, 298; MMPI-2 means and standard deviations by race or ethnicity, 191*t*, 192*t*. *See also* International formats of test measures

Exaggerated symptom pattern, 56*f*, 56–57, 57*f*, 58*f*

Explosive Behavior (component scales): adolescent (A-ang$_1$), 299*t*; adult (ANG$_1$), 148*t*

Extreme responding, 318

Eyde, L., 361

F (Infrequency) scale: adolescent testing and, 44; all-False pattern and, 42; assessment indicators, 195; interpretation of, 44–47, 46*f*, 47*t*, 153; MMPI-A and, 9, 13, 228*t*, 228, 237–40, 241*t*. *See also* F$_b$ (Infrequency Back) scale of MMPI-2; F$_p$ (Psychopathology Infrequency) scale

F$_1$ subscale, 240, 241*t*

F$_2$ subscale, 240, 241*t*

Factor scales. *See* A (Anxiety) supplementary scale; R (Repression) scale

Fairbank, J. A., 170

Fake-good profile, 54*f*, 54–55

Fake response sets, 227, 233, 238–39

False negative results, 215. *See also* Fake response sets

FAM (Family Problems) content scale: external correlates, 137, 145, 146*t*, 162

FAM$_1$ (Family Problems) component scale, 148*t*

FAM$_2$ (Familial Alienation) component scale, 148*t*

Familial Alienation (component scales): A-fam$_2$ (adolescent), 299*t*; FAM$_2$ (adult), 148*t*

Familial Discord (A-fam$_1$) component scale, 299*t*

Familial Discord (Pd$_1$) subscale, 72; adolescent interpretation, 259*t*

Family problems: critical MMPI-2 items and, 181*t*; critical MMPI-A items and, 309*t*; as factor in adolescence, 260, 278

Fang, L.: on test instructions, 17

F$_b$ (Infrequency Back) scale of MMPI-2, 47–48, 48*t*, 228

Fears (FRS) content scale, 139*t*6-2, 139, 148*t*

Filsinger, E. E., 6, 162

Finger, M.: on computerized testing, 24

Fink, A., 17

Finn, S. E., 197, 325, 366

Fishburne, F., 361

Five Factor Model, 174

Fixed responding, 242–45, 244*f*, 245*f*; case illustrations of, 242–45, 244*f*, 245*f*; MMPI-A and, 234–36, 235*f*

F–K (Dissimulation) index, 48–49; MMPI-2 interpretation of, 48–49; MMPI-A interpretation of, 240–41, 241*t*

Fm scale, 76

Forbey, J. D., 311

Fordyce, W., 64

Foreign languages and MMPI measures, 224, 368–69

Forensic studies, 196; classification of criminal offenders, 176–77; forensic assessment case, 337, 344–45*f*, 346*f*, 347*f*, 348–51*f*; forensic scale elevations study, 198, 349*f*; Minnesota Report for Forensic Settings, 337, 344–45*f*, 346*f*, 347*f*, 348–51*f*

Formats of test measures: abbreviated, 24–25; audiocassette, 23; computerized, 23–24, 25; paper and pencil, 20

Form AX (experimental) booklet, 4–5, 136

Form TX (experimental) booklet, 4–5, 8

Forsyth, R.: complex decision model, 332–33

Four-point code types, 99

F_p (Psychopathology Infrequency) scale, 48, 49f, 49t, 228

Franzen, M. D., 46

FRS (Fears) content scale, 139t6-2, 139, 148t

FRS$_1$ (Generalized Fearfulness) component scale, 148t

FRS$_2$ (Multiple Fears) component scale, 148t

Gallagher, R. W.: on F scale, 46

Galluci, N. T.: inpatient adolescent studies, 238, 250, 251, 254, 256, 262, 263, 268, 304, 305, 306

Gambling (pathological): MAC-R elevation and, 156

Gantner, A. G., 304

Garfinkle, P. E., 73

Gastrointestinal Complaints component scales: A-hea$_1$ (adolescent), 299t; HEA$_1$ (adult), 148t

Gender and test measures, 189; adult-adolescent differences in test measures, 210, 211–12, 213f, 214f, 215f, 216f; gender role scales, 77–78; means and standard deviations for men and women, 191t, 192t; ungendered norms, 189

Gender in adolescent test measures, 219–20, 225, 253t; A-aln scale and, 283; A-ang scale and, 285, 286t, 300; A-con scale and, 287, 288; A-fam scale and, 294; A-lse scale and, 288; Pd$_4$ scale and, 258; scale 1 (Hs) of MMPI-A and, 252; scale 2 (D) of MMPI-A and, 253–54, 255–56t; scale 4 (Pd) of MMPI-A and, 322; scale 5 (Mf) of MMPI-A and, 261; scale 6 (Pa) of MMPI-A and, 263, 264t; scale 7 (Pt) of MMPI-A and, 263; scale 8 (Sc) of MMPI-A and, 265, 266t; sexual abuse history and, 321–22

General Health Concerns (component scales): A-hea$_3$ (adolescent), 299t; HEA$_3$ (adult), 148t

Generalized Fearfulness (FRS$_1$) component scale, 148t

Gianetti, R. A., 62

Gilbertstadt, H., 90, 102, 103

Gino, A., 171

Glaser, R., 73

Goldberg, L. R., 174

Goodstein, L. D., 78

Gordon, R. A., 62

Gottesman, I. I., 156, 216

Gottfried, A. W., 37

Gough, H. G., 49–50, 90, 93, 169, 170

Graham, John R., 4, 5, 62, 77, 78, 100; on content

scales of MMPI-2, 7–8, 73, 135; on the D scale, 68; on the F scale, 45; inpatient studies, 6, 67, 137, 200; on MAC and MAC-R scales, 156, 304; on MMPI-2 code types, 34–35, 102, 103; psychiatric inpatient studies, 64, 67, 70, 82, 87, 90, 198, 348; on Scale 5 (Mf), 77, 78

Grayson, H. M., 177

Greene, R. L., 52, 62, 64, 78, 79, 159, 183, 231; alcohol treatment setting studies, 6, 160

Griffin, R., 102, 103

Grossman, L. S. (1990), 46, 182

Grove, W., 103

Gumbiner, J., 12

Guthrie, G. M., 73, 81

Gynther, M. D., 45, 103, 190

Haertzen, C. A., 73

Halbower, C. C., 103, 331

Hall, G. S., 191

Haller, D. L., 8, 14, 232

Hallucinations, 310t, 318

Hammond, J. A., 46

Han, K., 167; on the S scale, 52

Hanlon, T. E., 87

Harkness, A. R., 174, 307

Harlow, T.: on litigation cases, 70

Harper, J. F., 37

Harris, R. E., 61–62

Harris-Lingoes subscales, 61–62, 194; interpretation of, 62, 94, 96–97; validity for adolescents, 251

Hathaway, S. R., 50, 51, 63, 71; adolescent testing and norms, 8, 209, 213, 214, 220, 230, 260, 262, 263; on content scales, 65, 76, 83, 93; delinquency indicators, 219, 256, 260; Hathaway system of coding, 32; MMPI scale development, 1–3, 11, 14, 30, 32, 217, 219

HEA (Health Concerns) scale, 140, 141t6-5, 148t; all-False patterns and, 44; chronic pain and, 137

HEA$_1$ (Gastrointestinal Symptoms) component scale, 148t

HEA$_2$ (Neurological Symptoms) component scale, 148t

HEA$_3$ (General Health Concerns) component scale, 148t

Heart disease: Ho scale and, 167

Hedlund, J. L., 62

Higgins, G., 73

Hill, H. E., 73

Hispanic adolescent case illustration (Tony): content scales, 298–302, 301t; Minnesota Report, 337, 356f, 358f, 359–61f, 362–57; supplementary scales, 312t, 312–14; test summary, 326, 326–29, 327f, 328t, 329f; validity scales, 237f, 245–47, 246f

Hispanics: adolescent studies, 224–25; MMPI-2 means and standard deviations for (comparative), 191*t*, 192*t*. *See also* Ethnic and cultural factors

Hjemboe, S.: marital distress study, 6, 74, 137, 145, 162

Ho (Hostility) supplementary scale, 167*t*, 167, 195; case illustration (Mr. E.), 168*f*, 168–69

Hoeglund, T., 189

Hoffman, H., 73

Hostetler, K., 62

Hostility (Ho) supplementary scale, 167*t*, 167, 195; case illustration (Mr. E.), 168*f*, 168–69

Hs (Hypochondriasis) standard scale: all-False pattern and, 42; assessment indicators, 195; chronic pain and, 64; descriptors and interpretation of, 65, 66*t*; empirical research on, 63–65, 64*f*; item content, 63; K scale and, 50; MMPI-A (adolescent) interpretation, 252, 253*t*

Hulsey, T. L., 177

Hy (Hysteria) standard scale, 68; all-False pattern and, 42; descriptors and interpretation, 71, 72*t*; empirical research on, 70; item content, 68–70; MMPI-A (adolescent) interpretation, 254, 255–58*t*, 256, 257–58*t*; validity in adolescents, 254

Hy₁ (Denial of Social Anxiety), 69; adolescent interpretation, 257*t*

Hy₂ (Need for Affection), 69; adolescent interpretation, 256, 257*t*

Hy₃ (Lassitude-Malaise), 70; adolescent interpretation, 257*t*

Hy₄ (Somatic Complaints), 70; adolescent interpretation, 258*t*

Hy₅ (Inhibition of Aggression), 70; adolescent interpretation, 256, 258*t*

Hypomania, acute mood state, 195. *See also* Ma (Hypomania) standard scale

Imhof, E. A., 307, 330

Imm (Immaturity) supplementary scale, 307

Impatience (TPA₁) component scale, 148*t*, 152

Imperturbability (Ma₃) subscale, 88; adolescent interpretation, 322

Inability to Disclose (A-trt₂) component scale, 299*t*

Indexes for the MMPI-2, 175–78

Infrequent response. *See* F_b (Infrequency Back) scale; F (Infrequency) scale

Inhibition, Defective (Sc₅), 86

Inhibition of Aggression (Hy₅), 70; adolescent interpretation, 256, 258*t*

Inpatient studies. *See* Psychiatric inpatient studies

International formats of test measures, 224, 368–69

International interpretation: F scale and, 46–47

Interpersonal Skepticism (A-aln₃) component scale, 299*t*

Interpersonal Submissiveness (A-lse₂) component scale, 299*t*

Interpersonal Suspiciousness component scales: A-cyn₂ (adolescent), 299*t*; CYN₂ (adult), 148*t*

Interpretive reports. *See* MMPI-2 interpretive report; MMPI-A interpretive report

Intoxication: elevated scales and, 318–20

Introversion: A-sod₁ component scale (adolescent), 291–92, 293*t*, 299*t*, 324; Psy-5 scale, 174*t*, 175; SOD₁ component scale (adult), 148*t*

Irritability (component scales): adolescent (A-ang₂), 299*t*; adult (ANG₂), 148*t*

Item Response Theory, 191–92

Iverson, G. L., 46

Jacobson, J. M., 311

Janus, M. D., 217

Jaynes, G., 137

Jeffrey, T.: military personnel study, 6

Johnson, M. E., 142, 176

Jortner, S., 67

Juvenile delinquency. *See* Delinquency

Kabacoff, R. I., 176

Kaemmer, Beverly, 4

Kaloupek, D. G., 171

Kammeier, J. M., 73

Kamphuis, J. H., 197

Katz, M. M., 6

Keane, T. M., 170, 171

Keller, L. S.: chronic pain study, 64, 70, 137, 177

Kelly, C. K., 99

King, G. D., 99

Kleman, R., 137

Klump, K., 222

Knight, J., 87

Kopper, B. A.: inpatient studies with adolescent MMPI correlates, 251, 268, 278, 283

Koss, M. P., Koss-Butcher critical items set, 177, 179–80*t*

Kowal, D., 361

Kroll, L. S., 229

K scale: all-False pattern and, 42, 44; correction, 30, 31, 51; defensive profile and, 55*f*, 55; interpretation of, 50–52, 52*t*; of MMPI-A, 228*t*, 232*t*, 232–33. *See also* F–K index (Dissimulation)

Kubany, E. S., 171

Kwan, K. L., 193

L (Lie) scale: all-False pattern and, 42; interpretation of, 50, 51*t*; MMPI-A and, 228*t*, 230–31, 232*t*

Lachar, D., 50, 191; Lachar-Wrobel critical items set, 178, 180–81*t*

Lack of Drive (component scales): A-dep₃ (adolescent), 299*t*; DEP₁ (adult), 148*t*

Lack of Initiative (A-las₂) component scale, 299*t*

Language factors: reading requirements for test measures, 192–93, 246, 318; translations and translators for test measures, 224, 368–69

Lassitude-Malaise (Hy₃) subscale, 70; adolescent interpretation, 257*t*

Lebow, B. S., 103

Lees-Haley, P. R., 198

Legan, L., 156

Levenson, M. R.: alcohol abuse–related studies, 6, 156

Lewandowski, D., 73

Lewinson, P. M., 87

Lichtenberg, P. A., 64

Lie (L) scale: all-False pattern and, 42; interpretation of, 50, 51*t*; MMPI-A and, 228*t*, 230–31, 232*t*

Lilienfeld, S. O., 6, 73, 137

Lilly, R. S., 77

Lim, J., 52, 193

Linear T scores, 6, 60

Lingoes, J., 61–62

Litigation test situations, 46, 70, 188, 198

Litz, B. T.: studies of veterans with PTSD, 6

Lloyd, P., 137

Loevinger, J., 174, 307

Long, K. A., 78

Loper, R., 73

Lopez, I. R., 191

Low Achievement Orientation (A-las₁) component scale, 299*t*

Low Motivation (A-trt₁) component scale, 299*t*

Low self-esteem: 4-8/8-4 code type and, 121–22, 122*t*; 6-8/8-6 code type and, 123–24, 125*t*

LSE (Low Self-Esteem) content scale, 137, 148*t*

LSE₁ (Self-Doubt) component scale, 148*t*

LSE₂ (Submissiveness) component scale, 148*t*

Lucio, E. M., 193; on the 6-8/8-6 code type, 124

Ma (Hypomania) standard scale: all-True pattern and, 41; descriptors and interpretation, 88, 90–91, 92–93*t*, 342, 351*f*, 354; empirical research on, 90; item content, 90; K scale and, 50; MMPI-A (adolescent) interpretation, 267–68, 269–70*t*, 270–71

Ma₁ (Amorality), 88

Ma₂ (Psychomotor Acceleration), 88

Ma₃ (Imperturbability), 88; adolescent interpretation, 322

Ma₄ (Ego Inflation), 88

MAC (MacAndrew Alcoholism) scale, 155–56. *See also* MAC-R (MacAndrew Alcoholism Revised) scale

MacAndrew, C., 155

MAC-R (MacAndrew Alcoholism) scale-Revised, 9; case illustration (Mr. Gabriel), 157–59, 158*f*; empirical studies of, 156–57; interpretation of, 155*t*, 157*t*, 157, 158, 159; for MMPI-A, 303–4, 304*t*, 312, 323–24. *See also* Alcohol abuse

Mail-in scoring of test measures, 26, 334

Malingering: F scale and, 46

Malloy, P. F., 170

Marital distress, 6, 37, 74. *See also* FAM (Family Problems) content scale; Marital Distress (MDS) supplementary scale

Marital Distress (MDS) supplementary scale, 7, 162, 163*t*; case illustration (Mr. and Ms. Levin), 163*f*, 163, 164*f*, 165–67, 167*f*

Marks, P. A., 8, 14, 100, 102, 103, 232; on adolescents and the MMPI, 212–14, 216, 217

Mayo Clinic study, 331–32

McCann, J. T., 226, 227, 239

McCrae, R. R., 174

McCulley, E., 200

McIntyre, S. C., 73

McKee, M. G., 90

McKenna, T., 156

McKinley, J. C., 1–3, 11, 30, 51, 63, 71, 83, 182

McMinn, M. R., 330

McNulty, J. L., 100, 174, 307, 308

MDS (Marital Distress) supplementary scale, 7, 162, 163*t*; case illustration (Mr., Ms. Levin), 163*f*, 163, 164*f*, 165–67, 167*f*

Medley, D. M., 167

Meehl, P. E., 51, 93, 169, 170; developing actuarial tables, 102, 331; development of K scale, 50

Megargee, E. I., 176–77, 335; classification system for criminal offenders, 45, 176–77

Mental Dullness (D₄) subscale, 67; adolescent interpretation, 256*t*

Meshcda, T., 87

Meyers, L. S., 93

Mf (Masculinity-Femininity) standard scale, 17–18, 60; adolescent gender differences, 261; adolescent interpretation, 260–62, 262*t*; descriptors and interpretation, 78–80, 80*t*; empirical research on, 78; item content, 77–78; MMPI-A (adolescent) version, 248

Military personnel: studies in, 6

Miller, K., 17, 62, 102, 156, 159, 160, 175

Minnesota Report, 230; for adolescents (MMPI-A), 337, 356*f*, 358*f*, 359–61*f*, 362–57; Adult Clinical System, 336, 337*f*, 337–38, 338*f*, 339*f*; Alcohol and Drug Treatment Program, 336–37, 340*f*, 340–44, 341*f*, 342–43*f*; evaluations of, 335–37, 361–63, 363t; for Forensic Settings, 337, 344–345f, 346f, 347f, 348–51f; Personnel Selection System, 336, 352, 353f, 354f, 355f, 358–59

Minority differences on MMPI-2. See Ethnic and cultural factors

Misanthropic Beliefs component scales: A-cyn$_1$ (adolescent), 299t; CYN$_1$ (adult), 148t

Misunderstood (A-aln$_1$) component scale, 299t

MMPI: adolescents' profile interpretation, 214–22, 221t; development of original, 1–3, 11, 30, 83, 182; norms for adolescents, 214–17, 215f, 216t; original sample, 3–4

MMPI-2: development of, 11, 608; experimental Form AX used in developing, 4–5, 136; features of, 10t; normative sample, 6, 7, 9–10; profile stability, 199; scale construction, 3; "subtle keys" to, 182–83; test administration, 12, 15–18, 20–25, 21f; translations and translators for, 224, 368–69; ungendered norms format, 189. See also Computerized interpretive reports based on test measures

MMPI-2 interpretive report: base-rate frequencies, 197–98; case illustration (Alice), 200–208, 201f; clinical diagnostic assessment, 199–200; educational factors, 190; ethnic and cultural factors, 190–93, 191t, 192t; extratest information in, 187–88; goals and presenting symptoms, 203–4; history and referral, 202–3; integrative scale descriptor approach, 186–87, 187t8-1; interpersonal relations assessment, 196–97, 205–6; personal observations, 202; profile stability, 199; self-control and acting out assessment, 195, 205; setting and test-taking attitude, 188–89, 193; social class factors, 190; substance abuse problems assessment, 196; symptoms and behaviors assessment, 193–95, 204–5; treatment planning, 187t8-2, 200, 206–8; validity appraisal, 294. See also Critical items

MMPI-2/MMPI-A formats: abbreviated, 24–25; audiocassette, 23; computerized, 23–24, 25; paper and pencil, 20

MMPI-A, 78; abbreviated format of, 24–25; age-appropriate adolescent norms for, 219; alternative test formats, 20–25, 22f; congruence with MMPI-2, 9–11, 10t; development of, 6, 8–11, 189, 220, 258; experimental Form TX used in developing, 4–5, 8; features and advantages of, 10t, 222–25, 223t; feedback session, 325–26; F scale not used with, 9, 13; item content and omissions, 220, 230; K correction not used with, 31; norms and normative sample, 8–10, 224–25; redundant information in, 316; test

administration, 12, 18–20, 19–20t, 20–25, 22f, 226; translations and translators for, 224, 368–69; T-score ranges and score conversion, 13, 22f, 229, 239–40. See also Computerized interpretive reports based on test measures

MMPI-A interpretive report: case illustration (Tony), 326, 326–29, 327f, 328t, 329f; clinical diagnostic assessment, 324–25; extratest information, 318, 319f, 320; integrative scale descriptor approach, 315–18, 317t, 319f; interpersonal relations assessment, 324; school problems, 323; substance abuse problems assessment, 323–24; symptoms and behaviors assessment, 320–21; validity appraisal, 318, 320

Moldin, S. O., 87, 200

Monachesi, E. D.: adolescent testing and norms, 8, 209, 213, 214, 220, 230, 260, 262, 263; on delinquency indicators, 219, 256, 260; on Pt scale, 83–84; on So scale, 93; on standard scale development, 11, 14, 24, 209, 217

Moreland, K. L., 358

Morfitt, R.: on test instructions, 17

Mrad, D. F., 176

Muller, B., 358

Multiple Fears (FRS$_2$) component scale, 148t

Munley, P. H., 137, 171

Munoz, R.: cross-cultural studies, 192–93

Murray, J. B., 78

Naïveté (Pa$_3$) subscale, 80–81; adolescent interpretation, 263, 264t

National Computer Systems (NCS), 39, 224, 334

Native Americans: MMPI-2 means and standard deviations for men (comparative), 192t; MMPI-2 means and standard deviations for women (comparative), 192t

Naylor, C., 332–33

Need for Affection (Hy$_2$) subscale, 69; adolescent interpretation, 256, 257t

Negative attitudes toward school: A-sch$_2$ component scale, 299t

Negative Emotionality/Neuroticism Psy-5 scale, 174t, 175

Negative Peer Group Influences (A-con$_3$) component scale, 299t; interpretation, 274, 287–88, 289t, 298, 328t, 371

Nelson, L., 67

Neurological Symptoms (component scales): A-hea$_2$ (adolescent), 299t; HEA$_2$ (adult), 148t

Neurotic triad. See Scale 1 Hypochondriasis (Hs); Scale 2 Depression (D); Scale 3 Hysteria (Hy)

Nezami, E.: cross-cultural studies, 193

Nichols, D., 52, 231

Normative samples, 198

Norms for adolescents, 4, 8, 12–15, 19; debate over adult/adolescent MMPI-score differences, 210–20, 221t; norms for MMPI-A, 219, 254

Null, C., 142

OBS (Obsessiveness) content scale, 140t, 140, 153

Oetting, E. R., 103

Offord, K. P., 3–4, 216–17

Older subjects: elevated scores in D, Pd, Si scales noted, 189; study of older men, 6, 156

One-point code types. See Single-point code types

Ones, D.: on computerized testing, 24

Onstad, J., 358

Osborne, D., 3–4

Ota, K. Y., 87

Pa (Paranoia) standard scale, 80–81; all-True pattern and, 41; descriptors and interpretation, 82, 83t; empirical research on, 81–82; item content, 81; MMPI-A (adolescent) interpretation, 162–63, 264t

Pa₁ (Persecutory Ideas) subscale, 81; adolescent interpretation, 263, 264t

Pa₂ (Poignancy) subscale, 81; adolescent interpretation, 264t

Pa₃ (Naïveté) subscale, 80–81; adolescent interpretation, 263, 264t

Palacios, H., 124

Pancheri, P., 47

Panic disorder case illustrations (Alice): clinician's interpretive report, 200–208, 201f; code types, 133–34; computerized interpretive report, 337–38, 338f, 339f; content scales, 153–54, 154f; profile validity, 59, 59f; standard scales, 97f, 97–98; supplementary scales, 184–85

Panton, J. H., 73

Paranoid Ideation (A-biz₂) component scale, 299t

Paranoid ideation in adolescents: critical items, 310t

Pd (Psychopathic Deviate) standard scale, 71; ASP scale and, 73–74; assessment indicators, 195, 322, 342, 348f, 351f; behavioral problems and, 73–74; descriptors and interpretation, 74–75, 75t; empirical research on, 73–74; item content, 71–73; K scale and, 50; MMPI-A (adolescent) interpretation, 256, 258, 259–60t, 260, 322; older subjects' elevated scores in, 189; validity with adolescents, 251

Pd₁ (Familial Discord) subscale, 72; adolescent interpretation, 259t

Pd₂ (Authority Problems) subscale, 72; adolescent interpretation, 260t, 260, 271

Pd₃ (Social Imperturbability) subscale, 72; adolescent interpretation, 260t, 260

Pd₄ (Social Alienation) subscale, 72–73; adolescent interpretation, 258, 260t

Pd₅ (Self-Alienation) subscale, 73; adolescent interpretation, 251, 260t, 260, 322

Pearson, J. S., 331

Peña, L. M., 212

Penk, W., 87

Perry, J., 62, 102, 331

Persecutory Ideas (Pa₁) subscale, 81; adolescent interpretation, 263, 264t

Personal Data Sheet (Woodworth), 177

Personality Psychopathology 5 (PSY-5) scales: of MMPI-2, 173–75, 174t; of MMPI-A, 307–8, 308t

Personnel screening, 17–18; case illustration (Eva), 336, 352, 353f, 354f, 355f

Personnel Selection System, Minnesota Report, 336, 352, 353f, 354f, 355f, 358–59

Persons, R. W., 100

Peterson, B. L., 167

Peterson, C. D., 77

Petzel, T. P., 45

Phobias: FRS scale and, 139t6-2, 139

Physical abuse history: A-ang scale and, 285, 286t; scale 4 (Pd) in MMPI-A and, 322

Physical Malfunctioning (D₃) subscale, 66; adolescent interpretation, 256t

Poignancy (Pa₂) subscale, 81; adolescent interpretation, 264t

Pope, K. S.: on litigation cases, 46, 70, 198

Posttraumatic Stress Disorder (PK) supplementary scale, 170–71, 171t7-8

Postuma, A. B., 37

Prescott, C. A., 156

PRO (Alcohol and Drug Problem Proneness) supplementary scale, 305–6, 307t, 312t, 312, 323–24

Profile codes. See Code types

Profile prototype, 193–94

Profiles based on test measures, 27f, 28f, 29f, 30f, 31f; extent of definition of, 349f, 364–65; plotting of, 26, 30–32; stability of, 199; submerged profile, 376. See also MMPI-2 interpretive report; MMPI-A interpretive report; Validity of profiles

Profile spike, 99

Psy-5 (Personality Psychopathology 5) scales of MMPI-2, 173–75, 174t; Aggressiveness, 174t, 174–75; Disconstraint, 174t, 175; Introversion, 174t, 175; Negative Emotionality/Neuroticism, 174t, 175; Psychoticism, 174t, 175

Psy-5 (Personality Psychopathology 5) scales of MMPI-A, 307–8, 308t; Aggressiveness, 308t, 308, 314, 329; Disconstraint, 308t, 314; Introversion, 174t, 308t; Negative Emotionality/Neuroticism, 308t, 308; Psychoticism, 308t

Psychiatric inpatient studies: of adolescents (Arita and Baer), 277–78, 280, 281, 283, 285, 292; of adolescents (Galluci), 238, 250, 251, 254, 256, 262, 263, 268, 304, 305, 306; Arbisi and Ben-Porath, 344–49, 348f; Ben-Porath, Butcher, and Graham, 6, 67, 137; elevated scores in, 198; Graham and Butcher, 64, 67, 70, 82, 87, 90, 198; NCS sample, 348f

Psychomotor Acceleration (Ma₂) subscale, 88

Psychomotor Retardation (D₂) subscale, 66; adolescent interpretation, 254, 255t

Psychopathology, serious, 199, 350f; 3-8/8-3 code type and, 118, 119t; 4-6/6-4 code type and, 118–20, 120t; 6-8/8-6 code type and, 124; 1-2-3 code type and, 128–30, 130t; assessing in adolescents, 211–12; case illustration (random respondent), 242, 243f10-4

Psychosis: acute mood state, 195

Psychoticism (Psy-5) scale, 174t, 175

Psychotic symptomatology (component scales): A-biz₁ (adolescent), 299t; BIZ₁ (adult), 148t

Pt (Psychasthenia) standard scale, 83–84; all-True pattern and, 41; assessment indicators, 195, 338; descriptors and interpretation, 84–85, 85t; empirical research on, 84; item content, 84; K scale and, 50; MMPI-A (adolescent) interpretation, 263, 265t

Quereshi, M. Y., 137

R (Repression) scale: MMPI-A version, 306–7, 313, 375; supplementary scale, 173t7-11, 173

Race. See African Americans; Ethnic and cultural factors

Random responding: case illustrations, 242, 243f

Reading requirements for test measures, 192, 246, 318

Regts, J. M., 162

Re (Social Responsibility) supplementary scale, 170, 171t7-7

Restandardization Project, 4–6, 7, 30, 68, 81, 90, 172, 178, 189, 213

Reyes-Lagunes, I., 193

Rice, J. P., 87, 200

Rierdan, J., 87

Rogers, R., 46, 238, 239–40

Roper, B. L., 25

Rosen, A., 87

Rouse, S. V.: on substance abuse assessment, 17, 62, 102, 156, 159, 160, 175

S (Superlative Self-Presentation) scale, 52–53, 53t; defensive profile and, 55f, 55; S₁ (Beliefs in Human Goodness), 52:, 53; S₂ (Serenity), 53; S₃ (Contentment with Life), 53; S₄ (Patience/Denial of Irritability), 53; S₅ (Denial of Moral Flaws), 53

Saccuzzo, D. P., 73

Salekin, R. T., 46

Sc (Schizophrenia) standard scale, 85–86; adolescent gender differences in (MMPI-A), 265, 266t; all-True pattern and, 41; descriptors and interpretation, 87–88, 89t; empirical research on, 87; item content, 86–87; K scale and, 50; MMPI-A (adolescent) interpretation, 250, 263, 265, 266–67t, 322; psychotic processes and, 318; scale elevation and clinical assessment, 195, 198, 322, 338, 348f, 349f

Sc₁ (Social Alienation), 86; adolescent interpretation, 266t

Sc₂ (Emotional Alienation), 86; adolescent interpretation, 266t

Sc₃ (Lack of Ego Mastery, Cognitive), 86; adolescent interpretation, 267t

Sc₄ (Lack of Ego Mastery, Conative), 86; adolescent interpretation, 267t

Sc₅ (Lack of Ego Mastery, Defective Inhibition), 86

Sc₆ (Bizarre Sensory Experiences), 87; adolescent interpretation, 267t

Scale 1 Hypochondriasis (Hs): all-False pattern and, 42; assessment indicators, 195; chronic pain and, 64; descriptors and interpretation, 65, 66t; empirical research on, 63–65, 64f; item content, 63; K scale and, 50; MMPI-A (adolescent) interpretation, 252, 253t

Scale 2 Depression (D), 60, 65; assessment indicators, 195; descriptors and interpretation, 68, 69t; empirical research on, 67f, 67–68; item content, 66–67; MMPI-A (adolescent) interpretation, 253–54, 255–56t, 266–67t; older subjects' elevated scores in, 189; validity for adolescents, 253

Scale 2 subscales: adolescent interpretation of, 254, 255–56t, 322; D₁ (Subjective Depression), 66; D₂ (Psychomotor Retardation), 66; D₃ (Physical Malfunctioning), 66; D₄ (Mental Dullness), 67; D₅ (Brooding), 67

Scale 3 Hysteria (Hy), 68; all-False pattern and, 42; descriptors and interpretation, 71, 72t; empirical research on, 70; item content, 68–70; MMPI-A (adolescent) interpretation, 254, 255–58t, 256, 257–58t; validity in adolescents, 254

Scale 3 subscales: adolescent interpretation, 256, 257–58t; Hy₁ (Denial of Social Anxiety), 69;

Hy$_2$ (Need for Affection), 69; Hy$_3$ (Lassitude-Malaise), 70; Hy$_4$ (Somatic Complaints), 70; Hy$_5$ (Inhibition of Aggression), 70

Scale 4 Psychopathic Deviate (Pd), 71; ASP scale and, 73–74; assessment indicators, 195, 322, 342, 348f, 351f; behavioral problems and, 73–74; descriptors and interpretation, 74–75, 75t; empirical research on, 73–74; item content, 71–73; K scale and, 50; MMPI-A (adolescent) interpretation, 256, 258, 259–60t, 260, 322; older subjects' elevated scores in, 189; validity with adolescents, 251

Scale 4 subscales: adolescent interpretation, 251, 258, 259–60t, 260, 322; Pd$_1$ (Familial Discord), 72; Pd$_2$ (Authority Problems), 72; Pd$_3$ (Social Imperturbability), 72; Pd$_4$ (Social Alienation), 72–73; Pd$_5$ (Self-Alienation), 73

Scale 5 Masculinity-Femininity (Mf), 17–18, 60; adolescent gender differences, 261; adolescent interpretation, 260–62, 262t; descriptors and interpretation, 78–80, 80t; empirical research on, 78; item content, 77–78; MMPI-A (adolescent) version, 248

Scale 6 Paranoia (Pa), 80–81; all-True pattern and, 41; descriptors and interpretation, 82, 83t; empirical research on, 81–82; item content, 81; MMPI-A (adolescent) interpretation, 162–63, 264t

Scale 6 subscales: adolescent interpretation, 263, 264t; Pa$_1$ (Persecutory Ideas), 81; Pa$_2$ (Poignancy), 81; Pa$_3$ (Naïveté), 80–81

Scale 7 Psychasthenia (Pt), 83–84; all-True pattern and, 41; assessment indicators, 195, 338; descriptors and interpretation, 84–85, 85t; empirical research on, 84; item content, 84; K scale and, 50; MMPI-A (adolescent) interpretation, 263, 265t

Scale 8 Schizophrenia (Sc), 85–86; adolescent gender differences in (MMPI-A), 265, 266t; all-True pattern and, 41; descriptors and interpretation, 87–88, 89t; empirical research on, 87; item content, 86–87; K scale and, 50; MMPI-A (adolescent) interpretation, 250, 263, 265, 266–67t, 322; psychotic processes and, 318; scale elevation and clinical assessment, 195, 198, 322, 338, 348f, 349f

Scale 8 subscales: adolescent interpretation, 266–67t; Sc$_1$ (Social Alienation), 86; Sc$_2$ (Emotional Alienation), 86; Sc$_3$ (Lack of Ego Mastery, Cognitive), 86; Sc$_4$ (Lack of Ego Mastery, Conative), 86; Sc$_5$ (Lack of Ego Mastery, Defective Inhibition), 86; Sc$_6$ (Bizarre Sensory Experiences), 87

Scale 9 Hypomania (Ma): all-True pattern and, 41; descriptors and interpretation, 88, 90–91, 92–93t, 342, 351f, 354; empirical research on,

90; item content, 90; K scale and, 50; MMPI-A (adolescent) interpretation, 267–68, 269–70t, 270–71

Scale 9 subscales: adolescent interpretation, 322; Ma$_1$ (Amorality), 88; Ma$_2$ (Psychomotor Acceleration), 88; Ma$_3$ (Imperturbability), 88; Ma$_4$ (Ego Inflation), 88

Scale 0 Social Introversion (Si), 60, 91, 251; descriptors and interpretation, 93–94, 95t; empirical research on, 93; gender differences in adolescents, 268, 269t, 270; item content, 91; MMPI-A (adolescent) interpretation, 268, 270, 271t, 324; MMPI-A (adolescent) version, 248–49, 249t; older subjects' elevated scores in, 189

Scale 0 subscales: Si$_1$ (Shyness/Self-Consciousness), 271t; Si$_2$ (Social Avoidance), 271t; Si$_3$ (Alienation—Self and Others), 271t

Schill, T., 137

Schizophrenia: 6-8/8-6 code type and, 124; 6-9/9-6 code type and, 126

Schoenfeld, L. S., 177

Schofield, W., 84

School problems: A-sch scale, 294, 296t, 296, 371; component scales, 299t

Schretlen, D., 46

Schroeder, H. E., 77

Schwartz, G., 34–35

Scoring the MMPI-2 and MMPI-A: computer scoring, 26; computer scoring (in office), 334; conversion of MMPI-A scores, 13; error types, 376; hand scoring, 25–26; mail-in scoring, 26, 334

Scotti, J. R., 171

Seelen, J., 46, 70, 198

Seeman, W., 8, 14, 100, 102, 103, 232

Self-Alienation (Pd$_5$), 73; adolescent interpretation, 251, 260t, 260, 322

Self-Depreciation (component scales): A-dep$_2$ (adolescent), 299t; DEP$_3$ (adult), 148t

Self-doubt (component scales): A-lse$_1$ (adolescent), 299t; LSE$_1$ (adult), 148t

Serkownek, K., 77

Sewell, K. W., 46

Sexual abuse history: A-ang scale and, 285, 286t, 300; A-fam scale and, 294; assessment of (adolescent case), 321–22; MMPI-A Psy-5 Aggressiveness and, 314; scale 8 of MMPI-A and, 265, 266t

Shaevel, B., 12

Shaffer, J. W., 87

Shekelle, R. B., 167

Sherwood, N. E., 147, 297, 298

Shimunkas, A. M., 45

Shondrick, D., 192

Short forms of test measures, 24–25

Shyness (A-sod$_2$) component scale, 299t

Shyness/Self-Consciousness (Si$_1$) subscale, 271t

Si (Social Introversion) standard scale, 60, 91; descriptors and interpretation, 93–94, 95t; empirical research on, 93; gender differences in adolescents, 268, 269t, 270; item content, 91; MMPI-A (adolescent) interpretation, 268, 270, 271t, 324; MMPI-A (adolescent) version, 248–49, 249t; older subjects' elevated scores in, 189

Si$_1$ (Shyness/Self-Consciousness), 271t

Si$_2$ (Social Avoidance), 271t

Si$_3$ (Alienation—Self and Others), 271t

Sieber, K. O., 93

Silver, R., 51

Sines, L. K., 51

Single-point code types, 99

Skehan, M. W., 64

Sleep disturbances, 2-8/8-2 code type and, 113–14, 115t

Sletten, I. W., 103

Smith, R., 34–35

Snyder, D. K., 162

Social Alienation (Pd$_4$) subscale, 72–73; adolescent interpretation, 258, 260t

Social Alienation (Sc$_1$) subscale, 86; adolescent interpretation, 266t

Social Avoidance (Si$_2$) subscale, 271t

Social Discomfort (SOD) scale, 145t6-12, 145; component scales, 148t

Social Imperturbability (Pd$_3$) subscale, 72; adolescent interpretation, 260t, 260

Social Introversion (Si) standard scale, 60, 91; descriptors and interpretation, 93–94, 95t; empirical research on, 93; gender differences in adolescents, 268, 269t, 270; item content, 91; MMPI-A (adolescent) interpretation, 268, 270, 271t, 324; MMPI-A (adolescent) version, 248–49, 249t; older subjects' elevated scores in, 189

Social Isolation (A-aln$_2$) component scale, 299t

Social Responsibility (Re) supplementary scale, 170, 171t7-7

Social withdrawal: 8-9/9-8 code type and, 128–29, 129t; 1-2-3 code type and, 128–30, 130t

Society for Personality Assessment, 330

SOD (Social Discomfort) content scale, 145t6-12, 145; component scales, 148t

SOD$_1$ (Introversion) component scale, 148t

SOD$_2$ (Shyness) component scale, 148t

Somatic Complaints (Hy$_4$) subscale, 70; adolescent interpretation, 258t

Song, W. Z., 47

Spanier, G. B., 6, 162

Stability of profiles, 199

Stafford, K., 192, 198, 349f

Standard scales, 60–62, 94, 372, 96f, 96t; adult-adolescent differences in, 213f, 213–17, 214f, 215f, 216f; case illustration (Alice), 97f, 97–98; case illustration (Ann), 94, 96f, 96t

Standard scales of MMPI-A, 235f; case illustration (Tony), 270–72, 272t; interpretation of, 249–52, 252t; items and omissions in, 248–49, 249t. See also by scale, e.g., Scale 1 Hypochondriasis (Hs)

Stein, K. B., 160, 172, 191, 238, 239, 240

Strenger, V. E., 156

Structure Interview of Reported Symptoms (SIRS), 239–40

Sturges, L. V., 171

Subcultural effects. See Ethnic and cultural factors

Subjective Depression (D$_1$) subscale: adolescent interpretation, 255t, 322

Submissiveness (LSE$_2$) component scale, 148t

Substance abuse: 2-4-7/2-7-4 code type and, 130–31, 131t; assessing with MMPI-2 scales, 196; high MAC-R score associated with, 156; Psy-5 Disconstraint scale and, 175; Weed et al. studies of, 6, 30, 51, 159, 160, 167, 183, 304. See also Alcohol abuse

Suicidal Ideation (component scales), A-dep$_4$ (adolescent), 299t; DEP$_4$ (adult), 148t

Suicide risk: code types associated with, 111, 112t, 115t, 116; critical items associated with, 178, 179t, 309t

Suicide risk in adolescents, 322–23; A-aln scale, 283; A-dep scale, 280, 279, 281t, 294; A-las scale, 291t, 291; A-lse scale, 288, 290t; A-sod scale, 292; D$_1$ subscale, 254, 255t, 322; Imm (Immaturity) scale, 307; Kopper et al. study of, 251, 268, 278, 283; Ma$_3$ subscale, 322; Pd$_4$ subscale, 258; Pd$_5$ subscale, 322; scale 2 (D), 322; scale 4 (Pd), 322; scale 7 (Pt), 263; scale 8 (Sc), 265; scale 9 (Ma), 267–68, 269t, 322

Superlative Self-Presentation (S) scale. See S (Superlative Self-Presentation) scale

Supplementary scales: case illustration (Alice), 184–85; case illustration (Tony), 312t, 312–14; cautions about, 178, 182; development of, 2, 155, 178–79, 303; evaluating new, 183–84; "subtle keys" for, 182–83. See also AAS (Addiction Acknowledgment) scale; APS (Addiction Potential) scale; Ho (Hostility) scale; MAC-R (MacAndrew Alcoholism-Revised) scale; MDS (Marital Distress) scale

Suppressor (K score). See K scale

Suspicion/mistrust: acute mood state, 195

Swensen, C. O., 64

Swenson, W. M., 3–4, 331

Taft, R., 73
Tellegen, A., 3, 189, 233–34; development of
    uniform T scores, 6–7, 30, 224
Terman, L. M., 76
Test administration, 12, 15–18, 20–25, 21*f;*
    MMPI-2, 12, 15–18; MMPI-A, 12, 18–20,
    19–20*t*
Test feedback, 325–26, 331, 366
Test instructions, 16–18
Test scoring and score conversion, 13
Test selection, 12–15
Test settings, 188–89, 196, 198
Test-taking attitudes, 135, 193; test instructions
    and, 16–18
Thompson, J., 191
Three-point code types, 99; 1-2-3 code type, 128–
    30, 130*t*; 2-4-7/2-7-4 code type, 130–31, 131*t*;
    2-7-8 code type, 131–32, 133*t*
Timbrook, R., 45, 102, 183
Tinius, T., 192
Tonnsager, M. E., 366
TPA (Type A Behavior) scale: external correlates,
    137; interpretation of, 143–44, 144*t*
TPA₁ (Impatience) component scale, 148*t*, 152
TPA₂ (Competitive Drive) component scale, 148*t*
Translations of test measures, 224, 368–69
TRIN (True Response Inconsistency) scale:
    MMPI-2 interpretation, 40–41, 41*t*; MMPI-A
    interpretation, 225, 228*t*, 233–36, 235*f*, 236*t*,
    318
TRT (Negative Treatment Indicators) content
    scale: external correlates, 137; interpretation
    of, 136, 146–47, 147*t*
Trull, T. J., 175
Tsai, J.: cross-cultural studies, 191–92
T scores: adolescent-adult differences on original
    MMPI, 213*f*, 213, 214*f*; linear T scores, 6, 60;
    MMPI-2 ranges, 7, 10, 38–39, 193–94, 195,
    198; MMPI-A ranges and score conversion,
    13, 22*f*, 229, 239–40, 254, 275; percentile rank
    and values, 374; uniform T scores, 6–7, 30–
    32, 60
TSC scales, 172
Two-point code types, 99; 1-2/2-1 code type,
    104–5*t*, 104–5; 1-3/3-1 code type, 106, 107*t*;
    1-4/4-1 code type, 106–8, 108*t*; 1-8/8-1 code
    type, 108, 109*t*; 1-9/9-1 code type, 109, 110*t*;
    2-3/3-2 code type, 109–10, 111*t*; 2-4/4-2 code
    type, 110–11, 112*t*; 2-7/7-2 code type, 112–13,
    114*t*; 2-8/8-2 code type, 113–14, 115*t*; 2-9/9-2
    code type, 114–16, 116*t*; 3-4/4-3 code type,
    100, 116–17, 117*t*; 3-6/6-3 code type, 117, 118*t*;
    4-6/6-4 code type, 118–20, 120*t*, 212; 4-7/7-4
    code type, 120, 121*t*; 4-8/8-4 code type, 121–
    22, 122*t*, 198, 348*f*, 349*f*, 351*f*; 4-9/9-4 code

type, 122–23, 124*t*, 342; 6-8/8-6 code type,
    123–24, 125*t*; 6-9/9-6 code type, 125–26, 126*t*;
    7-8/8-7 code type, 127, 128*t*, 338; 8-9/9-8 code
    type, 128–29, 129*t*
Type A Behavior (TPA) scale: coronary
    disease and, 167; external correlates, 137;
    interpretation of, 143–44, 144*t*; subscales,
    148*t*, 152
Tyron, Stein, and Chu (TSC) scales, 172

Ungendered norms, 189
Uniform T scores, 6–7, 30–32, 60

Validity of profiles: all-True or all-False pattern,
    38, 41–44, 42*f*, 43*f*; case illustration (Alice),
    58–59, 59*f*; catastrophic life events and, 318;
    defensive profile, 55*f*, 55–56; exaggerated
    symptom pattern, 56*f*, 56–57, 57*f*, 58*f*; fake-
    good profile, 54*f*, 54–55; inconsistent
    responding, 38, 39–41; item omissions, 38,
    39; MMPI-2 profiles, 37–39, 38*f*; MMPI-A
    profiles, 251; random responding, 44–50;
    Superlative Self-Presentation scale and, 52–
    53; test defensiveness and, 50–52
Validity scales, 4, 9, 376; of MMPI-A, 226–29,
    228*t*; case illustration (Lisa), 236–37, 237*f*;
    case illustration (Tony), 237*f*, 245–47, 246*f*.
    See also F (Infrequency) scale; K scale; L (Lie)
    scale; TRIN; VRIN
Veltum, L., 171
Veterans studies of MMPI-2 correlates: Arbisi,
    170–71, 198, 348*f*; Litz, 6
Vincent, K. R., 102
Violent behavior: 3-4/4-3 code type and, 116;
    threatened assault critical items, 179–80*t*
VRIN (Variable Response Inconsistency) scale:
    MMPI-2 interpretation, 39–40, 40*t*3-2;
    MMPI-A interpretation, 225, 228*t*, 241–42,
    242*t*, 318

Waller, N. G., 174, 191
Walsh, S., 137
Wang, T., 137
Warbin, R. W., 45
Waring, E. M., 73
Watts, D., 45
Wauck, L. A., 87
Weathers, F. W., 171
Weed, N. C.: substance abuse studies, 6, 30, 51,
    159, 160, 167, 183, 304
Well-defined code types, 100–101, 212–13
Well-defined versus poorly defined profiles, 349*f*,
    364–65
Welsh coding system, 32–34, 33*f*; modifications
    of, 34–35

Welsh, G. S., 32, 76, 77, 172, 173; on test-retest
    reliability, 62, 101
Welsh scales. *See* A (Anxiety) scale; R
    (Repression) scale
Wenk, E., 191
Wetter, M. W., 52, 231
Wiener, D. N., 182
Wiggins, J. S., 135
Williams, Carolyn L., 4, 7–8, 73, 135; 62, 78, 213;
    on adolescent interpretation, 62, 210–11, 222,
    275; on MMPI-A content scales, 136, 238, 273,
    281, 283, 284, 285, 293, 297,
Williams, R. B., 167, 182

Wolfson, K. T., 303
Woodworth, R. S., 177
WRK (Work Interference) scale: external
    correlates, 137; interpretation of, 146*t*6-14,
    146; 136
Wrobel, T. A., 62, 178, 180–81*t*, 252, 254, 261, 268

Yandell, R. J., 90

Zager, L. D., 176
Zald, D. R., 103
Z scores, 376

James N. Butcher is professor of psychology at the University of Minnesota and the author of numerous articles and books on the MMPI instruments. He served on the MMPI-2 Restandardization Committee and is the MMPI consultant to the University of Minnesota Press. He has conducted the workshop series Symposia of Recent Developments in the Use of the MMPI for thirty-five years.

Carolyn L. Williams is professor of epidemiology in the School of Public Health at the University of Minnesota. Her work on the MMPI instruments focuses on the MMPI-A. She is co-author, with James N. Butcher, Yossef Ben-Porath, and John Graham, of *MMPI-A Content Scales: Assessing Psychopathology in Adolescents* (Minnesota, 1992).